The Official America Online® for Windows Tour Guide

by Tom Lichty

Second Edition

The Official America Online® for Windows Tour Guide, Second Edition

Library of Congress Cataloging-in-Publication Data

Lichty, Tom
The official America Online for Windows tour guide / Tom Lichty.--2nd ed.
p. cm.
Includes index.
ISBN 1-56604-128-7
1. America Online (Videotex system) 2. Microsoft Windows (Computer file)
I. Title.
QA76.57.A43.L523 1994
004.69--dc20 94-38637
CIP

Book design: Marcia Webb
Cover design: IMAGE Communications; adaptation: John Nedwidek
Index service: Nancy Guenther
Technical review: Tim Barwick, Marshall Rens, Kelly Richmond: America Online
Editorial staff: Angela Anderson, Laura Bader, Walter R. Bruce, III, Tracye Giles, Pam Richardson
Production staff: Patrick Berry, Cheri Collins, John Cotterman, Bill Hartman, Dan Koeller, Dawne Sherman
Proofreaders: Martin Minner, Valeria Nasir

Second Edition 20 19 18 17 16 15 14 13 12 11 10
Printed in the United States of America

Ventana Press, Inc.
P.O. Box 13964
Research Triangle Park, NC 27709-3964
919/544-9404
FAX 919/544-9472

Limits of Liability and Disclaimer of Warranty

The author and publisher of this book have used their best efforts in preparing the book and the programs contained in it. These efforts include the development, research and testing of the theories and programs to determine their effectiveness. The author and publisher make no warranty of any kind, expressed or implied, with regard to these programs or the documentation contained in this book.

The author and publisher shall not be liable in the event of incidental or consequential damages in connection with, or arising out of, the furnishing, performance or use of the programs, associated instructions and/or claims of productivity gains.

Although the author and publisher of this book have consulted with staff of America Online, Inc. with regard to use and operation of the America Online® Service, this book is the work of the author and publisher, and not of America Online, Inc. America Online, Inc. makes no warrranty of any kind, express or implied, with regard to the accuracy, completeness, or usefulness of any information contained in this book. Users of the America Online Service should consult America Online Inc.'s Terms of Service (available online) for the complete provisions governing limitation of liability and disclaimer of warranties in connection with the use of the America Online Service.

Trademarks

About the Author

Tom Lichty recently retired to devote full-time energies to research and writing. He is author of six computer books, including *Design Principles for Desktop Publishers* (voted Book of the Year by the Computer Press Association in 1988), *America Online's Internet for Windows* and *The Official America Online Membership Kit & Tour Guide* (Windows and Macintosh versions). Tom lives at the base of Oregon's Mount Hood, where he specializes in the design, desktop publishing and online communications fields of the computer industry. His Internet mailing address is majortom@aol.com.

Acknowledgments

Oh sure, I want to acknowledge people like Laura Bader, Tim Barwick, Mary Daffron, George Louie, Luis Montel, Bill Hartman, Marshall Rens, Pam Richardson, Kelly Richmond, Kathy Ryan, Matt Triplet, Matt Wagner and Elizabeth & Joe Woodman: they're the heart and soul of this book's production and editorial teams and without their assistance there would be no book.

Special thanks goes to Jennifer Watson, who coordinated the update of this book with expedience, professionalism and aplomb. Santa never had a better elf.

Most of all I want to acknowledge the thousands of readers (nearly 5000 at last count) who have written to me with comments and suggestions for improvements to the first edition. I read every message, and many of the suggestions are woven into this book's manuscript. Thus, this book is truly a community project. We all have reason to be proud of that.

—Tom Lichty

Contents

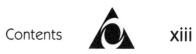

Foreword

I first got interested in online services in the early 1980s. I didn't know much about them then, but I knew enough to realize that they had a lot of potential. So when I bought my first personal computer in 1982, I decided to buy a modem and get online. This proved to be a very frustrating experience. It took me several months before I had all the equipment properly configured and was able to connect for the first time. Once I got connected, I found the services themselves hard to use and expensive. Nevertheless, despite all the hassles and shortcomings, I thought it was amazing that such a wealth of information and services were out there, waiting to be tapped into.

That was more than a decade ago. When we founded America Online, Inc., our objective was simple: to make online services more accessible, more affordable, more useful and more fun for people like you and me. America Online now serves more than a million customers and is the nation's fastest-growing online service.

Our success has been driven by a constant focus on making the power of online services accessible to everyone. In designing America Online, we worked hard to make it very easy to use. We didn't want people to have to read a book in order to get connected, so we made the software easy to install and easy to use. As a result, people are usually up and running with America Online in less than 15 minutes.

Although we've done a good job of making the process of connecting to America Online hassle-free, we still have a problem: once you're connected, what do you do? America Online has grown so quickly, and now contains so many different services, finding the services that best meet your specific needs can be a bit of a challenge.

That's where this book comes in. Think of it as your personal tour guide, helping you get the most out of America Online. It highlights a wide range of useful and fun services, so you can begin enjoying America Online immediately. After you're comfortable with the basics, it will take you to the next step by explaining some of the more advanced capabilities that are built into the service.

When Ventana Press first contacted us about publishing an America Online book, we thought it was a great idea. Our members had been asking for a book for some time, so we knew there was interest. And we felt that by working with an independent publisher, we'd end up with a better book than if we tried to write it ourselves.

Ventana's choice of Tom Lichty as the author was inspired. Tom had written a number of popular computer books, so he knew how to communicate information in an interesting and humorous manner. (A lot of computer books are deathly dull; Tom's are funny and engaging.) And since Tom was a novice user of online services, we felt his insightful observations as a novice would help others get the most out of America Online.

When the first edition of this Tour Guide was published in 1992, it got raves from readers, so this new, expanded version—highlighting our broader array of services (including Internet access), and introducing you to our new Main Menu and multimedia look—is certain to be even more popular.

As you'll soon discover, America Online is more than easy-to-use software and a collection of useful and fun services. It's a living, breathing "electronic community" that comes alive because thousands of people all across the country don't just passively read the information that scrolls by on their screens, they get involved and participate, exchanging ideas on hundreds of topics. We provide the basic framework; beyond, that, America Online is shaped by the collective imagination of its participants.

A new interactive communications medium is emerging, and it will change the way we inform, educate, work and play. America Online is at the forefront of this exciting revolution. Come join us, as we work together to shape this new medium.

Steve Case, President, America Online, Inc.
AOL E-Mail Address: SteveCase

CHAPTER 1

Starting the Tour

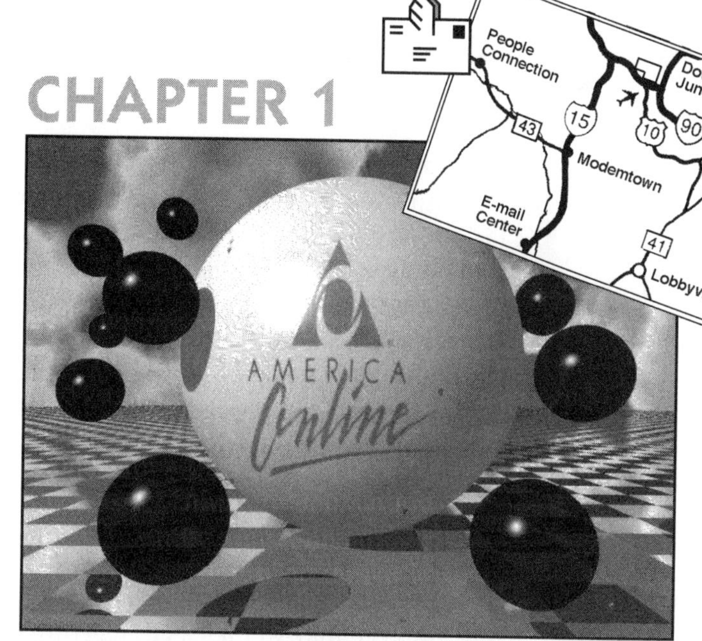

I'll never forget my first visit to the San Diego Zoo. I took the whole family. The cabby who drove us there told us to take the tour bus immediately upon arrival. After that, he reasoned, we would have an idea of how the zoo was organized and know what exhibits we would want to visit. We took his advice and hopped on the bus first thing.

The San Diego Zoo's buses are of the double-decker variety, and we sat on the top deck, baronially surveying the fauna below. The tour guide—wise San Diegan that he was—sat down below, out of the sun and away from the family of miscreants who shared the top deck with us, littering it with profanity, malcontent children and various artificially sweetened beverages. We never saw the tour guide, but we heard him. In anticipation of the Odious Family Robinson, the zoo had installed a megaphonelike loudspeaker on the top deck that immersed us in tsunamis of sound capable of drowning out not only the complaints of small children, but the bellows of elephants and screeches of orangutans alike. We left the tour at the first stop, wondering if our insurance covered auditory prosthetics.

With that preamble, allow me to welcome you to the *America Online Tour Guide*. I have good news: you won't encounter any orangutans, megaphones or tickets on this tour. You won't even see a bus. No signs will warn you to keep your hands and feet inside, and artificially sweetened beverages are permitted.

Frontispiece graphic: "Fantasy AOL Spheres," by Gwydian (Mike Wiseman). Use the keywords: File Search and then the criterion: AOLSPHER.GIF.

You can take this tour without ever leaving home or fraternizing with miscreants; and though I'm a tour guide, I'm here for your singular employ. I will endeavor to inform, entertain and enlighten—forever vigilant and always *sotto voce*. When the tour has concluded, you're welcome to explore on your own, secure in your familiarity with the territory and the attractions therein.

Best of all, the territory we're about to explore is every bit as diverse and wondrous as the San Diego Zoo. It's always at your fingertips, and about the most threatening creature you'll find here is a mouse.

What Is America Online?

This question isn't as easy as it seems. A term like "America Online" doesn't give many clues as to its composition. We can safely deduce its country of origin (it's in America, all right: Vienna, VA, to be exact—just outside Washington, DC; see Figure 1-1). But what's this "online" business? The word's not even in the dictionary.

Figure 1-1: America Online nestles snugly in this office building in the Virginia forests just outside Washington, DC.

You can define America Online in many ways. It is, after all, a great many things. It offers abundant resources: the latest news, weather reports, stock quotes, movie and book reviews, databases to research things as diverse as wine or hardware prices, online discussions of everything from politics to system software—even a service for reserving airline tickets, rental cars and hotel rooms.

America Online (AOL) is also an electronic mail (e-mail) service. You can use AOL to exchange e-mail with nearly anyone who uses e-mail, regardless of whether they are a fellow AOL member. If they don't use e-mail, you can use AOL to send them a fax. If they don't use fax, you can use AOL to send them printed mail via the US Postal Service.

America Online is an Internet gateway. The Internet is a vast superset of AOL itself, incorporating thousands of other communications systems from around the world similar to AOL. The extent of a thousand AOLs is almost incomprehensible, but that's what the Internet is, and AOL offers an elegant way of getting there.

America Online is also a community. In Chapter 9, "Entertainment," I compare AOL to the small Oregon town where I live. People are friendly here. They say hello when they pass you on the street, they invite you to their house for a chat, and they go out of their way to be of assistance. AOL does all these things: Instant Messages allow people who are online at the same time to say hello and hold "passing on the street" conversations; Chat Rooms are electronic "rooms"—public or private—where groups of members hold real-time conversations about subjects of their choosing; and Members Helping Members is a message board where members help one another with questions regarding AOL.

But how does all this communication take place? I can recall when I bought my first CD player. It offered more features than a 1973 Cadillac, and it sounded like the Boston Symphony on the bridge of my nose.

At first I was enamored with its technology. CDs were new to me. The player's booming bass and crisp treble commanded my respect; its aurora borealis of indicator lights illuminated my curiosity, and its scores of controls rivaled those of the Starship Enterprise. In the end, however, it's the music I enjoy. Mozart, Haydn, Vivaldi—these are my companions, and I treasure their company the most.

America Online is much the same. At first, ignoring the technology is difficult, but AOL is people—and in the end, you will treasure their company the most.

I am going to pursue the definition of AOL much as one might pursue any new technological acquisition. Over the next few pages, we'll allow its technology to dazzle us, but in the end it will be the community—the people who await us on AOL—who are the true reward.

It's a Telecommunications Service

Now there's a polysyllabic mouthful: "telecommunications." As the term is used here, telecommunications refers to two-way communications via telephone lines. A phone call, in other words, is a form of telecommunicating. Telephone lines are good for things other than phone calls. Fax machines use telephone lines to transfer documents; video phones use them to transmit pictures; and *modems* use them to transfer computer data (more about modems in the next chapter). I'm not talking about expensive, dedicated telephone lines here—I'm talking about the very same telephone lines that are already in our homes and offices.

Now we're getting somewhere. If you have a computer and I have a computer and we each have modems, we can use our existing telephone lines to connect our computers to one another. Once connected this way, our computers can exchange data: text, graphics, sounds, animation—even other computer programs.

Of course, you have to be at your computer and I have to be at mine—at the same time—and we have to know how to make our computers talk to one another, and we have to check for errors encountered in the transmission, and I'm just me and you're just you, and there's only so much computer data two people can exchange with one another before the whole thing gets to be pretty dull.

What we need is a *service* that will store our data so that we don't have to be at our computers at the same time. Instead of calling your computer, I have my computer call the service and store my data and messages there. When you're ready for that data, you can instruct your computer to call the service and retrieve the data at your convenience.

As long as we're imagining a service, we might imagine it to automate all the electronic technicalities as well. If we imagine it right, the service can mediate communications between the two computers, check for errors (and fix them when they're encountered) and even dial the telephone.

And who's to say that you and I should have the service all to ourselves? We can let everyone else with a computer in on it as well, regardless of the type of computer they own. Carried to its extreme, this scenario might result in hundreds of thousands—millions, actually—of people utilizing the service, exchanging and storing thousands of computer files. Most of this data can be public rather than private, so the exchange becomes multilateral.

Which is precisely what telecommunications services—and AOL—are: a vast network of "members," each of whom uses a computer, a modem and a telephone line to connect with a common destination—to "go online." Members can exchange public and private files; they can send and receive e-mail; and members who are online at the same time can "chat" in real time—they can even play online games with one another.

And what does this service cost? The economies of scale allow expenses to be distributed among the members. Moreover, even though AOL is near Washington, DC, few members pay for long-distance calls. America Online has local telephone numbers in nearly every city in the contiguous United States. Even if you live in the sticks, chances are you can find a local number you can call, or one that's a "short" long-distance call away.

It's One Big Thunder-Lizard Computer

Another way of defining AOL is by describing its hardware. Coordinating thousands of simultaneous phone calls and storing tens of thousands of files requires one Thunder Lizard of a computer complex. No little Stegosaurus will do. We're talking Brontosaurus here, a beastie who relocates continents whenever he gets the urge to sneeze. Forget prefixes like kilo and mega. Think giga and terra. When they turn on the power to this thing, lights dim all along the Eastern seaboard.

Open Architecture

I hate to disappoint you, but America Online isn't a single Brontosaurus-sized mainframe; it is, in fact, a number of refrigerator-sized computers, each having more in common with the adaptable Velociraptor than a leviathan as benign as the Brontosaurus.

Figure 1-2: A few of the many systems that comprise the heartbeat of America Online. A number of manufacturer's products are represented here, each selected on the basis of its suitability to a specific task. The homogenization factor is open architecture, which allows all of these diverse systems to work in concert.

By employing a technique called open architecture, AOL is able to utilize hardware, software and communications systems from a variety of manufacturers, each optimized for a specific task. America Online's open architecture permits it to use the most powerful hardware running the fastest software. The open communication architecture runs on the fastest local area and the most powerful wide area networks. The open architecture is AOL's key to the scalability it needs to keep up with its meteoric growth and the unpredictable mutations of the telecommunications industry.

Common Carriers

If you wanted to send a package to a friend across the country, you could probably hop in your car and drive it there yourself. Compared to the alternatives, driving across the country would be a perilous journey and would cost a fortune.

More likely, you'd hire a *common carrier*—a service such as United Parcel Service or FedEx—to deliver the package for you. For a fraction of what it would cost you to do the job yourself, common carriers can do it more reliably, less expensively and much more conveniently.

For much the same reason, AOL hires common carriers to deliver goods to its members. And typical of AOL, it hires multiple common carriers to ensure reliability. SprintNet, a service of US Sprint, is the common carrier AOL most often uses in the United States. (Figure 1-3 shows SprintNet equipment at AOL.) Datapac, a subsidiary of Bell Canada, serves Canadian members. These common carriers offer *nodes*—local telephone numbers—in most cities in North America. They charge AOL for phone calls (placed or received) just as FedEx would charge you to deliver a package.

Figure 1-3: High-speed telecommunications equipment in use at America Online Headquarters.

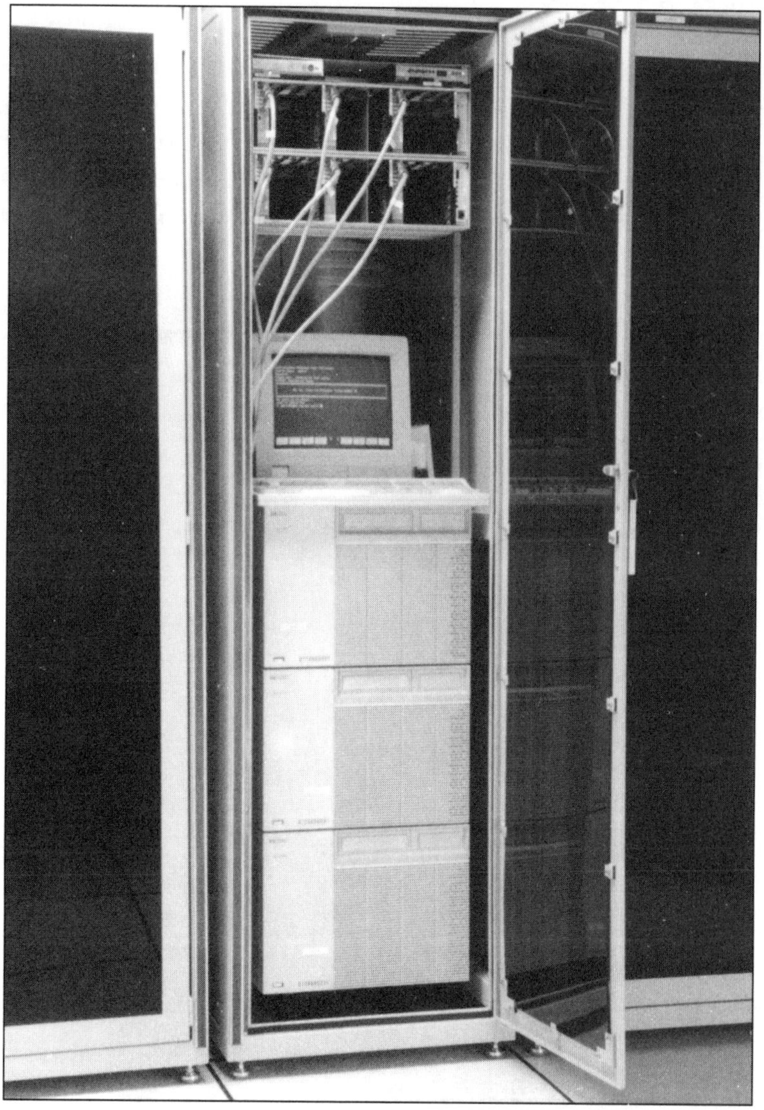

Again, the economies of scale operate to our advantage. Thousands of clients, of which AOL is only one, use these long-distance providers. Chances are when you're not using one of your local nodes, some corporate computer is phoning data to a parent mainframe in New Jersey or Chicago. The cost of this service is so insignificant that it's covered by your membership. No matter how many hours you're online per month, AOL never charges extra for the call. Indeed, the only connect charges are to those few members who have to make a long-distance call to reach a node.

It's Software Installed In Your Computer

Conceptualizing AOL as nodes and mainframe computers isn't very comforting. America Online is much more parochial than that. For many of us, AOL is software in our PCs—software that arrived on that little disk provided in The Official America Online Membership Kit. (Figure 1-4 shows the AOL logo.)

Figure 1-4: America Online's logo appears whenever you run the software installed on your PC.

That's more like it. The software you use on your PC to sign on to AOL more accurately represents the personality of the service than anything we've discussed so far. It makes noises, it's resplendent with windows and icons, and it automates those tasks and procedures that formerly were responsible for excluding most semi-normal people from using an online service.

Here's what I mean. Nearly every telecommunications program assumes you know how to set certain arcane but necessary attributes and protocols such as data bits, stop bits, parity or flow. Frankly, although I've used telecommunications software for years and though I have adjusted my data bits and parity, I have no idea what they are, and I have always been kind of nervous about shooting in the dark like that. America Online, on the other hand, uses its own custom software at both ends of the line. After you install the software on your PC (a simple process I describe in the next chapter), all the technicalities are coordinated by the host computer and your PC. They simply talk things over and make adjustments as required. This is as it should be. People shouldn't be asked to do these things; that's why we have machines. America Online's software simply has no controls for setting data bits, stop bits, parity or flow (see Figure 1-5). It's all taken care of for you.

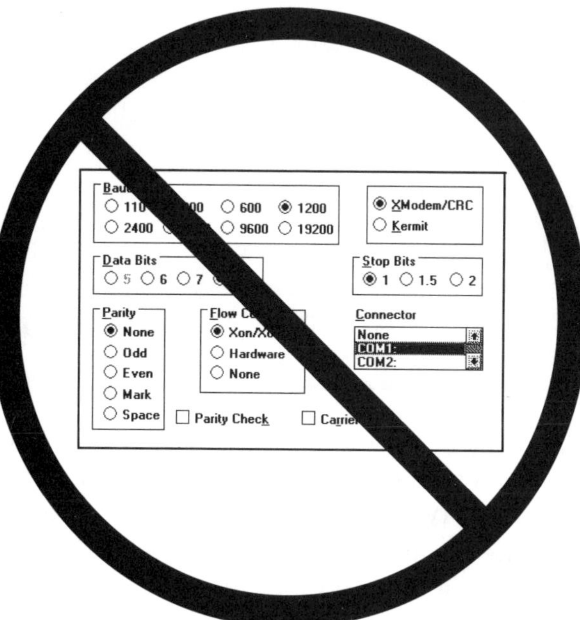

Figure 1-5: America Online's software never asks you to set (or even think about) data bits, stop bits, parity or flow.

Amazingly, the software is self-configuring. Whenever you sign on, a behind-the-scenes dialog transpires between your PC and the host computer. In effect, your PC says, "Hey host computer! Do you have any new features I should know about?" If new features are available, your PC requests them from the host computer and adds them to its version of the local software (the copy of AOL that resides on your hard drive). This capability is significant: at any point, AOL can add features to the service and incorporate them immediately. No new software releases have to be sent out. No interminable decimal places have to be added to the version number. That convenience means the AOL staff can add features whenever they please. No disk duplication and mass mailings are required. Upgrade costs to you are nonexistent, and they hardly amount to anything at AOL either. America Online's staff operates in an environment that encourages, rather than stifles, improvement. Perhaps best of all, you don't have to lift a finger to take advantage of whatever changes or additions AOL makes to its service. Just sign on as usual, and you immediately have the most recent version available. (See Figure 1-6.)

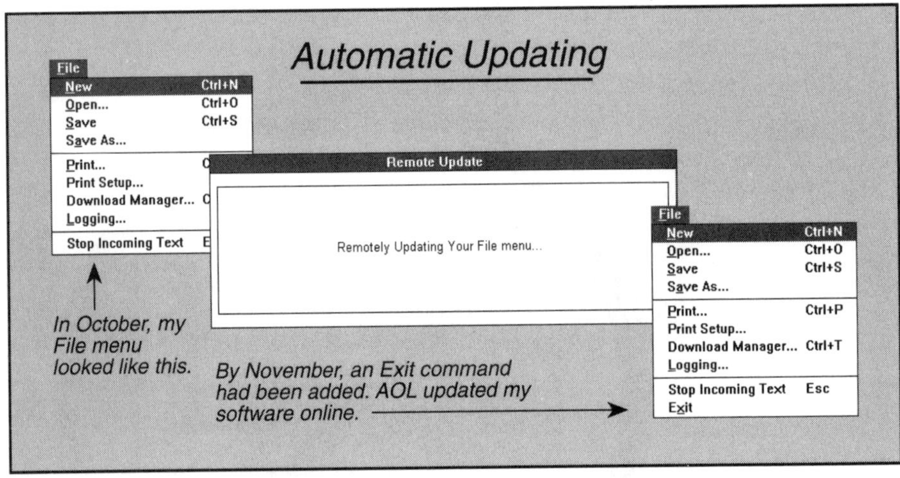

Figure 1-6: In November of 1992, during the early testing periods of the Windows software, AOL added the Exit command to the File menu. The update took place automatically and online. No disks were sent out. No costs were incurred. AOL simply got better.

We're getting closer to the mark. The phrase "user-friendly" is properly used to describe this service. America Online's Windows software is real Windows software: familiar, predictable and comfortable. The File menu says Open, Save, Close and Exit. Its windows have title bars and minimize buttons. It even takes advantage of all those esoteric Windows commands, such as Cascading and Minimizing.

Another unique aspect of the AOL for Windows software is its interface and communication strategy. Though it's highly graphical, none of those graphical elements are transferred to your PC online. Transferring graphics online takes time—much more than transferring text, for instance—which could make the service as sluggish as a hound in July. Instead, all of AOL's graphical components are stored on your hard disk. Only text is transferred. This capability makes AOL much faster than other graphically oriented services and saves you money in connect-time charges.

Here's the point: AOL is an advanced and aggressive telecommunications service that grows daily, and contains the features necessary to accommodate that growth. The software features I described previously reflect a progressive attitude, and that attitude is a better way of defining AOL.

It's a Resource

News, sports, weather—sure you can get them on radio and television, but not necessarily when you need or want them. You can get them in a newspaper, too; but it's going to cost the environment a tree or two, the pictures are fuzzy, and about all you can do with a newspaper you've read is throw it away (consult the Environmental Forum—clubs are described in Chapter 13, "Clubs & Interests"—for recycling information). America Online offers the news, sports and weather as well, available at your convenience and without sacrificing any trees. It's in electronic form, too; so you can file it, search it and include it in documents of your own.

This past winter, I kept tabs on China's nuclear testing in Today's News (discussed in Chapter 6), tracked the meager investments in my portfolio (discussed in Chapter 10, "Personal Finance") and monitored the progress of the Israeli/Palestinian peace accord while browsing the Newsstand (discussed in Chapter 7). I researched the purchase of a new hard disk for my computer in the Marketplace (discussed in Chapter 17) and actually bought that hard disk using Comp-U-Store. I booked both airplane and auto rentals for a trip to New Mexico using EAASY SABRE (discussed in Chapter 11, "Travel"). I constantly search the online video reviews before I rent a tape (the Entertainment Department is discussed in Chapter 9), and I check Wine & Dine Online (Chapter 13, "Clubs & Interests") for recommendations before I hazard the racks of wines at the shop down the street. Past issues of *PC World*,

National Geographic and *Smithsonian*, and even *CNN* are online for my review, as is *Compton's Encyclopedia* and the Gray Lady: the *New York Times*. I recently sold my old car after consulting AutoVantage (described in Chapter 17). As a professional member of the desktop publishing community, I constantly collect graphics (AOL has thousands of files online—described in Chapter 5, "Computing"; also see Figure 1-7), fonts (see Figure 1-8) and utilities, and the Desktop Publishing Resource Center is one of my favorite haunts.

In other words, you could describe AOL as a resource of almost infinite potential. You don't have to drive anywhere to use it; it's continuously maintained and updated; and it's all electronic—available for any use you can imagine. Many members find the resource potential alone ample justification for signing on to AOL, but to limit your participation this way would be a disservice to AOL and to yourself. Above all, AOL is people: friends, associates, consultants—even lovers. It's a resource all right, but it's also a community, and therein lies its greatest value.

It's a Community

I've taken the easy way out. Yes, AOL is a telecommunications service. Yes, it's the host computer. Yes, it's software in your PC; and yes, it's a resource. But that's like saying that Christmas is just another day of the year. There's much more to it than that. Christmas is reverence and good things; but for many of us, Christmas means people: family, friends and community. What really defines AOL is its people, as well. America Online is a *community*. My dictionary defines community as, "A social group sharing common characteristics or interests," and that is the best definition I can imagine for AOL.

As members, we have common interests, we all have computers, and we love to share. *That's* what AOL is all about. After a few weeks, the novelty of interconnection and graphical images wears off. After a few weeks, we stop wondering about the host computer and data bits. After a few weeks, we all discover the true soul of AOL, and that soul is its people.

Figure 1-7: Just a few of the over 25,000 graphics available in America Online's file libraries. ("Lise2," by David Palermo; "Dragonfly," from the Graphics Forum; and "High Tech Laurel & Hardy," by Lou Moccia.)

A Graphics Gold Mine

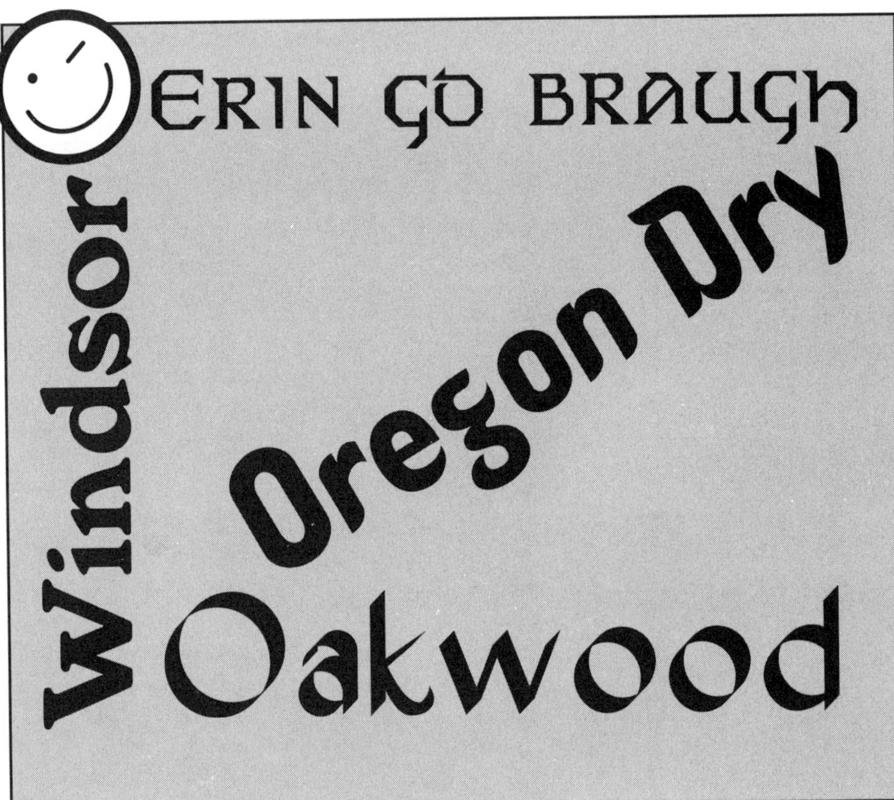

Figure 1-8: A quintet of fonts, all downloaded from the Desktop Publishing Resource Center. At top, Eire is by Paul Glomski; Oregon Dry is by Pat Snyder; Jim Pearson's Oakwood ProFont is particularly elegant; Brian Hendrix's Windsor is a traditional, Old World font; and Jonathan Macagba's Smiley Face is great for illuminating e-mail. Most are shareware and cost about $5 each.

When I first signed on to write this book, community was the last thing on my mind. I have been a telecommunicator for years. I thought I'd seen it all. Now, however, I spend as much of my online time corresponding with friends—new friends in every part of the country—as I do conducting research. In Chapter 4, I admit to getting despondent if I don't hear the familiar mail notification when the Welcome screen comes up. Throughout this book, I'll offer little tips on how to make friends online; follow these tips, and you'll become as much a part of this community as I am.

You really couldn't do much better.

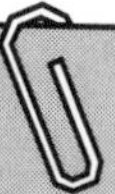

Steve Case

I have never asked AOL President Steve Case where he lives. It would surprise and disappoint me to learn that he doesn't live in the suburbs: Steve Case is a character study of the suburban next-door neighbor. He's a clean-cut, casual guy. He wears rumpled chinos, cotton sportshirts and no tie. He looks as if he's about to mow the lawn. He took me to lunch at the Ringmaster's Pub in the Barnum and Bailey building next door. (America Online's building is next door to the world headquarters of the Ringling Brothers Circus.) We had iced tea and sandwiches. That's Steve's idea of a business lunch.

Steve's personality is reflected everywhere at AOL. I've never seen a necktie or a closed office door during my visits there. More important, the people in the AOL offices reflect the spirit of community. They never use titles. No one wears ID badges, not even guests. Everyone calls everyone else by his or her first name. Conferences happen in hallways.

Steve's eyes sparkle when the conversation turns to community. He sends e-mail to every new member and hopes for a reply. He's the president of the company, yet he spends as much time conversing with members as he does with his staff. Everyone calls him Steve.

With Steve Case steering the ship, AOL remains, foremost, a community. All corporate decisions are based on that concept; every change benefits the community. That's the way Steve wants it to be. If he could have his way, he'd have us all out to Virginia for a barbecue on the green. You'd know who he was the moment you got there: he'd be the one turning burgers on the grill. You couldn't ask for a better neighbor.

How To Use This Book

The America Online Tour Guide serves two purposes: 1) it's the official documentation for the use of America Online; and 2) it's a guidebook for the explorer. As documentation, the book should be thoroughly indexed, strictly organized and pithy. As a guide, the book should offer entertainment, insight and advice. These goals are somewhat disparate, but not necessarily incompatible.

Fortunately, the people at AOL have an altruistic attitude toward the documentation for their service. *The America Online Tour Guide* is a book, not a manual. I'm an independent author, not a staff technical writer. And AOL chose a traditional publisher—Ventana Press—to produce and distribute this book; it's not an AOL production. I therefore have the autonomy and elbow room to explore the subject with you independently, thoroughly and candidly. The people at AOL are to be commended for their courage in choosing this path. It could be perilous. Confidence in their product, however, emboldens them, and rightfully so.

How To Use This Book as Documentation

As you no doubt already know, documentation can be dull. Few people take a software manual to the hammock for a lazy afternoon of reading. The universe of technical documentation is far from the universe AOL inhabits. America Online is diverse, abstract and personable—hardly documentation material. Nonetheless, I've included a number of organizational and reference tools to serve the documentation need.

Finding Answers

I want you to be able to turn to *The America Online Tour Guide* whenever you have a question about AOL. I want you to be able to find the answer to your question with a minimum of effort, no matter how many different places the subject may appear in the book. Pursuant to that, a number of tools are at your disposal:

- The *table of contents* lists titles, section heads and subheads for every chapter. When you need information on a specific subject, turn first to the table of contents. Nine times out of ten, it will be all you need.
- A thorough *index* appears at the end of the book, with references to subjects, procedures and departments. If the subject you're after doesn't appear in the table of contents, turn to the index.
- A listing of primary *keywords* is the first appendix item. Keywords are the interstate highway system at AOL. If you want to get somewhere in a hurry, use a keyword. As you discover places that appeal to you, grab your yellow pen and highlight the keyword corresponding to that location. Eventually, you'll commit a number of keywords to memory (or place them on your Go To menu, a process described in Chapter 13, "Clubs & Interests"), and the keyword appendix will have served its purpose.

- A *listing of Control-key combinations* follows the keywords list. Few people memorize every Control-key combination for every program they use, but most people memorize some. If you're an occasional (or frequent) user of Control keys (or if you'd like to learn a few shortcuts that will cut down on mouse use), refer to Appendix B of the book.
- A *glossary* of terms used in the book follows the appendices. The glossary is especially thorough in its inclusion of telecommunications terminology. I may never define "parity" in the text—with AOL, you never have to bother with it—but I want you to be able to find out what it means if you're curious.

Departmental Listings

Starting with Chapter 5, each chapter explores a department available online at AOL. If Entertainment is your game (forgive the pun), read Chapter 9. If you're interested in the Computing Department, read Chapter 5. America Online is infinitely too large and diverse to explore these departments thoroughly. Instead, I've attempted to capture the personality of each department with glimpses into a few areas of particular interest. Wherever possible, I offer insight into the department's features: where to find the really good stuff.

Subject Listings

Departments are also vehicles for exploring specific subject areas. In Chapter 13, I introduce the concept of the forum; in Chapter 5, we explore the subject of downloading. These subjects can be complex, and to document them without some relief could be as dry as white bread. Instead, I've made a sandwich of each technical subject, flavoring the presentation with the diversity of a department. This approach, I hope, will make for more effective documentation: if you're enjoying yourself, you'll learn more about the subject. Associating subjects with departments also provides a context that's practical rather than theoretical; learning by doing is always more effective than listening to a lecture.

A Documentation Strategy

My personal strategy for the use of software documentation is to first spend a half-hour browsing. With no specific need and in no particular order, I just thumb through the manual, trying to get a feeling for its contents and organization. I look for organizational signposts (chapter titles, icons, sidebars, heads and subheads); I peek at the index; I read a paragraph or two from sections that strike my fancy. This kind of random orientation buoys my confidence and orients my perspective.

If you're a new member and haven't yet installed the software or signed on, read Chapter 2, "Making the Connection," next. It's a "hand-holder," documenting every step of the installation and initial sign-on process. The chapter includes a suggested initial online session.

From then on—perhaps once a week—pick a department and tour it with me at your own pace. While we're there, we'll explore a procedural subject as well as the department itself. Each chapter should take about an hour. When we're finished, you will not only be familiar with the department, you'll learn about a feature that will make your online experience more productive and fun.

How To Use This Book as a Book

I would be flattered if you would read this book for the pleasure of it. As I spend time on AOL, I'm struck by its diversity. Last night I spent an hour contemplating the universe on the Online Home Companion (my favorite forum—forums are described in Chapter 13). This afternoon I visited the Lobby for some companionship. Tonight I plan to attend a Rotunda event (which we explore in Chapter 12, "People Connection"). Online visits are often unstructured. Your rhythm is syncopated and your interests wander.

I have tried to organize this *Tour Guide* in much the same fashion. I have liberally splashed gobbets of material throughout the book, often with no other intention in mind than to relieve the page of textual tedium. I want your thoughts to wander; I want to pique your curiosity; I want to delight and provoke and intrigue you (see Figure 1-9). That's what AOL does: it discourages linearity and encourages randomness. It demands your regard and rewards your return.

I hope this book does the same.

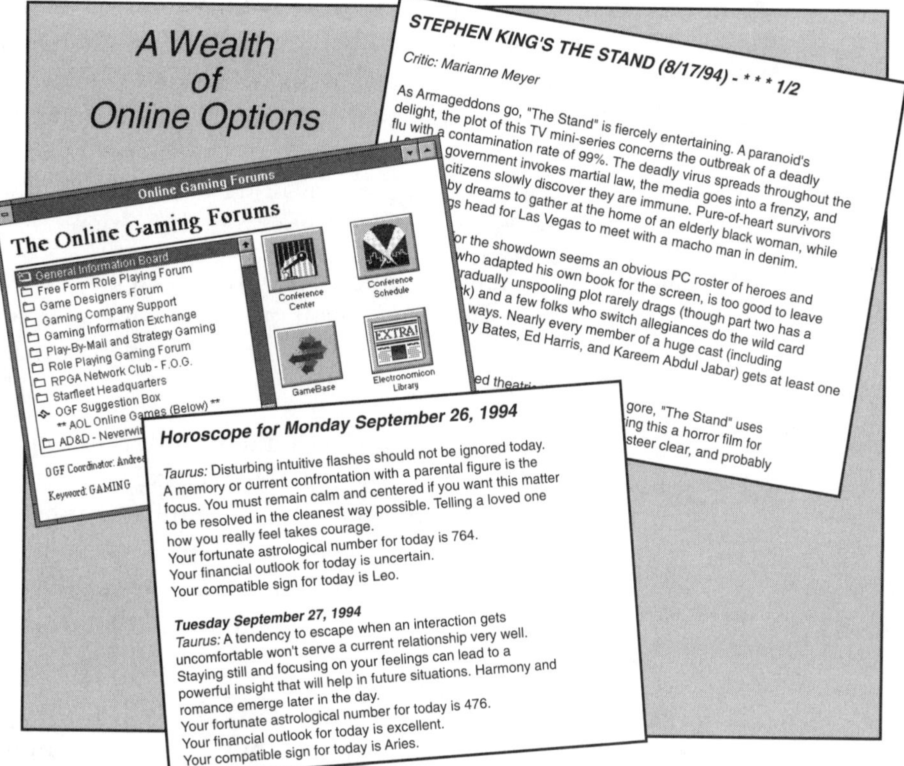

Figure 1-9: A video review, the title screen for the Online Gaming Forum and a daily horoscope. These examples are just a tiny slice of the spectrum of opportunity that awaits you on America Online.

Moving On

Are you comfortable? Our journey is about to begin. Reach into that pocket in the seat in front of you and pull out the program. Here's where we're about to go:

- Chapter 2, "Making the Connection," walks you through the setup and initial sign-on process. Just as it relieves you from worrying about the complexities of most of the other technical aspects of telecommunications, AOL automates most of the process of getting started as well, so Chapter 2 isn't too technical. You'll be up and running in no time.

- Chapter 3, "Online Help & the Members," serves as an introduction to the AOL software—especially all of its offers of help. We'll pull down menus and peek at dialog boxes. We'll do most of this work off line, but you'll need your PC (and a modem) handy. Eventually we'll sign on, visit the Lobby and get to know an online guide. Guides are usually there, waiting to help. We'll examine the members' directory and see if we can make a friend.
- Chapter 4 will teach you everything you need to know to master AOL's e-mail feature. We'll put some names into our Address Book, send (and receive) some mail, and attach a file to be uploaded to a friend.
- Chapter 5 goes for the heart: the Computing Department. We'll visit the Windows Forum, look over *PC World* magazine, catch up on the latest computing news and opinion, and solicit some assistance from a software vendor. Along the way, we'll explore the process of downloading files. We'll download a few for ourselves, decompress those that require it and perhaps upload a file in return.
- Chapter 6, "Today's News," reveals AOL's new news feature, including not only news, but business, entertainment, sports and weather. You can search them to find the stories of interest to you, and they're all updated on a continuing basis. We'll keep a log of our visit for review later, when we're off line and rested.
- Chapter 7 discusses the Newsstand. America Online features alliances with a number of contemporary magazines and newspapers, including *The Atlantic Monthly, Bicycling, Car & Driver, Consumer Reports, Chicago Tribune, San Jose Mercury, The New York Times, Time, Road & Track, Popular Photography, WIRED* and dozens of others. The Newsstand is where you'll find them all. You can search these articles too (including back issues), talk with the editors, and in many cases download the graphics that accompany the stories.
- Chapter 8 is dedicated to sports fans. In addition to baseball, basketball, football, hockey, tennis and golf, there are even games you can play yourself.

- Chapter 9, "Entertainment," is simply for the fun of it. We'll read a few movie reviews, peek at a cartoon or two, have a (virtual) beer at LaPub and play a game or two.
- Chapter 10 explores AOL's extensive Personal Finance Department. There we'll start our portfolio of investments (cash optional), consult Morningstar and Hoover's financial profiles, and consult Real Estate Online.
- Chapter 11 offers a break from the workaday world, as we visit the Travel Department. We'll consult the experts (and fellow travelers) before we plan our dream vacation, then we'll book our reservations and set up correspondence with other members before we leave.
- Chapter 12 explores People Connection. We'll wipe the sweat from our palms, walk into the Lobby and say hello. We'll check out a few of AOL's Chat Rooms and see who we can find there. Perhaps we'll visit the Center Stage and participate in a game show.
- Chapter 13, "Clubs & Interests," explores AOL's clubs. Perhaps we'll try Wine & Dine Online, the Environmental and Star Trek Forums, and BikeNet. We'll learn about forums, read a few messages and post one of our own.
- Chapter 14 introduces the Internet and AOL's "Internet Connection." In the telecommunications industry, AOL is to Walla Walla what the Internet is to the universe. Over 30 million people visit the Internet every day, downloading files, exchanging mail, and acquiring data. America Online is your key to this universe, *if* you know enough to keep from getting stuck in orbit. This chapter is your official Internet primer.
- Chapter 15 reveals one of the newest departments: "Kids Only." Prominent among the offerings is KOOL (Kids Only OnLine), but Disney is here, and KIDSNET, and games, and TIME for Kids.
- Chapter 16 is devoted to education. *Compton's Encyclopedia* is here, of course, but so is the Online Campus. Perhaps we'll enroll in a class, or enroll in a correspondence course through the International Correspondence Schools. We'll make a special visit to the Library of Congress as well.

- The Reference Desk is the subject of Chapter 17. The Career Center is here, along with Barron's Booknotes, the Bible and the CNN Newsroom.
- Chapter 18 introduces The Marketplace, where you can buy or sell anything from computers to cars. And *Consumer Reports* magazine—past issues and present—ensures an informed decision.
- Chapter 19 explores FlashSessions and the Download Manager. This chapter covers the heavyweight stuff, but it's also some of the best telecommunications software ever offered. Even if you never use it, you've got to read this chapter just to appreciate two of the high-end features AOL offers.
- Chapter 20 offers my ten best ten-best lists—the ten best tips for using AOL, the ten most frequently asked questions of the AOL customer support team, the ten best files for downloading—that kind of thing. You'll be among the online *illuminati* after you've finished this chapter.
- Five appendices conclude the book. A keyword listing offers warp-speed navigation through the AOL universe. The Control-key reference helps you Get It Done Fast; the Modems, Localities and CCL Files appendix is for the digitheads among us; an on-the-road reference serves those who take AOL to remote locations; and the Member's Preferences appendix shows you how to configure AOL just the way you want. At the end of the book, an extensive glossary defines all those cryptic terms that have become requisite adjuncts to the telecommunications lexicon.

You'd better fasten your seat belt. Sometimes the ride gets a little bumpy, and when I get to talking, I forget to steer—hand gestures and all that, you know. Don't worry: I haven't lost a passenger yet. Have your camera ready, you have lots of stuff to see. And relax. Smile a bit. You're five years old again and Christmas morning is only a turn of the page away....

CHAPTER 2

Making the Connection

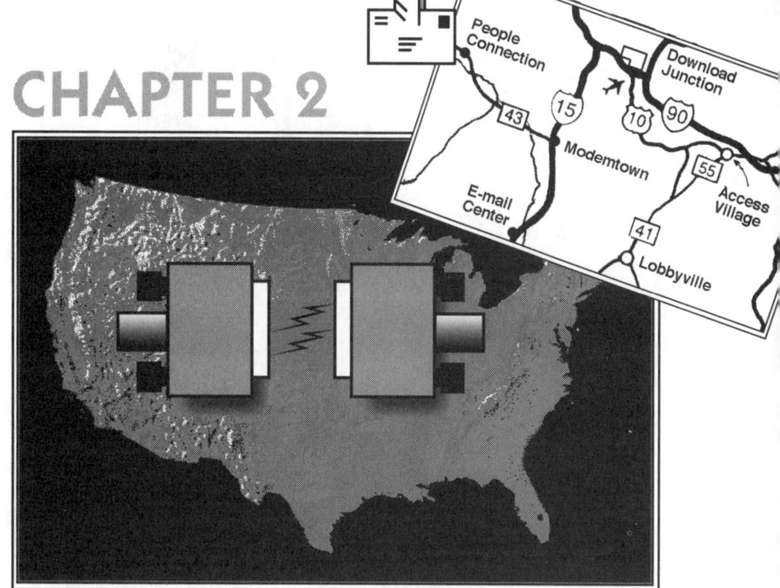

If you have never used America Online—if you have never even installed the software—this chapter's for you. It's written for the amateur, the novice—those who hold disks in their sweaty palms and wonder if they are stalwart enough to connect their PC to the outside world.

For most of us, computers are autonomous and independent. The only external device we've ever encountered is a printer. Our dialog with the computer has always been a singular one—isolated and solitary. We might personify our Macs. We might give them names and even voices, and we might think of their error messages and dialog boxes as communication, but we know better.

Computers don't think. Computers don't respond with imagination or indignation or intelligence. There are no threats to us here. Connecting to AOL will put human intelligence at the other end of the line. America Online isn't just a computer in Virginia named the host computer, it's people, and people online expect a dialog. People respond, with innovation and humor. This is not the isolation we have come to expect of our computers.

So far, our ordered universe has been predictable and familiar. Why mess with it?

Because there's more to life, that's why. Think of your first car, your first love, your first child. Each was shrouded in anxiety, and each was

---

Frontispiece terrain map by Gail P. Thelin and Richard J. Pike, published by the US Geological Survey. Superimposed are the connector icons from the AOL sign-on screen. The terrain map is online. Use the keyword: FileSearch, then search with the criterion: USGS.

resplendent with reward. We're talking about discovery here, and while the AOL opportunity might not rank with love and birth, it's an opportunity one should not deny.

Before you read any further, I want you to understand that this chapter describes the process of installing the AOL software and making the first connection with AOL itself. If you already have an established AOL account, then you probably won't need to read much of this chapter. Feel free to skim it or skip ahead to another part of the tour—I'll catch up with you soon enough.

Things You'll Need

Let's take inventory here. There are a few things you need before you can connect with America Online. No doubt you already have them, but let's be sure.

The Computer

You need a PC, of course. It has to be a 386 or better, capable of running Windows 3.1 or higher, which should already be installed and tested on your machine. A mouse is highly recommended too. Although most Windows programs operate without a mouse, doing so is like eating with your fingers: it's archaic, it's much more difficult than using the proper tool, and in many circles it's socially unacceptable.

You will need at least 4 megabytes of random access memory (4mb of RAM is Windows' minimum requirement) and a hard disk with 2.5mb of free space. You will also need a floppy disk drive capable of reading 3½-inch floppy disks. (If you purchased this Tour Guide as part of *The Official America Online Membership Kit,* a high-density 3½-inch AOL disk is included.)

Finally, a display system capable of displaying 256 colors is recommended. Your AOL software works with 16-color systems, but the presentation of the service is optimized for 256 colors. Refer to your Windows manual (or the manual for your video display adapter, if one is installed as an option) for information on how to change the number of colors your system displays.

I digressed. Essentially, any Windows-compatible machine will do. If yours isn't the latest model—if it doesn't have 435 horsepower and fuel injection and a 5-speed transmission—don't worry. The AOL software isn't picky. If computers were cars, AOL would run on a Yugo.

The Telephone Line

Speaking of telephone lines, you need one of those. Your standard residential phone line is fine. A multiline business telephone might be more of a challenge. What's really important is that your telephone plugs into a modular (RJ-11) telephone jack. It's the one with the square hole measuring about one-quarter inch on a side.

Whenever you're online, your telephone is out of commission. It's as if someone is on an extension phone, except that you'll never want to eavesdrop on an AOL session. The screeching sound that modems make when communicating with each other is about as pleasant as fingernails on a blackboard—and about as intelligible.

The Membership Kit

America Online membership kits come in a number of forms, but they all have two things in common: they include a disk and a certificate. *The America Online Membership Kit & Tour Guide* includes a disk, registration number and password in a little plastic pouch affixed to the inside back cover. Find the disk, the registration number and the password, and set them by your PC. Keep this book nearby as well.

Make a copy of the AOL disk right now. Use Windows' File Manager: the Copy Disk command is under the Disk menu. Once you've made the copy, put the original AOL disk away somewhere safe. You never know when you might need it again.

The Modem

A modem (short for *mo*dulator/*dem*odulator) is a device that converts computer data into audible tones that the telephone system can transmit. Modems are required at both ends of the line: the system at AOL's end has one too.

Modems are rated according to their data-transmission speed. If you're shopping for a modem, get one rated at 14,400 baud if you can. Modems rated at 14,400 baud are fast and are capable of extracting every bit of performance AOL has to offer. (If AOL doesn't offer 14,400-baud capability when you read this, be patient. It's in the works.) On the other hand, high-speed modems really only strut their stuff when you're downloading files (discussed in Chapter 19, "FlashSessions & the Download Manager"), and unless you do a lot of downloading you may never miss the higher speed. In other words, a 2400-baud modem might satisfy your needs if you don't plan on a lot of downloading. A 2400-baud modem, however, should be considered the minimum.

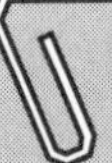

Baud Rates

The term *baud rate* refers to the signaling rate, or the number of times per second the signal changes. You might hear this term confused with *bits per second* (bps), which isn't entirely accurate. By using modern electronic wizardry, today's modems can transmit two, three, or four bits with each change of signal, increasing the speed of data transfer considerably. Since it takes eight bits to make a byte, a rate of 9600 bps means that anywhere between 1200 and 4800 bytes per second can be transferred. A byte is the amount of data required to describe a single character of text. In other words, a baud rate of 9600 should transmit at least 1200 characters—about 15 lines of text—per second.

Alas, the world is an imperfect place—especially the world of phone lines. If static or interference of any kind occurs on the line, data transmission is garbled. And even one misplaced bit can destroy the integrity of an entire file. To address the problem, AOL validates the integrity of received data. In plain English, this means that AOL sends a packet of information (a couple of seconds' worth) to your PC, then waits for the PC to say, "I got that!," before it sends the next packet. Validation like this means things run a little slower than they would without validation, but it's necessary. We're probably down to a minimum of 1000 characters per second once we factor in the time it takes to accommodate data validation.

Then there's noise. You've heard it: static on the line. If you think it interferes with voice communication, it's murder on data. Often your PC says, "That packet was no good—send it again," and AOL complies. The reliability of any particular telephone connection is capricious. Some are better than others. Noise, however, is a definite factor, and packets have to be re-sent once in a while. Now we're probably down to a minimum of 900 characters per second on a good telephone line on a good day—a little over 11 lines of text per second at 9600 bps.

In other words, a 14,400-bps modem isn't six times faster than a 2400-bps model, and a 2400-bps modem isn't twice as fast as one rated at 1200 bps. On the other hand, a 2400-bps modem doesn't cost twice as much as a 1200-bps model, and a 14,400-bps screamer doesn't cost six times as much as a 2400-bps pedestrian model. What I'm trying to say is in terms of baud per buck, 14,400 bps is your best buy.

I prefer modems with speakers and lights. Lights, of course, are only found on external modems, and external modems typically require an available serial port. If you have an internal modem, you won't need an available serial port (and you won't have any lights to watch). My modem has six or seven lights. I don't understand most of them, but they look important. The one marked RD (receiving data) is worth watching when you are downloading a file. It should stay on almost continuously. If, during a download, your RD light is off more often than it's on, you've got a noisy phone line or the system is extremely busy. Whatever the cause, it's best to halt the download (AOL always leaves a Finish Later button on the screen for that purpose) and resume it another time. That's why I advise buying a modem with lights: if you don't have them, how can you tell what's going on?

A number of PCs now offer internal modems: modems inside the PC itself. If you have an internal modem, you won't tie up a com port on the back of your PC (leaving it available for some other purpose), but you won't have any lights to watch either. Life is full of compromises.

If your modem is the external variety, it will need power of some kind. Some external modems use batteries, but most use AC power and plug into the wall. Be sure a socket is available.

Most important, be sure you have the proper cables. You need two: one to connect the modem to the PC (if the modem is external) and another to connect the modem to the phone jack. The modem-to-phone-jack cable bundled with many modems rarely exceeds six feet. If the distance between your modem and your phone jack exceeds that distance, you can buy an extension cable at a phone, electronics or hardware store. Extension cables are standard equipment and are inexpensive.

Few external modems include a PC-to-modem cable. You will probably have to purchase one if you're buying an external modem. Check your modem's manual to see if your modem requires a hardware-handshaking cable. If it does, it's essential that you use one, as it provides a more reliable connection at high speed.

You will also need the continued use of your phone, and will need to make some provision for that. It's less complicated if the modem has a jack for your phone. In that case, you can plug the modem into the phone jack, then plug the phone into the modem. The jacks on the back of the modem should be marked for this.

If your modem is internal, or if your external modem only has a single jack, and you want to continue using your phone as well as your modem, you might want to invest in a modular splitter, which plugs into the phone jack on your wall, making two jacks out of one. You plug your phone into one of the splitter's jacks and your modem into the other. Plugging both devices into the same jack won't interfere with everyday telephone communications; incoming calls will continue to go to your phone, just as they did before. You should be able to find a splitter at a phone, electronics or hardware store for less than $3.

If all this sounds like a lot of wires to keep track of and you have trouble plugging in a toaster, don't worry. Most modems come with good instructions, and the components are such that you can't connect anything backwards. Just follow the instructions and you'll be fine.

The Money

Before you sign on to AOL for the first time, there's something else you'll need: money. America Online wants to know how you plan to pay the balance on your account each month. Cash won't do. Instead, you can provide a credit-card number: Visa, MasterCard, American Express or Discover Card are all acceptable. So are many bank debit cards. Or have your checkbook handy: AOL can have your bank automatically transfer the funds if you provide the necessary numbers.

The Screen Name

We're almost ready, but right now I want you to get all other thoughts out of your mind and decide what you want to call yourself. Every AOL member has a unique screen name. Screen names are how AOL tells us apart. You must have one and it has to be different from anybody else's.

A screen name must be three to ten characters in length—letters or numbers. Hundreds of thousands of people use AOL, and they all have screen names of ten or fewer characters. Chances are the screen name you want most is taken, so have a number of alternates ready ahead of time, and prepare yourself for disappointment. Hardly anyone ever gets his or her first choice.

There's no going back, by the way. Once AOL accepts your initial screen name, it's yours as long as you remain a member. Although your account can have as many as five screen names (to accommodate other people in your family or your alter egos), your initial screen name is the one AOL uses to establish your identity. For this reason, your initial screen name can't be changed. Be prepared with a zinger (and a half-dozen alternates), or AOL will assign you something like TomLi5437, and you'll forever be known by that name. People have a hard time relating to a name like that.

MajorTom

I worked my way through college as a traffic reporter for an Oregon radio station. I was both reporter and pilot. It was a great job: perfect hours for a student, easy work and unlimited access to a flashy plane. It didn't pay much, but somehow that wasn't important—not in the halcyon days of bachelorhood.

I hate to date myself, but David Bowie was an ascending force on the music scene in those days. Impertinent, perhaps—a little too androgynous and scandalous for the conservative element of the Nixon era—but definitely a hit-maker. Our station played Bowie. On my first day, the morning-show disk jockey switched on his microphone and hailed "Ground Control to Major Tom"—a line from Bowie's *Space Oddity*—to get my attention. The name stuck. I was known as Major Tom from then on.

When the time came for me to pick my AOL screen name, it suggested TomLi5437 and I balked. How about just plain Tom? I asked. It's in use, said AOL. I tried four others and AOL continued to remind me of my lack of imagination. In desperation I tried MajorTom, and AOL accepted it. Once an initial screen name is accepted, there's no going back. I'm MajorTom on AOL now, and I will be forever more.

The Password

Oh yes, you need a password. Without a password, anyone knowing your screen name can log on using that name and have a heyday on your nickel. Passwords must be from four to eight characters in length, and any combination of letters or numbers is acceptable. You're asked for your password every time you sign on, so choose something easy for you to remember—something that's not a finger-twister to type. It should be different from your screen name, phone number, Social Security number, address or real name—something no one else would ever guess, even if they know you well.

A Case for Elaborate Passwords

In his book *The Cuckoo's Egg,* Cliff Stoll describes computer hackers' methods for breaking passwords. Since most computers already have a dictionary on disk—all spelling checkers use dictionaries—the hackers simply program their computers to try every word in the dictionary as a password. It sounds laborious, but computers don't mind. (Cliff Stoll and *The Cuckoo's Egg* are mentioned again in Chapter 3, "Electronic Mail." Look in the bibliography for the specifics on his book.)

In other words, I'm making a case for elaborate passwords here. Don't make it personal, don't use your Social Security number, don't write it down, and select something that's not in a dictionary. That'll foil the rascals.

Installing the Software

Finally, we're ready to get our hands dirty. Installing the AOL software is a straightforward process, since an installation program does all the work for you.

- Again, be sure you have at least 2.5 mb of space available on your hard disk, and be sure your PC has no trouble running Windows. Use the File Manager to disclose your free disk space.
- Assuming you made a copy of the AOL disk, insert that copy into your floppy disk drive. (The original AOL disk works just as well, but making—and using—a copy is just standard paranoid procedure.)
- Connect your modem to your PC and turn both of them on. Refer to your modem's instruction manual if you're not sure how to connect it.
- Start Windows using the Program Manager: choose Run from the Program Manager's File menu, enter A:SETUP (I'm assuming your floppy drive is drive A:), and click the OK button.
- A few minutes might pass as the Setup program determines the best way to install your software. It's looking at the amount of space on your hard disk, the communications port to which your modem is attached, and the modem itself. It's also looking for an

earlier version of the AOL software on your disk. If it finds one, it assumes you will want to retain all of your account information from that installation. This process can take a while. Don't let it worry you: the Setup program isn't making any changes to your machine during this time.

- Eventually, the Setup program's Welcome screen will appear (see Figure 2-1).

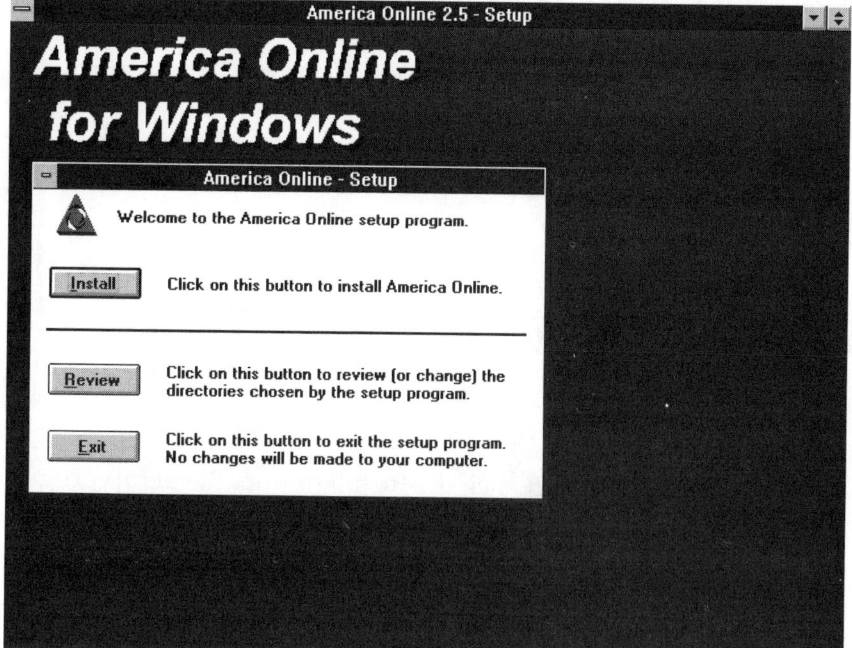

Figure 2-1: The Setup program s Welcome screen is displayed when Setup is loaded and ready to run.

- *Upgrader's Note:* If you're upgrading from a previous version of the AOL software, the Review button indicates where the Setup program found your previous version. It will use your preferences and data (address book, modem speed and type, screen names and artwork) from the previous installation once you verify the location of that installation.

- When you click the Install button, the Setup program asks where you want to place the AOL software. It assumes that you want to install the software in a C:\AOL25 subdirectory on your hard disk (see Figure 2-2). You can change this assumption by typing over the C:\AOL25 entry in the text box. As the message says, if you change anything be sure to include the drive letter and full path.

Note: You need not create the subdirectory prior to installation. The Setup program creates the subdirectory if it doesn't already exist.

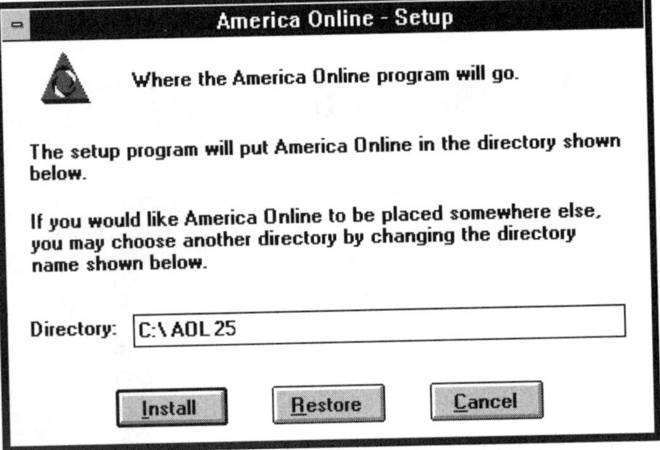

Figure 2-2: The Setup program assumes you want to install the software in a directory named C:\ AOL25. Accept the assumption if it's appropriate, or change the path (including the drive letter if necessary) in the text box.

Once you click the Install button, the Setup program does its work. This takes a couple of minutes. As it's working, a thermometer keeps you abreast of the program's progress (see the center window in Figure 2-3). The Setup program concludes with an announcement of its success (bottom window of Figure 2-3).

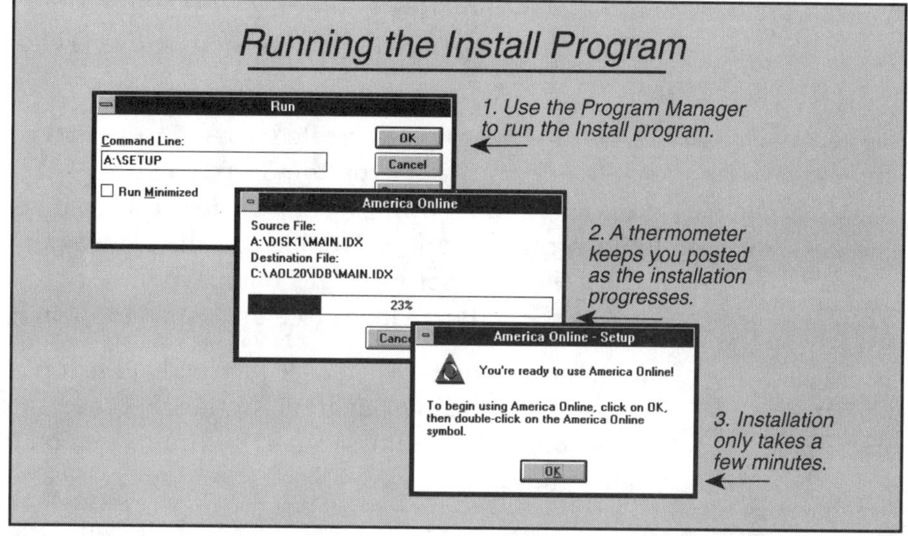

Figure 2-3: Installation of the America Online software takes only a few minutes.

There, you've done it. You've installed the software and you're ready to sign on. Eject the floppy disk, put it in a safe place and let's get on with it.

The Initial Online Session

The initial online session takes about 15 minutes. Be sure you have the time and uninterrupted access to the phone before you begin. You needn't worry about money: although you'll be online for a while, the setup process is accomplished on AOL's dime, not yours. You needn't worry about indelibility either: plenty of Cancel buttons are offered during the initial session. If you get cold feet, you can always hang up and start over.

Configuring the Telephone Connection

Before it can successfully make the connection, AOL needs to know a number of things about your telephone. It needs to know whether you have Touch Tone or rotary dialing, whether it needs to dial a nine (or something else) to reach an outside line, and whether a one should be dialed before the 800 number. Canadian members will need to supply additional information.

Your modem should be connected to the phone line and to your PC before you begin the initial online session, and everything should be turned on.

- The Setup program has created an AOL program group and left that window open on your desktop. You can resize and relocate the program group's window for a neater desktop if you wish—it's just like any other window. Double-click the America Online icon to launch the AOL software. A Confirmation screen will greet you as soon as the software loads (see the top window in Figure 2-4).

  Note: The assumptions you see pictured at the top of Figure 2-4 are derived from the investigation routine that the Setup program conducted when you first ran it. Your information probably won't match mine.

- A second screen greets you if you click the No button shown in the top window of Figure 2-4. Click that button (and make changes) only if it's necessary.
- A third screen verifies your modem and port settings (see the third screen in Figure 2-4). Again, the assumptions displayed here are the result of the Setup program's investigation routines. Here's a tip: even if your modem is Hayes compatible, click the Select Modem button and select your modem brand and model from the list that's pictured in the fourth window of Figure 2-4. Specificity pays under these circumstances.
- When you click the Set up America Online window's OK button, the application dials an 800 number to find a local access number for you. You will be able to monitor the call's progress by watching the window pictured at the bottom of Figure 2-4. Once you see the message that says "Connected at XXXX baud" (the baud rate is determined by the speed of your modem) you can be sure that your PC and modem are communicating properly. You can be sure that your modem and the telephone system are connected as well. If the AOL software found anything amiss prior to this point, it would have notified you and suggested solutions.

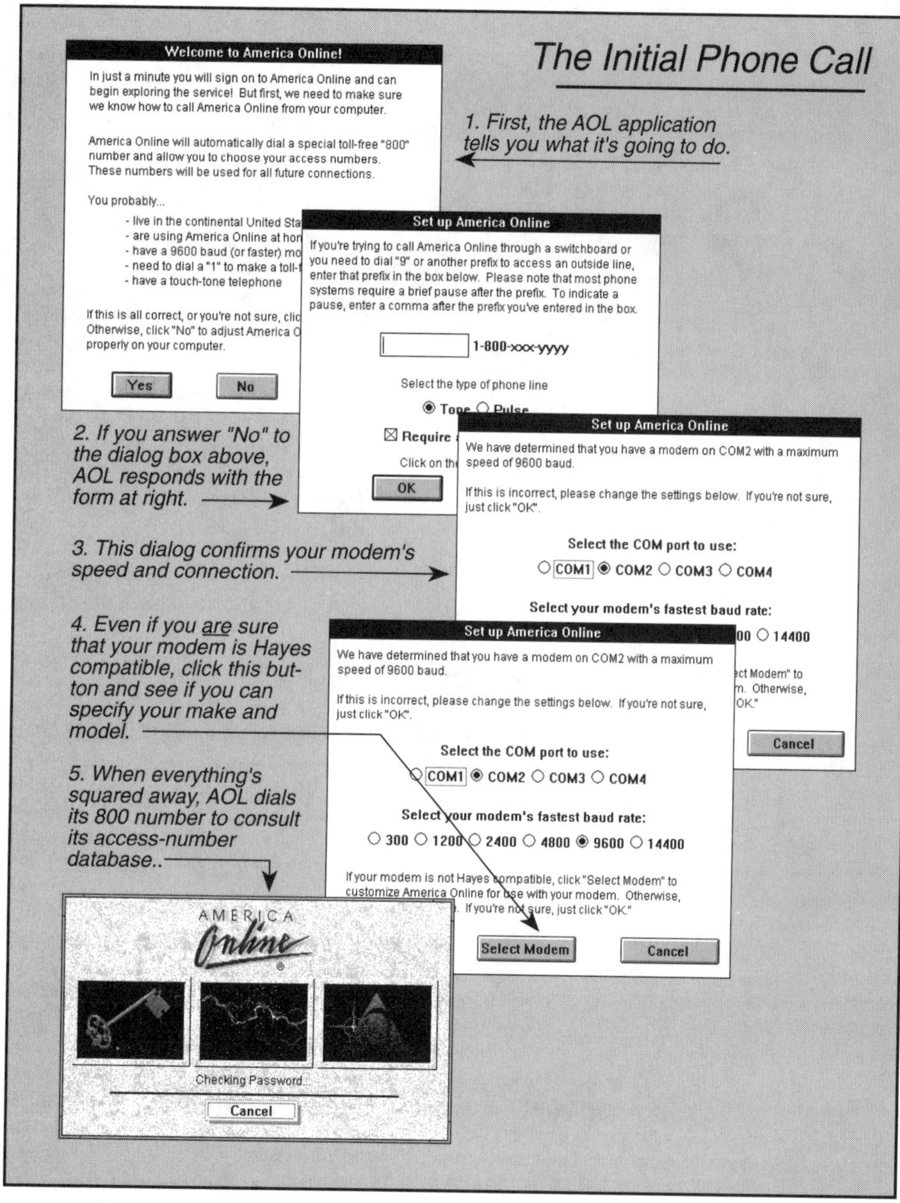

Figure 2-4: Read these screens carefully, make changes if they're necessary, and take advantage of the opportunity to specify your modem. Once you OK the Setup window, AOL dials an 800 number for the initial connection.

The Initial Phone Call

1. First, the AOL application tells you what it's going to do.

Welcome to America Online!

In just a minute you will sign on to America Online and can begin exploring the service! But first, we need to make sure we know how to call America Online from your computer.

America Online will automatically dial a special toll-free "800" number and allow you to choose your access numbers. These numbers will be used for all future connections.

You probably...

- live in the continental United Sta
- are using America Online at hon
- have a 9600 baud (or faster) mo
- need to dial a "1" to make a toll-f
- have a touch-tone telephone

If this is all correct, or you're not sure, clic
Otherwise, click "No" to adjust America O
properly on your computer.

Yes | No

2. If you answer "No" to the dialog box above, AOL responds with the form at right.

Set up America Online

If you're trying to call America Online through a switchboard or you need to dial "9" or another prefix to access an outside line, enter that prefix in the box below. Please note that most phone systems require a brief pause after the prefix. To indicate a pause, enter a comma after the prefix you've entered in the box.

[ ] 1-800-xxx-yyyy

Select the type of phone line

◉ Tone ○ Pulse

☒ Require

Click on th

OK

3. This dialog confirms your modem's speed and connection.

Set up America Online

We have determined that you have a modem on COM2 with a maximum speed of 9600 baud.

If this is incorrect, please change the settings below. If you're not sure, just click "OK".

Select the COM port to use:

○ COM1 ◉ COM2 ○ COM3 ○ COM4

Select your modem's fastest baud rate:

00 ○ 14400

ct Modem" to
n. Otherwise,
OK."

Cancel

4. Even if you are sure that your modem is Hayes compatible, click this button and see if you can specify your make and model.

Set up America Online

We have determined that you have a modem on COM2 with a maximum speed of 9600 baud.

If this is incorrect, please change the settings below. If you're not sure, just click "OK".

Select the COM port to use:

○ COM1 ◉ COM2 ○ COM3 ○ COM4

Select your modem's fastest baud rate:

○ 300 ○ 1200 ○ 2400 ○ 4800 ◉ 9600 ○ 14400

If your modem is not Hayes compatible, click "Select Modem" to customize America Online for use with your modem. Otherwise, . If you're not sure, just click "OK."

Select Modem | Cancel

5. When everything's squared away, AOL dials its 800 number to consult its access-number database..

AMERICA Online®

Checking Password...

Cancel

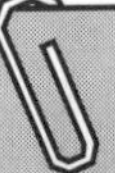

Isolating Connection Errors

Though they rarely do, things can go wrong during the connect process. The problem could be at your end (for example, the phone lines), or it could be at AOL's end. You can be sure the problem is at your end if you don't hear a dial tone (again, assuming your modem has a speaker) before your modem begins dialing. If you hear the dial tone, the dialing sequence and the screeching sound that modems make when they connect, you'll know everything is okay all the way to the common carrier (long-distance service) you're using. If your connection fails during the initial connect process, don't panic. Wait a few minutes and try again. If it fails a second time, call AOL Technical Support at 800-827-3338.

Selecting Your Local Access Numbers

Now you're connected to AOL and they're anxious to say hello. The initial greeting is friendly, if not a bit laconic (see the top window in Figure 2-5). The singular interest right now is to find some local access numbers for you. To do that, AOL needs to know where you are. It finds that out by requesting your area code.

- Using your area code, AOL consults its database of local access numbers and produces a list of those nearest you (see the second window in Figure 2-5). Look the list over carefully. The phone number at the top of the list isn't necessarily the one closest to you. Also, note the baud rates listed in the third column. Be sure the number you pick represents the baud rate you intend to use.
- If there isn't a local number listed for your area, you may have to pay long-distance charges to your telephone company in order to connect to AOL. (You'll know this is true if you have to dial a 1 before your access number in order to complete the call). Once the initial sign-on process concludes and you're online, press F1 and investigate AOL's database of access numbers again. You might find a number there after all.

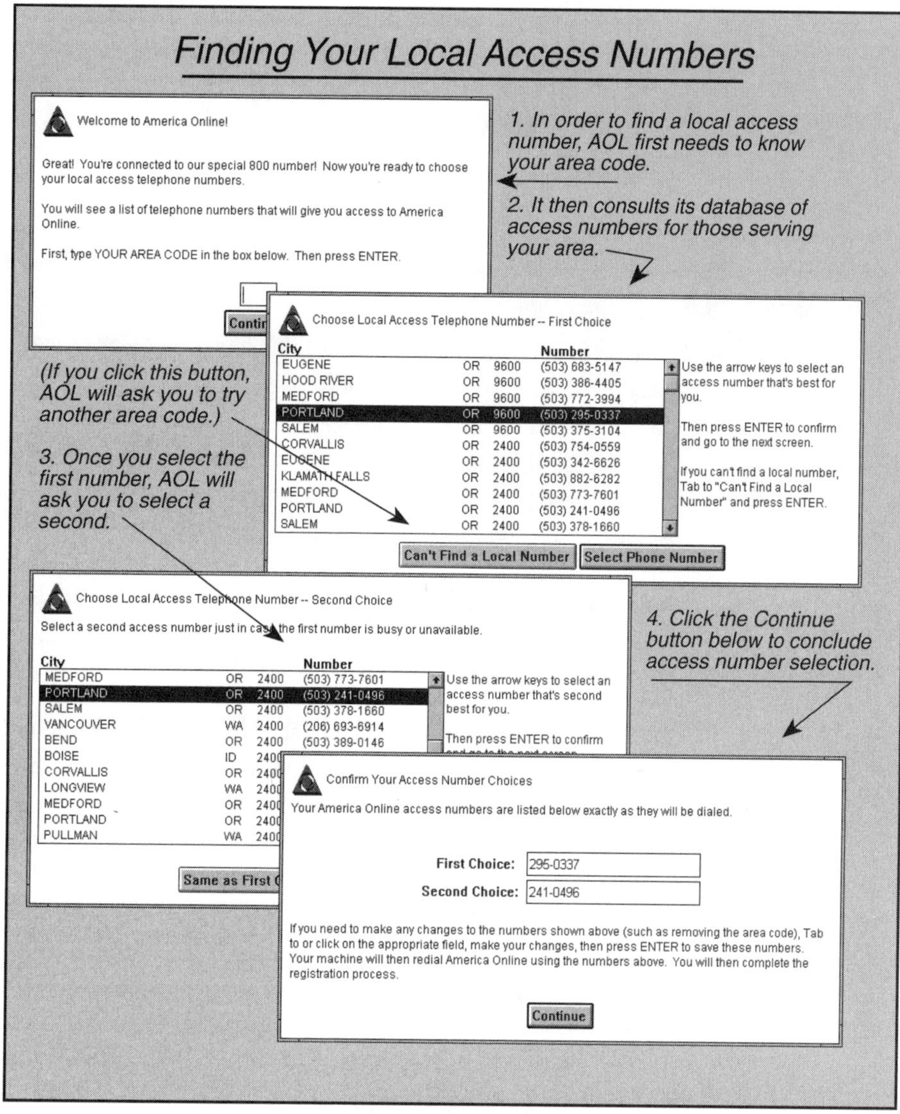

Figure 2-5: Using your area code, America Online attempts to select two local numbers for access to the service.

Finding Your Local Access Numbers

Welcome to America Online!

Great! You're connected to our special 800 number! Now you're ready to choose your local access telephone numbers.

You will see a list of telephone numbers that will give you access to America Online.

First, type YOUR AREA CODE in the box below. Then press ENTER.

Contin

1. In order to find a local access number, AOL first needs to know your area code.

2. It then consults its database of access numbers for those serving your area.

Choose Local Access Telephone Number -- First Choice

City			Number
EUGENE	OR	9600	(503) 683-5147
HOOD RIVER	OR	9600	(503) 386-4405
MEDFORD	OR	9600	(503) 772-3994
PORTLAND	OR	9600	(503) 295-0337
SALEM	OR	9600	(503) 375-3104
CORVALLIS	OR	2400	(503) 754-0559
EUGENE	OR	2400	(503) 342-6626
KLAMATH FALLS	OR	2400	(503) 882-6282
MEDFORD	OR	2400	(503) 773-7601
PORTLAND	OR	2400	(503) 241-0496
SALEM	OR	2400	(503) 378-1660

Use the arrow keys to select an access number that's best for you.

Then press ENTER to confirm and go to the next screen.

If you can't find a local number, Tab to "Can't Find a Local Number" and press ENTER.

Can't Find a Local Number | Select Phone Number

(If you click this button, AOL will ask you to try another area code.)

3. Once you select the first number, AOL will ask you to select a second.

Choose Local Access Telephone Number -- Second Choice

Select a second access number just in case the first number is busy or unavailable.

City			Number
MEDFORD	OR	2400	(503) 773-7601
PORTLAND	OR	2400	(503) 241-0496
SALEM	OR	2400	(503) 378-1660
VANCOUVER	WA	2400	(206) 693-6914
BEND	OR	2400	(503) 389-0146
BOISE	ID	240	
CORVALLIS	OR	240	
LONGVIEW	WA	240	
MEDFORD	OR	240	
PORTLAND	OR	240	
PULLMAN	WA	240	

Use the arrow keys to select an access number that's second best for you.

Then press ENTER to confirm

Same as First

4. Click the Continue button below to conclude access number selection.

Confirm Your Access Number Choices

Your America Online access numbers are listed below exactly as they will be dialed.

First Choice: 295-0337

Second Choice: 241-0496

If you need to make any changes to the numbers shown above (such as removing the area code), Tab to or click on the appropriate field, make your changes, then press ENTER to save these numbers. Your machine will then redial America Online using the numbers above. You will then complete the registration process.

Continue

- It's nice to have a secondary number as well. A secondary number (if available) is just that: a second number (the proper term is *node*—see the glossary) for your modem to call if the first one is busy (which happens rarely) or is bogged down with a lot of traffic (which happens more frequently). Interestingly, dozens of modems can use the same node at the same time by splitting the time available on that node into tiny packets. This is all very perplexing to those of us who think of phone lines as being capable of handling one conversation at a time, but it's nonetheless true. There is a limit, however, and when it's reached, AOL tries the second number. The third window in Figure 2-5 illustrates the screen used to select this alternate.

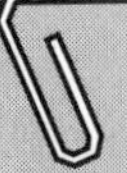

Slow Down!

If your first-choice access number provides high-speed (9600 baud or greater), make your second choice something slower. The number of high-speed incoming lines at AOL is limited, and when they're all in use, the host computer will instruct your software to hang up and try the alternate number. If the alternate is also rated at 9600 baud you'll have the same problem. Select a 2400-baud alternate. At least you'll get online.

- Finally, AOL offers the screen confirming your selections (pictured at the bottom of Figure 2-5).

The Temporary Registration Number & Password

Assuming you've clicked on Figure 2-5's Continue button, your PC will disconnect from the 800 number and dial your primary local access number. Once the connection is established, AOL presents the screen shown in Figure 2-6. This is where you must enter the registration number and password printed on your certificate. These are the temporary equivalents of the permanent screen name and password you'll soon establish. Enter the words and numbers carefully; they're usually nonsensical and difficult to type without error.

Your Name & Address

When you click the Continue button shown in Figure 2-6, AOL provides directions for using an online form like that shown in Figure 2-7. If you're not familiar with Windows, you'll want to read the directions carefully. If you've used Windows software before—even a little bit—you already know this stuff. It's traditional Windows protocol. *Hint:* Use the Tab key to move from field to field.

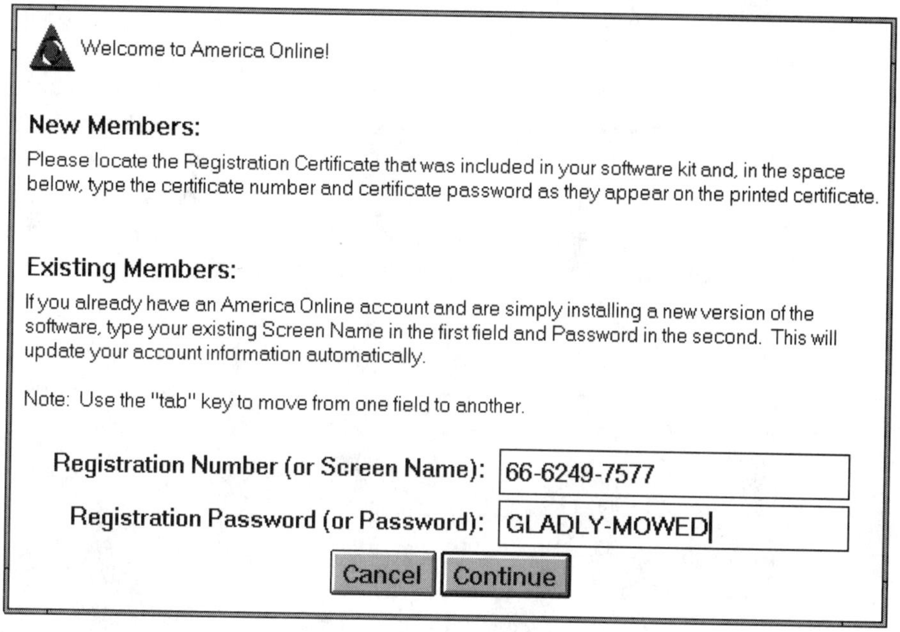

Figure 2-6: Enter your registration number and temporary password here. Be sure to type them exactly as they appear on your certificate

Welcome to America Online!

New Members:

Please locate the Registration Certificate that was included in your software kit and, in the space below, type the certificate number and certificate password as they appear on the printed certificate.

Existing Members:

If you already have an America Online account and are simply installing a new version of the software, type your existing Screen Name in the first field and Password in the second. This will update your account information automatically.

Note: Use the "tab" key to move from one field to another.

Registration Number (or Screen Name): 66-6249-7577

Registration Password (or Password): GLADLY-MOWED

Cancel | Continue

Once you've read the form-usage instructions, click the Continue button and AOL will ask you for some personal information (see Figure 2-7).

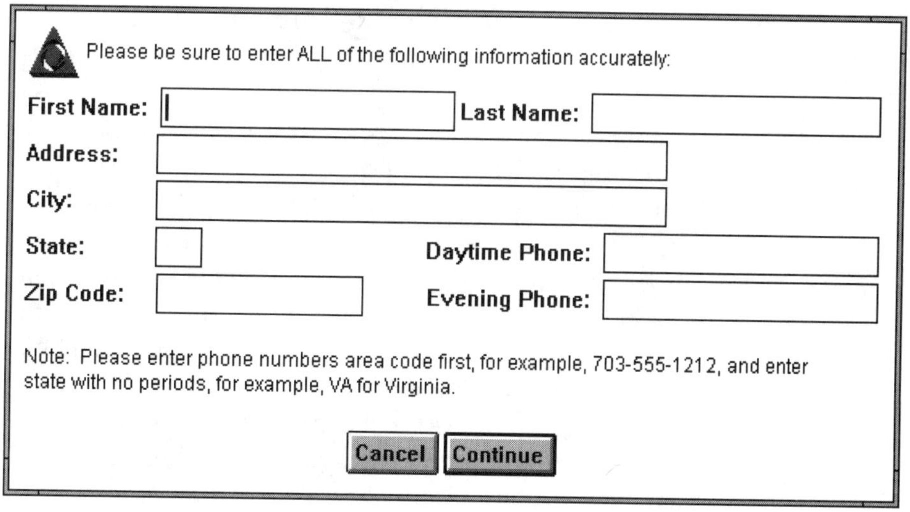

Figure 2-7: Provide your name, phone number(s) and address. Be sure to use the telephone-number format shown in the illustration.

Please be sure to enter ALL of the following information accurately:

First Name: **Last Name:**

Address:

City:

State: **Daytime Phone:**

Zip Code: **Evening Phone:**

Note: Please enter phone numbers area code first, for example, 703-555-1212, and enter state with no periods, for example, VA for Virginia.

Cancel | Continue

America Online uses this information to communicate with you off-line. Though AOL never bills members directly (we'll discuss money in a moment), and though this information is not available online to other members (member profiles—which is what other members see—are discussed in the next chapter), AOL occasionally needs to contact you off-line, and they use this information to do so. They might want to send you a disk containing a software upgrade, or perhaps you've ordered something from them (this book, for example) that needs to be mailed. That's what this information is for.

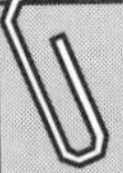

Your Phone Number

Your phone number becomes an important part of your record at AOL, not because anyone at AOL intends to call you, but because AOL's Customer Service Department uses this number to identify you whenever you call. Should you ever find the need to call, the first question Customer Service will ask is, "What's your phone number?" It's unique, after all, so Customer Service uses it to look up your records. It's an efficient method, but only if you provide the number accurately during your initial sign on.

Providing Your Billing Information

Let's be up front about it: America Online is a business run for profit. In other words, AOL needs to be paid for the service it provides. It offers a number of ways to accomplish this. VISA, MasterCard, Discover Card or American Express are the preferred methods of payment. Certain bank debit cards are also acceptable, although you will have to confirm their acceptability with your financial institution. If none of these works for you, America Online can also arrange to automatically debit your checking account. (There's a fee for this—more than a credit card costs you—so you might want this to be your last choice.)

When you click on Figure 2-7's Continue button, another screen appears, identifying AOL's connect-time rates. Read it carefully (you need to know what you're buying and what it's costing you, after all), then move on (see Figure 2-8).

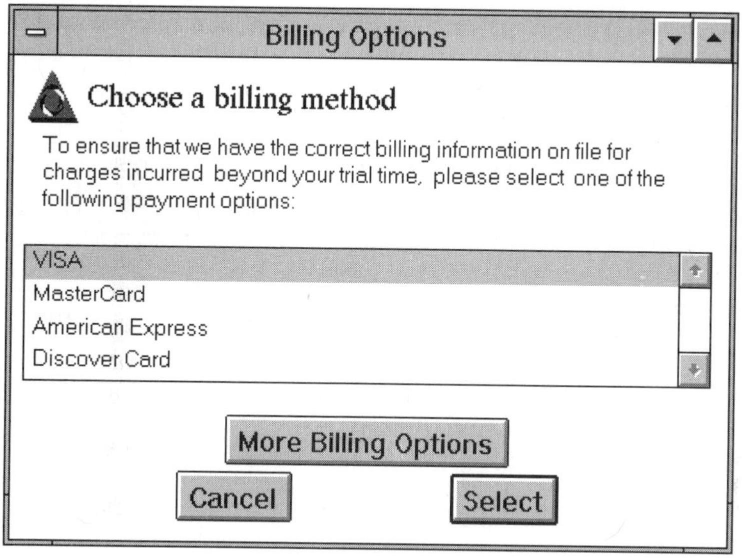

Billing Options

Choose a billing method

To ensure that we have the correct billing information on file for charges incurred beyond your trial time, please select one of the following payment options:

VISA
MasterCard
American Express
Discover Card

More Billing Options

Cancel Select

Figure 2-8: All major credit cards are welcome, and the More Billing Options button leads to information on debiting your checking account.

Figure 2-9 is an example of the billing information screen that lies under the buttons pictured in Figure 2-8. This is the VISA form, but the forms for MasterCard and Discover are about the same.

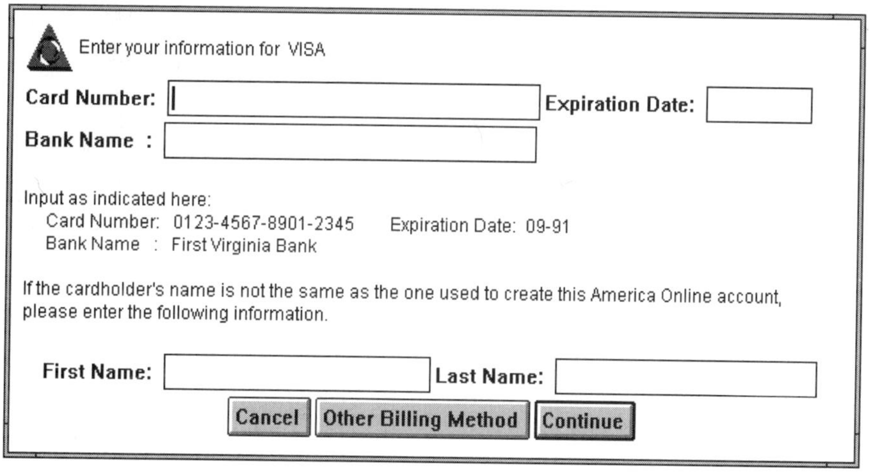

Enter your information for VISA

Card Number: **Expiration Date:**
Bank Name :

Input as indicated here:
Card Number: 0123-4567-8901-2345 Expiration Date: 09-91
Bank Name : First Virginia Bank

If the cardholder's name is not the same as the one used to create this America Online account, please enter the following information.

First Name: **Last Name:**

Cancel Other Billing Method Continue

Figure 2-9: The VISA form is about the same as those for MasterCard or Discover Card. Use the number formats described.

Choosing a Screen Name & Password

When you click on the Continue button in Figure 2-9, AOL provides a series of screens discussing the significance of screen names, concluding with the screen name input form, pictured at the top of Figure 2-10. Do you see the screen name it picked for me? This is an incentive to have your own alternates at hand.

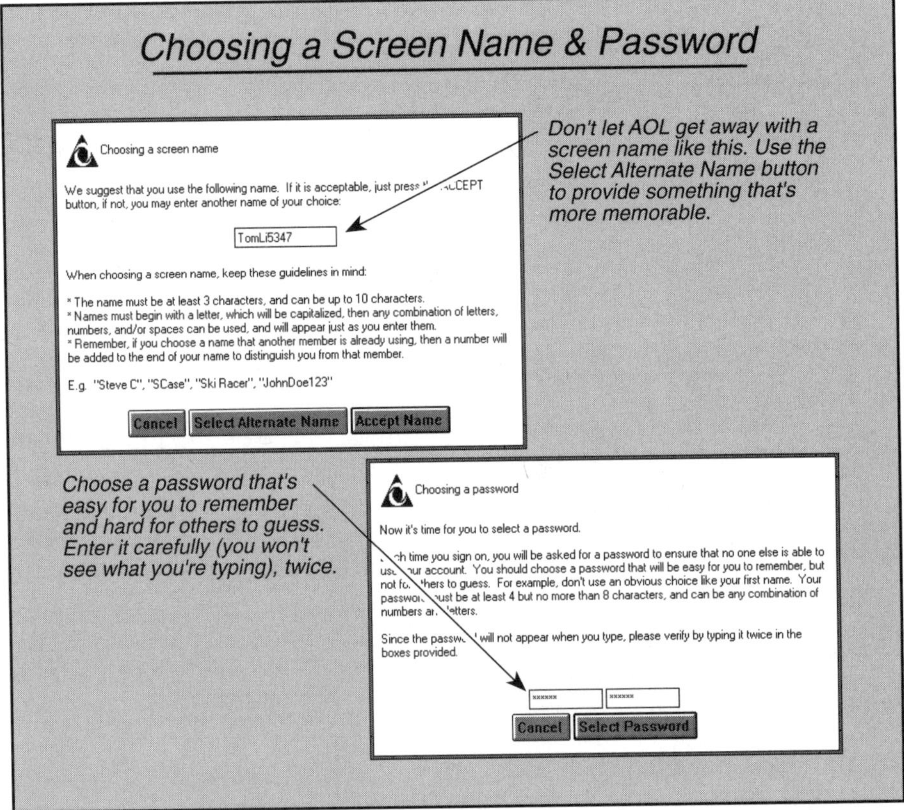

Figure 2-10: Conclude the registration process by entering your screen name and password.

Note that your password doesn't appear on your screen as you type it. Substituting asterisks for the letters of your password is a standard security precaution. You never know who's looking over your shoulder. America Online asks you to enter your password twice, to be sure you didn't mistype it the first time.

A Letter From the President

Now that you've successfully finished setting up and signing on, you enter the AOL service itself. No doubt the first thing that will happen is you'll receive an announcement that you have mail. To read the letter, choose Read New Mail from the Mail menu, or click on the little mailbox icon on the Toolbar (see top of Figure 2-11). The New Mail window appears, with mail from AOL President Steve Case selected. Click on the Read button and read what he has to say (see bottom of Figure 2-11).

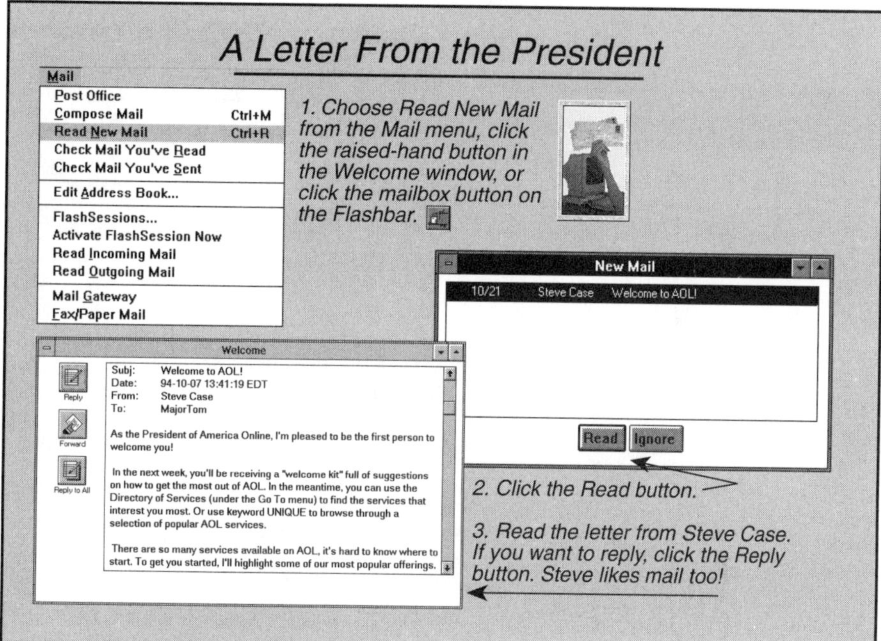

Figure 2-11: Your first activity online is to read a letter of welcome from AOL President Steve Case. How many times have you heard directly from the president of a company when you became a customer? How many times have you been invited to respond?

Where To Go From Here

Once you're online, you have the entire AOL universe to explore. The thought is both enticing and overwhelming. Here's what I suggest: spend a half-hour wandering around right after you read Steve's letter. You have quite a bit of free connect-time coming, so you don't have to worry about money. You will find all of the online departments' buttons along the Toolbar (see Figure 2-12). Find a department that interests you, then, without any particular agenda, explore that department and perhaps one other.

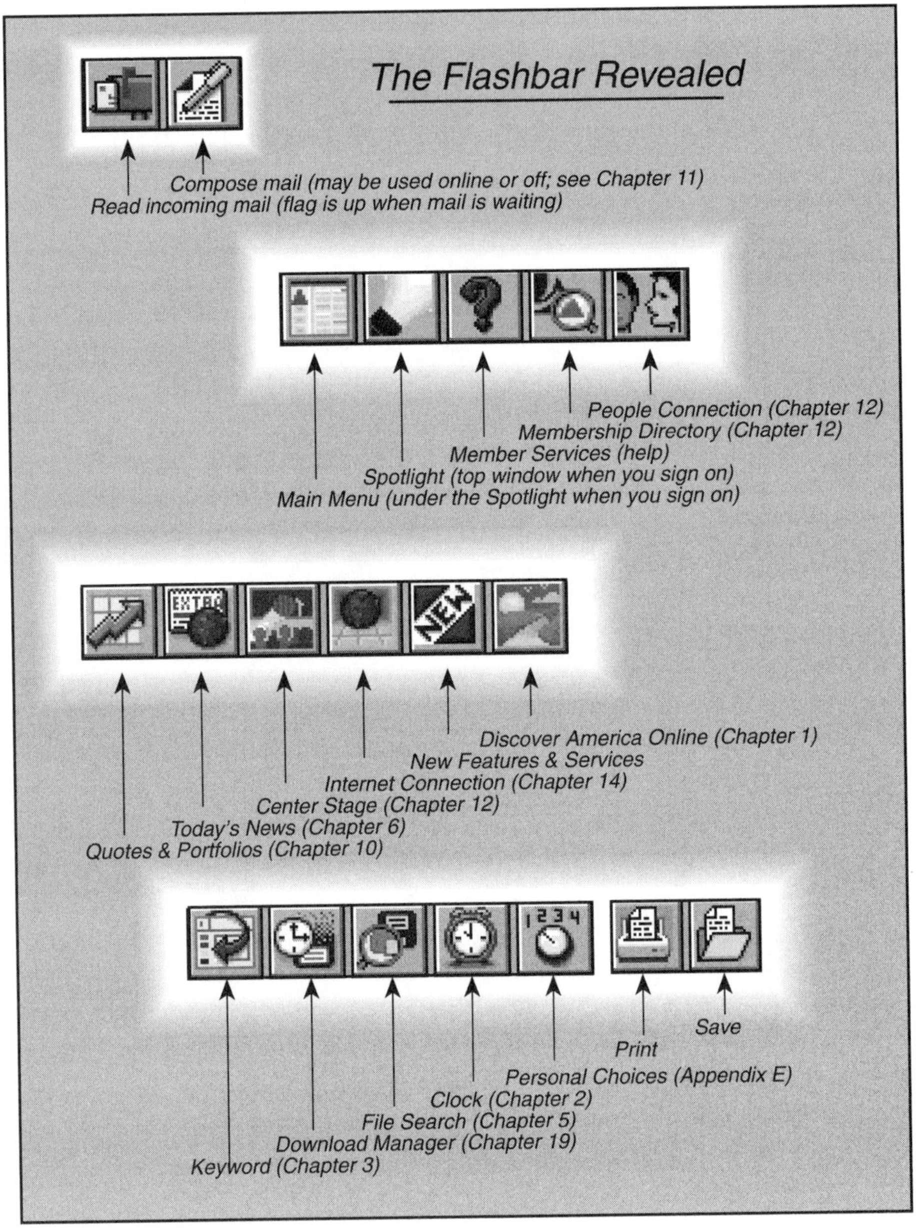

Figure 2-12: Here's your official key to the America Online for Windows Toolbar. You have my permission to photocopy it and tack it up near your computer.

The Flashbar Revealed

Compose mail (may be used online or off; see Chapter 11)
Read incoming mail (flag is up when mail is waiting)

People Connection (Chapter 12)
Membership Directory (Chapter 12)
Member Services (help)
Spotlight (top window when you sign on)
Main Menu (under the Spotlight when you sign on)

Discover America Online (Chapter 1)
New Features & Services
Internet Connection (Chapter 14)
Center Stage (Chapter 12)
Today's News (Chapter 6)
Quotes & Portfolios (Chapter 10)

Save
Print
Personal Choices (Appendix E)
Clock (Chapter 2)
File Search (Chapter 5)
Download Manager (Chapter 19)
Keyword (Chapter 3)

During this initial session, don't try to absorb the entire contents of AOL. Rather, wander aimlessly, getting a feeling for the nature of the AOL universe. Note how Windows-like it is. Everything is predictable and familiar—at least to a Windows user.

After a half-hour or so, you might want to sign off. Choose Exit from the File menu. Once the dust settles, turn to the chapter in this book that describes the department you just visited (review Figure 2-12 to cross-reference chapters with departments). Read that chapter, then sign back on and explore that department again. See if you can find the things I described in the chapter. Spend another half-hour at this.

Now you're on your own. Explore another department if you wish, or turn to Chapter 4, "Electronic Mail," and learn how to send mail to somebody. You'll probably get a response in a few days. People at AOL are very friendly. It really is a community.

Moving On

Speaking of the people online, that's one of the subjects covered in the next chapter, "Online Help & the Members." When you next have the time (I know how enticing AOL can be—you might never return to this book now that you're online), read on. We have many more things to talk about.

CHAPTER 3

Online Help & the Members

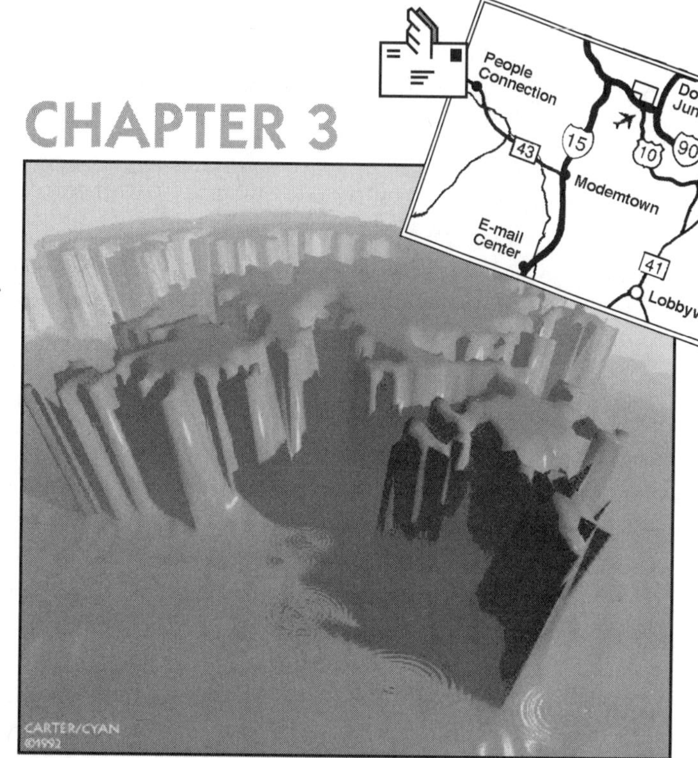

Sounds like a heavy-metal band: "Online Help & the Members." Dressed in black leather, with chains draped around their waists, Online Help & the Members take the stage accompanied by waves of cacophony and pandemonium. As in a jailbreak, spotlights sweep the auditorium, illuminating a mass of writhing supplicants below. The spotlights converge on Online as he wrests the microphone from its stand. An expectant hush fills the air. In a voice amplified by 2,000 transistors the size of hubcaps, he speaks: "America Online Customer Relations! May I help you?"

Getting Help

Much to my delight, software publishers have recently placed notable emphasis on providing users with help. The version of Microsoft Word I use, for instance, includes a help file measuring 1.8mb—larger than Word itself. The help file is right on my hard disk. All I have to do is tap on a couple of keys and there's the help I need: convenient, comprehensive and clear.

Frontispiece graphic by Chuck Carter/Cyan. The graphic was created in Infini-D using Phong shading with shadows. Use the keyword: File Search and the criterion: Phong shadows.

America Online is no different. Like all good software, AOL's help is always a simple keystroke away. America Online, however, has a unique advantage: since a good portion of AOL's help resides on the host computer, it can be updated any time. This means that AOL's help can be particularly responsive. If members are having trouble with a specific area, AOL can rewrite the help files to address the source of confusion. It's as if a Microsoft representative came to my home with a new help disk every time Word's help files needed to be changed.

There's a flaw in the plan, however. In order to access online help, I have to be online. While this isn't much of a restriction—online is the time I usually need help, after all—there are occasions when I would like to get help without signing on. What if I can't sign on? What if I'm traveling and need help finding an alternative number?

Altruistically, AOL offers both online and off-line help. One set of help files resides on your hard disk available at any time regardless of whether you're online. The other set of help files resides on the host computer. This set is the one that's constantly being updated. It's not just comprehensive, it's downright monumental. It's available whenever you're online, and—incredibly—it's free. Whenever you access AOL's online help area, the clock stops and you aren't charged for your time there.

Off-line Help

Let's talk about off-line help first. America Online's off-line help is especially configured to answer the kind of questions you'll encounter when you're disconnected from the service. How do I connect when I'm away from my usual location? What's the Customer Relations telephone number and when are they on duty? How do I sign up my friends?

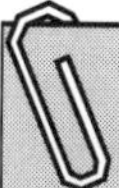

Getting Help: A Methodical Approach

If you have a question about AOL and require help, don't write to me! I'm just a writer, and everyone knows that writers don' know nuttin'.

Rather, I suggest you use the methods described below, in the order in which they appear. All of the topics mentioned are explained in detail later in this chapter.

1. Look up the topic in the index of this book to see if your question is answered here. I'd like to think that most of your questions will be answered this way.
2. Run the AOL software and choose Search for Help On... from the Help menu. In this chapter I refer to this kind of help as *off-line* help, since it's available when you're off-line (even though it's available online as well). Off-line help offers an extensive searchable list of topics and will often answer your question, especially if it has to do with the most commonly asked AOL questions.
3. Go online and click on the question-mark button on the Flashbar (the Flashbar is that bar of icons just under the menu bar). Alternatively, you could press Ctrl+K (which is how you prepare AOL to accept a keyword—we'll discuss keywords later in this chapter), then type Help. Click the Go button and click the Yes button in response to the "Are you sure..." message. This will take you to AOL's Member Services, a particularly comprehensive (and free) resource. There's a Member Services button on each department's screen as well. Look for them on the first page of each departmental chapter in this book.
4. Go online and use the keyword: MHM. This will take you to AOL's Members Helping Members message board. Post your question in the appropriate folder there. Within a day or so you will have a response to your question from another member. Peer help is often the best help you can find.
5. Go online and use the keyword: TechLive. This will take you to Tech Support Live, where you can consult AOL's Technical Support staff. This feature is free and open from 8 A.M. to 4 A.M. (Eastern time) seven days a week.
6. Ask a Guide. Sign on, choose Lobby from the Go To menu, and once you arrive, look around for someone with the word "Guide" in their name. Guides are a particularly friendly form of help, and they're on duty weekdays from 9 A.M. until 6 A.M. (Eastern time), 7 days a week, 365 days a year.
7. Send email to Customer Relations. Sign on and use the keyword: Help. In the Help window, click the "Email to the Staff" button. You'll hear back from them in a day or two.
8. If you're having trouble connecting or your problem is of a technical nature, call Technical support at 800-827-3338. They're open 6 A.M. to 4 A.M. (Eastern time), seven days a week. For other assistance contact Sales & Services. They may be reached 8 A.M. to 12 A.M. (Eastern time) Monday through Friday, and 12 P.M. to 9 P.M. Saturday and Sunday. It's a toll-free call in the U.S., and there's never any charge for support from AOL.

Accessing Help From the Help Menu

With Windows 3.0, Microsoft inaugurated a policy that was new to the industry at the time: a help application common to all programs. In the Windows environment, help is a separate program that's called by other programs when the user wants help. When you choose an item from AOL's Help menu, AOL starts the Windows help application. When you ask for help from Microsoft Word, the same thing happens. The help files themselves are different; the help application is the same (see Figure 3-1).

Figure 3-1: A familiar face: AOL's help utility looks and acts just like the help utility in any other Windows program.

This means there's no need to learn how to use the help feature over again for each application, since help is the same for all Windows applications. Because you only have to learn how to use it once, Microsoft felt confident in enhancing the Windows help application with a rich variety of features: bookmarks, jumps, copy and paste, printing, a search mechanism—even a Stay on Top command, so help is always only a mouse-click away.

America Online utilizes the Windows help application to its fullest. The AOL help file is very large, and there are plenty of jumps to cross-reference help topics with one another. Any help topic can be searched and printed; bookmarks can be placed to lead you back to topics of particular interest; an extensive list of tips and tricks is available; and even the Flashbar icons are pictured and identified in AOL's help feature (see Figure 3-2).

As is always the case with items that aren't grayed out on Windows menus, Help can be chosen at any time, whether you're online or off. These help topics are stored in a file on your hard disk, and as such don't require that you go online in order to access them; you just need to launch the AOL program and pull down the Help menu.

One of the topics on the Help menu is How to Use Help. If you've never used AOL's off-line help feature before, this is the place to start. Get to know help inside and out; become comfortable with it. Once you've gained that kind of confidence, you won't hesitate to use help the next time it's needed. If you think you already know how to use Windows help, here's a little test: can you make the help icon stay on top of all windows on the screen? If you don't know how, you haven't spent enough time exploring help.

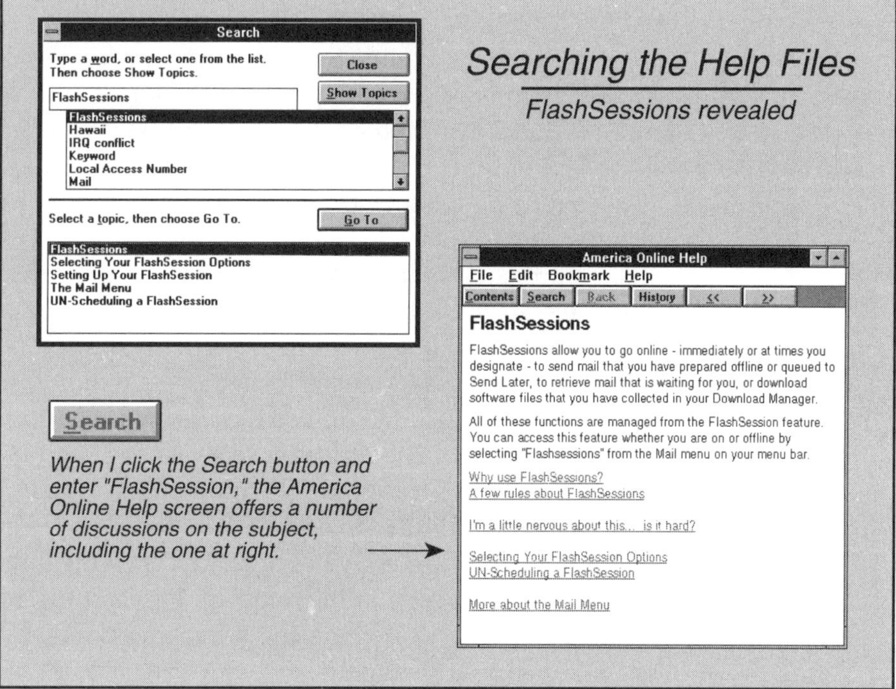

Figure 3-2: Searching America Online's help files for "FlashSessions," I discover plenty of resources. This information is available whether I'm online or off.

My wife is a medical student. She learned a long time ago that it's impossible to memorize all of the things she has to know to become a successful practitioner. The sheer magnitude of the task was dragging her down until she realized that all she really had to know was where to look for information, not all of the information itself. She has a well-organized library and knows which books discuss which topics. When she needs assistance, she goes to her library and gets help.

You should do the same. Don't worry about memorizing all of the petty details—for any computer program. Instead, learn how to use help. It will take 20 minutes and it will be the most productive 20 minutes you'll ever spend with your computer.

Online Help

America Online's online help is especially comprehensive. Moreover, since the online help file is stored on the host computer (and not on your hard disk) only one file needs to be updated when the online help files require changing. In addition to the help you get using the online files, AOL staff and members stand ready to help you as well. This is world-class help and its breadth is unique to AOL.

Members' Online Support

To access Members' Online Support, choose Member Services from the Members menu, click on the question-mark icon on the Flashbar (see Figure 3-3), click the Member Services button on all department screens and the Main Menu, or use the keyword: Help. You must be signed on for this: online help isn't stored on your hard disk, it's on AOL's host computer.

Just before you enter the Member Services area where Online Support resides, AOL flashes the message pictured in the middle of Figure 3-3. Unprovoked dialog boxes like this often spell trouble, I know, but not this one. America Online is trying to say that you're about to pass through the "free curtain" (to use the AOL vernacular) and that you won't be charged for the time you're about to spend in Member Services. That's a comforting thought: online help is free. You can spend all day perusing online help and AOL will never charge you a dime.

Once in the Member Services area, just click the large question-mark icon to enter Members' Online Support. Proceed through the confirmation message that you are entering a free area by clicking on the Members Online Support button.

Random Acts of Help

The next time you sign on to AOL, click the Flashbar's question-mark icon and venture into the Member Services and Members' Online Support areas. Once you're there, relax (the clock's not running) and explore this area casually. Poke around as you would at a flea market. Don't try to memorize anything. Get the feel of the place. Get to know what's there and where it's found. Consider this an exploratory mission without any particular agenda. After 20 minutes or so, move on to something else.

You will be amazed at what this kind of unstructured behavior can do for you. You will acquire a familiarity with the layout of the place, and you will gain confidence in the use of online help. Most importantly, the next time you need help, you won't hesitate to use the keyword. And that, in the long run, is perhaps the most productive attitude you can adopt toward the use of AOL.

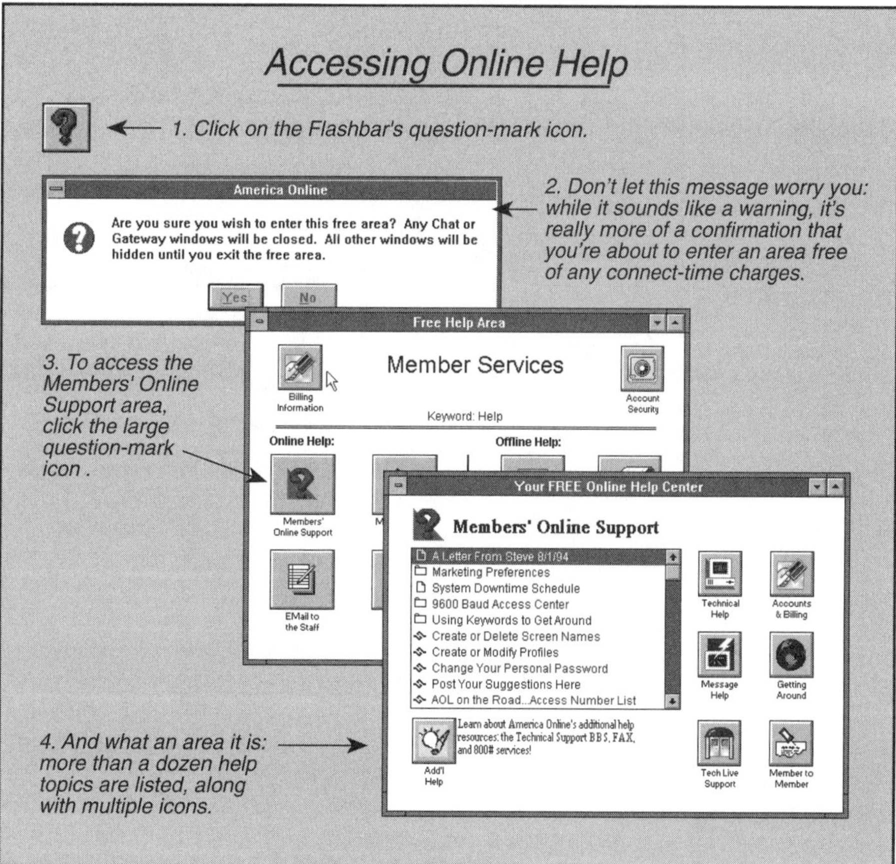

Figure 3-3: Online help is available whenever you're online by clicking the question-mark icon on the Flashbar. The best part: it's absolutely free.

The subjects pictured in the list box on the left side of Figure 3-3's lower window offer immediate answers for nearly anything you encounter while online. Each of these help topics can be saved, printed or both. The list of topics is extensive, and the detail offered within each topic is bountiful (see Figure 3-4).

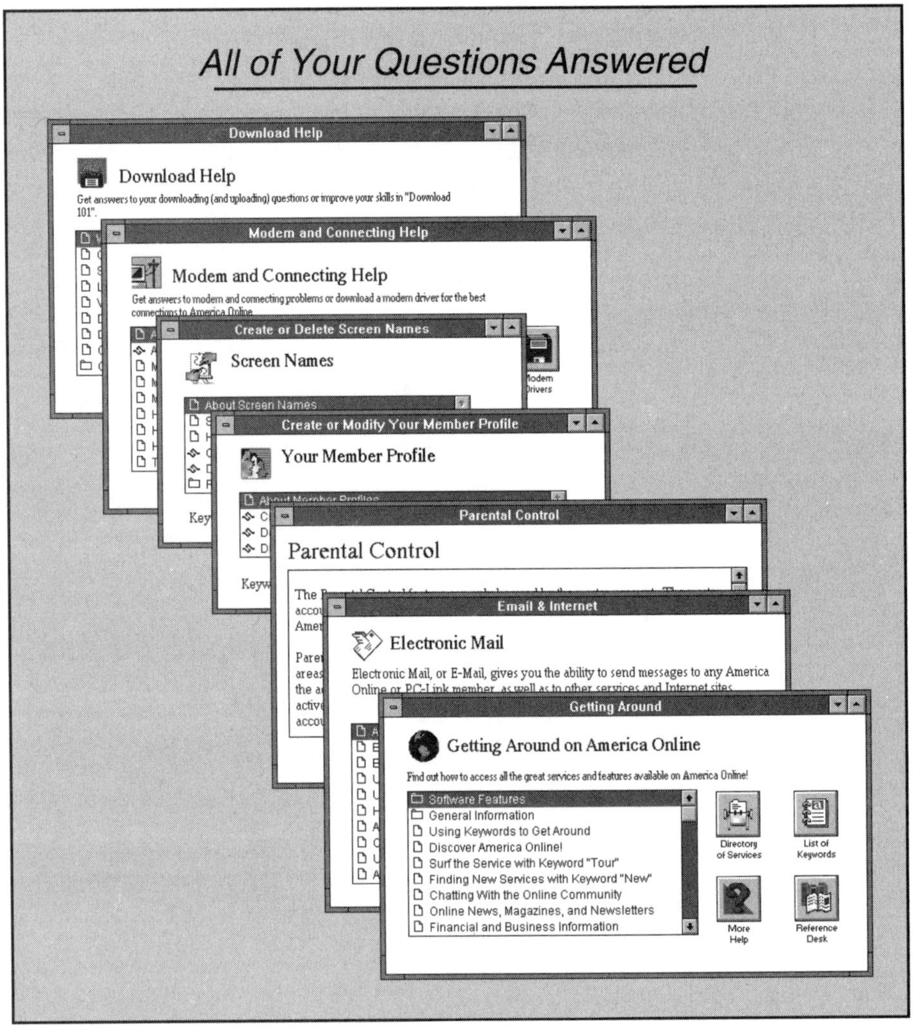

Figure 3-4: A few of the help topics available in the Members' Online Support area.

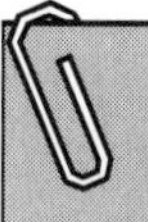

Help Grab-bag

Nearly every online help feature discussed in this chapter is available via the keyword: Help. It's a free area so get to know it well.

Saving Help

Although AOL's online help screens are primarily intended for you to read while you're online (there's no charge for the service, after all, so you can take your time), you might want to save a help topic or two on your disk. Doing so provides you with a text file that can be combined with other help files using a word processor, for instance, to create a comprehensive help manual.

To save a help topic that's on your screen, simply choose Save (or Save As—they're the same command in this context) from the File menu. America Online asks you what you want to name the file and where you want to save it. Provide the information it needs, and that help topic will be stored on your disk, ready for any purpose you might have in mind.

Printing Help

More likely, you'll want to print a help topic for ready reference. As you might expect, all you have to do is choose Print from the File menu. Printing from AOL works about like printing from any other Windows application. You'll receive the print dialog box associated with the printer you've selected via the Print Setup command under the File menu. Configure this dialog as you please and print. By the way, you can print just about any text file you read online, not just the help files. If you run across a file description or news article you want to print, just choose Print from the File menu—AOL will print whatever text is in the front-most (active) window.

The Directory of Services

Look again at Figure 3-4. In the Getting Around on America Online window, you'll find a little Rolodex icon representing the Directory of Services, a searchable database of information on all the services offered by AOL. Information for each service includes the following:

- the service's name,
- any keywords associated with that service (see sidebar),

- a menu path for access to that service,
- a description of that service, and
- a button to take you there.

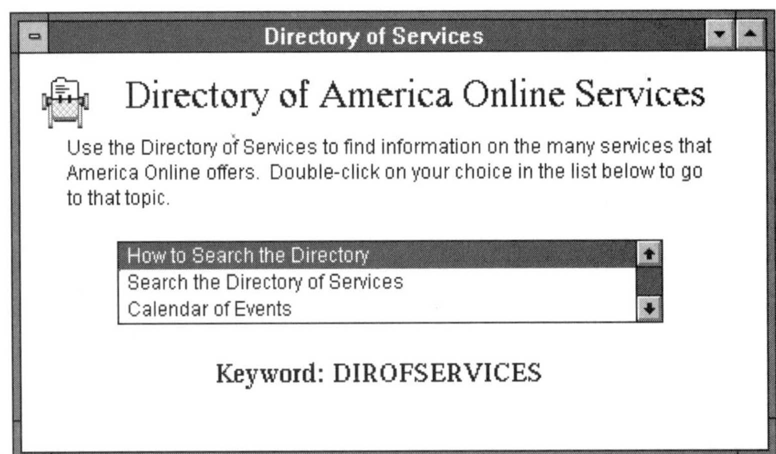

Figure 3-5: The Directory of Services offers a method of searching all the services America Online has to offer.

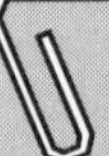

Keywords

Keywords are shortcuts to specific destinations within AOL. Without keywords, accessing the Microsoft Knowledge Base, for example, via menus and windows requires that I click the Computing button on the Main Menu, click Industry Connection, click Companies Listed A-Z, click the I-M button, double-click the Microsoft folder, and finally click on Knowledge Base. Whew! There's gotta be a better way.

And there is: keywords. The keyword for the Microsoft Knowledge Base is Knowledge Base. Once I know the keyword, all I have to do is choose Keyword from the Go To menu (or click the keyword button on the Flashbar) and enter Knowledge Base into the area provided. Instantly, AOL takes me directly to the Knowledge Base, bypassing all the steps in between.

A list of keywords is available in Appendix A of this book. Keywords are also available within the Directory of Services (discussed later), which you can search right in the Keyword window. Just enter your criterion where the keyword would normally go and click on the Search button.

Searching the Directory of Services

One of the most helpful features of AOL's online help is the Directory of Services. This is AOL's answer to the question: "I wonder if they have anything that addresses my interest in..." Are you interested in model airplanes? Search the Directory of Services. How about music, poetry or fine food? Use the Directory of Services.

I was having trouble with Microsoft Word the other day. Couldn't get it to do things I knew it was capable of doing. What to do? Call five friends on the phone and get their voice mail? Call Microsoft long distance and wait as they play bad Seattle radio while I'm on hold?

None of the above. I simply signed on and consulted the Microsoft Knowledge Base. The Knowledge Base is the summation of nearly everything Microsoft knows about its products, including answers from their technical support staff. It's updated periodically and released on CD-ROM. You can subscribe if you wish (if you have a CD-ROM player)—it's only $295 a year.

Or you can use AOL. America Online subscribes to the Knowledge Base and posts it online, complete with a search mechanism to find what you're after. If you forget Microsoft's keyword, use the Directory of Services to find it for you. That's just what I did the other day, and my question was answered within a few minutes (see Figure 3-6).

Note that the middle window in Figure 3-6 offers the keyword(s) for the Knowledge Base, its location (the menu path that gets you there) and its description. If it isn't what I need, the description saves me the trouble of going there. If it is what I need, not only do the keyword and location tell me how to get there quickly, a Go button is provided at the bottom of the window. Clicking on it will take me there in a flash.

Locating the Directory of Services

There are at least five ways to get to the Directory of Services. As shown in Figure 3-4, you'll find the directory's listing in the Getting Around in America Online window. Since you passed through the free curtain to get to Members' Online Support where this window is located, accessing the Directory of Services via Online Support is free. It's also in the Discover AOL area (keyword: Discover, or click the Discover AOL button on the Main Menu).

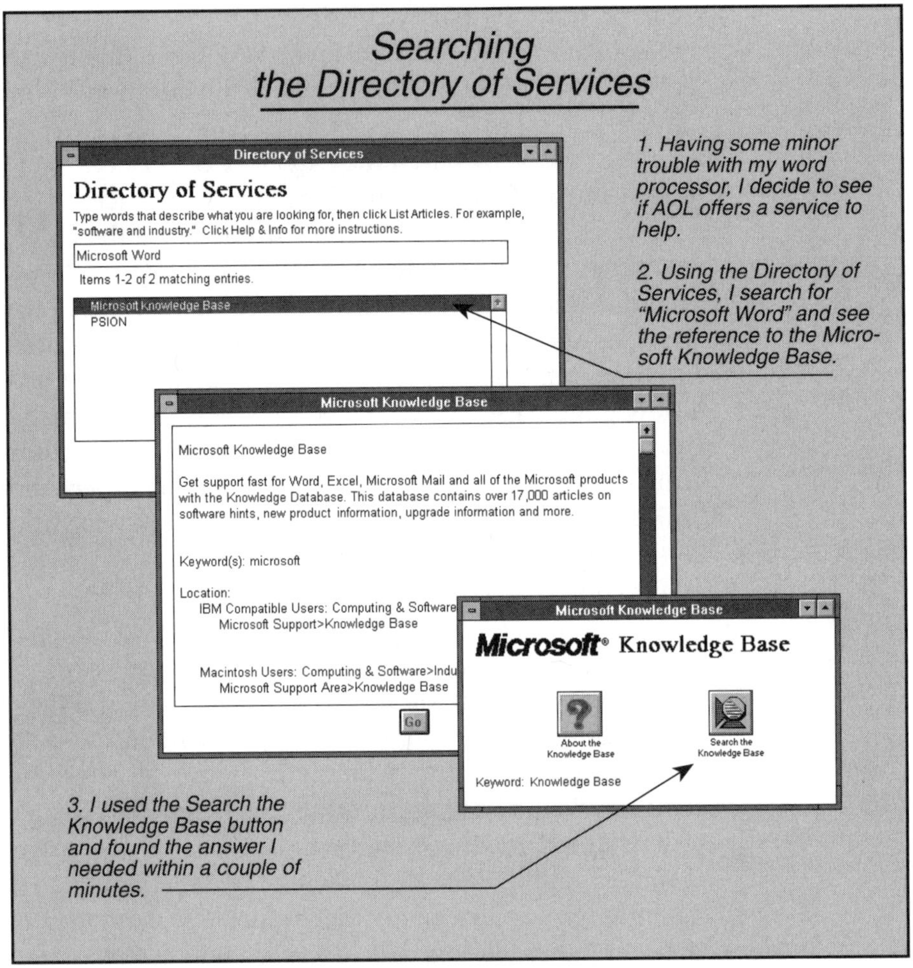

Figure 3-6: The Directory of Services found the Microsoft Knowledge Base for me, and the Knowledge Base had my answer.

Searching the Directory of Services

Directory of Services

Directory of Services

Type words that describe what you are looking for, then click List Articles. For example, "software and industry." Click Help & Info for more instructions.

Microsoft Word

Items 1-2 of 2 matching entries.

Microsoft Knowledge Base
PSION

1. Having some minor trouble with my word processor, I decide to see if AOL offers a service to help.

2. Using the Directory of Services, I search for "Microsoft Word" and see the reference to the Microsoft Knowledge Base.

Microsoft Knowledge Base

Microsoft Knowledge Base

Get support fast for Word, Excel, Microsoft Mail and all of the Microsoft products with the Knowledge Database. This database contains over 17,000 articles on software hints, new product information, upgrade information and more.

Keyword(s): microsoft

Location:
IBM Compatible Users: Computing & Software
Microsoft Support>Knowledge Base

Macintosh Users: Computing & Software>Indu
Microsoft Support Area>Knowledge Base

Go

Microsoft Knowledge Base

Microsoft® Knowledge Base

About the Knowledge Base

Search the Knowledge Base

Keyword: Knowledge Base

3. I used the Search the Knowledge Base button and found the answer I needed within a couple of minutes.

Alternatively, you can choose Search Directory of Services from the Go To menu, or use the keyword: Services. If you're not in the free area at the time, accessing the Directory via the Go To menu or via its keyword is on your dime, not AOL's. It's a little faster and more convenient than passing through the curtain, however; so you might wish to use it when you plan to spend only a moment or two there.

You can also access the Directory of Services through the Keyword window. Type Ctrl+K, enter your criterion and click on the Search button.

Tech Help Live

Let's talk about rooms for a moment. At AOL, a room is a place where a number of people gather to talk about a subject of common interest. There are classrooms, for instance, where you'll find a teacher and students (the Online Campus is discussed in Chapter 16, "Education"). There's the Lobby (the whisper-in-the-ear button on the Flashbar) where people go to mingle and meet other people. In fact, AOL offers scores of rooms, and we will explore a number of them in Chapter 10, "People Connection."

Look again at Figure 3-3. Do you see the button marked Tech Live Support? If you click that button, you'll eventually find yourself in a room with at least one Customer Service representative and probably a number of other members, all with questions regarding the service. Conversations in the room are real-time: you don't have to wait for replies. This isn't mail and it's not a message board; it's a room, and like real rooms in real buildings, people in rooms can hold real-time conversations.

There's a lot to be learned here. Not only do you receive answers to your questions immediately, you can "eavesdrop" on questions from other members as well—all at AOL's expense (don't forget that you're still in the free area).

Tech Live help is available from 8 A.M. to 4 A.M. seven days a week. If you need an immediate response, this is the place to find it.

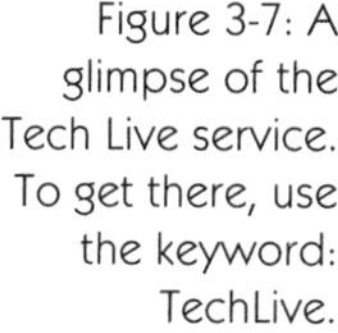

Figure 3-7: A glimpse of the Tech Live service. To get there, use the keyword: TechLive.

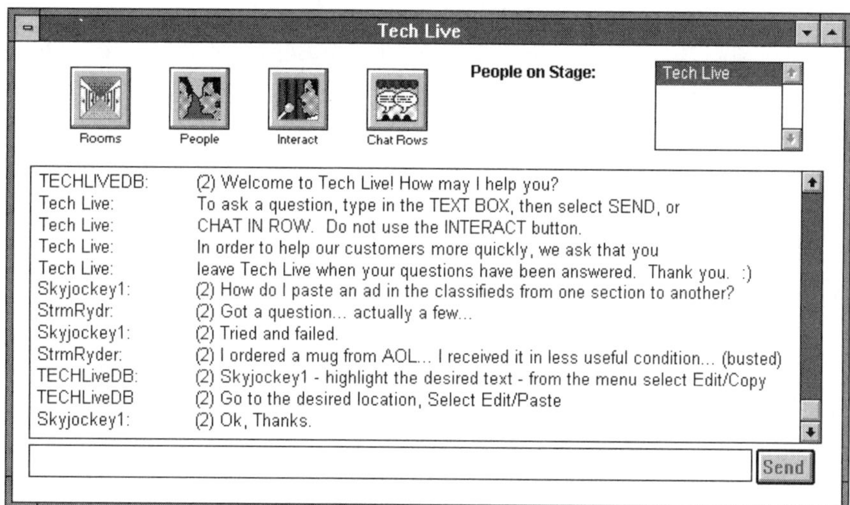

Jay Levitt

Fully one-third of AOL's business is email. AOL handles *half a million* pieces of mail a day—few post offices have that volume—and we all simply assume that each message will make it from sender to receiver without a hitch.

Which it does, thanks to Jay Levitt. Jay is AOL's Mail Guy. Few people are more pivotal to the service than the person in charge of the mail. Jay Levitt is so important that his screen name is "Jay." Even Steve Case doesn't have a first-name screen name. Jay does. In a little cubicle in the "engine room" of AOL, he sits surrounded by computer screens: a Mac, two HP workstations, a host terminal and two PDAs (Personal Digital Assistants: palmtop computers that many feel will become email's hingepins in the upcoming years). He plays these terminals like a keyboard musician at a rock concert—the fingers of his left hand a blur as they tap out commands to display instantaneous mail volume, while the right hand tickles one of the two mainframes that are dedicated to his imperative. All the while he carries on a conversation with me, popping witticisms like Victor Borge on a good night.

The rock musician analogy isn't far off the mark (though I doubt that you'd ever find him in leather and chains), for Jay Levitt is in his early 20s. *Just a kid!* Kid or not, he's a scholar, a prodigy and a gentleman. Most of all, he's one of the finest friends I made at AOL. Few could do as well.

Members Helping Members

On my IRS 1040 form, right there next to the word Occupation, it says "educator." I write books, teach classes and do some consulting. As an educator, I attend a number of conferences. Most of these conferences are academic, each featuring a number of speakers and seminar leaders.

Reflecting back on those conferences, I must admit that the greatest value I receive from them is not from the speakers or the seminars; it's from the other people attending the conference. My education occurs in the hallways and at lounge tables. People talking to people—peer to peer—that's where I find the Good Stuff.

America Online is no different. Some of the best help online is that received from other members. America Online knows that; that's why it provides Members Helping Members—a formalized version of peer support (Figure 3-8).

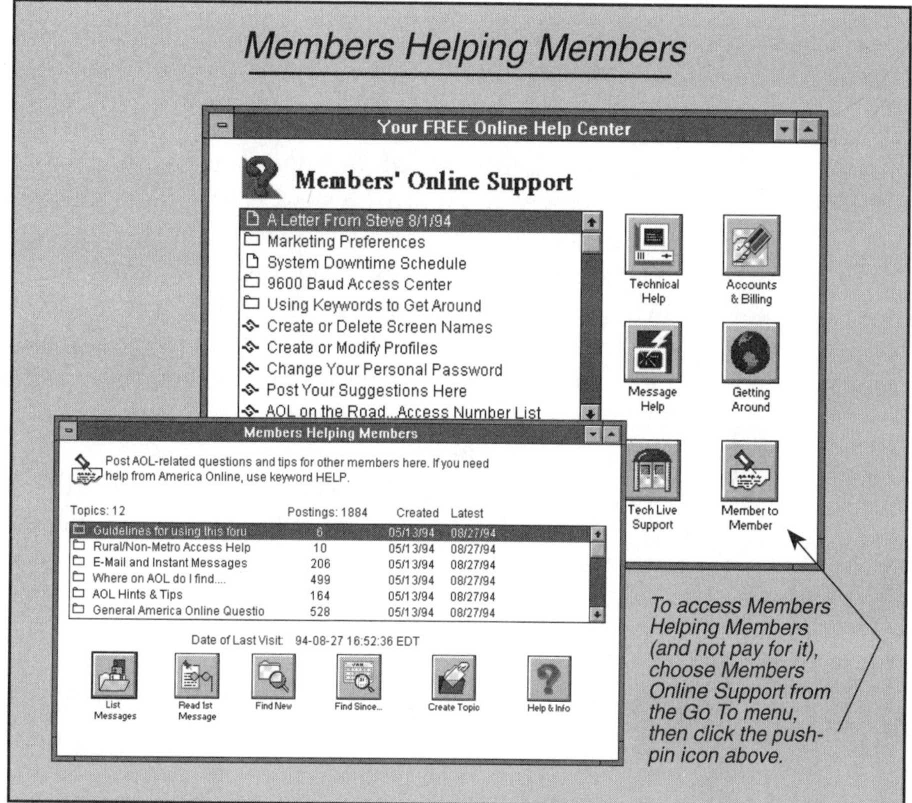

Figure 3-8: To access Members Helping Members, click the pushpin icon in the Members' Online Support window, or use the keyword: MHM.

To access Members Helping Members, either click the pushpin icon in the Members' Online Support window, or use the keyword: MHM. Unlike the Directory of Services, you'll pass through the free curtain regardless of how you choose to access this feature. In other words, it never costs you a dime to use Members Helping Members.

Message Boards

Members Helping Members is a message board. Although we'll discuss message boards in Chapter 6 ("Lifestyles & Interests"), the subject is worth a brief mention here as well.

Throughout AOL you'll see little pushpin icons. This is AOL's way of identifying message boards. A message board is analogous to the bulletin boards you see hanging in the halls of offices and academic institutions. People post things there for other people to see: postcards, lost mittens, announcements and messages. America Online's message boards are exactly the same (though you might not see lost mittens on AOL's boards).

Look again at Figure 3-8. Note how AOL's boards are organized by using folders. The bulletin board analogy weakens a bit here, but AOL's boards get a lot of messages (the Members Helping Members board pictured in Figure 3-8 has 1,884). Unless they're organized in some fashion, 1,884 messages posted on a single board would be chaotic and overwhelming. The solution is folders.

You can read all the messages in a folder, browse through them (viewing only their subjects, rather than the messages themselves), or specify only those messages that have been posted since a specific date. This is a very convenient message-reading system and is described in detail in Chapter 6.

For the time being, let's select a folder and read its messages. I picked the AOL Hints & Tips folder and found the series of messages pictured in Figure 3-9.

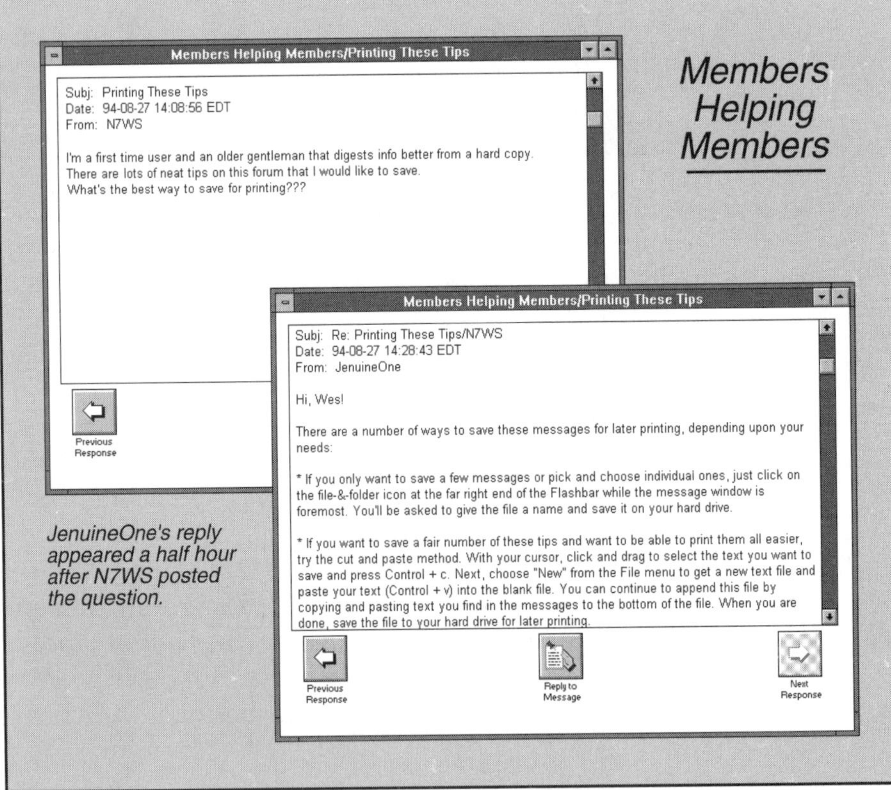

Figure 3-9: N7WS needed help on saving messages for later printing. JenuineOne was there to help.

The Value of Member Help

Look at the last message pictured in Figure 3-9. Not only does JenuineOne suggest three ideas for N7WS, she explains why and when each idea would work best. This is superb help, and it came from another member. The full text of the message from JenuineOne appears in Figure 3-10.

Figure 3-10: JenuineOne offers not one, but three solutions to a question.

JenuineOne's Message

```
Subj:  Re: Printing These Tips/N7WS
Date:  94-08-27  14:28:43 EDT
From:  JenuineOne

Hi, Wes!

There are a number of ways to save these messages for later
printing, depending upon your needs:

* If you only want to save a few messages or pick and choose
individual ones, just click on the file-&-folder icon at the far
right end of the Flashbar while the message window is foremost.
You'll be asked to give the file a name and save it on your hard
drive.

* If you want to save a fair number of these tips and want to be
able to print them all easier, try the cut and paste method. With
your cursor, click and drag to select the text you want to save and
press Control + c. Next, choose "New" from the File menu to get a
new text file and paste your text (Control + v) into the blank file.
You can continue to append this file by copying and pasting text you
find in the messages to the bottom of the file. When you are done,
save the file to your hard drive for later printing.

* If you want to save *all* the messages, use a log to capture
everything. To open a log, select "Logging..." from the "File"
menu and open a Session Log. Now all text you come across will be
captured and saved in the log, whether you read it all or not! When
you are done, go back to Logging and close the log. You can read and
print it right in AOL (if it isn't too big) or in a word processor.

I hope these ideas are helpful!

JenuineOne  O;>
```

Note another small detail: JenuineOne must have looked up N7WS's profile, as she addresses her message to "Wes." That's a nice touch. JenuineOne didn't have to do that, but it makes her message all the more personable.

I'm reminded of community again. Visiting a big city a few months ago, I was struck by the isolation that seemed to surround everyone I passed on the street. Perhaps it's a defense mechanism for dealing with high population density, but it seemed that everyone was in a cocoon, oblivious to everyone else. No one smiled. No one ever looked anywhere but straight ahead. Thousands of people jostled together yet none were talking. An incredibly lonely place.

On the other hand, in the little Oregon town where I live, there are no strangers. People stop on the street and say hello, swap some gossip and perhaps offer advice.

America Online is more like my little Oregon community. I spent years on other services and never felt like I belonged. I never got mail, I never contributed to a message board, and I never knew where to find help. It was like a big city to me and I was always anxious to leave. At AOL I'm walking the street in a small town on a sunny day and everyone is smiling. The first day I arrived at AOL, I got a letter from Steve Case. People like JenuineOne go out of their way to offer assistance. This is my kind of place. I'm at home here.

Guides

Guides are members chosen by AOL to serve as real-time assistants. Guides are like Members Helping Members, except there's no waiting. Have a question? Ask a Guide.

I recall an art gallery in Amsterdam. There were a number of Rembrandts there, hanging on the wall just like any other picture. No glass cases or protective Lexan—just those radiant Rembrandts, emancipated and free. A gentleman in uniform stood near. He wasn't a guard; the uniform wasn't that severe. He was a guide. He was a volunteer. He got to spend his days in a room full of the Rembrandts he loved and at the same time share his interest with other people. He explained the Rembrandts to us in a fatherly way, exhibiting a proprietorial regard for his fellow countryman's legacy.

Which is precisely what AOL's Guides are. They're members just like the rest of us—experienced members, with particularly helpful online personalities—but members all the same. They remain politely in the background, leaving us to our own explorations, silent unless spoken to. If we need help, however, Guides are always nearby, ready with friendly advice and information. If you have a question—any question at all—about AOL, its services or its policies, ask a Guide.

Like the guide in Amsterdam, you can identify Guides by their appearance: their screen names have the word "Guide" in them. If Figure 3-9's JenuineOne was to be a Guide (she should be), she would probably be "Guide JEN," or something like that.

Figure 3-11: A stop by the Lobby for some help from Guide MO.

A Night in the Lobby

MajorTom : Hi all!
Guide MO : Hey MajorTom :) ← *To help you follow what's going on, my part of the conversation appears in bold.*
Lthrneck : ::::getting out ostrich feather::::
Guide MO : Nononononono!!!
Lthrneck : ::::TICKLE, TICKLE::::
Guide MO : ::giggling::
Guide MO : Hey Cantoni!! :)
Cantoni : Hi MO!
Guide MO : Hiya NyteMaire :)
NyteMaire : Hiya MO :)
CountStixx : Maire!!!! {}{}{}{}{}{} ← *These are hugs for a new arrival in the Lobby.*
NyteMaire : {{{{{{Count}}}}}}} **
LovlyVix : Nyte {}{}{}{}{}{}{}{}{}{}{}{}{}{}
NyteMaire : {{{Vix}}}
LovlyVix : How are you Nyte?
NyteMaire : Getting crazy, and you? ;)
LovlyVix : Pretty good Nyte :)
MajorTom : Anybody know of a utility to convert JPEG to TIFF?
Guide MO : Let me check the libraries for you, T :) I always use Photoshop :)
PC Kate : <--trying to type while holding ice pack on face. :)
Lthrneck : ACK Kate, what happened?
Guide MO : Kate :(Dentist??
AFC Borg : Is the ice pack inside or outside the paper bag?
PC Kate : Lthr, had 3 hours of oral and sinus surgery yesterday. They say I should be able to eat again next Friday.
GWRepSteve : Alchemy would probably be the converter to use, MajorTom...
Lthrneck : Ouch! Kate!! {}{}{}{}{}{}{}{}
Lee123 : awww Kate. * to make it better..... ← *The asterisk is a kiss.*
LovlyVix : <--needs to go to dentist for Kates new diet :)
PC Kate : Vix, works real well... lost just under five pounds in 2 days. :)
LovlyVix : Perfect ...that would put me just where I want to be, Kate :)
Guide MO : MajorTom - I 'm sorry - I don't see what you need offhand, though I know we must have it here :/ ← *Chagrin.*
Guide MO : I'll check later and email you, if that's any help.
MajorTom : Thanks Guide. Appreciate it. I have a Plus. Can't run PhotoShop.
Guide MO : Ok - I just wrote a note to myself - I'll check for you when I get off shift at 9 and email you :)
MajorTom : Great! Thanks for the help. G'Night all! ← *I got an answer the next day.*
Guide MO : Night MajorTom :)

Figure 3-11 is a little hard to follow if you're not used to AOL's so-called chat rooms. Although chat rooms are discussed in Chapter 10 ("People Connection"), a little explanation seems in order here as well. Twenty-one people were in the room when I visited. Many were just watching (lurkers), but others seemed to be old friends. The room was full of "smileys" (turn your head counterclockwise 90 degrees and :) becomes a smile) and hugs. Smileys are discussed in Chapter 6, "Lifestyles & Interests," and Chapter 13, "Ten Best." The entire illustration is a "chat log" (see your File menu for the Logging command). Logs are discussed in Chapter 5, "News & Finance."

Chat rooms can be intimidating to the first-time visitor. Don't be shy. Jump right in with a Hello, look for the Guide's name, and ask your question. More important, note that I received one immediate answer to my question (from GWRepSteve, a member) and another the next day from Guide MO. I got just what I needed (Alchemy worked perfectly, and it's available online), and it only took 10 minutes.

Guides are on duty from 9 A.M. until 6 A.M. (Eastern time), 7 days a week, 365 days a year. To find a Guide, choose Lobby from the Go To menu, type Ctrl+L, click on the whisper-in-the-ear button on the Flashbar, or select the People Connection icon from the Main Menu.

Members

All of this talk about Guides and Members Helping Members might give you the impression that members play a significant part in the operation of AOL, and you're right. Members are much more than AOL's source of income: they're contributors (most of the files in the data libraries discussed in Chapter 7, "Computing & Software," are submitted by members), they're assistants, and, of course, they're the heart of the online community.

Since members play such an important role at AOL, it behooves us to spend a few pages discussing them: how to find them, the member profile, and how to be a better member yourself.

The Member Directory

America Online offers you the opportunity to post a voluntary member profile. Though I'll talk about profiles in a moment, the operative term in the previous sentence is "voluntary." America Online values the individual's privacy, and if you wish to remain secluded in the online community, you may do so. Those members who have completed a profile are listed in the Member Directory.

You can search for a member by real name, screen name or by profile. You might see a screen name online and wonder who is behind it: search the directory. You might wonder if a friend is signed up with AOL: search the directory.

One of the more interesting things you can do with the directory is to search for people with interests similar to yours. Once you've found them, you can send them mail (I discuss electronic mail in Chapter 4) and, perhaps, strike up a friendship. It's all part of the electronic community.

I, for instance, enjoy the beauty of my state. I live in Gresham, OR—just 13 miles from the Mount Hood National Forest where hundreds of square miles of virgin forest, lakes, trails and meadows await the explorer. Thinking I might find someone to share my interest, I search the Member Directory for members in my locality by using Gresham as my criterion (Figure 3-12).

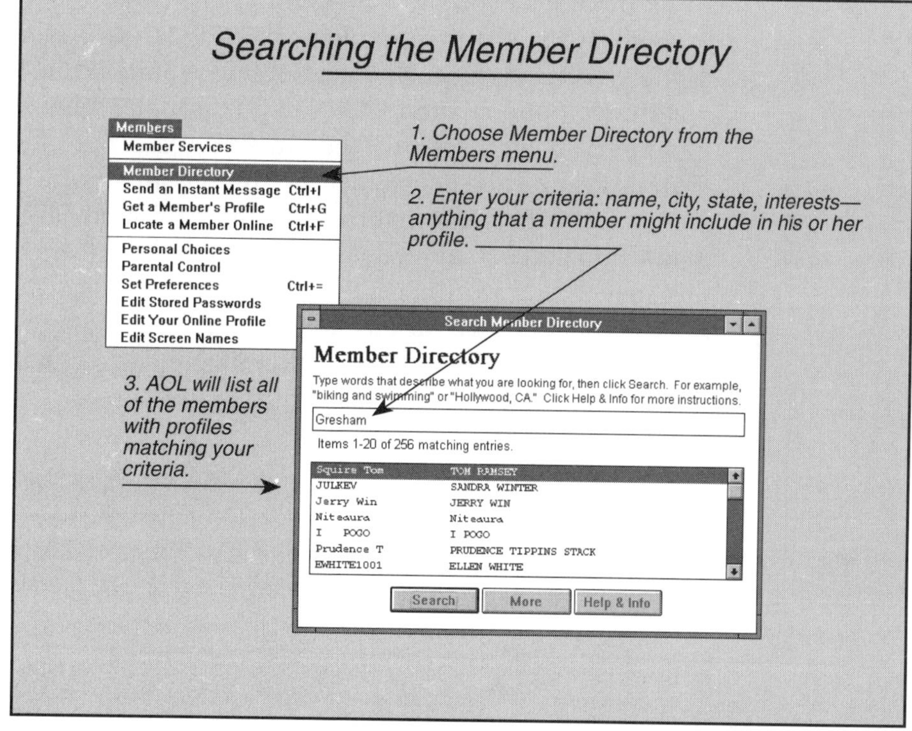

Figure 3-12: Much to my delight, 256 others from Gresham have posted their profiles. I'll send them some mail and see if they want to explore the forest someday.

Actually, Figure 3-12 is misleading. My search for "Gresham" omitted those members who live in other towns near Mount Hood National Forest. It also didn't include those members who have elected to omit their profiles. My guess is that there are thousands of AOL members from my area, many more than pictured in Figure 3-12.

To access the Members Directory, choose Member Directory from the Members menu, then double-click the Search the Members Directory option.

Member Profiles

As I mentioned a moment ago, member profiles are optional. If you elect not to complete a profile, your name won't show up in searches like the one described above.

If that's your preference, you cut yourself out of a number of opportunities to become involved in the online community. If you elect to post a profile (or if you've already posted a profile and want to edit it), AOL provides a couple of ways for you to do so.

Look again at the menu pictured in Figure 3-12. Note that one of the options listed there is Edit Your Online Profile. While this is one way to get the job done, a better way is to go through Members' Online Support. You've got to be signed on in either case, but Members' Online Support is free and choosing Edit Your Online Profile from the Members menu is not. Moreover, the Members' Online Support route offers a few options that aren't available from the Members menu. You can also use the keyword: Profile. Both routes pass through the free curtain.

The profile inquiry asks only a few questions about you. Take your time answering these (it's free, after all), and soon you'll have a profile as sterling and poetic as mine (Figure 3-14).

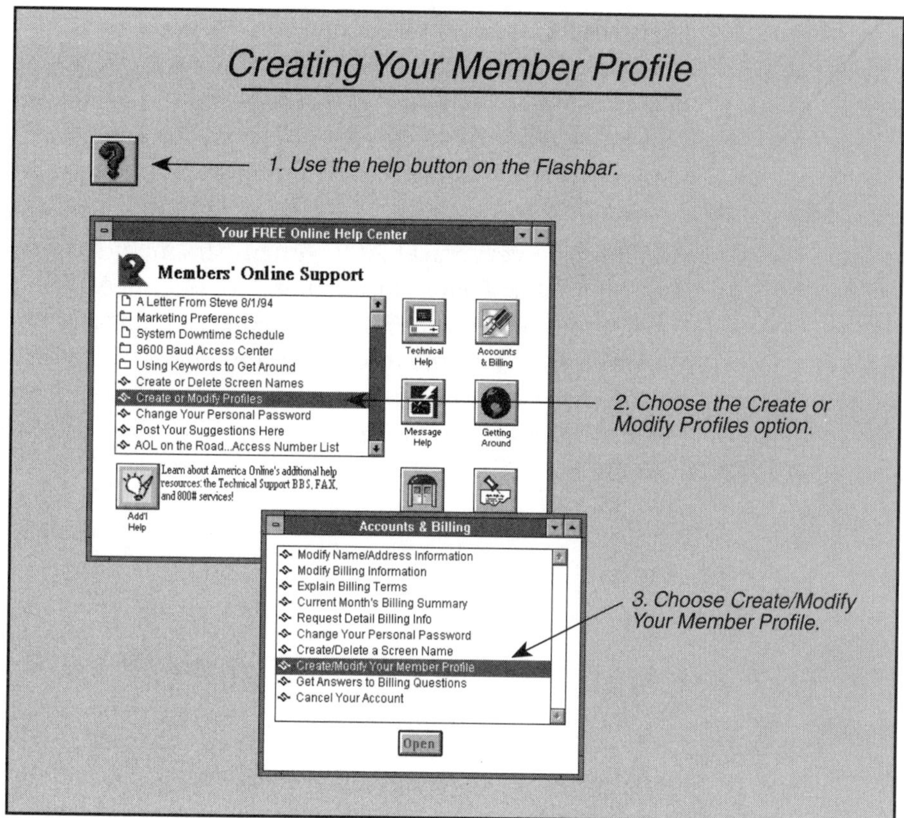

Figure 3-13: You can access your member profile by using the keyword: Profile; by choosing Edit Your Online Profile from the Members menu; or by using Members' Online Support (keyword: Help).

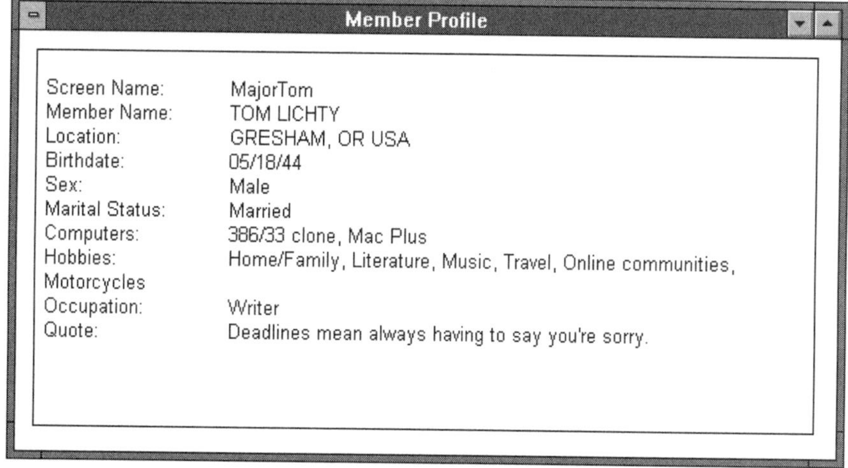

Figure 3-14: MajorTom's profile reveals all of my secrets.

Moving On

We've come a long way since the heavy-metal band took the stage at the beginning of this chapter. I hope your journey has been confidence-building for you. America Online offers more help—and more kinds of help—than any software I've known. It's online, it's off-line, it's the Customer Relations Department, it's Members Helping Members, and it's Guides. Everyone at AOL—members included—helps someone else sooner or later. That's comforting. Not only is AOL a community, it's a considerate community, where no one remains a stranger for long.

And now's the time to become a member of that community. The best way to do that is to send electronic mail to someone. Mail is the heart of the AOL community, and we'll explore it thoroughly in the next chapter.

CHAPTER 4

Electronic Mail

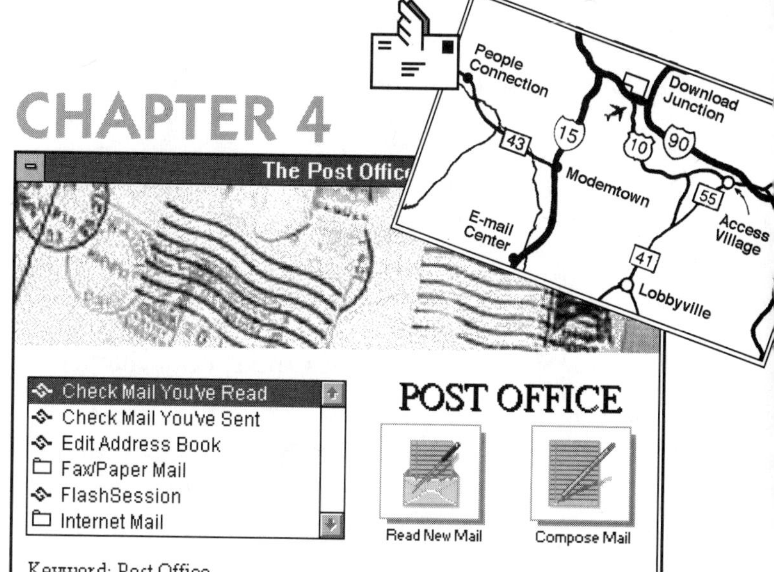

People my age remember the days when the phrase "the mail" meant only one thing. If you wanted to mail something, you handed it to the postman, you dropped it in a mailbox or you took it to the post office. There was no UPS, no fax, no FedEx, no e-mail and no Internet. There was only "the mail"—the US Postal Service—and a first-class postage stamp cost 3 cents.

The fast-moving information age we live in today requires alternatives such as package delivery, overnight letters, facsimile, voice mail and e-mail. Each has its place. Each offers something the others do not. Electronic mail offers immediacy, convenience, multiple addressing and automated record-keeping. Moreover, it's cheap—perhaps the least expensive of the bunch—and ecologically responsible. E-mail has all the makings of a darling, and it is just now entering its prime.

What Exactly Is Electronic Mail?

Electronic mail (*e-mail* for short) is simply mail prepared on a computer and sent to someone else who has access to a computer. There are lots of private e-mail networks—computers wired together and configured to send and receive mail. America Online is one of these. Many of these networks (including AOL) are connected to the Internet (the Internet is discussed in Chapter 14, "The Internet Connection;" Internet mail is

---

The frontispiece is of the AOL Post Office greeting screen. Most of the e-mail commands and resources can be accessed via this screen, or via the Mail menu. Use the keyword: PostOffice.

discussed later in this chapter), and you can send mail to (and receive mail from) the people across these networks.

Most e-mail systems share a number of common characteristics:

- Messages are composed of pure ASCII text. Fancy formatting, graphics and special characters aren't accommodated within messages.
- Because they're usually simple text, messages can be sent between dissimilar computers. You can communicate with people using Macs, Amigas, mainframes—even terminals (there are thousands on the Internet), which aren't really computers at all.
- The addressee must be known to the mail system.

Additional features are offered by some e-mail systems, including AOL:

- Messages can be replied to or forwarded to anyone, including people connected to networks outside of AOL. This includes commercial services such as Prodigy and CompuServe.
- Files can be attached to messages. In most cases, files are specific to a particular computer or operating system, so the receiving computer must be compatible with the sending computer in order to open the file. On the other hand, files can contain anything: graphics, formatted text, even sound and animation.
- Messages can be addressed to multiple recipients. "Carbon copies" can be sent to people other than the addressee, and "blind" carbon copies (copies sent without the other addressees' knowledge) can be specified as well.
- Messages need not be composed while you're online. Likewise, received messages need not be read while you're online. Any incoming message can be filed for later retrieval and read offline at your convenience. If you choose to reply, you can compose your reply offline as well. You need to sign on only to send and receive mail, a process that rarely consumes more than a couple of minutes online.

Why Use E-mail?

Nothing matches the convenience, immediacy and ecology of electronic mail. Composing a message amounts to nothing more than typing it; mailing a message is accomplished with a single click of the mouse; and AOL files a copy for you, automatically, on the host computers in Virginia. Archaic inconveniences such as envelopes and stamps are never required, and fax funny paper—an ecological disaster if ever there was one—never enters the picture. Indeed, paper of any kind is rarely used when mail is sent electronically.

America Online's e-mail service is an outstanding example of this communication medium. It does all the things e-mail should do, and adds enough features to make a mail carrier want to resign. You can compose mail off-line, send (and receive) it when you're away from your computer, address it to multiple recipients, send carbon copies (and blind carbon copies), attach files (to mail addressed to other AOL members), reply to mail received and forward mail to others at AOL or on the Internet. Mail can also be faxed or, if the recipient is really in the dark ages, even sent via the US Mail.

America Online obediently holds your mail until you're ready to read it, announces its availability every time you sign on and never sends you junk mail.

Perhaps best of all, about all you'll ever pay for this service is a nickel—maybe a dime if you're really pedantic. America Online doesn't charge extra for e-mail, even that sent to or received from the Internet. It's not exactly a return to the 3-cent stamp, but it's close.

A Circular Exercise

Before we get to the details, here's a little exercise just to show you how e-mail works. This exercise is somewhat futile: sending mail to yourself is a little like narcissism—a little less vainglorious perhaps, but no less futile. Nevertheless, do it just this once. Nobody's looking.

- With America Online up and running, sign on. Leave the In the Spotlight screen showing and choose Compose Mail from the Mail menu (or click on the pen-and-paper button on the Flashbar). A Compose Mail form will appear (see Figure 4-1).

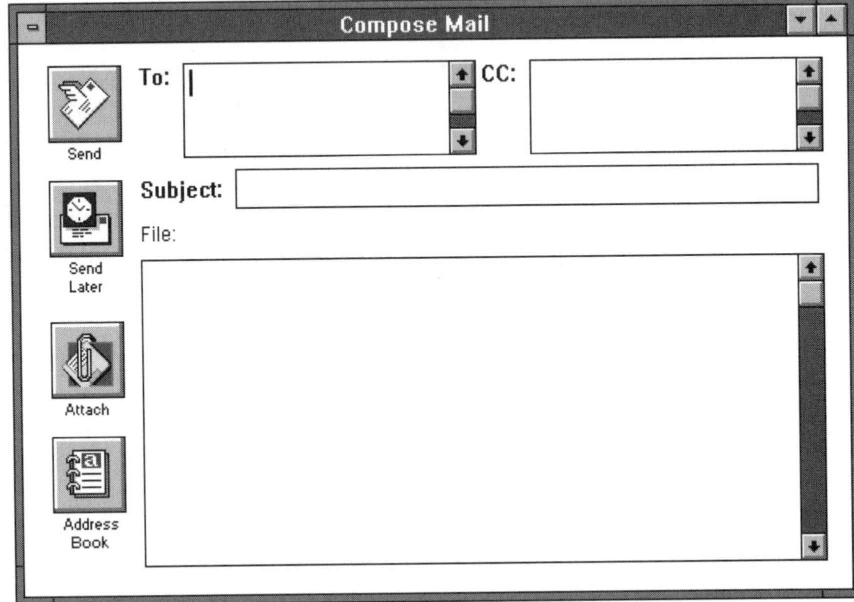

Figure 4-1: This window appears whenever you're about to compose some mail. AOL has already identified you as the sender; it's now waiting for you to identify the recipient.

- The insertion point is now flashing in the To text box, where you insert the screen name of the recipient. Type in your screen name. This is the futile part of the exercise—sending mail to yourself—but the rewards are immediate, and there will be no guessing as to whether the mail ever made it to the addressee.

No Accounting for Case

America Online screen names are not case-sensitive. MajorTom works no better than majortom. This is really comforting: I used to be obsessed with such details, worrying that imperfectly addressed mail would end up in electronic limbo somewhere. My anxieties were needless (as most are). Even if you misspell a screen name, AOL will notify you that there's no match for the address you've typed. There's no "dead mail" room at AOL.

- In the Subject text box, enter the word "Test" (without the quotes).
- Type something into the message text box. This is the narcissistic part. Don't overdo it. People will talk.
- Click the Send button.

Instantly, a voice announces "You've got mail!" (if your PC is equipped with sound). Even if you don't hear anything, the mail flag will pop up in the mail button at the far left of the Flashbar. There's a particular comfort in that. Mail moves around the AOL circuit quite literally at the speed of light. You'll never wonder again if your mail will get to its destination by next Thursday. It gets there the instant you send it.

Note also that two things have happened: (1) the little flag in the mailbox button on the Flashbar comes up; and (2) the "You Have Mail" button on the In the Spotlight Screen is now active (Figure 4-2).

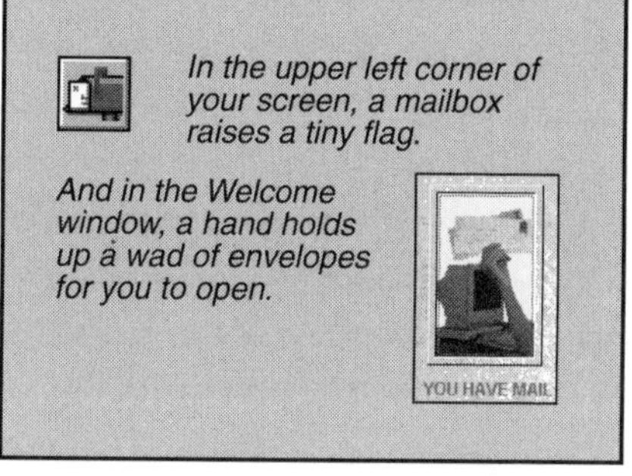

In the upper left corner of your screen, a mailbox raises a tiny flag.
And in the Welcome window, a hand holds up a wad of envelopes for you to open.
YOU HAVE MAIL

Figure 4-2: You've got mail! You get two doses of visual indication and one aural prompt every time mail is waiting for you at America Online.

- By now, the Compose Mail window has closed and you're back at the In the Spotlight screen. Click the "You Have Mail" button.
- The New Mail window appears (see Figure 4-3). This window is a little redundant when you only have one piece of mail waiting, but soon you'll be a Popular Person and dozens of entries will appear here every time you sign on.
- Double-click the entry, which represents the mail you sent a moment ago.
- The message window appears, with your message therein (see Figure 4-4).

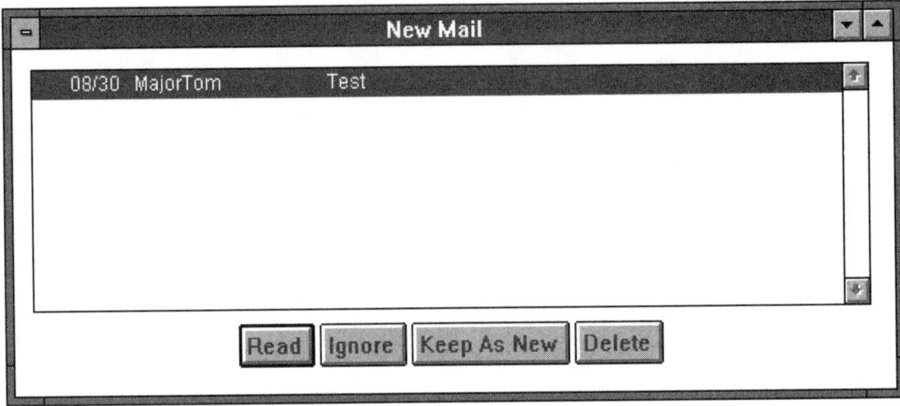

Figure 4-3: The New Mail window appears whenever you elect to read incoming mail.

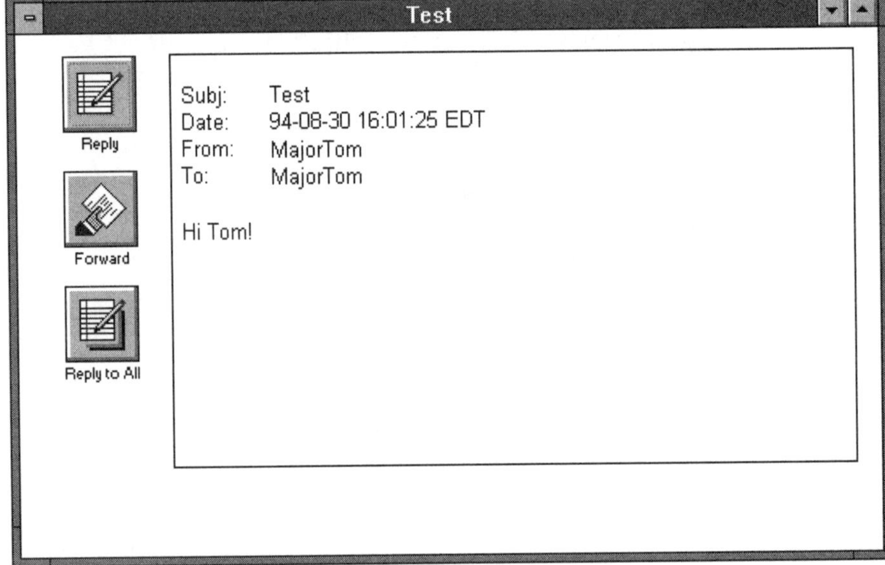

Figure 4-4: The mail is received. Note that you can forward or reply to this mail by simply clicking the appropriate button.

It's probably best for you to toss this mail now, before anyone sees what you've been up to. To throw it away, double-click its control menu (the little box in the upper left corner of the window) or press Ctrl+F4. I just wanted you to see how simple, fast and easy the process really is. That's the whole idea—above all, e-mail should be convenient, global and inexpensive, and AOL certainly makes it so.

The Mail Controls

Nearly all day-to-day mail activities are performed using the Mail menu or the Flashbar. You can compose and read mail using the two mail buttons on the Flashbar if you wish (they're the two at the extreme left: Read and Compose, in that order—review the Flashbar key in Figure 2-12), or you can choose the corresponding command from the Mail menu. The Mail menu also offers keystroke shortcuts for Compose and Read (Ctrl+M and Ctrl+R, respectively). (Some prefer AOL's Post Office screen—see the frontispiece—but we'll discuss the Mail menu here.) The single exception is the FlashSession, which we'll discuss in Chapter 19, "FlashSessions and the Download Manager." FlashSessions aren't for everybody, however: indeed, most seminormal people conduct all of their mail activities using the Mail menu (Figure 4-5) exclusively.

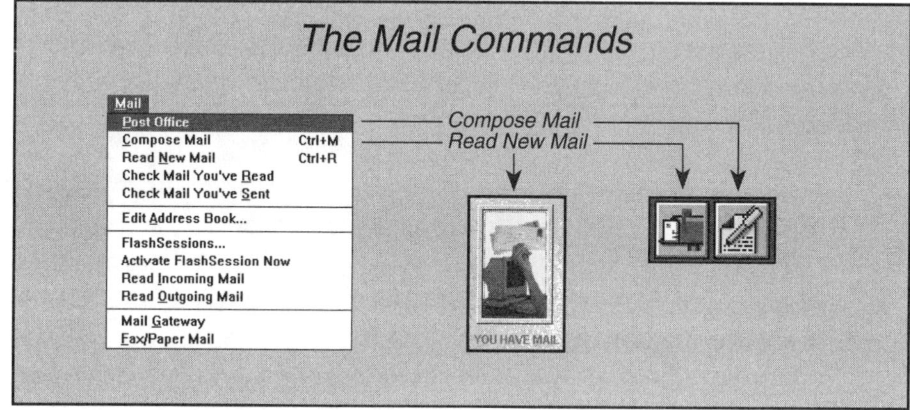

Figure 4-5: The Mail menu and buttons offer plenty of alternatives for your daily e-mail.

Composing Your Mail

An option near the top of the Mail menu is Compose Mail, which you choose whenever you want to send mail to someone. This option is available whether you're online or off; you can compose mail off-line and send it later—a feature I'll discuss in a moment.

When the Compose Mail command is issued, AOL responds with a Compose Mail Form (review Figure 4-1). Note the position of the insertion point in Figure 4-1. It's located within the To field of the window. America Online, in other words, is waiting for you to provide the recipient's screen name. Type it in. (If you don't remember the screen name, you can use your Address Book, which I'll discuss later in this chapter.)

You can send mail to multiple addresses if you wish. Simply include multiple screen names in the To field, separated by a comma and a space. You can place multiple names there (I have never discovered the maximum, but it must be large: note that the field is actually a scroll box). If you want to send mail to Steve Case and Tom Lichty, type "Steve Case, MajorTom" (without the quotes) in this box.

Press the Tab key and the cursor jumps to the CC (carbon copy) field. Here you can place the addresses of those people who are to receive "carbon copies" of your mail. Carbon copies (actually, they're called *courtesy copies* now—carbon paper being a thing of the past) are really no different than originals. Whether a member receives an original or a copy is more a matter of protocol than anything else. *Note*: Use only screen names in the To and CC fields. Do not put members' real names here.

Blind Carbon Copies

As is the case with the traditional "CC:" at the bottom of a business letter, the addressee is aware of all carbon copies. This is a traditional business courtesy.

On the other hand, you might want to send a copy of a message to another person without the addressee (or addressees) knowing you have done so. This is known as a "blind" carbon copy. To address a blind carbon copy, place the recipient's address in the CC field, *enclosing it in parentheses*. The parentheses are the trick. No one but the recipient of the blind carbon copy will know what you've done. The ethics of this feature are yours to ponder; its use, after all, is voluntary.

Press the Tab key to move the insertion point to the Subject field, and enter a descriptive word or two. *Note*: The Subject field *must* be filled in—AOL won't take the message without it.

Press the Tab key again. The insertion point moves to the message text area. Type your message there (see Figure 4-6).

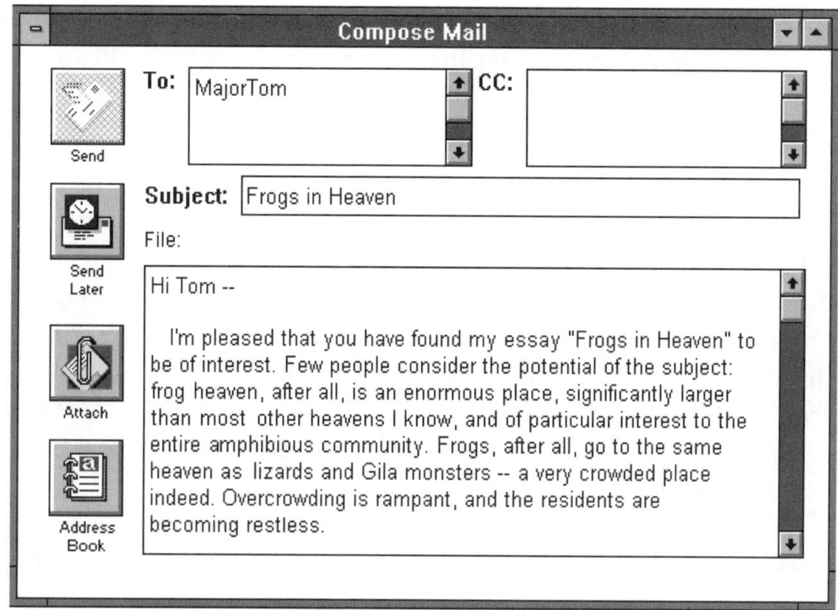

Figure 4-6: The completed message is ready to send. Click the Send button (if you re online) or the Send Later button (if you re not).

It's subtle, but note that the Send button in Figure 4-6 is dimmed: this message is being prepared off-line (see sidebar).

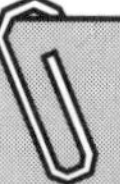

Preparing Mail Off-line

Consider preparing mail when you're off-line and the meter isn't running. You can linger over it that way, perfecting every word. When you complete a message, click the Send Later button. The next time you sign on, choose Read Outgoing Mail from the Mail menu, then click the Send All button.

Alternative Mail Sources

Occasionally, you might want to send a text file as mail. Perhaps it's a file you created with the New command (File menu), or a text file from a word processor, or one that you captured online. Regardless of the source, you can send a text file as mail (rather than as a file) by simply cutting and pasting.

Any text that can be copied via Windows' Copy command (the Copy command is under the Edit menu of most Windows software) can be pasted into the text field of the Compose Mail form. Add a subject and an addressee, click on Send and it's done.

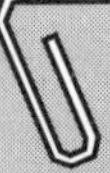

A Pain in the Neck

Because there's no eye contact or voice intonation in e-mail messages, sometimes it's necessary to punctuate your conversation with textual "smileys," as they're called. Smileys clarify the sender's intention when it might otherwise be misinterpreted. The phrase, "Just as I thought, Billy Joe: there are no forks in your family tree," could be interpreted as slander. Follow it with a smiley, however, and most members will understand your attempt at depraved humor: "Just as I thought, Billy Joe: there are no forks in your family tree. ;)"

The semicolon-close parenthesis combination at the end of the sentence above is a wink. Turn your head 90 degrees counterclockwise and you'll see a little "smiley face" with its right eye winking. It's a pain in the neck, but it's better than making enemies.

Below are some of the more common smileys. Some people use them more than others, but most everybody does occasionally.

:)	Smile
;)	Wink
: D	Laughing out loud (also abbreviated LOL).
: (	Frown
: /	Chagrin
{}	Hug (usually plural: {{{{{}}}}} Why hug just once?)

These are the smileys I see most often online. There are scores of others. I've seen : # (lips are sealed), : & (tongue tied), : [(pout), : * (kiss) and : 0 (yell). But my favorite is : p (sticking out tongue). See Chapter 20, "Ten Best," for more smileys.

All of this is a little like those inane yellow smiley faces that punctuated the '70s, but it's justified here. Misinterpretation of text is easy; smileys help clarify the meaning. Go ahead: smile at someone today. :)

This technique is especially useful for those who prefer to use a word processor to compose messages. Word processors feature spelling checkers and productivity tools that AOL's Compose Mail utility does not offer. If you prefer to use your word processor for mail composition, go ahead. When you're finished with your document, select and copy it, run the AOL software, and paste into the text field of the Compose Mail window. Since fancy formatting (nearly *all* formatting, really: fonts, type sizes, appearance attributes such as italics—that kind of stuff) contained in a word-processing document is lost or altered when pasted into an AOL mail window, you should prepare your mail without any formatting, regardless of how feature-laden your word processor may be.

Checking Mail You've Sent

Occasionally you might want to review mail you've sent to others: "What exactly did I say to Billy Joe that caused him to visit the Tallahatchee Bridge last night?"

Even if you don't file your mail (a subject addressed later in this chapter), AOL retains everything you send for at least one week. You can review any sent mail by choosing Check Mail You've Sent from the Mail menu. America Online responds by displaying a listing of all the mail you've sent recently. Choose the mail you want to know about from that list, and click the Read button to review what you've sent (see Figure 4-7).

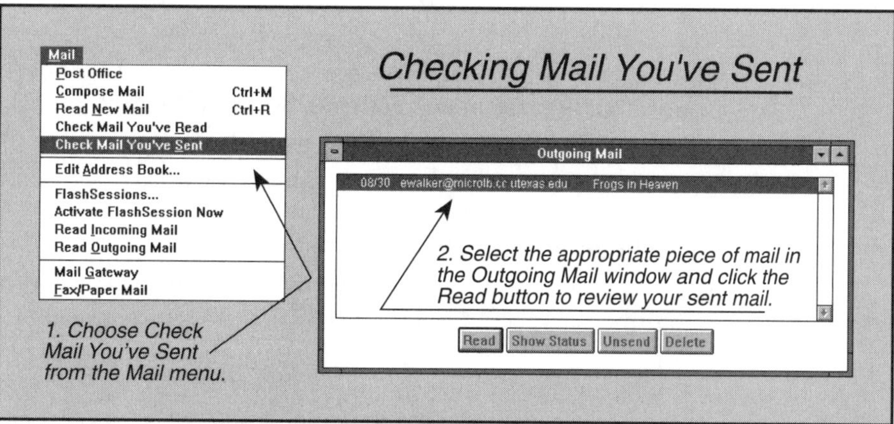

Figure 4-7: You can reread any mail you've sent by using the Check Mail You've Sent command.

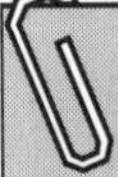

Online Only

The Check Mail You've Sent and the Check Mail You've Read commands are *only* available when you're online. This mail is stored on AOL's machines, not yours; you have to be online to access data stored there.

As you're reading your sent mail, you can select and copy it, then paste it into other documents (see the Copy & Paste sidebar if you're not familiar with this process). This works especially well for reminder notices, clarifications and nagging. It could save you some typing as well: you might need to send a message that's a near-duplicate of one you sent four days ago. Rather than retyping text from the old message, reopen it using Check Mail You've Sent under the Mail menu, copy the sections you need, and paste them into a new message window.

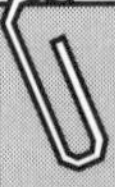

Copy & Paste

If you're not yet familiar with your PC, here's a brief lesson in copying and pasting: Select mail messages by clicking somewhere within them and choosing Select All from the Edit menu. To copy the selection, choose Copy from the Edit menu. This puts the selected text on the Windows Clipboard—its internal memory—where it's ready for use elsewhere. To paste text into another document, Open that document (File menu), click the mouse at the location where you want the text to go, then choose Paste from the Edit menu.

Buttons in the Mail You've Sent Window

A number of buttons appear across the bottom of the Outgoing Mail window pictured in Figure 4-7; each serves a specific purpose.

The Read Button

Select a piece of mail from the list, then click the Read button to read that message. This function was discussed a few pages back.

The Show Status Button

The Show Status button tells you when the recipient (or recipients, if the mail was sent to more than one address) read the message. This is a great way to see if someone has read a message you've sent. This only applies to mail sent to another AOL member, however: if the mail was sent to an Internet address (Chapter 14, "The Internet Connection," discusses the Internet), there's no way for AOL to know if the mail was read. The Show Status button will return "Not applicable" under these conditions.

The Unsend Button

The Unsend button allows you to retrieve mail you have sent from the mailboxes of all recipients, as well as from your Mail You've Sent list. To unsend a piece of mail, highlight the mail you wish to unsend and click the Unsend button. Certain conditions, however, will disable this feature:

- If any addressee has an Internet mail address.
- If any recipient has read that piece of mail (excepting you, even if you were on the addressee list).
- If any recipient has a fax or US Mail address.

If you close the Outgoing Mail window with an unsent message showing, it will be permanently deleted from the AOL archives: it won't show up on your Outgoing Mail list when you check it again. If you want to modify or save an unsent message, double-click it while it's still showing, then either modify it (and resend it if you wish), or copy and paste it into some other document. *Then* you can Unsend it.

The Delete Button

This button simply removes the selected piece of mail from your Outgoing Mail list. It does *not* affect the message's destiny: AOL will still deliver it. It's really a feature for people who send *lots* of mail and prefer to keep their "Check Mail You've Sent" lists short.

Reading New Mail

The third option on the Mail menu—Read New Mail—refers to mail you've just received. I don't use this menu item. To me, mail is like Christmas morning: I can't wait to get to it. Immediately after hearing that I have mail, I click the "You Have Mail" button (pictured in Figure 4-2) and start unwrapping my presents.

Nevertheless, there are those who don't share my enthusiasm. That, I suppose, is why AOL provides this menu option. When it's chosen, America Online presents the New Mail window (Figure 4-8).

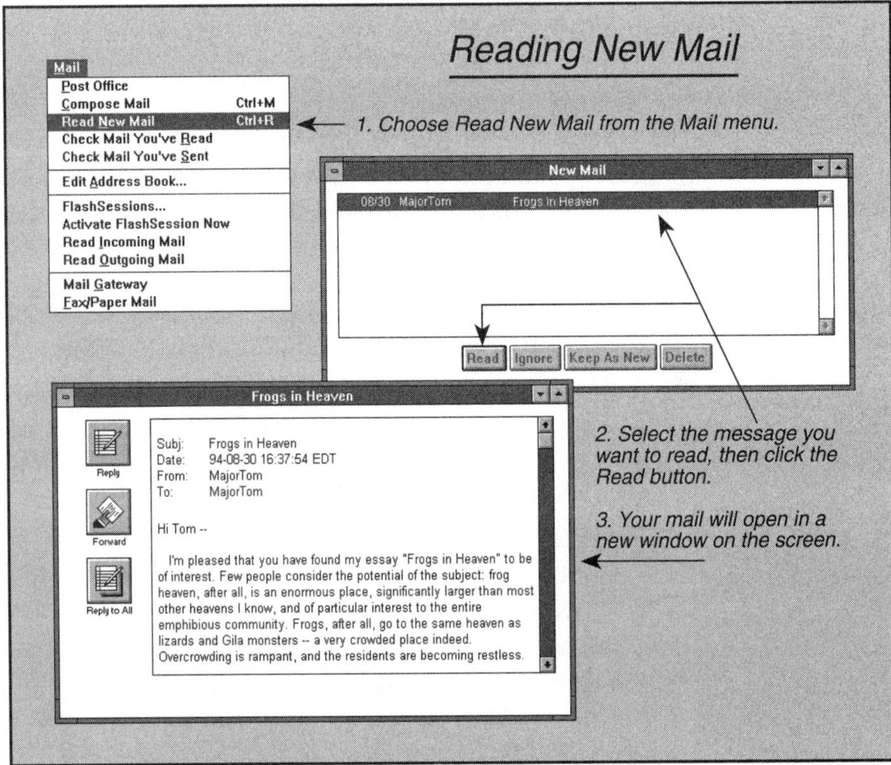

Figure 4-8: Reading new mail can be accomplished with the mailbox button on the Flashbar, the "You Have Mail" button in the Welcome window, by pressing Ctrl+R, or by choosing Read New Mail from the Mail menu.

Though Figure 4-8 shows only one unread piece of mail, a number of pieces might appear here. If more than one shows up, they'll appear in the order in which they were received at AOL. The oldest mail will be at the top, the most recent at the bottom. In other words, to read your mail in chronological order from oldest to most recent, read your messages from top to bottom.

Buttons in the New Mail Window

A number of buttons appears across the bottom of the New Mail window pictured in Figure 4-8. They can be confusing at first, so a discussion of their use is in order.

Read

This button displays the selected piece of mail on the screen for reading. It's the default button: double-clicking an entry on the list does the same thing.

Ignore

This option will move a piece of mail directly into your Old Mail list without your having to read the mail, in effect "ignoring" that piece of mail. If the sender issues a status check, he or she will see the word "Ignored" beside your screen name. Be sure that's what you want the addressee to see if you use this command.

Keep as New

Clicking this button will return the selected piece of mail to your New Mail list after you've read it. The mail is, however, still considered *read* as far as other members' status checks are concerned. In other words, if someone checks the status of a piece of mail that you read then kept as new, they will see the time you read the mail, regardless of whether you kept it as new or not.

Delete

This feature allows you to permanently remove a piece of mail from your New Mail mailbox. It will not appear on the Old Mail list either (I'll discuss the Check Mail You've Read command in a moment). Status checks performed by other members on deleted mail say "Deleted." Compare this button with the Ignore button mentioned earlier.

Printing and Saving Mail

You can print or save any piece of mail that occupies the front-most (active) window by choosing the appropriate command from the File menu. If you choose Print, AOL will display a dialog box identifying your Windows default printer (as selected through Windows' Control Panel). Choose OK to print or change to another installed printer through the Setup button.

If you choose Save (or Save As—in this context they're the same command), AOL responds with the traditional Save As dialog box. Give your mail a name and use the .TXT extension. It will be saved as a standard text file and you will be able to open it with not only AOL's software, but any word processor (or text editor such as Windows Notepad).

Alternatively, you can select and copy any mail appearing on your screen. Now you can open any text file on your disk (or start a new one via the New command under the File menu) and paste your mail into that file.

You can also paste copied AOL text into other Windows applications' files if you wish. There are a number of ways to file mail, and I'll describe some of them in the Gorilla Food section of this chapter.

Remember Size

Those of you more fortunate than I might find the placement of AOL's windows to be restricting. My PC has a standard 14-inch screen. To my benefit, the defaults for size and placement of AOL's windows have been determined with 14-inch screens in mind. In other words, if you have a larger screen, a few of AOL's windows may congregate in the upper left corner. If that is your predicament, you'll be happy to discover the Remember Window Size Only and Remember Window Size and Position commands under the Window menu (see Figure 4-9).

Window
Cascade Shift+F5
Tile Shift+F4
Arrange Icons
Close All
Exit Free Area
Remember Window Size and Position
Remember Window Size Only
Forget Window Size and Position
√ 1 Welcome, MajorTom!

Figure 4-9: Super VGA users with large screens should investigate the Remember commands under the Window menu.

If you have a large-screen PC and want to permanently relocate a window, simply situate the window to your satisfaction, then choose Remember Size and Position from the Windows menu. From that moment on, the window will pop back into your preferred position and size, every time it's used. As you might expect, the Remember Size Only command remembers only the window's size but leaves its *location* up to AOL. Whether you're a minimalist or a maximalist, you will like this command.

Forwarding Mail

Once you have read your mail, you can forward it, reply to it or throw it out. Each of these options is accomplished with a click of the mouse. To forward a piece of mail, simply click the Forward button pictured in Figure 4-10. America Online will respond with the slightly modified Compose Mail window that appears in the middle of Figure 4-10.

Figure 4-10: Forwarding mail is as easy as clicking a button, identifying the recipient and typing your comments.

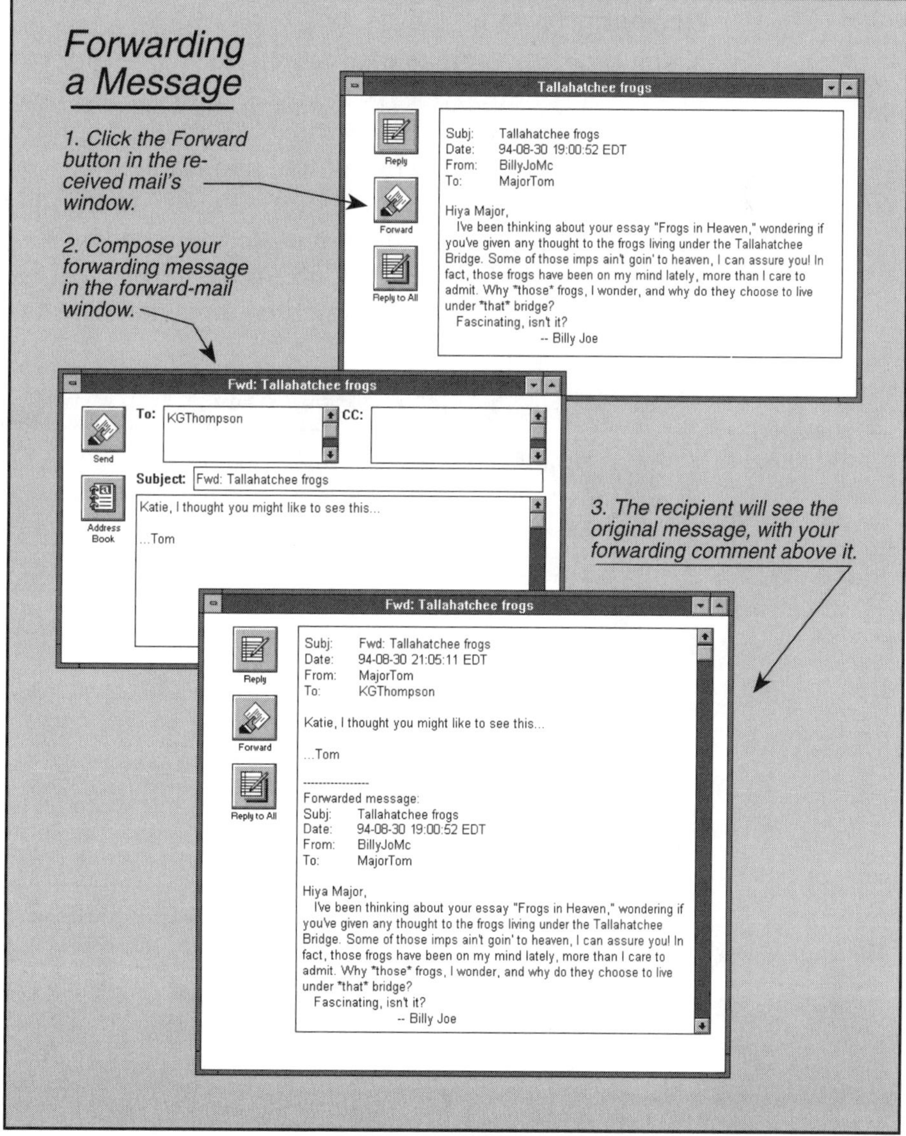

The middle window pictured in Figure 4-10 is where you enter your forwarding comment and the address of the person who is to receive the forward. The new recipient then receives the forwarded mail with your comment preceding it. America Online clearly identifies forwarded mail by including a line at the top of the message that declares it as forwarded mail and identifies the person who did the forwarding (see the bottom window in Figure 4-10).

Replying to Mail

You'll probably reply to mail more often than you forward it. Actually, all the Reply button does is call up a Compose Mail window with the To and Subject fields already filled in with the appropriate information (see Figure 4-11). Aside from these two features, a reply is the same as any other message. You can modify the To and CC fields if you wish, and discuss any subject that interests you in the message text. You can even change the Subject field or remove the original recipient's screen name from the To field, though this somewhat defeats the purpose.

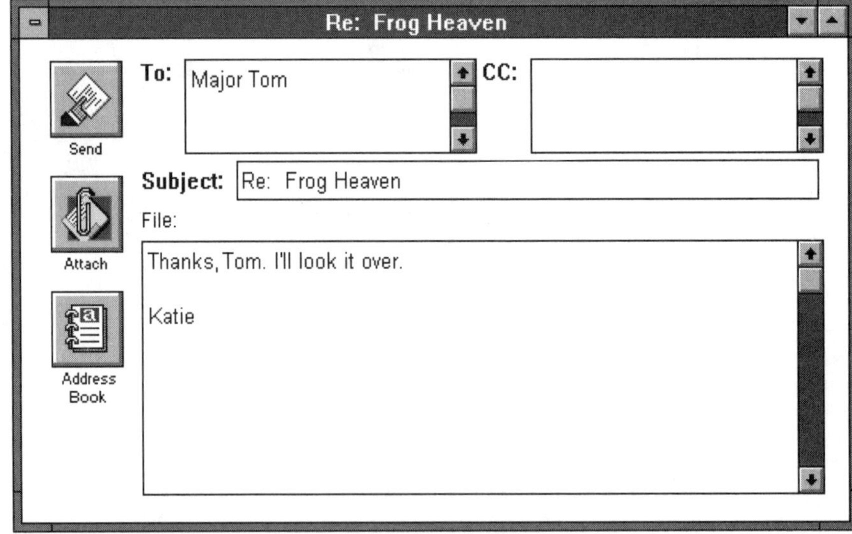

Figure 4-11: The reply window. The Subject and To fields are already completed for you; all you have to do is provide the message.

Replying to All

Look once again at the lower window in Figure 4-10. Note that there are two reply buttons, including one marked Reply to All. Reply to All allows you to reply to everyone who was sent a message, including any carbon copy addressees. In other words, you have your choice of replying only to the original sender (Reply button) or to everyone who receives a message (Reply to All button).

Note: Reply to All does not reply to blind carbon copy addressees. The rule here is, Reply to All replies to all whose screen names are visible in the Mail window. If you don't see a name (which would be the case if someone received a blind carbon copy), that person will not receive your reply.

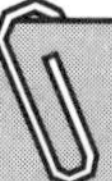

Replying with a Copy of the Original

Some people get lots of mail. Steve Case, for instance, gets hundreds of pieces a day. For Steve's benefit, I always include a copy of his original message when I reply. I do this to help him remember the subject of our discussion. Rather than copy and paste his message into a Reply window, I use the Forward button. Remember that forwarded mail includes a copy of the original message along with your comment. This little trick also works when you want to reply to a very old message the sender might not recall.

Because a copy of the original message gets sent with the reply, using the Forward button is an inefficient way of handling mail. More significantly, AOL has to store much more data. America Online's storage problems, however, are not our concern. The people at AOL are gonna love me for telling you about this.

Checking Mail You've Read

We all forget things now and again: "What did I promise to get my mother for Valentine's Day?" That's why AOL provides the Check Mail You've Read option under the Mail menu. When you choose this command, AOL responds with the Old Mail window (see Figure 4-12).

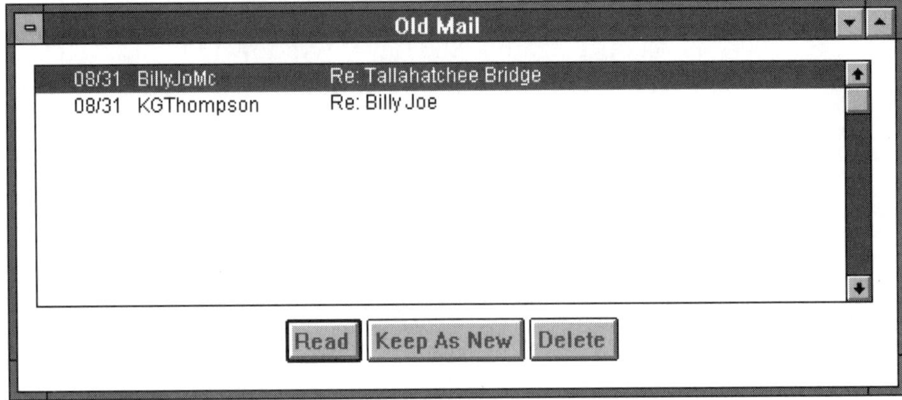

Figure 4-12: The Old Mail window lists all of the mail you have read, just in case you forget.

There are no surprises here. Double-click any message in the window to reread it. Reread mail can be forwarded and replied to just like any other mail.

The Address Book

America Online provides an address book just like the address book next to your telephone. In effect, AOL's book is a cross-reference, listing people's real names and their corresponding screen names. My recommendation is that you use the Address Book, even if you only have a name or two to put there now. Eventually you'll have scores of entries in your book, and you will be glad they're there.

Adding a Name to the Address Book

No one memorizes screen names. Screen names are eccentric composites of letters and numbers like "MikeQ4506," which AOL's sign-on software cooks up for each new member, or something clever like "DerringDo," which the member creates later when AOL's default screen name becomes insufferable. Either way, most screen names are eminently forgettable. That's why AOL provides an Address Book.

Of course, before you can use the Address Book you have to put some names there. It's easy. Online or off, choose Address Book from the Mail menu and AOL will provide the Address Book editing window pictured in Figure 4-13.

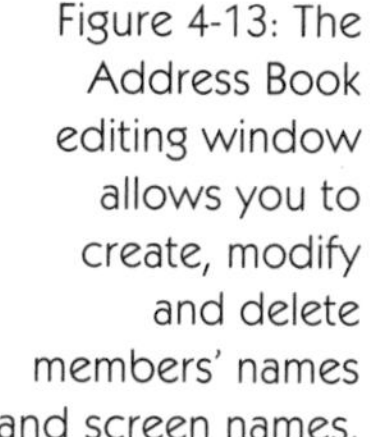

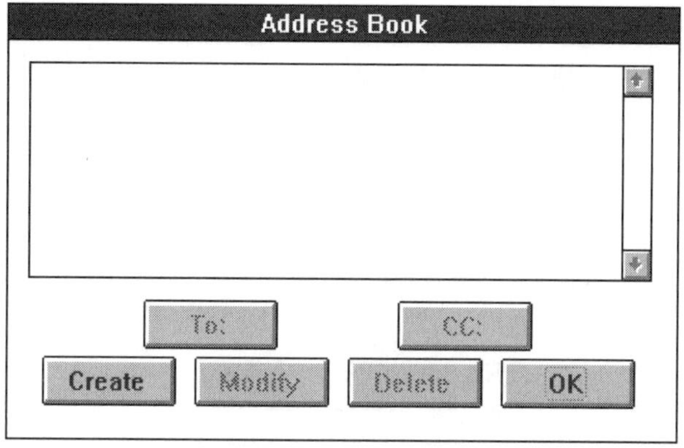

Figure 4-13: The Address Book editing window allows you to create, modify and delete members' names and screen names.

To add an entry to your Address Book, click the Create button. America Online will provide the editing form pictured in Figure 4-14.

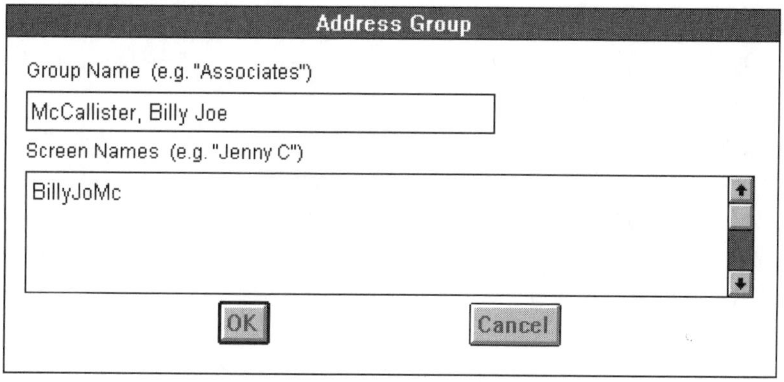

Figure 4-14: The Address Book editing form.

Place the person's real name in the Group Name field, then place their AOL or Internet address in the Screen Names field. The next time you choose Address Book from the Mail window, the name will appear there (see Figure 4-15).

Now you are ready to use the Address Book whenever you prepare mail. Look again at Figure 4-1. Do you see the button in the lower left corner marked Address Book? If your Address Book is current, you can use it to look up people's addresses and plug them into the To and CC fields of the Compose Mail window. Whenever a Compose Mail form is displayed on your screen, all you have to do is click that button. From then on, it's only a matter of clicking the mouse.

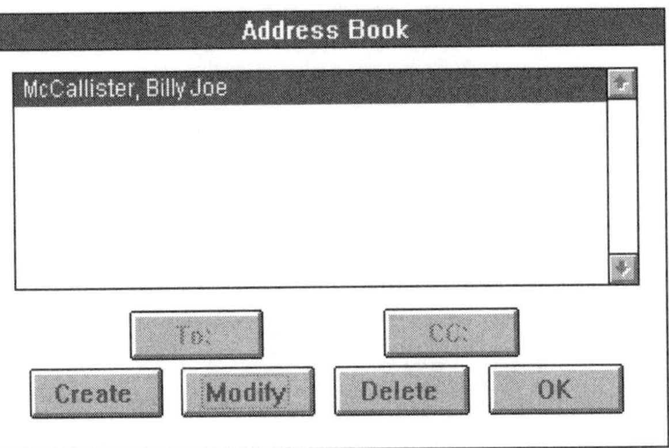

Figure 4-15: The Address Book now contains the new entry.

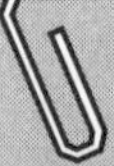

Multiple Accounts

If you look again at Figure 4-14, you'll notice that there's room for multiple addresses in the Screen Names field. In fact, the word "screen names" appears, not "screen name." You might wonder why.

Imagine that you're participating in an online discourse of frog heaven with three other esteemed theologians. Nearly every piece of mail on the subject has to be sent to all three of them. In this situation, you might want to create an entry in your Address Book called Froggers, and list all three addresses—with commas between each address—in the Screen Names field. Once you have done so, all you have to do is select Froggers from your Address Book to send them mail.

Gorilla Food

Okay, you e-mail Thunder Lizards, here's your raw meat. Read this section and you'll take your place among the e-mail *illuminati*. Mortals will climb mountains to seek your wisdom; the masses will genuflect as you pass by; your aura will illuminate the northern sky.

Mail-filing Strategies

A while back I mentioned that e-mail to me is like packages on Christmas morning. I look forward to it with great anticipation. I descend into a pit of depression if a voice doesn't say "You've got mail!" when I sign on. Consequently, I have developed a cadre of online friends, and correspond with them regularly. This means that I get a lot of mail.

I send and receive 20 or more pieces of mail a day. With that much mail coming in, finding a place to file that mail is critical. I need fast, convenient, electronic access to it. I copy and paste messages frequently, so a paper filing system just won't do. I am also an environmentalist, another reason why paperless e-mail appeals to me. My e-mail filing system is the bedrock of my online activities.

You might be facing the same need. Because of the Christmas-morning quality of AOL's e-mail system, lots of people get lots of mail, and lots of people need to be thinking about a filing system. Now's the time to bring the subject into the open.

Saving Mail in FlashSessions

Though I'll discuss FlashSessions in Chapter 19, you've no doubt noted the FlashSessions option in the Mail menu. If you choose this option, you can have AOL sign on and retrieve your mail.

Mail retrieved this way can be reviewed online or off by choosing Read Incoming Mail from the Mail menu. It remains available for review until you delete it. (AOL adds a Delete button to the reviewed mail's window when mail is accessed this way.)

If you don't delete it, the incoming mailbox can serve as your mail repository. This method is extremely convenient, but it has a few flaws:

- It's effective only if you keep a small number of messages on file. Mail stored this way can't be categorized, and the list eventually becomes too long for convenient access.
- While filing mail you've read this way is easy, filing mail you've *sent* isn't (unless you send carbon copies to yourself).
- Additional incoming mail from FlashSessions (I'll discuss FlashSessions in Chapter 19) is filed here, and mixing new FlashSession mail with old mail can become confusing and troublesome.

Nevertheless, if you don't intend to file much mail, and if you carbon-copy yourself when necessary, and if you don't intend to use FlashSessions, this might be the most convenient method of them all.

The Mail Folder

I have created a directory (a Windows "folder") named "Mail" on my hard disk (directory-creation instructions are available in your Windows manual—look under "File Manager"). It's not buried inside another directory; it's right off the root directory of my hard drive. I never have to spend much time searching for it, and it consolidates all of my mail into one place for convenient backup.

This folder has to be organized in some way. Probably the simplest strategy is to save all your mail in your Mail folder as it arrives, piece by piece. Every time you read a new piece of mail, choose Save As from the File menu and save the mail in the folder. While this might work if you don't get much mail, it regresses to anarchy after a dozen or so files have accumulated. A File Manager screen of such a scenario appears in Figure 4-16.

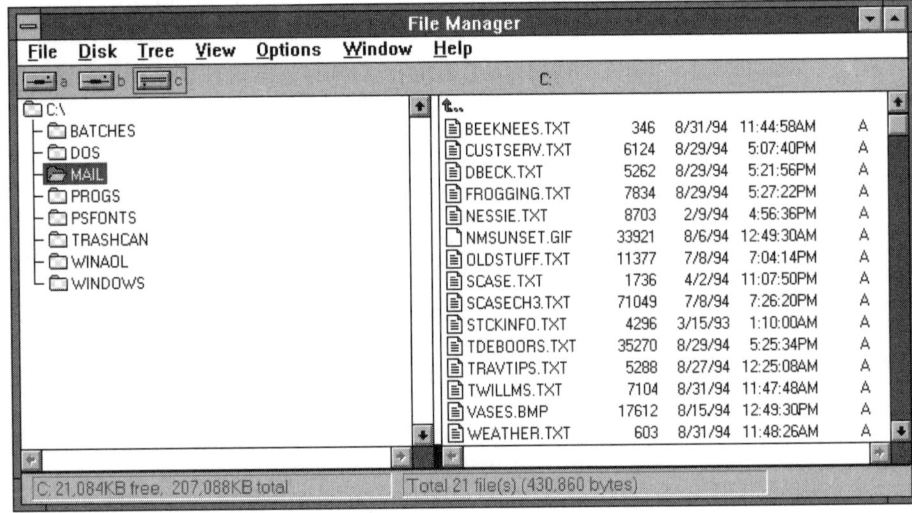

Figure 4-16: A file-based mailing system can become confusing when mail starts to accumulate.

A Single-file Strategy

Note: All of the strategies mentioned from here on require an understanding of the Windows Cut, Copy and Paste commands. If you are not familiar with these commands, review the sidebar on page 82.

If your mail is infrequent, a single file might prove beneficial. Instead of a Mail *folder*, try a Mail *file* instead. (Use the New command under AOL's File menu to create a new file.) Each time you receive a piece of mail, read it, then select and copy it. Use the Open command under the File menu to open your Mail file, scroll to the bottom, paste and save. You can store 50 or more pieces of mail this way before the file becomes so large that it's unwieldy. Advantages to this method include the following:

- Only one file needs to be managed; only one file must be opened to access all your past mail; only one file needs to be backed up.
- Mail appears in chronological order.
- Comments and replies appear in context—there's no need to search your disk for the mail that provoked SuzieQ to say "You yahoo! I hope your stack overflows!" If you've been consistent, the offending statement is nearby—probably just above Suzie's malediction.

On the other hand, AOL limits the size of text files to about 24k. If your Mail file exceeds this amount, AOL won't be able to store it. Windows Notepad won't help either; its file-size limitation is even worse than AOL's. This is a severe limitation.

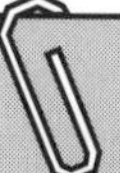

File the Header Too

Most of the filing strategies described here rely on the storage of not only received mail, but mail you've sent as well. All you need to do is copy each piece of mail you send and paste it into the appropriate file. Here's a tip: choose Check Mail You've Sent from the Mail menu and open the mail to be copied from there. Mail retrieved this way contains AOL's header information—date, time, CCs and blind CCs—the retention of which should be considered a necessity in any mail filing system. If you simply copy text from the message field of a Mail window before you send it, your file won't contain all this information.

A Date-based Strategy

Alternatively, consider a date-based strategy. This method is essentially the single-file strategy with a file for each month of activity. A greater volume of mail can be accommodated this way, and old material can easily be copied to a floppy for archiving (see Figure 4-17).

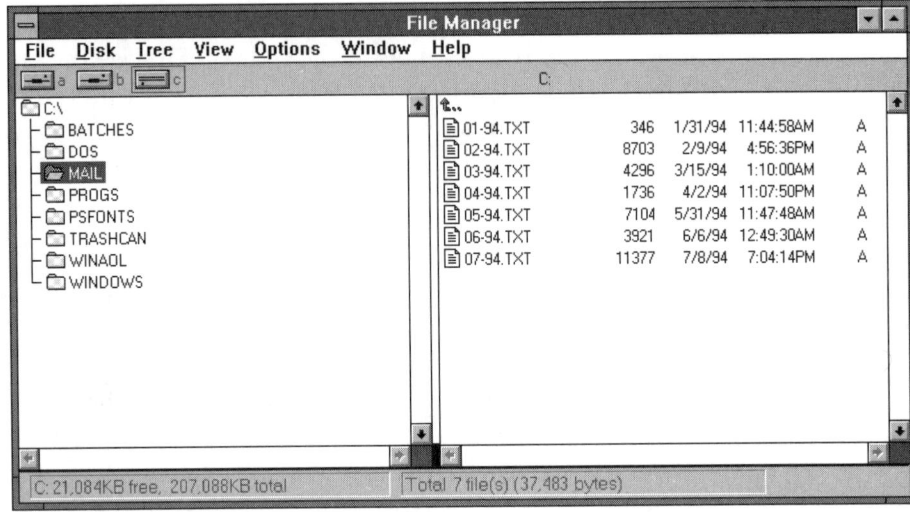

Figure 4-17: The date-based strategy accommodates a greater volume of mail.

A People-based Strategy

I receive too much mail for the single-file method, and I never remember dates. The strategy I use is people-based. Inside my Mail folder are dozens of files, each named after a person with whom I regularly correspond (see Figure 4-18).

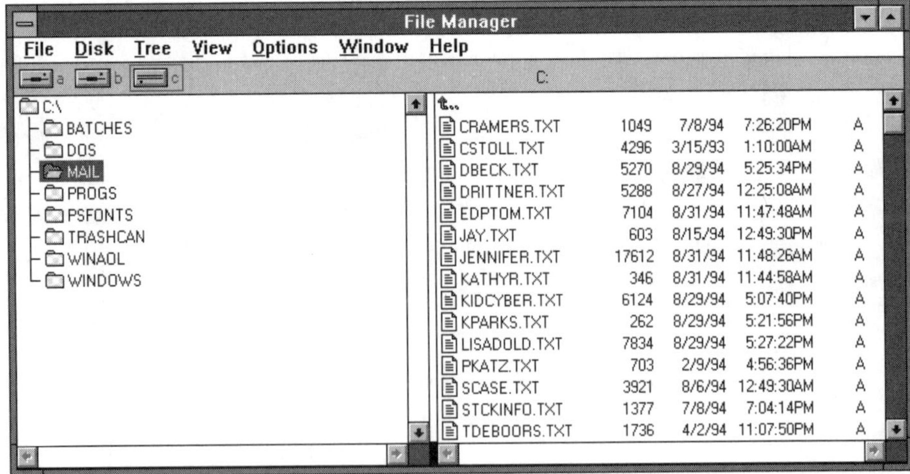

Figure 4-18: The list of files in my Mail directory, arranged and sorted by name.

Each person's file contains all the messages I've sent to and received from that person in chronological order. Again, I include mail I've sent as well as received, as discussed in the sidebar.

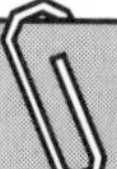

Searching Text Files

At the moment, my Mail folder contains over 2mb of data, representing thousands of pieces of mail. Just yesterday, a reader sent me a piece of mail saying, "Thanks, Tom." That's all it said. It was sent by someone with the AOL screen name GeorgeD12. No offense intended, George, but I get a lot of reader mail, and I had no idea why I was being thanked.

I really hate to throw away mail like that. Maybe I did something really nice for George. Maybe George sent the mail to the wrong person. Maybe he meant to tell me to jump in a lake. I had to know.

The solution was *Hunter*, a little Windows shareware program from Peter Eddy. Hunter's purpose in life is simple: I tell it what to look for and where to look and it looks inside of every file for whatever I'm after. This it does in the background while I work on something else. I told Hunter to look for the word "George" in the c:mail path and I went back to work on my manuscript. Sure enough, a few minutes later (yes, minutes, not seconds: Hunter ambles rather than scrambles) my PC beeped and there was a list of all files with the word "George" in them. Sure enough, GeorgeD12 was there in my FANMAIL file. I had forwarded a message for him to a member whose screen name he didn't know. He didn't want me to jump in a lake after all.

Hunter is available online at AOL. Use the keyword: FileSearch, then the criterion: Hunter. Pay the shareware fee if Hunter is useful to you.

A Subject-based Strategy

If your online mail relates better to a number of subjects, this might be a better method for you. Perhaps you use AOL to plan your travels. You might have developed some acquaintances in the Travel Club. You might be receiving confirmations from EAASY SABRE, AOL's travel reservations service. Or you might be clipping articles from Wine & Dine Online, the excellent restaurant, food and wine forum. If this is the case, you might develop a number of files for each of your destinations.

These strategies can be combined, of course, and they aren't the only ones. There are no doubt scores of others. What I'm trying to do is convince you of the importance of filing your mail. Decide upon a method, set it up to your satisfaction, and maintain it faithfully. You'll become a better citizen of the e-mail community if you do.

Internet Mail

As much as Steve Case and his fellow shareholders would prefer it, not everyone is a member of AOL. Some receive their mail via the Internet (which we'll discuss in Chapter 14, "The Internet Connection"); others prefer AOL's competition (which, as you might suppose, this book doesn't discuss).

We're still 10 chapters away from Chapter 14, so discussing Internet mail is somewhat premature. But this *is* the mail chapter after all, and e-mail is a big part of the Internet, so an Internet e-mail discussion follows.

For the time being, understand that the Internet is a worldwide interconnected network of networks, each of which is similar to AOL. Something like 30 million people use the Internet, and you can send mail to (or receive mail from) any one of them via AOL.

Internet Addresses

To identify an Internet addressee, the format paul_williams@oregon.uoregon.edu is used. Everything to the left of the at sign (@) in an Internet address is the user's name (paul_williams, in the example). Internet user names aren't subject to the 10-character limit AOL screen names are, so they can become quite elaborate. Everything to the right of the @ sign is the addressee's *domain*—the name of the network the addressee is using (oregon.uoregon.edu in the example—a computer network at the University of Oregon). Our domain is AOL, which is known as aol.com on the Internet. My Internet address, then, is the combination of my screen name, an @ sign, and AOL's domain name—or majortom@aol.com. Note that Internet addresses appear in all lowercase letters: that's the way it always is on the Internet.

The Directory of Internet Users

Users come and go on the Internet like nighttime talk-show hosts. There are 30 million of them, after all, and thousands come and go every day. Keeping a directory of them would be nearly impossible.

"So what," you say. "There are well over 30 million telephone users in this country and they're all listed in directories." Your point is well taken, but the telephone system is composed of a number of coordinated authorities (the baby Bells), each charged with the responsibility of publishing phone books. Not so with the Internet. No one's charged with the responsibility of maintaining Internet member directories. Those that exist are produced voluntarily, and these volunteers all have lives beyond their spare-time member directories.

In other words, there's no accurate, up-to-the-minute, all-inclusive Internet membership directory. There are a few online directories, but they're more like a Who's Who of Internet users than a comprehensive directory. In other words, you must have the *exact* address for someone you intend to address via the Internet. You'll have to obtain those addresses from a source other than AOL or the Internet: there's no Internet membership directory to consult.

Here's a tip: keep a written record of your important Internet addresses. Don't just put them in your AOL address book (you might need an address when you're away from your machine, and AOL's software stores your address book on your hard disk), and don't trust them to memory (few people remember the alphabet soup of Internet addresses accurately). If you carry an old-fashioned (hardcopy) address book with you, that's the best place to keep your Internet addresses.

Sending Internet Mail

Internet e-mail is composed and sent conventionally. To address an Internet user, simply place the recipient's Internet address in the To field of the Compose Mail form (see Figure 4-19).

Once you click the Send button (or once you run a FlashSession containing outgoing Internet mail), your outgoing mail is sent on the 'Net without delay.

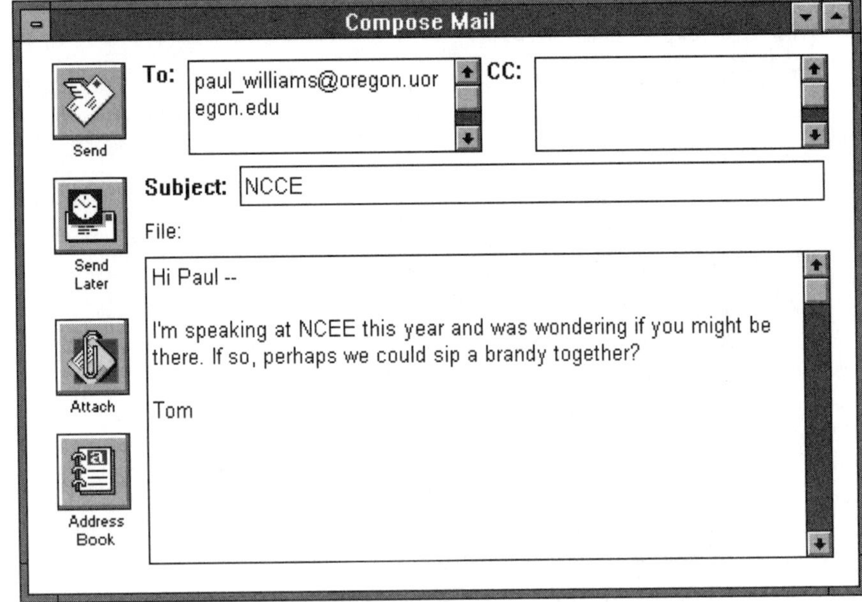

Figure 4-19: Sending mail via the Internet requires entries in the To, Subject and Message fields. You can't leave any of them blank.

Undeliverable Mail

Because of the complexity of Internet addresses, you might occasionally misaddress a piece of Internet mail. Fortunately your fallibility has been anticipated in the form of the Internet "postmaster." Should you include a nonexistent domain or user name, the postmaster will intercede and send the mail back to you. It's no problem, really, as the postmaster sends back the body of the message as well (see Figure 4-20). All you have to do is select and copy the message text, paste it into a new mail window, enter the proper address and re-send the mail. Your mail won't end up in some kind of Internet dead letter box: the Internet postmaster always delivers.

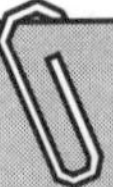

Daemons

Look at the sender's address in Figure 4-20. Isn't that a vicious sounding word: daemon? My dictionary defines the word as a "subordinate deity." In this context, however, a daemon (pronounced demon) is an innocuous little Unix program—one that's usually transparent to the user—which is anything but a deity, subordinate or not. PCs have daemons too (though we don't call them that); perhaps the most familiar example is the PrintMonitor—the background program that spools the print output from your applications to your printer.

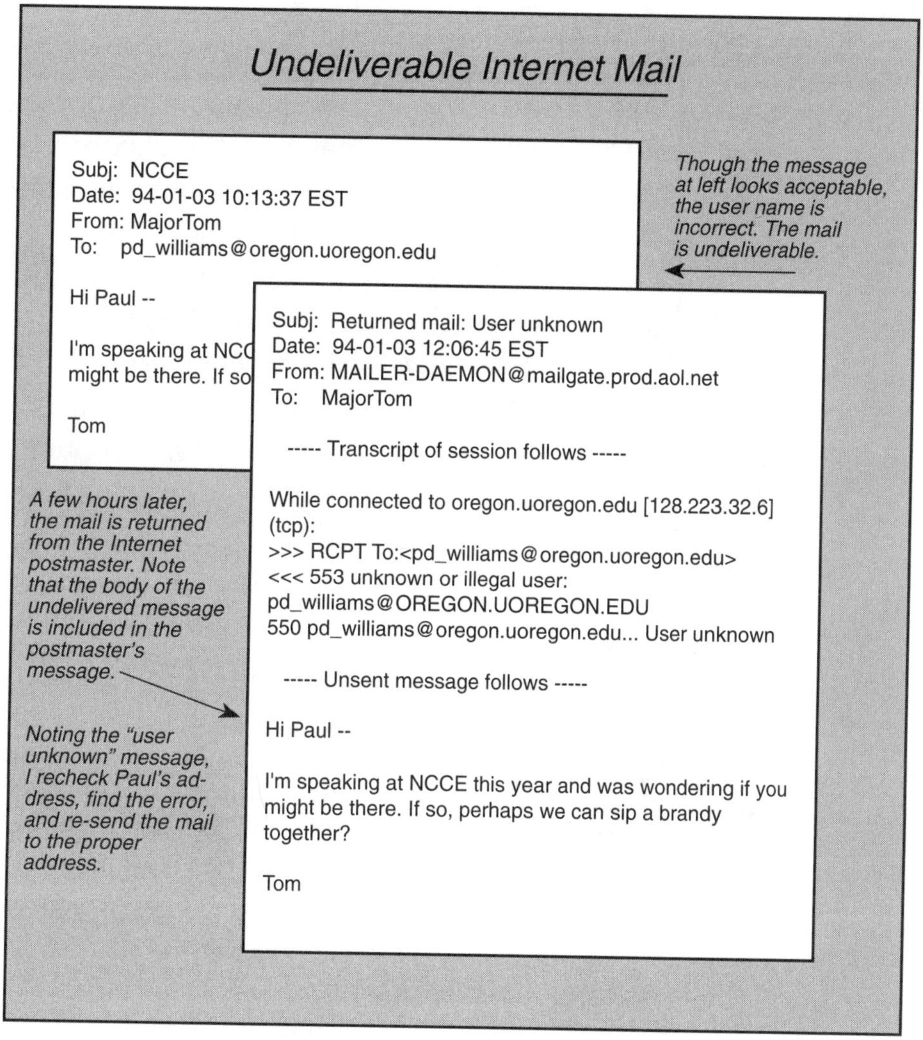

Figure 4-20: At top, a misaddressed Internet mail message looks as good as any other, but a few minutes later I receive the User unknown message pictured in the center window. Note the inclusion of my message s text in the postmaster s message in the bottom window. When I later copy and paste the mail into a new mail window (and fix the address), the mail will be delivered satisfactorily.

Undeliverable Internet Mail
Subj: NCCE
Date: 94-01-03 10:13:37 EST
From: MajorTom
To: pd_williams@oregon.uoregon.edu
Hi Paul --
I'm speaking at NCC
might be there. If so
Tom
Though the message at left looks acceptable, the user name is incorrect. The mail is undeliverable.
Subj: Returned mail: User unknown
Date: 94-01-03 12:06:45 EST
From: MAILER-DAEMON@mailgate.prod.aol.net
To: MajorTom
----- Transcript of session follows -----
While connected to oregon.uoregon.edu [128.223.32.6] (tcp):
>>> RCPT To:<pd_williams@oregon.uoregon.edu>
<<< 553 unknown or illegal user: pd_williams@OREGON.UOREGON.EDU
550 pd_williams@oregon.uoregon.edu... User unknown
----- Unsent message follows -----
Hi Paul --
I'm speaking at NCCE this year and was wondering if you might be there. If so, perhaps we can sip a brandy together?
Tom
A few hours later, the mail is returned from the Internet postmaster. Note that the body of the undelivered message is included in the postmaster's message.
Noting the "user unknown" message, I recheck Paul's address, find the error, and re-send the mail to the proper address.

Sending Mail to Other Commercial Services

To reach a few of the more common Internet-connected commercial services, use the address formats shown in Figure 4-21.

Note: CompuServe addresses must show a period (rather than CompuServe's traditional comma) between the fifth and sixth numbers. That's because AOL separates the addresses of multiple recipients with commas. If AOL encounters a comma in a CompuServe account number, it will try to send the mail to two addresses.

Figure 4-21: Use these address formats to reach users on other commercial services.

Service name	Example
AppleLink	name@applelink.apple.com
AT&T Mail	name@attmail.com
CompuServe	12345.678@compuserve.com
Delphi	name@delphi.com
GEnie	name@genie.geis.com
MCI Mail	name@mcimail.com
NBC Nightly News	nightly@nbc.com
Prodigy	name@prodigy.com
The White House	president@whitehouse.gov, or vice-president@whitehouse.gov

Receiving Internet Mail

Internet mail is received like any other AOL mail: it's announced when you sign on and you can read it by clicking the "You Have Mail" button on the Welcome screen. The only way you'll know it's Internet mail is by looking at the sender's address, which will be an Internet address. You'll also see the Internet "header" at the end of the message. Reading Internet headers is a little like reading the Bible in its original Hebrew: enlightening perhaps, but not requisite to effective use of the medium.

A few notes regarding received Internet mail:

- If you want to give your Internet address to someone else (it's very impressive printed on your business cards), remove any spaces, change everything to lowercase, and follow it with @aol.com. As I mentioned earlier, my Internet address is majortom@aol.com. Steve Case's Internet address is stevecase@aol.com.

- America Online's maximum e-mail message length is around 28k. (It's actually more than that but AOL reserves a small overhead space for forwarding comments.) If someone on the Internet sends you a message longer than that, AOL will cut it up and deliver it to you as multiple pieces of mail. Use a word processor to re-assemble the pieces.

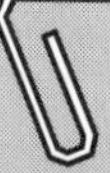

Internet Mail Trivia

Actually, this isn't trivia at all. I was trying to attract your attention with a sidebar. If you're an Internet mail user, this is Really Important Stuff:

- The maximum message length for outgoing Internet mail is 24k, or about 15 pages of text. If you must send a message longer than that, use a word processor to cut your mail into pieces.
- If you use a word processor to prepare outgoing Internet mail, be sure to save the file in a text-only format (most word processors offer this option) copying and pasting into a new mail form. The text-only file format will strip all character and paragraph formatting from your message. Don't try to send formatted word processing files as e-mail over the Internet.
- Don't use any special characters (like copyright symbols or the "smart quotes" offered by some word processors) in Internet mail. If a character requires the use of the Alt key, it's off-limits.
- Don't use the Attach button for outgoing Internet mail. The Internet simply doesn't accommodate attachments.
- Some of the services listed in Figure 4-21 charge their members for Internet mail, both incoming and outgoing. Keep that in mind when sending mail to these people: they might not appreciate the gesture.
- America Online doesn't charge you anything extra for Internet mail, sent or received. If you're counting your blessings, add that to the list.
- If you're going to use Internet mail frequently, go to your local bookstore and buy a copy of *A Directory of Electronic Mail !%@:: Addressing & Networks* (see the bibliography). You'll be a better citizen of the Internet community if you do.

- America Online offers plenty of help with Internet e-mail, including a message board and an avenue for communication with the AOL Internet staff. Use the keyword: MailGateway to explore this feature.

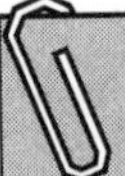

Use Internet Mail Appropriately

Don't send e-mail to fellow AOL members using their Internet address. In other words, don't send mail to majortom@aol.com when you can simply send mail to majortom. Tagging an AOL member's address with "@aol.com" forces the mail to go all the way out on the Internet and bounce around in cyberspace for a couple of hours before it returns. It also makes it difficult for the recipient to reply without doing the same. If the addressee is an AOL member, his or her screen name is the best address for efficient mailing.

Attaching Files to Messages

Understand that we've finished our discussion of Internet mail. This is a new topic. As I mentioned a few pages back, you can't attach files to Internet mail.

Also understand that we're not talking in the abstract here: files are files. On the PC, files can include text, graphics, data, sound, animation, even programs. Any of these files can be attached to a piece of e-mail. When mail is received with an attached file, the file is then downloaded in its native format, which is astounding.

File transmission requires elaborate protocols and error checking. Not a single bit, nibble or byte can be displaced. Most other telecommunications services require you to decide upon one of many cryptic protocols with names like XModem and Kermit. You also have to determine the number of data bits, stop bits and the parity setting your system needs. All told, of the 50 or so potential configurations for file transfer, usually only one of them will work in a given situation.

Forget all of that. You need not become involved. America Online handles it all invisibly, efficiently and reliably. If you want to send a file, all you have to do is click the Attach button (review Figure 4-1) and AOL will take care of it from there.

Tip: If you're a traveler and you take your PowerBook with you on the road, send e-mail to yourself, attaching important files that you've constructed while away from the office. America Online will hold them for you until your return. If something untoward should happen to your data while you're on the road, you can download your files when you return. It's cheap insurance.

Figure 4-22 follows a telecommunicated file from beginning to end. The journey spans half a continent—from Oregon to Mississippi—but only costs pennies.

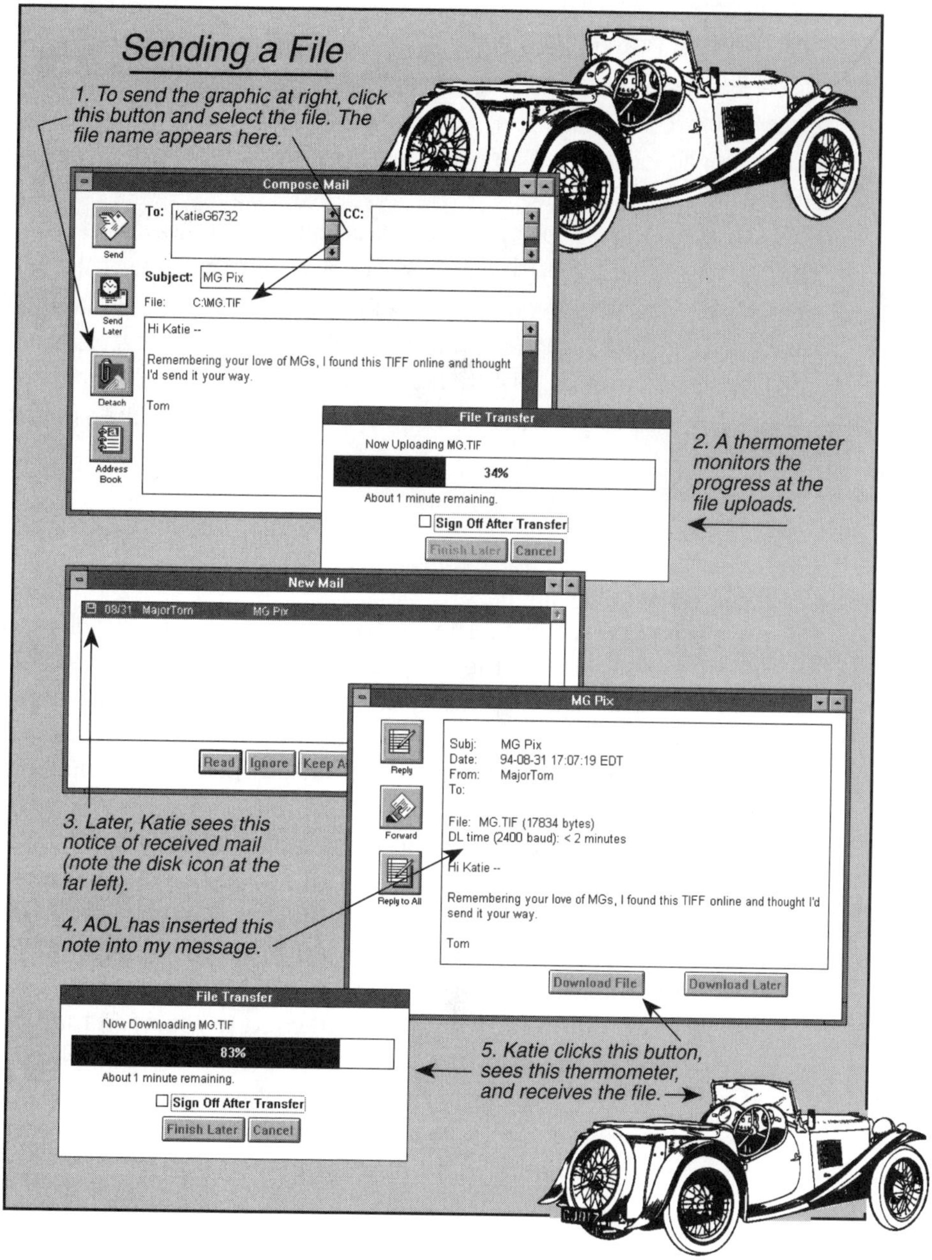

Figure 4-22: Sending an MG across the country is as easy as clicking a mouse. (Illustration by Rich Wald. Keyword: File Search, then use the criterion: Classic Cars.)

Sending a File

1. To send the graphic at right, click this button and select the file. The file name appears here.

Compose Mail

To: KatieG6732

CC:

Subject: MG Pix

File: C:\MG.TIF

Hi Katie --

Remembering your love of MGs, I found this TIFF online and thought I'd send it your way.

Tom

Send

Send Later

Detach

Address Book

File Transfer

Now Uploading MG.TIF

34%

About 1 minute remaining.

Sign Off After Transfer

Finish Later Cancel

2. A thermometer monitors the progress at the file uploads.

New Mail

08/31 MajorTom MG Pix

Read Ignore Keep As

3. Later, Katie sees this notice of received mail (note the disk icon at the far left).

4. AOL has inserted this note into my message.

MG Pix

Subj: MG Pix
Date: 94-08-31 17:07:19 EDT
From: MajorTom
To:

File: MG.TIF (17834 bytes)
DL time (2400 baud): < 2 minutes

Hi Katie --

Remembering your love of MGs, I found this TIFF online and thought I'd send it your way.

Tom

Reply

Forward

Reply to All

Download File Download Later

File Transfer

Now Downloading MG.TIF

83%

About 1 minute remaining.

Sign Off After Transfer

Finish Later Cancel

5. Katie clicks this button, sees this thermometer, and receives the file.

Use Attached Files Appropriately

Before the recipient can do anything with an attached file, it has to be downloaded, saved and (usually) viewed with some kind of program other than AOL itself. This is something of a nuisance for the recipient. In other words, don't send attached files when a simple e-mail message will do.

You might be tempted, for instance, to send a word processing file instead of a conventional message to another member. Perhaps the message is long, or you want to format it, or you just prefer your word processor over AOL's text editor. Resist the urge. America Online can handle e-mail messages up to 28k in length (about 15 pages), no one expects fancy formatting when it comes to e-mail , and you can always send unformatted word processing files by copying them and pasting them into a Compose Mail window. Attached files should never be sent when simple messages will do.

Attaching a File

You can attach a file to e-mail messages. To attach a file to an e-mail message, click the Attach button in the message's window. America Online will respond with the sequence of windows pictured in Figure 4-23.

When you click the Send button pictured in the bottom window of Figure 4-23, you trigger the sequence of events pictured in Figure 4-22. America Online will hold the mail and the file until the addressee is ready to read the mail and download the file. If you address the mail to multiple recipients—even if they're receiving carbon copies or blind carbon copies—each will be afforded the opportunity of downloading the file.

And downloading files attached to received mail *is* optional. Though the MG Pix window pictured in step 4 of Figure 4-22 offers both Download File and Download Later buttons, the recipient might elect to ignore them both. (Keep that in mind if you ever receive mail with attached files you don't want.)

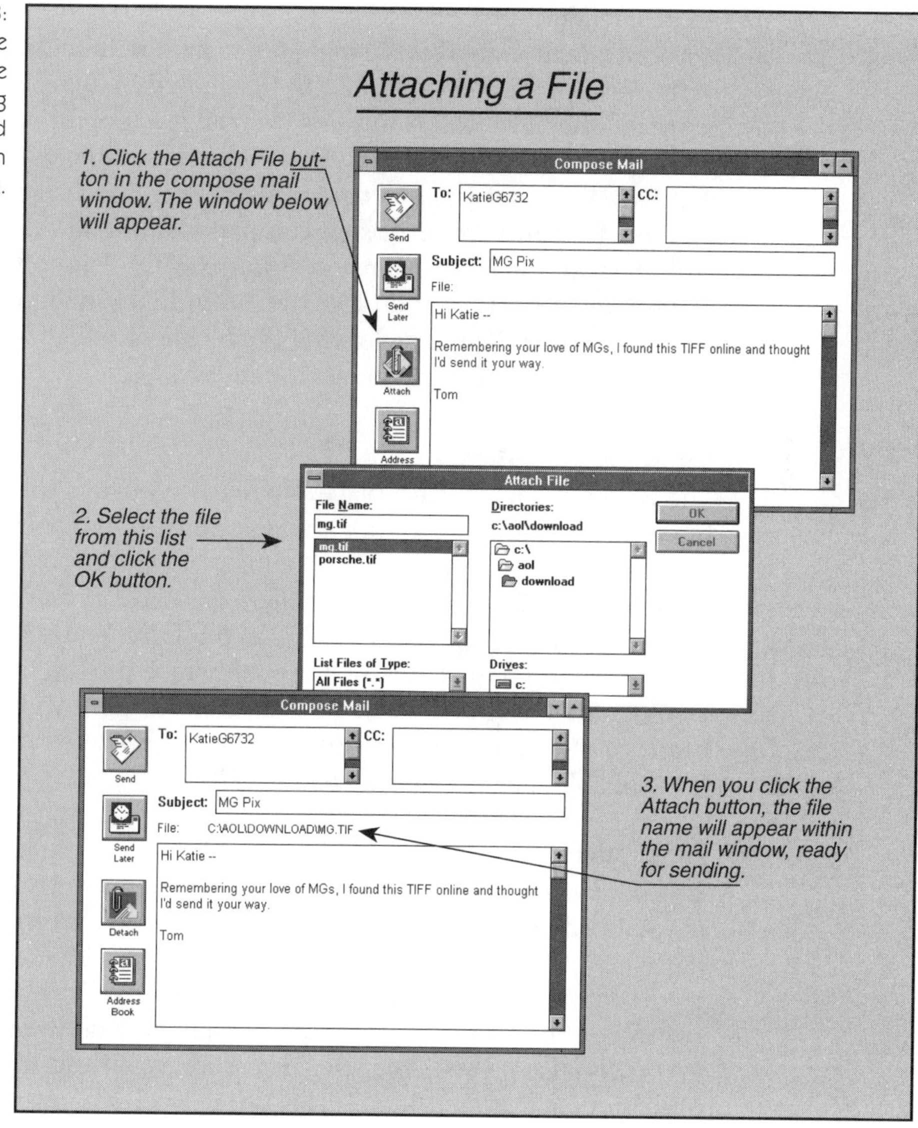

Figure 4-23: Attaching a file amounts to little more than clicking a button and locating the file on your disk.

Attaching Multiple Files

You can attach more than a single file to an e-mail message if you wish, in the form of a *ZIP archive*. PKZIP (discussed in detail in the next chapter—the "PK" is the author's initials) is a tool for compressing (and decompressing) files. Your AOL software is capable of *unzipping* files that have been compressed using PKZIP.

The AOL software unzips (decompresses) files attached to e-mail with the .ZIP filename extension automatically. The software may make a new directory and place the individual (unzipped) attached files within that directory, leaving the recipient with both the Zip archive *and* the directory on his or her disk.

E-mail Alternatives

The world is not a perfect place. No one can always correctly predict the weather, computers don't always address envelopes reliably, and *some* people still aren't online. What if you want to communicate with these heathens? You could write them a letter, but that requires paper, an envelope, a stamp and a trip to the mailbox. You could phone them, but an answering machine will probably take the call (and your money as well, if it's long distance). You could try telepathy or ask Scotty to beam you there, but these are emerging technologies and you know how reliable they are (remember *The Fly*?).

Paper Mail

Instead, use AOL to send 'em a letter. All you have to do is prepare normal e-mail and include a special address (see Figure 4-24). A few days later, a real paper letter in a real paper envelope will arrive at your specified destination, looking for all the world like you typed it yourself. The cost for this service is somewhere between the cost of a first-class stamp and a long-distance phone call; and it's no more difficult than sending e-mail. This brings such a convenience to communicating that it almost eliminates procrastination.

Speaking of procrastination, when was the last time you wrote your mother?

Figure 4-24: Sending a message via US Mail involves completing return and mailing address forms before confirmation.

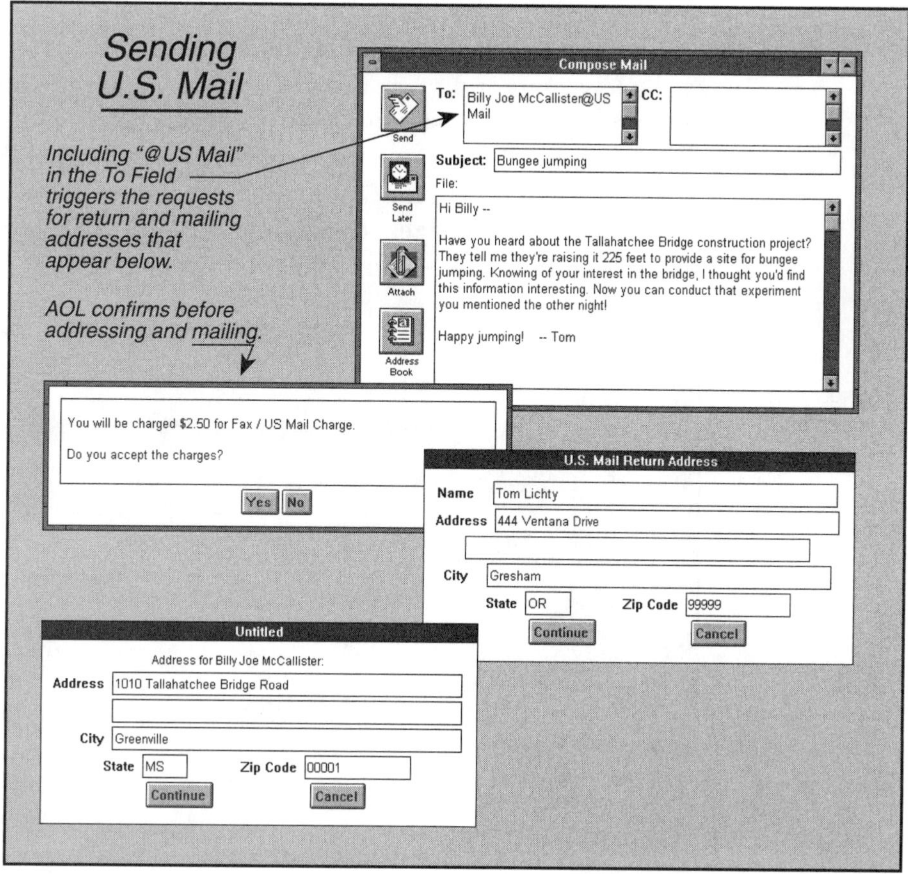

Note that the only difference between sending regular e-mail and sending US Mail is the address. If AOL sees @usmail in an e-mail address, it automatically triggers the address request dialogs you see pictured in Figure 4-24.

Note: ZIP codes are required, and AOL verifies that they match the cities in both the return and mailing addresses. If they don't, you will receive an "invalid US Mail address" error and be sent back to the offending entry.

Sending a Fax

Perhaps your mother owns a fax machine (doesn't everyone?). You can save a few cents and a few days over paper mail by sending her a fax instead. Again, AOL stands ready to serve, even if you don't own a fax machine yourself. The process is no more complicated than sending paper mail—or e-mail for that matter (see Figure 4-25). Again, an @ sign in an address triggers the dialog. Within a few minutes of sending fax mail, AOL sends e-mail to you confirming the transmission of the fax message.

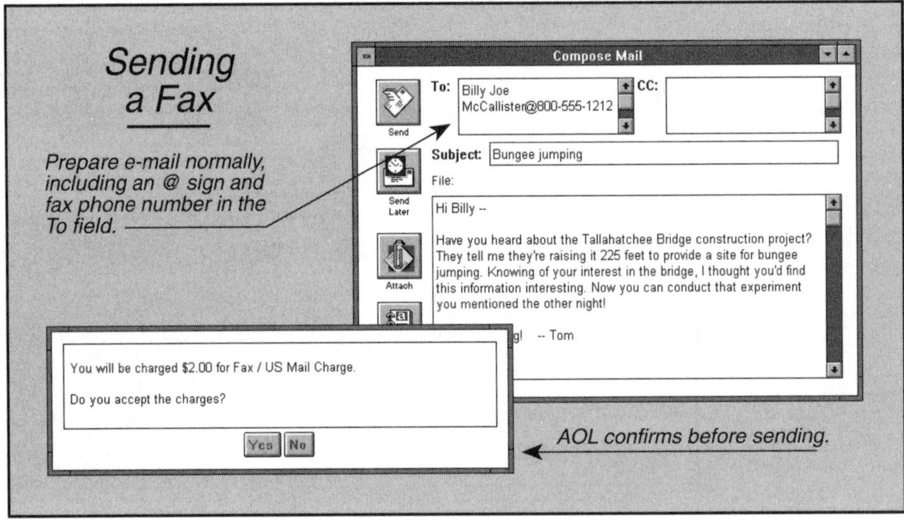

Figure 4-25: Fax mail differs little from normal e-mail.

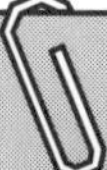

The Fine Print

Fax and paper mail can be sent to multiple addresses. Complete the To field just as you would for e-mail, separating the recipients' names with commas. You'll be charged for each address, however.

- All charges are billed to your AOL account.
- Paper mail requires ZIP codes.
- Fax addressee names cannot exceed 20 characters, including spaces and punctuation. Paper mail addressee names are limited to 33 characters.
- You can't attach files to fax or paper mail messages. Both services are plain text only.
- Both fax and paper mail messages wrap to 70 characters on a line. Fax pages contain a maximum of 60 lines. Paper mail messages contain 40 lines on the first page (to make room for the address) and 53 lines on all others.
- Forced page breaks may be declared: Type ">>> PAGE BREAK <<<" (without the quotes) on a line by itself. This works for both fax and paper mail.
- Paper mail is limited to four pages. Fax mail is limited to 24k.
- Include your real name (not your screen name) in the text of both fax and paper mail.
- In either case, you'll receive a confirmation identifying all charges before AOL sends your mail (refer again to Figures 4-24 and 4-25). If, after reviewing the charges, you decide you don't want to send the mail or the fax, you can cancel at that point. You will also receive a confirmation (via e-mail from AOL) that your fax has been transmitted a few minutes after you click the Send button.

Moving On

As it has been described, AOL's e-mail facility is impressive work. It holds your mail for you, even after you've read it. It allows you to send courtesy copies. It provides access to the Internet, fax and the US Post Office. Best of all, it rarely costs you any more than your monthly AOL membership fee.

But e-mail isn't everything AOL has to offer. America Online is also composed of departments—14 of them to be exact. We'll begin our departmental exploration with the Computing Department, the subject of the next chapter.

The Colossus of Memnon was erected in the 14th century B.C. by the Egyptian king Amenhotep III. The Colossus is composed of two seated stone figures each measuring 38 feet high. If they ever stood up, they would tower over every structure in Washington, DC, including AOL's four-story office building a few miles away. While King Kong was satisfied with only one Faye Wray in the palm of his hand, it would take six Faye Wrays to fill a Colossus hand—and there are four of them.

In size, the colossus of departments at AOL is Computing & Software. All other departments pale in comparison—mere King Kongs, pebbles in the sandals of a colossus like the Computing Department. Exploring a colossus takes a while, but that's what we'll do when you turn the page....

CHAPTER 5

Computing

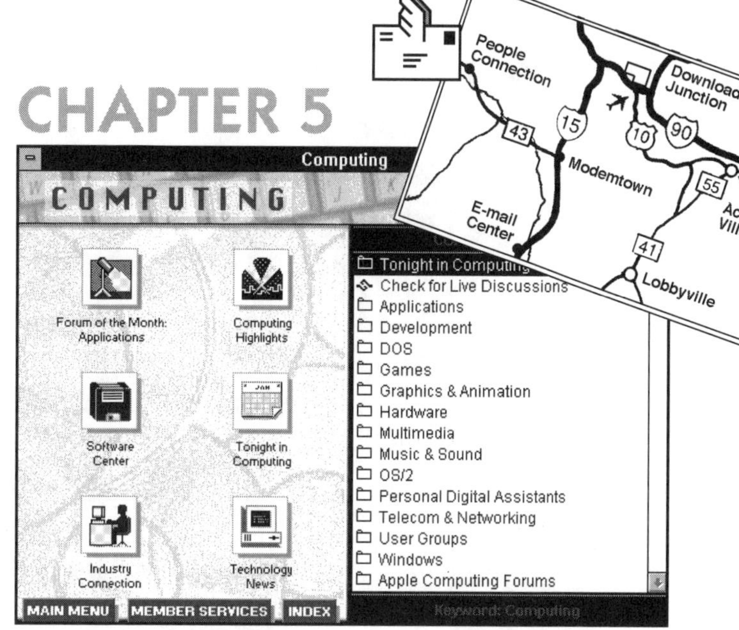

If you love your PC, if it beckons with an alluring radiance when you walk into the room, if you find yourself inventing tasks to do, such as optimizing your hard disk and changing your wallpaper twice a day, you're going to love this department. The Computing Department is the consummate carnival—an opiate, a tabernacle, a jubilation for Windows weirdoes.

In fact, even if you're not a Windows fanatic, you'll spend a lot of time here in the Computing Department. There are thousands of files here—fonts and graphics in particular—that will appeal to even the casual Windows user. And if you need help with either your PC or the software you run on it, the Computing Department is ready to oblige. There are stimulating forums here, ranging from the fundamental to the existential. This place is as rife with opportunity as a sunny Saturday in August, and you can enjoy it any day of the year. To get in use the keyword: Computing, or click the department's icon in the Main Menu window.

The Computing Department's main window serves as this chapter's frontispiece graphic. To reach the Computing Department, use the keyword: Computing.

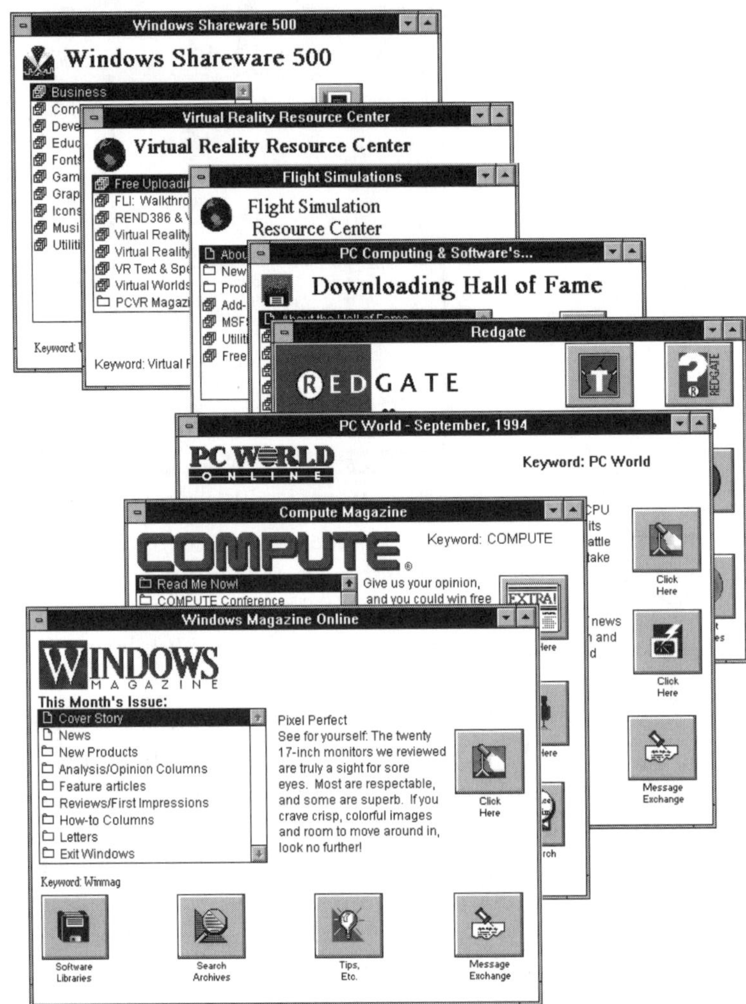

Figure 5-1: The consummate toy store: the Computing Department offers a boundless universe of resources (keyword: Computing).

The Windows Forum

There's so much great stuff here, it's hard to know where to begin. Probably the most fertile field for those of us who use Windows is the Windows Forum itself. You can either choose the forum from the main Computing Department window pictured in the frontispiece to this chapter or use the keyword: Windows Forum.

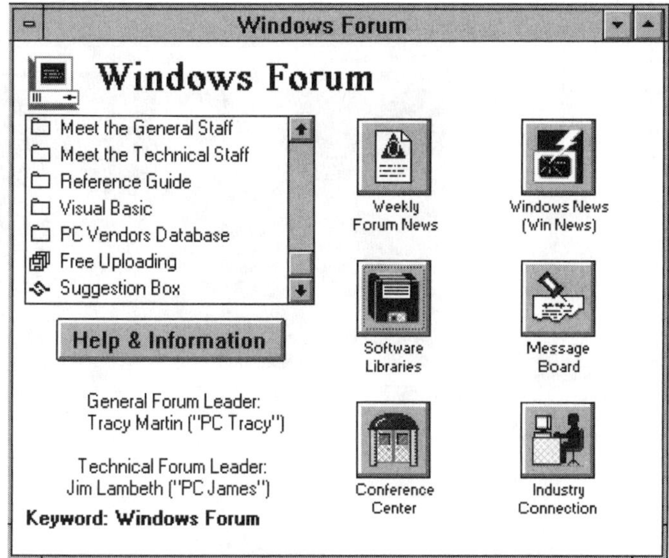

Figure 5-2: The Windows Forum offers programs, fonts, games, graphics, demos, utilities—even sounds. A bounty among the bountiful.

Top Picks

One of the places I like to visit regularly is the Top Picks area, available in the software libraries. It lists the files available for downloading that the Forum Leader has elected to feature. When I investigated Top Picks this afternoon, I found four files that seemed interesting (see Figure 5-3).

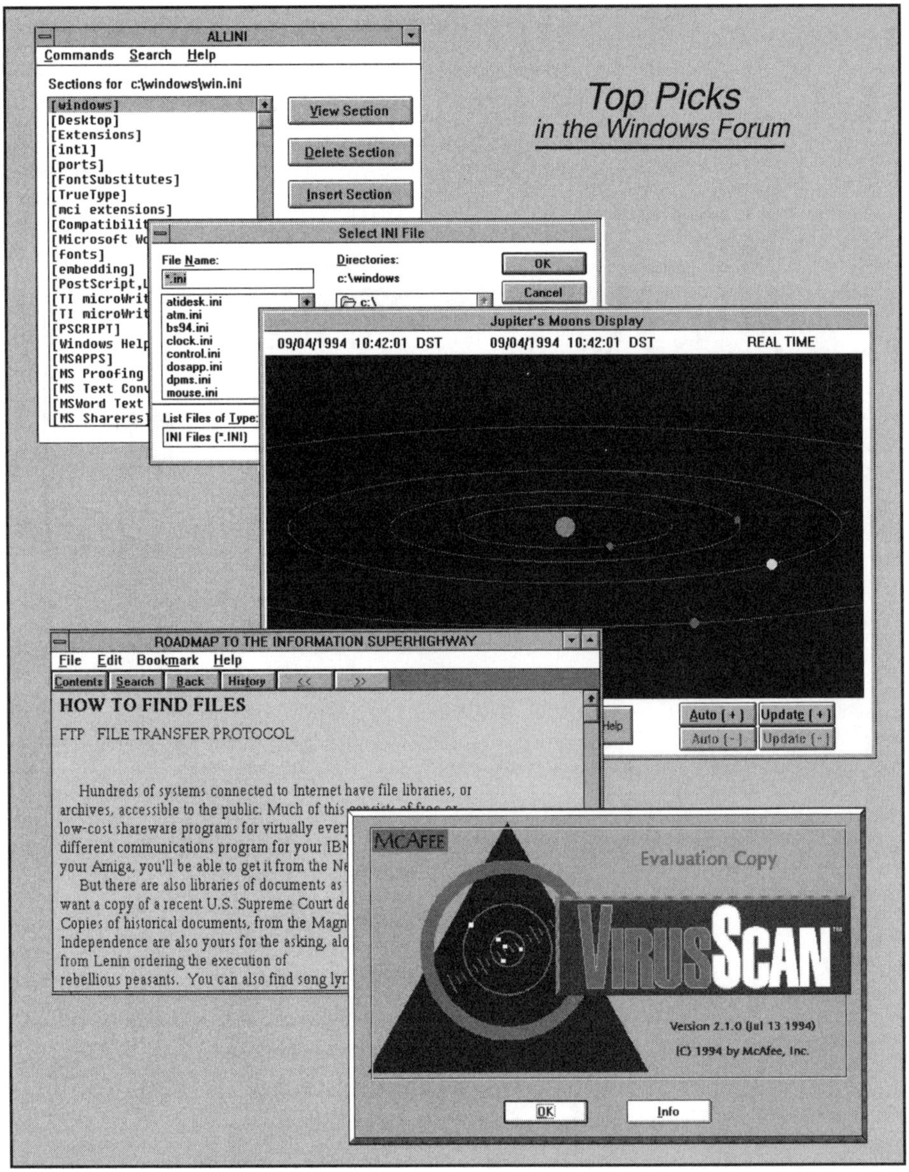

Figure 5-3: Four of the Windows Forum's top picks for downloading. From the top, "AllIni" by Ken Partridge (a handy .ini file editor); "Hubble Space Telescope" by Gene W. Lee (views celestial events in real time on your screen); "Internet Roadmap" by Lighthouse Productions (lots of Internet information in Windows help format); and "Anti-Virus SCAN" by Chris McAfee (thorough and updates are posted online).

Top Picks
in the Windows Forum

The programs pictured in Figure 5-3 are a few of the Top Picks for September 1994—the month during which I'm writing this chapter. I say that because files come and go on AOL, and some of those pictured in Figure 5-3 might be gone or replaced by the time you read this. If you have an interest in a file I've mentioned and can't locate the file online, try searching with generic search criteria. Instead of searching for "WSC-210E.ZIP," search instead for "Anti-Virus SCAN" (file names change; program names usually don't), or just "virus" (generic searches are best if they don't produce too many "hits"). To search AOL's library of files, use the keyword: FileSearch.

Fonts

Fonts are the chocolate of computing: you can never have enough. To many of AOL's members, fonts are the most tempting downloads AOL offers. They're relatively small (most download in a minute or so at 9600 baud) and inexpensive. Most of these fonts are shareware or freeware; the shareware fees rarely exceed $15. Best of all, they enhance your documents with personality and individuality, like icing on a cake. Chocolate icing, of course. Yum.

Windows fonts come in two flavors: TrueType and PostScript (the forum calls these "ATM" fonts). Most general Windows users seem to prefer TrueType, though desktop publishers prefer PostScript. Neither group could ask for much more than these extensive Windows Forum offerings. Researching this chapter, I found more than 190 PostScript Windows fonts online. I didn't bother to count the TrueType ones, but there were just as many, or more. In addition, a number of Macintosh-to-Windows font converters were available, meaning that the entire Macintosh desktop-publishing font library (keyword: MacDTP) is accessible as well. We're talking about thousands of fonts here. If fonts are chocolate, AOL is the passkey to the Godiva kitchens (Figure 5-4).

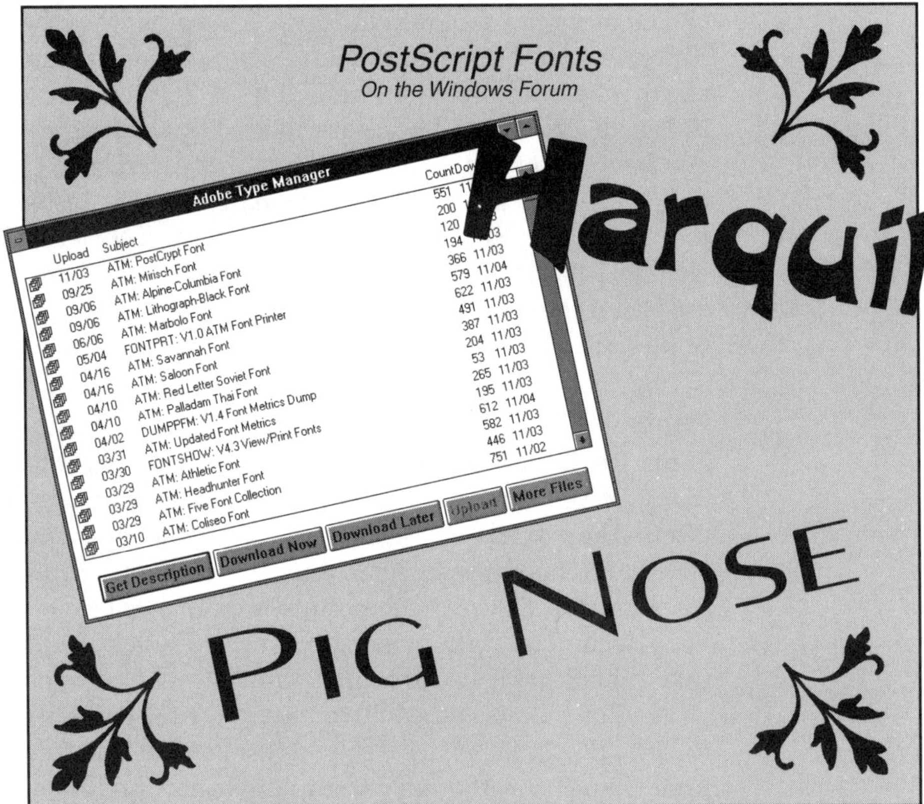

Figure 5-4: Three fonts from the Windows Forum: "Harquil;" "Pig Nose," a Peignot-like font by DavidTeicht; and "Fleurons," by Stephen Moye (the flower in each of the four corners). The inset lists only 13 of the scores of PostScript fonts available in the Windows Forum.

Visual Basic & the Forum Libraries

Many Windows users get so inspired with ideas for new Windows programs, they decide to try writing their own. Enter Microsoft's Visual Basic, a fertile programming environment providing both amateur and professional software creators access to all of Windows' features (such as pull-down menus, dialog boxes and graphics). This environment for developing Windows-based programs has generated a lot of interest in the past few years. Ideas for possible applications often surface in a Windows Forum chat, then travel over to the PC Development Forum (keyword: PCDevelopment), where staff specialists help people use Visual Basic (or other programming languages such as C, C++, and Pascal) to implement their ideas. Visual Basic help and samples are found in both a library and a message board shared by the Windows and PC Development Forums.

In fact, programs in the Windows Forum's libraries range from the trivial to the profound, offering a wealth of graphics, sound files, games, utilities and text help to assist you in customizing your Windows environment.

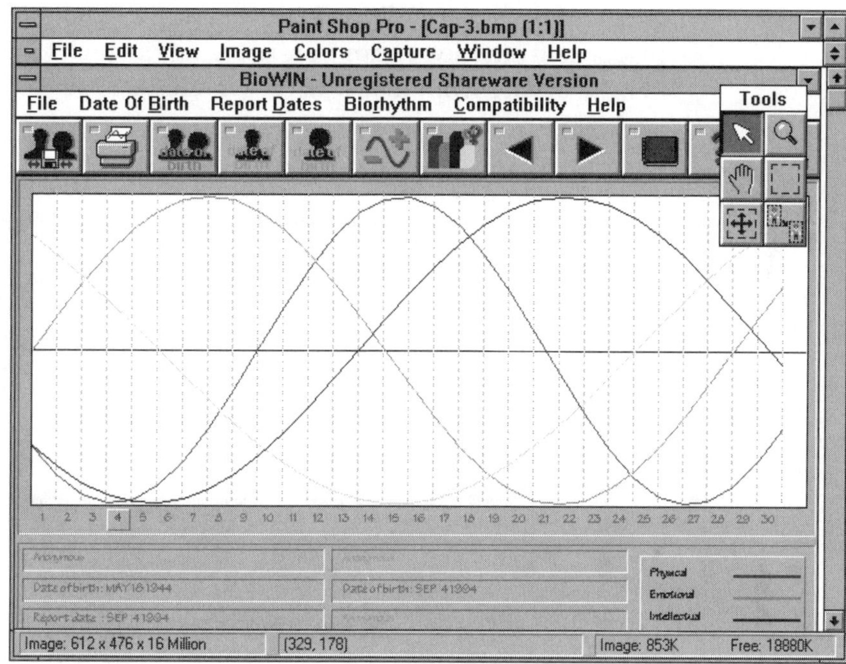

Figure 5-5: Two shareware programs available in the Windows Forum. Within "Paint Shop Pro" (by Robert Voit and JASC, Inc.) is "BioWin," a biorhythm charting program by Greg Kasy, written in Visual Basic.

Industry Connection

Windows users sometimes need help with hardware or software, which leads us directly into a discussion of the Windows Forum's Industry Connection. There are a number of ways to accommodate problems with your computer:

- Worry at the problem, trying solutions as they come to mind. This might take a week.
- Look up the solution in the manual (if you can remember where you put it). This usually takes half a day.

- Call the publisher's or manufacturer's customer support line—which can involve 20 minutes on hold (listening to a bad radio station playing commercials for stores in a city 3,000 miles away), then several days waiting for someone to return your call.
- Or you can sign on to AOL, type in the publisher's keyword and post your question. Within 24 hours you will not only receive a response from the vendor you're trying to reach (Figure 5-6), but helpful advice from fellow users who have experienced the same problem.

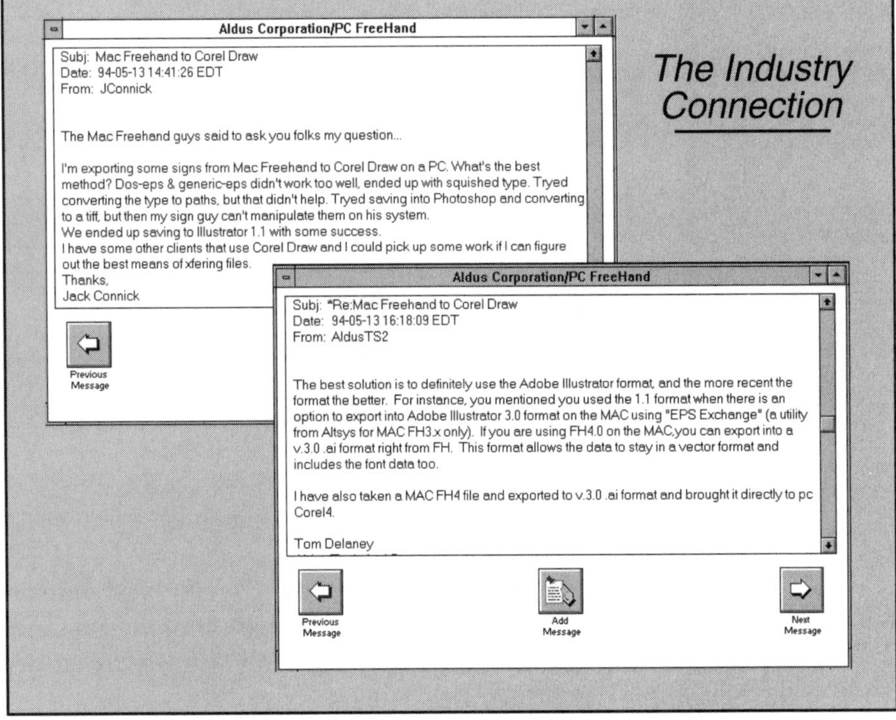

Figure 5-6: No waiting on hold: post your question online and read the technical support team's response at your convenience a few hours later.

No Place for Vilification

Look again at JConnick's question in Figure 5-6. He identifies the complexity of his problem (including the need to cross from the Mac to the PC platforms) and even the steps he has already taken to address the situation. He resisted the temptation to take his frustration out on the manufacturer. Instead, he is concise, specific and nonantagonistic.

If we all communicated our problems this courteously—no matter how frustrating and agonizing the problems might be—we'd be more likely to receive prompt, courteous responses like AldusTS2's. Requesting industry support is not the proper occasion to demonstrate our expertise or shower abuse on those who are trying to help us.

Prepare your question in advance, before you sign on. Include the hardware brand name, software version number, system configuration, additional boards—these kinds of things. Spend a few moments checking your message for clarity, brevity and courtesy. Sign on and post your message only after it has passed this kind of scrutiny. You can prepare a message off-line, away from a message board, by choosing New from the File menu (or press Ctrl+N). After you have prepared the message, select it all and copy it. Now sign on and find the message board you want, then paste your message into the form used for posting messages on the board. The Select All, Copy, and Paste commands are all under the Edit menu.

The service that provides this solution is AOL's Industry Connection (Figure 5-7). More than 300 vendors currently maintain message boards on AOL, and each board is checked every day—often more frequently than that—by the respective vendor. Not only is excellent vendor support found here, but peer support, libraries of accessories and updates, announcements from the industry and tips from other users are also at your disposal.

Software libraries usually round out the company support area online. These libraries boast a variety of programs for downloading, including patches, demo versions, diagnostic tools, and hardware and software drivers—programs that would otherwise only be available directly from software manufacturers.

Figure 5-7: A scene from "The Secret of Monkey Island," a demo from the Lucasfilm Games Forum serves as the background for this montage of windows from the Industry Connection. More than 300 companies offer support via America Online.

The Forums

Perhaps the busiest forums on AOL are found in the Computing Department. This industry is a moving target, and those who try to keep it in their sights seek information with eagerness that borders on the fanatical. The Computing Department offers forums for every level of computer enthusiast, from beginners to developers, and those forums are extremely popular.

I think it's appropriate, then, that we steal a peek at a few. Although we've already looked in on the Windows Forum, I want you to realize the breadth of this department—to expand your horizons. Perhaps you will discover something that interests you in the process.

The DOS Forum

DOS is the software everyone loves to hate, yet it's the system in place on tens of millions of computers worldwide. It's without a doubt the most widely used software on earth. The DOS Forum's 27 libraries house thousands of files; message boards allow users and staff to help one another; and 5 live conference sessions meet each week to address the needs of novice and veteran DOS users. Click on the Forum Update icon from the main DOS Forum menu to see the complete meeting schedule, which is continuously updated and covers events up to a month in advance.

The DOS Forum's message boards are a haven for the perplexed DOS user. Want to know how to configure EMM386, increase your PATH limit, or unstick your Shift key? You'll find the answers on the DOS Forum's message boards.

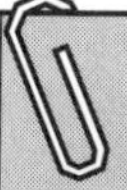

Finding Leadership Online

If you've ever wondered who's in charge of running the forums, you've probably run into the answer to your question if you spend much time online: the Forum Leader. Forum Leaders are responsible for the day-to-day management of the forums in their charge. But forum life online is so busy that each Forum Leader maintains a staff of forum assistants and consultants, usually selected from the general membership on the basis of their expertise in a given area. The Forum Leader, consultants and assistants work as a team to provide technical support, answer member inquiries, process file uploads and help direct forum conferences. You can identify forum personnel quickly by looking for one of these three prefixes on a screen name: PC (Forum Leader), PCA (Forum Assistant) or PCC (Forum Consultant). (AFL prefixes denote Forum Leaders for the Mac and Apple II forums.) Look for these folks when you have a question, and you'll likely find that the forum staffer will bend over backward to help you.

Perhaps the DOS Forum's greatest asset is its fast emergency assistance to members who install a new piece of hardware or software, only to find their computers suddenly don't function as they should. It's not uncommon to find a DOS staffer online well after midnight, helping to rescue a damaged config.sys file, long after most company support hotlines have closed for the day.

Certainly of equal value to beginning and advanced users alike is the DOS Forum's extensive library of files, ranging from command enhancers to full-scale disk managers. During a browse the other day, I discovered utilities to fix the aforementioned sticking Shift key problem, optimize a hard disk and align DR DOS with Windows. Because there are so many files, a single library would be unwieldy. Instead, 30 libraries are offered, each housing hundreds of individual files (see Figure 5-8).

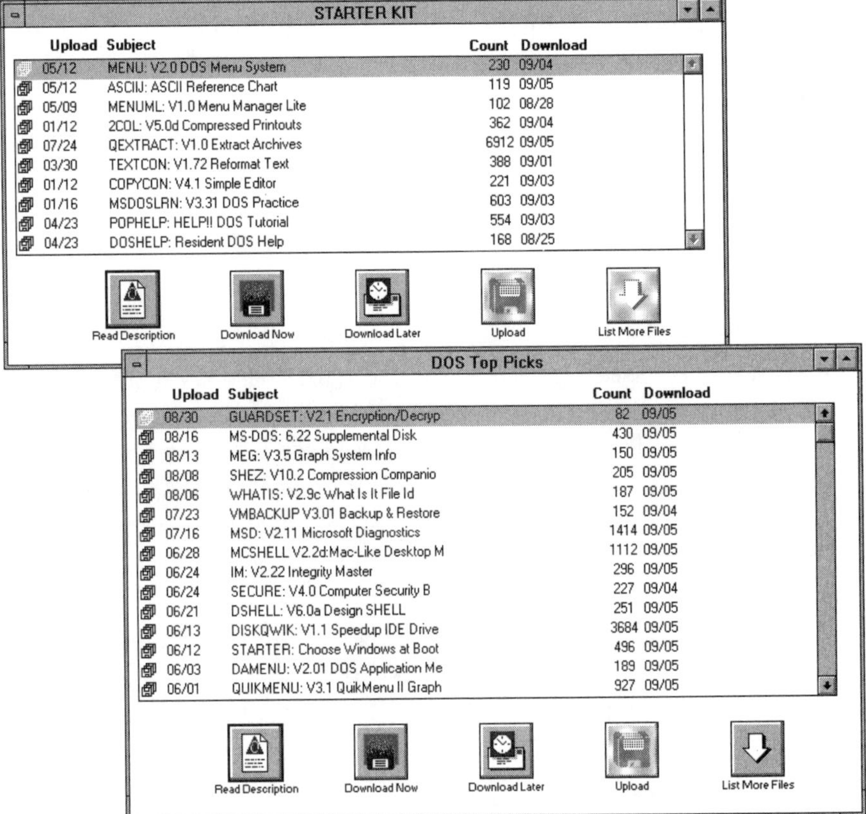

Figure 5-8: Two of the DOS Forum's software libraries: Top Picks and the Starter Kit. There are 28 other libraries, each housing hundreds of files.

The PC Graphics & Animation Forum

Imagine having access to over 10,000 graphics files, with more being added every day. Imagine a database of these files, searchable by keywords, author names and file names. Imagine reviews of graphics software, tips from graphics experts and a comprehensive manual describing the ins and outs of online graphics. This, of course, is the PC Graphics & Animation Forum (keyword: Graphics).

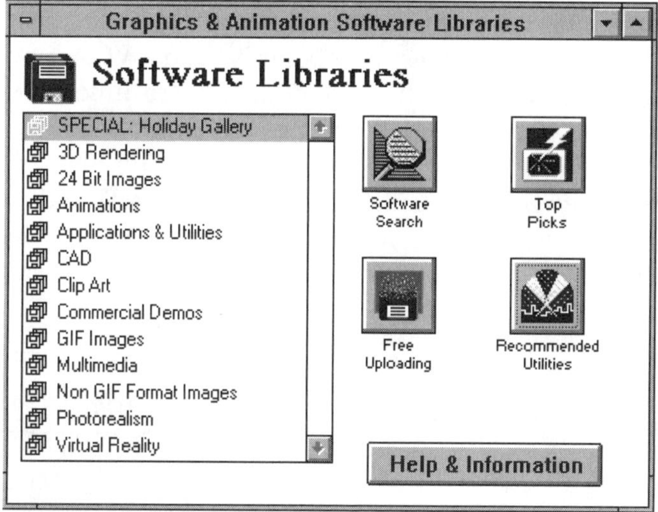

Figure 5-9: The Graphics Forum offers 15 categories of graphics files and utilities, ranging from simple line art to complex ray-traced animations.

The Graphics Forum's libraries are even more prodigious than those of the DOS Forum. At this writing, over 50 topical libraries populate the forum, and like the DOS Forum, a searchable database allows you to search the thousands of files for subject matter that meets your needs. There's a Start Up Library for the novice, a Graphics Reference Guide for the inquisitive, scores of message boards, and a Graphics Meeting Room where public conferences are held nearly every weeknight at 9:30 (Eastern time). To attend, use the keyword: Graphics, then click the Conference Center button. Here's the weekly calendar:

- Monday: The Graphics Conference, with a new topic or guest each week.
- Wednesday: The evening CAD Conference for engineers, architects and other users of computer-aided design systems.

- Thursday: The Artists' Studio.
- Friday: The Animation Conference.

Mention of that last conference—the Animation Conference—reminds me that this is the PC Graphics & Animation Forum, and I would be doing the forum a disservice by not mentioning animation. As it turns out, any PC capable of running Windows is capable of running most of the animations posted in the animation library of the forum. All you need is an animation-viewing program (there's a one-minute, public-domain download from AutoDESK—aaplay.zip—in the forum's library that does the job nicely) and a VGA monitor. While high-quality animation files are huge, they're almost mystical. I can't show you one here, but believe me, you won't believe you're watching a PC when you see your first animation. Try tyranrex.zip by Ero W. It's a lengthy download, but when that chromium Thunder Lizard stomps across you screen, you'll never think of your PC (or T-Rex) the same way again.

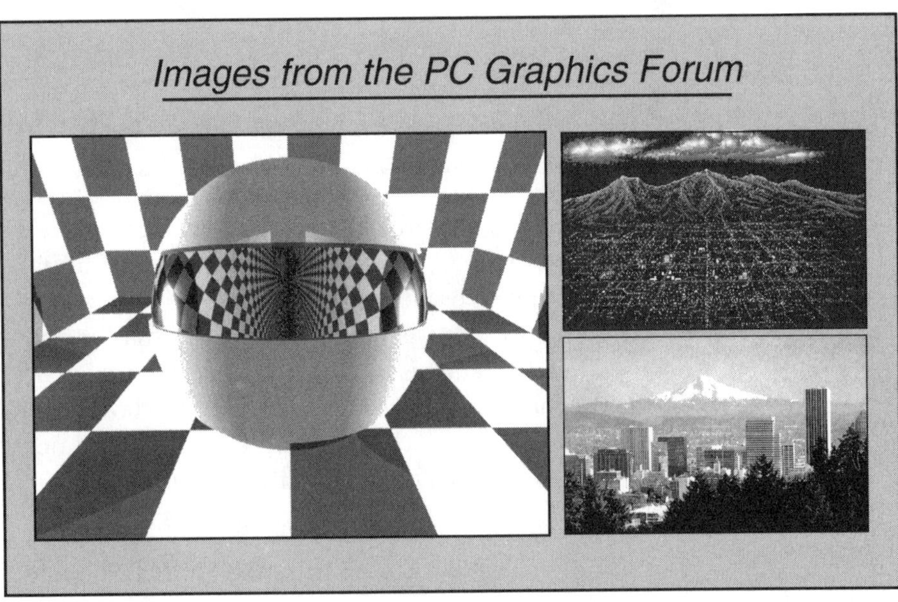

Figure 5-10: Three of my favorite graphics from the PC Graphics & Animation Forum. At left, "Sphere" by Gwydian; top right, "Portland" by DiGino; and bottom right, "City," posted by PC John. To locate these graphics, use the keyword: FileSearch, then specify the title or the artist.

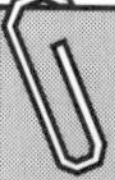

No place for chauvinism

Only half the graphics available online reside in the PC Graphics & Animation Forum. An equal number await the adventurous in the—dare we say it?—Macintosh Graphics Forum (keyword: MacGraphics). This sister forum is just as plentiful as the PC forum, and many of the graphics there are in GIF or JPEG format, meaning they can be viewed and used on almost any PC with your AOL software. Even those graphics in the MacGraphics Forum that are saved in Macintosh-specific formats are accessible with the proper software (see Chapter 20, "Ten Best," for my favorite graphic conversion programs). So go ahead, slip into the MacGraphics Forum, and check out the files that reside there. No one will ever know, and I promise I won't tell anyone I sent you there.

The PC Games Forum

If all this talk of operating systems, Windows interfaces and GIF conversions is starting to sound like more work than fun, then a visit to the PC Games Forum—a place that takes fun seriously—is in order (keyword: PC Games).

Be prepared for temptation, because this forum's libraries are better stocked with glorious adventure, arcade, board, gambling, simulation and role-playing gameware than the most abundant software store (Figure 5-11).

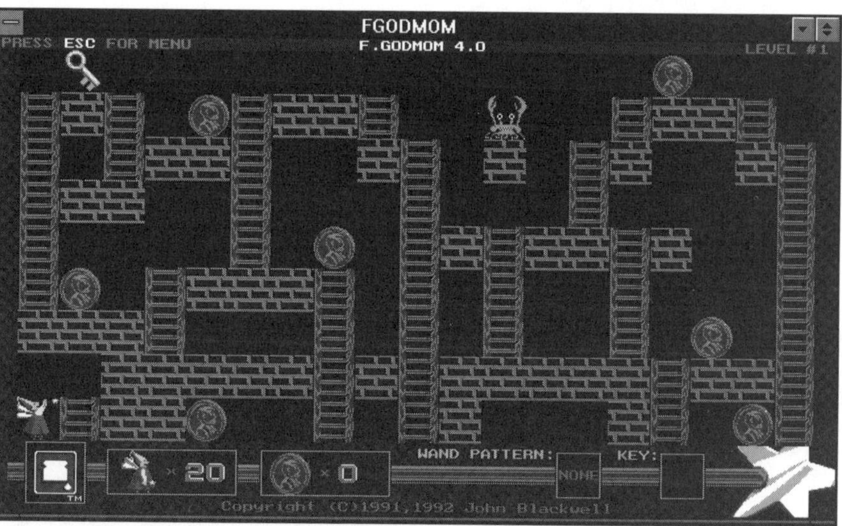

Figure 5-11: "Fairy Godmom" by John Blackwell. For the price of a single movie ticket, Godmom offers hours of shareware entertainment.

Don't let the shareware tag on most of these files fool you. Although the games online usually cost much less than their commercial counterparts, many of them sport better visual and adventure effects than even some of the top-rated mainstream games. The temptations continue in the forum's nightly conferences and message boards, where participants exchange clues and reviews of the hottest new game releases. You'll come away from your first night's session determined to spend the week's grocery budget on the latest game packages from the Games' Top Picks library.

There are no age restrictions here, as you'll discover when you see preteens raving over chess and Mahjongg selections, while more mature types race to grab the latest high-octane arcade battle.

Click the Industry Connection button from the PC Games main menu, and discover special areas resplendent with gaming jewels. The Apogee support area is a favorite, offering supreme graphics and challenges at unbeatable shareware prices. Apogee offers a game for every taste: Word Rescue is great fun for very young players while Castle Wolfenstein 3-D is rated PC (for "profound carnage"). Interplay, another noted game producer, also has a support area here offering demo versions of its most popular PC titles, including BattleChess, Star Trek: 25th Anniversary and SolWin (not one, but three Solitaire games for Windows). In fact, you will find demo versions of many popular games from a host of different companies. For more on games, you might want to review Chapter 9, "Entertainment," where several popular games are featured.

While I have highlighted some of my favorite PC forums, you should check out the other great forums online, including Development, PC Music & Sound, Hardware, PC Applications, PC Telecom, and the Help Forum. The keyword: TITF is an invaluable tool to forum regulars and beginners alike. TITF stands for "Tonight in the Forums." It gives you a comprehensive list of computer conferences held online each night. You can even click on Check for Active Rooms to see which conference rooms have sessions in progress and then enter one right from where the keyword: TITF takes you.

What is Shareware?

Two major channels exist for the distribution of computer programs and data. The traditional commercial channel involves publishers, distributors and retailers. Each must make a living, thus each adds a bit to the cost of the product. There's a considerable distance between the people who use the material and the people who actually create it.

The alternative distribution method is referred to as shareware. The shareware method is usually a direct connection between the user and the person who created the program. Shareware programs and data are posted on telecommunications services like AOL where they can be downloaded whenever we, the users, please. Shareware can also be distributed among individuals or through users' groups without fear of recrimination. Every piece of shareware I have ever seen avidly encourages this kind of distribution.

Shareware is usually complete. If you download a shareware program, you get the complete program—not a "crippled" version—and (usually) documentation as well. You can try it out for a few weeks before you decide to buy. If you decide to keep it, the author usually requests that you send money. Since the money is sent directly to the author—no publishers, distributors, or retailers are involved—shareware can cost much less than commercially distributed software. The author's share is all you pay for shareware, and the author's share is a very small portion of the total cost of the software distributed through commercial channels.

The shareware model also provides a direct channel for communication between user and author. If you have a complaint or a suggestion for improvement, send email to the author. Chances are you'll get a reply. This is a significant feature: to whom do you send mail if you think your car or your refrigerator can be improved? And do you really think they will ever reply?

While most shareware authors request financial remuneration, a few simply give their material away (freeware), or request a postcard from your city or town (postcardware), or a donation to a favored charity.

The shareware concept only works if users pay, and payment is voluntary. Sadly, only about 10 percent of the people who use shareware programs actually pay for them. This is undoubtedly the biggest fault in the shareware concept. The potential that shareware offers is especially rewarding for us the users, but only if we honor the honor system that's implicit in the shareware concept. In other words, if you use shareware, pay for it, and encourage others to do the same.

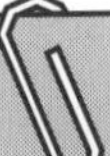

Tim Barwick

Tim Barwick gazes at the woods outside his window, just a few minutes from downtown Washington, DC. Red squirrels scamper up deciduous trees, reveling in the springtime sunshine. The forest's contrast to the rush hour chaos on Route 7 a half-mile away somehow reflects Tim's contrast to the hubbub at AOL. Originally a member, then a forum leader, then the Department Head of the Computing Department, now the Manager of the Product Development team, Tim personifies contrast. The contrast is heard rather than seen: a native of England, Tim speaks with an old-world elegance that hardly conforms to the frenzied, neological industry he helps shape.

As Manager of Product Development, Tim serves as liaison between the members and the people who write the software that's installed in our computers. Tim, in other words, is the staple in the customer-satisfaction recipe.

Tim's old-world heritage is reflected in his management philosophy: he is champion for the rank and file. His philosophy is reflected in today's AOL software. "I know it's corny," Tim says, "but customer satisfaction is paramount. We listen to our users, and many of the features we now offer are the result of end-user suggestions." The shape, the feel—the spirit of the service didn't result from a white paper drafted by directors or advisory committees. AOL is our progeny. Tim Barwick sees to that.

Downloading Files

The most popular aspect of the Computing Department is its extensive collection of software. All it takes is a browse through the libraries: the number of times a file has been downloaded is shown beside each file's name, and most of those numbers exceed 100. Let's say there are 60,000 files in the Computing Department. A hundred downloads for each of 60,000 files equals 6,000,000 downloads. *Six million!* But that's just the Computing Department. Over 60,000 files reside elsewhere within AOL, spread across the service like flowers in a meadow. Members graze this meadow, downloading bouquets of files and smiling. People must be on to something here.

It might be appropriate, then, to spend a few pages discussing downloads: what they are, where they are and how to get one for yourself.

What Is Downloading?

Simply put, downloading is the process of transferring a file from AOL's host machines to a disk in your computer. Files can be programs, utilities, drivers, fonts, graphics (many of the graphics in this book have been downloaded), sound, animation and, of course, text. In fact, this whole book has been downloaded: using attachments to AOL's email, I uploaded the manuscript to AOL (more about uploading later), and the publisher downloaded it back to me after it was edited. (Attachments and email are discussed in Chapter 4.)

A Downloading Session

Perhaps the best way to explain downloading is to download a file for you and explain the process as it's happening. With all of this talk about 60,000 files, how do you find the good stuff? Frankly, the best strategy is to buy a copy of the *Windows Shareware 500* (see sidebar) and refer to it when you're in the mood for something new. The book comes with enough online time and shareware on disk to pay for itself, and it's the reference for Windows shareware.

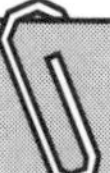

The Windows Shareware 500

The trouble with shareware is there's so much of it. If you downloaded every utility, graphic, and font that sounds interesting, you would spend the rest of the century online. Even reading descriptions can become laborious.

We need to know what's good and what's better; we need to know what's compatible with our machines; we need to know where to find shareware online; and we need to know what the shareware fees are. What we need is a guide. Someone who has seen it all and is willing to share opinions with us.

Would I bring it up if such a service wasn't available online? The Windows Shareware 500 Forum is based on the book of the same name by John Hedke. As the title suggests, the book lists 500 shareware packages available online, ranks each one, specifies their prices, and identifies things like compatibility, version numbers, and the authors' names and addresses.

If you use shareware, this is the place to start.

Finding a File

Before you can download a file, you've got to find it. This could be a horrendous task were it not for AOL's searchable database of online files. The database is only a keyword away.

Begin by clicking the disk-and-magnifier button on the FlashBar, or by entering the keywords: FileSearch (see Figure 5-12). There are lots of other ways to find files for downloading on AOL, but this is the most effective.

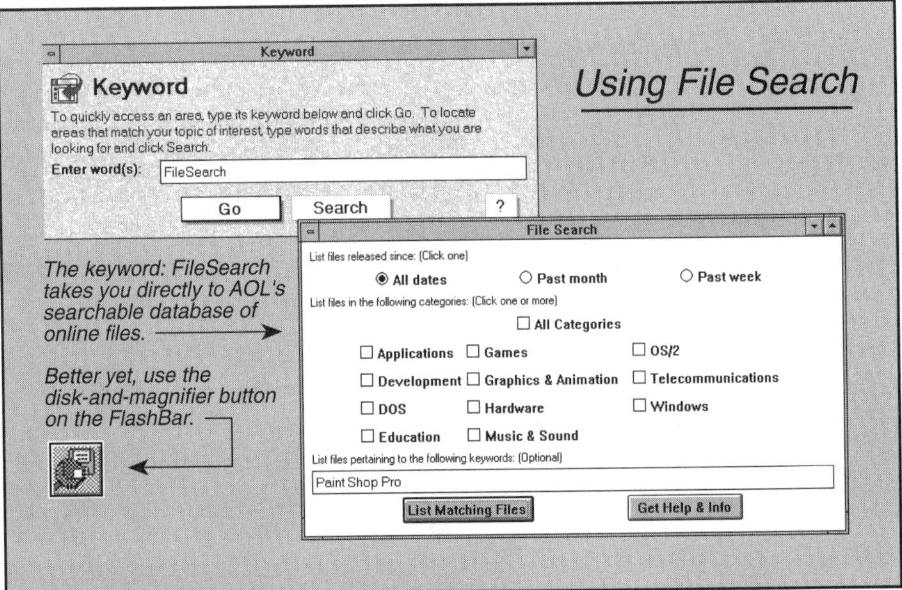

Figure 5-12: The disk-and-magnifier button on the Toolbar or the keyword: FileSearch take you directly to a database of files stored on AOL. There you can enter specific criteria to help you find exactly the file you want.

My search criterion was specific. Only four files match the criterion (and three of them are the Paint Shop Pro program, posted in different places). This isn't always the case. Often, many files will match a given criterion and you'll have to scroll through the results to find the one you want.

When I click the Read Description button, AOL provides a complete description of the file (see Figure 5-13). This intermediary step is critical. There are lots of things I need to know about this file before I choose to download it.

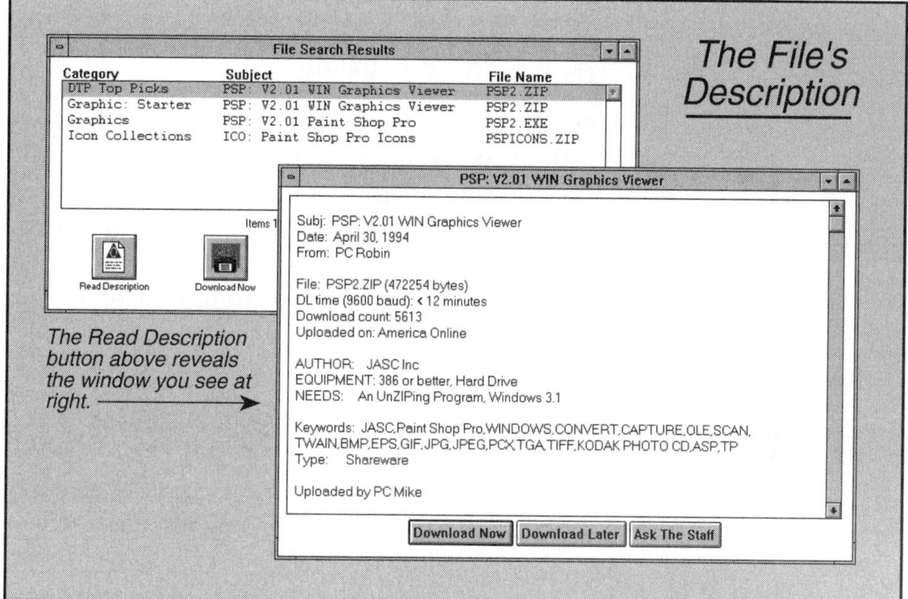

Figure 5-13: It s a good idea to read a file s description before you download it.

The Online File Database

Use of the keyword: FileSearch is a convenient way to search all of AOL's libraries with one command. The keyword cuts across forums and departments to provide access to all the files currently available online. This method assigns the file-searching task to the host computer rather than to your PC, and the host computer searches very quickly—rarely taking more than a few seconds to search the more than 60,000 files available.

Look again at the File Search dialog box pictured in Figure 5-12. Two categories of check boxes are provided, allowing you to specify only those files that have recently been uploaded (the Past week option is great for finding only new files), or only those files that fit certain criteria.

More important, a text box is also available within the File Search dialog. Here you can specify your own criteria. Words entered here are matched against keywords appearing in the following areas:

- the person who uploaded the file,
- the file's name,

- the subject line, and
- keywords assigned to the file.

There are three special words you can use in a match phrase: *and*, *or*, and *not*. I might receive dozens of matches to the search phrase "Versailles," most of which would be references to the city, not the font. The search phrase "Versailles *and* font," on the other hand, narrows the search. (The *and* modifier is the default, by the way. Whenever more than one word appears in a search phrase, AOL assumes there's an *and* between them. Thus the phrase "Versailles and font" is the same as the phrase "Versailles font.")

Perhaps you want the Utopia font as well as the Versailles font. Here is where the or modifier comes in. The phrase "Versailles *or* Utopia" finds either one.

The *not* modifier excludes material matching the criterion that follows it and narrows the search. The phrase "Versailles *not* France" would provide a listing of all references to Versailles that aren't associated with the city in France.

Combining modifiers can be unclear. The phrase "Versailles or Utopia and font" is ambiguous. Do we mean "Versailles, or Utopia and font," or do we mean "Versailles or Utopia, and font"? The solution is found in the use of parentheses. The phrase "(Versailles or Utopia) and font" says, look for Versailles or Utopia, excluding everything but fonts from either category. It pays to be specific.

When the File Search dialog box opens, we can enter our criterion: Paint Shop Pro (again, refer to Figure 5-12). In this case, we know the name of the program we want to find. That's not always the case, and AOL can accommodate myriad search strategies to deal with the alternatives.

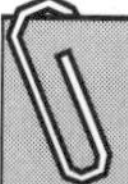

The Software Center

As you can imagine, the computing forums are like the seashore: familiar each time you visit, but the minutiae are never the same. Keeping up with the metamorphoses would be a nuisance were it not for the PC Software Center (keyword: Software). Think of it as a staging area for your journey into the PC Computing and Software Forums.

Of particular interest is the center's database listing for all of the files online in the Computing Department. All you need to do is download the database each week: AOL provides a public domain database program that you can download to search the database listings off-line. It sure beats poking around while the clock's running.

To download the database, use the keyword: FileSearch and the criterion: AOLDBF. You'll find both the program and the database listings by doing so. Download the program once. Download the listings each week as they're updated.

Reading a File Description

Let's look at Paint Shop Pro's file description in its entirety (Figure 5-14).

The Subject, From and File lines are all searchable criteria. Don't confuse the From line with the Author line. The From line contains the name of the person who uploaded the file. That person is often a Forum Leader or an Assistant, not the author. Note that the File line not only includes the file's name but its size as well.

The file date is used when you specify "Past month" or "Past week" in the File Search dialog box.

The download time is AOL's best guess as to how long it will take to download the file. This time is estimated based on the baud rate at which you're currently connected. If you're connected at 9600 baud, the estimate is based on that baud rate. This number is only an estimate. If you signed on during a peak usage period (around 9 P.M. [Eastern time] is a peak usage period), this number might be slightly optimistic. If you're signed on at 4 A.M., this number will be pessimistic. I downloaded Paint Shop Pro, which AOL estimates as a 12-minute download, in less than 10 minutes during a mid-morning session at 9600 baud.

Figure 5-14: A wealth of information is found in file descriptions.

Paint Shop Pro's File Description

```
Subj:  PSP: V2.01 WIN Graphics Viewer
Date:  April 30, 1994
From:  PC Robin

File:  PSP2.ZIP (472254 bytes)
DL time (9600 baud): < 12 minutes
Download count: 5613
Uploaded on: America Online

AUTHOR:     JASC Inc
EQUIPMENT: 386 or better, Hard Drive
NEEDS:      An UnZIPing Program, Windows 3.1

Keywords:  JASC,Paint Shop Pro,WINDOWS,CONVERT,CAPTURE,OLE,SCAN,
TWAIN,BMP,EPS,GIF,JPG,JPEG,PCX,TGA,TIFF,KODAK PHOTO CD,ASP,TP
Type:       Shareware

Uploaded by PC Mike

See GRAPHICS HELP & INFO (ABOUT GIF & GIF VIEWERS) on the main menu of this
forum for Paint Shop Pro installation instructions.

PSP (Paint Shop Pro) is THE recommended viewer for WINDOWS. Paint Shop Pro
supports the file formats; GIF, JPG (JPEG), PCX, TGA, TIFF, BMP, CLP, CUT,
DIB, EPS, IFF, IMG, JAS, JIF, LBM, MAC, MSP, PCD (Kodak Photo CD), PIC, RAS,
RLE, WMF and WPG. Paint Shop Pro is a Windows program that will allow you to
work with multiple images at a time. With Paint Shop Pro you can display,
convert, alter, scan and print images. In addition, it is a screen capture
utility. Paint Shop Pro includes a batch conversion for those large
conversion jobs.

Scan your images directly into Paint Shop Pro using any TWAIN-compliant
scanner. Make your adjustments, then save the image to exactly the file type
you will need.

Add image support to your other applications with Paint Shop Pro's OLE server
support.

Paint Shop Pro displays images in many ways, including zooming in and out.
Altering the image includes flipping, mirroring, rotating in one-degree
increments, resizing, resampling, cropping, adding a border and 19 standard
filters. Paint Shop Pro supports user defined filters to allow you to create,
edit, delete and apply your own filters. You can also work with the colors of
an image by adjusting the brightness/contrast, highlight/shadow, gamma
correction and red/green/blue. Alter the colors by greyscaling, solarizing
and creating a negative. Palette manipulation allows you to change individual
color values, save and load palettes. Change the image type by increasing or
decreasing the color depth.

Winner - 1992 Shareware Industry Awards

Downloads for previous version: 35,600

INSTALLATION DOCUMENTATION: README.TXT
```

The Download Count is a rough indication of the file's popularity. If you're looking for a graphic of a cat, for instance, and 40 files match your search criteria, you might let the number of downloads (review Figure 5-13) direct you. Often, however, the number of downloads is more reflective of the catchiness of a file's name or description than of its content.

The Equipment and Needs lines are critical: if your PC isn't up to the task, or if you need special software, it's nice to know before you download the file. For instance, you'll need an unzipping program to unzip Paint Shop Pro, and the Needs line informs you of this. (America Online unzips automatically, by the way, so Paint Shop's needs are met by your AOL software.)

Keywords are those that provide matches when you enter your own search criteria. Read these. They offer valuable insight as to how to word your search phrases.

Note: In this context, a keyword is a word assigned to a shareware file that is used to help categorize and describe it for easy search and retrieval. These are separate from and can't be used by AOL's navigational keyword function (accessed by typing Ctrl+K or by clicking the keyword button on the FlashBar).

The description itself is provided by the person who uploaded the file. Paint Shop Pro's description, for instance, indicates that a documentation file unzips with the program, and that the documentation is in textual format. In other words, I will probably be able to open the documentation using Notepad or Write.

Before being posted, each file uploaded to AOL is checked for viruses by one of the forum's personnel. None escape this level of security.

File descriptions can be saved for later reference. Choose Save from the File menu before you close the description window. America Online will ask where you want to store the description, which it stores in ASCII text format. All the text that you read on your PC's screen is formatted this way, and it can be read off-line (after you've saved it to a separate file) with any word processor or the AOL software (just choose Open from AOL's File menu).

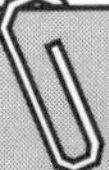

Using the Fastest Local Access Number

As I mentioned in Chapter 1, AOL employs the services of a variety of long-distance services. When you first sign on to AOL, AOL's host computers consult their database of telephone numbers in your locale and assign one of them as your primary AOL calling number. They will also assign an alternate number in case the first number is busy or having problems.

The most effective way to judge downloading efficiency is to use a modem with indicator lights. One of them should be marked "receive data" or "RD." This light will stay continuously lit or almost so during an efficient download. Inefficient downloads are indicated when this light flashes on and off like a digital clock that needs to be set. Usually this condition is caused by a heavy load on the host computer. Calling back at a different time of day usually solves the problem.

If calling back at a different time of day doesn't solve the problem, try the alternate number. Here's how:

- If the sign-on screen isn't showing, choose Set Up & Sign On from the Go To menu.
- Click the button marked Setup.
- Two major segments dominate the Setup screen, marked First Choice and Second Choice. If these two numbers are rated at the same speed (9600 baud, for example), try reversing the numbers and services. Be sure to reverse them both! Failure to swap both numbers and services is one of the most common errors people make when they fiddle with this screen.
- Sign on again and try out your setup.

Remember, the description's downloading time is an estimate. However, if your downloads reliably exceed this estimate, you might have a problem. If neither calling back at a different time of day nor swapping services improves your downloading time, send an email message (I discussed email in Chapter 4) to Customer Support. Sometimes they're aware of a service problem in your area and can set your mind at ease.

The Downloading Process

Once you've read a file's description, you might decide to download it. This is the easy part: all you have to do is click on the Download Now button. (The Download Later button is discussed in Chapter 19, "FlashSessions & the Download Manager.")

Remember that downloading is the process of transferring a file from AOL to a disk in your computer. In other words, you're going to have to decide where to put the file. The destination can be either a hard disk or a floppy disk, and that's the next decision you'll be asked to make (Figure 5-15). Pick a disk and a folder, then click the button marked Save.

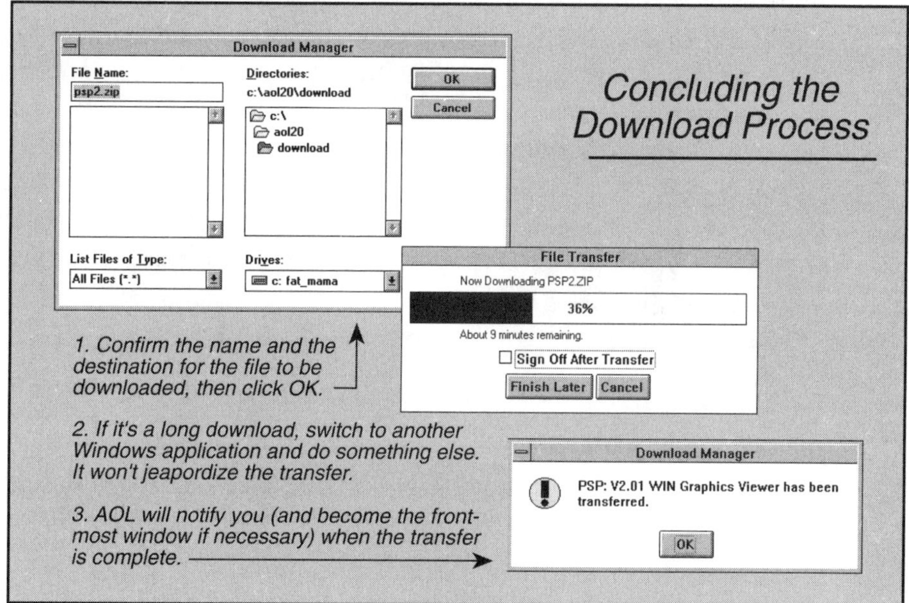

Figure 5-15: The download process is automatic once you've determined the file's name and destination.

When you click the Save button, the downloading process progresses predictably, monitored by the on-screen thermometer pictured in Figure 5-15. When the download is completed, you'll be notified both aurally (if your PC is equipped to play sound) and visually (see the message pictured in the third window in Figure 5-15).

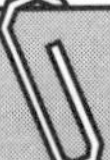

File Names & Destinations

Look again at Figure 5-15 and note the proposed file name. If you want to use a file name other than the one proposed, all you have to do is select the proposed name (if it isn't selected already) and start typing. I don't recommend this, unless the proposed file name conflicts with one already on your disk. The file's documentation, for instance, might refer to the file by name; if you change the name, the reference might be unclear. Forum discussions might refer to the file's original name. If you search for an update to the file, you'll need to refer to it by its original name. So use the original name unless you have a good reason not to.

I also recommend you download to floppy disks rather than your hard disk. Have a few formatted floppies at your side, and specify one when you encounter the dialog pictured at the top of Figure 5-15. I suggest this strategy for two reasons related to safety: (1) Downloaded files might conflict with your PC. It's very rare, but these conflicts could corrupt the disk that contains the file. (2) Downloaded files could contain a virus. As I mentioned, AOL's files are checked for viruses before they're posted, but new viruses are dreamed up every day, and one could conceivably sneak through. Though this potential is also remote, it's better to be safe than sorry. I'll show you how to find virus detection software online in a moment.

Saving to floppies imposes only a slight penalty on downloading time. Though floppy disks are slower in reading and writing than hard disks, the primary limiting factor during the downloading process is baud rate. The additional time required to download Paint Shop Pro to a floppy is about 10 seconds.

File Formats

The number of potential file formats for downloaded files is staggering. Fortunately, some standards and conventions help to organize the confusion.

All downloadable files for the PC follow DOS naming conventions. DOS file names consist of up to eight characters, a period and a three-character file name extension, such as psp20.zip. Though the eight-character limit is stifling (eight characters are hardly enough for a descriptive file name), the three-character extension is particularly useful. All you have to do is look at a DOS file's extension to see what kind of file it is. DOS file names ending in .xls are Excel worksheets, for instance. Those ending in .txt are text files and are readable by most word processors and text editors, including the AOL software itself.

Those ending in .zip are files compressed using the PKZip utility (more on PKZip later in this chapter). And those ending in .tif are TIFF graphic files.

The chart pictured in Figure 5-16 identifies some of the common DOS file name extensions and their meanings. File format compatibility differs from program to program. PageMaker, for instance, reads most of these formats except the compressed ones. Excel, on the other hand, can only read TXT, WKS and Excel formats. Read the documentation that came with your software to determine which formats you should use.

Figure 5-16: Filename extensions for some of the most common file formats you'll find online.

Filename Extensions

Textual formats

TXT	Unformatted ASCII text
RTF	Rich Text Format
DOC	Microsoft Word, WordPerfect

Graphic formats

BMP	Windows bitmaps
TIF	Tagged-image file format
GIF	Graphic interchange format
PCX	PC Paintbrush, Windows Paintbrush
WMF	Windows Metafile
EPS	Encapsulated PostScript

Compressed formats

ZIP	PKZip (AOL unzips automatically)
JPG	Joint Photographic Experts Group
SEA	Self-Extracting Archive
SIT	StuffIt (Macintosh)

Other formats

PM*	PageMaker (* = version number)
XLS	Excel worksheet (XLC = Excel chart)
WKS	Lotus 1-2-3 worksheet (also WK1)
FLI	AutoDESK Animator

Look again at Figure 5-16. Four compressed formats are identified there, and they require further explanation.

Why compress files? There are three good reasons: (1) compressed files are much smaller than uncompressed files and thus take significantly less time to download; (2) compressed files require less storage space; and (3) compressed files are often stored in an archive (several files compressed into a single file). Archives are a convenient way of grouping multiple files for storage and downloading.

Amazingly, compressed files can be reduced to only 20 percent of the original size; yet when they're decompressed, absolutely no data is lost. I don't know how they do that. Smoke and mirrors, I suppose.

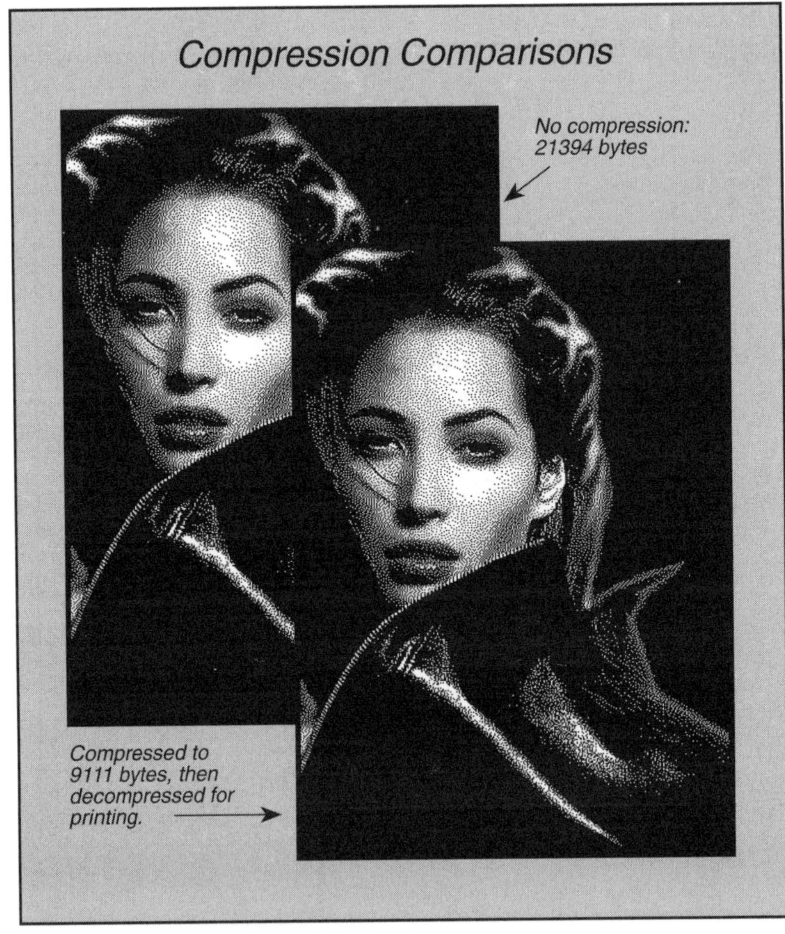

Figure 5-17: The original image on the left measures 21,394 bytes. The image on the right was compressed to 9,111 bytes (43 percent of the original), then decompressed for printing. No data was lost; both pictures are identical. (Scanning and retouching by David Palermo.)

Figure 5-17 indirectly identifies a problem common to all compressed images: they're useless until decompressed. The compressed image in Figure 5-17 couldn't be included in the illustration until it was decompressed. In other words, you must have decompression software before you can use compressed images. That's the bad news. The good news is that you already have decompression software: it's part of the AOL software package installed on your PC.

PKZip

A shareware program called PKZip is responsible for a great deal of the file compression encountered in the PC environment. PKZip can compress (or zip, as it's called) a single file or a multitude of files into a single file—the archive. PKZip archives are identified by the .zip file name extension.

Like all archives, PKZip archives must be decompressed (unzipped) before use, and, incredibly, that happens automatically when you use AOL. If compression is done with smoke and mirrors, automatic decompression must be done with smoke and mirrors and the eyes of a newt. Whatever the technique, it works—and we're the beneficiaries.

When your AOL software downloads a file with .zip in its file name, it makes a note to itself to unzip the file immediately after you sign off. (You must have this option in effect. Choose it using Set Preferences on the Members menu). An unzipped copy of the file appears on your disk after decompression, ready for use. Your AOL software also automatically decompresses any files with the .arc (for "archive") file name extension.

America Online only gives you the unzipping part of PKZip. While you can use your AOL software to unzip any file with the .zip file name extension (just choose Open from AOL's File menu), if you want to zip your own files, you'll need your own copy of PKZip. Fortunately, PKZip is available online: use the keyword: FileSearch , then search for PKZip. You'll find a number of files meeting the criterion; be sure you get the latest. PKZip is shareware. If you like the program, pay the shareware fee and you can use it indefinitely with a clear conscience.

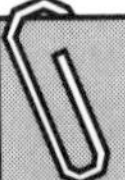

WinZip

As great as PKZip is, it's not Windows software. In fact, PKZip steadfastly clings to the archaic DOS interface of command lines and obtuse, exacting syntax. Though a number of shell programs came along—programs that wrapped up PKZip in a pretty Windows interface—they were usually slow and they all required PKZip. The double shareware fees—one for PKZip and one for the shell—were an insult; until WinZip came along.

In its latest incarnation, WinZip is fully self-contained and does its work effectively, without the need for PKZip. It's fully compatible with PKZip, it's almost as fast—quite a compliment—and it's easy to use. Perhaps best of all, WinZip offers an extensive help file for those few occasions when you need it.

Use the keyword: FileSearch and search with the criterion: WinZip. It's a superior alternative.

Self-extracting Archives

You now know all about Zips, but there is another type of archive you'll find online: the *self-extracting archive*. Just as the name implies, these are archives which decompress themselves when you run them (use Program Manager or File Manager). Self-extracting archives even look like DOS programs because they usually end with the .exe file name extension. But so do many uncompressed files, so check the download's description.

For example, let's say you find a file online called dummit.exe, and you see this line in the file description:

```
This file is self-extracting, requiring 112,500 bytes.
```

That tells you dummit.exe is a self-extracting archive, and it clues you in to how much room (how many bytes) it will take up on your disk when you extract it. You would download it just like any other file; but, because it's self-extracting, AOL's automatic decompression feature won't work here. That's not a worry. All you need to do is select dummit.exe using File Manager, then choose Run from File Manager's File menu. The files contained within dummit.exe will decompress themselves (if there are more than one; it might be a single file), and you're ready to run the program according to the instructions contained in the online file description.

StuffIt

While PKZip is the file compression standard for PCs, a program called StuffIt is the standard for the Macintosh platform. Instead of being zipped and unzipped, StuffIt files (followed by the .sit extension) are "stuffed" and "unstuffed." A number of files suitable for use on either platform—graphics, mostly—were originally constructed on Macintoshes and are stuffed rather than zipped. (This is beginning to sound like a recipe for baked turkey: First stuff, then zip the carcass, then bake at 350 degrees for four hours . . .)

Stuffed files won't decompress themselves automatically on a PC, nor are they self-extracting archives. To use them, you have to acquire unstuffing software. My favorite is a program called UNSTUFF. I forgive its DOS command-line interface because it's written by the people who wrote StuffIt, so compatibility is assured. UNSTUFF is available as freeware on AOL. Use the keyword: FileSearch, then search for UNSTUFF.

JPEG

The newcomer on the block of file compression formats is JPEG, formulated by the Joint Photographic Experts Group to establish a compression standard for large graphics files and full-motion video and sound. JPEG is often used to compress high-resolution color or black-and-white TIFF files. By removing some of the less-than-vital color information here and there, files compressed using JPEG can accomplish dramatic size reductions. But once this data is gone, it's lost forever. Consequently, JPEG is said to be a *lossy* compression method. All of the other file compression methods I have mentioned are *lossless*, meaning no loss in information is encountered in the compression process.

Lossy compression would never do for text: dropping a character or two here and there would be catastrophic. On the other hand, lossy compression for bitmapped graphics (the kind produced by scanners, in particular) isn't much of a problem. After all, who will notice if a bit of information 1/300 of an inch across is light blue instead of medium blue? In fact, most files subjected to lossy compression techniques are hard to tell from the original. If you're willing to accept some minor data loss, you can achieve much higher compression levels than with lossless compression. Your AOL software can read most JPEG files.

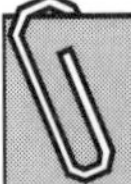

Once is Enough

Your AOL software will save graphics in the JPEG format as well as open them. Since some loss of information is involved, however, you don't want to repeatedly open, then save JPEG files. If you intend to make changes to a graphic, make them all before you save the graphic using the JPEG format. A JPEG save should be your last save for any particular image.

Uploading Files

With all this talk about downloading, it's easy to forget that before a file can be *down*loaded, it first must be *up*loaded. Pursuant to its community spirit, AOL depends on its members for most of its files—members like you and me. Uploading isn't the exclusive realm of AOL employees and forum staff, nor is it that of the super-nerds. Most of the files you can download from AOL—I'd guess over 90 percent—have been uploaded by members, using PCs just like yours.

Earlier I defined downloading as "the process of transferring a file from AOL's host machines to a disk on your computer." Uploading is just the reverse: the process of transferring a file from a disk on your computer to AOL's host computer. Once received, it's checked for viruses and the quality of its content, then it's posted. The process rarely takes more than a day: upload a file on Monday and you'll probably see it available for downloading Tuesday morning.

The Uploading Process

Begin the uploading process by visiting the forum where your file seems to fit. If it's a graphic, post it in the PC Graphics Forum. If it's poetry, post it in the Writers Club. Once you're in the forum, select the library that's the most appropriate place for your file (if there's more than one library in the forum) and click on the Upload File button. (Some forums have an icon marked Submit a File; use this icon if it's available.)

Recently I uploaded a magazine article to the Writers Club. When I clicked on the Upload button, I received the Upload File Information form pictured in Figure 5-18. You'll encounter this form every time you upload a file to AOL.

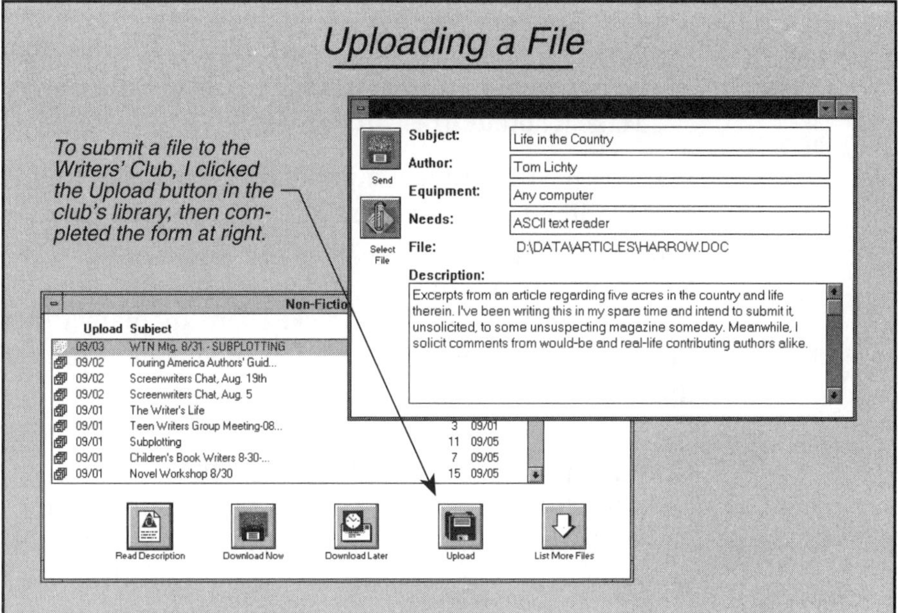

Figure 5-18: You'll be asked to fill out the Upload File Information form for every file you upload to America Online.

The Upload File Information Form

All too often, uploaders fail to complete the Upload File Information form adequately. This form "sells" your file to other members, and what you have to say about it determines whether a member will take the time to download it. Here are some hints for creating accurate, useful and compelling descriptions of files you upload.

- The Subject field should be descriptive and catchy, in that order. Look at the window in the foreground of Figure 5-18. Do you see how the subjects are listed there? The subject line is your headline. If you want members to read your story, hook 'em with a really great subject line.
- The Equipment line should identify any special equipment required to access the file. A 24-bit graphic requires a 24-bit color card; VGA won't do.
- The Needs line is where you specify the particular software application or program that's required to access your file. An Excel worksheet, for instance, requires the Excel spreadsheet program.
- The Description field is where you get specific. Here you differentiate your file from others that might be similar. If you're submitting

a program, you should include the version number. Be specific and persuasive: you're selling your file here. Think about what you would want to read if you were considering downloading the file. Make it sound irresistible.

If you're submitting a number of related files, or if your file's size exceeds about 20k, compress it (or them) using PKZip or something equivalent. This saves downloading time and is the polite way to offer your material. Archives should generally be smaller than 720k, so they'll fit on a single floppy disk. There are many different versions of PKZip. Ask your Forum Leader what version is preferred before you upload.

Concluding the Uploading Process

America Online's by-now familiar thermometer will keep you entertained while the upload is under way, followed by a dialog box announcing your success. The time spent uploading your file will be credited back to you. Though you might not see the credit before you sign off, it will appear soon thereafter.

To check your billing information, use the keyword: Billing. A day or so after your upload is completed, you should see a note crediting your account with any time you have spent uploading files. The billing area is free, so you won't be charged for whatever time you spend online checking your account's billing information.

Moving On

This has been a long chapter steeped in technicalities. We've explored the largest department on the service and peeked at a few of its forums. We've downloaded files, archived files, unstuffed files and uploaded files. We've even explored criteria phrases for the searching of online databases. For making it this far, you deserve a gold star.

You also deserve a break from technicalities—a break which I offer in the next chapter. We're about to explore Today's News, another extremely effective use of the online medium.

Best of all, you won't have to wait for "film at 11," or the morning paper, or even news on the hour. America Online's news is available whenever you want it, and it's never stale. It's as current as news can be, and it's only a page away....

CHAPTER 6

Today's News

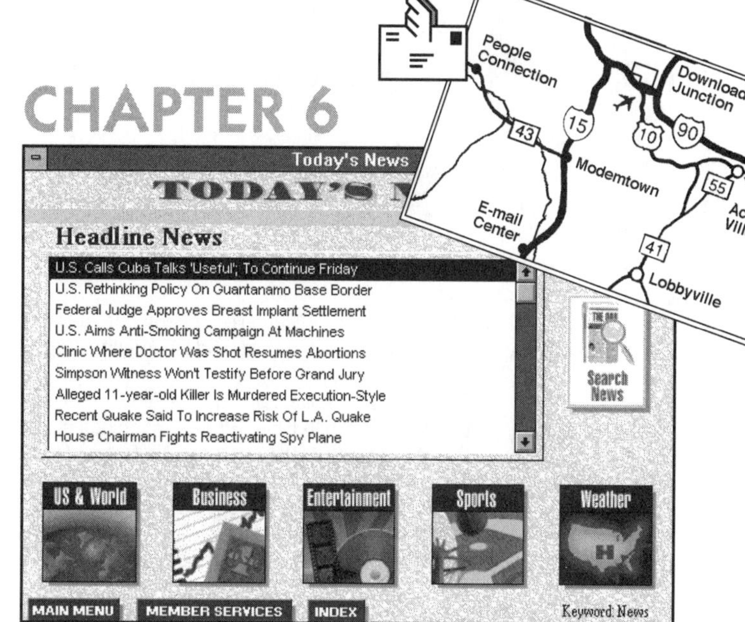

Eighty years ago, people got their news from newspapers. At best, newspapers offered the news once a day—a small inconvenience considering the urgency with which events occurred back then. Radio emerged 70 years ago, offering the potential of immediate, "on the scene" coverage. But there were no pictures, and you had to be listening when the news was broadcast or you missed it. Forty years ago, television brought pictures, but even today you're at the mercy of TV scheduling if you want the latest.

Have you considered online news? It's immediate (updated perpetually), it has pictures, and it's available at your convenience: there's no broadcast schedule that must be observed. (There are no commercials either!)

America Online is aware of its prerogative, and a recent redesign of the service (see the frontispiece and use the keyword: News) emphasizes the potential.

Top Stories

Look again at the frontispiece above. That list of stories you see at the left of the window is always current and changes as events change. These are the stories that lead the news; the online "front page." To read any of the stories featured there, simply double-click the headline (see Figure 6-1).

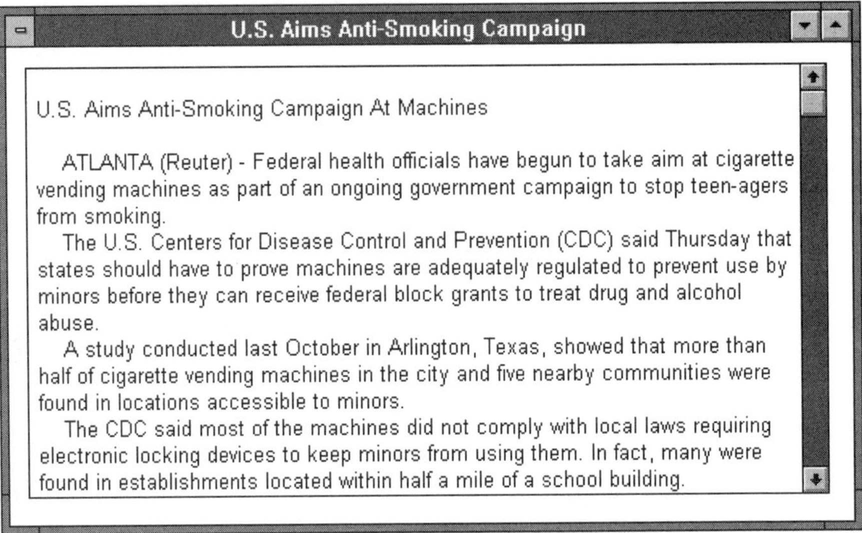
U.S. Aims Anti-Smoking Campaign

U.S. Aims Anti-Smoking Campaign At Machines

ATLANTA (Reuter) - Federal health officials have begun to take aim at cigarette vending machines as part of an ongoing government campaign to stop teen-agers from smoking.

The U.S. Centers for Disease Control and Prevention (CDC) said Thursday that states should have to prove machines are adequately regulated to prevent use by minors before they can receive federal block grants to treat drug and alcohol abuse.

A study conducted last October in Arlington, Texas, showed that more than half of cigarette vending machines in the city and five nearby communities were found in locations accessible to minors.

The CDC said most of the machines did not comply with local laws requiring electronic locking devices to keep minors from using them. In fact, many were found in establishments located within half a mile of a school building.

Figure 6-1: By double-clicking the fourth lead story pictured in the frontispiece, the complete text of the story is displayed. I can now read, save or print it.

Keeping a Log

While articles like those pictured in Figure 6-1 are informative, invaluable, and often fascinating, reading them online is not. I prefer to absorb information like that at my leisure, when the online clock isn't running.

The solution is found in AOL's Log feature. When a log is turned on, all text appearing on your screen is recorded on your disk. You can zip through an online session without delay, letting articles flash across your screen with the tempo of an MTV video. Then, when you've accessed what you need, sign off and review the log. Any word processor will open a log file, as will your AOL software: just choose Open from the File menu.

Now that I've read the paragraph above, I feel compelled to make a disclaimer: some things such as portfolios offer their own saving routines; others, such as the EAASY SABRE gateway [discussed in Chapter 11] may have to be copied and pasted into a new document for saving. Generally speaking, the logging feature logs articles—AOL text files—for later review.

To start a log, choose Logging from the File menu. In the Logging window, open a Session Log by clicking the Open button in the lower part of the window. America Online will display a standard file-open dialog box complete with a suggested file name and location (Figure 6-2). Change what you want, then click Save. From then on, all the text you see onscreen will be saved on your disk.

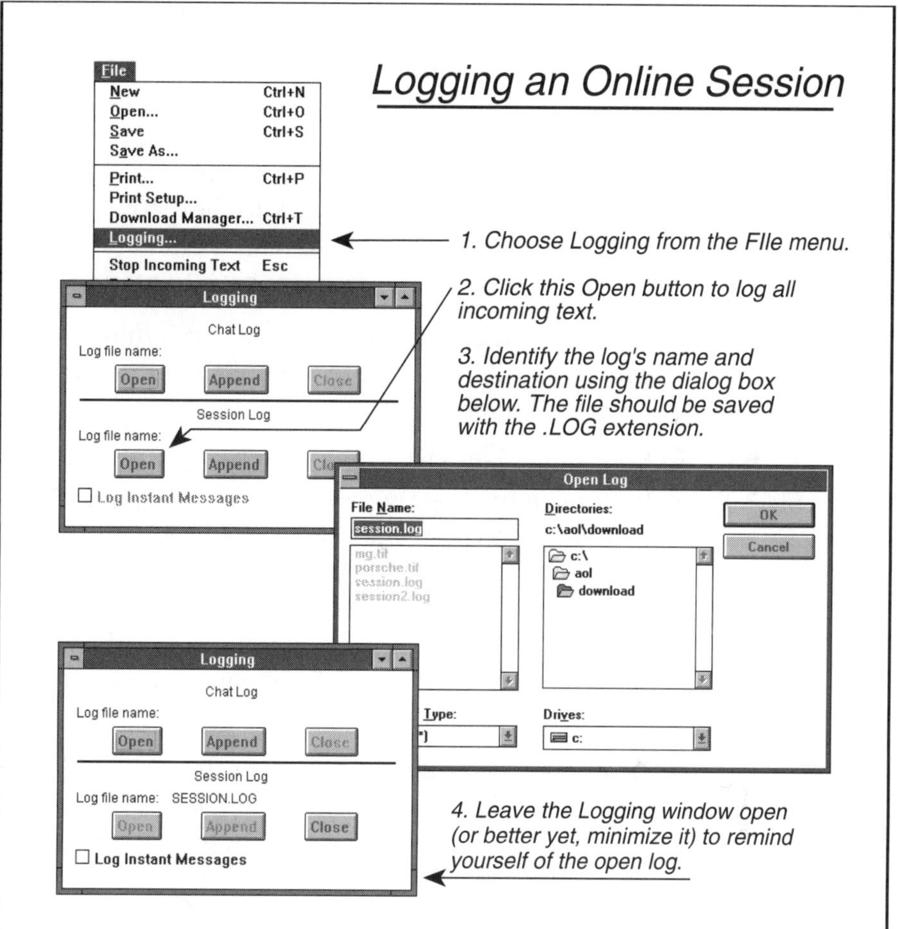

Figure 6-2: Log files capture on-screen activity to disk for later review.

Saving Articles

Whenever an article appears on your screen in the front-most window, it's available for saving on a disk. To save an article (news or otherwise—I'm talking about any article, at any time), just choose Save from the File menu. You'll see a standard Windows file-save dialog box, where you can change the article's suggested name, and determine its location. (This saving procedure goes for graphics also—see "Downloading" in Chapter 5, "Computing.")

Saved articles are pure text and can be opened with any word processor. You can open saved articles with AOL's software as well—whether you're online or off—by choosing Open from the File menu.

A few notes regarding logs:

- To capture the complete article in your log you must double-click (open) the article's headline while you're online, and allow AOL to complete the article's transmission to your PC (be sure it's complete: if the More button is active, there's more to follow). When the hourglass cursor changes back to the arrow cursor, transmission is complete. You don't have to read it online—you don't even have to scroll to the end of it—you just have to receive it in its entirety.
- Log files can be unlimited in size, but if they exceed 30K, the AOL software will be unable to open them. Use a word processor to open the larger log files.
- You can always close the log or append an existing one with the buttons in the Logging window (refer again to Figure 6-2). This is handy when you want to toggle your log on and off: you can use the Close and Append buttons as you would the pause button on a tape recorder, capturing the material you want and excluding what you don't want. The Logging window works while you're off-line as well, so you can start a log even before you sign on. You'll never miss a thing that way.
- If you look carefully at the bottom window in Figure 6-2, you will note two types of logs. The Session log is the one that captures articles such as those discussed in this chapter; it doesn't capture chats and instant messages (which I'll discuss in Chapter 12, "People Connection").

Printing Articles

You can print any article that appears in AOL's front-most window. This is best done off-line, when the clock's not running. Again, use the File menu. Choose Print and you'll see your PC's standard printing dialog box. Make any changes that are necessary to the print configuration and click OK. America Online will print the article to your PC's currently selected printer. (Refer to your Windows manual for a complete description of Windows printing procedures.)

Searching the News

Look again at the frontispiece for this chapter. On the right-hand side of the window you'll see an icon labeled "Search News." This is an extremely powerful tool.

It's powerful because it searches not only the world news, but also business, entertainment, sports and even weather. If you know of a subject that's in the news and you want to know more, click this icon.

Look at Figure 6-3. Searching for the word *Virus*, AOL finds 14 stories in the news, ranging from computer viruses to President Clinton's health plan. Along the way, AOL even found a business item ("Gilead Sciences Announces Fiscal 1995 First Quarter..."). Since my true interest was in the International Anti-(Computer) Virus competition in Holland, I narrowed my search by using the criterion: Computer Virus and conducted the narrower search (four "hits") pictured in the lower window of Figure 6-3.

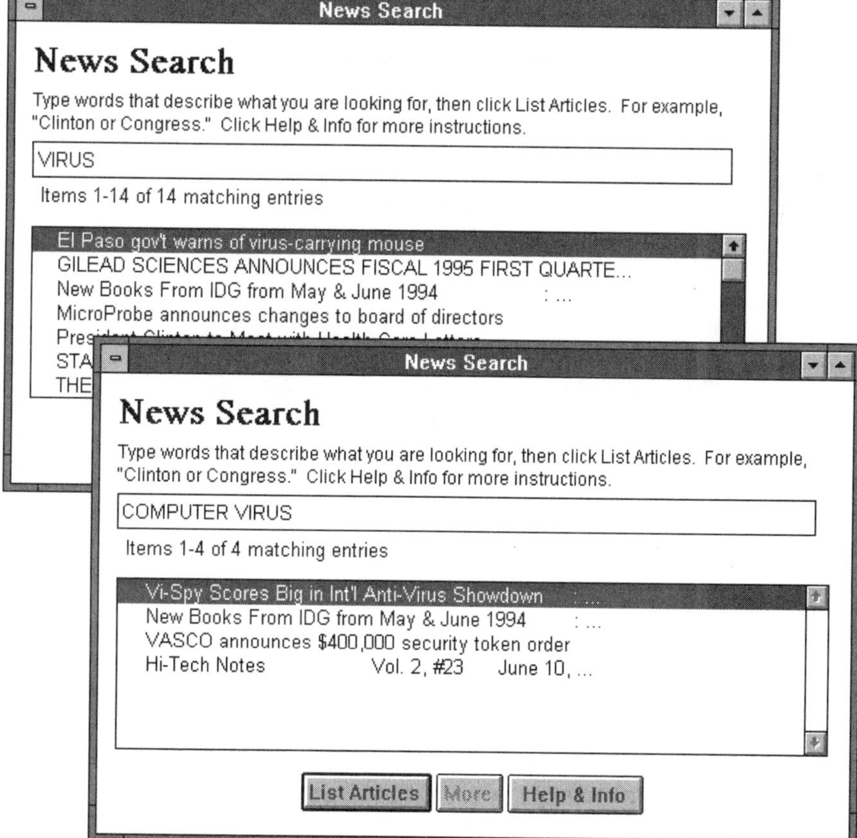

Figure 6-3: Using the criterion: Virus, I receive 14 "hits" in an America Online news search. By specifying *Computer Virus*, I narrow my search to four hits, a much more manageable number.

Specifying effective search criteria for AOL's database searches takes a bit of practice and a working knowledge of Boolean operators. You'll find a discussion of database searches in Chapter 13, "Clubs & Interests."

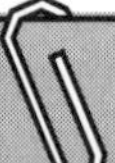

No Criteria

Here's a little trick you might find revealing: conduct a news search with no criteria whatsoever. Press the space bar to place nothing more than a space in the criteria field (where the words *Virus* and *Computer Virus* appear in Figure 6-3), then click the List Articles button.

This tells AOL to search for anything, and it will find every article in today's news. Typically, you'll see two to four thousand of them: an indication of the extent of the Today's News Department. America Online subscribes to Reuters among others. Few news sources are this extensive.

US & World News

America Online's top stories and News Search features access every news article on file in the Today's News Department—3,200 of them on the day I researched this chapter. If you prefer a more structured approach to your daily news, use the buttons arrayed across the bottom of the Today's News window.

The leftmost of those buttons is labeled "US & World," leading you to an organized presentation of the day's world news (see Figure 6-4). Use the keyword: USNews if you want to access this feature directly.

The buttons at the bottom of the Today's News window are analogous to the sections of your daily newspaper. They're especially useful if you're just browsing the news, with no particular interests in mind other than a general subject area.

Figure 6-4: The US & World News feature structures world news into regions to facilitate browsing. By selecting the "Russia/CIS" entry in the main US & World News window, I'm presented with a half-dozen associated news stories.

Business

Don't confuse today's business news with the Personal Finance Department found elsewhere on AOL. The business news offered in the Today's News Department is just that: the news—today's most recent business news from around the world. Investing advice, stock market timing charts, mutual funds and analysis are all discussed in Chapter 10, "Personal Finance."

Like the US & World News area, the Business News area brings a coherent structure to an expansive number of news articles, with categories ranging from Media & Leisure to High Technology (see Figure 6-5).

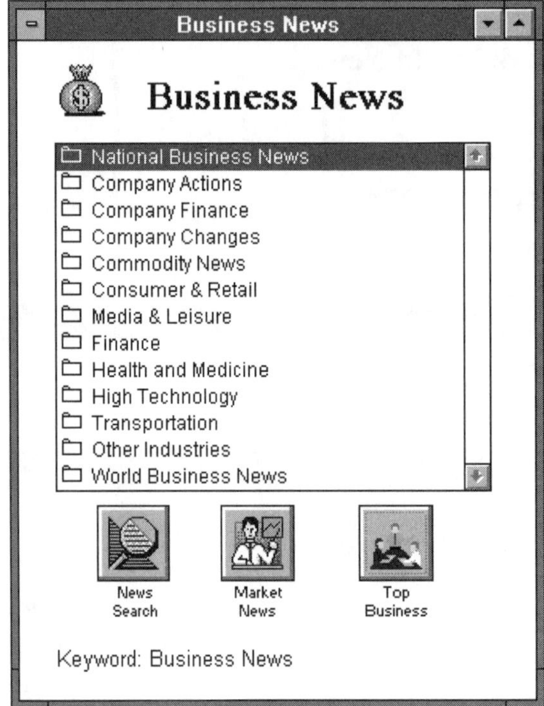

Figure 6-5: The Business News section offers 13 categories of news. Double-click any folder to browse that category.

Market News

Look again at Figure 6-5. Do you see the icon labeled Market News? This is the direct route to AOL's equivalent of the stock market charts of your daily newspaper (see Figure 6-6). All the information you expect in your newspaper is here, with one significant difference: AOL's stock market information is current and updated constantly during periods of stock market activity.

Top Business

If you look again at Figure 6-5 you'll see an additional icon on the bottom, "Top Business." Click this icon to reveal the business news "lead stories": the top stories—not of the day, but of the moment (Figure 6-7).

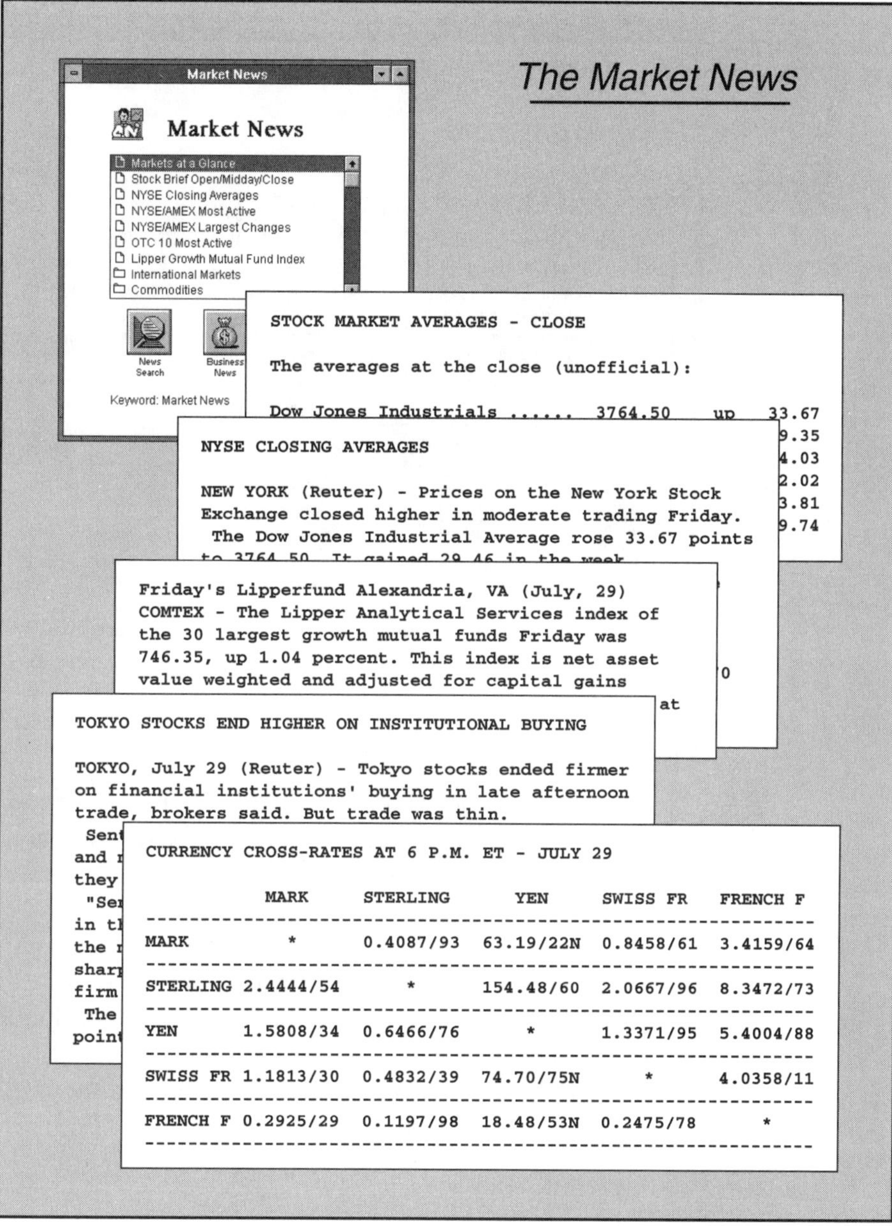

The Market News
Market News
Market News
Markets at a Glance
Stock Brief Open/Midday/Close
NYSE Closing Averages
NYSE/AMEX Most Active
NYSE/AMEX Largest Changes
OTC 10 Most Active
Lipper Growth Mutual Fund Index
International Markets
Commodities
News Search
Business News
Keyword: Market News
STOCK MARKET AVERAGES - CLOSE
The averages at the close (unofficial):
Dow Jones Industrials ...... 3764.50 up 33.67
NYSE CLOSING AVERAGES
NEW YORK (Reuter) - Prices on the New York Stock
Exchange closed higher in moderate trading Friday.
The Dow Jones Industrial Average rose 33.67 points
Friday's Lipperfund Alexandria, VA (July, 29)
COMTEX - The Lipper Analytical Services index of
the 30 largest growth mutual funds Friday was
746.35, up 1.04 percent. This index is net asset
value weighted and adjusted for capital gains
TOKYO STOCKS END HIGHER ON INSTITUTIONAL BUYING
TOKYO, July 29 (Reuter) - Tokyo stocks ended firmer
on financial institutions' buying in late afternoon
trade, brokers said. But trade was thin.
CURRENCY CROSS-RATES AT 6 P.M. ET - JULY 29
MARK STERLING YEN SWISS FR FRENCH F
MARK * 0.4087/93 63.19/22N 0.8458/61 3.4159/64
STERLING 2.4444/54 * 154.48/60 2.0667/96 8.3472/73
YEN 1.5808/34 0.6466/76 * 1.3371/95 5.4004/88
SWISS FR 1.1813/30 0.4832/39 74.70/75N * 4.0358/11
FRENCH F 0.2925/29 0.1197/98 18.48/53N 0.2475/78 *

Figure 6-6: America Online's Market News rarely trails the NYSE ticker by more than 20 minutes during trading. To get there in a hurry, use the keyword: MarketNews.

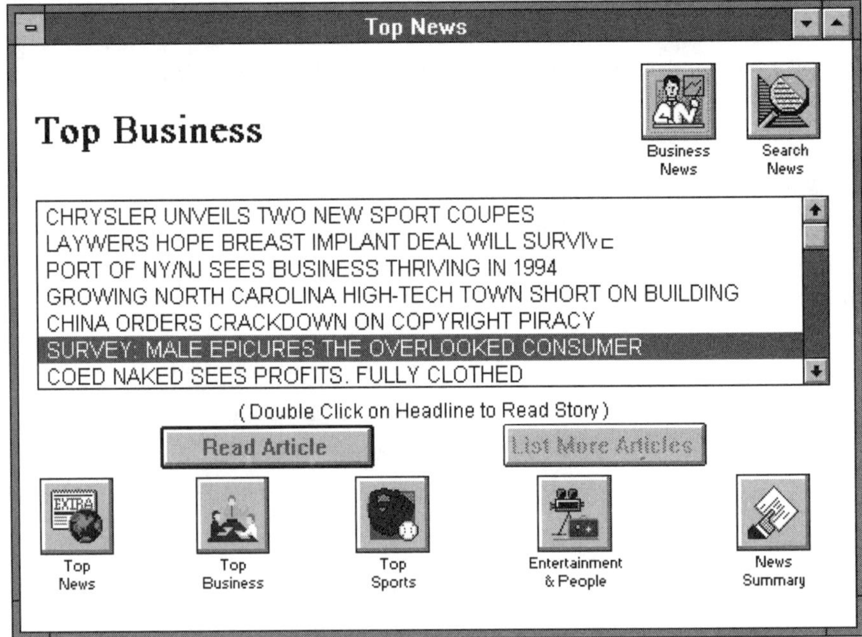

Figure 6-7: A select number of the day's key business news stories are featured in the Top Business section.

Entertainment

Can you recall an occasion when you purchased a product and were pleasantly surprised when you got more than you bargained for? If you're interested in news from the entertainment field, AOL might be just one of those events.

I say this because without fanfare, the Entertainment section of Today's News is primarily composed of articles from *Variety*, the preeminent industry magazine that profoundly influences people in the entertainment capitals of our nation.

It's posted each day on AOL. All you have to do is click the Entertainment button in the Today's News window (Figure 6-8).

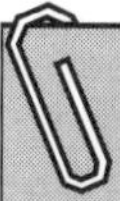

Male Epicureans

With a full-time medical student for a wife, I've become the chef and houseboy at home, a complete role reversal for both of us after 20 years of conjugal conventionalism. I was intrigued, then, when I saw the "Male Epicures the Overlooked Consumer" headline pictured in Figure 6-7. The story (quoted below) tells me I'm far from alone. I never thought of myself as an "overlooked consumer," but I'm willing to be patronized the next time I step into a cooking store.

> SURVEY: MALE EPICURES THE OVERLOOKED CONSUMER
>
> NEW YORK (Reuter) - Picture this — a kitchen, pots simmering on the stove. Someone is chopping ingredients for a gourmet meal. Expect this to be a woman?
>
> Wrong. Chances are very good that the chef, and the purchaser of the wine, the china and the espresso machine, is a man.
>
> A recent study shows men, either as part of families or alone, are in large numbers buying household goods and foods and consider themselves knowledgeable and interested....
>
> Although women are consistently targeted by advertisers and marketers as the primary household purchaser, men are shopping, cooking and giving parties, the statistics show.
>
> According Shifrin Research, a public opinion research firm, men who enjoy food and wine—epicures—make up 30 percent of the adult male population.
>
> And, according to the survey for Food and Wine magazine, men who like to cook at home and eat in restaurants appear to be as involved in buying food as women in general....

You see? It's about time people start taking us seriously. Now, anyone for macaroni and cheese?

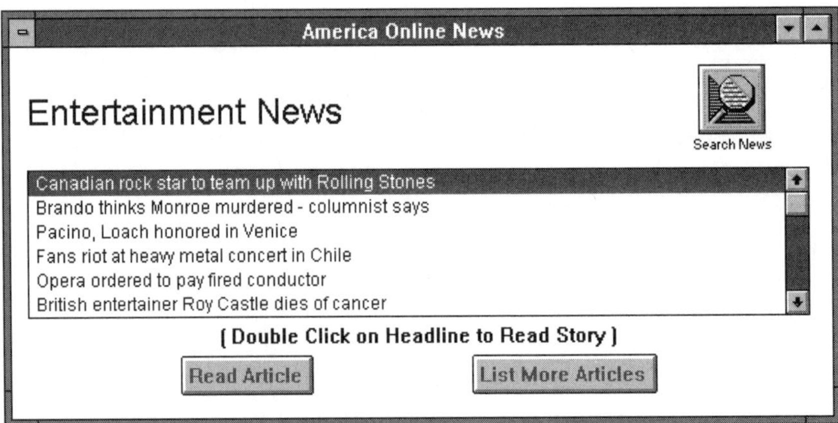

Figure 6-8: The Entertainment section of Today's News features news of the entertainment industry, most of which is drawn from *Variety* magazine.

This is one of AOL's best-kept secrets. *Variety* magazine is the entertainment industry's Bible, and now you know where to find it.

There's Much More

Don't confuse the Entertainment and Sports sections of the Today's News Department with the Entertainment and Sports Departments themselves. America Online offers much more than is described here for entertainment patrons and sports fans. This chapter discusses today's entertainment and sports *news*; the Entertainment and Sports *Departments* are discussed in Chapters 8 and 9.

Sports

The button marked Sports at the bottom of the Today's News window leads you to Sports News (keyword: SportsNews), pictured in Figure 6-9.

Most of the buttons that surround the window in Figure 6-9 change with the season, but two remain where you see them: Top Sports (a compilation of the lead sports stories of the hour) and Highlights. Clicking the Highlights icon takes you to the Sports Highlights section where, among other things, you'll find Sports Headlines.

Figure 6-9: Sports News offers not only the top stories, but routes to the sports discussion boards, sports headlines, and various topical sports news areas.

I mention Sports Headlines because I want to share a strategy with you. There's a lot of sports news on AOL. You probably won't have the time to read every story. If you're like me, you have a few stories you're following and you want to know about them first.

For this you should use News Search. No matter where you are, use the keyword: NewsSearch, and search for the subjects—sports or otherwise—that interest you.

But that's a somewhat monochromatic strategy. Following one or two sports stories to the exclusion of others ignores the abundance of sports events that transpire every day. Many of these might interest you as well.

Here's my strategy: click the Highlights icon pictured in Figure 6-9, then examine the Sports Headlines (Figure 6-10). The headlines are extensive and ideal for browsing. Once you find a headline that intrigues you, use News Search to find (and read) the story behind the headline.

Figure 6-10: In conjunction with America Online's News Search facility, Sports Headlines offers an effective method for pursuing the sports news of your choice.

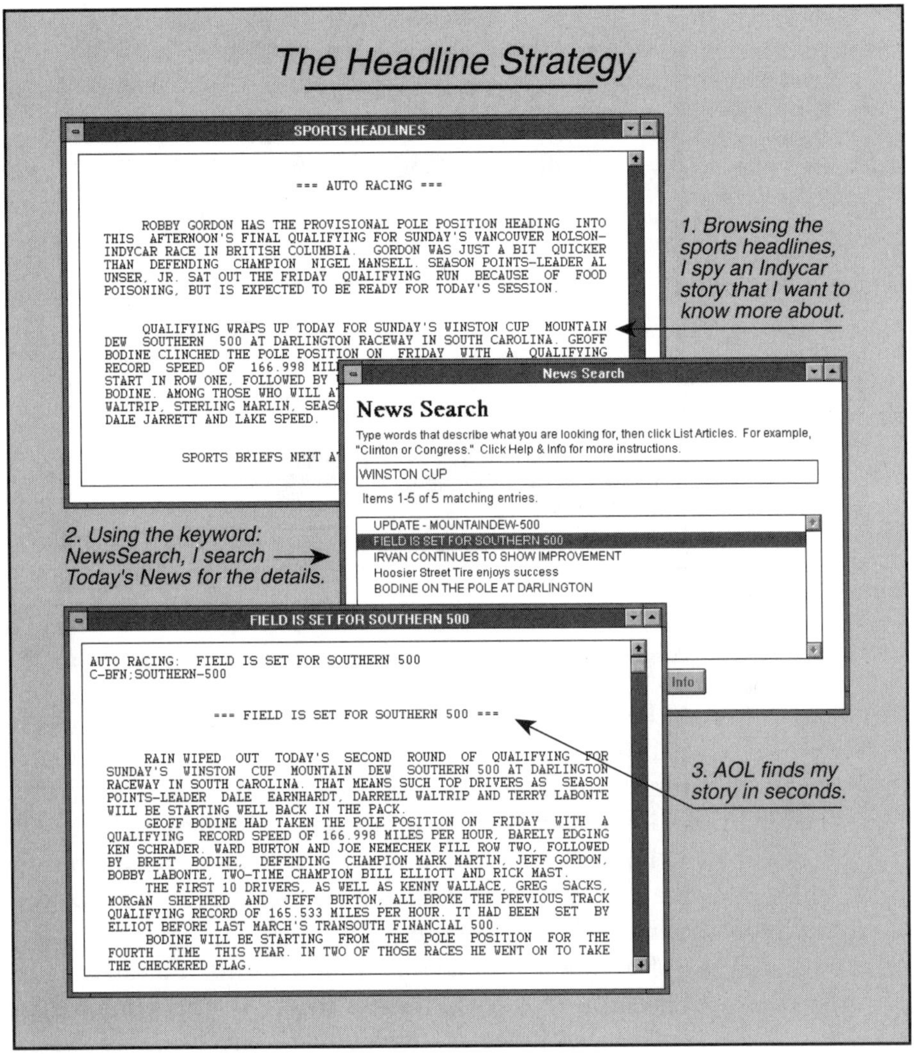

The Headline Strategy

SPORTS HEADLINES

=== AUTO RACING ===

ROBBY GORDON HAS THE PROVISIONAL POLE POSITION HEADING INTO THIS AFTERNOON'S FINAL QUALIFYING FOR SUNDAY'S VANCOUVER MOLSON-INDYCAR RACE IN BRITISH COLUMBIA. GORDON WAS JUST A BIT QUICKER THAN DEFENDING CHAMPION NIGEL MANSELL. SEASON POINTS-LEADER AL UNSER, JR. SAT OUT THE FRIDAY QUALIFYING RUN BECAUSE OF FOOD POISONING, BUT IS EXPECTED TO BE READY FOR TODAY'S SESSION.

QUALIFYING WRAPS UP TODAY FOR SUNDAY'S WINSTON CUP MOUNTAIN DEW SOUTHERN 500 AT DARLINGTON RACEWAY IN SOUTH CAROLINA. GEOFF BODINE CLINCHED THE POLE POSITION ON FRIDAY WITH A QUALIFYING RECORD SPEED OF 166.998 MIL
START IN ROW ONE, FOLLOWED BY
BODINE. AMONG THOSE WHO WILL A
WALTRIP, STERLING MARLIN, SEAS
DALE JARRETT AND LAKE SPEED.

SPORTS BRIEFS NEXT A

1. Browsing the sports headlines, I spy an Indycar story that I want to know more about.

News Search

News Search

Type words that describe what you are looking for, then click List Articles. For example, "Clinton or Congress." Click Help & Info for more instructions.

WINSTON CUP

Items 1-5 of 5 matching entries.

UPDATE - MOUNTAINDEW-500
FIELD IS SET FOR SOUTHERN 500
IRVAN CONTINUES TO SHOW IMPROVEMENT
Hoosier Street Tire enjoys success
BODINE ON THE POLE AT DARLINGTON

Info

2. Using the keyword: NewsSearch, I search Today's News for the details.

FIELD IS SET FOR SOUTHERN 500

AUTO RACING: FIELD IS SET FOR SOUTHERN 500
C-BFN;SOUTHERN-500

=== FIELD IS SET FOR SOUTHERN 500 ===

RAIN WIPED OUT TODAY'S SECOND ROUND OF QUALIFYING FOR SUNDAY'S WINSTON CUP MOUNTAIN DEW SOUTHERN 500 AT DARLINGTON RACEWAY IN SOUTH CAROLINA. THAT MEANS SUCH TOP DRIVERS AS SEASON POINTS-LEADER DALE EARNHARDT, DARRELL WALTRIP AND TERRY LABONTE WILL BE STARTING WELL BACK IN THE PACK.

GEOFF BODINE HAD TAKEN THE POLE POSITION ON FRIDAY WITH A QUALIFYING RECORD SPEED OF 166.998 MILES PER HOUR, BARELY EDGING KEN SCHRADER. WARD BURTON AND JOE NEMECHEK FILL ROW TWO, FOLLOWED BY BRETT BODINE, DEFENDING CHAMPION MARK MARTIN, JEFF GORDON, BOBBY LABONTE, TWO-TIME CHAMPION BILL ELLIOTT AND RICK MAST.

THE FIRST 10 DRIVERS, AS WELL AS KENNY WALLACE, GREG SACKS, MORGAN SHEPHERD AND JEFF BURTON, ALL BROKE THE PREVIOUS TRACK QUALIFYING RECORD OF 165.533 MILES PER HOUR. IT HAD BEEN SET BY ELLIOT BEFORE LAST MARCH'S TRANSOUTH FINANCIAL 500.

BODINE WILL BE STARTING FROM THE POLE POSITION FOR THE FOURTH TIME THIS YEAR. IN TWO OF THOSE RACES HE WENT ON TO TAKE THE CHECKERED FLAG.

3. AOL finds my story in seconds.

Weather

Naturally, AOL is resplendent with weather information. This is where the online medium really excels. America Online's weather is not only always up to the minute, it's also graphic and colorful.

The primary Weather window (see Figure 6-11) not only offers access to the day's weather news (check here before traveling or when the weather is particularly interesting), forecasts (updated continuously and organized by state), and boards (lots of experts hang out here: post questions freely), it also offers a route to the color weather maps, and that's where the fun begins.

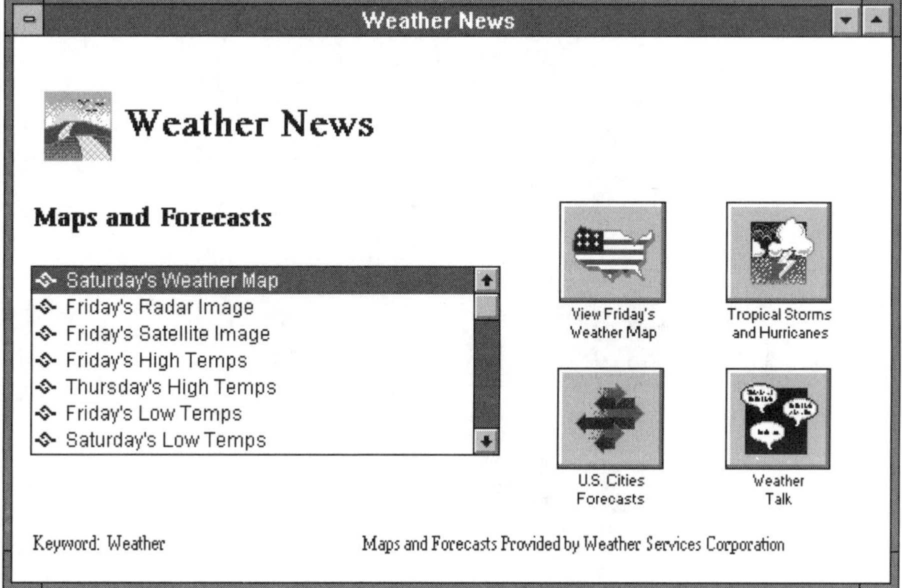

Figure 6-11: America Online's primary Weather window offers a wealth of current weather information, including maps.

The maps are provided by Weather Services Corporation, which provides forecasting and consultation services for *USA Today*, among others. Those colorful weather maps on the back page of *USA Today* are derived from the same data that's available on AOL when you use the keyword: Weather.

The precipitation, jet stream and tropical outlook maps are released between 10 A.M. and 11 A.M. (Eastern time) each day; the temperature bands for the next day will be available between 6 P.M. and 7 P.M. (see Figure 6-12).

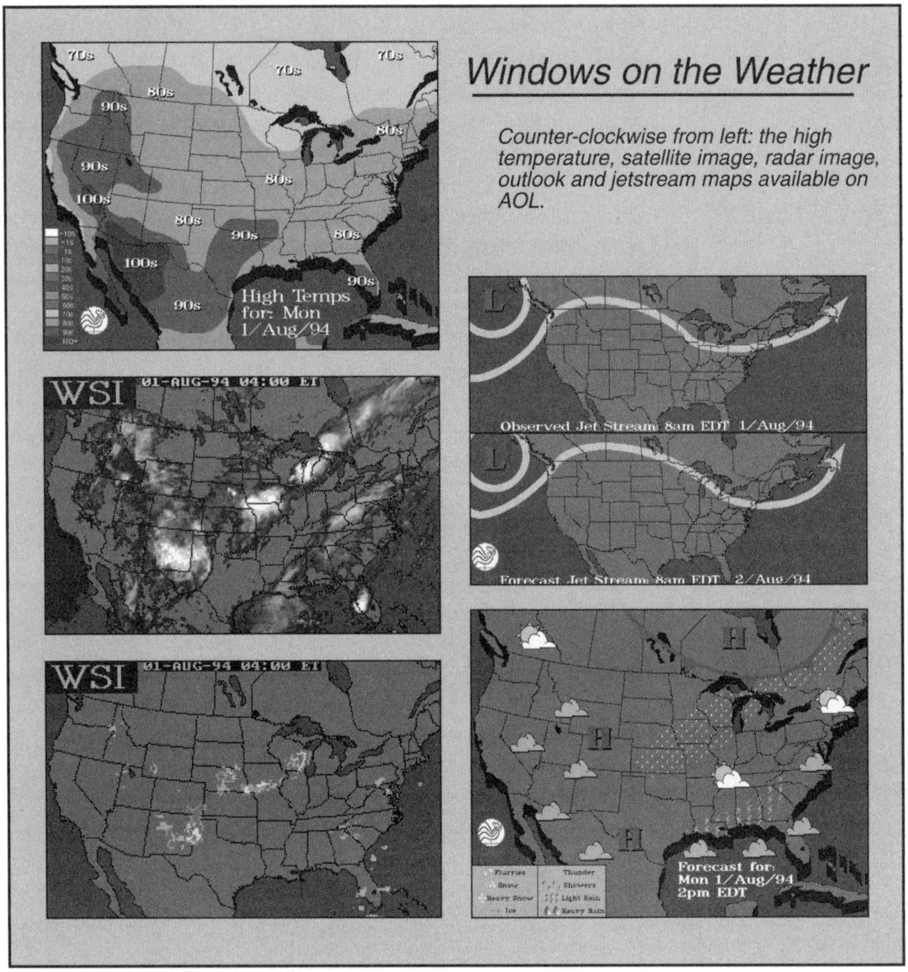

Figure 6-12: You'll have to imagine it here, but each of these maps displays in 16 colors and downloads in less than a minute. To get to them quickly, use the keyword: WeatherMaps.

No special software is required for viewing these maps: simply double-click any listing, read the description if you wish, then click the Download Now button. If you're using Version 1.5 (or later) of the AOL software, the maps will be displayed onscreen as they're downloaded. None of them takes more than a minute to download at 9600 baud; they'll display satisfactorily even if you don't have a color monitor (or printer); and the files are always available for viewing after you've downloaded them (even after you sign off) by choosing Open from the File menu.

For a detailed description of the downloading process, read Chapter 5, "Computing," and review Figures 5-9 and 5-13.

Moving On

The online medium is a newcomer to the dissemination of the daily news. We've developed the habit of seeking the news in our papers or broadcast media.

The online medium, however, boasts immediacy, comprehensiveness and independence. America Online's news is updated constantly, it never needs to cater to time or space constraints, and there are no advertisers to oblige. More people are discovering this inherent advantage every day. If you follow the news, try this medium for a month and compare.

The list of those who embrace the online medium for the dissemination of news includes the broadcast and print media themselves—many of which appear on AOL. There are so many, in fact, that they now have their own department, the Newsstand, where publications as diverse as *SPIN, HOME, TIME* and even the Gray Lady herself—*The New York Times*—have found a home. It's a diverse and stimulating place, and we begin its exploration on the next page. . . .

CHAPTER 7

The Newsstand

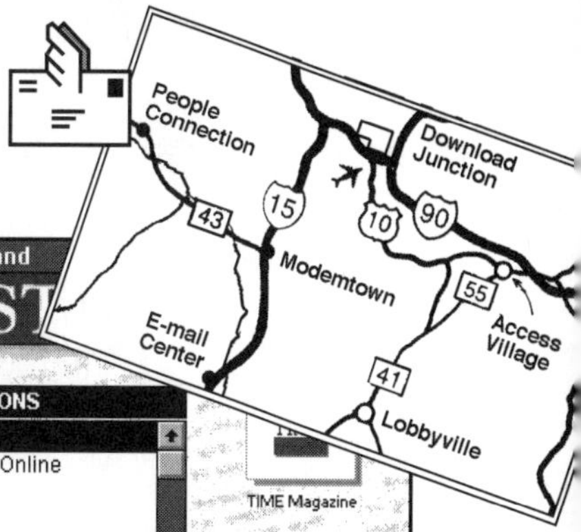

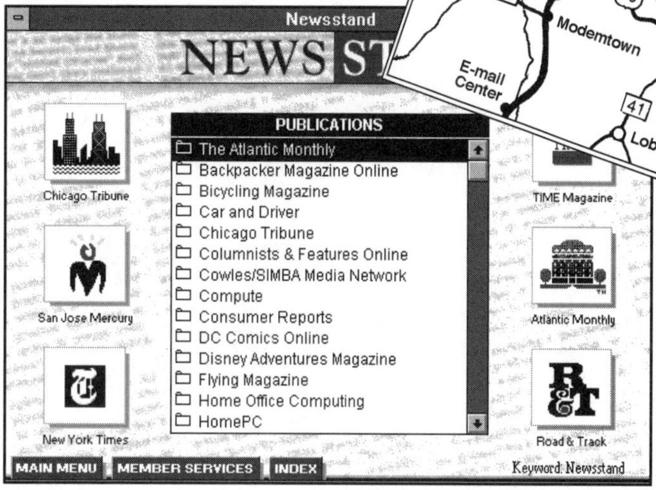

I alluded to the online medium's superiority for the dissemination of journalistic material in the previous chapter. Immediacy was the primary benefit cited there, but the online medium has another significant journalistic benefit: capacity.

Most magazine readers value the printed medium, but if you're like me, you've given up on filing past issues. After a few months, most of my magazines go into the trash. Naturally I regret trashing them soon thereafter, for it's then that I decide to review something I saw in that issue that just contributed to the landfill over the hill.

I have good news, periodical patrons: you can ignore those magazines, because AOL now has the Newsstand, where you can read current issues, save articles, download files and even talk to the editors online. Perhaps best of all, most of AOL's online publications provide database access to past issues. Chances are, if you search for a subject of interest, it's there. That's what I mean by the benefit of capacity.

PC World Online

There's so much great stuff in the Newsstand, it's hard to know where to begin. One thing I know we all have in common is our PCs, thus PC World Online (see Figure 7-1) is probably a place to begin.

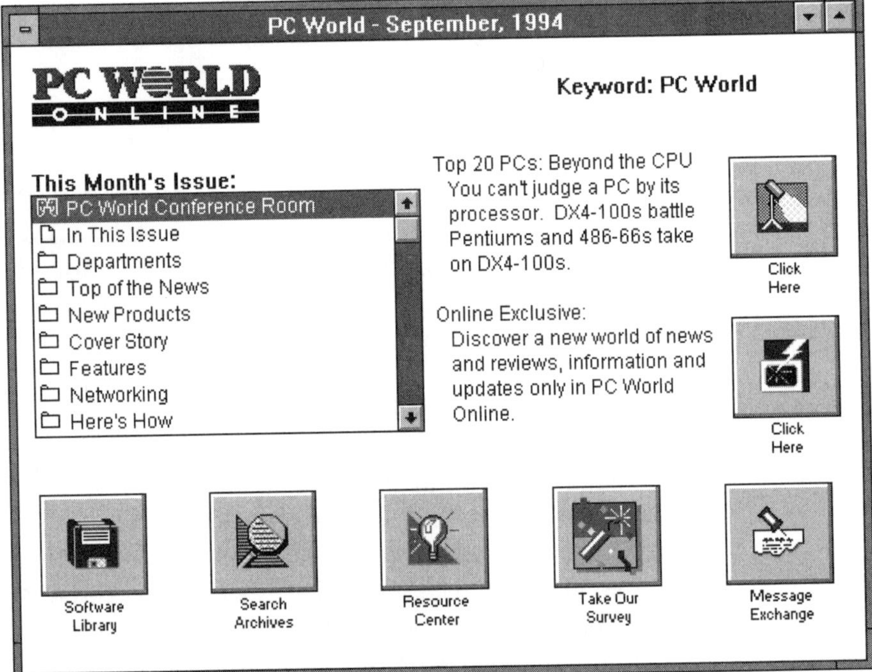

Figure 7-1: Everything but the ads: nearly all the current issue of *PC World* is online, plus past issues and software libraries. Use the keyword: PCWorld to get here.

I visit *PC World* once a month without fail, and every time I contemplate a purchase—hardware or software—I consult the reviews. A few months ago I researched the availability of a triple-speed CD-ROM drive. A brief search of past issues produced an announcement of a price drop on just the device I needed (Figure 7-2).

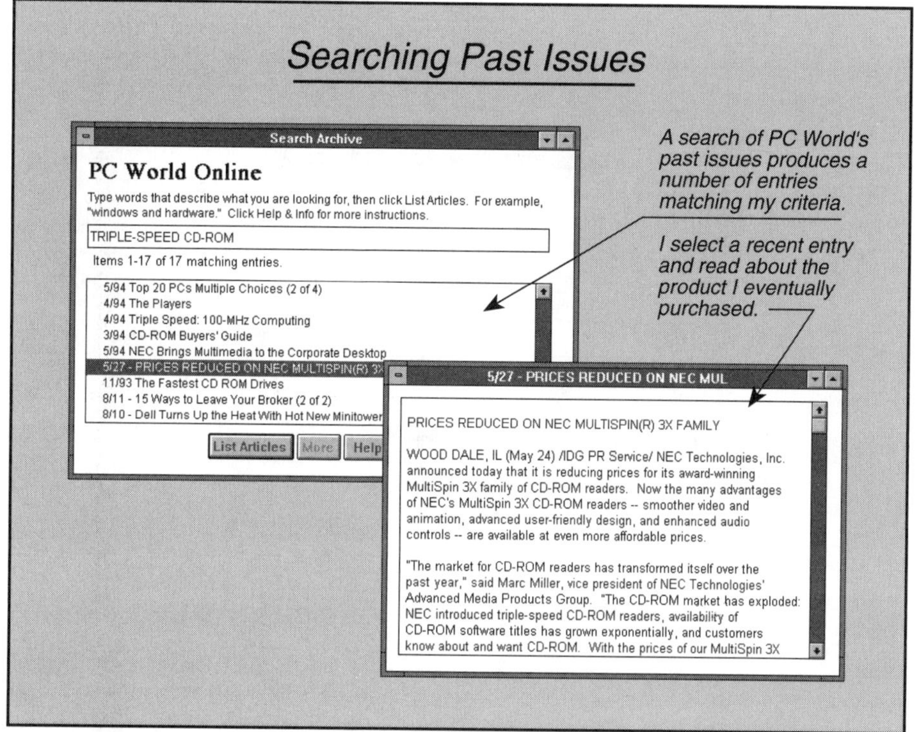

Figure 7-2: Searching past issues of *PC World*, America Online found an article describing the CD-ROM drive I eventually purchased.

While the ability to search past issues is a primary feature of PC World Online, hundreds of news stories, reviews and files are also available—all searchable, and all in a form that you can use for inclusion in documents of your own. In addition, a special section called Message Exchange features message boards that put you in touch with *PC World's* editorial staff, and a library of files offers indices to past issues, macros and programs (Figure 7-3).

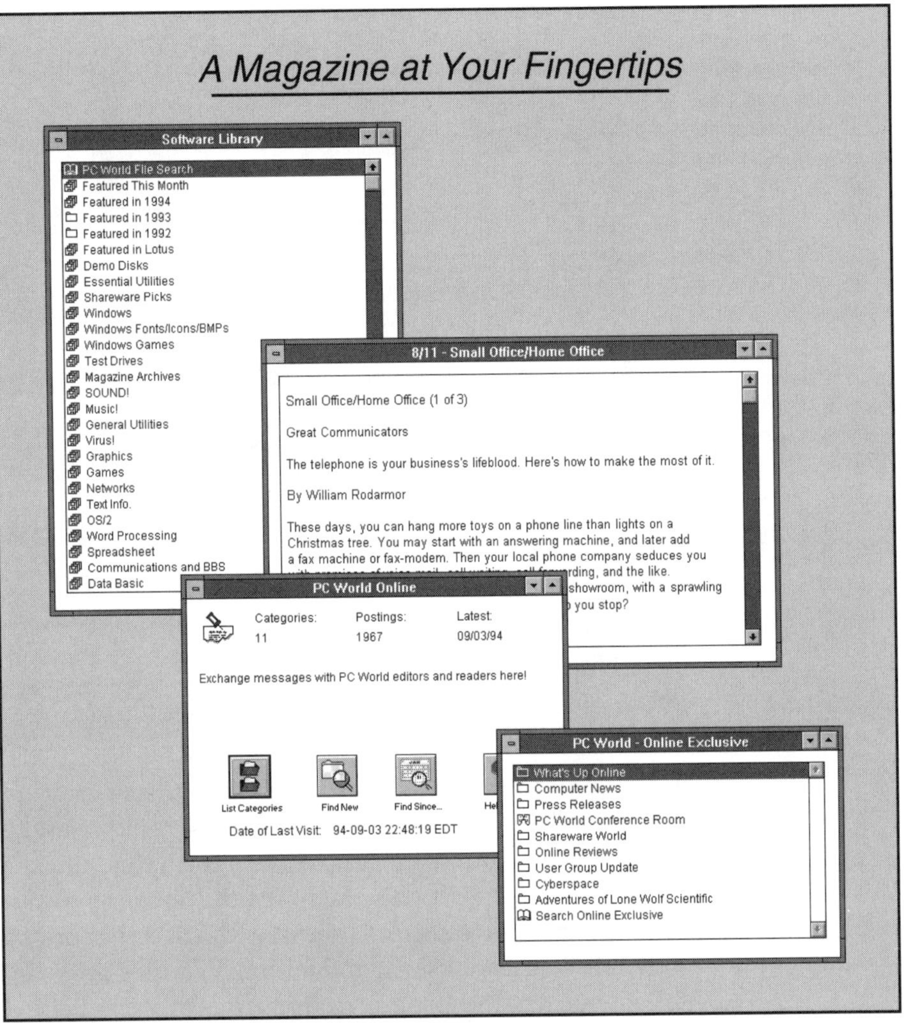

Figure 7-3: A software library, feature stories, a question-and-answer message board and an exclusive area full of online information round out PC World Online.

A Magazine at Your Fingertips

Software Library

PC World File Search
Featured This Month
Featured in 1994
Featured in 1993
Featured in 1992
Featured in Lotus
Demo Disks
Essential Utilities
Shareware Picks
Windows
Windows Fonts/Icons/BMPs
Windows Games
Test Drives
Magazine Archives
SOUND!
Music!
General Utilities
Virus!
Graphics
Games
Networks
Text Info.
OS/2
Word Processing
Spreadsheet
Communications and BBS
Data Basic

8/11 - Small Office/Home Office

Small Office/Home Office (1 of 3)

Great Communicators

The telephone is your business's lifeblood. Here's how to make the most of it.

By William Rodarmor

These days, you can hang more toys on a phone line than lights on a Christmas tree. You may start with an answering machine, and later add a fax machine or fax-modem. Then your local phone company seduces you

PC World Online

Categories: 11 Postings: 1967 Latest: 09/03/94

Exchange messages with PC World editors and readers here!

List Categories Find New Find Since...

Date of Last Visit: 94-09-03 22:48:19 EDT

PC World - Online Exclusive

What's Up Online
Computer News
Press Releases
PC World Conference Room
Shareware World
Online Reviews
User Group Update
Cyberspace
Adventures of Lone Wolf Scientific
Search Online Exclusive

Windows Magazine Online

I subscribe to both *Windows* and *PC World* magazines. For a couple of years I intended to allow one of the subscriptions to lapse, but I found that I depended on both of them equally and simply couldn't let go of either one.

Imagine my delight, then, when *Windows* magazine appeared online several months back. This magazine's presence is substantial: everything from the printed version is included online, and an extensive library of files for Windows users complements the textual material, including games, drivers, utilities, sounds and music.

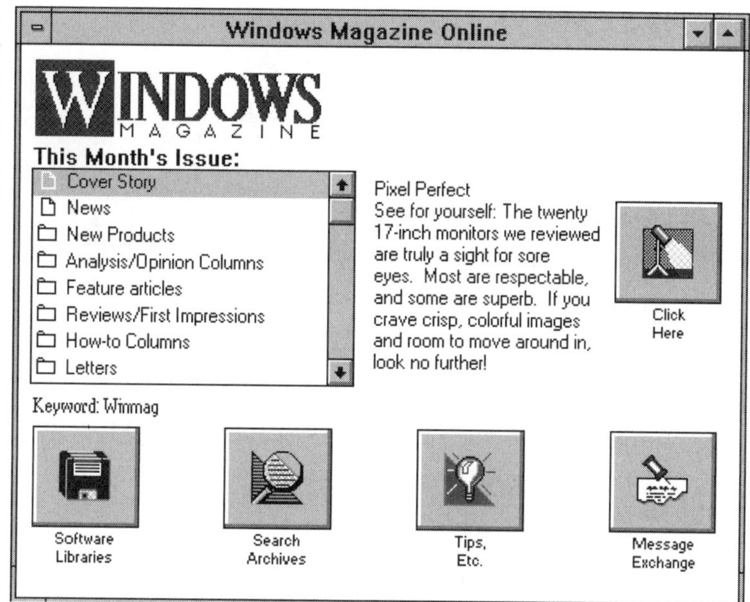

Figure 7-4: *Windows* magazine offers a relevant complement of information and resources for the Windows user.

Enumerating the features offered by this forum would be redundant: the *Windows* and *PC World* magazine forums are similar in design and presentation. Like the magazines themselves, however, the forums differ in content. Duplication is minimal. Each complements the other. Just as I elected to continue my subscriptions to both magazines, so it is with the forums: you gotta have both.

The *Windows* magazine forum offers a unique feature of significant note: a library of programs written by the staff of the magazine. There are scores of programs here, including the industry-standard *WinTune,* a performance-measuring utility with exhaustive reporting features (see Figure 7-5).

Figure 7-5 reveals a real-world example of the value of online support for the computer user. My new machine was acting erratically—one of those nagging problems that left no signature and refused exact identification. I used WinTune to isolate the problem, and with the results traveled to the Gateway forum (keyword: Moo) to see if anyone there had a solution.

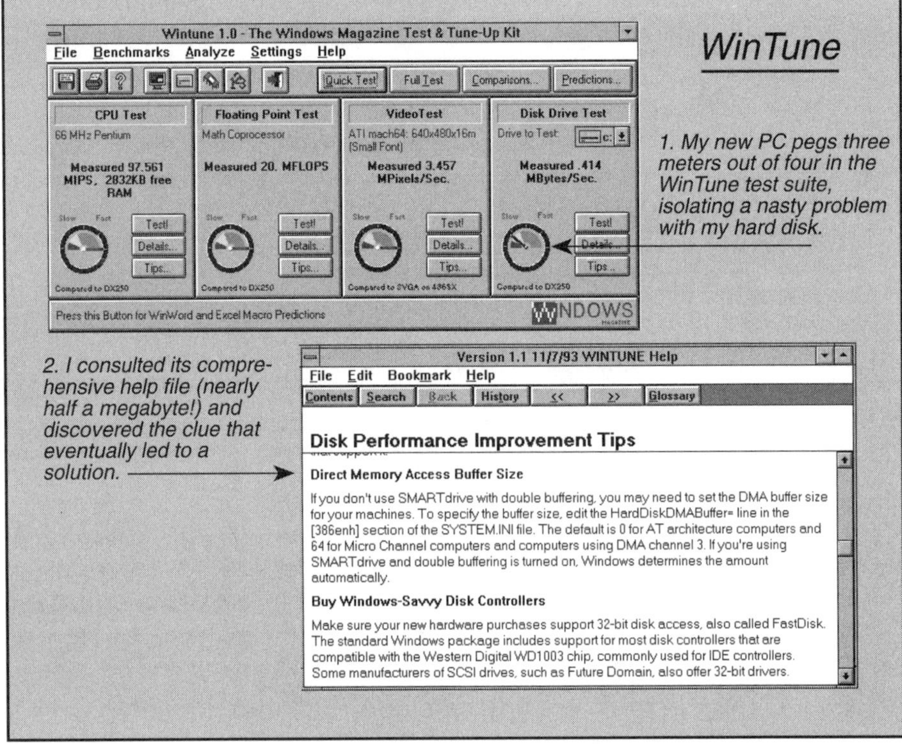

Figure 7-5: WinTune measured the performance of my new PC and found a nasty problem with my hard disk. A review of the program's exhaustive help file offered some solutions.

Sure enough, many others had experienced the same problem. The solution turned out to be an improved driver for my Western Digital hard drive, something which Gateway conveniently posted on AOL. I downloaded the driver, installed it, and improved my hard disk's performance *by a factor of 20* in just a few minutes. This I did at night on a holiday weekend, when no other resources were available (or necessary, as it turned out). I have Windows Magazine Online (and Gateway) to thank for my redemption.

TIME Online

Now here's a bold experiment: *TIME* magazine not only posts its latest issue before it reaches many (non-virtual) newsstands, it also posts stories online from its international editions—stories that aren't available in the domestic version of the magazine. The people at *TIME* even post stories that fail to make either edition due to space or time constraints. TIME Online (see Figure 7-6) is the only place you'll find these stories.

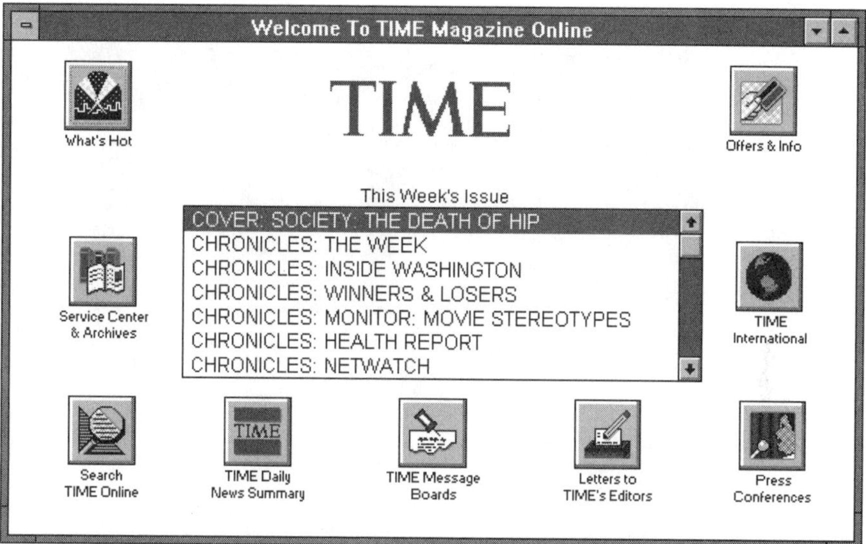

Figure 7-6: TIME Online is an experiment in which the world's oldest and largest news magazine plugs into the world's newest and fastest-growing medium.

The text of the current issue appears online each Sunday by 4 P.M. (Eastern time). The text of the stories that appear in *TIME*'s international editions appear each Wednesday.

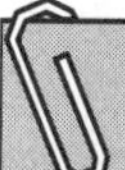

TIME versus CLOCK

Veteran AOL members have no doubt noted one significant change in the service. The keyword: Time no longer produces the online clock. Lots of people depend on that clock to tell them how long they've been online, but when *TIME* came online, the keyword was reassigned to the magazine. If you want the online clock, use the new keyword: Clock or simply press the clock button on the Flashbar.

There's more. Every day, TIME Online posts a feature, at least once a day, called TIME Daily News Summary, where TIME's view of the day's breaking news is offered, along with pointers to message board topics and relevant archived material. Some pictures from the magazine are available in the Daily News Summary archives, plus extra material that's not printed. You'll find others are in the Other Pictures Library in the Service Center & Archives. You'll find the current cover picture in the TIME Covers Library in the Service Center, too.

Figure 7-7: *TIME* magazine's covers are available each week in GIF and JPEG formats. Your America Online software will open them for viewing.

You can search past issues, of course, and send letters to the editors. WHAT'S HOT lists the best of TIME Online's articles and messages, and TIME Press Conferences are real-time online interviews with newsmakers, authors, moviemakers and *TIME* staffers.

This is online journalism at its best. It represents an optimistic alliance between print and electronic media, and it's only available on AOL via the keyword: TIME.

@times

Don't confuse *TIME* magazine with *The New York Times. The Times* is a newspaper; *TIME* is a magazine. About the only thing they share in common is America Online.

One of the great strengths of *The Times* is its cultural coverage and criticism. For decades, readers have relied on *The Times* critics for guidance in choosing everything from books to videos. Now, with @times, thousands of Times reviews—movies, videos, books—are available in one place (see Figure 7-8).

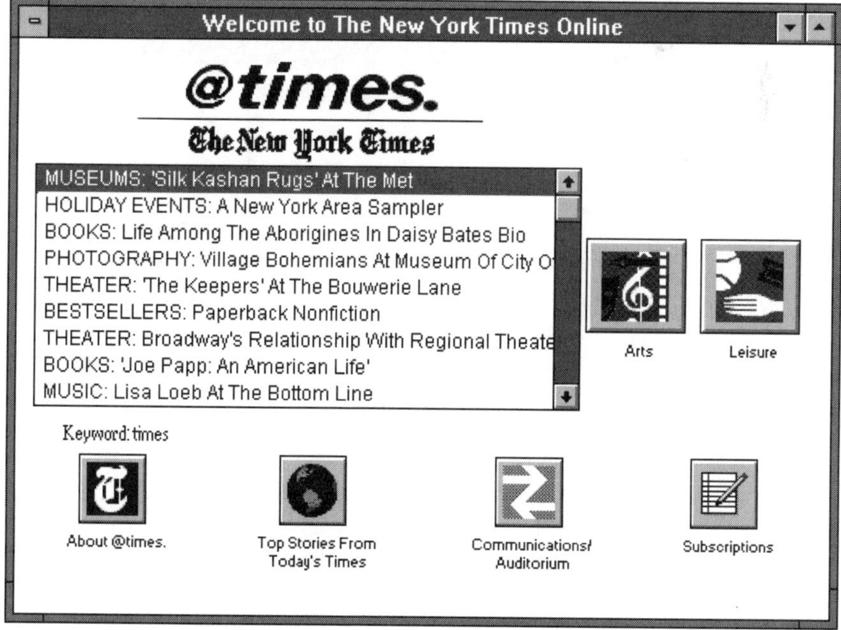

Figure 7-8: @times offers, among other things, the *crème de la crème* of *The New York Times:* its entertainment and arts features. To get there in a hurry, use the keyword: @times.

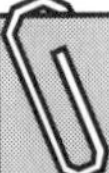

Data on Demand

Screens such as that pictured in Figure 7-8 are abundant with graphics and interface components. Think of it: in the Newsstand alone, there are scores of publications, each with a screen as complex at that offered by @times.

If all these visual effects were stored on the host computer and fed downline every time you visited a section of the service, AOL would seem as slow as the building of the pyramids. On the other hand, if all of these components were stored on your disk, your AOL directory would be as vast as the inside of Pharaoh's tomb.

There's a compromise, and it's called *Data on Demand* (or *DOD*, among AOL's *cognoscenti*).

Here's the trick: only a few of AOL's special graphics are stored in your AOL software when you first install it. When you initially visit an area such as @times or OMNI Magazine Online, the additional components for that area are downloaded—automatically—to your disk. The download occurs only once—during the first visit to an area—and it's accompanied by a notification similar to that pictured in Figure 7-9.

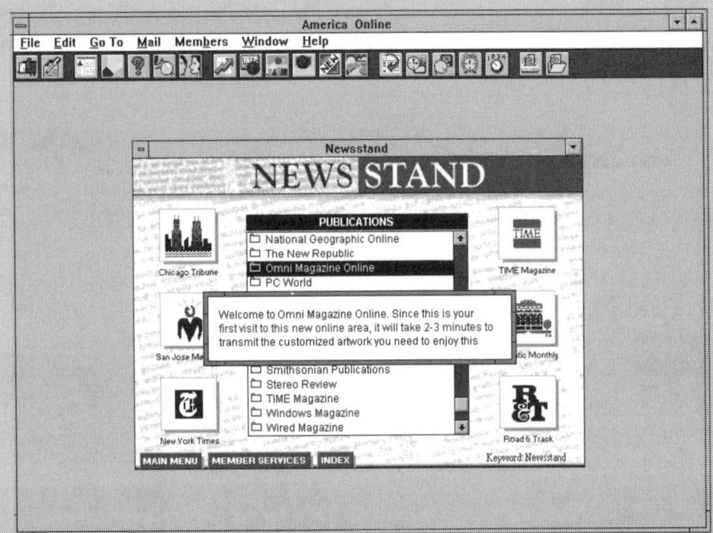

Figure 7-9: A DOD download occurs the first time you visit an area such as OMNI Magazine Online.

The theory is that each of us visits an abridged number of areas on the service—no one visits every one—so each of us accumulates a set of graphics customized to our personal interests. It's an effective solution to a somewhat unappeasable problem.

Look for *The New York Times Best Seller List* here, along with *The Times* weekday book, video, and movie reviews. @times also features the top international and domestic news, business and sports stories. These stories appear before they're printed in the paper: articles from the next day's newspaper begin appearing after 11 P.M. Sunday to Friday nights, and after 9 P.M. on Saturdays.

Chicago Online

When I first visited AOL's headquarters, the staff was particularly optimistic about a newly launched service called *Chicago Online.* At that time, Chicago Online represented two significant strategies that made the inauguration of the Newsstand auspicious, and which today offer a glimpse into the future of online journalism.

The first strategy is that of a stand-alone, municipal communications service. Chicago Online is a parochial service, optimized for the people of Chicago, by the people of Chicago. It has its own message boards, chat rooms, news, sports and weather (plenty of the latter, actually). In a way, Chicago Online is like a local newspaper. The nation has *USA Today* and *The Wall Street Journal*, and Chicago has the *Chicago Tribune.* The nation has AOL and Chicago has Chicago Online. Neither precludes the need for the other. Nearly every community in the country has its own newspaper; we might someday all have our own little online areas as well. After all, local communications channels are as much a part of the community as national ones. America Online knows that, and that's why they're moving forward with Chicago Online (see Figure 7-10). (For additional evidence of the potential of this alliance, visit the Mercury Center, an online publication of the *San Jose Mercury.* Use the keyword: Mercury to get there.)

The second strategy is that of the *strategic alliance.* Chicago Online is the product of an alliance between the *Chicago Tribune* and AOL. The *Tribune* gains a communications channel that's significantly more bilateral (and less costly) than a daily newspaper, and AOL gets a test bed for another avenue in the electronic community. Perhaps best of all, we all get to observe the formative moments of a new communications medium. Ecologically speaking, the "electronic newspaper" (or something like it) will soon be a necessity, and this alliance represents the exploration of that potential by two of the most progressive representatives of the electronics and newspaper industries. There's lots of hope here, for all of us.

Figure 7-10: Chicago Online offers a potential glimpse of future telecommunications and a banquet of sustenance for the online appetite as well.

But enough existentialism. The *Chicago Tribune* is no lightweight when it comes to information, after all. There's a wealth of practical information for us outlanders. Check out Gene Siskel's *Flick Picks* (and Dave Kehr, Roy Leonard, and Sherman Kaplan's reviews), Ed Curran's *Technogadgets* and the *Chicago Tribune Cookbook* Online. Chicago Online isn't a half-hearted experiment in alternative media, it's a mature, expansive and resourceful communications medium. Give it a half-hour of your time. It will reward you eloquently.

Moving On

There are scores of publications in the Newsstand. Many cater to specific interests; others serve more general needs. Be sure to check out *Bicycling Magazine, New Republic, OMNI Smithsonian, WIRED* (mentioned in Chapter 14, "The Internet Connection"), *Popular Photography, Saturday Review, Worth,* and any others that appeal to you. This place is a quarry of priceless literary nuggets, and you pay nothing extra for access to it.

For many, literature is a staple of life. Sports, then, is no doubt its condiment. Shall we sprinkle a bit of it on AOL? Turn the page. . .

CHAPTER 8

Sports

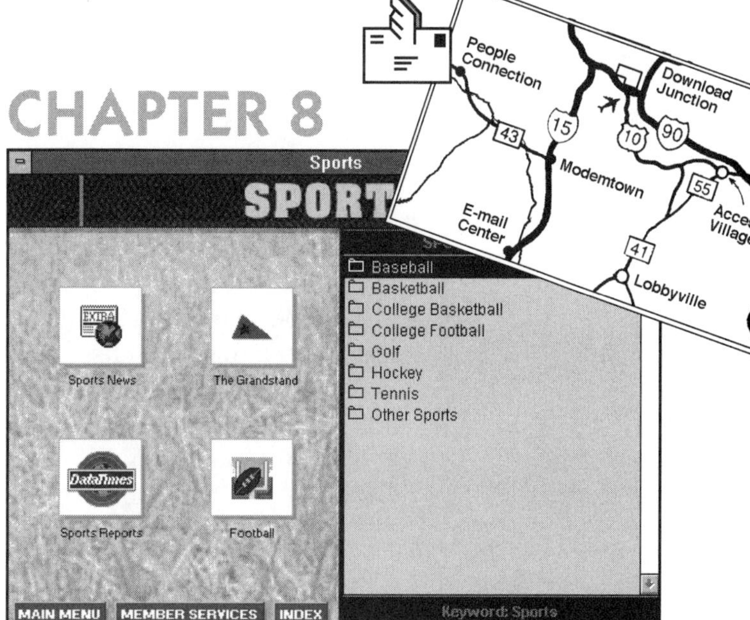

A friend of mine brought a smile to my face when she related a story about her boyfriend. In something of a reversal of stereotypes, *she* is the computer fanatic of the two; until recently, he had no interest whatever in the subject.

He does, however, have a keen interest in sports. She discovered the Sports Department on the first day she signed on to AOL. Grabbing him by the hair (I'm taking some creative license here, but I kind of like the reverse Cro-Magnon image), she sat him down in front of the screen and made him explore the department with her. In minutes he was using the mouse, typing messages and downloading files. He had never used a computer before, and now she can't get him away from it.

Ah, but now who will slay the giant mastodon and protect the cave from the wily saber-toothed tiger?

The News

I discussed Sports News in Chapter 6, "Today's News," so I won't spend much time on the subject here. Note, however, that the Sports News icon in the upper left corner of the Sports Department's main window (see Figure 8-1) leads to the same categories of sports news

---

The Sports Department offers sports news, sports message boards, sports files and Fantasy League games. To get there, click the Sports option on AOL's Main Menu, or use the keyword: Sports.

that appear in the scroll list in the main window. In other words, if you're here to browse the news, save yourself a mouse click or two and browse the stories from the main Sports window rather than from the icon.

On the other hand, the Sports News icon does lead to the news-searching mechanism discussed in Chapter 6. If you're seeking information on a specific subject and you're not in the mood for browsing, use this method of searching AOL's database of current sports articles. Click the Highlights icon.

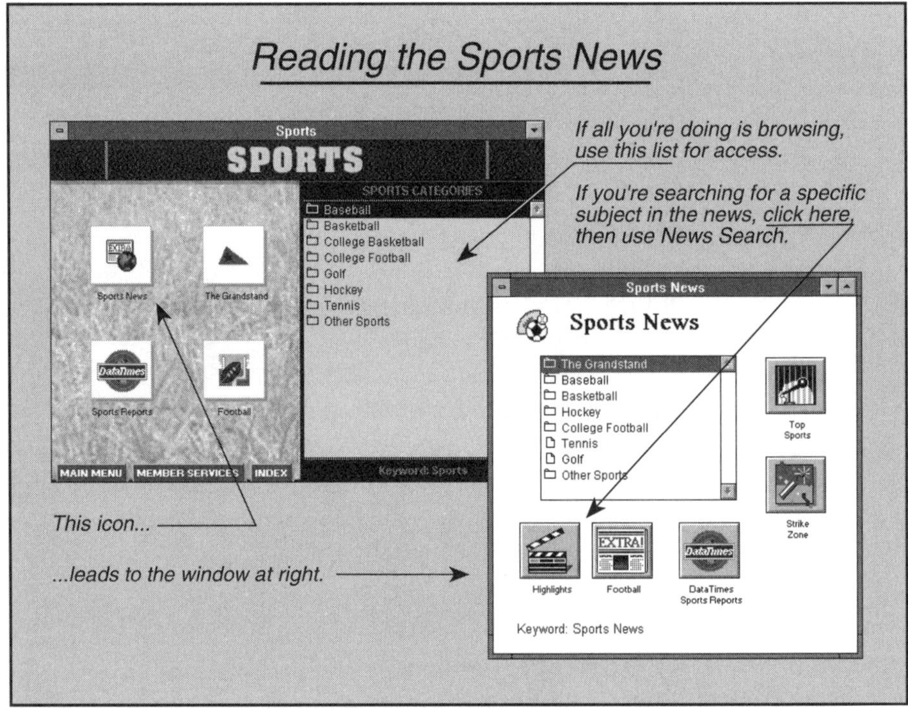

Figure 8-1: The main Sports Department window and the Sports News window duplicate content.

The Grandstand

If you enjoy sports, you'll love the Grandstand (use the keyword: Grandstand; it's the most effective way of getting there). America Online's homage to the sports enthusiast is current, relevant and vast (Figure 8-2). In the interest of sports widows everywhere, however, I suggest moderation. The walls of prehistoric caves the world over are riddled with pictographs of smashed keyboards and fractured computer screens. It's not a pretty sight.

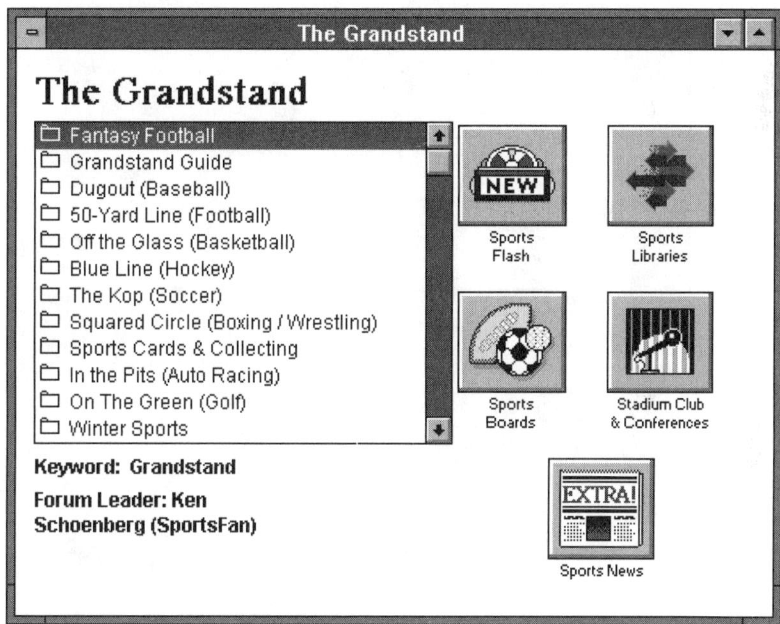

Figure 8-2: The Grandstand offers something for every sports enthusiast.

While investigating the Grandstand the other day, I downloaded a Microsoft Excel spreadsheet file that offered plenty of features for World Cup soccer fans (part of which is pictured in Figure 8-3). I also discovered an online club dedicated entirely to baseball cards, providing news, price polls and conferences for collectors throughout the nation.

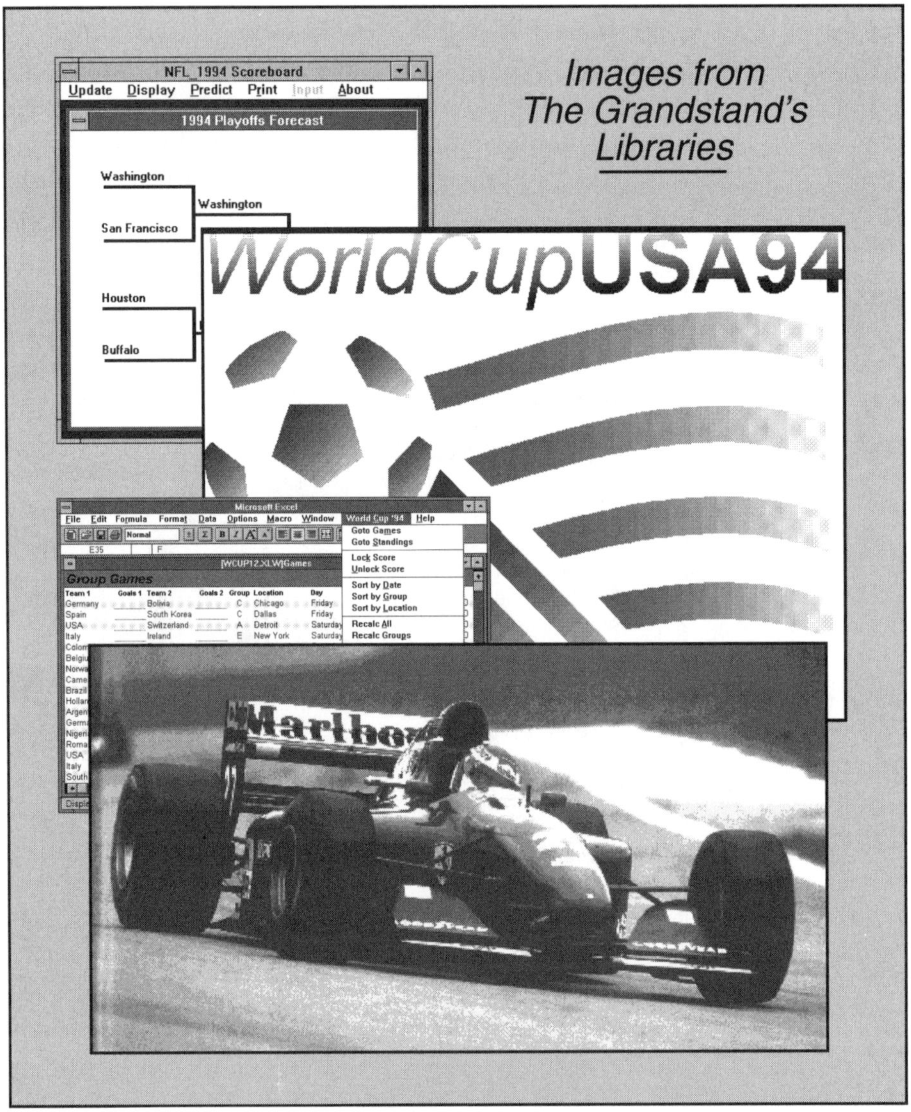

Figure 8-3: A quick browse through the Grandstand turns up a picture of a Ferrari 412 T1 uploaded by Nigel Mans, a rendition of the NHL World Cup logo created by RobyBaggio, a World Cup tracking spreadsheet for Microsoft Excel by Robert Piller, and a little application called NFL by Tom Kerr that tracks football games and makes predictions.

Sports fans like to talk about their interests with other sports fans. Sports talk is especially rewarding when it's carried on with people who aren't directly within your sphere of acquaintance, especially with people who live all over the country. If this sounds appealing, consider visiting the message boards. Just click on the Sports Boards icon on the right side of The Grandstand window or open the folder of the sport that interests you (Figure 8-4).

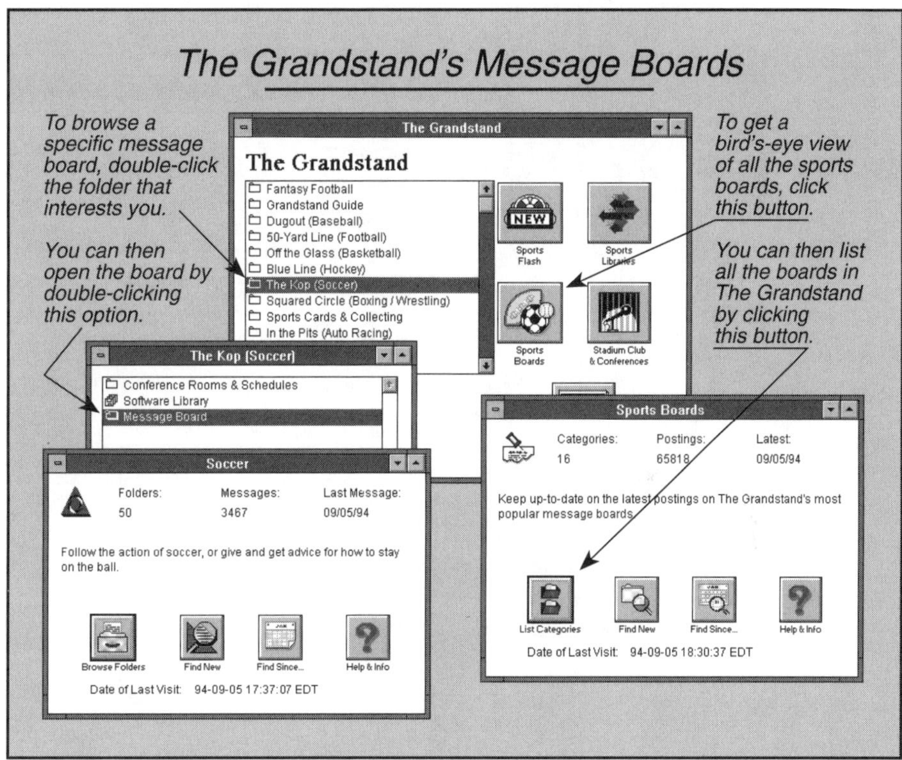

Figure 8-4: Browse your favorite sport's message board or take them all in. Either way, you'll find a wealth of information.

Messages on the sports boards are diverse and occasionally unexpected. Consider the thread of messages I found on the Hockey board (pictured in Figure 8-5). When was the last time you not only received a timely answer to a technical question but were given a frank review from a fellow member?

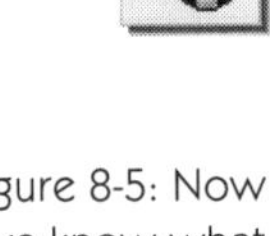

Figure 8-5: Now we know what hockey enthusiasts do in the summer: they play hockey—on their PCs.

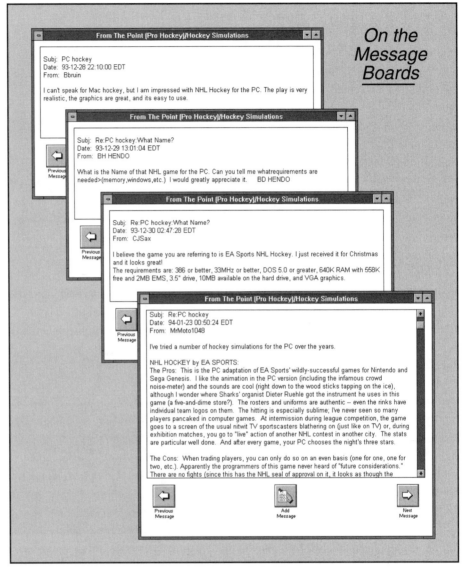

Message boards are wonderful things, but getting to know how to use them effectively takes a little learning. Assistance is provided in Chapter 13, "Clubs & Interests."

Perhaps the most interesting aspect of the Grandstand is its assortment of fantasy teams assembled by members—make-believe teams made up of real players in the sport. The Grandstand Fantasy Baseball

League (GFBL), for example, is modeled after "Rotisserie League Baseball," as described in the book of the same name by Glen Waggoner (Bantam Books). Team owners (that's us—the members of AOL) draft 23 players from the available talent in the American or National Leagues. The players' actual big-league performances are used in computing the standings of the GFBL team. Standings (see Figure 8-6), stats, newsletters and other league information are found in the message and library sections of the GFBL, and members watch them fanatically. Double-click any of the folders in the scroll box of the Grandstand's main window to access the leagues.

Figure 8-6: The end-of-July standings of the GFBL National League. Kornbread's Krumbs seem to be pulverizing the competition.

Fantasy Baseball

GFBL National League K   Backporch Baseball '94 by UofDWare
07/31/94   League Standings   Page 1

Team Name	Total	BA	HR	RBI	STL	ERA	WIN	SAV	RAT
Kornbread's Kru	77.0	11.0	11.0	11.0	9.0	10.0	11.0	3.0	11.0
Legal Eagles	66.0	12.0	5.0	8.0	1.0	12.0	7.0	9.0	12.0
Black Labs	65.5	8.0	6.0	10.0	11.0	9.0	8.0	5.5	8.0
Wolverines	64.5	10.0	7.5	9.0	7.5	11.0	4.0	5.5	10.0
Cunctating Mast	57.0	7.0	12.0	12.0	10.0	6.0	5.0	4.0	1.0
Trolley Dodgers	52.0	2.0	2.0	1.0	12.0	7.0	12.0	10.0	6.0
Hebron Settlers	46.0	1.0	3.0	2.0	3.0	8.0	9.0	11.0	9.0
Master Batters	45.0	5.0	7.5	7.0	7.5	2.0	10.0	1.0	5.0
Hell Razors	43.0	9.0	1.0	4.0	6.0	3.0	1.0	12.0	7.0
P.A.'s	43.0	6.0	10.0	6.0	5.0	4.0	6.0	2.0	4.0
Clutchers	37.0	4.0	9.0	5.0	2.0	5.0	2.0	7.0	3.0
Team Terrific	28.0	3.0	4.0	3.0	4.0	1.0	3.0	8.0	2.0

Moving On

The Sports Department is one that's slated for significant change during the next few months, much of which might be in effect by the time you read this book. Of particular interest is DataTimes News Reports, which will offer an extensive library of sports stories from sources such as the *Washington Times*, the *Orange County Register*, the *San Francisco Chronicle* and the *Seattle Post-Intelligencer*. DataTimes will offer an alternative to the news-searching mechanism described at the beginning of this chapter (which will be relocated to the Other Sports folder in the main Sports department window), with more opinion and even broader interests. To get to DataTimes, either click its icon in the main Sports department window, or use the keyword: DT Sports.

The Sports Department doesn't have a franchise on games, however. Consider the Entertainment Department, where games (along with television, radio, movies, books, music, cartoons, columnists and critics) abound.

Sounds like an interesting place. Turn the page and let's see what it has to offer.

CHAPTER 9

Entertainment

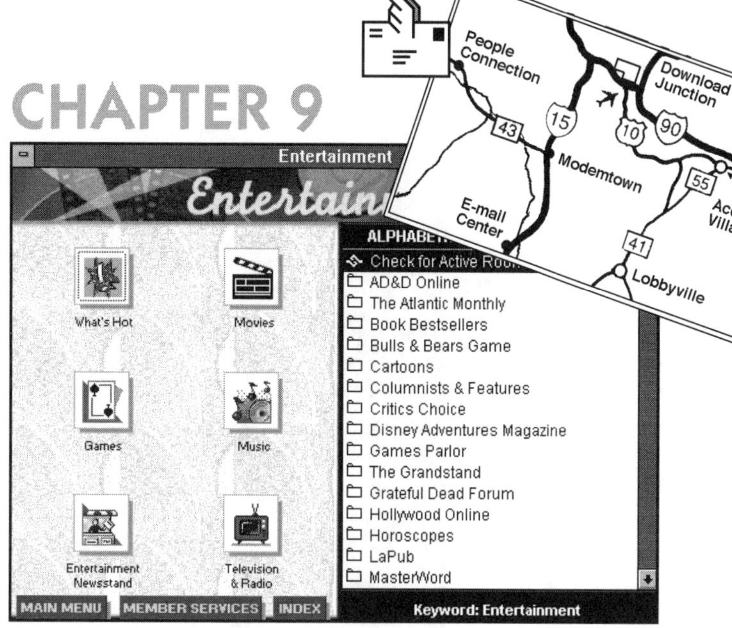

I've made many online friends over the years, and I've developed ongoing philosophical discussions with a few of them: it's my brain food and I enjoy it.

The other day a friend and I were discussing some of the significant changes in the American lifestyle over the past 100 years. Our conclusion: three major developments have changed that lifestyle forever: (1) the automobile, (2) the computer, and (3) the media.

That last development is the one that brings us to the subject of this chapter: Entertainment. Imagine entertainment when there were no movies, no videos, no television, no magazines, and very few books! What did those people do with their time? They certainly didn't hang around AOL's Entertainment Department.

That opportunity, it would appear, is uniquely ours. And it's one you're not going to want to miss. This place is rife with the spangles of technoglitter.

What's Hot

You'll want to begin your Entertainment Department visits here. The contents of What's Hot (note its icon in the frontispiece above) change constantly, listing a practical number of timely entertainment topics (see Figure 9-1).

The Entertainment Department not only offers a banquet of riches for watchers, readers and listeners, it also provides an avenue of communication with the writers, stars and producers. It's an exposition for multimedia habitues, and it's available via the Main Menu or the keyword: Entertainment.

Figure 9-1: As I write this chapter, NBC, CSPAN, Court TV, and MTV are What's Hot. (Helen Hunt and Paul Reiser of NBC's *Mad About You* appear in the background. Their graphic is filed in the NBC libraries.)

Critics' Choice

Critics' Choice (see Figure 9-2) is actually a multimedia syndicate, specializing in entertainment reviews. You'll find their reviews not only on AOL, but in newspapers as well. Their mission is to serve as a provident guide to entertainment—a mission they fulfill admirably. Use the keyword: Critics.

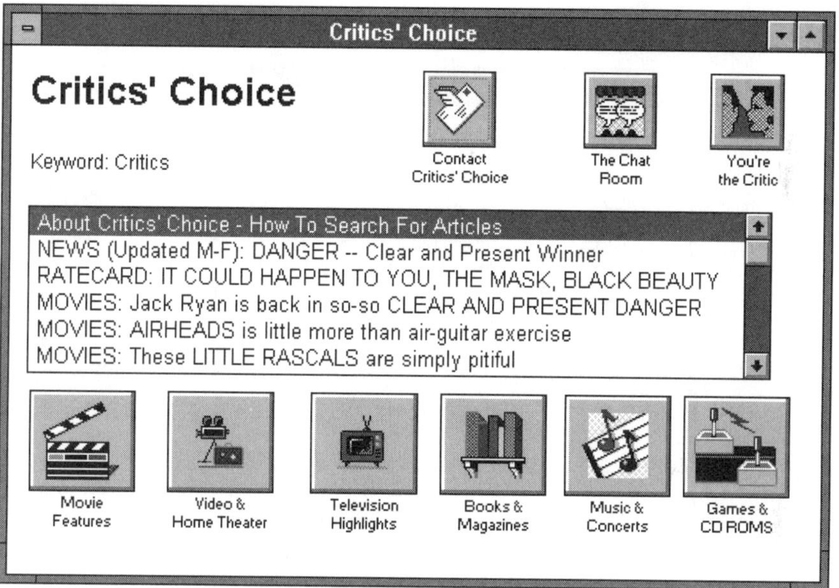

Figure 9-2: Though there are lots of places to find reviews of books, television, videos and movies online, I prefer Critics' Choice.

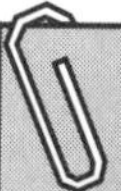

A Review of Online Reviews

While Critics' Choice is AOL's sovereign source of media reviews, you'll find a number of others. *Hollywood Online* (discussed later in this chapter) is one, *The New York Times* and the *Chicago Tribune* (discussed in Chapter 7, "The Newsstand") are a couple of others. The *San Jose Mercury-News* offers reviews as well (keyword: Mercury), and so does *TIME* (keyword: TIME).

The Afterwards Coffeehouse (keyword: Art) discusses art, the *Atlantic Monthly* (keyword: Atlantic) and *Saturday Review* (keyword: Saturday) magazines review a wide variety of media, and RockLink (keyword: RockLink) reviews music. Try each one of these services: that's the only way to find the reviewers whose preferences match yours.

The RateCard (third item in the list box in Figure 9-2) is especially convenient if you're intending to see a movie. Reviews from *The New York Times, Playboy, Gannett News Service, Mercury News,* National Public Radio, *Chicago Tribune* and *USA Today* are all summarized in the RateCard, as are the venerable Gene Siskel and Roger Ebert. Though many of these reviewers are found elsewhere on the service, they're all collectively quoted here: a handy feature for moviegoers (see Figure 9-3).

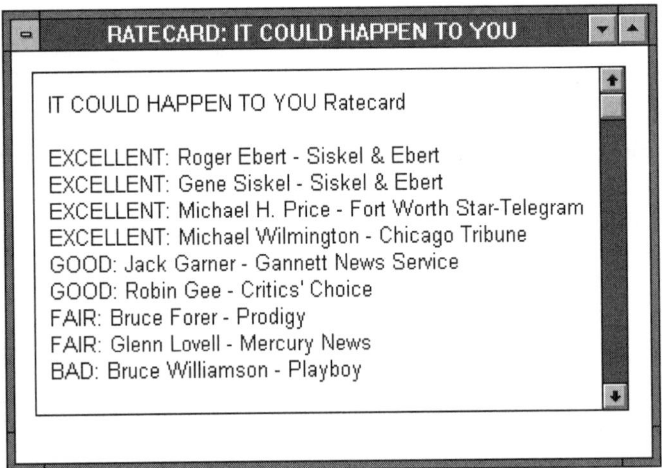

Figure 9-3: The RateCard is a quick way to see what the reviewers have to say about the current crop of movies.

The remainder of Critics' Choice offers consummate, relevant reviews of all of today's media (see Figure 9-4). As you examine Figure 9-4, note the Coming Soon feature in the movies section and the Laserdisc Report in the video section. The television section offers descriptions of this week's episodes for nearly all shows; the magazine section describes the feature stories of dozens of popular magazines; the music section offers a gift guide; and the games section offers strategies and tips.

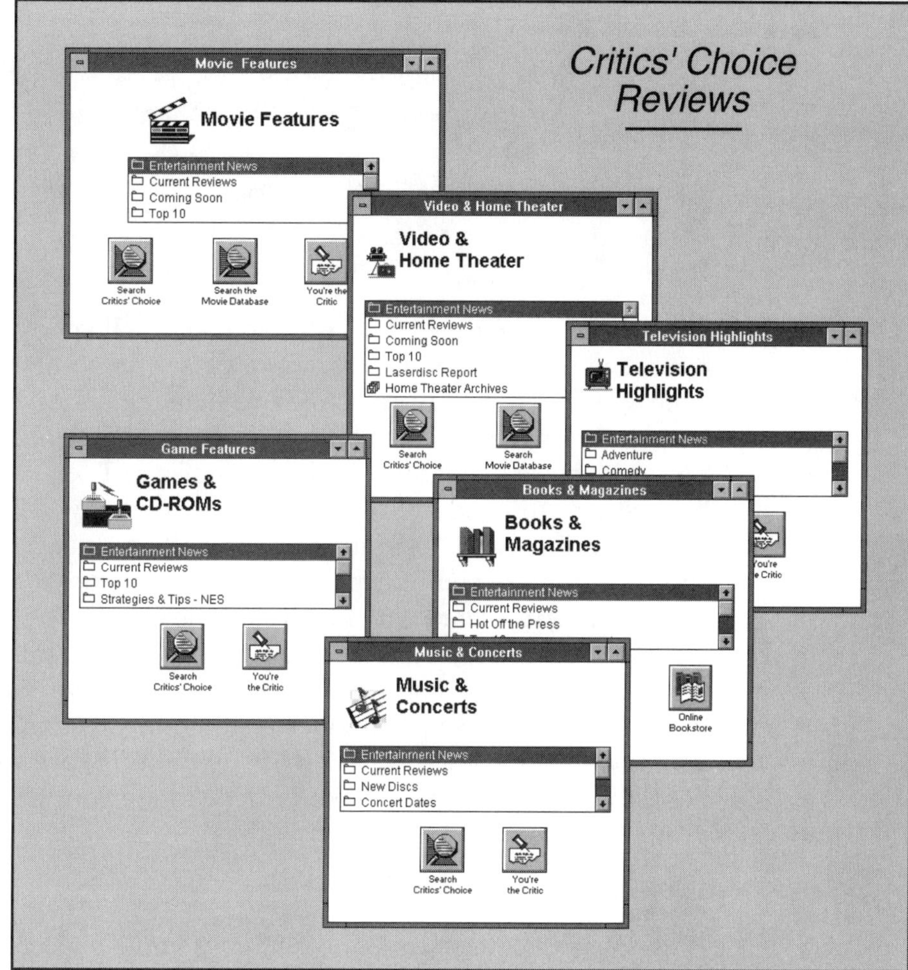

Figure 9-4: The contents of Critics' Choice. Nearly every current attraction is reviewed, and all reviews are searchable.

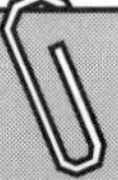

Search Tips

All of the reviews in Critics' Choice are searchable—just click any of the search icons pictured in Figure 9-4. Want to see a really great movie: search for "4STAR." Want to take the kids to a matinee? Search for "MPAAG." Want a review of a Scott Turow novel? Search for "thriller and legal." Searching methods are described in "About Critics' Choice," available from the area's main screen.

Don't forget the Critics' Choice video reviews. If you're like me, you can spend hours in a video store and leave with nothing to show for it. Unless I know what I want before I walk in the door, I become a tremulous enormity of indecision after 10 minutes of video-store browsing. The video store in my town is about the size of Texas. It's hard to browse in a store the size of Texas. Either you know what you want or you're swallowed by the immensity of it all, wandering aimlessly in a labyrinth of racks and little plastic boxes where the exits are known only to the pubescent knaves who staff the place.

Critics' Choice is an operative example of the potential that online services represent today. The Critics' Choice database is vast, and no place gathers the arsenal of reviewers that the RateCard does. Before you buy the popcorn; before you fire up the VCR; before you visit a bookstore or record shop, make Critics' Choice your first stop.

Hollywood Online

Hollywood Online offers all of the things you'd expect from its title: pictures of your favorite stars from the Pictures and Sounds library, cast and production notes in Movie Notes, and talk on the Movie Talk message board (see Figure 9-5).

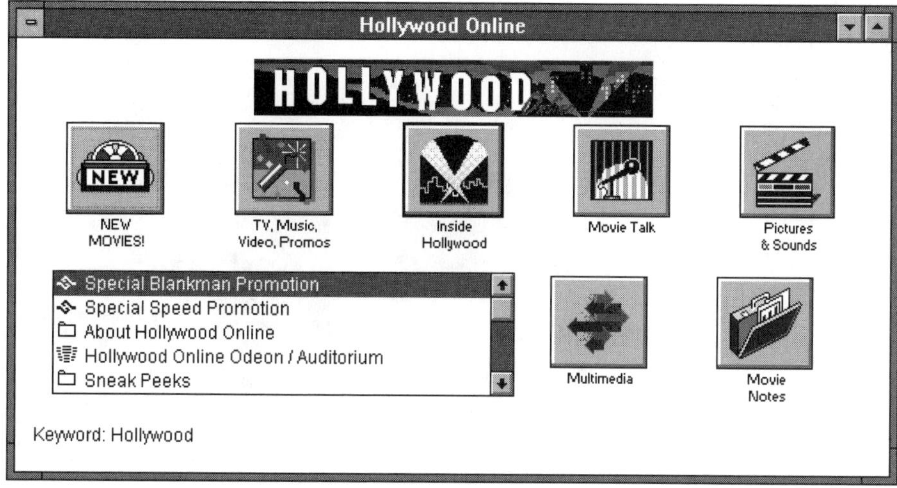

Figure 9-5: Hollywood Online is a prototype of online multimedia resources—and it's available now via the keyword: Hollywood.

Two other things, however, fascinate me: (1) you can download sneak previews of selected motion pictures before they're released, and (2) multimedia figures heavily in Hollywood Online's contents. Film clips are complete with color, sound and animation; and interactive "kits" provide an opportunity to browse a film's contents, allowing you to replay scenes that interest you and skip those that don't.

Still pictures, posters and sound clips are available here as well, and most of them download in less than two minutes at 9600 baud (Figure 9-6).

Be sure to check out Joey Berlin's "Inside Hollywood" (Figure 9-7). His long list of credits includes *The Los Angeles Times*, *New York Newsday* and the *New York Post*. He also writes the nationally syndicated newspaper columns "Film Close-Up" and "Pop Talk" for the Copley New Service.

Figure 9-6: Against a backdrop poster from "The Next Karate Kid" starring Hilary Swank, I've pasted clips of Harrison Ford in "Clear and Present Danger," Bridget Fonda in "It Could Happen to You," and Jim Carrey in "The Mask." They're all available in the Pictures & Sounds library of Hollywood Online.

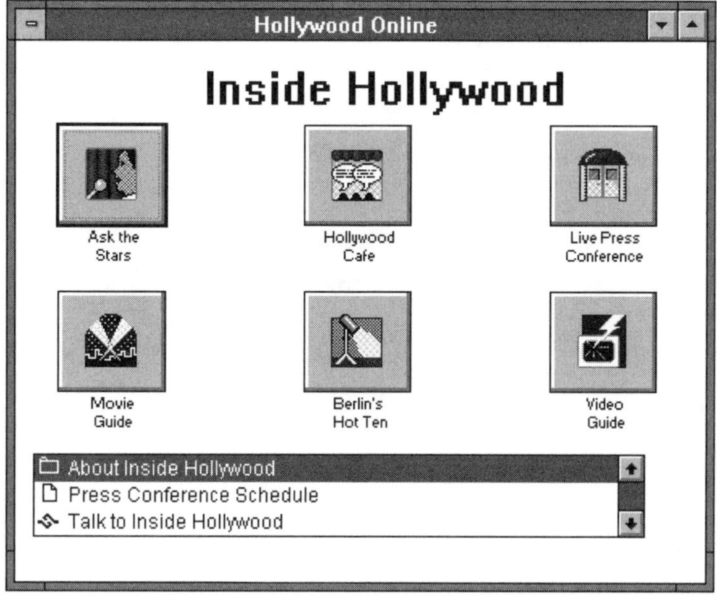

Figure 9-7: Joey Berlin's Inside Hollywood is your pipeline to glitterdom.

Book Bestsellers

Two features in Book Bestsellers are of particular interest. The first is the bestseller lists (Figure 9-8), compiled by *The Wall Street Journal*. These lists serve as an alternative to the lists that appear in *The New York Times* (discussed in Chapter 7, "The Newsstand"). Compare them: the differences are occasionally enlightening.

The second feature is the reviews, compiled by Kirkus Reviews of New York. These reviews appear before the books become available at book stores and libraries. Kirkus hires independent reviewers, so the reviews are often more diverse than those appearing in The Times. Again, compare for yourself, and—if you are a true literati—give thanks that AOL offers alternatives such as this.

Don't forget the Book Bestseller boards! This is the place for your reviews—often the most incisive of all.

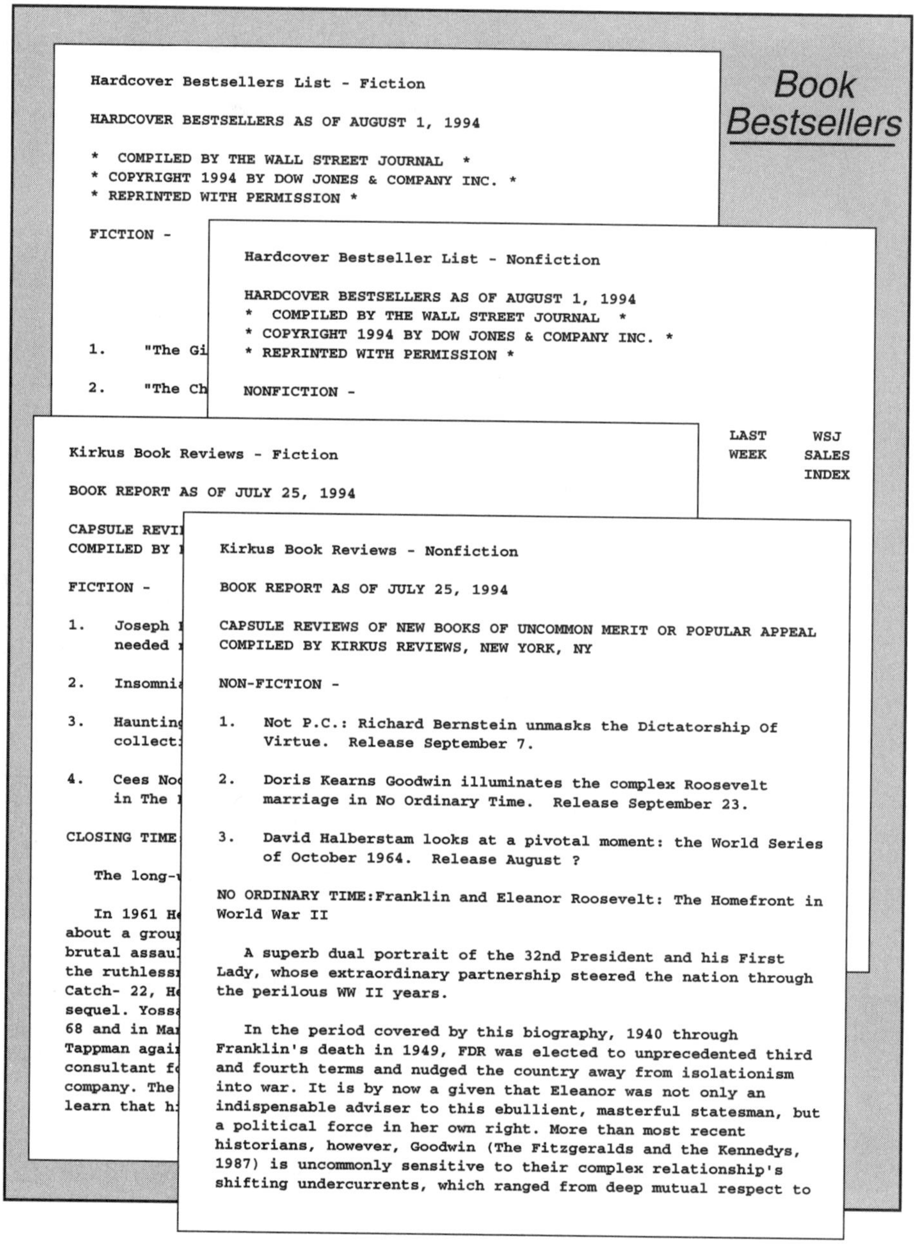

Figure 9-8: The bestseller lists and reviews found in Book Bestsellers. To get here quickly, use the keyword: Books.

Book Bestsellers

Hardcover Bestsellers List - Fiction

HARDCOVER BESTSELLERS AS OF AUGUST 1, 1994

* COMPILED BY THE WALL STREET JOURNAL *
* COPYRIGHT 1994 BY DOW JONES & COMPANY INC. *
* REPRINTED WITH PERMISSION *

FICTION -

1. "The Gi

2. "The Ch

Hardcover Bestseller List - Nonfiction

HARDCOVER BESTSELLERS AS OF AUGUST 1, 1994
* COMPILED BY THE WALL STREET JOURNAL *
* COPYRIGHT 1994 BY DOW JONES & COMPANY INC. *
* REPRINTED WITH PERMISSION *

NONFICTION -

LAST WEEK | WSJ SALES INDEX

Kirkus Book Reviews - Fiction

BOOK REPORT AS OF JULY 25, 1994

CAPSULE REVI
COMPILED BY

FICTION -

1. Joseph
needed

2. Insomni

3. Hauntin
collect

4. Cees No
in The

CLOSING TIME

The long-

In 1961 H
about a grou
brutal assau
the ruthless
Catch- 22, H
sequel. Yoss
68 and in Ma
Tappman agai
consultant f
company. The
learn that h

Kirkus Book Reviews - Nonfiction

BOOK REPORT AS OF JULY 25, 1994

CAPSULE REVIEWS OF NEW BOOKS OF UNCOMMON MERIT OR POPULAR APPEAL
COMPILED BY KIRKUS REVIEWS, NEW YORK, NY

NON-FICTION -

1. Not P.C.: Richard Bernstein unmasks the Dictatorship Of Virtue. Release September 7.

2. Doris Kearns Goodwin illuminates the complex Roosevelt marriage in No Ordinary Time. Release September 23.

3. David Halberstam looks at a pivotal moment: the World Series of October 1964. Release August ?

NO ORDINARY TIME:Franklin and Eleanor Roosevelt: The Homefront in World War II

A superb dual portrait of the 32nd President and his First Lady, whose extraordinary partnership steered the nation through the perilous WW II years.

In the period covered by this biography, 1940 through Franklin's death in 1949, FDR was elected to unprecedented third and fourth terms and nudged the country away from isolationism into war. It is by now a given that Eleanor was not only an indispensable adviser to this ebullient, masterful statesman, but a political force in her own right. More than most recent historians, however, Goodwin (The Fitzgeralds and the Kennedys, 1987) is uncommonly sensitive to their complex relationship's shifting undercurrents, which ranged from deep mutual respect to

Cartoons

Let's take a little survey. What's the first section you read when you pick up the Sunday paper? If you're like me, you read "the funnies" before anything else. Often they're the *only* thing I read, depending on how dreary the world has been that week.

America Online is particularly rich in cartoons, and you don't have to wait until Sunday morning to enjoy them. A number of nationally acclaimed cartoonists contribute to AOL each week including:

- Charles Rodriguez, who produces cartoons regularly for *MacWEEK* magazine; his work has appeared in *Stereo Review* and *National Lampoon* as well. His "CompuToons" are computer-related and available only on AOL.
- Mike Keefe, a nationally syndicated cartoonist based in Denver. Mike and his cartoons are featured in Chapter 19, "FlashSessions & the Download Manager."
- Peter Oakley, who began drawing pictures on his Macintosh Plus in 1987 using MacPaint software. He now lives in Seattle, where he's a full-time cartoonist drawing for a number of publications, including AOL's own "Modern Wonder" cartoon series.

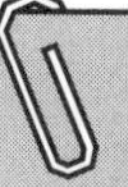

The Cartoonist's Life

The cartoonist's life seems like an easy one. All you have to do is sketch a funny picture, then send it off to a magazine and wait for a big check to come back in the mail.

Peter Oakley knows better. On the subject of the cartoonist's life he writes, "The truth is that magazine cartooning is extremely competitive, there are hundreds of remarkably talented cartoonists out there, and few of us are what you would call famous. And because I am doing something new, there was considerable resistance to 'computer-generated' cartoons in the traditional pen-and-ink cartoon market. Of course, the most comfortable home for these cartoons is on the computer, and so it was just a matter of time before they would show up on a telecommunications network. [America Online] is the first national network to host a regular cartoon feature, and I am glad 'Modern Wonder' has found a home here."

Figure 9-9: Three 'toons from the Cartoon Forum: "Heavy Fog," by Theresa McCracken; "Whistle," by Charles Rodriguez; and "Crash and Burn," by Peter Oakley. New cartoons are posted weekly in the Entertainment Department.

As you might assume by looking at Figure 9-9, cartoons from members are available as well, and there's a lively discussion on the Toon Talk message board involving all who find an interest in cartooning.

Columnists & Features Online

Columnists & Features Online is the best way to read provocative newspaper columnists and communicate with them online (see Figure 9-10).

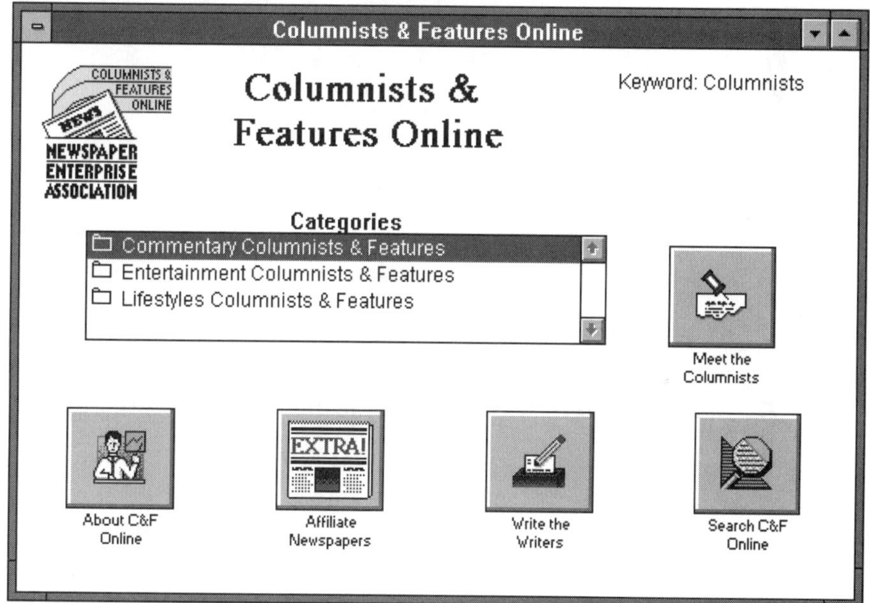

Figure 9-10: Columnists & Features Online offers current material as well as an extensive, searchable library. Use the keyword: Columnists.

The Newspaper Enterprise Association (NEA) syndicates distinguished writers and political columnists to newspapers nationwide, including the 29 (a number that's sure to grow) featured on AOL (see Figure 9-11).

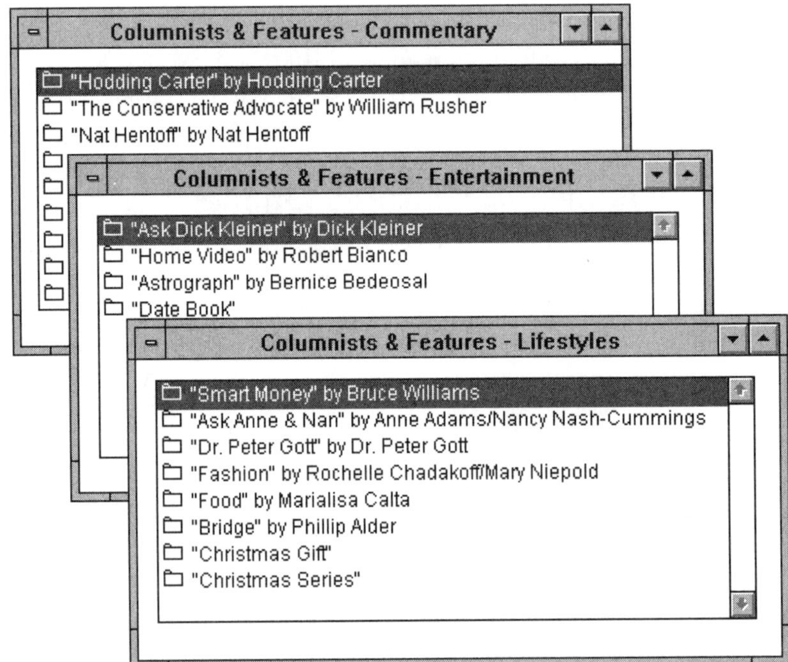

Figure 9-11: A sample of the columnists available via America Online, assembled for bilateral discourse via Columnists & Features Online.

The text of each column appears the same day it is released to the newspapers and remains online for a week. After that, past columns are posted in the library and can be searched using standard AOL criteria. Some of the columnists include:

- Hodding Carter III, State Department spokesman for Jimmy Carter's administration, offers sharp opinions on today's issues from the perspective of a respected insider and noted partisan of strong, active government.
- "The Conservative Advocate" by William Rusher. Written by the former publisher of *National Review*, "The Conservative Advocate" jabs and lampoons liberals and the left, mixing humor and political commentary in this popular voice of the American right.
- "Environment" by J.D. Hair. The president of the National Wildlife Federation, J.D. Hair offers insightful reports and timely accounts of current environmental concerns, covering all aspects of natural resource protection.

- Nat Hentoff. One of the foremost authorities on the First Amendment, Nat Hentoff's column, which originally appears in The Washington Post, examines how legislative decisions affect our basic freedoms to speak, write, think and assemble.
- "Saints And Sinners" by George Plagenz. A personal look at family values and spiritual issues from an ordained minister and news veteran.
- Ian Shoales. Amusing social commentary from this popular National Public Radio and *San Francisco Examiner* humor columnist.
- Martin Schram. Politics with a liberal perspective from this frequent commentator for CNN's *The Capital Gang*.
- Joseph Spear. An advocate for the average American, Spear offers witty, insightful political commentary.
- "Home Video" by Robert Bianco. Up-to-the-minute reviews of home video releases from this *Pittsburgh Post-Gazette* journalist.
- "Smart Money" by radio personality Bruce Williams. Gives incisive answers to personal finance questions.
- "The Tax Adviser" by George Smith. Advice for year-round tax planning from an experienced CPA.
- "Wheels" by Peter Bohr. Advice on keeping your car in shape from this contributing editor to *Road & Track*.
- "Ask Anne & Nan" by Anne B. Adams and Nancy Nash-Cummings. Household hints from two expert problem-solvers and National Public Radio personalities.
- Dr. Peter Gott. Medical advice from this practicing physician and patients' rights advocate.
- "Fashion" by Rochelle Chadakoff and Mary Martin Niepold. Trends and tips on the latest fashions, plus interviews with leading designers.
- "Food" by Marialisa Calta. Witty observations and easy-to-prepare recipes from this well-known food journalist.

- "Astrograph" (horoscope) by Bernice Bede Osol. What's in the stars for you? You'll find it in "Astrograph," one of the most popular astrology columns in America.

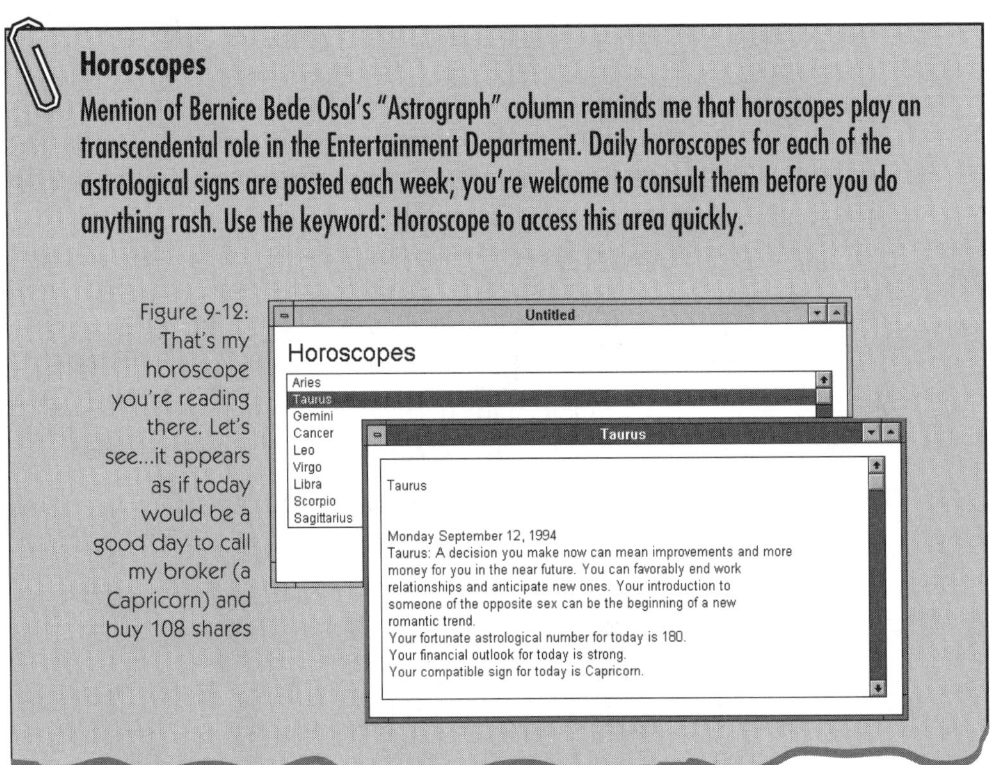

Horoscopes

Mention of Bernice Bede Osol's "Astrograph" column reminds me that horoscopes play an transcendental role in the Entertainment Department. Daily horoscopes for each of the astrological signs are posted each week; you're welcome to consult them before you do anything rash. Use the keyword: Horoscope to access this area quickly.

Untitled
Horoscopes
Aries
Taurus
Gemini
Cancer
Leo
Virgo
Libra
Scorpio
Sagittarius
Taurus
Taurus
Monday September 12, 1994
Taurus: A decision you make now can mean improvements and more money for you in the near future. You can favorably end work relationships and anticipate new ones. Your introduction to someone of the opposite sex can be the beginning of a new romantic trend.
Your fortunate astrological number for today is 180.
Your financial outlook for today is strong.
Your compatible sign for today is Capricorn.

Figure 9-12: That's my horoscope you're reading there. Let's see...it appears as if today would be a good day to call my broker (a Capricorn) and buy 108 shares

The Grateful Dead Forum

In Chapter 1, I mentioned my preference for classical music. Stephen King might do his writing while rock and roll plays at 120 decibels, but I write to Mozart. I'm not a purist, however. As an Oregonian and a former "radical" of the '60s, I confess a liking for the Grateful Dead. The Dead are especially fond of Oregon, and they exhibit that fondness with an annual visit to Eugene, a Mecca for Deadheads if there ever was one.

Two years ago while I was writing the first edition of this book, the Grateful Dead was just another board on the RockLink Forum. It was a crowded board—its messages always numbered around 500—but just a board nonetheless. The other day when I looked in on the Dead I discovered they had a forum of their own (Figure 9-13). Something peculiar is going on here. This band is older than color TV, yet it provokes one of the most active areas on AOL today.

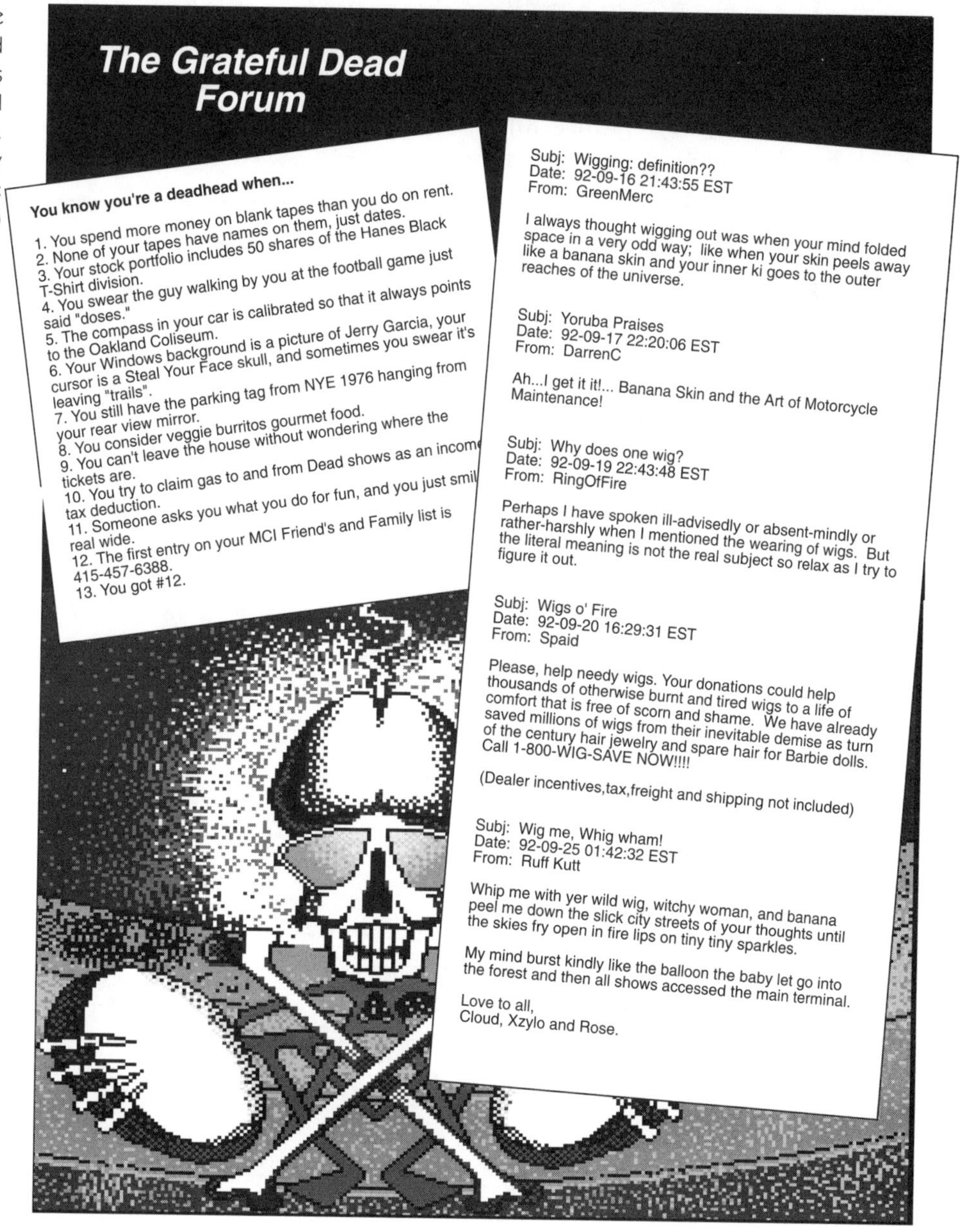

Figure 9-13: The Grateful Dead Forum defies rational interpretation. (Text significantly edited by the author.)

The Grateful Dead Forum

You know you're a deadhead when...

1. You spend more money on blank tapes than you do on rent.
2. None of your tapes have names on them, just dates.
3. Your stock portfolio includes 50 shares of the Hanes Black T-Shirt division.
4. You swear the guy walking by you at the football game just said "doses."
5. The compass in your car is calibrated so that it always points to the Oakland Coliseum.
6. Your Windows background is a picture of Jerry Garcia, your cursor is a Steal Your Face skull, and sometimes you swear it's leaving "trails".
7. You still have the parking tag from NYE 1976 hanging from your rear view mirror.
8. You consider veggie burritos gourmet food.
9. You can't leave the house without wondering where the tickets are.
10. You try to claim gas to and from Dead shows as an incom tax deduction.
11. Someone asks you what you do for fun, and you just smil real wide.
12. The first entry on your MCI Friend's and Family list is 415-457-6388.
13. You got #12.

Subj: Wigging: definition??
Date: 92-09-16 21:43:55 EST
From: GreenMerc

I always thought wigging out was when your mind folded space in a very odd way; like when your skin peels away like a banana skin and your inner ki goes to the outer reaches of the universe.

Subj: Yoruba Praises
Date: 92-09-17 22:20:06 EST
From: DarrenC

Ah...I get it it!... Banana Skin and the Art of Motorcycle Maintenance!

Subj: Why does one wig?
Date: 92-09-19 22:43:48 EST
From: RingOfFire

Perhaps I have spoken ill-advisedly or absent-mindly or rather-harshly when I mentioned the wearing of wigs. But the literal meaning is not the real subject so relax as I try to figure it out.

Subj: Wigs o' Fire
Date: 92-09-20 16:29:31 EST
From: Spaid

Please, help needy wigs. Your donations could help thousands of otherwise burnt and tired wigs to a life of comfort that is free of scorn and shame. We have already saved millions of wigs from their inevitable demise as turn of the century hair jewelry and spare hair for Barbie dolls. Call 1-800-WIG-SAVE NOW!!!!

(Dealer incentives,tax,freight and shipping not included)

Subj: Wig me, Whig wham!
Date: 92-09-25 01:42:32 EST
From: Ruff Kutt

Whip me with yer wild wig, witchy woman, and banana peel me down the slick city streets of your thoughts until the skies fry open in fire lips on tiny tiny sparkles.

My mind burst kindly like the balloon the baby let go into the forest and then all shows accessed the main terminal.

Love to all,
Cloud, Xzylo and Rose.

The Trivia Club

One of the most active chat rooms on AOL (we'll discuss chat rooms in Chapter 12, "People Connection") is the Trivia room. This is one of the two places where trivia addicts get their fix.

The other is the Trivia Club (keyword: Trivia), where the Trivia Teaser (see Figure 9-14) is offered each day. Free time is awarded once a month to the highest three scorers in each trivia game. The Club's library has profiles of some great triviots, sounds for use in the chat room games, and graphics of some of the staff and players.

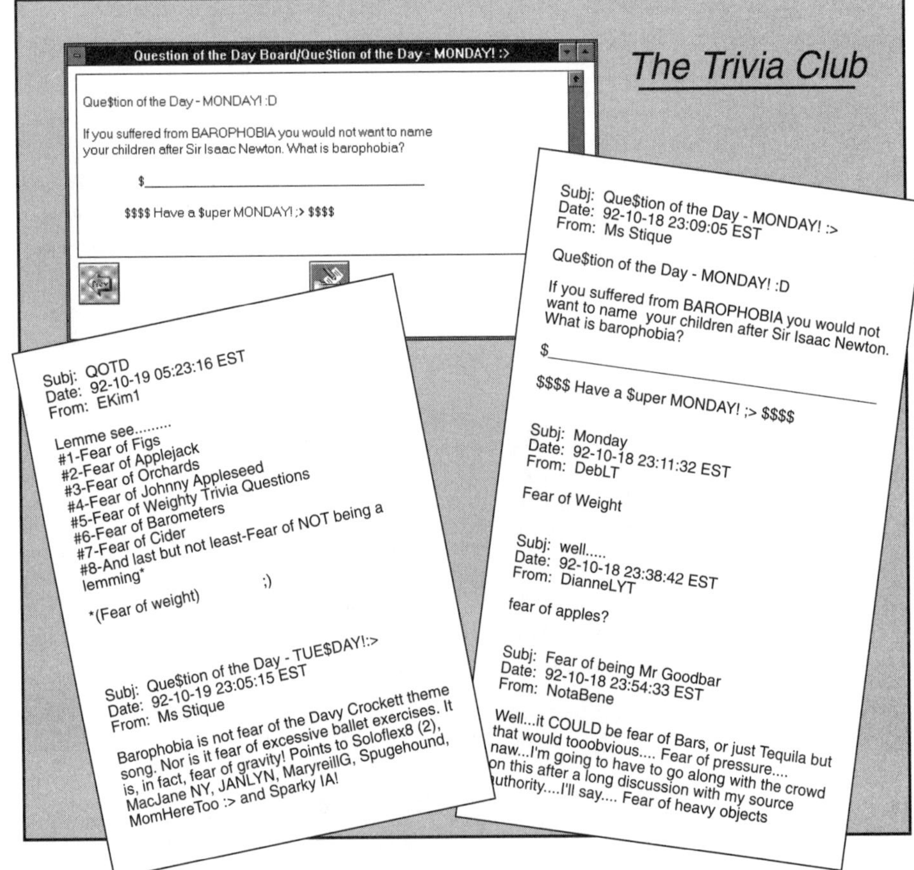

Figure 9-14: You've gotta be fast to win in the Trivia Club's Trivia Teaser. The correct answer was posted in just over two minutes after the question was published.

The Online Gaming Forums

There's a world of game players who find the Online Gaming Forums (keyword: Gaming) to be their hermitage, the place where games are paramount and challenges are eternal. It is here where knights slay dragons, space voyagers conquer aliens, and residents of the late 20th century scratch their heads in bewilderment. You owe it to yourself to try an online game if you never have: the challenge of playing with remote competitors—unseen and unknown—isn't quite matched by any other. And if you get hooked, the Online Gaming Forums stand ready to nourish your obsession (see Figure 9-15).

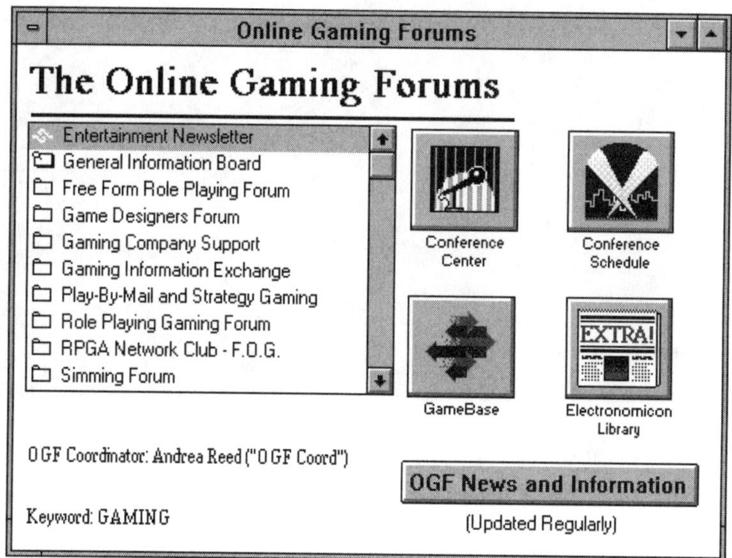

Figure 9-15: Role-playing, free-form and play-by-mail games abound on the Online Gaming Forums.

Neverwinter Nights

Neverwinter Nights is an online Advanced Dungeons & Dragons (AD&D) fantasy role-playing game. There's no other online experience quite like it; and there's no better way to play AD&D than with real people in real time, in a medium that combines color, sound, graphics and unbounded intellectual stimulation.

Neverwinter Nights is played using its own software, which you must purchase and install on your hard drive (a minor investment which I'll describe in a moment). Once that's done, you sign on, enter the Neverwinter Nights Forum (keyword: Neverwinter), then start the Neverwinter Nights software that resides on your hard drive (see Figure 9-16). Windows and AOL disappear, and the land of Lord Nasher, Neverwinter's brave leader, assumes control. Great treasures can be found here. And if you and Nasher succeed in returning peace to the region, bounty can be yours.

Figure 9-16: AD&D's title screen greets you with flashy colors and a catchy tune. It's here that the adventure begins.

Spectacular sound and 3D graphics are provided by the Neverwinter Nights software on your hard disk. Anyone who has played the game can tell you that there's nothing lightweight about Advanced Dungeons & Dragons. America Online is aware of this and graciously provides a number of AD&D experts to help whenever you need it. At the top of the list are the official Neverwinter Nights AD&D staff members—easily recognizable by the "NW" or "NWA" in front of their names.

Neverwinter Nights Software

To play Neverwinter Nights, you will need special software which can be either downloaded free of charge or purchased. For those who just want to take a peek inside Neverwinter Nights, use the keyword: Neverwinter and click on NWN Software Download Center. The download is free (you will pass through the free curtain on your way to the download area), and you'll find complete instructions posted detailing how to download and install the software. If you find Neverwinter Nights intriguing (and you will), you can also purchase the software, which comes complete with original game disks, manuals, reference guides and special access privileges. To buy Neverwinter Nights software, click on Order Neverwinter Nights Software. The software package costs $14.95 for AOL members and includes everything you need to play the game. In addition, you'll be able to download any upgrades to the Neverwinter software at no cost other than your normal connect charge. The program will be shipped via UPS within two weeks of ordering. It's worth the wait.

When I tried out the game, I was a little overwhelmed by its immensity until I happened upon NW Arwen (AD&D Online NWN Coordinator) and Trollsbane (a fellow member). They kindly showed me some of the ropes (there are a lot of them). They let me follow them around; helped me acquire gold, treasures and weapons; cast spells upon my character to make it stronger and less vulnerable to the terrible beasts it met along the way; and saved my character's life on more than one occasion. This isn't special treatment: anyone who needs help only has to ask. People are incredibly helpful and congenial here. There's a New Members area and a Lounge where you can relax and get to know other players. Either one is fertile ground for members new to the game who need help.

Neverwinter Nights provides a degree of interactivity and realism that entices the new member and challenges the veteran player. Many people join AOL solely for access to this game—it's *that* good. While you may not be as fervertly committed as this, you should at least explore this remarkable realization of the telecommunications medium.

RabbitJack's Casino

If you love the roll-the-dice excitement of Atlantic City and Las Vegas but you don't have the time (or money) to travel to those gambling meccas, you might want to visit RabbitJack's Casino, where you'll find all your favorite games, including bingo, poker and blackjack.

Established by RabbitJack, the famous online gambler, the casino is now run by RabbitJill, who promises everyone a good time tempting fate at the wheel of fortune. To play this game, use the keyword: Casino, and click on the Free Casino Software Library to download

RabbitJack's Casino (see Chapter 5, "Computing & Software" for instructions on how to download). As with the Neverwinter Nights software, the download is free, and you'll find complete instructions posted in the casino detailing how to download and install the software.

The casino works much like an America Online chat room, with a number of people at a table or in a row at a given time. You receive 250 chips upon entering the casino and 250 more each day you visit. You can transfer some of your chips to a pal, or borrow some if you're down on your luck. But don't worry, the chips are only in fun—this is one casino where you'll never wish you hadn't bet it all on that last hand (Figure 19-17).

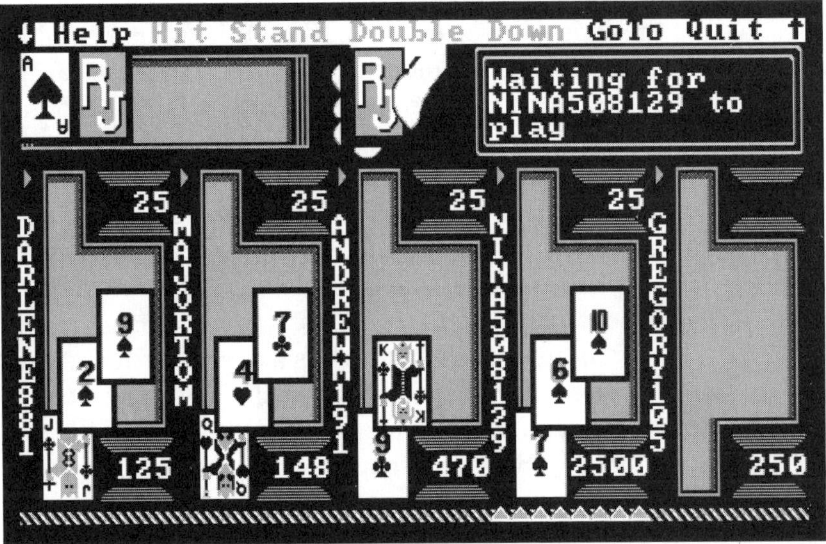

Figure 19-17: Major Tom isn't doing too well at RabbitJack's Blackjack table. He's down to $148 and sliding. However, he is holding 21. Things may be looking up. (They weren't: ten minutes later I was heading for home, disgraced and insolvent.)

Moving On

From the trivial to the profound, we now make the not inconsiderable transition to the world of the Personal Finance Department. Lots of people subscribe to AOL for financial purposes alone, and AOL rewards them with relevant (and current) information, and advice from professionals and fellow investors alike. Grab your checkbook and turn the page. . . .

CHAPTER 10

Personal Finance

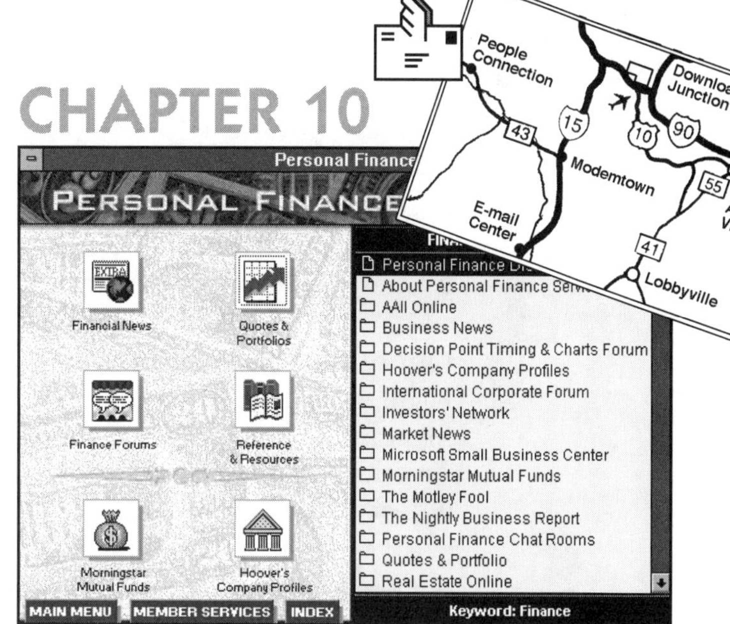

Have you ever seen those little radios that pick up weather reports? I use one every day. It's tuned to the local National Oceanic and Atmospheric Administration (NOAA) station, which broadcasts nothing but the weather, 24 hours a day. These gadgets are the ideal information machine: always current, always available and nearly free. Now if I could only find a similar source for financial information.

Aha! What about AOL? If there ever was a machine for instant financial news, this is it. Unlike television or radio, AOL's market information is available whenever you want it: there's no waiting for the six o'clock news or suffering through three stories (and four commercials) that you don't want to hear before they get around to the one you do. Unlike newspapers, AOL's financial news is always current. It's not this morning's news, it's this minute's news. It's current, it's always available and it's almost free.

I wonder if Ted Turner knows about this?

Your Personal Stock Portfolio

Let's begin this chapter with a financial exercise. This one is risk-free, but nonetheless, quite real. A portfolio of investments is a fascinating thing to follow and nourish, even if it's only make-believe. And if you want to add

The Personal Finance Department is an anchorage for investors in the sea of financial bedlam. There's financial data here in plenty, and it's pertinent, precise and never more than 15 minutes old. Click the Personal Finance button on the main menu, or use the keyword: Finance.

some real punch to it, AOL offers a brokerage service. You can invest real money in real issues and realize real gains (or real losses).

Whether you intend to invest real cash or funny money, join me as we create a personal portfolio of stocks and securities.

Quotes & Portfolio

Begin the journey by clicking the Personal Finance button on the Main Menu, or by typing Ctrl+K and entering the keyword: Finance. America Online responds by transporting you to the Personal Finance department (see Figure 10-1).

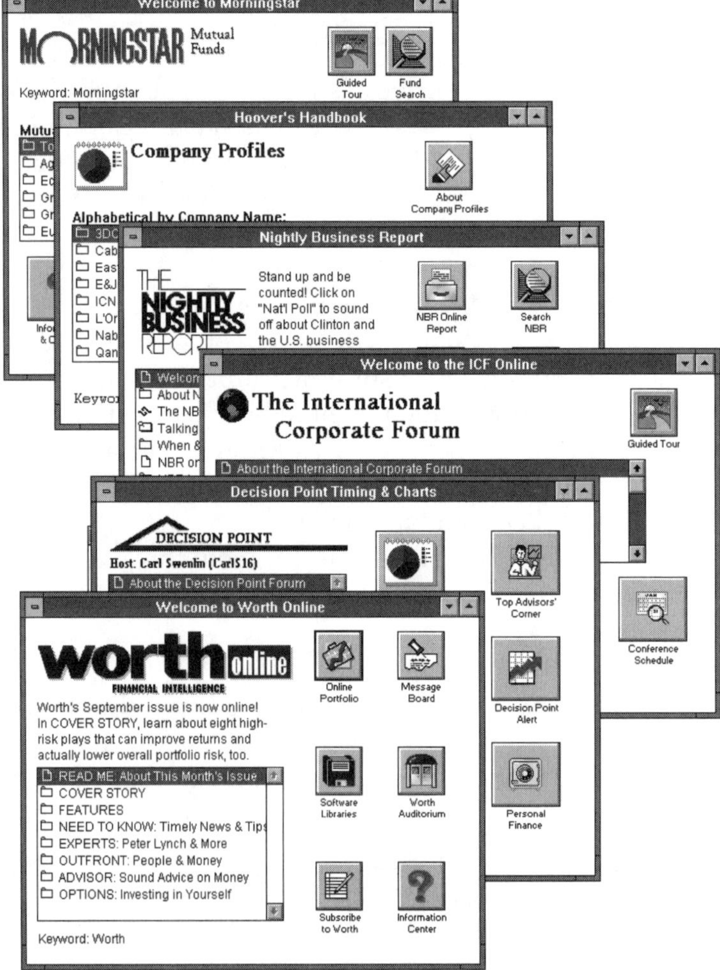

Figure 10-1: America Online might be the perfect financial information machine: it's always current and it's available 24 hours a day.

A wealth (pun intended) of financial information awaits you here, as does opportunity. You cannot only seek counsel on your investments, you can actually buy them here, and maintain a portfolio as well. And that, for the moment, is our focus. Click the icon labeled Quotes & Portfolios, and let's invest our surplus cash (see Figure 10-2).

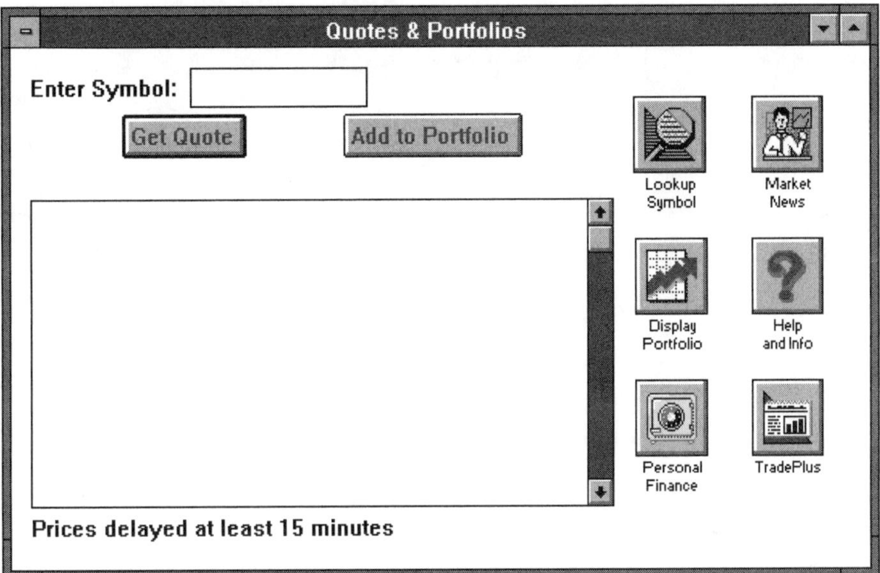

Figure 10-2: The Quotes & Portfolios window allows you to access market news, look up an issue, build a portfolio and actually buy and sell issues. It's available from the main window of the Personal Finance window, through the jagged-arrow button on the Flashbar, or use the keyword: Quotes.

The Quotes & Portfolio section of the Personal Finance Department is a comprehensive financial information service equaled by few others in the telecommunications industry and available on AOL without surcharge. The only thing you pay when you're visiting here is your normal connect-time charges. America Online is connected to the financial centers of the world via high-speed telephone lines, providing financial information updated continuously during market hours on a 15-minute (minimum) delay basis.

Finding a Stock Symbol

America Online is waiting for us to enter a stock symbol. Stock symbols are those abbreviations you see traveling across the Big Board in a stockbroker's office. What shall we buy? Since it's something that we all have in common, let's look up AOL. America Online is a publicly traded issue, after all, so we should offer a reference to it here.

But what's AOL's symbol? Hmmm . . . Let's try the Lookup Symbol icon. When you click that icon and follow the path pictured in Figure 10-3, we discover that AMER is the symbol for America Online.

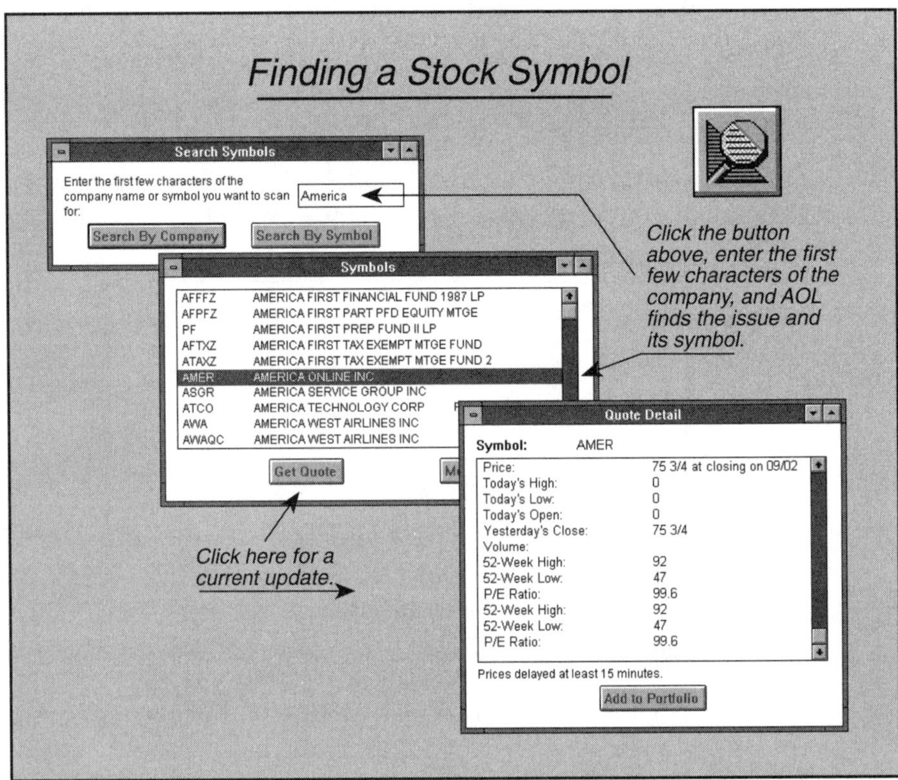

Figure 10-3: Don't know the symbol for an issue? Let America Online look it up for you.

Once you have the symbol, enter it into the box indicated in Figure 10-3 and click on the Get Quote button. The results are pictured in Figure 10-3's scroll box.

Building the Portfolio

Note the current price, then click on the Add to Portfolio button. America Online responds with the dialog box shown in Figure 10-4.

Figure 10-4: Enter the current price and the number of shares, then click OK. The "investment" will be added to your portfolio.

Portfolio Information

Symbol: AMER

Number of Shares: 100

Purchase price: 55 1/4

Leave both "Number of shares" and "Purchase price" blank to exclude from portfolio value calculation.

OK Cancel

Since this is only make-believe, buy as many shares as you'd like. Don't worry: AOL doesn't share your portfolio with anyone, and you won't be charged any special fees for this exercise; it's a private matter between you and your computer.

My portfolio consists of the AOL investment I've just described, plus additional investments in IBM, Apple Computer (no favorites here) and Intel. Whenever I want to know how my portfolio is doing, I use the keyword: Portfolio, and view the window pictured in Figure 10-5.

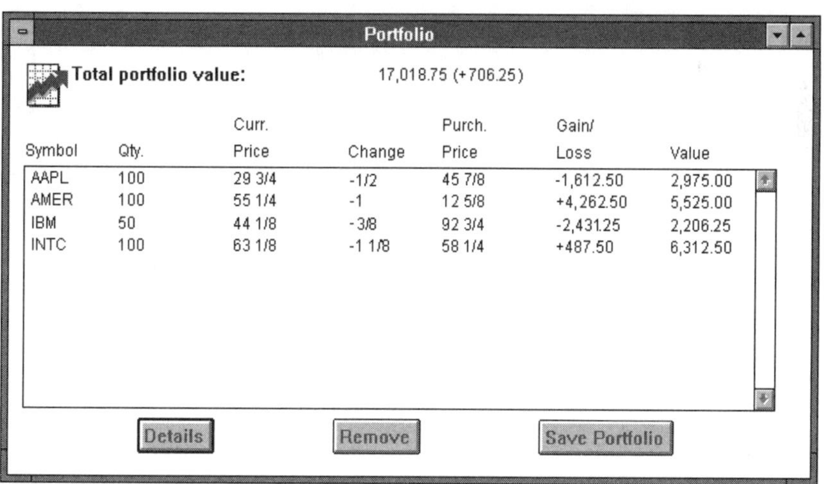

Portfolio

Total portfolio value: 17,018.75 (+706.25)

Symbol	Qty.	Curr. Price	Change	Purch. Price	Gain/ Loss	Value
AAPL	100	29 3/4	-1/2	45 7/8	-1,612.50	2,975.00
AMER	100	55 1/4	-1	12 5/8	+4,262.50	5,525.00
IBM	50	44 1/8	-3/8	92 3/4	-2,431.25	2,206.25
INTC	100	63 1/8	-1 1/8	58 1/4	+487.50	6,312.50

Details Remove Save Portfolio

Figure 10-5: My "fantasy portfolio" includes shares in Apple Computer, America Online, IBM and Intel. If only it was real. . .

Charting the Portfolio

One of the little-known features offered by AOL is its ability to save portfolios on a disk, providing fuel for electronic spreadsheet programs like Microsoft's Excel (see Figure 10-6).

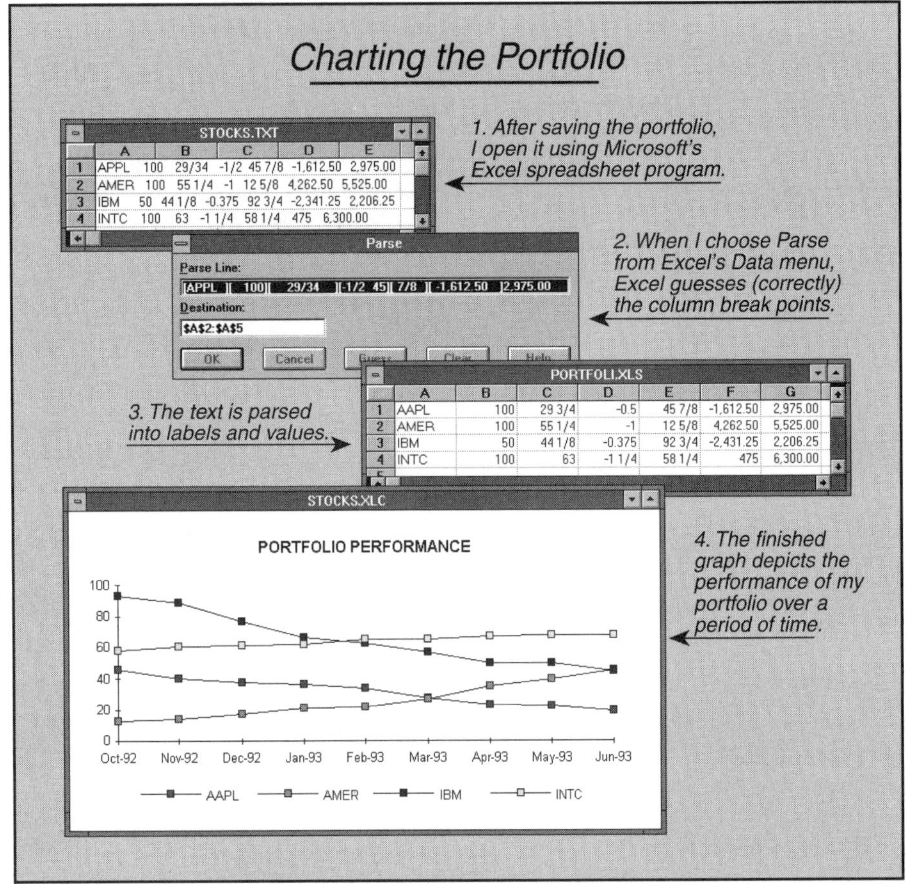

Figure 10-6: By saving my portfolio and using Excel's data parsing feature, I can graph my portfolio's performance over time. If you're an Excel user, read the sidebar for instructions.

To save a portfolio, click the Save Portfolio button in the Portfolio window (again, refer to Figure 10-5). America Online will then guide you through a standard Windows file-save procedure. The file is saved as ASCII text, but most standard spreadsheet programs have parsing features that can convert ASCII text into spreadsheet cells for easy graphing.

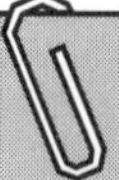

Graphing Instruction Manual

Although this is not an Excel manual, so many readers have written asking me to explain the charting procedure that I'll explain it—briefly—here:

1) Open a historical worksheet of your portfolio's investments' prices over time. If such a worksheet doesn't already exist, make a new one. The leftmost column of this worksheet should contain the issues' stock symbols; each column to the right thereafter should contain dates and selling prices for your investments. The topmost row should be reserved for dates, which you will enter. These instructions tell you how to save the current selling prices.

2) Use Excel to open the portfolio text file you saved via the instructions in the text. The data displayed will probably have to be parsed: Excel usually opens portfolio files without parsing.

3) To parse the data, select the cells in column A representing your issues. Don't select any of the cells to the right, or above or below these cells.

4) Choose Parse from Excel's Data menu. Excel will guess where to parse the data. It's always right. Click OK.

5) Select the column of information representing the current prices for your portfolio and copy them.

6) Use the Window menu to switch to your historical worksheet and paste the data into the appropriate cells. Enter the date in the blank cell above the data you've just pasted.

7) Save the worksheet before you quit. If you wish, use traditional Excel charting methods to construct the chart shown in Figure 10-6.

The TradePlus Gateway

Though you can pretend all you want, eventually you're going to want to make some investments, and that's what TradePlus is for. To get there, click the TradePlus icon displayed in Figure 10-2. Eventually you'll enter the gateway displayed in Figure 10-7. Interestingly, there is no keyword (at the moment) for this service.

Figure 10-7: The TradePlus gateway. It's here that you can buy and sell investments online.

```
Gateway Host

L15166

        - Welcome to E*Trade -
        - Copyright 1983-94 -
- 11:38 PM EDT  9/05/94 3885.58 -15.9

New games have begun and will
run thru Friday, 9/30.

- The Main Menu is Menu # 1 -
***  TYPE NUMBER TO SELECT  ......

Input:                                   Send
```

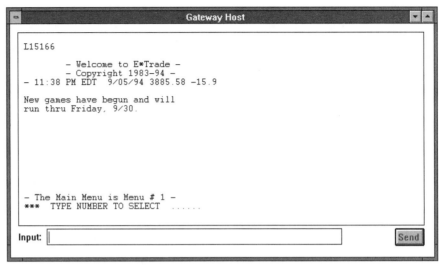

TradePlus is the home for the market investor. During trading hours, TradePlus tracks NYSE, AMEX and NASDAQ advances, declines and volume; Dow Jones indices (price, change, high, low); Standard & Poor's Index (put volume, call volume, ratio); most active issues; and percentage gainers and losers. TradePlus also monitors stock, options and commodities prices—all continuously updated on a 15-minute delay basis.

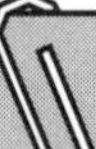

Gateways

The TradePlus gateway is only one of a number of gateways offered by AOL. The word, however, begs for definition. A gateway is a passage to another computer system, independent of AOL. Once you "enter" a gateway, AOL becomes passive and all communication occurs with the remote system. Most of these systems are textual (rather than graphical) and offer a menu-based interface similar to that pictured in Figure 10-7. America Online's graphical interface—utilizing the mouse, pull-down menus and windows—isn't very common in the online universe. Thousands of machines use the TradePlus system, and few offer the graphical potential your PC does. The TradePlus system has to serve them all, so its interface is structured around the lowest common denominator—the textual interface. You'll return to the AOL interface as soon as you exit the gateway; don't let the seemingly antiquated nature of the textual interface bother you.

You can buy and sell stocks online via TradePlus as well. The brokerage firm of Quick & Reilly offers discounted commissions and insures accounts up to $2.5 million. You will be assigned a personal broker and an automated portfolio management account. The portfolio management system maintains all your personal records and automatically updates your portfolio every time you buy or sell. Brokerage records are available online 24 hours a day, 7 days a week.

And, except for the commission you pay if you buy and sell real stocks online, all of this is free. You pay only your normal connect-time charges to AOL.

The Bulls & Bears Game

Regardless of whether you choose to invest real money, you're always welcome to participate in AOL's Bulls & Bears game. (The game is available via the keyword: BullsAndBears). Players invest $100,000 in game money in stocks or options of their choice. The game automatically maintains your portfolio, reflecting trading activity and current prices. Each month, contestants with the top three best-performing portfolios win free online time. There's no better education for the would-be investor, and the rewards are real, even if the investments are not.

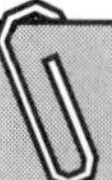

Escape

Many of the articles offered online are lengthy. And sometimes after reading the first few sentences of an article, you will find it's not what you're after. What do you do? Wait while the hourglass cursor spins on your screen, mocking your impatience?

Indeed not. You use the AOL command that means STOP! It works nearly everywhere on AOL and it's especially useful when long articles or lists threaten to make morning molasses out of your Derringdo DX-2.

This important command is, of course, Escape. Whenever you want to interrupt something, press Esc. It works for long articles, ponderous downloads, dreary mail and ceaseless searches. It's especially valuable when a sluggish sign-on sequence portends a noisy line and a need for redialing. It inspires a feeling of omnipotent power, and it will become your best online friend. Keep it in mind.

Morningstar Mutual Funds

I began investing a couple of years ago. I located a broker—Dave is his name—with whom I found mutual trust, and in whom I found a kindred soul. Trading through him has never been stressful.

As I would expect, Dave is extremely knowledgeable about the market—especially mutual funds and bonds, which is where I've done most of my investing. I asked him one day where he got his information. "Morningstar," he said. "It's an interdictory association," he said obliquely. That evening I looked up the meaning of the word "interdictory" and felt that I was right privileged to walk among the ranks of the plutocracy.

Then I peeked around AOL and found Morningstar there, complete with User's Guide and Guided Tour (see Figure 10-8). The plutocracy had come to the proletariat and the plutocrats didn't even know. Now I read Morningstar just as Dave does—and I don't tell him that I do. Kindredness warrants cynicism when my money's involved.

Hoover's Business Resources

Morningstar isn't the only investor's reference available on AOL. If your investing interests exceed mutual funds and bonds, investigate Hoover's Business Resources (keyword: Hoovers). Hoover's collection of searchable database includes profiles of over 1,100 of the largest, most influential, and fastest-growing public and private companies in the world. In addition, monthly updates on these and 6,200 other major companies are provided. They've even got business rankings from a number of perspectives and industry profiles. The voice is lively and interesting; the data is pertinent to every investor; and the price—free of surcharges to AOL members—is as affordable as old clothes used to be.

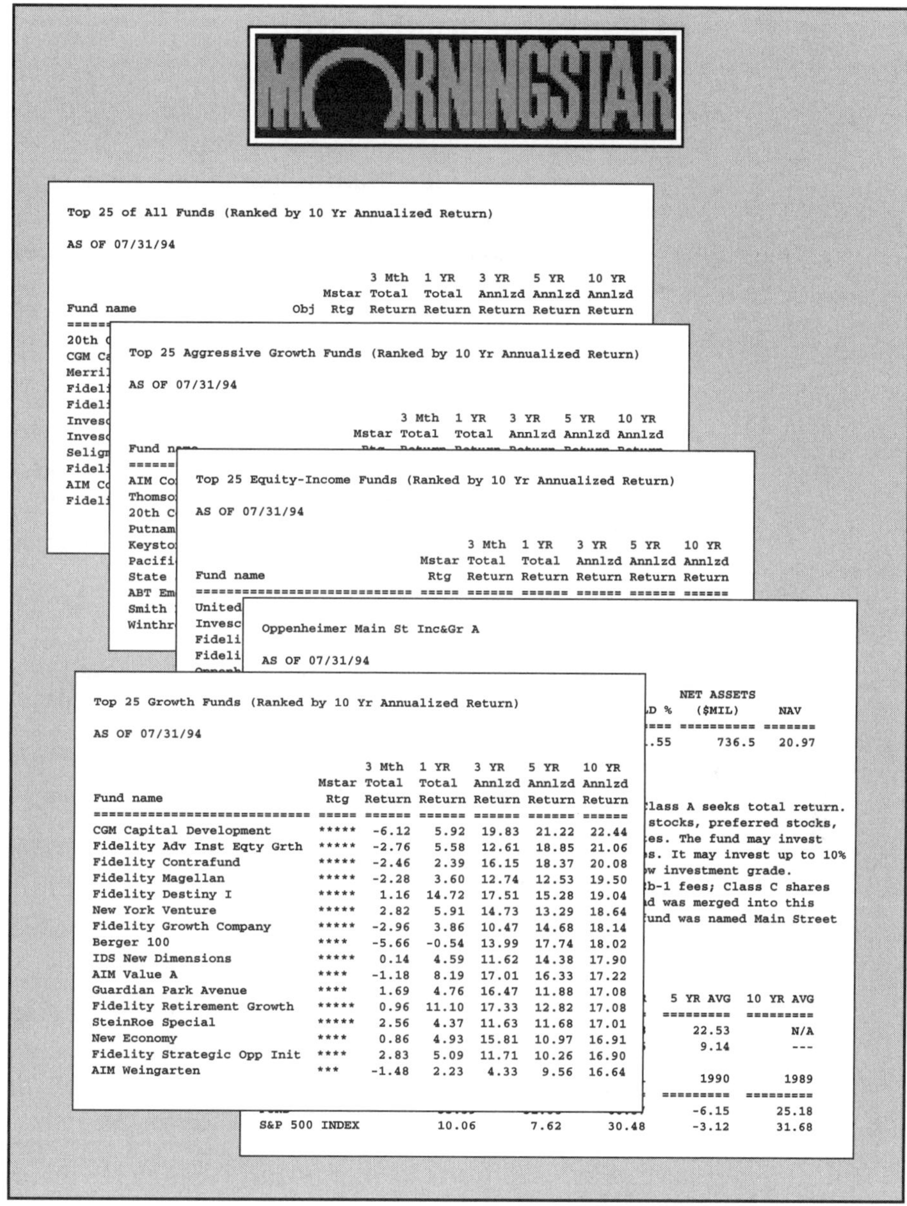

MORNINGSTAR
Top 25 of All Funds (Ranked by 10 Yr Annualized Return)
AS OF 07/31/94
Top 25 Aggressive Growth Funds (Ranked by 10 Yr Annualized Return)
AS OF 07/31/94
Top 25 Equity-Income Funds (Ranked by 10 Yr Annualized Return)
AS OF 07/31/94
Oppenheimer Main St Inc&Gr A
AS OF 07/31/94

Top 25 Growth Funds (Ranked by 10 Yr Annualized Return)

AS OF 07/31/94

Fund name	Mstar Rtg	3 Mth Total Return	1 YR Total Return	3 YR Annlzd Return	5 YR Annlzd Return	10 YR Annlzd Return
CGM Capital Development	*****	-6.12	5.92	19.83	21.22	22.44
Fidelity Adv Inst Eqty Grth	*****	-2.76	5.58	12.61	18.85	21.06
Fidelity Contrafund	*****	-2.46	2.39	16.15	18.37	20.08
Fidelity Magellan	*****	-2.28	3.60	12.74	12.53	19.50
Fidelity Destiny I	*****	1.16	14.72	17.51	15.28	19.04
New York Venture	*****	2.82	5.91	14.73	13.29	18.64
Fidelity Growth Company	*****	-2.96	3.86	10.47	14.68	18.14
Berger 100	****	-5.66	-0.54	13.99	17.74	18.02
IDS New Dimensions	*****	0.14	4.59	11.62	14.38	17.90
AIM Value A	****	-1.18	8.19	17.01	16.33	17.22
Guardian Park Avenue	****	1.69	4.76	16.47	11.88	17.08
Fidelity Retirement Growth	*****	0.96	11.10	17.33	12.82	17.08
SteinRoe Special	*****	2.56	4.37	11.63	11.68	17.01
New Economy	****	0.86	4.93	15.81	10.97	16.91
Fidelity Strategic Opp Init	****	2.83	5.09	11.71	10.26	16.90
AIM Weingarten	***	-1.48	2.23	4.33	9.56	16.64

Figure 10-8: Morningstar offers data, publications and software for analysis of over 3,800 mutual funds, closed-end funds, variable annuities, variable life, variable universal life, Japanese equities, and American Depository Receipts. Use the keyword: Morningstar.

The Decision Point Forum

Now we're getting serious. The Decision Point Forum provides a platform and materials to help you learn, refine and profitably utilize technical analysis skills and market timing information. You're encouraged to assimilate information and opinions, then arrive at your own conclusions. There are no magic systems here, only aids that help you make your own decisions. And there are plenty of them:

- The buy/sell signals generated by the forum's timing models are summarized in the Decision Point Alert, updated each week on Saturday mornings.
- Each market day the forum posts chart tables of the 150 stocks and 160 mutual funds that they're following. Featured are four proprietary timing models that can help you identify stocks that might be in the beginnings of a new trend. Two-year charts are provided for the stocks and funds in this portfolio.
- There are message boards, where you can post questions and exchange ideas with other members regarding the technical condition of the market and the stocks you own or follow.
- There is a vast collection of chart libraries (see Figure 10-9) containing files of stock, mutual fund, and market indicator charts. These are updated each week.
- A collection of historical data files of market indicators and indexes is available for download in the database libraries so that you can construct your own charts. This data is also updated weekly.
- A collection of essays/articles covering various subjects is available in the reading libraries. Of particular importance is the "Timing Model Documentation"—a thorough explanation of how to use the timing models found elsewhere in the forum.
- The Top Advisors' Corner features comments by prominent stock market advisors.
- The Investor's Resource Center lists sources of investing information, products and services.

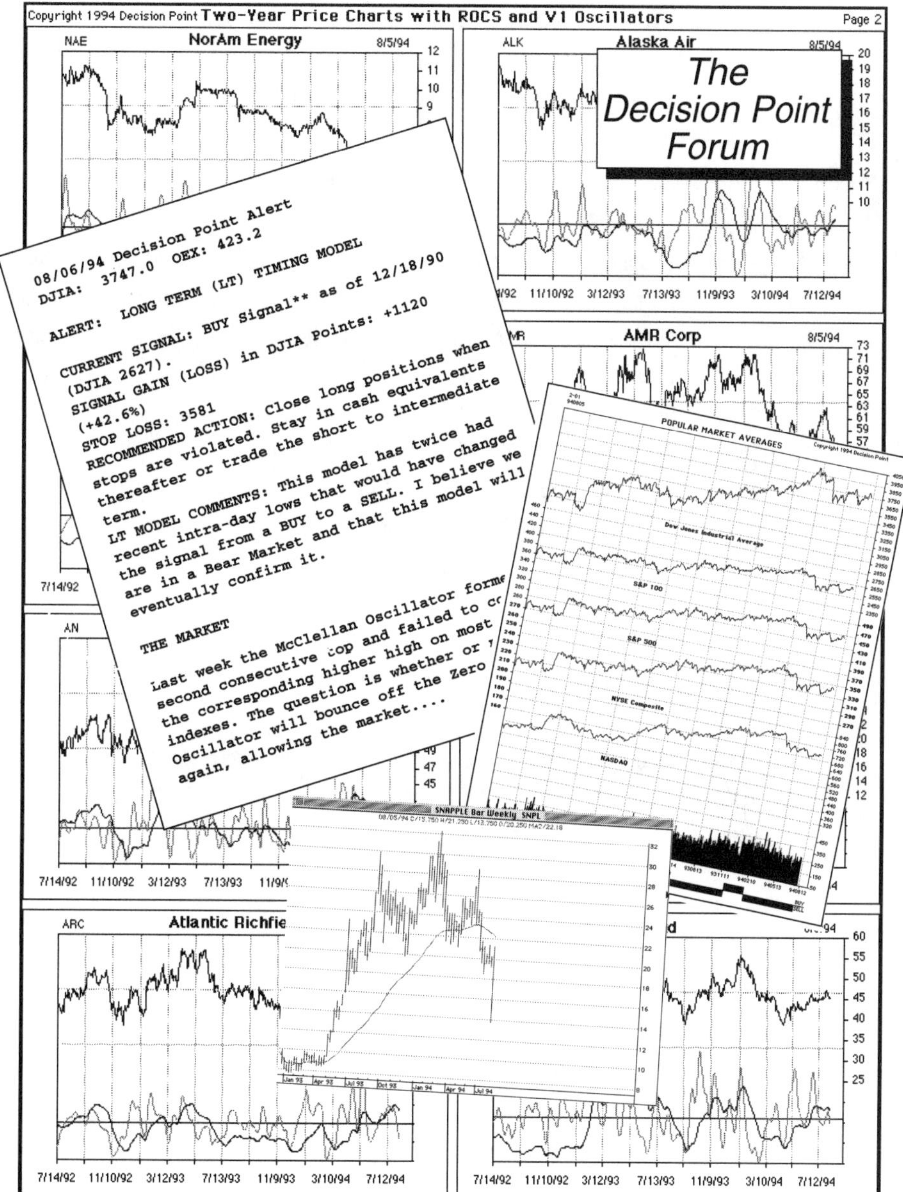

Figure 10-9: The Decision Point Forum is the home of America Online's stock market charts. There are hundreds of them here, and they're all available for downloading and viewing with your America Online software.

If you're a serious investor—or if you've considering investments in the stock or mutual funds markets, the Decision Point Forum should be a frequent stop in your AOL journey.

Free of Extra Charges

Most commercial online services offer some of the news and finance features found on AOL. None offers them all, however, and none offers them at the price AOL charges: nothing beyond the normal connect-time charges. This is unique to AOL. In this industry the word "premium" usually translates to "extra charge." Aside from sending the occasional fax or piece of mail via the US Post Office (which is discussed in Chapter 3, "Electronic Mail"), you will rarely find an extra charge for any of the services AOL offers. With all the money you save, perhaps you can invest in the stock market or buy a small business. If you do, AOL stands ready to help—at no extra charge, of course.

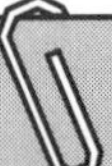

***Worth* Magazine**

No serious investor should conclude an AOL journey without exploring the articles of Worth Online, the electronic version of *Worth* magazine, the magazine of financial intelligence. Here you can download current and past articles written by such Wall Street experts as Peter Lynch, Graef Crystal, Gretchen Morgenson, Bob Clark, Jim Jubak and John Rothchild. It's available in the main Personal Finance window, or by using the keyword: Worth.

Real Estate Online

If I'm ever again in the market for real estate, this is the first place I'll go for information. Real Estate Online, AOL's real estate forum, offers tips on buying a home, information on mortgage loans, property listings in all 50 states and a comprehensive collection of articles for reading (see Figure 10-10).

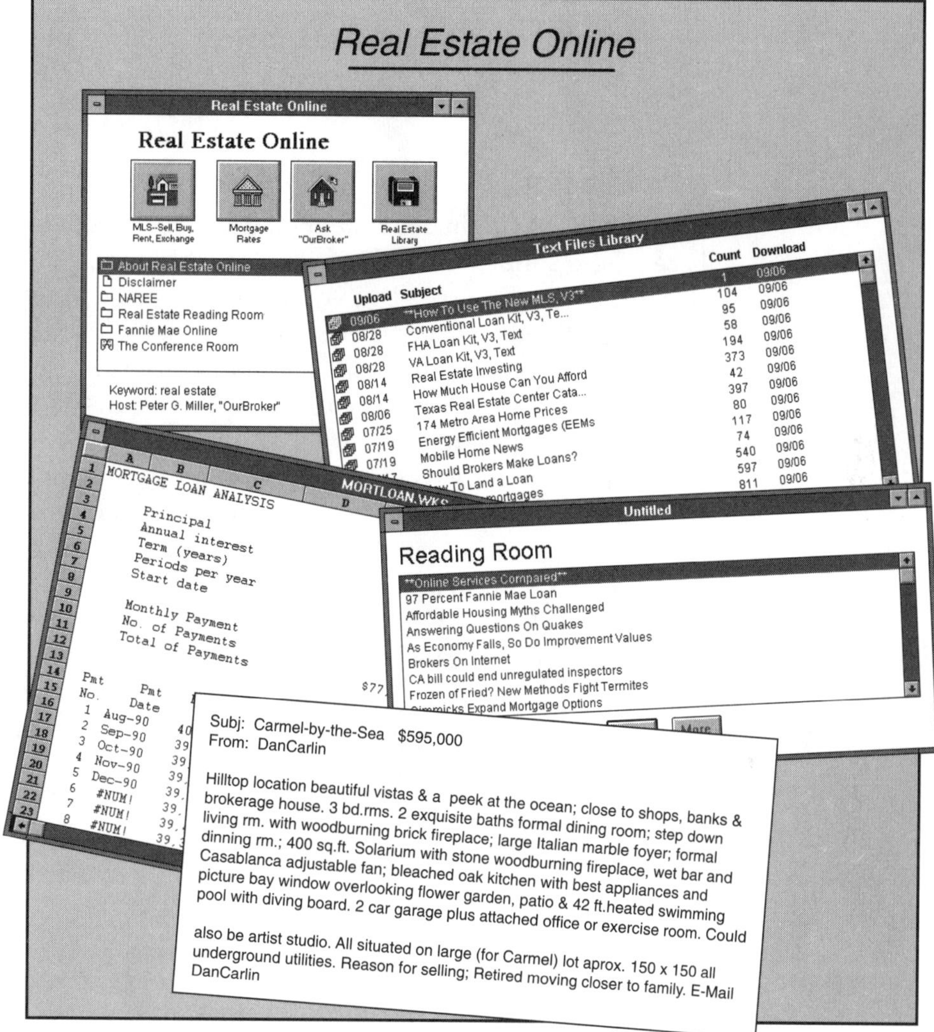

Figure 10-10: Real Estate Online offers everything a home buyer (or seller) will ever need. In a 15-minute visit, I found more than a dozen articles for reading, a library of PC programs—including a mortgage loan analysis spreadsheet for Excel—and an alert regarding changes in FHA loan limits.

The person responsible for this wealth of information is Peter G. Miller, author of six real estate books, two of which were on the top-10 best-selling nonfiction book list during the summer of 1992. Miller's forum features weekly commentaries, home prices and trends in all 50 states, current mortgage rate listings and a board featuring properties for sale. You'll find handy financial programs in the library, and an "Ask Our Broker" board where you can obtain answers to those sticky real estate questions that simply can't be asked of brokers or agents who are involved in a transaction. Few personal transactions equal the monetary significance of buying or selling a home, and the real estate forum is one of the few unbiased sources of information available. It's as near as your computer (keyword: Real Estate).

Moving On

It's a disservice to the Personal Finance Department to end this chapter here. There's much more than I've described, and I don't want you to misinterpret my emphasis. I've tried to present the diversity of features offered by the department, not a listing of its best stuff.

Moreover, this department is scheduled for some major changes, most of which will appear before you receive this book. Buying and selling publicly-traded issues will change significantly, many of the portfolio commands will be improved (hint: check out Worth magazine's portfolio feature), new and improved news services are scheduled for inauguration soon, and the Motley Fool (keyword: Fool) is offering exceptional guidance for the new investor.

Too much time in the Personal Finance Department, however, can lead to information overload. By now you probably need a break. How about a respite: a cruise perhaps, or a journey to a land where no one has gone before. In Chapter 11, "Travel," we'll do just that.

CHAPTER 11

Travel

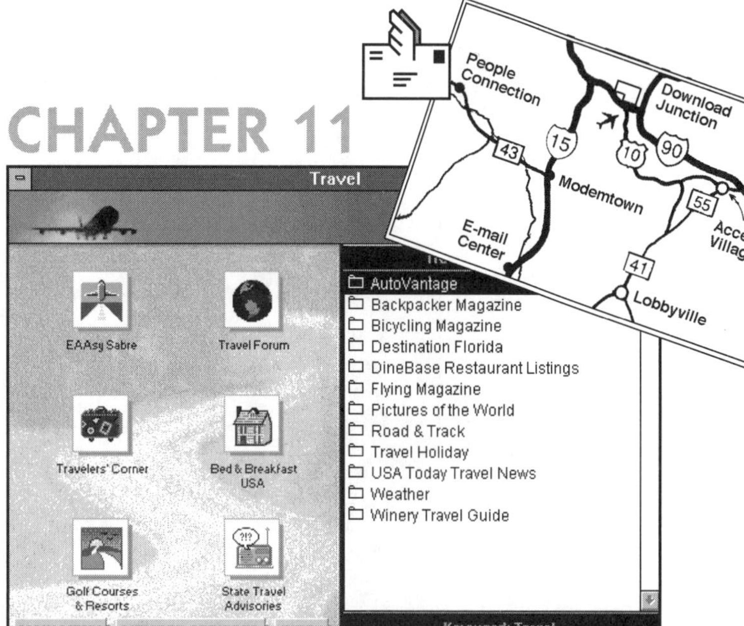

Who hasn't indulged in the "If I had a million dollars. . ." fantasy? My favorite is travel: South America, the British Isles, a blue water cruise, the Orient Express. . .

Heck, I'd be happy if someone just gave me a ticket to Tucumcari.

Of course, fantasies require money. That's why they're fantasies. If you want money-optional indulgences, try AOL's Travel Department. Not only can you indulge your fantasies here, you can actually commit them. You can book airline, car and hotel reservations; you can consult with other travelers before you depart; you can even buy a car. This place can really get expensive if you give it a chance. You'd better hide your credit card before you read any further.

As is so often the case, the montage of features in Figure 11-1 is incomplete, and we don't have space here to explore the entire department. If you're a traveler, get to know this department: it will add to the richness of your adventure, and more than likely reduce its cost.

The Travel Department is AOL's all-in-one travel venue. You can learn about your destination here, make your lodging and travel reservations, and even download pictures of it—all without leaving your keyboard. It's a must for the intrepid traveler. Click the Travel button on the Main Menu, or use the keyword: Travel.

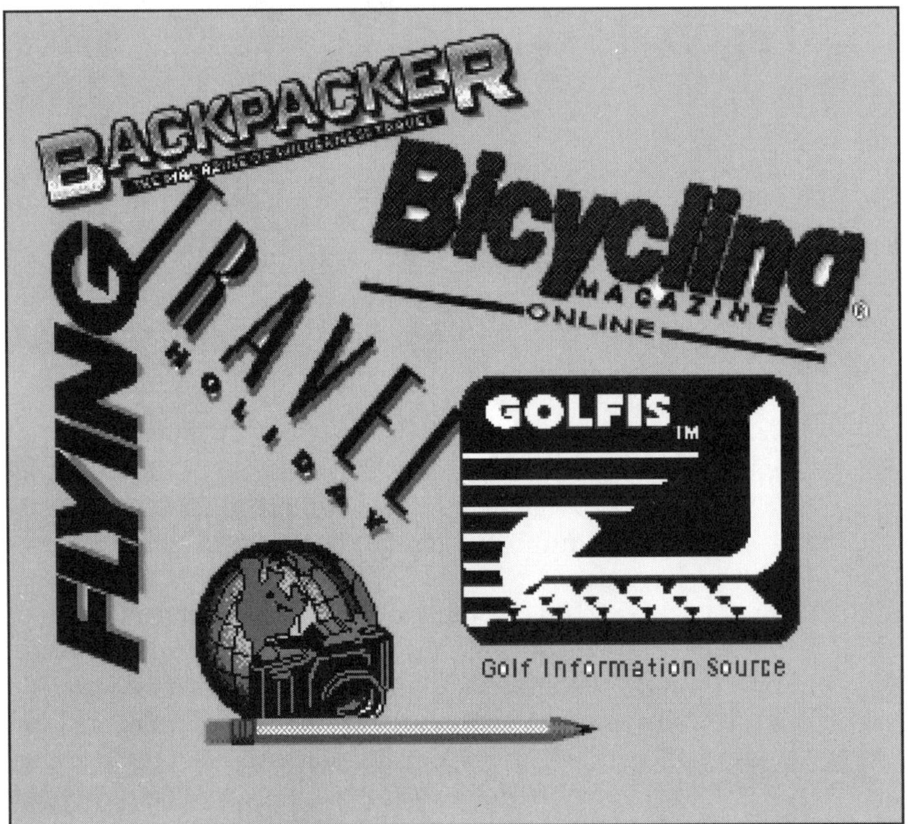

Figure 11-1: Logos for a few of the services you'll find in the Travel Department.

The EAASY SABRE Gateway

Here's another example of a gateway, though in this case we have a textual interface for it. American Airlines's SABRE reservations system is one of the few centralized travel reservations systems in America. As such, it's used by travel agents and airline reservation counters as well as AOL members. When you enter the EAASY SABRE gateway, you actually log on to the Sabre computer itself. America Online's computer network remains relatively passive until you exit the gateway.

Sabre software is designed to run on travel agents' terminals. Most travel agents use simple, text-only terminals, and Sabre reflects that simplicity. There are no graphics here: no windows, no pull-down windows, no dialog boxes—just the basics. You can put your mouse aside. You converse with the Sabre host (the term *host* refers to a remote computer to which your machine is connected) by responding to old-fashioned menus and arcane slash commands. /E, for instance, means Exit.

Being a professional system, Sabre is in no way abbreviated. Not only can you make airline reservations (on *any* airline, not just American), you can reserve automobiles and hotels as well (see Figure 11-2). Indeed, EAASY SABRE allows you to make reservations on over 350 airlines, reserve a room at over 27,000 hotels, or rent a car at any of nearly 60 car rental companies worldwide. . .all from your computer.

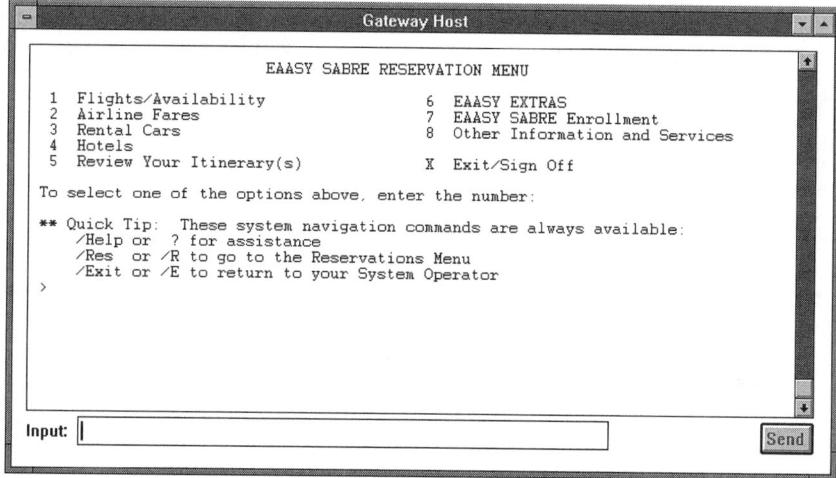

Figure 11-2: EAASY SABRE may not be pretty, but it's comprehensive, immediate, and oh-so-useful.

The first time my travel agent found out I was using Sabre, she was incredulous. She couldn't believe I was using my standard telephone line to access it, or that I was paying nothing but my normal AOL connect-time charges to use it. Not only is EAASY SABRE easy to use, it's a bargain as well.

Perhaps best of all, you don't have to be a SABRE member to poke around the EAASY SABRE system. Membership *is* required to make reservations, however, and becoming a member is easy. You don't have to be Someone Important, and membership doesn't cost a dime.

Finding a Flight

One of my favorite jaunts is a trip to North Carolina in the spring. They have some delectable cuisine there (to say nothing of the mint juleps), it's a comely place, and the natives talk with a lilt that could melt even

Jack Palance's heart. (Did I mention that my publisher is there too? And that they usually pay for the trip? It's amazing how a travel allowance can make a place seem suddenly endearing.) Let's use EAASY SABRE to see if there's a flight that will get me there (Figure 11-3).

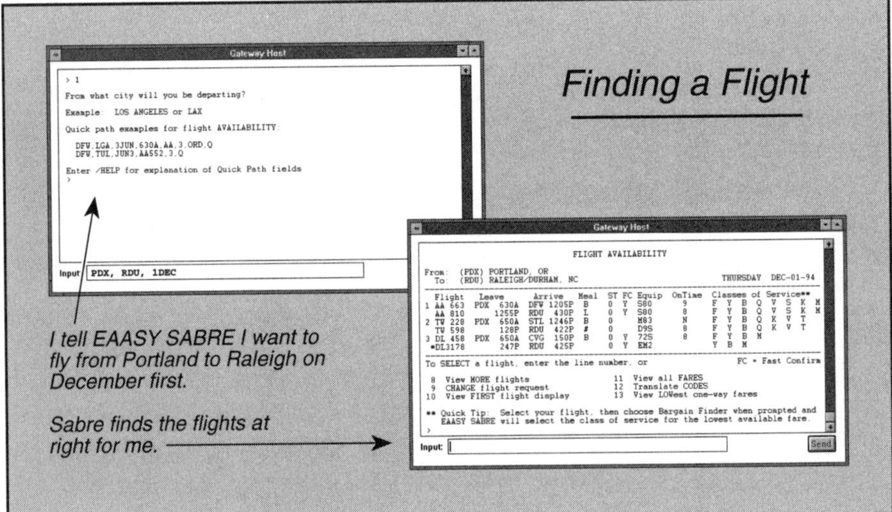

Figure 11-3: All I have to do is identify where and when I want to travel; EAASY SABRE supplies the how.

There are four points I should make about Figure 11-3. One, I didn't have to use the departure, destination and date codes (PDX, RDU, 1DEC) that you see in the top window. I could have answered the questions in plain English, one at a time, and SABRE would have determined my need. Two, EAASY SABRE found something like sixteen flights that met my criteria, though only three appear in Figure 11-3's lower window. Three, I can see how reliable each flight has been recently by looking at the On Time column. And four, I specified a date of December 1. Who wants to wait 'til spring?

Finding the Cost

Another 10 minutes on the system reveals the cost of not only the airline tickets, but the car rental and hotel as well (see Figure 11-4). These rates differ drastically (especially for car rentals, all of which offer essentially the same service), and Sabre practically begs you to do some comparison shopping.

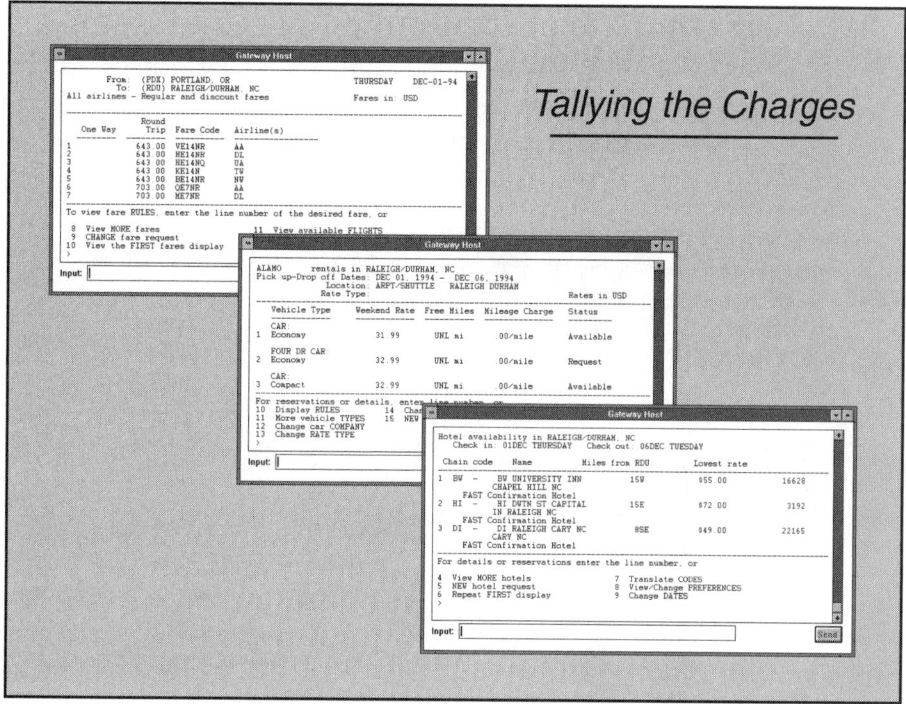

Figure 11-4: Let's see: $650 for the flight, $33 for the car and $55 a night for the hotel. North Carolina, here I come!

Booking the Reservations

Before you can book reservations, you need to sign up for a "membership" in EAASY SABRE. Though it sounds formal, membership amounts to little more than providing your credit card number and mailing address. As I mentioned before, membership in EAASY SABRE is free. Once you're a member, booking airlines, cars and hotels is an online event. EAASY SABRE establishes an itinerary for that trip (which you can review and print at any time), and within a few days provides confirmation numbers and (in the case of airline reservations) mails the tickets to you.

Not only is membership free, so is browsing the system. You pay only your normal AOL connect charges. Even if you don't plan to go anywhere, no one will tattle if you indulge in a little fantasy traveling. It's a great cure for the wintertime blues; and who knows, maybe you too will visit the beautiful Raleigh-Durham area of North Carolina. Sip a mint julep while you're there: there are none better in the South.

The Travel Forum

As long as we're in a traveling mood, let's check out the Travel Forum. Articles, message boards and a library offer a wealth of information and tips for the domestic or world traveler (see Figure 11-5).

Figure 11-5: The Travel Forum offers packing tips, a Bargain Box, great programs like Geoclock that show the current time in terms of daylight around the world, and much more.

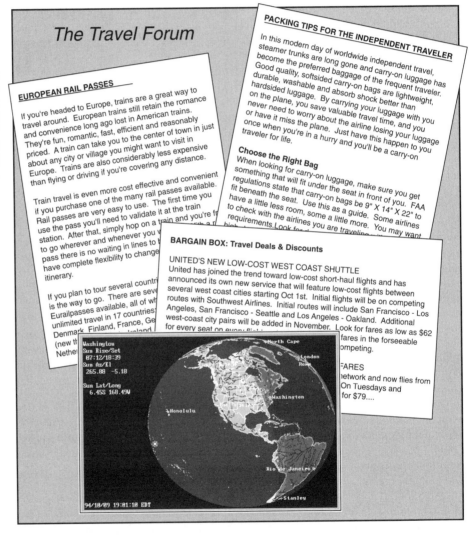

The Travel Forum

EUROPEAN RAIL PASSES

If you're headed to Europe, trains are a great way to travel around. European trains still retain the romance and convenience long ago lost in American trains. They're fun, romantic, fast, efficient and reasonably priced. A train can take you to the center of town in just about any city or village you might want to visit in Europe. Trains are also considerably less expensive than flying or driving if you're covering any distance.

Train travel is even more cost effective and convenient if you purchase one of the many rail passes available. Rail passes are very easy to use. The first time you use the pass you'll need to validate it at the train station. After that, simply hop on a train and you're f

PACKING TIPS FOR THE INDEPENDENT TRAVELER

In this modern day of worldwide independent travel, steamer trunks are long gone and carry-on luggage has become the preferred baggage of the frequent traveler. Good quality, softsided carry-on bags are lightweight, durable, washable and absorb shock better than hardsided luggage. By carrying your luggage with you on the plane, you save valuable travel time, and you never need to worry about the airline losing your luggage or have it miss the plane. Just have this happen to you once when you're in a hurry and you'll be a carry-on traveler for life.

Choose the Right Bag

When looking for carry-on luggage, make sure you get something that will fit under the seat in front of you. FAA regulations state that carry-on bags be 9" X 14" X 22" to fit beneath the seat. Use this as a guide. Some airlines have a little less room, some a little more. You may want to check with the airlines you are traveling

BARGAIN BOX: Travel Deals & Discounts

UNITED'S NEW LOW-COST WEST COAST SHUTTLE

United has joined the trend toward low-cost short-haul flights and has announced its own new service that will feature low-cost flights between several west coast cities starting Oct 1st. Initial flights will be on competing routes with Southwest Airlines. Initial routes will include San Francisco - Los Angeles, San Francisco - Seattle and Los Angeles - Oakland. Additional west-coast city pairs will be added in November. Look for fares as low as $62

Washington
Sun Rise/Set
07:12/18:39
Sun Az/El
265.88 -5.18
Sun Lat/Long
6.45S 168.49W
North Cape
London
Washington
Honolulu
Rio de Janeiro
Stanley
94/10/09 19:01:10 EDT

Are you looking for a romantic hideaway for your getaway weekend? Check the cruise message board. If you're looking for the best itinerary for your train trip through Europe, check the World Traveler message board. If you're traveling overseas, check out the U.S. State Department Travel Advisories, and the Forum's special events with travel experts. In-depth articles cover topics such as "How to find hotel discounts" and "Should I buy trip cancellation insurance?"

Travel plans, perhaps above all else, benefit from peer support. The Travel Forum is where you can solicit the advice of peers and pros alike. No travel plans are complete until you talk to those who have been there. For this purpose, check the Travel Forum's message boards. Lots of people travel, and most who do like to talk about it. Their comments are candid and relevant, and because it's a message board, everything is current.

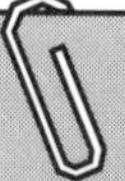

Getting Bumped

Ever been at a gate, waiting to board a flight, when the agent announces over the loudspeaker that the flight was overbooked and would anyone like to give up their seat? Usually some kind of motivation is included in the announcement, and the motivation is often lucrative. People with time on their hands can profit from these situations, as the (edited) thread of Travel Forum messages below indicates. . .

```
Subj: How to get bumped                    91-05-04 14:12:14 EDT
From: William40
```

```
Taking a long trip and you want to get bumped and have the time to
enjoy the experience? It's fun. Check all possible routes to your
destination. Make a list of all flight segments on all routes. Ask for
the load factors on each flight for each flight segment that is how
many seats have been booked. Divide this number by the total number of
seats available on each flight. Airlines always book more reserva-
tions than available seats because of no-shows. The number of avail-
able seats divided by the number of booked seats is the probability
that the flight is oversold. Multiply the probabilities for all of the
flight segments for each route and book your reservations on the route
which gives you the greatest probability of being bumped. Simple.
```

Subj: bumped 91-05-05 14:52:13 EDT

From: Fred44

It's not so complicated. And it's even more complicated.

Best flights are Fri & Sun night, pre holiday. Thanksgiving is the busiest. William40 idea is interesting and may produce the best mathematical model...but the carrier can substitute a larger or smaller aircraft at any time, for any reason. Therefore this model can fail.

A better way to determine "Actuals" (load) is to call reservations and indicate that you are an airline employee pass riding. The agent will tell you how difficult or easy it will be to get on board. If you are trying to get bumped you want to hear an answer like "impossible". That would be a good indicator.

I've managed to get bumped twice in one day (once from CO and then from AA) but it's not that easy. I wrote a newspaper article on a fellow who got bumped 26 times in one year.

Tip-o-the-wings to ya,

Fred44

Subj: airfare secrets 93-11-06 02:17:12 EST

From: Jeremy12

I used to be an airline ticket agent. One aspect of bumping overlooked here involves the 'history' of each particular flight. Every flight has its own history of no-shows and oversales, differences exist between even two flights on the same route, same airline but different days and times, and time of year. Some flights are authorized to be oversold to even twice their capacity at certain times of year. While it is obvious that holiday periods and weekends usually provide more occasion for bumping, it is not an exact science and formulas are not reliable.

Travelers' Corner

Don't confuse the Travel Forum with Travelers' Corner. Though the two serve similar purposes, there's a subtle but significant difference in their focus.

Arnie Weissmann began planning for an around-the-world journey in the early 1980s. To his frustration, he couldn't find information about his destinations. He knew how he was traveling, he knew what his costs were going to be, and he knew what to pack and how to dress. What he needed were friends, chaperones who were familiar with his destinations to tell him what to do, how to behave, how to find the good stuff, and how to avoid the bad. He needed what the Travelers' Corner calls 'destination profiles' (see Figure 11-6). The Travel Forum, in other words, concentrates on planning, transportation, and reservations. The Travelers' Corner focuses on what to do once you arrive. You should become familiar with both.

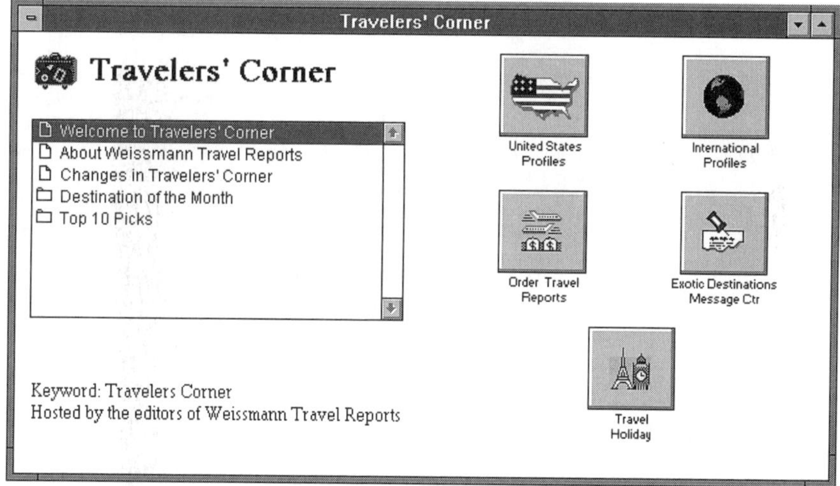

Figure 11-6: The Travelers' Corner offers destination information for thousands of locations around the world.

Look also at the Top 10 Picks and Destination of the Month features. If you're ready for travel but not sure where you want to go, the insights here are invaluable (see Figure 11-7).

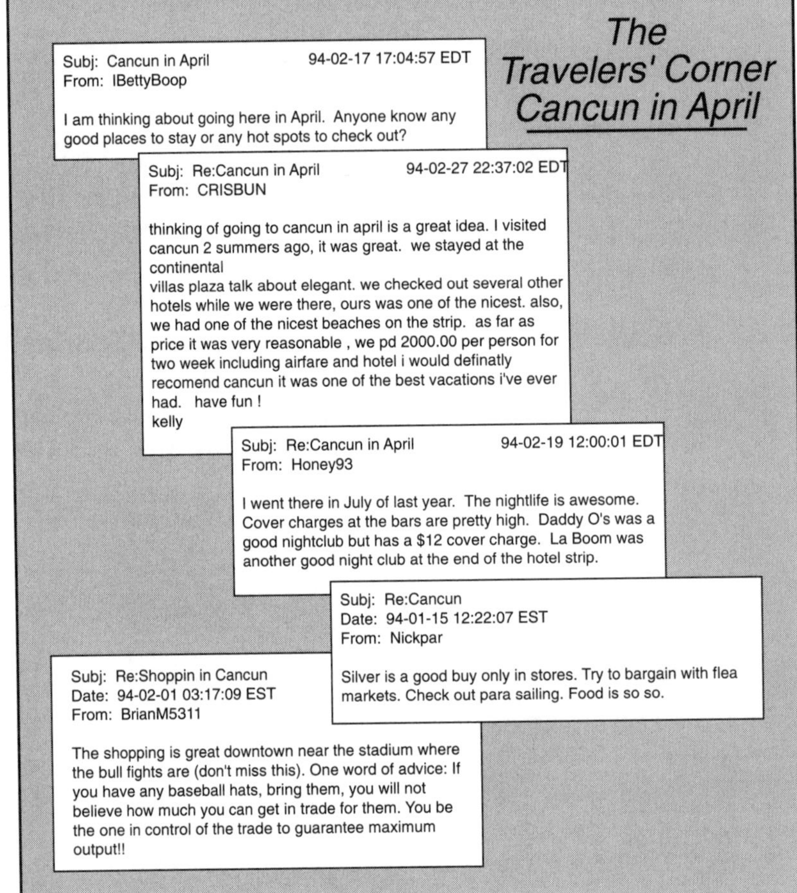
The Travelers' Corner
Cancun in April

Subj: Cancun in April 94-02-17 17:04:57 EDT
From: IBettyBoop

I am thinking about going here in April. Anyone know any good places to stay or any hot spots to check out?

Subj: Re:Cancun in April 94-02-27 22:37:02 EDT
From: CRISBUN

thinking of going to cancun in april is a great idea. I visited cancun 2 summers ago, it was great. we stayed at the continental
villas plaza talk about elegant. we checked out several other hotels while we were there, ours was one of the nicest. also, we had one of the nicest beaches on the strip. as far as price it was very reasonable , we pd 2000.00 per person for two week including airfare and hotel i would definatly recomend cancun it was one of the best vacations i've ever had. have fun !
kelly

Subj: Re:Cancun in April 94-02-19 12:00:01 EDT
From: Honey93

I went there in July of last year. The nightlife is awesome. Cover charges at the bars are pretty high. Daddy O's was a good nightclub but has a $12 cover charge. La Boom was another good night club at the end of the hotel strip.

Subj: Re:Cancun
Date: 94-01-15 12:22:07 EST
From: Nickpar

Silver is a good buy only in stores. Try to bargain with flea markets. Check out para sailing. Food is so so.

Subj: Re:Shoppin in Cancun
Date: 94-02-01 03:17:09 EST
From: BrianM5311

The shopping is great downtown near the stadium where the bull fights are (don't miss this). One word of advice: If you have any baseball hats, bring them, you will not believe how much you can get in trade for them. You be the one in control of the trade to guarantee maximum output!!

Figure 11-7: IBettyBoop was considering Cancun in April. She posted a single message and received not only the responses she requested, but some beneficial tips as well.

AutoVantage

Somewhere a few pages back I mentioned that most telecommunications services are textual in nature and much more difficult to use than AOL. With AutoVantage, I have an opportunity to show you what I mean. The moment you enter AutoVantage, everything changes. Gone are the attractive windows, menus and dialogs to which you've become accustomed. Even the mouse is essentially inactive. A window appears instead, populated with nothing but text (see Figure 11-8).

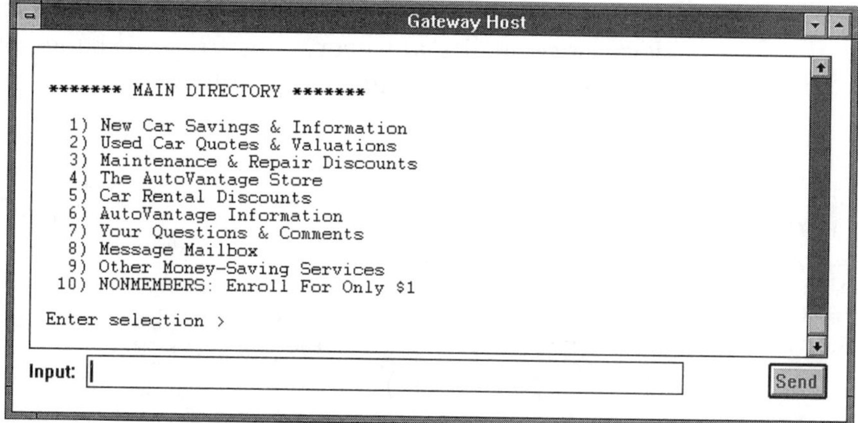

Figure 11-8: Textual interfaces aren't much fun and are generally more difficult to learn, but in the case of AutoVantage, it's worth the trouble.

AutoVantage is one of the few premium services (one for which an extra fee is charged) available to AOL members: its annual fee of $49 entitles you to the following:

- New car summaries that detail a model's features, pros and cons, specifications, available options, sticker and dealer prices, and road test highlights.
- Used car pricing onscreen, instantly, from the vast nationwide used car AutoVantage database. This service gives you the estimated selling and trade-in prices, an overview of the model, bargaining tips and recall history for any car up to 20 years old (see Figure 11-8).
- New cars at a discount. AutoVantage will arrange for you to purchase a car at a local dealer. On the average, a member who purchases a car this way saves $2,000, though savings vary, of course, with make and model.
- Locate nearby service centers online. AutoVantage members are able to access a list of all participating service centers within a 50-mile radius. Each listing highlights the address, phone number, contact name and discount offer made by the servicing agency. You can search by type of service, type of car needing service or the service center name.

- Prenegotiated national discounts. Savings of 10 to 20 percent off the local price on virtually everything from oil changes, tune-ups and transmissions to auto glass and body repair.

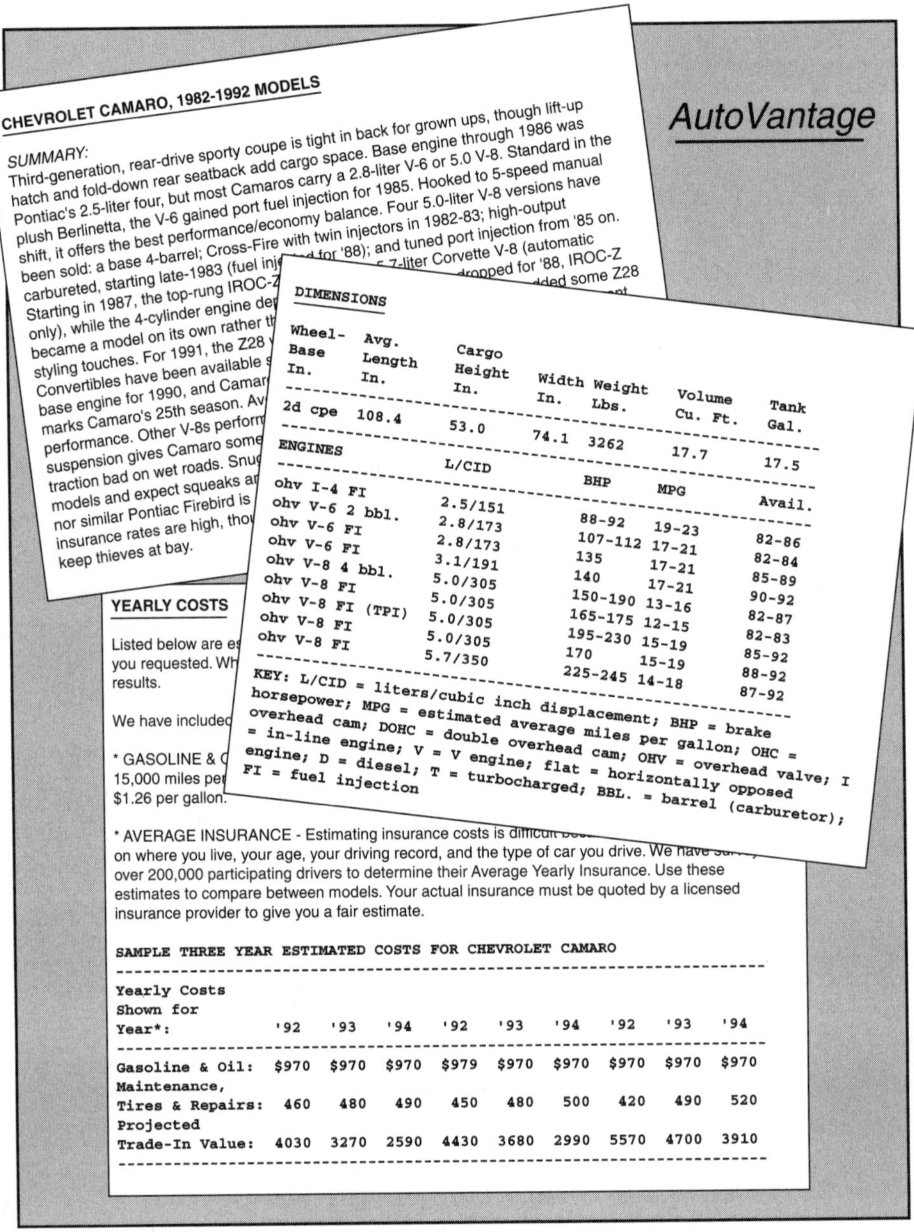

Figure 11-9: "Psst: Hey Buddy! Wanna buy a used Camaro?" Before you do, check out AutoVantage.

AutoVantage

CHEVROLET CAMARO, 1982-1992 MODELS

SUMMARY:
Third-generation, rear-drive sporty coupe is tight in back for grown ups, though lift-up
hatch and fold-down rear seatback add cargo space. Base engine through 1986 was
Pontiac's 2.5-liter four, but most Camaros carry a 2.8-liter V-6 or 5.0 V-8. Standard in the
plush Berlinetta, the V-6 gained port fuel injection for 1985. Hooked to 5-speed manual
shift, it offers the best performance/economy balance. Four 5.0-liter V-8 versions have
been sold: a base 4-barrel; Cross-Fire with twin injectors in 1982-83; high-output
carbureted, starting late-1983 (fuel inj... for '88); and tuned port injection from '85 on.
Starting in 1987, the top-rung IROC-Z ... 5.7-liter Corvette V-8 (automatic
only), while the 4-cylinder engine de... dropped for '88, IROC-Z
became a model on its own rather th... dded some Z28
styling touches. For 1991, the Z28 ...
Convertibles have been available ...
base engine for 1990, and Camar...
marks Camaro's 25th season. Av...
performance. Other V-8s perform...
suspension gives Camaro some...
traction bad on wet roads. Snu...
models and expect squeaks a...
nor similar Pontiac Firebird is ...
insurance rates are high, tho...
keep thieves at bay.

DIMENSIONS

	Wheel-Base In.	Avg. Length In.	Cargo Height In.	Width In.	Weight Lbs.	Volume Cu. Ft.	Tank Gal.
2d cpe	108.4		53.0	74.1	3262	17.7	17.5

ENGINES	L/CID	BHP	MPG	Avail.
ohv I-4 FI	2.5/151	88-92	19-23	82-86
ohv V-6 2 bbl.	2.8/173	107-112	17-21	82-84
ohv V-6 FI	2.8/173	135	17-21	85-89
ohv V-6 FI	3.1/191	140	17-21	90-92
ohv V-8 4 bbl.	5.0/305	150-190	13-16	82-87
ohv V-8 FI	5.0/305	165-175	12-15	82-83
ohv V-8 FI (TPI)	5.0/305	195-230	15-19	85-92
ohv V-8 FI	5.0/305	170	15-19	88-92
ohv V-8 FI	5.7/350	225-245	14-18	87-92

KEY: L/CID = liters/cubic inch displacement; BHP = brake horsepower; MPG = estimated average miles per gallon; OHC = overhead cam; DOHC = double overhead cam; OHV = overhead valve; I = in-line engine; V = V engine; flat = horizontally opposed engine; D = diesel; T = turbocharged; BBL. = barrel (carburetor); FI = fuel injection

YEARLY COSTS

Listed below are es... you requested. Wh... results.

We have included...

* GASOLINE & O... 15,000 miles per... $1.26 per gallon.

* AVERAGE INSURANCE - Estimating insurance costs is difficult ... on where you live, your age, your driving record, and the type of car you drive. We have ... over 200,000 participating drivers to determine their Average Yearly Insurance. Use these estimates to compare between models. Your actual insurance must be quoted by a licensed insurance provider to give you a fair estimate.

SAMPLE THREE YEAR ESTIMATED COSTS FOR CHEVROLET CAMARO

Yearly Costs Shown for Year*:	'92	'93	'94	'92	'93	'94	'92	'93	'94
Gasoline & Oil:	$970	$970	$970	$979	$970	$970	$970	$970	$970
Maintenance, Tires & Repairs:	460	480	490	450	480	500	420	490	520
Projected Trade-In Value:	4030	3270	2590	4430	3680	2990	5570	4700	3910

Premium services are scarce on AOL. So are textual interfaces. Nonetheless, AutoVantage might well pay for itself through the money you'll save on regular maintenance and service, and it certainly pays for itself the first time you buy or sell a car—it's probably the second-largest financial transaction of our lives (for the largest—real estate—see Chapter 10, "Personal Finance"), and most of us know very little about the business. If all this makes you a little nervous (and it should), investigate AutoVantage. It helps to even the score.

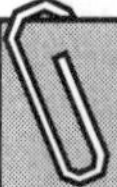

Your Wallet is Safe at AOL

All of this talk about premium services, buying cars and booking airline tickets may make you a little squeamish: "Does my AOL membership obligate me for anything beyond the standard monthly fee and connect charges?" No, not at all. All of the additional-expense items I've discussed in this chapter are voluntary—not at all requisite to membership in AOL. This is the Travel Department, after all, and most travel is discretionary. . .and an additional expense.

Pictures of the World

Before I conclude this chapter, I must call your attention to Pictures of the World (keyword: Pictures). Carl and Ann Purcell are freelance photographers whose work appears in newspapers and magazines around the world. In a word, their work is magnificent. It's especially radiant when it's displayed on a high-resolution color screen. I'm not the only one with this opinion: when I last checked this forum, nearly 3,000 people had downloaded the Purcells' image of the Golden Gate Bridge!

America Online is sprinkled with spangles of magnificence, like evening gowns at the Academy Awards. But unlike the Academy Awards, you have to look around to find AOL's spangles. Pictures of the World is one of them.

Figure 11-10: The perfect scene for the conclusion of the travel chapter. The couple with the dog in the moonlight is one of thousands of images available in the Pictures of the World forum.

Moving On

The Travel Department is one of the most utilitarian features AOL offers. A few hours spent here can save you hundreds of dollars and hours of frustration once you're on the road. Visit this place before your next vacation. As Karl Malden says: "Don't leave home without it."

Planning, however, is one thing. There's a lot to be learned from spontaneous experiences as well, especially those involving a lively exchange of views and experiences among people of widely varying backgrounds and interests. People Connection is the real-time headquarters of AOL, and it's a journey of sorts itself. Like all journeys, however, it's best to travel prepared. Your tour guide for People Connection begins on the next page. . . .

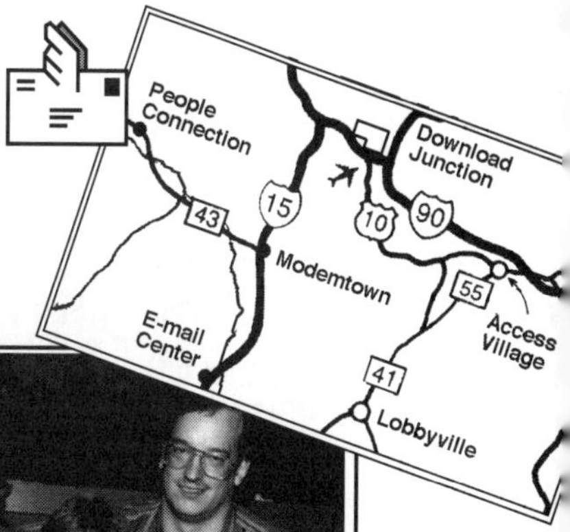

CHAPTER 12

People Connection

People Connection is the real-time headquarters of AOL. This is not the home of message boards and e-mail: communication here is as immediate as a telephone conversation. Unlike telephone conversations, however, with People Connection any number of people can be involved.

People Connection is the heart of the AOL community. It is here you make the enduring friendships that keep you coming back, day after day. Here, in a "diner," you can order a short stack and a cup of coffee, and talk over the weekend ahead. You can also sip a brew in a "pub" after a long day on the job. There are "events" here as well, where you can interview eminent guests and hobnob with luminaries.

Doesn't that sound like a community to you? This isn't couch-potato entertainment, this is *interactive* telecommunication—where imagination and participation are contagious and the concept of community reaches its most eloquent expression.

It sure beats reruns.

Proving that AOLers do exist in real life, a photo of seven members at the Las Vegas AOL gathering in January 1994. Top row (L to R): Trevayne, NealnJanet (2 people). Bottom row (L to R): WaterLily, CaNurse, Vrroom, Kunphuzed.

This photo (along with thousands of others) appears in the Gallery, a feature of the People Connection. To get to People Connection, press Ctrl+L, or click the People Connection button in the Main Menu window.

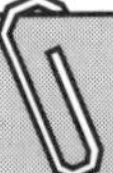

A Haven for Shy People

America Online is a haven for shy people. Shy people usually like other people, and they're likable themselves; they just don't do well with strangers. Most shy people want to make friends—and all friends were once strangers—but they aren't very adept at doing it.

This is why shy people like AOL. Nobody can see them online, nobody seems to notice if they don't talk much, and if they're uncomfortable, they can always escape at any time—just by signing off. Perhaps best of all, if you're a shy person, you can use a *nom de plume* and no one will even know who you are. There's a bit of masquerade ball in People Connection: you can wear the mask of a different screen name and be whatever or whomever you want. There's something comforting yet exciting about those possibilities.

Shy people can begin the AOL journey in a "safe" place like a forum, where no one's the wiser when they read a few forum messages or download a file or two. The next step would be to make an online friend and exchange some mail. Regardless of the path taken, it takes some time to work up the courage to venture into People Connection, since that invariably means ending up in a room full of strangers. This is not where shy people feel their most comfortable.

The irony is that shy folks love People Connection once they become acquainted with it. It's the perfect outlet for years of pent-up sociability. I'm a shy person. It took me months to work up to People Connection. Yet now it's one of my greatest rewards. I go there whenever I have time. You will too, once you get the hang of it.

The Lobby

Unlike the other departments we've explored, a visit to People Connection requires first passing through the "Lobby." The Lobby is one of AOL's so-called *chat rooms,* where real people communicate in real time. No messages are left here. There are no files to download. America Online's Lobby is similar to the lobby of a hotel: it's an area people pass through, often on their way to some other destination. Every so often, people bump into an acquaintance, or just sit there a moment to rest.

Entering the Lobby

To begin our People Connection adventure, click the whisper-in-the-ear button on the Flashbar, choose People Connection from the Main Menu window, choose Lobby from the Go To menu, use the keyword: Lobby, or press Ctrl+L. No matter which method you use, you will soon find yourself in the Lobby (see Figure 12-1).

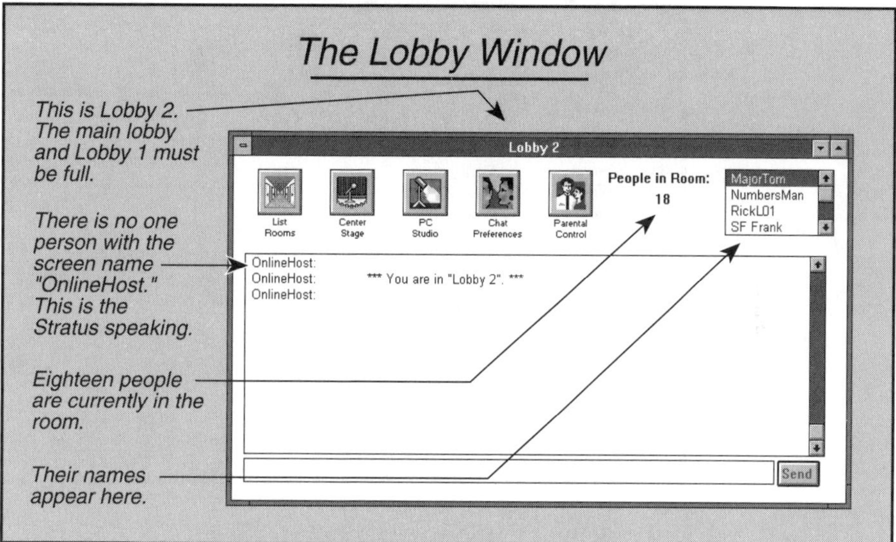

Figure 12-1: The Lobby screen seems empty just after I enter.

Note that the message in the chat room window pictured in Figure 12-1 says "You are in Lobby 2." When I entered the Lobby, AOL routed me to Lobby 2. This happens whenever traffic on the system is heavy. When the main Lobby reaches capacity (rooms are considered filled when they contain 23 members), AOL places people in the secondary lobby—Lobby 1. It too must have filled by the time I arrived, so I got placed in Lobby 2. Note that it was also approaching capacity, so new arrivals were about to be routed into yet another lobby. This isn't uncommon. There are often a dozen or more lobbies in operation at any one time.

Also note that of the 18 people in Lobby 2 at the time, a few of their names appear in the scroll box in the upper right corner of Figure 12-1's window. My preferences are set to arrange these names alphabetically (we'll discuss chat room preferences later on). Your scroll box may list the members in the order they appear.

Finally, note that there is no text in the main (conversation) portion of the window other than the announcement telling me where I am. The only true conversation appearing here occurs after my arrival, and

I have just walked in the door. That situation changes the moment I speak (see Figure 12-2).

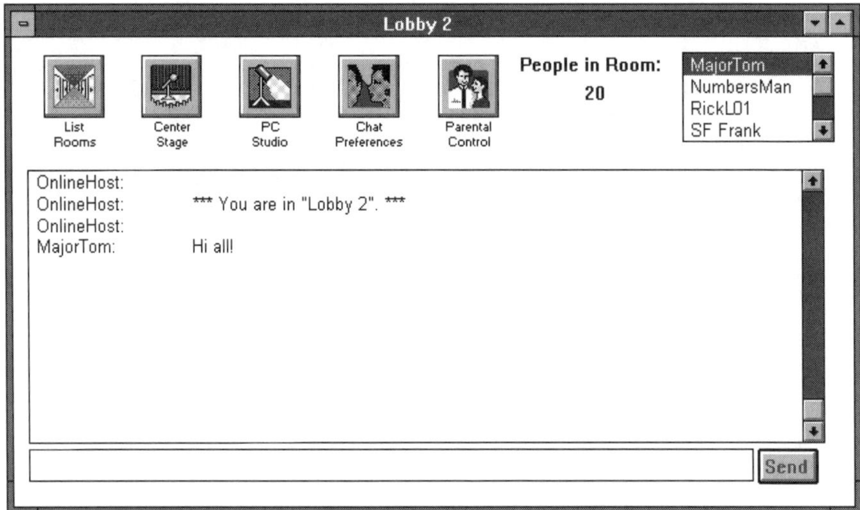

Figure 12-2: No matter how shy you're feeling, say hello when you enter a room.

Look again at Figure 12-2. This lobby is active today. People are rushing through it with hardly a pause. By the time I've said hello, in a matter of seconds, two more people have arrived. America Online's lobbies are something like a hotel lobby just after a large meeting has let out: people are scurrying everywhere. (This is particularly true during periods of heavy usage. The session pictured occurred on a Sunday morning. America Online is almost always busy on the weekends.)

Seconds later, a conversation has begun (see Figure 12-3).

Though I became immediately involved in a conversation, don't feel obligated to do so yourself. It's perfectly all right to say hello, then just watch for a while. In fact, I recommend it: it gives you a chance to adapt to the pace of the conversation—to get to know who is in the room and what they're like. Lobbies are good for this. They're lobbies, after all. It's perfectly natural for people to sit in a lobby and watch other people.

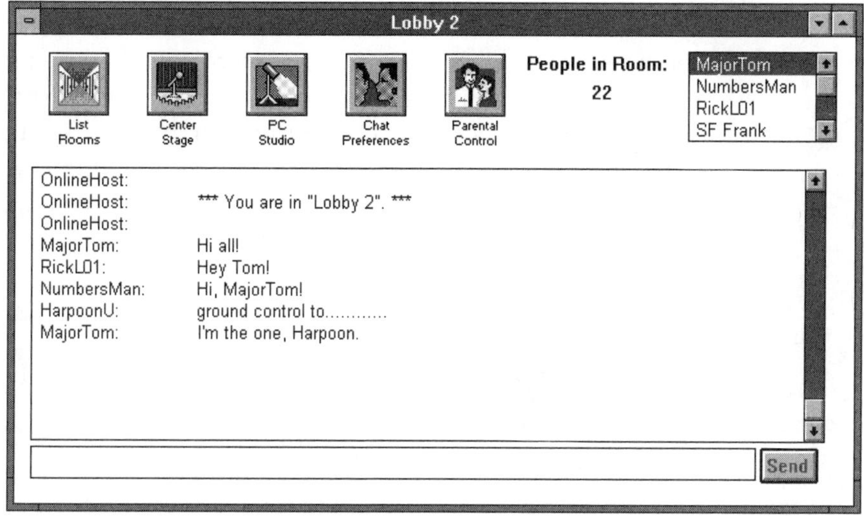
Lobby 2
List Rooms
Center Stage
PC Studio
Chat Preferences
Parental Control
People in Room:
22
MajorTom
NumbersMan
RickL01
SF Frank
OnlineHost:
OnlineHost: *** You are in "Lobby 2". ***
OnlineHost:
MajorTom: Hi all!
RickL01: Hey Tom!
NumbersMan: Hi, MajorTom!
HarpoonU: ground control to............
MajorTom: I'm the one, Harpoon.
Send

Figure 12-3: Catchy screen names come in handy when you first enter a room.

Guides

To carry my hotel lobby analogy a bit further, you might find a "concierge" there—a *Guide*—to answer your questions. Like a real-life hotel concierge, AOL's Guides are chosen for their knowledge of the territory and their friendly personalities. Watch the conversation for a while. No doubt you'll soon see someone with the word "Guide" in his or her screen name. More likely, a Guide will welcome you to the room.

Take a moment to look back at Figure 3-11. Do you see the Guide there? She welcomed me the moment I walked into the room and went out of her way to be of assistance. This is the way all Guides tend to be.

Guides are on duty from 9 A.M. to 6 A.M. (Eastern time), seven days a week. Since I already discussed them in Chapter 3 ("Online Help & the Members"), I won't go over their function again. But if you would like to review that section, turn back to that chapter (see page 64).

Exploring Other Public Rooms

As is the case with hotel lobbies, you won't want to stay in AOL's lobbies indefinitely. Lots of other rooms await you, where conversations are more focused and residents less transitory. These rooms can be great fun; all you have to do is find the one that suits you best.

The Event Rooms Guide

Room exploration should not be done randomly. The method I recommend is to become familiar with the event rooms before you enter them. To do this, click the PC Studio icon. It's the "spotlight" icon pictured in Figure 12-3. The PC Studio window opens with its selection of options. Double-click What's Happening This Week, then double-click Event Rooms Guide (see Figure 12-4).

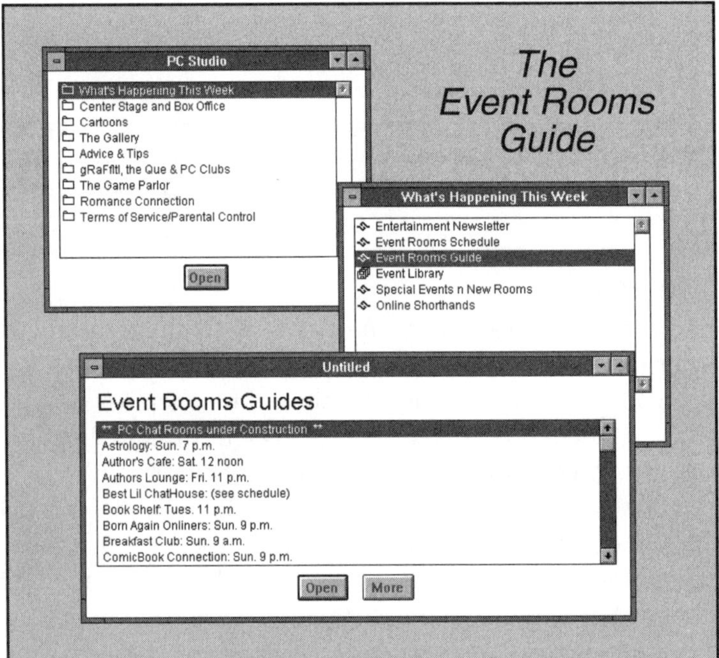

Figure 12-4: Become familiar with the Event Rooms Guide before you spend time in People Connection.

Many of the rooms available on AOL at any particular moment are spontaneously created by members. While spontaneous rooms can sometimes be entertaining and fun, they lack the focus found in the regularly scheduled event rooms. Event rooms are populated by hosts and regulars—people who have developed an online camaraderie and whose patter is familiar and neighborly. Hosts keep the conversation on track and offer a familiar "face" to anyone who visits. Hosts and regulars aren't cliquish, however; you're never made to feel unwelcome in one of AOL's event rooms. At this writing, 33 event rooms are listed (a number that's sure to change), ranging from the Best Lil ChatHouse to Parents R Us (see Figure 12-5). Shall we drop in on one?

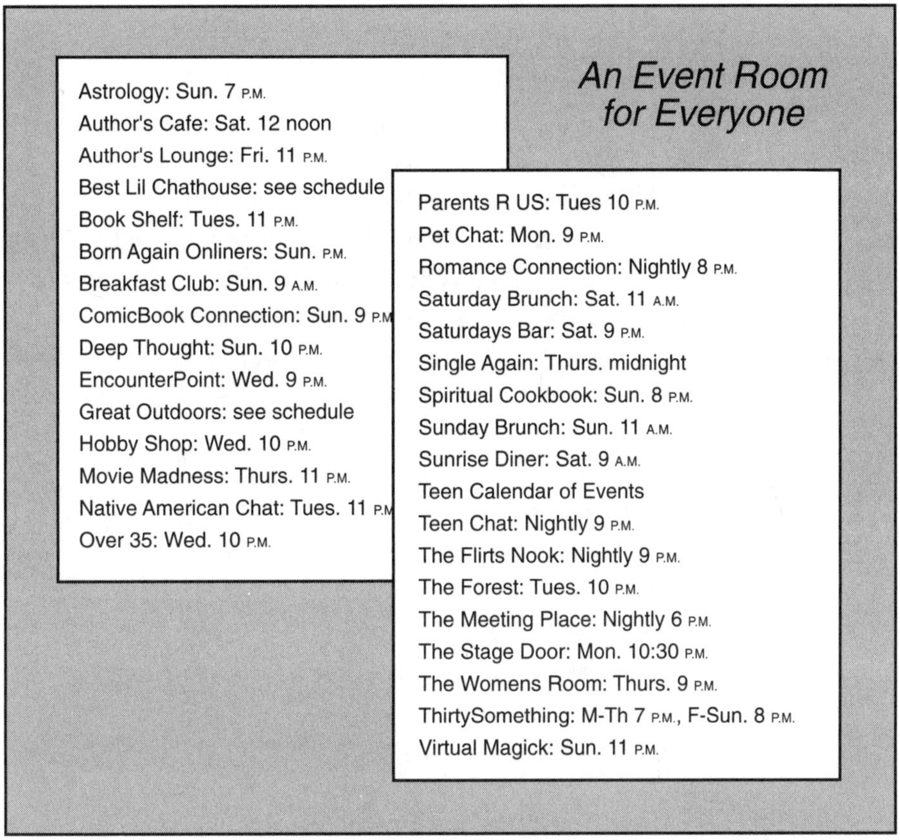

Figure 12-5: Thirty-three event rooms are scheduled this week. Double-click any one for a description.

An Event Room for Everyone
Astrology: Sun. 7 P.M.
Author's Cafe: Sat. 12 noon
Author's Lounge: Fri. 11 P.M.
Best Lil Chathouse: see schedule
Book Shelf: Tues. 11 P.M.
Born Again Onliners: Sun. P.M.
Breakfast Club: Sun. 9 A.M.
ComicBook Connection: Sun. 9 P.M
Deep Thought: Sun. 10 P.M.
EncounterPoint: Wed. 9 P.M.
Great Outdoors: see schedule
Hobby Shop: Wed. 10 P.M.
Movie Madness: Thurs. 11 P.M.
Native American Chat: Tues. 11 P.M
Over 35: Wed. 10 P.M.
Parents R US: Tues 10 P.M.
Pet Chat: Mon. 9 P.M.
Romance Connection: Nightly 8 P.M.
Saturday Brunch: Sat. 11 A.M.
Saturdays Bar: Sat. 9 P.M.
Single Again: Thurs. midnight
Spiritual Cookbook: Sun. 8 P.M.
Sunday Brunch: Sun. 11 A.M.
Sunrise Diner: Sat. 9 A.M.
Teen Calendar of Events
Teen Chat: Nightly 9 P.M.
The Flirts Nook: Nightly 9 P.M.
The Forest: Tues. 10 P.M.
The Meeting Place: Nightly 6 P.M.
The Stage Door: Mon. 10:30 P.M.
The Womens Room: Thurs. 9 P.M.
ThirtySomething: M-Th 7 P.M., F-Sun. 8 P.M.
Virtual Magick: Sun. 11 P.M.

One of my favorites is the Authors' Cafe, which meets every Saturday at 1 P.M. (Eastern time). You never know who'll turn up—familiar writers visit it regularly. America Online is a favorite haunt for writers, partly because of the Writers' Club (keyword: Writers) and partly because of its unique chat rooms such as the Authors' Cafe. The morning I visited, Tom Clancy dropped by, unscheduled and unannounced. The log of his appearance appears below. Typical of a chat room, smileys and shorthand abound. The symbol :) is a smile and :(is a frown (turn your head 90 degrees counterclockwise); and "LOL" means "laughing out loud." These can be modified with semicolons (winks) or D's (open-mouth smiles).

D P Gumby: Hi Tom!! :)
Tom Clancy: Good morning, Gumby
Tom Clancy: and Rosey

D P Gumby: Hey Tom..... you should think about joining us at the Allentown Bash!

Tom Clancy: when's the party?

D P Gumby: We've got about 100 onliners coming to the Bash.... it's gonna be a blast! :)

D P Gumby: August 21-23.... in Allentown PA!

Tom Clancy: busy then—doing something with Johns Hopkins

Tom Clancy: their summer camp for kids with cancer

ROSEY DAWN: Got any new books close to being released, Tom???

Data Dump3: <— showing a prospective customer the service :D

Tom Clancy: sorry, Rosey, no. I just came to terms with Putnam for #7, which I now have to write :(

Gleeful: Hiya Prospective Customer..;D

Data Dump3: Mornin' Tom :D

D P Gumby: I'll be first in line for it, Tom! :)

ROSEY DAWN: Oh well, anticipation makes it even better!

Tom Clancy: hello, Dump

Gleeful: lol Tom...you sold it and you haven't written it yet?? :D

Tom Clancy: that's normal

ROSEY DAWN: Heck, Glee—I'd *buy* it too — just knowing Tom is going to write it

Tom Clancy: the advance money is the literary equivalent of a gun to the head

Gleeful: Tom...doesn't that put a lot of pressure on you tho???

D P Gumby: I think, based on past performance...we can assume it'll be a good investment on behalf of the publisher

Tom Clancy: pressure....what do you think?

Tom Clancy: they pay you $XM, and you have to deliver a product, from inside your head, that's worth $XM

ROSEY DAWN: What's in your head, Tom, is worth at least $XXXXX

D P Gumby: Or more! :)

Tom Clancy: thanks, ma'am, I'd like to think so

Gleeful: awww Tom...You'll be just fine...just ask us..we know..D

Data Dump3: Sheesh Tom, I would hate to run around w/ a price on my head....let alone in it!!! ;D

Tom Clancy: don't worry, all writers are scared at this stage

Tom Clancy: we're SUPPOSED to be insecure, but not as badly as actors are

D P Gumby: That's a good point, Tom.. i do a lot of theater.. and it's awfully frightening sometimes!!

Tom Clancy: I speak a lot, and I always get stage fright

D P Gumby: they say the best of them do, Tom...

Tom Clancy: there's no dishonor in it, it happened to Olivier, too

Tom Clancy: it's a thoroughly crummy way to earn a living, but you do it because you love it, and because you have to do it

Gleeful: Have to Tom??

Tom Clancy: yeah, it's my mission in life, it's what I do

Rich OO: Money is a great motivator. :)

Gleeful: Tom...do you give a lot of talks??

Tom Clancy: quite a few, yes

Rich OO: Tom..I always draw a blank til the speech is over,,,I have no idea what I've said. :)

Gleeful: Are books usually the subject or something else, Tom?

Tom Clancy: me, too, Rich

Tom Clancy: Glee, I just get up there and ramble

Tom Clancy: All my speaking money goes to my kids' school

Gleeful: Good place for it to go.;D

ROSEY DAWN: Will you run for President, Tom????

GATEWAY: You have my vote, Tom!

Tom Clancy: Rosey, do I LOOK that STUPID?????

Gleeful: See ya'll later!! I have an appt to keep..;D

Gleeful: Tom..it was nice to meet you..:D

AFC Doug: <— off to jump out of an airplane. :D

Tom Clancy: don't forget the chute, pal

D P Gumby: Time for me to run... see y'all later! Take care, Tom!

Tom Clancy: see ya

ROSEY DAWN: well—time for me to be productive!

ROSEY DAWN: take care all!!!!! nice seeing you again, Tom

Tom Clancy: Bye, all

The Event Rooms Schedule

The Event Rooms Schedule is posted in the PC Studio along with the Event Rooms Guide. Look again at the center window in Figure 12-4: do you see the schedule there? Double-click it to view it. The week's schedules are pictured in Figure 12-6.

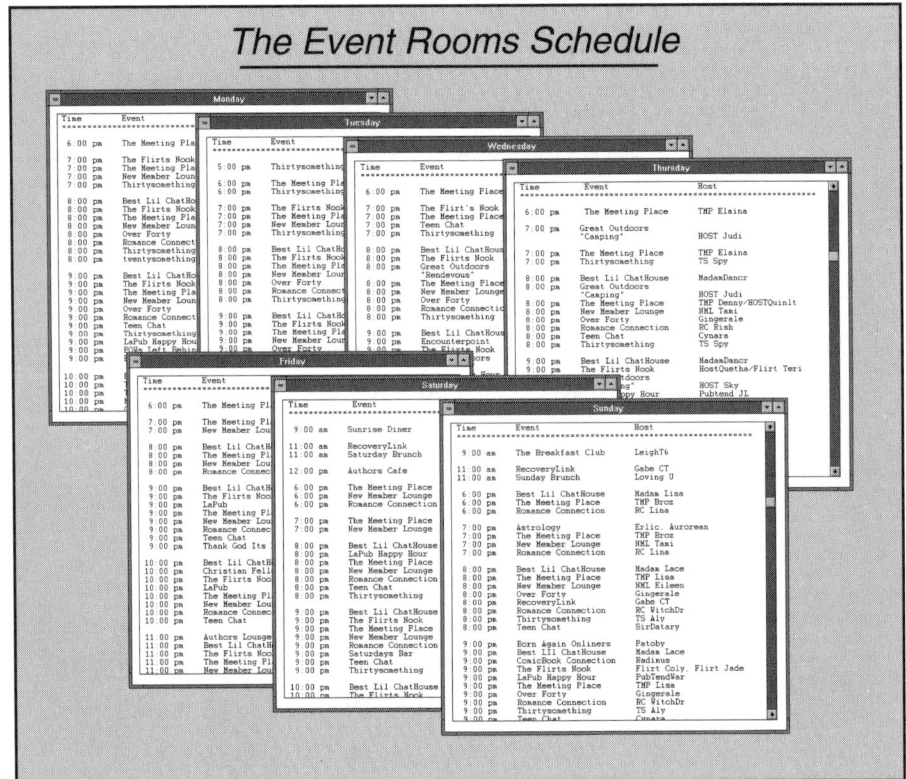

Figure 12-6: The Event Rooms Schedule for the week. Use this schedule along with the Event Rooms Guide to plan your visits.

There are three things I need to mention about the schedule in Figure 12-6:

- These schedules are only shown in part and they are subject to change. By the time you read this book, the schedules you see in Figure 12-6 will probably be out of date. Check it for yourself. Print it if you wish (choose Print from the File menu when the schedule is on the screen).

- No matter how current it might be, the Event Rooms Schedule lists only those events in the People Connection Department and not those scheduled by individual forums or clubs. Red Dragon Inn, for instance, is an Online Gaming Forum chat room, and it isn't mentioned in the Event Rooms Schedule at all. Consult individual clubs (see Chapter 13, "Clubs & Interests," for a discussion of clubs) for their chat rooms and schedules, or use the keyword: TITF (Tonight in the Forums) to see what's about to happen.
- Note the names of the hosts in Figure 12-6. Each of the Event Rooms is hosted, and that is a matter of significance. The hosts' duties include keeping the conversation going, selecting topics, aiding members who have questions (not to the degree that the Guides do, but aid nonetheless), and making sure all members have an enjoyable time—including the shy ones. Events rooms are sponsored by AOL; each room and its host has to go through a trial period before the room is added to the schedule. Though a number of rooms are simply opened by members (and don't appear on the schedule), you can be assured of certain standards of behavior when you visit an event room, and most of the credit goes to the host.

Finding Other Rooms

You can always tell which other rooms are available at any particular moment by clicking the Rooms icon at the top of any chat window (review Figure 12-2 for Lobby 2's window). When you click that icon, you'll see the window pictured in Figure 12-7.

Seventeen rooms are listed in Figure 12-7 and the More button (at the bottom of the window) is active. In fact, more than 146 rooms were available when I visited. Note that the lobby is filled to capacity (again, 23 is the maximum for a room: must have something to do with the fire marshal), so there must be other lobbies hidden beneath the More button. I can go into any room by double-clicking it, or I can get a list of all the people in a room (without going in) by selecting the room, then clicking the People button at the bottom of the window.

The Active Public Rooms window in Figure 12-7 only lists the *active* public rooms—rooms with people in them. Often, public rooms are available and no one is in them. A listing of these rooms is available by clicking the Available Rooms button (see Figure 12-8).

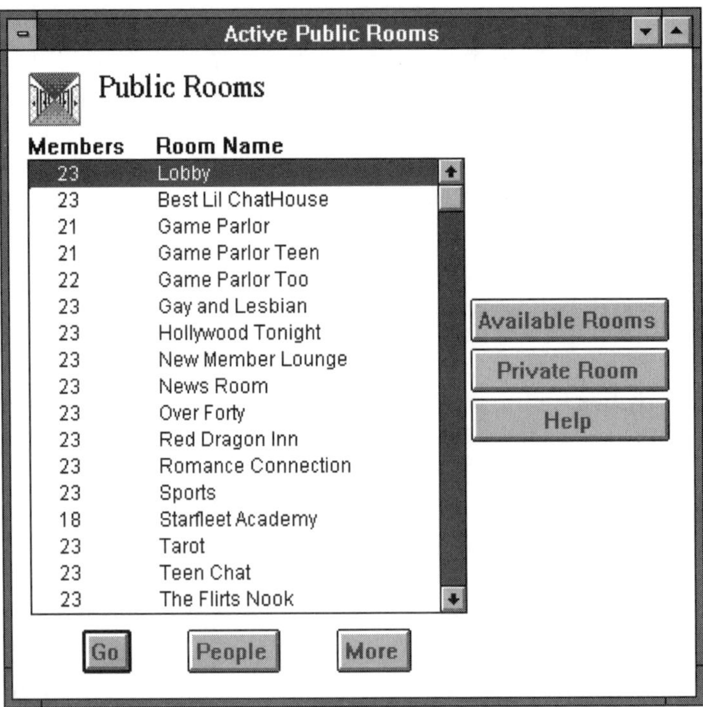

Figure 12-7: A Public Rooms list appears whenever you click the Rooms icon in a chat window.

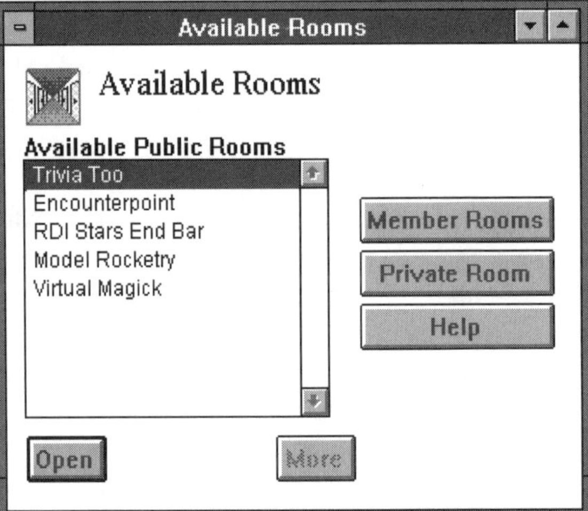

Figure 12-8: The Available Public Rooms window lists only those available rooms which are currently unoccupied.

Three Kinds of Rooms

People who are new to AOL often have trouble understanding the three kinds of rooms AOL has to offer. Each serves a different purpose. Entering one without an understanding of what's inside is a bit like opening meeting room doors in a large hotel: some might welcome you enthusiastically, others might make you feel unwelcome, and still others might be engaged in conversations that are of no interest to you whatsoever.

- *Public rooms* are created and named by AOL to reflect their conversational focus. Some of these are hosted; some are not. So far, public rooms are all we've discussed.
- *Member rooms* are named and created by members (see Figure 12-9). Member rooms are rarely hosted, though Guides might occasionally visit them. Conversations in member rooms are usually unmonitored and their topics range from the sublime to the scurrilous.
- *Private rooms* are created and named by members. Their names never appear on any of the lists you can see. I'll discuss private rooms in a few moments.

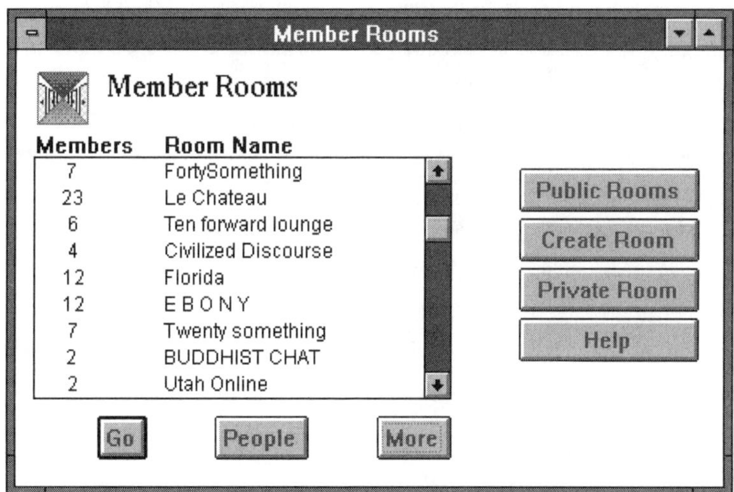

Figure 12-9: Member rooms are created by members and are not hosted. You can create one of your own whenever you wish using the Create Room button.

Note that Figure 12-9 contains a Create Room button. Anyone who wishes can create a member room—to talk about a specific topic, or no particular topic at all. You can create your own member room (in which case its title will appear in the window pictured in Figure 12-9), or, if an existing member room topic appeals to you, highlight the room and click the People button first (see the bottom of the window in Figure 12-9). You can tell a lot about a room by seeing the names of the people who are there.

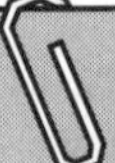

Parental Control

We've discussed it before: AOL is a community. On a political level, communities range from socialism to anarchism. But in this country we think of something in between. There *is* a government, after all, but it's not authoritarian; people do pretty much as they please, within certain bounds.

Our politics are reflected in our families: we seek a balance between despotic authority and profligate anarchy. Parents struggle with this balance: equanimity is elusive. Nowhere is this more evident than in matters of censure.

Every parent adopts a personal level of censorship: that's as it should be. Recently, however, the media have offered their assistance: all motion pictures are rated, many television cable companies offer selective channel blocking, a rating system is emerging for video games, and AOL offers a feature called *Parental Control* (keyword: Parental Control.)

Parental Control can only be used by the master account. The master account is the permanent screen name that was created during your first sign-on to AOL. Parental Control enables the master account holder to restrict—for other names on that account—access to certain areas and features available online. It can be set for one or all screen names on the account; and once it is set for a particular screen name, it is active each time that screen name signs on. Changes can be made only at the master account level, and therefore, only by the person who knows the master account's password.

Refer to Figure 12-10: the master account holder can set any or all of the following four Parental Control features:

- *Block instant messages* turns off all Instant Messages to and from the screen name. (We'll discuss Instant Messages later in this chapter.)

More

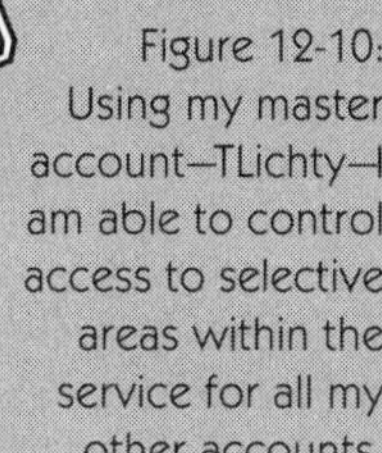

Figure 12-10: Using my master account—TLichty—I am able to control access to selective areas within the service for all my other accounts.

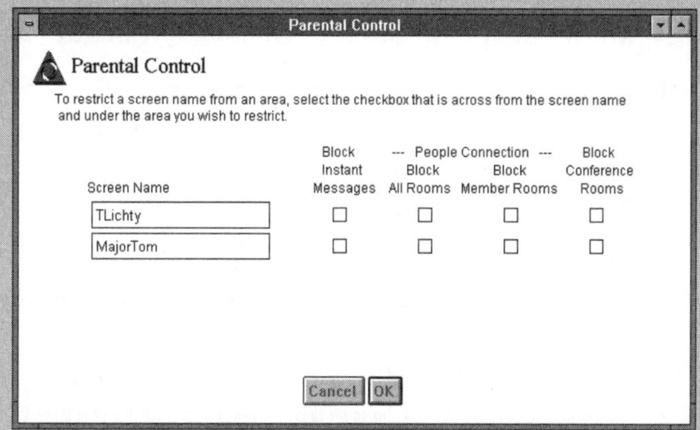

- *Block all rooms* blocks access to People Connection.
- *Block member rooms* only blocks access to the member-created rooms within People Connection.
- *Block conference rooms* blocks access to the special-interest rooms found throughout AOL, such as the classrooms in Education, the technical forums in Computing, and the Neverwinter Nights role-playing game in Entertainment.

The Parental Control feature is an elective, not an imperative. Use it if you want; ignore it if you wish. That's a level of intervention that accommodates any parental attitude, and that's the way most of us prefer to have it.

The New Member Lounge

If you're new to chat rooms, you should start at the New Member Lounge. It meets every evening starting at 8:00 P.M. (Eastern time). Before you enter this or any room, however, it helps to know some of the basic protocol.

- If you intend to stay in a room for a while, say hello when you enter.
- Don't type in uppercase. That's shouting.
- Speak when spoken to, even if you say nothing but "I don't know."

- Use a screen name containing your first name or a nickname. Talking to "TLic7563" is like talking to a license plate. "MajorTom" allows people to call me "Major," "Tom" or "T."
- Keep a log of your first few chat room visits by choosing Logging from the File menu (logs are discussed in Chapter 6, "Today's News "). Review the log off-line when your session has concluded. You'll learn a lot about chats this way.
- Learn your shorthands and smileys, if for no other reason than to figure out what people are doing when they type something like "{{{{{{{{{{{{**}}}}}}}}}}}}}" or "ROFLWTIME." To find shorthands online, choose Online Shorthands from the What's Happening This Week window pictured in Figure 12-4 or use the keyword: Shorthands. Smileys are also discussed in Chapter 3, "Electronic Mail," and again in Chapter 20, "Ten Best."
- There are no stupid questions. Guides, hosts and members love to help. If you're made to feel stupid or unwelcome in a room, visit another.

Private Rooms

Private rooms are the same as public rooms except that they don't appear in any of the rooms windows. Private rooms can hold as many as 23 people and are established by members. There's no way to see a list of private rooms. You'll never know about a private room unless you create one of your own or someone invites you into theirs.

Look again at Figure 12-9. The Private Room button pictured there allows you to create or visit a private room. When you click this button, AOL asks you for a room name. If you enter a name and the room already exists, AOL takes you into that room. If it doesn't exist, AOL creates it and takes you there. If you create a room, the only people who can enter it are those who know its name.

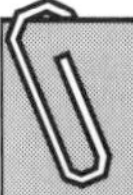

Online Conference Calls

Consider the private room as an alternative to the conference call. We don't tend to think of them that way; but private rooms are essentially mechanisms whereby people from around the country can hold real-time conferences. America Online's private rooms are much less expensive than the phone company's conference calls, and participants can keep a log of the conversation for review once the conference has concluded (see Chapter 6, "Today's News," for a discussion of logs). Conferences are often more productive when participants have to write what they say (makes 'em think before they speak) and vocal inflections don't cloud the issue.

To hold a private-room conference call (or to simply meet some friends for a chat in a private room), tell the participants the name of the room and the time you want to meet beforehand, then arrive a few minutes early and create the room. Instruct the participants to enter the Lobby (Ctr+L gets you there in a hurry) when they sign on, click the Rooms icon, click the Private Room button, then type in the name of your room. Try it: it's in many ways superior to a conference call—and cheaper to boot.

Chat Room Technique

It's easy to participate in an online chat. All you need to do is read other members' comments and type your responses, then press the Enter key (or click the chat window's Send button) when you want to send your own comment. But if you plan to spend a lot of time chatting online, here are a few techniques that might come in handy while you're visiting a chat room.

Cut & Paste

Remember that AOL's windows can be resized and relocated anywhere on the screen. First, size the chat window down to leave a small open area on your screen. Now choose New from the File menu and size the resulting Untitled window to fit the open area (see Figure 12-11). Use the Untitled window as a scratch pad. Make notes and jot responses there. If you want to send a note as a chat comment, copy it from the Untitled window, paste it into the comment box and click Send.

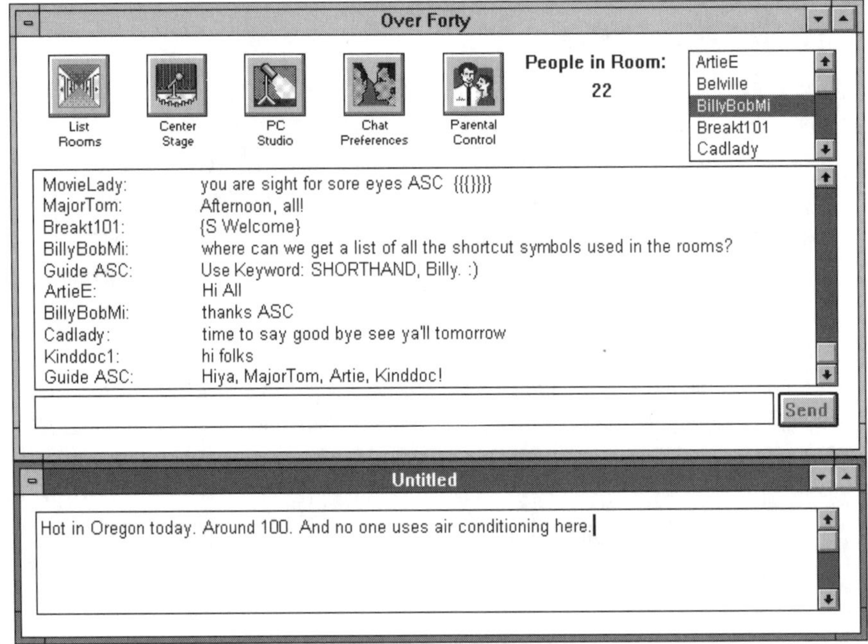

Figure 12-11: Two windows on my screen: at top, Over Forty; below, Untitled, where I'm scribbling notes that can be copied later to the top window. I can also use the Untitled window to paste material copied *from* Over Forty for saving later to disk.

Getting Information About People in a Room

You can find out about anyone in a chat room by double-clicking the appropriate member's name in the scroll box with the names in it (review Figure 12-3). By double-clicking BillyBobMi's name, I am provided with three options. I can communicate directly with him, afford him special handling, or look up his profile (see Figure 12-12).

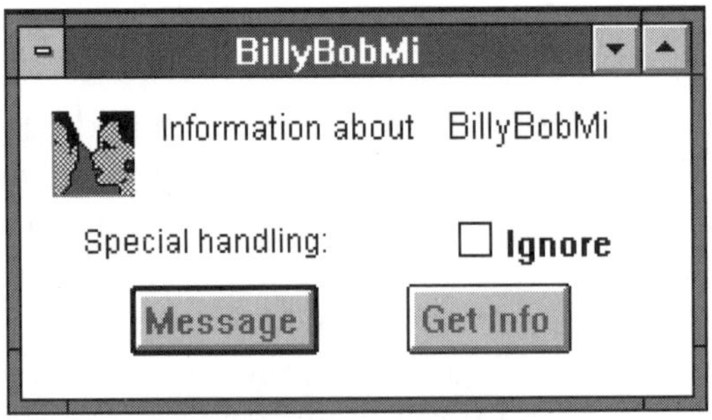

BillyBobMi
Information about BillyBobMi
Special handling: Ignore
Message
Get Info

Figure 12-12: By double-clicking BillyBobMi's name in the names area of a chat window, I receive this dialog box.

If you want to know more about a specific person, click the Get Info button pictured in Figure 12-12. If that person has completed a profile (profiles are discussed in Chapter 3, "Online Help & the Members"), everything they want you to know about them will appear on your screen.

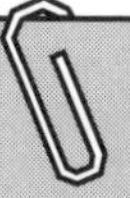

The Gallery

If you want to know even more about a person, check out the Gallery (keyword: Gallery). Members can send their photographs to a scanning service and the electronic result is posted in the Gallery, or they can post scans of their own. There's a search button, so you don't have to look through long listings. Steve Case is there; so am I. Printed gallery photos make great trading cards: "I'll trade you one Steve Case for two MajorToms...."

Sending an Instant Message

Look again at Figure 12-12. See the button marked "Message"? If I wanted to send an Instant Message to BillyBobMi, I could click that button. Only BillyBobMi would see it; the other people in the room would be none the wiser. This feature is especially handy, since you will often want to "whisper" privately to someone in a chat room. We'll discuss Instant Messages in a few moments.

Excluding Members

Investigate the Ignore button pictured in Figure 12-12. When rooms become full and everyone is talking, it can be difficult to follow what's going on. Often, three or four conversations are going on at the same time. If you wish to exclude a member's comments (or those of all the members in a conversation in which you're not interested), click the Ignore button. From then on, that member's text will not appear on your screen.

Chat Room Sounds

As long as we're talking about little-used commands, look again at Figure 12-11, and note the Preferences icon at the top there. The Preferences command allows you to change your chat room preferences and enable chat room sounds. You can send these sounds just as you send text; people in the room will hear the sound just as they would read the text. There are a couple of caveats, however:

- Your PC needs a sound card and speakers. Though Microsoft offers a speaker driver for Windows that allows your PC's internal speaker to play sounds and music, the driver is incompatible with AOL's software.

- Almost any sound card and speaker combination will work, but if you're buying, buy the best you can afford. Although AOL's not talking, you can be sure that elaborate multimedia stuff is on the way, and it will make extensive use of sound.

- Only PCs so equipped (and Macintoshes) can send and receive chat room sounds. Members using other types of machines will only see the sound's name in the chat room window. (Look again at Figure 12-11: do you see the word {S WELCOME} there? That's a sound.

- Both the person sending the sound and those who want to hear it must have the sound already installed on their hard disk. America Online doesn't transmit the sound file when you send a sound (sending the actual sound itself would take too long using a modem) but rather a notification to play the sound. Members' machines will play the sound only if they have the sound on file.

- The only sound files that work in chat rooms are those that end with the filename extension .WAV. You already have a number of them: take a look at your WINDOWS and WAOL directories. To broadcast a sound in a chat room, type a line matching the format below, then click the chat window's Send button. (See WlkinDude's "FanFare" example in Figure 12-13.) {S WELCOME.WAV}. Notice that the entire command is enclosed in braces {}, and that it begins with a capital S (a lowercase s won't do). There's a space after the S then the name of the sound. The .WAV filename extension is optional in the command.

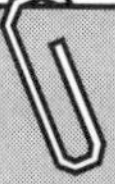

Finding & Installing Sounds

Hundreds of sounds are available online, where they're referred to as "waves" due to their .WAV filename extension. For a listing of them all, use the keyword: PC Music, then browse the WAV Sounds library. A library of Mac sounds is available in the Macintosh Music and Sound Forum (keyword: MMS) . To convert Macintosh sounds to WAV format, I use one of the many utilities available from the PC Music and Sound Forum. I use "Makin' Waves," from Geoff Faulkner (file search using the criterion: Faulkner), but there are lots of others available.

Once you have downloaded (or converted) a WAV file, move or copy it to your WAOL subdirectory. From then on, it's available in chat situations by following the directions above.

Chat Preferences

America Online offers a number of preferences which allow you to customize the behavior of the chat window (see Figure 12-13).

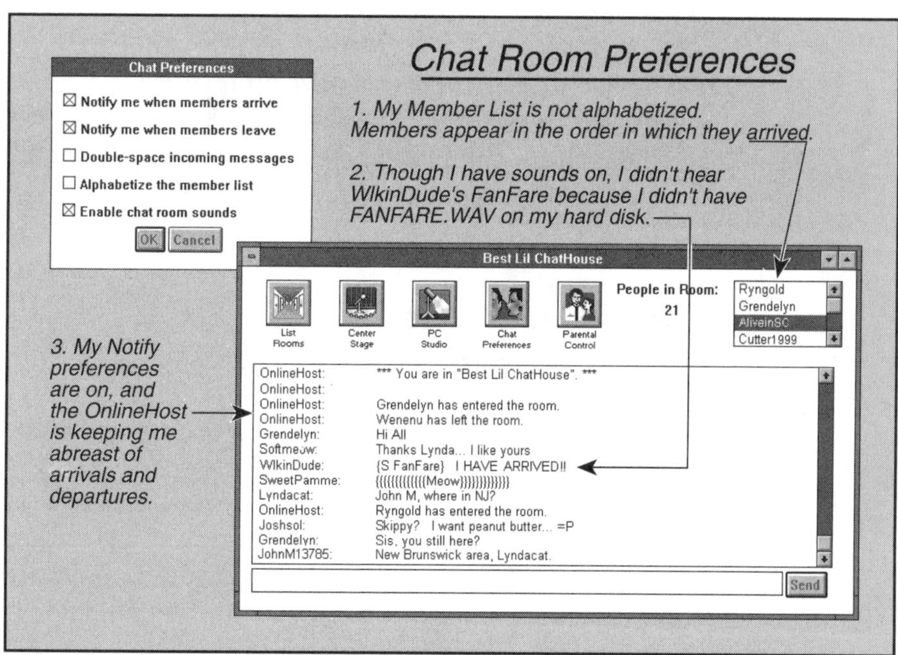

Figure 12-13: Chat room preferences allow you to customize the behavior of the chat window.

- The first two options—the *Notify* preferences—allow you to see the names of arriving members. This is handy if you don't want to watch the names scroll box with an eagle eye for comings and goings in the room. Hosts and guides use this feature so they can say hello to all new arrivals. It clutters the screen in busy rooms like lobbies, however. Let the amount of traffic in the room determine whether these preferences should be on or off.
- The next option—*Double-space incoming messages*—simply makes the screen easier to read. It limits the amount of text the window can display, however.
- The *Alphabetize* preference alphabetizes the list of member names in the scroll box in the upper right corner of the chat window. If this preference is off, the names appear in the order in which the members arrive in the room, with the most recent at the top. Sorting this list in chronological order is handy if the Notify preferences are turned off. On the other hand, it's easier to locate a specific member if the list is alphabetized. The choice is yours.
- *Enable chat room sounds* turns on the sound feature I discussed a few pages back. Turn this feature off if your PC can't play sounds. Subaudible chirps from the piezoelectric transducer trying to say "Big Hug!" can be very distracting (and a little melancholic if you're feeling neglected at the moment).

Instant Messages

An *Instant Message* is a message sent to someone else online. Don't confuse Instant Messages with e-mail. Unlike e-mail, both the sender and the recipient have to be online at the same time for Instant Messages to work.

As I mentioned earlier, an Instant Message sent to someone else in a chat room is something like whispering in class, though you'll never get in trouble for it. You'll probably encounter Instant Messages most often when you're in a room. It's then, after all, that other people know you're online. Instant Messages aren't limited to chat rooms, however: they work whenever you're online, wherever you might be.

A moment ago, I suggested a private room as an alternative to conference calls. You might also consider Instant Messages as alternatives to long-distance phone calls. Pam Richardson (my primary contact at Ventana Press) and I need to have a number of discussions nearly every day. Unfortunately, Pam is in North Carolina and I am in Oregon—we're about as far away from one another as we can be without being in different countries. Instead of making long-distance telephone calls across the country and four different time zones, we have agreed on mutual times to go online, and now we "talk" without worrying about the cost. All we pay is our normal connect-time charge. A conversation we had the other day appears in Figure 12-14.

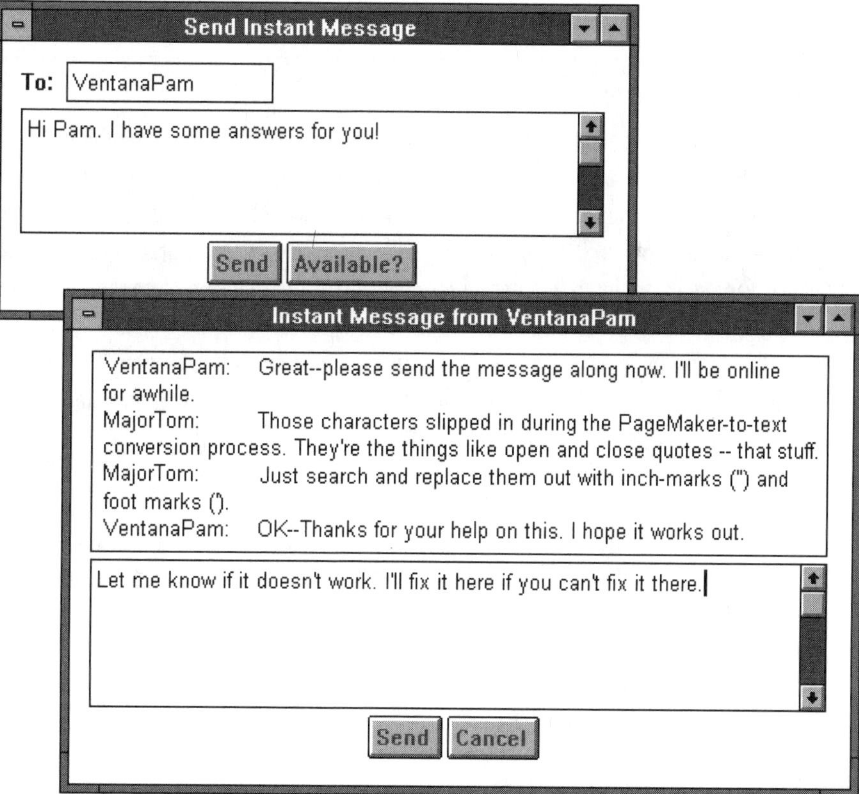

Figure 12-14: The Instant Message window contains a running log of our conversation in the upper text box along with the response I'm composing in the lower one.

- To send an Instant Message, choose Send an Instant Message from the Members menu or type Ctrl+I. Enter the recipient's screen name and your message where appropriate and click Send, as pictured in the upper window in Figure 12-14. After that, a running log of the conversation is maintained in the Instant Message window, the lower window in Figure 12-14.
- Before you send an Instant Message, use the Available? button in the upper window pictured in Figure 12-14, or the Locate a Member Online command under the Members menu. If the recipient isn't online when you send an Instant Message, AOL tells you and you'll have to wait for another opportunity. (If a member is not available online, consider sending e-mail instead. Electronic mail is discussed in Chapter 4.)

Available or Locate?

The Available? button in the Send Instant Message window does the same thing as the Locate a Member Online command under the Members menu. I prefer the button. Most of the time, if a member is online you're going to want to say hello, right? If you discover the member online via the Locate command and want to say hello, you have to call up the Send Instant Message dialog box anyway; but in the period of time it takes to produce that box, you might lose your opportunity.

OK, it's a small matter, and locating members online isn't like locating pike: they aren't liable to disappear in a matter of seconds. Nonetheless, it's one less command to learn, and every time you don't use the Available? button, you'll wish you did.

- Figure 12-14's lower window has been enlarged from the default. Like all of AOL's windows, the Instant Message window can be sized as you please. If you want to change the size of a window permanently, choose Remember Window Size Only from the Windows menu after you have sized the window to your satisfaction.

- You cannot receive or send Instant Messages while in a free area such as Members' Online Support. America Online closes any open Instant Message windows when you enter a free area.
- Determine where the intended recipient is before sending an Instant Message by clicking the Available? button in the Send Instant Message window. This feature tells you if the recipient is online, and if so, whether he or she can receive Instant Messages. It also tells you if a member is in a chat room, in which case you might want to go to that room rather than send an Instant Message.
- If the recipient is online but unable to receive an Instant Message, AOL tells you—after it unsuccessfully tries to deliver the message.
- Instant Messages are accompanied by a "tinkerbell" sound (assuming your machine is equipped to play sounds), and the Instant Message window becomes the front-most window on your screen. The Set Preferences command under the Members menu allows you to change these options, but most people prefer the high degree of priority Instant Messages receive without changing their preferences.
- You can log Instant Messages (handy for "phone call"-style Instant Messages such as those I exchange with Pam) by choosing Logging from the File menu.
- If you don't want to be disturbed by Instant Messages, you can turn them off at any time by sending an Instant Message to "$im_off" (without the quotation marks, with the dollar sign, and always in lower case). Include a character or two as text for the message; otherwise AOL will respond with a "cannot send empty Instant Message" error. A single character will do. To turn Instant Messages back on, send an Instant Message to "$im_on."

Center Stage

Center Stage is America Online's unique theatre district, offering four special "auditoriums:" *Coliseum, Odeon, Globe,* and *Rotunda*. Auditoriums are the format AOL uses to present special guests or to offer "game shows" for members to play.

Typically, members attending a Center Stage auditorium event sit in "rows" of seats in the audience. Each row has a limited number of seats. This is how AOL accommodates a large audience of members without exceeding its own 23-member room capacity. Your chat window contains the text of everything that's happening on stage, along with comments from other members in your row (but not from members in other rows). You can change rows if you like, as long as there's an empty seat in that row, and you can turn off the comments of members in your row if they're distracting.

Provision is usually made to submit questions or comments to the people on-stage. The event's host receives your message and (optionally) delivers it to the guest for a response.

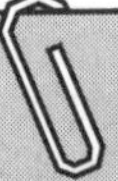

Virtual Romance

Robin Williams writes wonderful little books for computer users. Her book *The PC Is Not a Typewriter* (published by Peachpit Press) should be on every PC user's shelf. Robin is the penultimate romantic: she's charmed by the Byronic, the poetic, the courtly. She writes:

"There was a letter in my mailbox. I didn't recognize the name of the sender. The letter quoted Macbeth, 'Tomorrow and tomorrow and tomorrow creeps in this petty pace from day to day, to the last syllable of recorded time....' The writer complained of a gloomy evening in Atlanta, wet and dark and lonely. I realized this person had probably done a search for users who mentioned an interest in Shakespeare in their bios. So I sent a letter back, which included, 'Hey, lighten up. Macbeth's dysfunctional. I know a bank where the wild thyme blows, where oxlips and the nodding violet grows.'

"We exchanged several other short letters. He was a 24-year-old son of a minister. I was a 37-year-old single mother of three, pure heathen. It was easy to be friends because neither of us expected anything from the other.

"One late night I was hanging around in the lobby. I had only been connected to America Online for about a month, so I was still learning the etiquette and the conventions of online

socializing. I heard a tinkling sound, as if someone threw fairy dust at me. On the screen was my first Instant Message, and it was from my friend. We sent a few messages back and forth, then he suggested we go to a private room. I had no idea what a private room was at that time, nor was I aware of what private rooms are generally used for. So I innocently tripped along with him to a room.

"I remember the feeling that night so clearly because it gave me a brief glimpse into the power of virtual reality. Meeting him in the lobby that night was as if I saw him across the floor of a crowded room. He winked at me, nodded his head toward the hallway, and we snuck out and met in the corridor. We tiptoed down the hall and slipped into an empty room. It was very innocent; we chatted about our lives, history, philosophy, religion. I was so involved in this conversation that took place in the computer's nether world of digital bits and analog streams that when my neighbor walked into my room I jumped. I felt like she had intruded on a very personal moment, as if I had been caught in a dimly lit room, holding hands.

"Somehow, over the months, this unlikely relationship took an unexpected romantic turn. When I received a letter telling me how he had reached up with his left hand, reached into his fantasy, and pulled me down beside him, when he said, 'I would trade my loneliness for the warmth of her laughter; she would trade her nightgown for the cloak of a young man's affection,' when I found emotions raging in me that fought between my brain and my heart, I realized there were facets to human nature that this new medium of communication was going to expose in new and different ways. It was going to be an interesting summer."

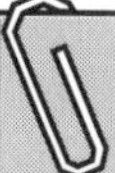

Amy Arnold

David Bowie enjoyed his appearance on AOL's Center Stage so much that he would prefer all of his celebrity appearances to be conducted that way in the future. Garth Brooks felt that more of his personality emerged during his online interview than in any other medium. After converting so many souls himself, the Reverend Billy Graham became the convert half an hour into his Center-Stage appearance.

The online medium's impersonality—the same hindrance that necessitates smileys and offbeat acronyms like ROTFLOL in chat rooms—works in favor of the online interview. Bowie claimed that reduced to text on screen, "The words don't yell at you." There's no interviewer personality with which you may clash; people don't talk back with the vehemence they use in

telephone talk shows; and you can conduct the interview from the comfort of your home—in your bathrobe if you please. (Indeed, my last online appearance was conducted in my dining room, with a plate of sauerkraut and a bottle of beer at my side.)

The person in charge of Center Stage—AOL's "theater district"—is Amy Arnold. Another team player who has come up through the ranks, Amy recruits the guests who have filled her four auditoria to capacity recently—something that rarely happened before she took over.

Her achievement is the result of unparalleled enthusiasm and an optimistic vision for her medium. Amy sees the AOL of the near future as the most appropriate vehicle for the interview, celebrity or not. It's a scaleable medium, and one that's particularly malleable. It's in its infancy, after all, and emerging technologies will bring a tidal wave of multimedia interview techniques, integrating graphics, video and sound into an intimate, one-on-one dialog that one-way telecommunications simply can't deliver.

Interestingly, no one has ever said no when Amy calls, in spite of the fact that she offers no pay. Interviewees are voluntary and eager, even if they are Billy Graham or Garth Brooks. Something's going on here; we're fortunate that we have Amy Arnold keeping an eye on it for us.

Center Stage event schedules are posted each day and are available by using the keyword: Center Stage (see Figure 12-15). You'll find dates, times, locations and descriptions for all Center Stage events in the Center Stage Box Office.

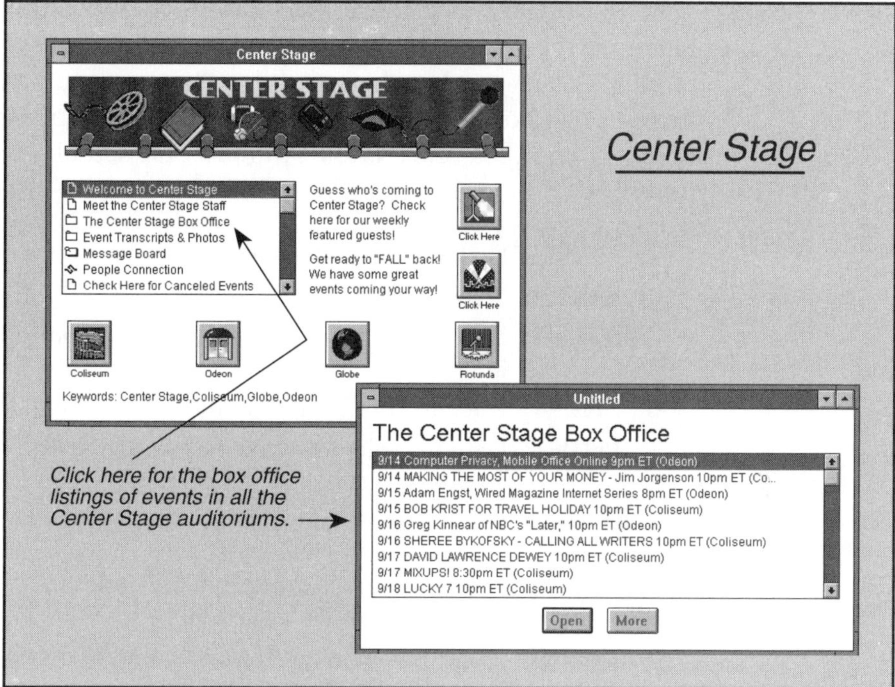

Figure 12-15: The Center Stage Box Office lists all upcoming events. Double-click any one for details.

Rules for the Coliseum game shows are available by double-clicking any game show announcement pictured in Figure 12-15. Read them before you take part in a game. Game shows are often profitable: winning contestants are awarded free connect time.

As I mentioned a moment ago, the Center Stage auditoriums are often used to present special guests to members. Two of those featured were Jerry Pournelle and Michael Banks, co-authors of *Pournelle's PC Communications Bible* (see the particulars in my Bibliography). The book is a sometimes-opinionated guide to getting online and what to do after you're there.

Jerry Pournelle is probably one of America's most famous computer users, best-known for his "Chaos Manor" columns in *Byte* magazine. He has been an enthusiastic computer user since the late 1970s and is one of the first writers to use a word processor for writing. He's also well known as a science fiction writer with several bestsellers to his credit.

Michael A. Banks is the author of more than two dozen science fiction novels. He is best known to computer users as the author of *The Modem Reference* and for his monthly "Online" column in *Computer Shopper*. The host for this particular Center Stage appearance was LouiseL. The "person" named OnlineHost is actually the host computer.

LouiseL: Hi, Jerry and Mike! I've been looking forward to meeting you!

BANKS2: Thanks!

JEPournell: hello — this is the first time I've been on AOL. I like the interface!

LouiseL: Let's find out what our audience has on their minds.

Question: Dr. Pournelle, will there be a sequel to *Go Tell The Spartans* or another novel in Falkenberg's Mercenary Legion series?

JEPournell: Funny you should ask. On my desk now I have the manuscript to *Prince of Sparta.* It needs some rewrite, because what I have is Stirling's draft from my outline and our discussion, but it will soon be turned in.

Question: Jerry, how has your role as "voice for the computer user" changed in the last two years?

JEPournell: Well, not sure it *has* changed much. I try to write for the people who *use* these things, but do it in a way that lets the technoweenies understand what I'm saying in hopes they'll pay attention and make things happen... I also try to get around to all kinds of things that may interest people in the future.

Question: Jerry how many computers are scattered around Chaos Manor?

JEPournell: We have four Macs: a Quadra, a IIfx which is temporarily not in service because both the color and the monochrome monitor are attached to the Quadra, then there is Roberta's SE, and Richard has a new Classic II, which will be the subject of a column on "outfitting a Classic II" in probably the June *Byte.* I'll have shareware sources and recommendations for commercial software, and like that. We also have a tt330 Atari, and three '486 machines running Windows. And Roberta has a 386/33. There are probably a couple of other machines, including some CP/M systems but they aren't in use... That enough?

Question: Will you be able to "rehabilitate" the CoDominium history in light of the current flux in Soviet affairs?

JEPournell: Don't know. It was a pretty good prediction at the time. Now I don't know precisely what's happening over there and no one else does. But it's possible that there will be some new developments. But no, I think the CoDominium has just become a parallel universe sort of like if the South had won the Civil War.

BANKS2: <applause> (Good idea...parallel universe—not the South winning.)

LouiseL: What is that I see coming up?

OnlineHost: It's time for a special audience prize!

LouiseL: What is the prize, Jerry and Mike?

BANKS2: A copy of *Pournelle's PC Communications Bible.*

LouiseL: WOW! That sounds great—which wish I could win! Who's the winner of that great prize?

OnlineHost: The lucky winner is Paratroop!

BANKS2: Congrats, 'troop!

Question: When is the sequel to *The Mote In God's Eye* going to be released? :)

JEPournell: *Hah!* My wife is mildly unhappy because I am on line here instead of writing the final chapter of that book. *Moat Around Murcheson's Eye* is done but for the last chapter and I am writing that here at the beach.

Question: How close does Mr. Pournelle think *Fallen Angels* could be to reality?

JEPournell: Well *Fallen Angel* was social satire, and not all things in it are likely but it's all 'possible' in that same way that 1984 is possible.

Question: Dr. Pournelle, how distinct for you are your science fiction and computing careers? Are they two sides of the same coin or is one an escape from the other?

JEPournell: I grew up in WW II and read science fiction about computers but they were all *big* things, and not terribly powerful. Mr. Heinlein wrote about computers that looked like the only ones he'd ever seen which were Navy mechanical analog fire-control systems. Van Gogt had a planet-sized computer. So did Asimov. Of course sf writers should have remembered the speed of light meaning that faster is smaller, but what the heck. Then suddenly we could buy a computer more powerful than anything the writers had dreamed of! And in 1954 I had to see ILIAC which was the biggest and most powerful in the world, and suddenly again I could buy something a lot more powerful. So I got it. And that machine, *Ezekial*, is now on display in the Smithsonian in Washington (go visit him, he gets lonesome)...

LouiseL: Looks like our time is up, folks! Thanks so much for being here, and thanks, Mike and Jerry, for a great time!

Moving On

Many of those who are new to AOL sidestep People Connection at first. Perhaps it's too intimidating. Perhaps they're shy. Whatever the reason, it's a shame. People Connection is the heart of the AOL community. It is here that you finally stop thinking of AOL as an electronic service and begin thinking of it as people. In the search for community, People Connection is where you find the bounty.

Speaking of bounty, do you have a hobby? Perhaps you have an interest: cooking comes to mind, or bicycling. Hobbies and interests are best enjoyed when there are others around with the same penchant: you can share your ideas with them and hear of theirs.

The trouble is, people with similar interests are sometimes hard to find—but not if you look around AOL. There are nearly a million of us here now, and with a numbers like that, there's bound to be a few who share your interests.

The place to investigate is the Clubs & Interests Department, and it's coming up next.

CHAPTER 13

Clubs & Interests

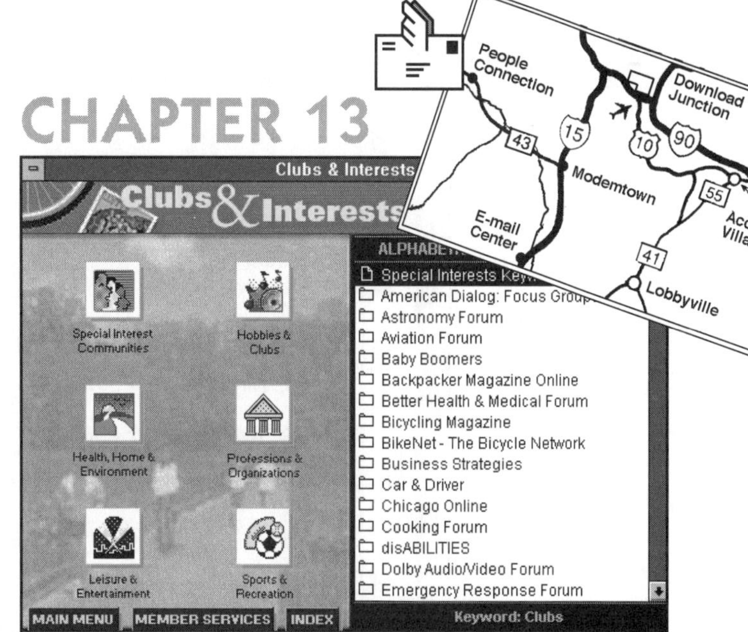

If we were to award prizes to AOL's departments, Clubs & Interests would win the Size Prize. No other department is this large; no other department offers such diversity; no other department represents the potential Clubs & Interests does. If you have an interest, there's probably some place here that serves it (see Figure 13-1).

The Index

Look again at the frontispiece for this chapter. Like all department screens, this one offers a little button at the bottom marked "Index." The Clubs & Interests index is especially important because it serves as a roadmap to the largest department in the system.

That's what indexes are: roadmaps. And like all roadmaps, AOL's indexes are best perused on paper.

Try this: click the Clubs & Interests Index button, then choose Print from the File menu. America Online will offer a standard Windows Print dialog box, then send the index to your printer. (Be prepared: the Clubs & Interests Index was 19 pages when I printed it!)

Do this for each department on the service, then file the printouts in a three-ring binder with an indexing tab for each department. When you're finished, you'll have a convenient, printed roadmap to the entire service. I've one right here next to my keyboard. It's probably my most frequently used reference.

The Clubs & Interests Department is AOL's gateway to everything from astronomy to wine. African Americans, Hispanics, gays and professional groups all find homes here. This place is as multiethnic as Ellis Island and as variegated as a harlequin's tights. Click the Clubs & Interests button on the Main Menu or use the keyword: Clubs.

Figure 13-1: A few of the many clubs in the Clubs & Interests Department. There are scores of others.

While the size of the Clubs & Interests Department is good for you, it's not so good for me: there's no way I can do this department justice. It's too large for that, and frankly, descriptions of special interests are a bit like puppies at a picnic: lots of dynamic, but they're not necessarily welcome at everyone's plate.

Instead, I'm going to use this department as an opportunity to describe three fundamental AOL tactics: searching online databases, reading message boards and multitasking while downloading.

Clubs Defined

Before we begin our tactical didactic, it might be best if I formally define the word *club*. The Clubs & Interests Department is primarily composed of clubs, after all. We need an example, one that's familiar to all and resplendent with people, goodies and activity.

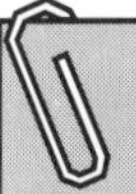

Nomenclature Evolving

The term *club* is an evolving one at AOL. Only a few months ago, AOL's preferred term was *forum*. Other telecommunications services call them *roundtables* or *bulletin boards*. Club is probably the best description: the term *forum* has formal Grecian overtones, the term *roundtable* doesn't include things like libraries of files, nor does *bulletin board*.

Lately, AOL has become especially fond of *cross-pointing*. Look again at the bottom window in Figure 13-1: cross-pointers to OMNI Magazine Online, DC Comics, and the Sci-Fi Channel appear there, none of which are part of the Science Fiction & Fantasy Club per se, but each might be found in a "clubhouse," so each appears here.

Club implies membership, however, and membership usually implies membership fees. Don't worry: there are never any membership fees for AOL's clubs. Join 'em if and whenever you wish; you're always welcome.

The perfect candidate is Wine & Dine Online. You'll find Wine & Dine Online among the listed features in the scroll box of the Clubs & Interests main window, or by using the keyword: Wine. This is a particularly refined club, one that every epicure should visit (see Figure 13-2).

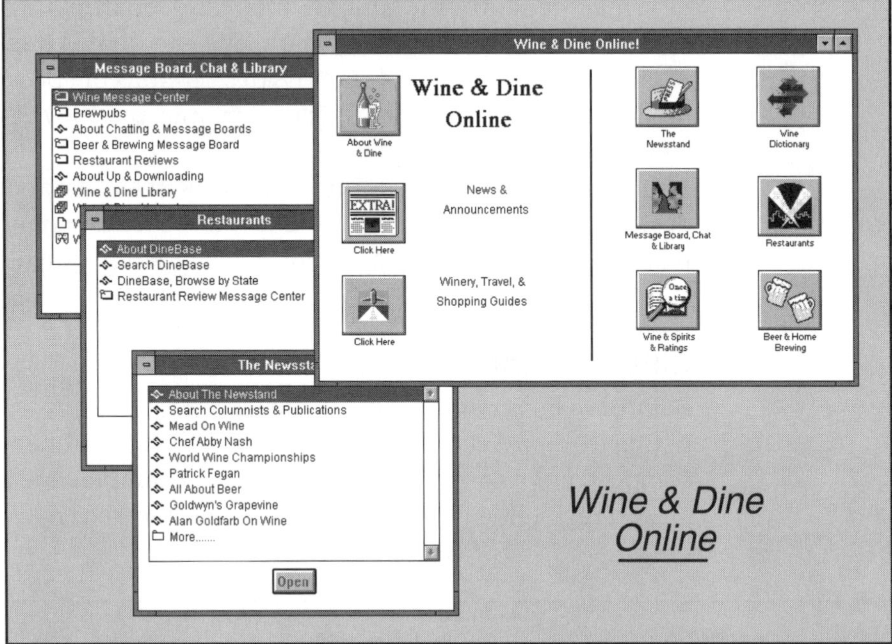

Figure 13-2: Wine & Dine Online offers articles, folders, message boards and a library of files.

I picked this club because its composition is fairly representative of most clubs on AOL—a little more resplendent than some, perhaps, but representative nonetheless. The primary club window contains nine icons, some of which are detailed in Figure 13-2. What I want you to notice in the illustration are the icons. We see so many of them while we use our PCs that we tend to overlook them; but that's not wise when you're exploring clubs.

Reference Materials

Look carefully at the icons in the subsidiary windows of Figure 13-2. The little page icons with turned-down corners represent *articles*. Double-click article icons to read them. The folder icons hold collections of articles, grouped by subject. The "linking" icon holds the article groups themselves. The "facing faces" icon is a chat room (which we discussed in Chapter 12, "People Connection"). Icons with pushpins are message boards, and the disk icons represent libraries. Let's discuss these one at a time.

Articles

Let's begin our exploration of this club by double-clicking the option labeled "Goldwyn's Grapevine" (see Figure 13-3).

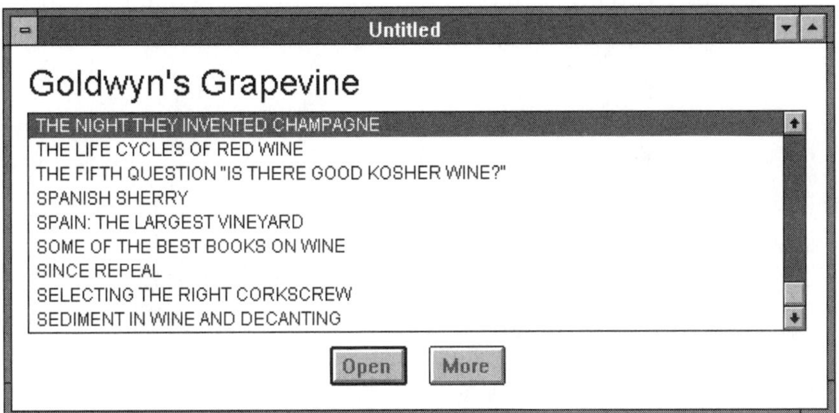

Figure 13-3: Lots of good reading here.

Nine articles appear in this window. Double-click any one of them to open it. The article entitled "The Night They Invented Champagne" piques my interest. Let's look it over (Figure 13-4).

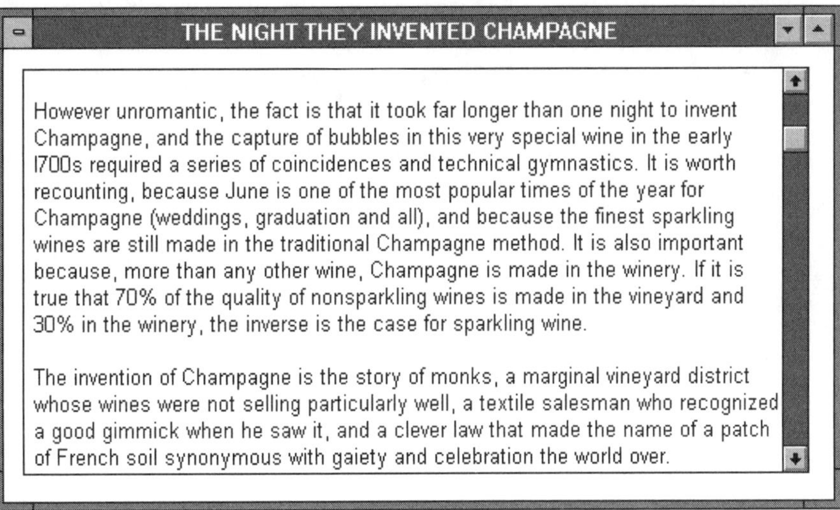

Figure 13-4: It's a long story, and good reading—especially if you like champagne.

The article pictured in Figure 13-4 was written by Craig Goldwyn, editor of Wine & Dine Online and president of the Beverage Testing Institute, Inc. He has published hundreds of articles as the wine critic for the *Washington Post* and the *Chicago Tribune*. A more notable authority is hard to find, and Craig's always available to answer your questions and provide advice. His screen name is "Goldwyn."

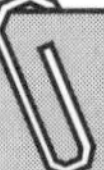

It Wasn't a Night at all

The story pictured in Figure 13-4 goes on to recount the complete history of Champagne (with a capital *C*—only the United States uses the term generically).

As it turns out, the Champagne district in northern France isn't the best place to grow grapes. The soil is less than ideal (*champagne* means "chalky white soil"), and the growing season is short—Champagne grapes often don't mature with enough sugar for winemaking. Champagne winemakers of yesteryear would often add cane sugar to feed the yeast.

Unfortunately, the Champagne district is gripped by cold weather by the time the grapes are harvested and the yeast hibernates most of the winter. When things warm up in the spring, the yeast wakes up and conducts a second fermentation, inundating the wine with excessive carbonation. The French called this *vin fou*, meaning "crazy wine."

And they loved it. Parisians traveled 90 miles to obtain it—no small feat in the seventeenth century. The wine was rare too—the bottles kept blowing up in the cellars and the wine that survived was precious stuff indeed.

The local monks, whose livelihood depended on winemaking, tried to prevent the profits from going down the sewers. One of these monks was Dom Perignon at the Benedictine Abbey of Hautvillers. He began to experiment with plugs cut from cork bark, invented a way to tie them down with string, and beefed up the thickness of the bottles. Only then did champagne become a successful commercial product.

Today the most precious champagne of them all—from the prestigious Moet-Hennessy house of spirits—carries his name.

Searching Online Databases

The searchable database is unique to the telecommunications industry. It's a benefit that simply can't be matched anywhere else. Searchable databases are perpetually maintained with not only the latest information but archived items as well. They can be searched without having to leave your keyboard. They arrive in the form of plain text, ready to be included in other documents or printed. Searchable databases are fast, immediate and usually extensive. America Online offers more than 70 of these databases; when you see one (look for the "linking" icon such as that next to "Dinebase" in Figure 13-2), take a few minutes to explore it—it's always worth the time.

Here's an eloquent example: The database of wines offered in Wine & Dine Online is probably the largest of its kind available to the public. Thousands of wines are listed here, along with prices and ratings from the Beverage Testing Institute. This is an excellent tool for cutting through a mystique that prospers on the obscurity of unfamiliar names and the bewilderment of heterogeneous prices.

I need a wine for tonight's dinner. Always the parochial Northwesterner, I'd like an Oregon wine if one's available. Before I go shopping, however, I consult Wine & Dine Online's wine database (see Figure 13-5).

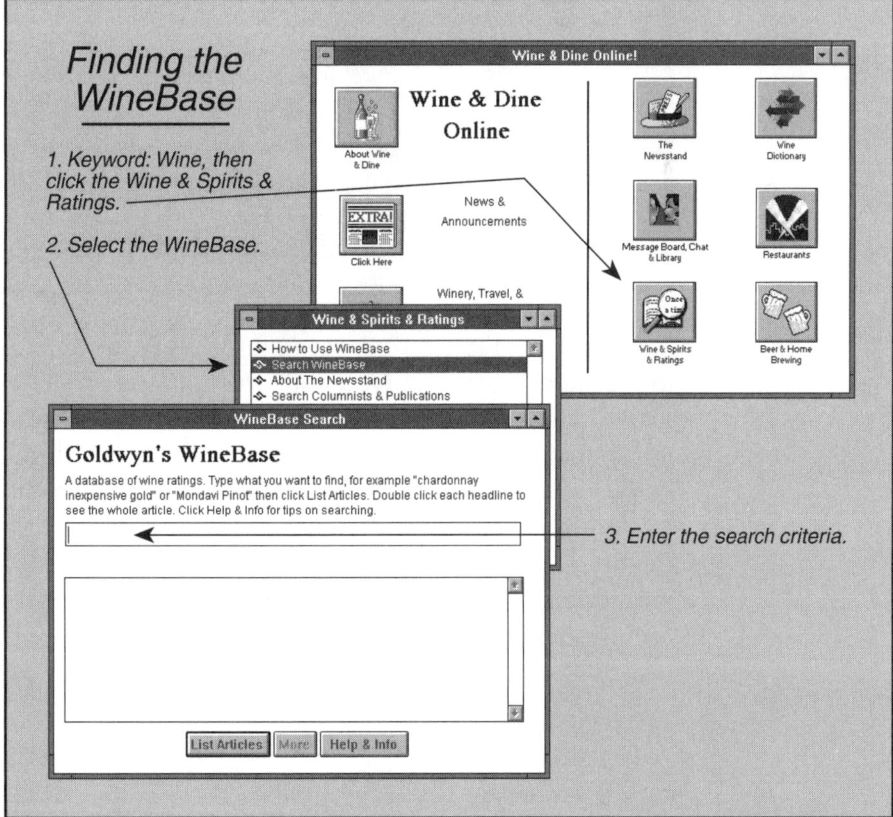

Figure 13-5: Become an instant enologist. Impress your friends with your wisdom and frugality. Look it up on America Online.

Note the "linking" icon in the Wine & Dine Online window of Figure 13-5. That's one of AOL's ways of identifying a searchable database. You'll also see the "open book" icon used to designate databases. Significant riches are available here almost instantly. That's a good thing: my dinner guests will be arriving shortly. I type in the criterion "Oregon" as a search criterion (see Figure 13-6).

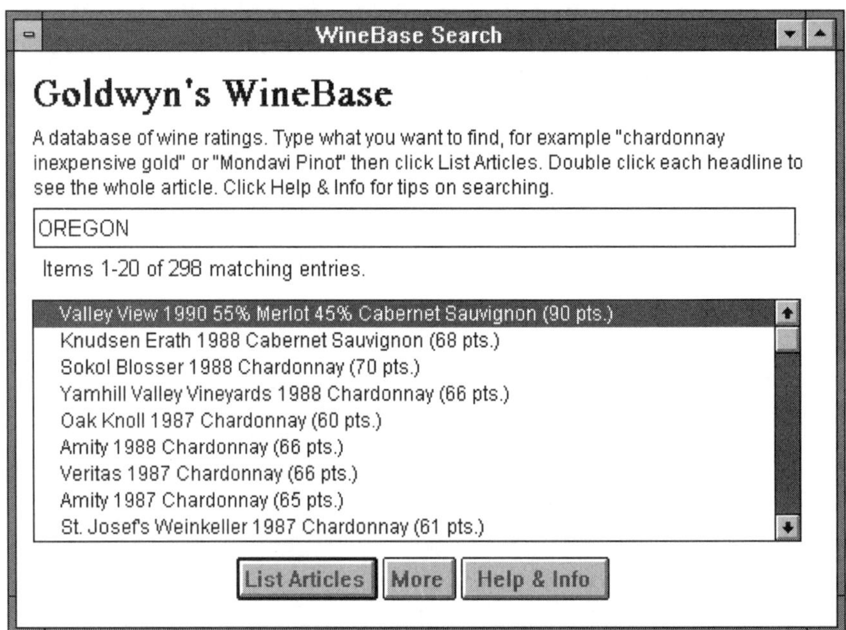

Figure 13-6: A search on the criterion "Oregon" produces 298 wines, far too many from which to make my decision.

Looking at Figure 13-6, I see that WineBase contains 298 references to the state of Oregon. Note that only 20 references have been downloaded to my PC, of which 9 appear in the scrollable window pictured in Figure 13-6. Note also that a button marked "More" appears at the bottom of the window. If I wanted to view more choices, I would use this button to see the remaining 278 wines, 20 at a time (see sidebar). By the time I read through that many listings, my guests will have departed in a pique, unfed and without libation, muttering disparaging remarks about AOL and my preoccupation with the PC.

The "More" Button

Look again at Figure 13-6's window. Do you see the button marked "More?" It's amazing how often this button is overlooked. As discussed in the text, my search based on the criterion "Oregon" was very inefficient. The WineBase found 298 entries matching that search criterion. While I thought I was looking for a product produced in limited numbers, the WineBase surprised me with the breadth of its knowledge of Oregon wines.

Rather than spend my online time listing all 298 entries, AOL chose only to download the first 20 (a safe assumption, since I would probably want to narrow my search), and offer them in Figure 13-6's scrolling window. Since matching entries remained, AOL activated the More button. If I wanted to see more than the first 20 entries, I'd click that button and AOL would send another 20; clicking again would result in another 20 entries and so on.

Don't overlook this button! It's not unique to the WineBase—many AOL windows have one—and if it *is* overlooked, lots of opportunities are missed.

I need to refine my criteria. It's a warm fall afternoon and I'm in the mood for a cool white wine. A chardonnay would be nice (see Figure 13-7).

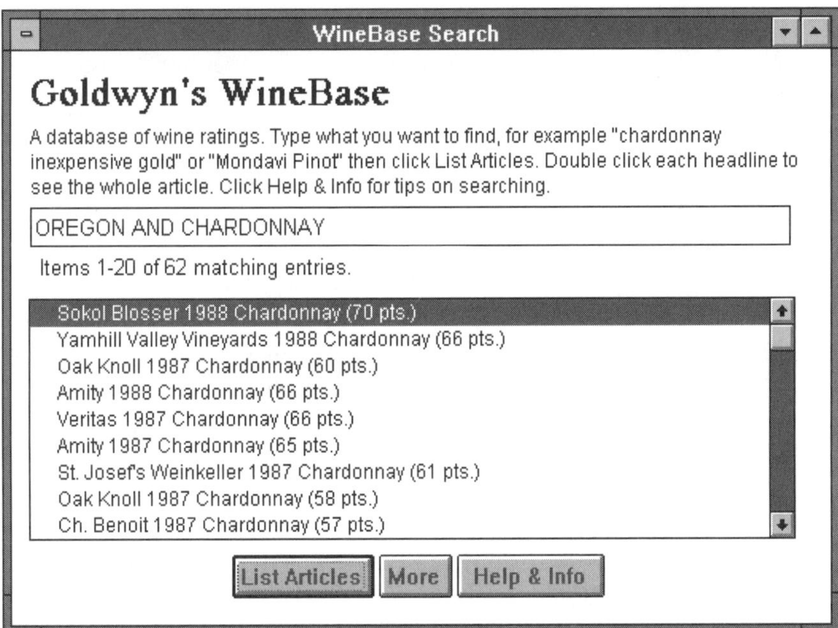

Figure 13-7: By using the word "and," I'm able to refine the search criteria.

Notice the criteria in Figure 13-7. By saying "Oregon *and* chardonnay," I'm able to exclude all wines that don't meet both criteria. I've narrowed it down to 62 wines, but that's still too many to sift through before my guests arrive. And these are important guests. People I want to please. Only the best will do. WineBase includes references to medals each wine might have won: bronze, silver, gold or platinum. I can exclude the no-medal wines as well as the bronze-medal wines with some *or* criteria (see Figure 13-8).

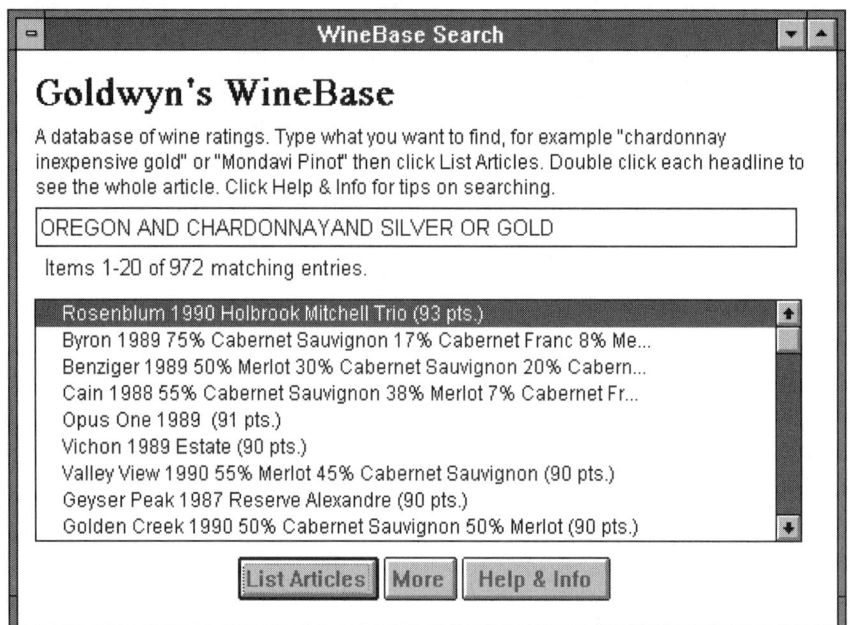

Figure 13-8: Improper use of *or* criteria is worse than specifying no criteria at all.

Uh oh! More than 900 matches! A mistake has been made. This is a problem similar to an algebraic statement such as "x = 5 plus 2 times 7." What's the value of x: 49 or 19? Do you first add the 5 and the 2, then multiply? Or do you multiply first, then add? WineBase has the same problem. It seems to be interpreting my criteria as "Oregon and chardonnay and silver—or gold, or platinum."

The solution is the same as the solution for mathematical expressions—parentheses. The answer to the statement "x = 5 plus (2 x 7)" is specific, as are the criteria in Figure 13-9.

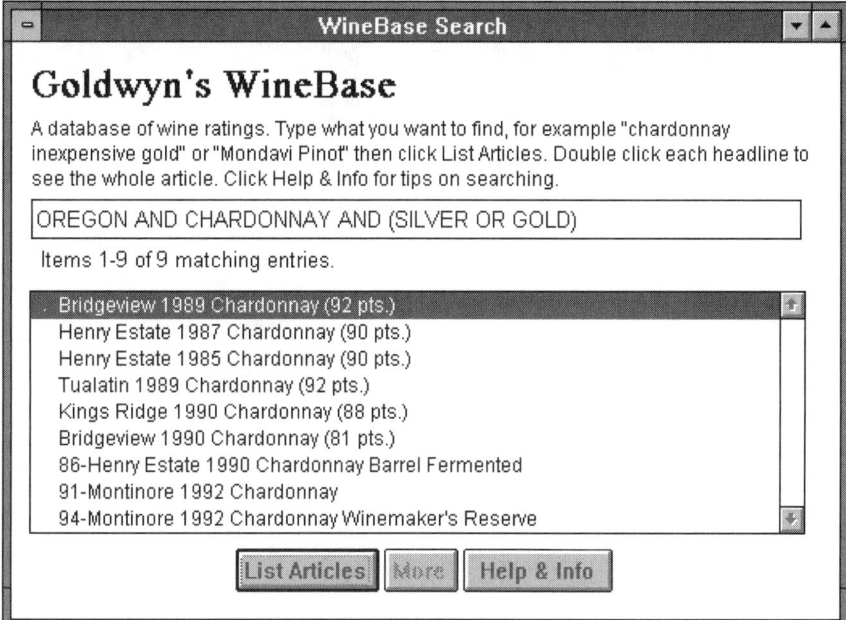

Figure 13-9: That's more like it. Nine wines is just the right number from which to choose. I'll take the list to the store and be back by the time my guests arrive.

Actually, the selection of wines at the shop I frequent is especially comprehensive. I suspect they will have all nine of the wines listed in Figure 13-9. Rather than pick one at random, I'll poll the database further. A double-click Montinore 1992, for instance, produces the description pictured in Figure 13-10.

Reviewing all nine listings takes about 10 minutes. Indeed, the whole process only required about 15 minutes from sign on to sign off. Our dinner guests will be astounded with my enological expertise and entranced by my erudite conversation. Naturally, I'll take all the credit, though WineBase properly deserves it.

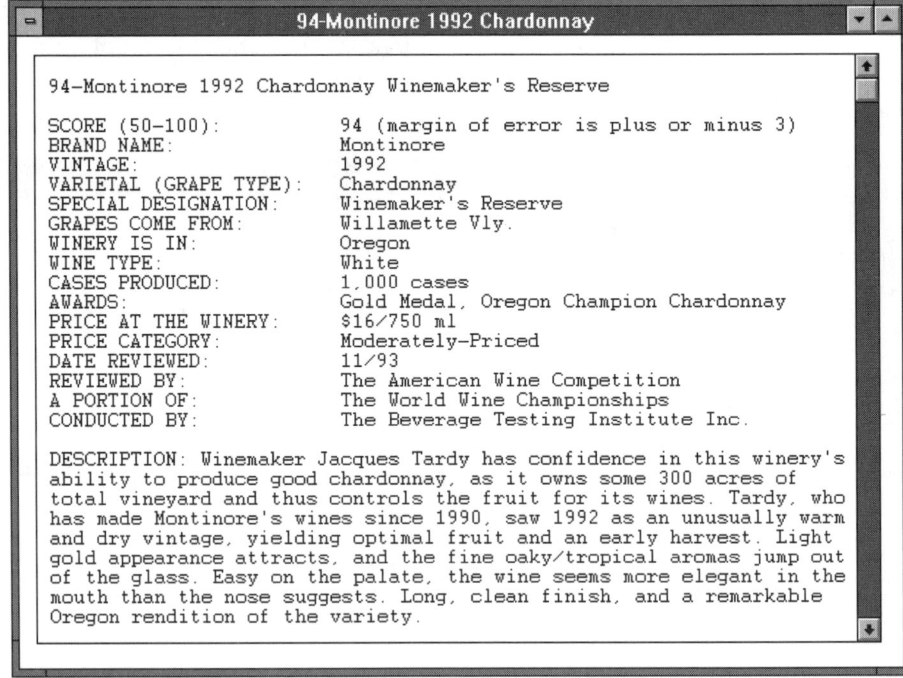
94-Montinore 1992 Chardonnay

94-Montinore 1992 Chardonnay Winemaker's Reserve

SCORE (50-100):	94 (margin of error is plus or minus 3)
BRAND NAME:	Montinore
VINTAGE:	1992
VARIETAL (GRAPE TYPE):	Chardonnay
SPECIAL DESIGNATION:	Winemaker's Reserve
GRAPES COME FROM:	Willamette Vly.
WINERY IS IN:	Oregon
WINE TYPE:	White
CASES PRODUCED:	1,000 cases
AWARDS:	Gold Medal, Oregon Champion Chardonnay
PRICE AT THE WINERY:	$16/750 ml
PRICE CATEGORY:	Moderately-Priced
DATE REVIEWED:	11/93
REVIEWED BY:	The American Wine Competition
A PORTION OF:	The World Wine Championships
CONDUCTED BY:	The Beverage Testing Institute Inc.

DESCRIPTION: Winemaker Jacques Tardy has confidence in this winery's ability to produce good chardonnay, as it owns some 300 acres of total vineyard and thus controls the fruit for its wines. Tardy, who has made Montinore's wines since 1990, saw 1992 as an unusually warm and dry vintage, yielding optimal fruit and an early harvest. Light gold appearance attracts, and the fine oaky/tropical aromas jump out of the glass. Easy on the palate, the wine seems more elegant in the mouth than the nose suggests. Long, clean finish, and a remarkable Oregon rendition of the variety.

Figure 13-10: The database record for a single wine reveals its price, awards, and ranking.

Message Boards

Not all clubs feature databases, and not all members require access to one. Fortunately, there's much more to AOL's clubs than databases. These are clubs, after all. People gather in clubs to discuss subjects of mutual interest and to learn more about their field. They might conduct some database research while they're online as well; but people make a club, and people make AOL's forums.

America Online's message boards are the electronic analog of the old familiar cork board and pushpins. Message boards (call them "boards") are especially appropriate to online clubs. One of the unique advantages clubs offer is convenience: you can drop in any time of the day or night, read the messages and post your replies.

Most of us visit our favorite clubs every time we sign on, and anxiously read all the messages posted since the last time we visited. The feeling is remarkably immediate, and withdrawal sets in after about three days absence. In other words, boards are addictive—but that's part of the fun.

Editing the Go To Menu

Once you've found a club to your liking, you might want to visit it every time you sign on. Rather than navigate a stack of menus or type a keyword, give the club a place on your Go To menu. Items at the bottom of the Go To menu are under your control; you can add or delete any one you please. The only requirement is that the item must have a keyword.

Let's say you've become an active participant in the Cooking Club. To add it to your Go To menu, follow the procedure illustrated in Figure 13-11.

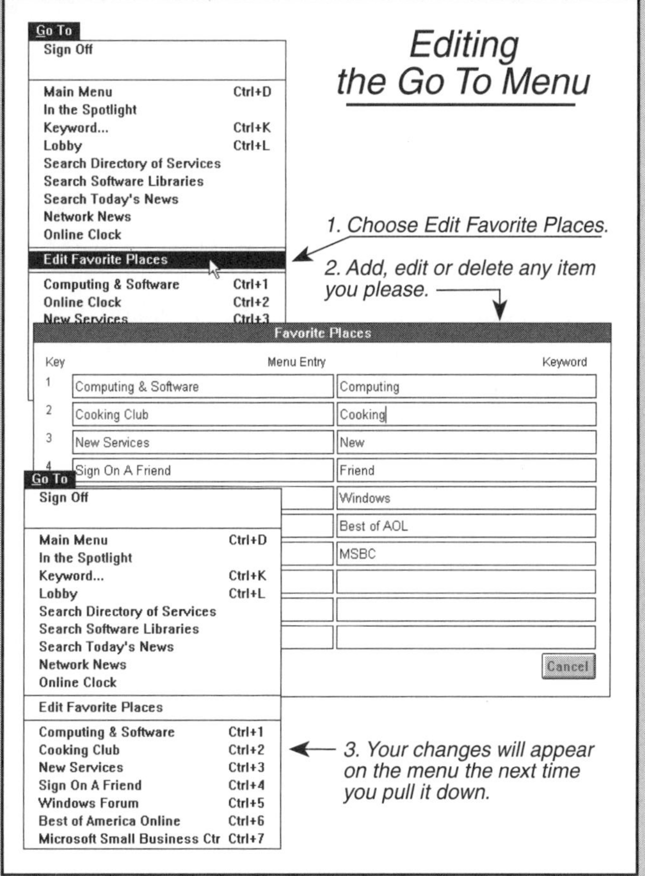

Figure 13-11: Adding menu items is accommodated via the Edit Favorite Places command.

More

Note that there are a total of ten positions that you can customize on the Go To menu, and that mine only has seven active. You don't have to have all ten positions filled if you don't want to, nor do you have to use those which AOL initially provides. You can change any item (select it and type over), or delete items (select the item, then use the Backspace key on your keyboard). Changes made to the Go To menu are unique to that computer, by the way, and not to any particular screen name. They won't appear when you're using another machine.

Once a club has been added to the Go To menu, all you have to do to get there is choose it from that menu. My Go To menu contains the names of the places I like to check every time I'm online. By choosing each one in order, I never neglect to visit places I'm likely to forget.

Reading Messages

One of my favorite clubs in the Clubs & Interests Department is the Cooking Club (keyword: Cooking). These folks like their food, and their library of recipes (The Kitchen Closet) ranges from elegant appetizers to tantalizing desserts. The Cupboard offers articles and reviews of cookbooks and cooking software, and The Kitchen (a chat room, a topic we discussed in Chapter 12) opens each Sunday evening at 8:00 P.M. (Eastern time) for a cooking class, new recipes and lively camaraderie. (This is an especially nonthreatening chat room by the way. If you're new to chat rooms you might try this one first: there's very little aggression among people who spend their Sundays sipping sherry and discussing soufflés.)

But I'm getting ahead of myself. I've chosen this club because it's an excellent example of message boards. In fact, it has three of them. Everyone eats food, after all, and most of us who eat it aren't shy when it comes to talking about it. For this discussion, we'll examine the Cooking Club's recipe-exchange board, The Cookbook (see Figure 13-12).

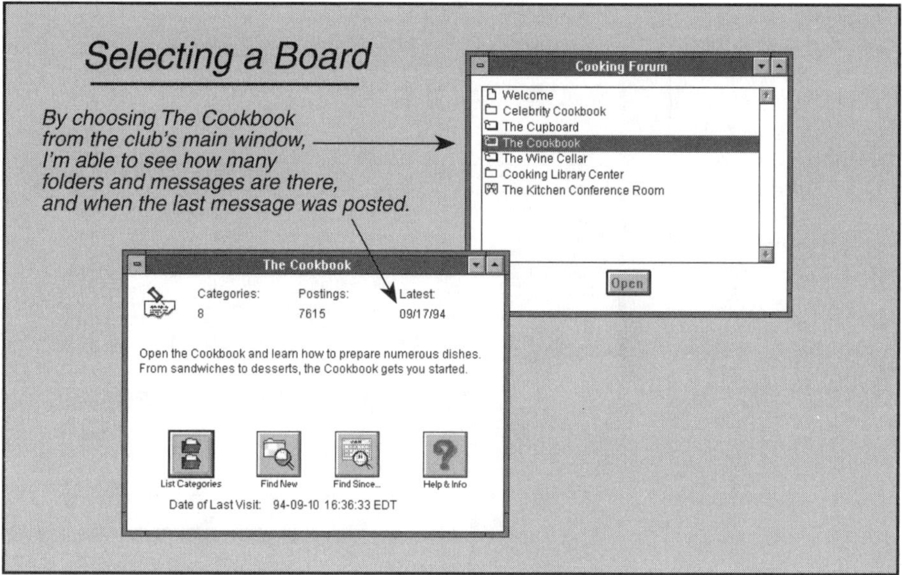

Figure 13-12: Type the keyword: Cooking to open the Cooking Club's main window, then double-click The Cookbook to visit the board.

Four icons appear across the bottom of The Cookbook window: List Categories, Find New, Find Since and Help & Info. We'll examine each of these, beginning with the one marked List Categories (see Figure 13-13). Since this is a complex board—it's a cookbook after all, and cookbooks are typically large and organizationally complex—a click on Figure 13-12's List Categories icon produces a list of categories (the top window in Figure 13-13), each of which is followed by a list of *topics*. The Desserts category, for instance, is further subdivided into more specific topics (Pound Cakes, Candy and Confections, and so on). Note that Figure 13-13's top window offers no Create Topic icon: these categories were established by the forum leader and can't be changed. The second window offers a Create Topic icon, and its topics represent the specificity that's typical of the members' interests. In this board, the categories are the staff's creation; the topics belong to the members. While this is a little anarchistic, it's also democratic; and that's the way message boards should be. If you feel like making a comment that's off the subject, use the Create Topic icon to make a new folder for it.

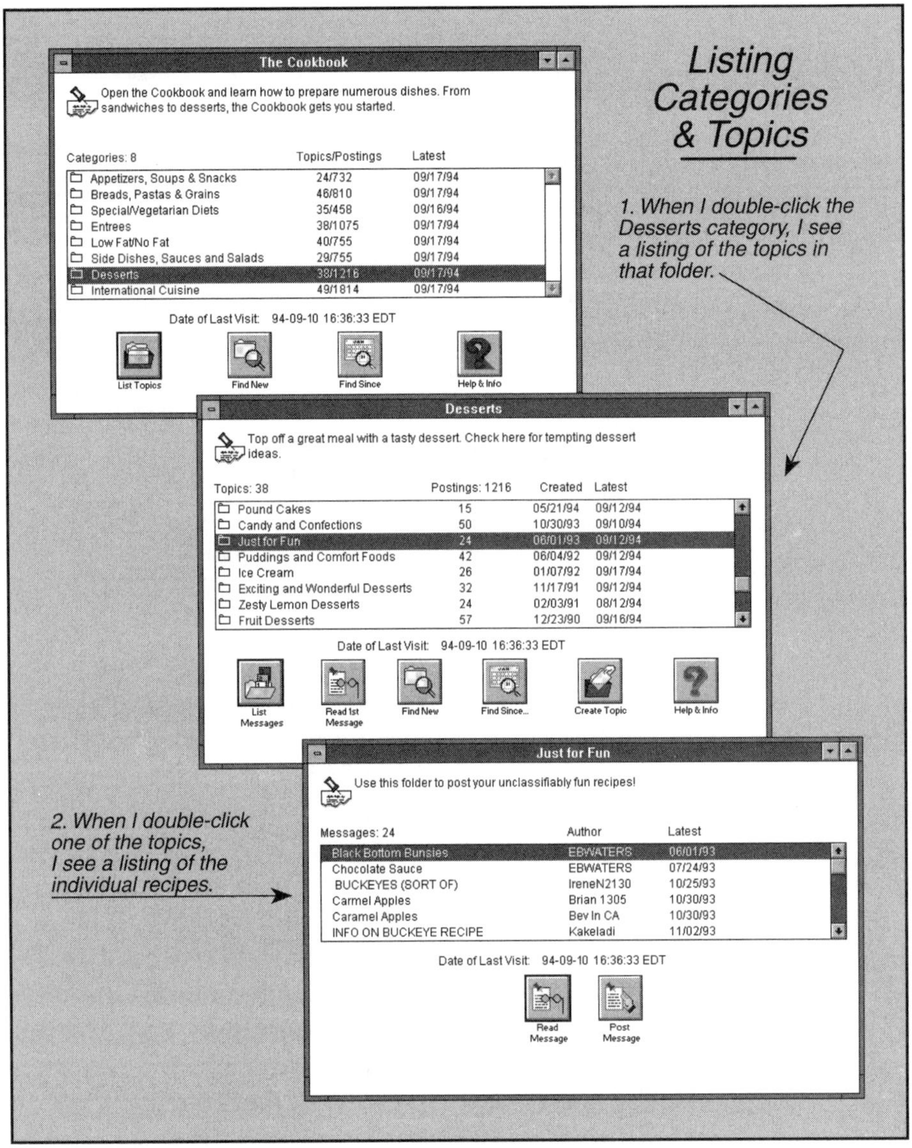

Figure 13-13: The eight categories posted on The Cookbook's recipe board are followed by up to fifty member topics. Each topic folder contains a number of individual recipes.

Listing Categories & Topics

The Cookbook

Open the Cookbook and learn how to prepare numerous dishes. From sandwiches to desserts, the Cookbook gets you started.

Categories: 8	Topics/Postings	Latest
Appetizers, Soups & Snacks	24/732	09/17/94
Breads, Pastas & Grains	46/810	09/17/94
Special/Vegetarian Diets	35/458	09/16/94
Entrees	38/1075	09/17/94
Low Fat/No Fat	40/755	09/17/94
Side Dishes, Sauces and Salads	29/755	09/17/94
Desserts	38/1216	09/17/94
International Cuisine	49/1814	09/17/94

Date of Last Visit: 94-09-10 16:36:33 EDT

List Topics | Find New | Find Since | Help & Info

1. When I double-click the Desserts category, I see a listing of the topics in that folder.

Desserts

Top off a great meal with a tasty dessert. Check here for tempting dessert ideas.

Topics: 38	Postings: 1216	Created	Latest
Pound Cakes	15	05/21/94	09/12/94
Candy and Confections	50	10/30/93	09/10/94
Just for Fun	24	06/01/93	09/12/94
Puddings and Comfort Foods	42	06/04/92	09/12/94
Ice Cream	26	01/07/92	09/17/94
Exciting and Wonderful Desserts	32	11/17/91	09/12/94
Zesty Lemon Desserts	24	02/03/91	08/12/94
Fruit Desserts	57	12/23/90	09/16/94

Date of Last Visit: 94-09-10 16:36:33 EDT

List Messages | Read 1st Message | Find New | Find Since... | Create Topic | Help & Info

2. When I double-click one of the topics, I see a listing of the individual recipes.

Just for Fun

Use this folder to post your unclassifiably fun recipes!

Messages: 24	Author	Latest
Black Bottom Bunsies	EBWATERS	06/01/93
Chocolate Sauce	EBWATERS	07/24/93
BUCKEYES (SORT OF)	IreneN2130	10/25/93
Carmel Apples	Brian 1305	10/30/93
Caramel Apples	Bev In CA	10/30/93
INFO ON BUCKEYE RECIPE	Kakeladi	11/02/93

Date of Last Visit: 94-09-10 16:36:33 EDT

Read Message | Post Message

The bulletin board metaphor is distorted a bit here. Individual messages aren't normally posted on boards; *folders* are posted on boards (the messages themselves are inside the folders). Look again at the left-hand window in Figure 13-12: this board is currently holding over 7,000 messages. If all 7,000 were posted independently, the board would be a mess. You would never find a thing. The board's nested folders are merely organizational tools intended to help you locate topics of interest to you.

To read the messages placed in a folder, double-click the folder. By double-clicking the Just for Fun topic folder in Figure 13-13's center window, we reveal the twenty-four recipes listed in the Just for Fun window at the bottom of that illustration. Although only six recipes can be seen listed in the window, you can scroll down to view the other eighteen.

To read all of the messages in a folder, double-click the first one, then use the Next Message icon (see Figure 13-14) to sequentially display the rest.

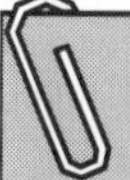

Log Those Messages

Reading messages is one of the most time-consuming activities AOL offers. Rather than read messages online, save a log of them (I discussed logs in Chapter 6, "Today's News") as they download to your PC. Let them scroll off your screen as fast as they can; do not try to read them while you're online. When you have finished the session, sign off, open the log (choose Open from AOL's File menu, or open it with a word processor) and read it at your leisure. You can always add messages to boards by signing back on again.

Reading Every Message in a Folder

Desserts/Just for Fun

Subj: Black Bottom Bunsies
Date: 93-06-01 15:57:42 EDT
From: EBWATERS

Black Bottom Bunsies

1 1/2 C all purpose flour
1 tsp. baking soda
1/2 tsp. salt
1 C sugar

Previous Message | Add Message | Next Message

Subj: Black Bottom Bunsies
From: EBWATERS

Black Bottom Bunsies

1 1/2 C all purpose flour

Sprinkle top

Makes 5 dozen

Subj: Chocolate Sauce 93-07-24 18:13:44 EST
From: EBWATERS

Chocolate Sauce

Subj: BUCKEYES (SORT OF) 93-10-25 12:28:33 EST
From: IreneN2130

2 cups peanut butter
1 stick melted butter
2 cups powdered sugar

Subj: Carmel Apples 93-10-30 10:08:24 EST
From: Brian 1305

I am trying to make carmel apples because I can't eat chocolate. If anyone has any suggestions for those or any other tasty non chocolate desserts, please send some to Brian 1305. Thanks

Subj: Caramel Apples 93-10-30 21:36:03 EST
From: Bev In CA

Caramel Apples

5 medium apples
1 cup granulated sugar
3/4 cup dark corn syrup
1 cup cream
2 Tablespoons butter
1 teaspoon vanilla
coarsely chopped nuts (optional)

Wash apples, remove stems, and stick skewers into stem ends of apples. Cook sugar, syrup, cream, butter, and vanilla to firm-ball stage, 245F. Do not stir. Remove from heat. Dip apples into syrup; spoon syrup over apples to cover completely. Remove apples; hold skewer between palms of hands and spin for a moment to cool caramel. If desired, roll in coarsely chopped nuts. Place apples upright on waxed paper.

The Next Message icon is the key to reading all messages. Every message will offer one except the last.

Brian's morning plea for help was answered that evening.

Figure 13-14: Once you have read the first message in a folder, click the Next Message icon to read the remaining messages in the order of their posting.

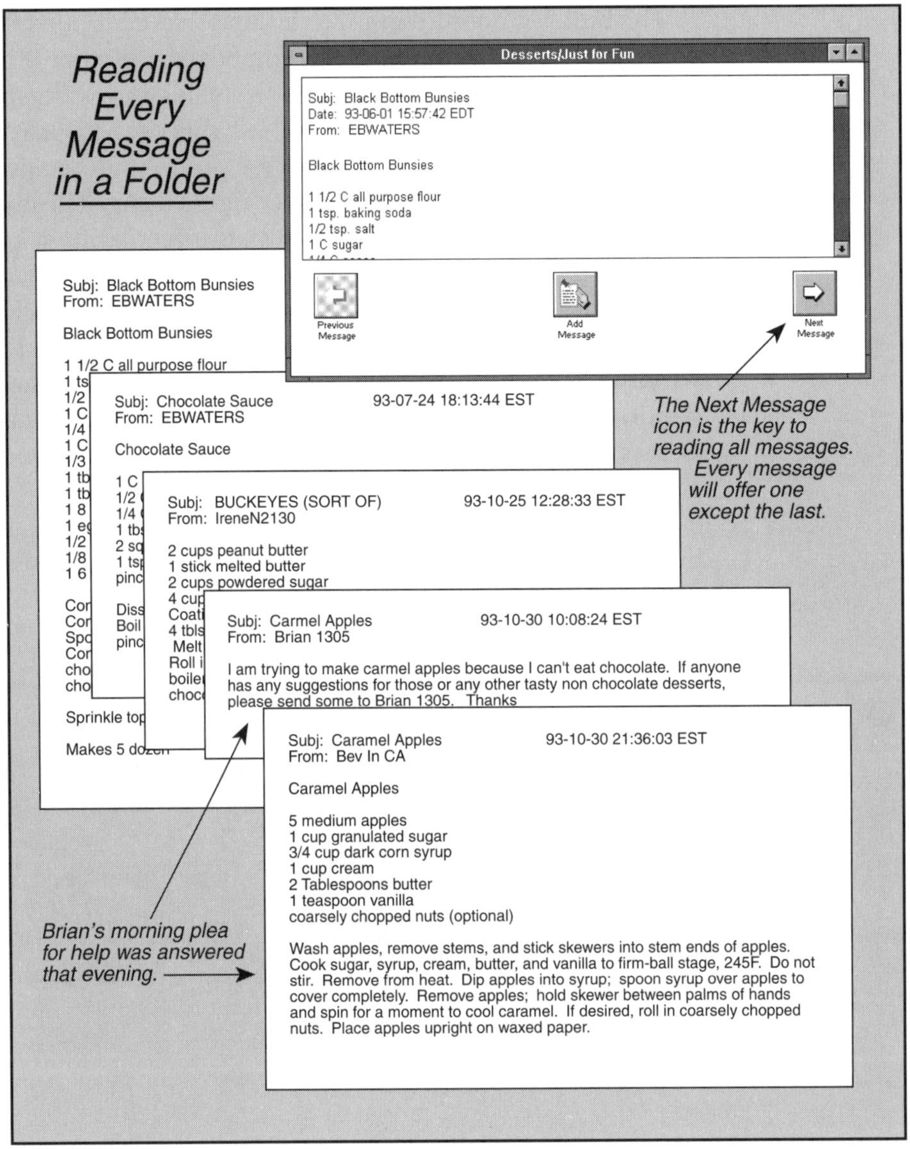

Browsing, Finding & Reading Messages

I need to take a side trip here. The verbs *browse, find* and *read* have particular, unequivocal meanings when it comes to message boards; it's important that you understand how to use them. Think of a public library: you might go to the library simply to pass the time. You walk in and browse, picking up a book here and there as different titles strike your fancy. On another day, you might visit the library with a specific title already in mind, in which case you go straight to the card files and find that particular book. Regardless of how you come across a book, you eventually want to sit down and read it, page by page.

America Online attaches the same meanings to these verbs. Look again at the Desserts window at the center of Figure 13-13. Six icons parade across the bottom of the window, representing variations on the three verbs we're discussing.

The List Messages icon displays the folder's message subjects, authors and dates, not the messages themselves (see the Just for Fun window at the bottom of Figure 13-13). The List Messages feature is like browsing through the books in a library: they're similar concepts. The leftmost icon (List Messages, in this case) is the default: if you double-click a folder, you'll see the list that appears in the lower window of Figure 13-13.

Clicking the Read First Message icon produces a window displaying the first message in the folder (see the top window in Figure 13-14).

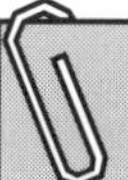

The Subject Line

As you read through this section, note the role played by the messages' subject lines. A subject line like "Comment" doesn't illuminate its contents very well. Alternatively, the subject line "Chocolate Sauce" clearly summarizes the content of the message and intrigues the reader. Spend a moment thinking about subject lines when you post your own messages; they're significant.

This might be a board you read often. You might visit it every time you sign on. If you do, you can go right to the Find New icon, which displays only those messages posted since you last visited (see Figure 13-15).

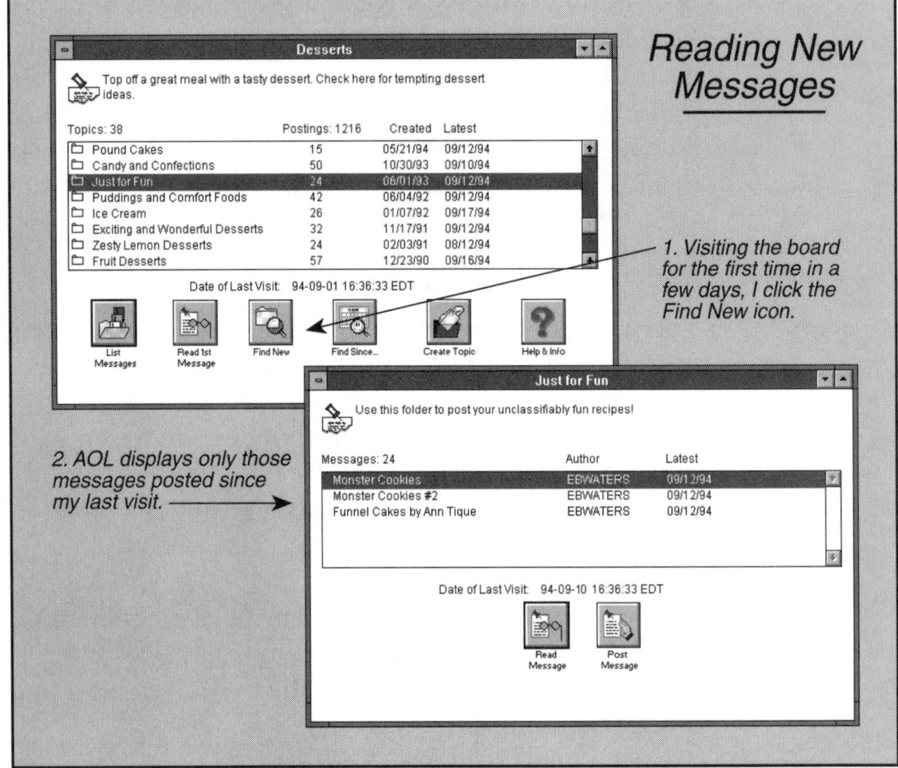

Figure 13-15: Only new messages appear when you click the Find New icon. You can read them, add to them, or list all of the messages in the folder.

Note the Post Message icon at the bottom of Figure 13-15. This is how you add messages to the folder. All you need to do is click the icon, enter the subject and text of your message, then click Post to submit your effort. Your message will be added to the folder immediately. I'll discuss this further in a moment.

Most boards contain hundreds of messages. No matter how interested in the subject you might be, it's doubtful you'll want to read every message the first time you visit a board. Or maybe you've been away from the board for a few months and don't want to be deluged with all the messages posted since your last visit. These are two of the reasons why AOL provides the Find Since icon (see Figure 13-16).

It took me months to figure out just how the List Messages, Find and Read icons work. I hope this little discussion saves you the trouble. Regardless, find a board that interests you and start reading its messages. Start with just one or two folders, read the last week's worth of messages, and become familiar with the subject and the people. When you feel confident, post your own messages. It is at that moment—

when you have joined the fray—that message boards start to get really interesting. This is part of the fun; don't deny yourself the opportunity.

Your Personal Date

Your personal "date of last visit" is marked the instant you visit a board. This implies two things: (1) No matter how many (or how few) messages you read while visiting a board, none of the messages posted prior to that visit are displayed when you next click the Find New icon; and (2) If anyone (including you) posts a message on a board while you're reading, that message will appear when you next click the Find New icon.

Note that I'm talking about *boards* here, not folders. If a board contains 600 messages in 24 folders and you read one message in one folder, none of the remaining messages will show up the next time you click the Find New icon, in any folder on the board. This is a significant subtlety. Don't let it trip you up.

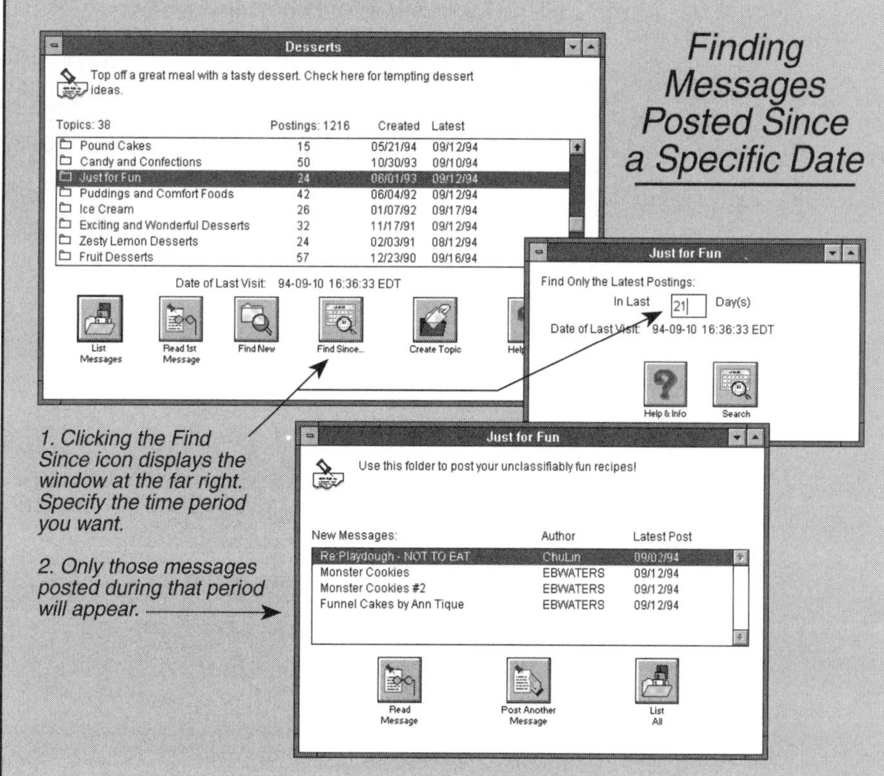

Figure 13-16: The Find Since icon allows you to specify the extent of a message list.

Posting Messages

A moment ago, I suggested you post your own messages. It might help if we review that process. There is not much to it: take a look at Figure 13-17.

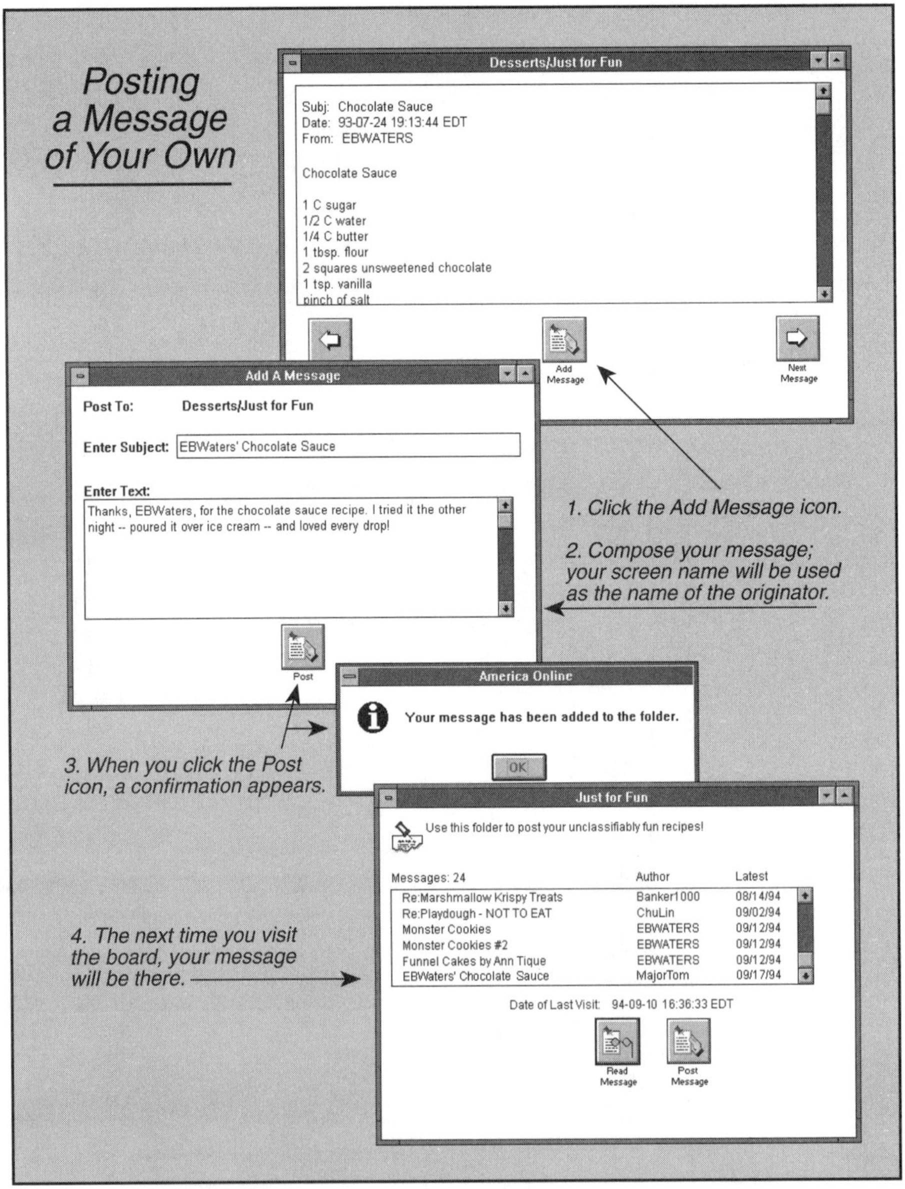

Figure 13-17: Posting your own message is as simple as clicking an icon.

Posting a Message of Your Own

Desserts/Just for Fun

Subj: Chocolate Sauce
Date: 93-07-24 19:13:44 EDT
From: EBWATERS

Chocolate Sauce

1 C sugar
1/2 C water
1/4 C butter
1 tbsp. flour
2 squares unsweetened chocolate
1 tsp. vanilla
pinch of salt

Add Message
Next Message

Add A Message

Post To: Desserts/Just for Fun

Enter Subject: EBWaters' Chocolate Sauce

Enter Text:
Thanks, EBWaters, for the chocolate sauce recipe. I tried it the other night -- poured it over ice cream -- and loved every drop!

Post

1. Click the Add Message icon.

2. Compose your message; your screen name will be used as the name of the originator.

America Online

Your message has been added to the folder.

OK

3. When you click the Post icon, a confirmation appears.

Just for Fun

Use this folder to post your unclassifiably fun recipes!

Messages: 24	Author	Latest
Re:Marshmallow Krispy Treats	Banker1000	08/14/94
Re:Playdough - NOT TO EAT	ChuLin	09/02/94
Monster Cookies	EBWATERS	09/12/94
Monster Cookies #2	EBWATERS	09/12/94
Funnel Cakes by Ann Tique	EBWATERS	09/12/94
EBWaters' Chocolate Sauce	MajorTom	09/17/94

Date of Last Visit: 94-09-10 16:36:33 EDT

Read Message
Post Message

4. The next time you visit the board, your message will be there.

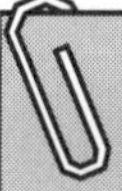

Online Etiquette

If you want to be heard, if you want replies to your messages, and if you want to be a responsible online citizen, you should comply with a few rules of telecommunications etiquette. Since Emily Post and Miss Manners haven't yet spoken on the subject (now that I think about it, Emily Post *has* spoken on the subject, and we'll discuss her in the next chapter), we'd best discuss it here.

- Post messages only when you have something to say, phrase the subject header effectively, and be succinct. The best messages have provocative headers and pithy prose. If your message fills more than a screen of text—if it requires a trip to the scroll bar to read—edit it.
- Stick to the subject. If the folder you're participating in is entitled "Weasels in Wyoming," don't discuss armadillos in Arizona.
- If your message wanders, summarize before responding. You might quote a previous posting (do so in brackets: "When you said <I really prefer Macintosh> were you talking about apples or Apples?"). This will help others stick to the topic.
- Don't post chain letters, advertisements or business offers unless the board was created for it. And never send junk mail to unsuspecting recipients.
- HEY YOU! CAN YOU HEAR ME??!! (Did I get your attention? Did you like the way I did it?) All caps are distracting, hard to read and arrogant. Use all caps only when you really want to shout (and those occasions are rare). For emphasis, place asterisks around your text: "I *told* you he was a geek!"
- Do not issue personal attacks, use profanity or betray a confidence. If criticism is specifically invited, remember that there is no vocal inflection or body language to soften the impact and remove the potential for misinterpretation. E-mail is a better forum for criticism than boards are.
- For the same reason, subtleties, double entendres and sarcasm are rarely effective.
- Avoid emotional responses. Think before you write. Once you've posted a message, you can't take it back.
- Remember your options. Some replies are better sent as mail than as messages. If you're feeling particularly vitriolic, send mail to the perpetrator. This saves face for both of you.

Posting effective messages is something of an art. Messages like "Me too," or "I don't think so" don't really contribute to a board. Before you post a message, be sure you have something to say, take the time to phrase it effectively and give it a proper subject header.

Threaded Boards

Some boards offer *message threading*: messages arranged so that you can elect to read responses to a specific message. Compare this with the Read First Message command pictured in Figure 13-16. Reading the first message displays the first message on a board with the option to read all of the remaining messages on the board as well.

Threaded message boards allow you to choose to read only the replies to a specific message. This is especially appropriate where the subject of a specific folder is likely to be broad and its messages are numerous and varied. To examine a threaded board, let's visit the Pet Care Club (use the keyword: Pets). A number of veterinarians from universities and private practices visit this board regularly, some of whom are on the board's staff. If you have pets—dogs, cats, reptiles, birds, even farm animals—this is a club you will want to visit often (see Figure 13-18).

Until now, threaded boards look just like unthreaded boards. But look what happens when I double-click the folder labeled "Cat Behavior" (Figure 13-19).

Look carefully at Figure 13-19: a Responses column appears, identifying the number of responses that have been posted to any particular message. A new List Responses icon appears at the bottom of the window as well.

Now watch what happens when I double-click the "Mean cat" posting (Figure 13-20).

Figure 13-18: The Pet Care Club offers boards for not only dogs and cats, but for farm animals, fish—even reptiles.

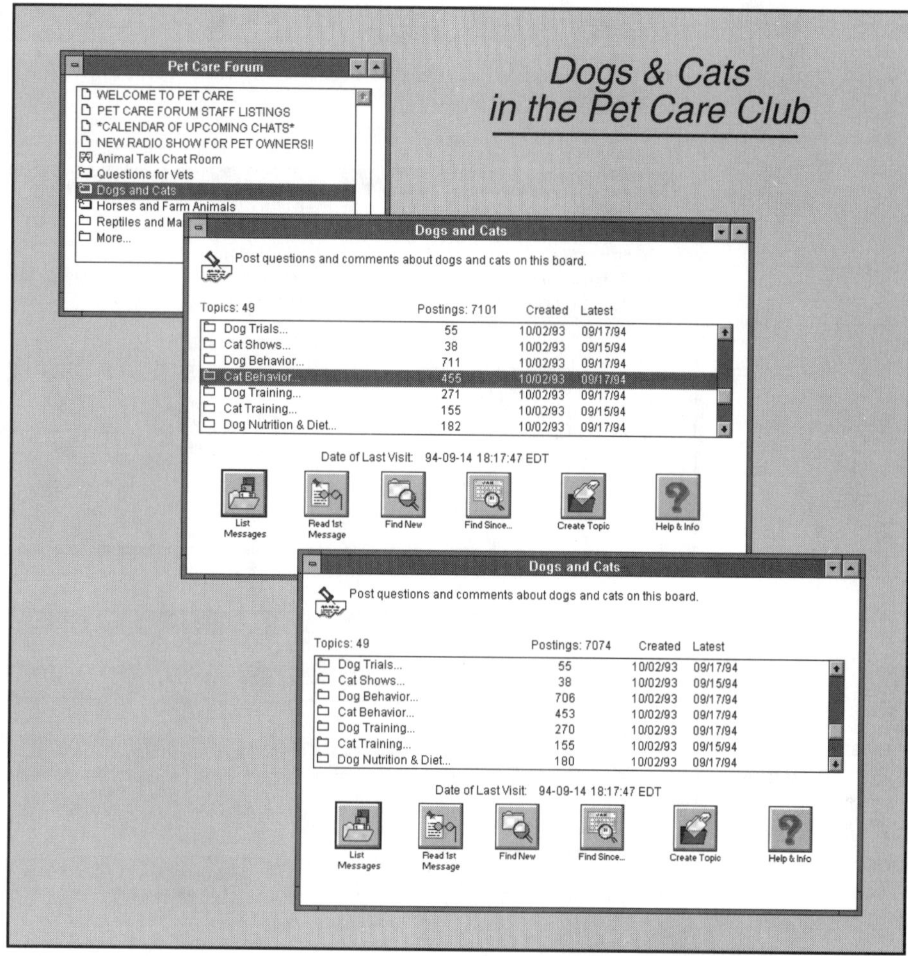

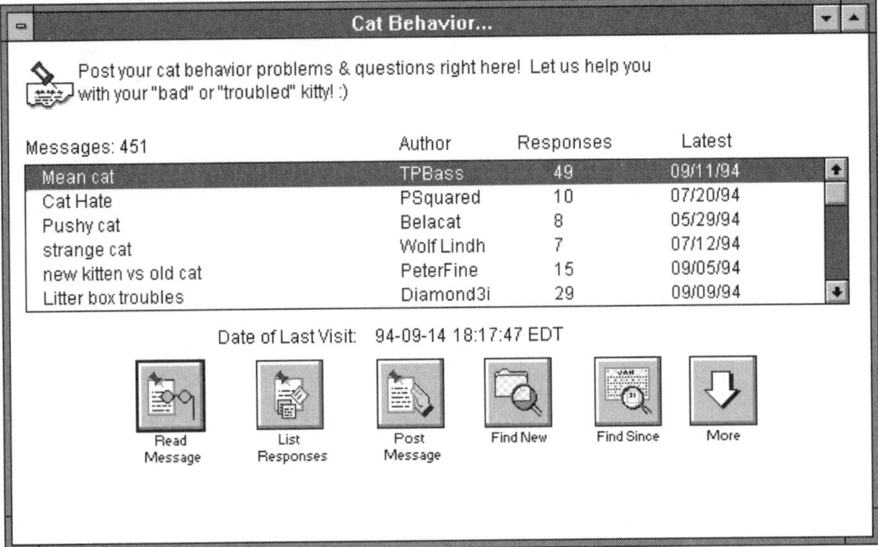

Figure 13-19: Threaded boards offer a Responses column and a List Responses icon at the bottom of the window.

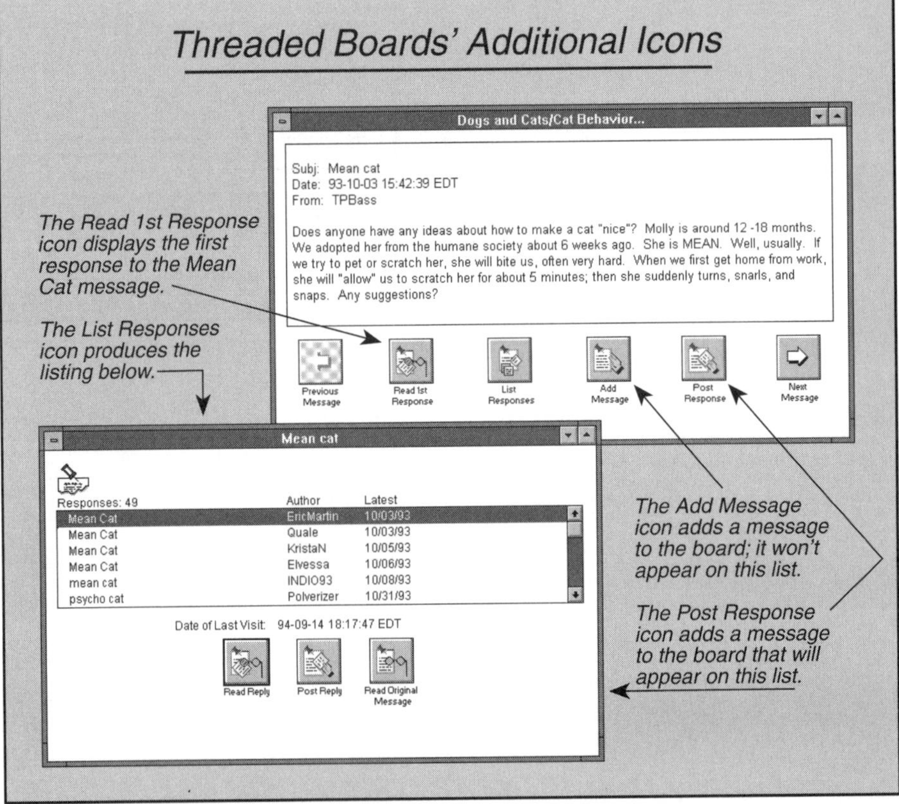

Figure 13-20: Note how the list of responses to the "Mean cat" message provides me with the opportunity to post a reply or reread the original message in case I've forgotten a detail.

The Read 1st Response and List Responses icons are new to the message window, as is the Post Response icon. When I click the List Responses icon I see a listing of only the responses to the "Mean cat" message. This provides a method by which I can stick to the "Mean cat" subject, and not wander all over the board.

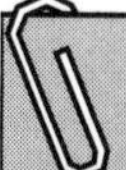

Proper Replies

Be sure you post replies to messages properly. Look again at the upper window in Figure 13-20: two reply icons appear there—Add Message and Post Response. The Add Message icon simply adds a message to the board; the added message is posted independently and not identified as a response to any other message. A message posted via the Post Response icon will appear as a response in a list of responses, similar to those pictured in the lower window of Figure 13-20. It's not just a matter of semantics; it's an organizational imperative. Give consideration to your replies on threaded boards: post them where they're most appropriate.

Not all boards are threaded. Some lend themselves to threading, some don't. Some of my favorites aren't threaded and I'm glad: threading discourages the kind of browsing that favored boards merit. Don't look upon an unthreaded board as old-fashioned or anarchistic. Welcome them, and celebrate their diversity.

Libraries

Libraries are collections of computer files, and the libraries in Clubs & Interests are especially bountiful. For the sake of discussion, I have chosen Star Trek: The Club (keyword: Trek). This is a particularly imaginative club, offering not only libraries of information, but simulations as well. "Starfleet Academy" (a role-playing chat room spinoff of the Star Trek club) meets every evening and "boldly goes where none have gone before."

Libraries consist of files, and files are available for downloading to your computer. The library in the Star Trek club contains text files, graphics files and even a few animations. Text and graphics files are usually generic and can be viewed with the appropriate software on any type of computer. Animation files are more computer-specific. If you're not sure whether you have the appropriate hardware or software needed to use a file, double-click the file's name to get a description of it. Under the headings "Needs" and "Equipment," you'll find out what you need to take advantage of that particular file.

Although downloading was discussed in Chapter 5 "Computing," a review seems in order here. Figure 13-21 describes the process.

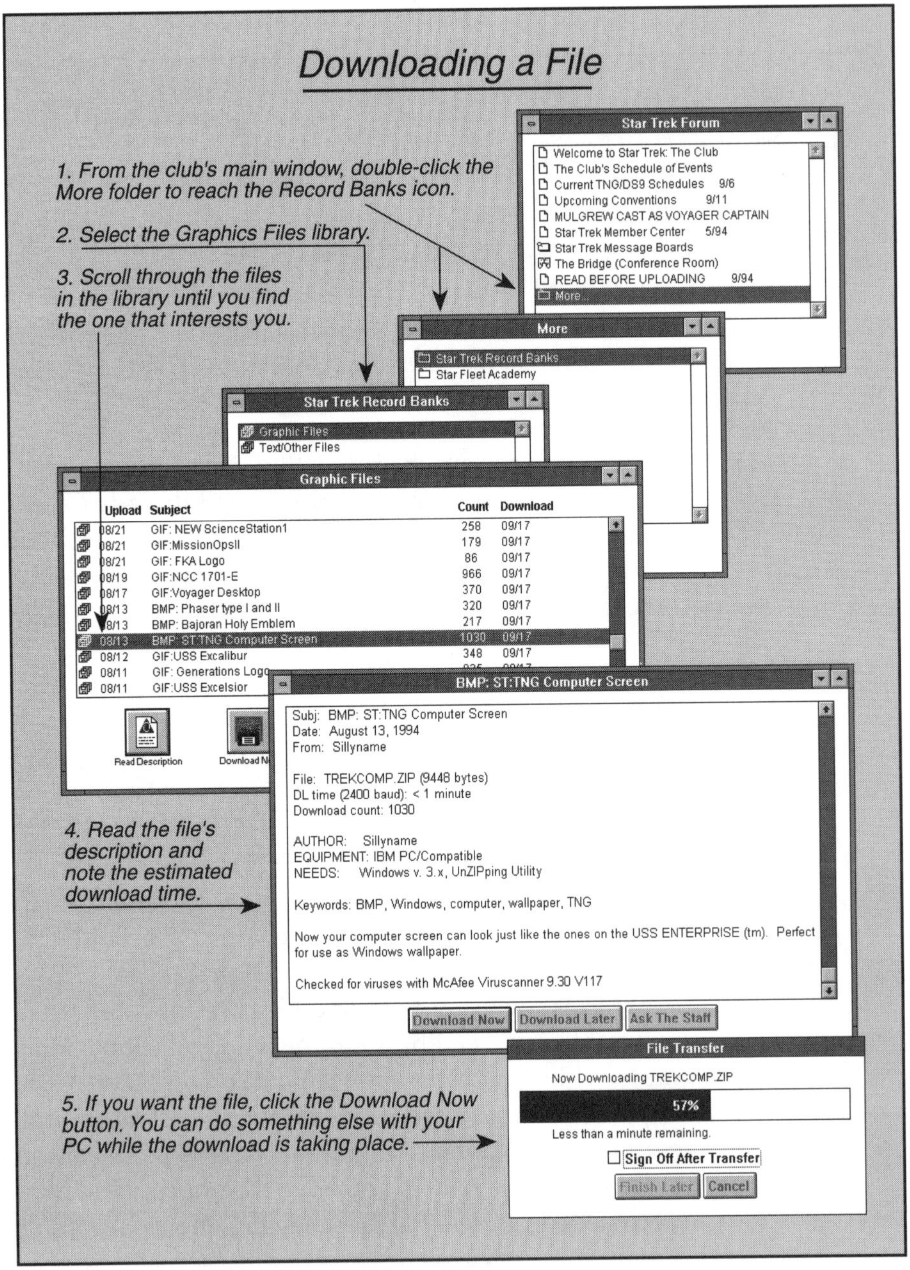

Figure 13-21: A quick glimpse of the file downloading process. Downloading is discussed in Chapter 5 "Computing."

Downloading a File

1. From the club's main window, double-click the More folder to reach the Record Banks icon.

2. Select the Graphics Files library.

3. Scroll through the files in the library until you find the one that interests you.

Star Trek Forum
Welcome to Star Trek: The Club
The Club's Schedule of Events
Current TNG/DS9 Schedules 9/6
Upcoming Conventions 9/11
MULGREW CAST AS VOYAGER CAPTAIN
Star Trek Member Center 5/94
Star Trek Message Boards
The Bridge (Conference Room)
READ BEFORE UPLOADING 9/94
More...

More
Star Trek Record Banks
Star Fleet Academy

Star Trek Record Banks
Graphic Files
Text/Other Files

Graphic Files

Upload	Subject	Count	Download
08/21	GIF: NEW ScienceStation1	258	09/17
08/21	GIF:MissionOpsII	179	09/17
08/21	GIF: FKA Logo	86	09/17
08/19	GIF:NCC 1701-E	966	09/17
08/17	GIF:Voyager Desktop	370	09/17
08/13	BMP: Phaser type I and II	320	09/17
08/13	BMP: Bajoran Holy Emblem	217	09/17
08/13	BMP: ST:TNG Computer Screen	1030	09/17
08/12	GIF:USS Excalibur	348	09/17
08/11	GIF: Generations Logo		
08/11	GIF:USS Excelsior		

Read Description
Download N

BMP: ST:TNG Computer Screen

Subj: BMP: ST:TNG Computer Screen
Date: August 13, 1994
From: Sillyname

File: TREKCOMP.ZIP (9448 bytes)
DL time (2400 baud): < 1 minute
Download count: 1030

AUTHOR: Sillyname
EQUIPMENT: IBM PC/Compatible
NEEDS: Windows v. 3.x, UnZIPping Utility

Keywords: BMP, Windows, computer, wallpaper, TNG

Now your computer screen can look just like the ones on the USS ENTERPRISE (tm). Perfect for use as Windows wallpaper.

Checked for viruses with McAfee Viruscanner 9.30 V117

Download Now | Download Later | Ask The Staff

4. Read the file's description and note the estimated download time.

File Transfer
Now Downloading TREKCOMP.ZIP
57%
Less than a minute remaining.
Sign Off After Transfer
Finish Later | Cancel

5. If you want the file, click the Download Now button. You can do something else with your PC while the download is taking place.

Nearly every club at AOL offers a library of files, and many of the libraries are searchable. While the essence of any club might be colloquy and networking, the availability of an elegant library adds considerable value to the experience. Where would a club like the Star Trek club be without Star Trek goodies?

Multitasking

America Online offers three ways to download files: (1) You can simply click the Download Now button and sit in front of your machine like a fossil, watching all the excitement the thermometer provides; (2) You can queue files for downloading and wait until the end of your online session (or for another part of the day) and download then. This is a function of the Download Manager, which we'll discuss in Chapter 19; or (3) You can do something else with your PC while the download concludes in the background, like write that letter you owe to your mother or pay the bills (see Figure 13-22).

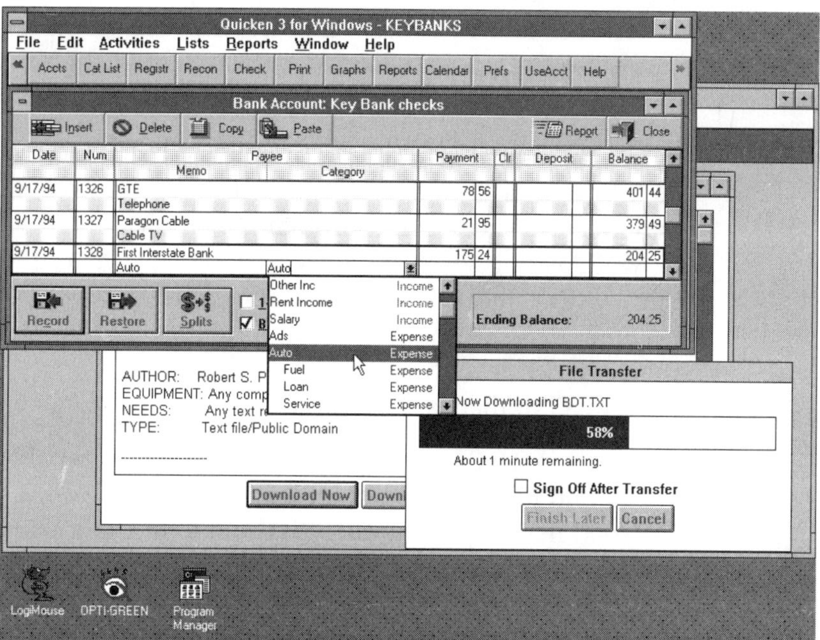

Figure 13-22: In the foreground I'm using Quicken to pay my household bills. My America Online software is downloading a graphic in the background. Neither process interferes much with the other, even on a slow machine.

The process of doing more than one thing at a time with your computer is known as *multitasking*, and it might come as a surprise to you (many veteran AOL members are ignorant of this feature) to discover that your AOL software offers true multitasking capabilities: start a download, then go off and do something else with your PC.

Here's how it's done:

- Ideally, start the software you intend to use during the download before you sign on. I started Quicken, for instance, before I began the online session pictured in Figure 13-22.
- If you haven't done so already, start your AOL software. It isn't important which software starts first. The AOL software, however, will have to occupy the front-most window in order for you to sign on.
- Sign on, locate the file you want to download, and start the downloading process by clicking the Download Now button pictured in Figure 13-21.
- Once the download thermometer appears (pictured in 13-21), press Alt-Esc to invoke the Windows Task List. If the program you want to use isn't already loaded, switch to the Program Manager to load it, then do as you please.

Use the other application normally. When the download concludes, AOL will once again become the active (front-most) window and announce its success in completing the task.

Multitasking seems a bit magical to me, and at first I didn't trust it, but it works. In three years I've never had a download go bad or a file become corrupted because of a multitask problem. In fact, I'm writing this sentence as a download is underway.

With all of that said, a few caveats are in order:

- Version 2.5 (but not the earlier versions) is capable of multitasking within itself. Once a download has begun, you can compose and send mail, visit forums—just about anything you can do when you're not downloading. Be aware, however, that performance might be sluggish, and that tasks involving other downloads (or uploads) may not function at all.
- Some software doesn't tolerate multitasking very well, especially software that relies heavily on disk activity or your computer's

central processing unit. Games are notoriously unfriendly to the multitasking environment.

- If you've got them, watch the lights on your modem. If the Receive Data (RD) light goes out or flickers badly while you're multitasking, you're asking too much of your PC. Run a FlashSession instead.

SeniorNet Online

My disclaimer at the beginning of this chapter notwithstanding, there's one club that I must mention. SeniorNet (the parent organization to SeniorNet Online) grew out of a research project begun in 1986 at the University of San Francisco to determine if computers and telecommunication could enhance the lives of older adults—in this case, adults who are 55 or older.

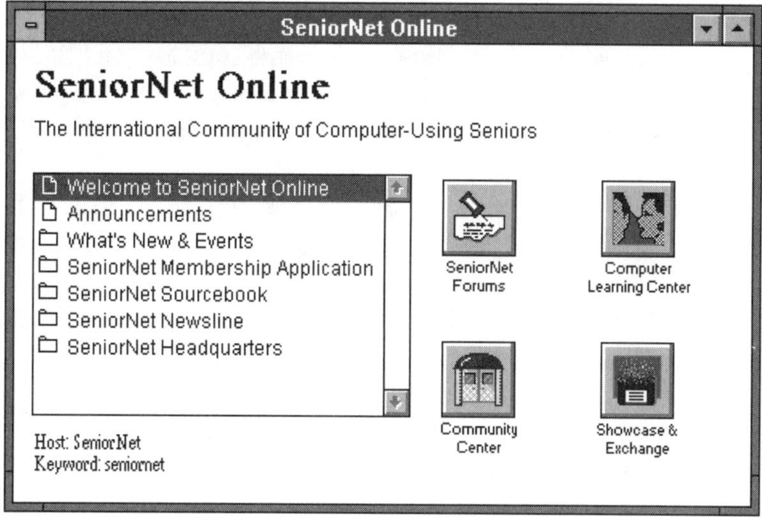

Figure 13-23: SeniorNet Online is home to over 5,000 SeniorNet members worldwide. Use the keyword: SeniorNet.

Though access to SeniorNet Online is afforded to any AOL member, those who qualify for and join SeniorNet receive a number of other benefits including:

- Unlimited SeniorNet Online access.

- Discounts of 25 to 50 percent on selected magazines and books.
- Significant discounts on computer hardware and software.
- *Newsline*, SeniorNet's quarterly newsletter. Each issue includes step-by-step computer workshops, computer product reviews, computer tips, and other articles of interest to computer-using seniors.
- Discounted admission to the national SeniorNet conference. The 1993 conference was held in Hawaii.

SeniorNet Online's boards are especially well-spoken and appropriate to the membership. Topics range from wellness to writing, and hundreds of postings appear every day. When I last visited, over *twenty thousand* messages were available. This might be the most active forum on AOL.

The History of the World

Peeking at the SeniorNet libraries the other day, I happened across this gem from history teacher Richard Lederer. Richard has pasted together the following "history" of the world from certifiably genuine student bloopers collected by teachers throughout the United States. Read carefully: you might learn something!

"The inhabitants of ancient Egypt were called mummies. They lived in the Sarah Dessert and traveled by Camelot. The climate of the Sarah is such that the inhabitants have to live elsewhere, so certain areas of the dessert are cultivated by irritation. The Egyptians build the Pyramids in the shape of a huge triangular cube. The Pyramids are a range of mountains between France and Spain.

"Without the Greeks, we wouldn't have history. The Greeks invented three kinds of columns—Corinthian, Doric and Ironic. They also had myths. A myth is a female moth. One myth says that the mother of Achilles dipped him into the River Stynx until it become intolerable.

"Achilles appears in the Iliad, by Homer. Homer also wrote The Oddity, in which Penelope was the last hardship that Ulysses endured on his journey. Actually Homer was not written by Homer but by another man of that name.

More

"Socrates was a famous Greek teacher who went about giving people advice. They killed him....

"In midevil times, most of the people were aliterate. The greatest writer of the time was Chaucer, who wrote many poems and verses and also wrote literature. Another tale tells of William Tell who shot an arrow through an apple while standing on his son's head.

"The Renaissance was an age in which more individuals felt the value of their human being. Martin Luther was nailed to the church door at Wittenberg for selling papal indulgences. He died a horrible death, being excommunicated by a bull....

"It was an age of great inventions and discoveries. Gutenberg invented the Bible. Sir Walter Raleigh invented cigarettes. Sir Francis Drake circumcised the world with a 100-foot clipper....

"Delegates from the original thirteen states formed the Contented Congress. Thomas Jefferson, a Virgin, and Benjamin Franklin were two singers of the Declaration of Independence. Franklin had gone to Boston carrying all his clothes in his pocket and a loaf of bread under each arm. He invented electricity by rubbing cats backwards and declared, 'A horse divided against itself cannot stand.' Franklin died in 1790 and is still dead."

Surely you know more now than you did a few minutes ago, even though I've cut more than half of the article in the interest of brevity. If you want it all, snoop around in the SeniorNet libraries. There's great reading to be found there.

Speaking of Seniors, the American Association of Retired Persons is the nation's oldest and largest organization of older Americans, with a membership of more than 33 million. AARP's motto, "To serve, not to be served," and its vision statement, "Bringing lifetimes of experience and leadership to serve all generations," are supported by its newest endeavor: AARP Online (see Figure 13-24).

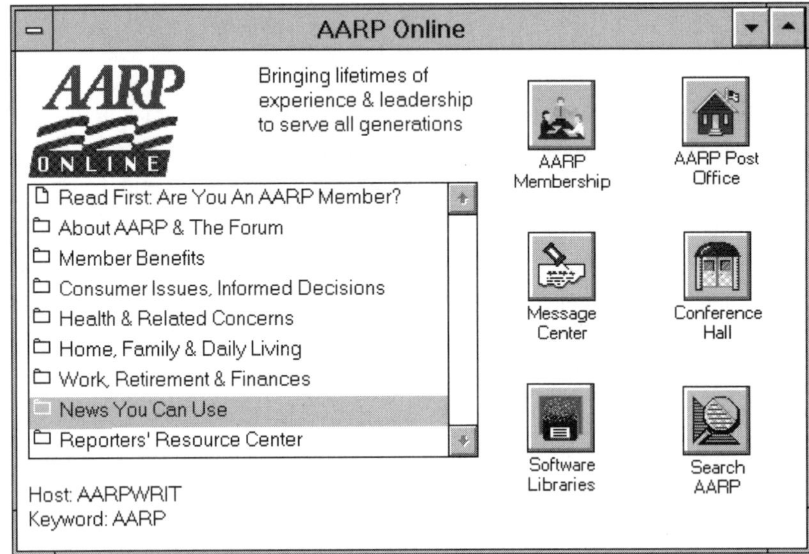

Figure 13-24: AARP Online offers extensive resources for Americans aged 50 and over.

AARP Online's consumer, health and home issues areas are especially comprehensive, but the message boards offer the greatest potential. This is a forum for older Americans—AARP members or not—to discuss issues or, perhaps more importantly, make the acquaintance of others with similar interests. Use the keyword: AARP to open this door of opportunity.

Moving On

America Online's Clubs & Interests Department might seem vast, and it is. But AOL's clubs are analogous to the range of clubs in any community, real or virtual: they're just the clubs in that community. One community does not equal a universe, no matter how large.

There are thousands of other online communities beyond those offered by AOL, scattered around the surface of the earth like cloves in an orange pomander. This universe of communities and the clubs within them is wired together via a protocol called the Internet, and the Internet's features—clubs and all—are available to any AOL member free of any charges beyond AOL's normal rates.

The Internet is vast and it can be intimidating. But not if you have a good guide. And you do. Just turn the page....

CHAPTER 14

The Internet Connection

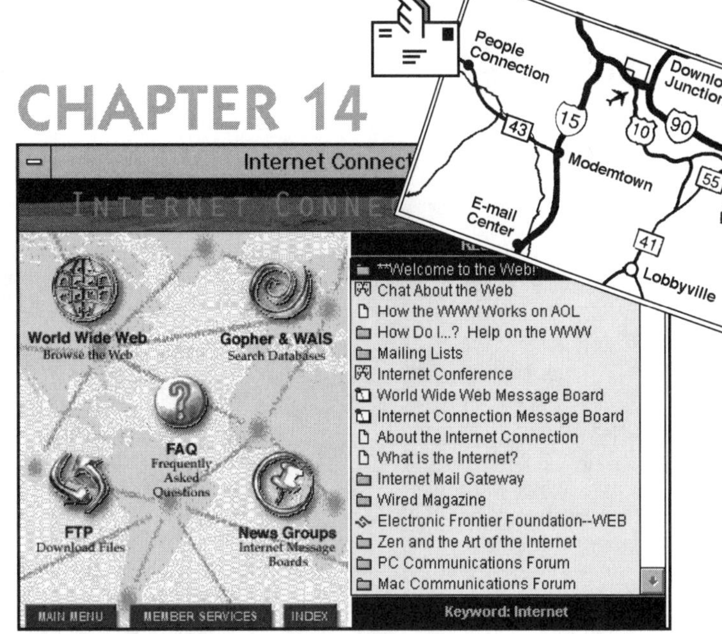

I saw television for the first time in 1954. We lived in a small town at the time, and the nearest station was over 100 miles away. The TV man—a shaman in his time—erected an immoderate antenna atop our roof and left us with a round, grainy black-and-white picture in our living room that would change our lives forever. We received one channel.

Years later, another TV guru—this one more closely connected with snake oil than shamanism—took away our antenna and replaced it with a magic cable. We received 35 color channels and started paying for the privilege.

Yet another TV man visited our home years later—more intellectual than the others, he dressed in a white lab coat and used words like "azimuth" and "latitude"—and planted a microwave dish in our backyard. Now we have more channels than the summer sky has stars, and the content of most of these channels is about as stratospheric.

I'm warming up to a discussion of the Internet. Before America Online, your computer was like a one-channel television set: functional and perhaps even entertaining, but a relic nonetheless. Connecting to AOL is not unlike connecting your TV to the cable: an ocean of opportunity is suddenly available, inconceivably vast at first, but finite nonetheless.

The Internet Connection is your gateway to the universe of online information. Why stay home when you can cruise the InfoBahn? Use the keyword: Internet to get there.

Figure 14-1: The InfoHighway RestStop is an ongoing, informal forum in AOL's People Connection. The graphic was created by OddManOut, who says "If you . . . enjoy good palaver, then you're welcome at the RestStop." Click the whisper-in-the-ear button on the FlashBar (for People Connection), then check the active rooms for the InfoHighway RestStop.

Now imagine connecting your computer not just to AOL, but to thousands of other computer networks, many with forums, e-mail and thousands of files to download. It's not unlike the wonder you might feel while gazing at summer stars—each a sun, many with planets—except the Internet's stars are attainable. The Internet takes you there.

A Superset of AOL

The Internet, then, is a superset of AOL. It's everything AOL is—forums, mail, files to download, chats—only bigger. Much bigger. AOL is less than 5 million people in less than 5 countries; the Internet is as many as 50 million people in over 100 countries. No one owns it, it has no central facility, there are no assigned Guides or Terms of Service. And there's no Steve Case. An advisory committee is at the helm, but its concerns are primarily technical and its members are all volunteers.

Now that I read the previous paragraph, I hasten to add that there's no "it," either. The Internet isn't a singular entity. It's comprised of scores of independent networks—some military, some academic, some commercial—all interconnected. Indeed, these *inter*connected *net*works are the very basis of the Internet name.

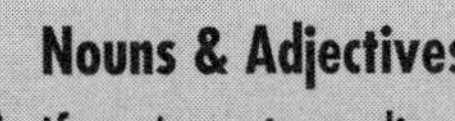

Nouns & Adjectives

If you're going to live in the neighborhood, you're going to have to speak the language. Used as a noun, the Internet is referred to as "the Internet." One would never say "Send me a message on Internet"; it would have to be "Send me a message on *the* Internet."

Used as an adjective, the article is dropped. It's "Internet mail," not "the Internet mail."

If you really want to speak in the vernacular, just call it "the Net," and refer to yourself as a "Netter." That'll keep 'em guessing.

Military Preparedness

The best way to define the Internet is to examine what it was: like democracy, the Internet is best understood by observing its past.

Most importantly, the Internet began as a military contrivance. Most Net users know this, but many have never grasped its significance. The Internet's early military credentials have more to do with what it is today than any other factor.

The Internet is a collection of millions of independent computers, or hosts. Most hosts are in turn connected to other computers via different kinds of networks, forming domains. Hosts are identified to one another on the Internet by their domain names (actually, they're identified to one another by the numeric equivalents of domain names). AOL's domain name is aol.com. The whole thing is called the Domain Name System, and you can find out more about domain names in the "Internet Addresses" section a little later in this chapter.

Using leased, high-speed telephone lines (not modems), each domain is wired to at least one other domain on the Net, and often more. The slowest of these telephone lines operates at 56 kbps—more than five times faster than a 9,600-baud modem. Many domains maintain a constant connection to the Net. They don't sign on and off as we do with AOL; they're online all the time.

A simplified map of this arrangement might look like that pictured in Figure 14-2.

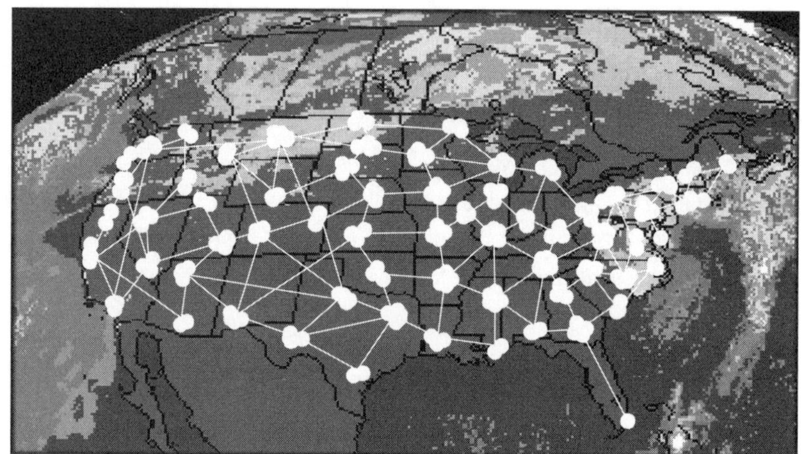

Figure 14-2: The Internet extends around the globe as a web of independent domains, interconnected round-the-clock by dedicated, high-speed telephone lines.

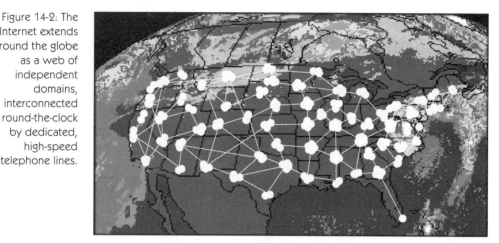

Don't interpret either Figure 14-2 or 14-3 literally. I drew the white lines, and they're not intended to represent literal Internet or AOL nodes (especially since all I've included is the US mainland—a politicocentric decision if there ever was one). It would take a map the size of a picture window to display all of these nodes. While there might be such maps somewhere, this isn't their place. (The image of the continent is from the GEOS satellite. Use the keyword: Weather, then investigate the color weather maps.)

Compare the Internet strategy with that of AOL. America Online consists of a host computer system (in Virginia) and thousands of client computers (our PCs). While the Internet strategy looks like a web, the AOL strategy looks more like a star (see Figure 14-3).

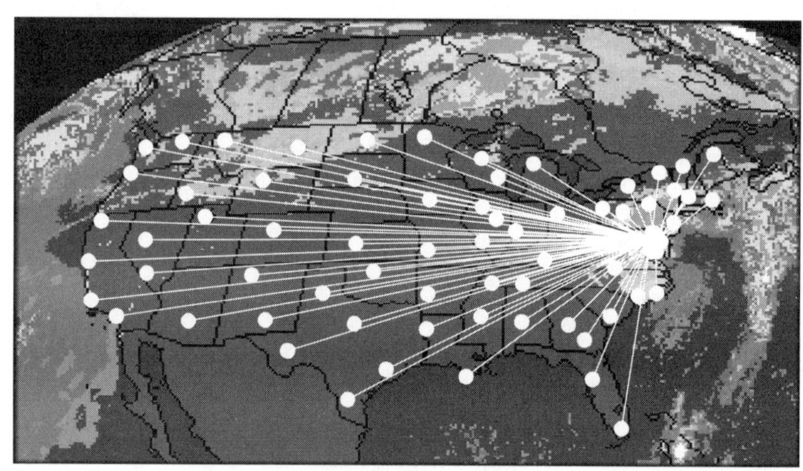

Figure 14-3: America Online's star-like network consists of a host computer and thousands of intermittently connected clients.

Now the military part: look again at Figure 14-3. If Ace Excavation were to dig up a fiber-optic cable in Vienna, Virginia, most of us would be without AOL—a disheartening experience. On the other hand, if a backhoe unplugged a domain in the Internet, communications would simply be routed around it. Indeed, a large percentage of the Net's domains could be eliminated, and the Net would still function.

Forever prepared, the Defense Department commissioned the Advanced Research Projects Agency (ARPA) to configure a computer network that would accommodate just such a possibility. This happened in the late 1960s; the network was called the ARPANET.

Academic Anarchy

By the early 1980s, educators discovered the value of sharing research information and computing resources through interconnected computers—especially supercomputers, which are precious as platinum. The educators weren't interested (much) in security; their interest was access. Their computers held vast amounts of data and, true to form, they wanted to share that information objectively, without bias, with anyone in the community who wanted access.

ARPANET was a possible answer, but there were fundamental differences in the military and academic attitudes. The academic community elected instead to develop its own network, which it called NSFNET—named for the National Science Foundation, the academics' primary source of funding. Significantly, NSFNET used the same networking strategy ARPANET used: interconnected domains, randomly distributed around the globe. Most of these computers were at colleges and universities; none were subject to any form of central control. The result could have been dysfunctional anarchy, but by definition a computer network implies some form of universal protocol: electronic standards that define how computers communicate. The result is best described as *consensual anarchy*, whereby everyone marches to his or her own drum, but all agree on a common route for the parade.

And that's how the Internet is today: an agglomeration of independent domains drawn from both ARPANET and NSFNET (now both phased out), each owned by organizations that are independent of one another, interconnected by high-speed data lines, and not subject to any form of central control. There's no central data storage, either. Data are scattered about the Net like dyed eggs on Easter Sunday: hidden in faraway places, waiting for discovery. It amazes me that the thing even exists—it's one of the few working models of functional anarchy today, and it works extremely well.

WIRED Magazine

WIRED is the "magazine of the digital generation"—covering interactive media, the networking community and the toys of technology. Started in early 1993, *WIRED* has quickly ascended to the vanguard of the literary aristocracy. Its design is precocious, its content acerbic, its language offensive. The information age has few perspectives that can match *WIRED*'s insight, candor or irreverence, and none can match them all.

Best of all, *WIRED* is available online at AOL. Only past issues are available—you'll have to visit your newsstand for the latest edition—but *WIRED*'s content isn't so timely that it becomes obsolete in a month or two. If this chapter interests you and you're not yet a *WIRED* devotee, read this magazine. Use the keyword: WIRED.

Until recently, military and academic users comprised most of the Internet community. It might have been an anarchistic community, but it was also a very exclusive club. Things have changed. Commercial accounts were allowed access in the early 1990s, opening the door to millions of everyday computer users like you and me. Now all of us with AOL accounts are offered Internet access. And there's no extra charge.

Internet Addresses

Before we go any further, we need to discuss Internet addresses. I touched on them briefly in Chapter 4, but they deserve more than that. They're really not much different from the addresses used by the US mail, though rather than being sent to you at your home, Internet mail is sent to your *domain*. Domain or domicile, they're the same thing: they're the places where you receive mail.

International Top-Level Domains

When my friend Kyoko writes to me from Japan, the address she places on the envelope goes from the specific to the general: she starts with my name and ends with "USA," in the format *name/address/city/state/usa*.

International Internet addresses are exactly the same. At the far right you'll find the name of the country. This is called the *top-level domain.* Figure 14-4 identifies the abbreviations for some common international top-level domains.

Figure 14-4: Country abbreviations are the top-level domain of international Internet addresses.

Abbreviation	Country
au	Australia
at	Austria
ca	Canada
dk	Denmark
fi	Finland
fr	France
de	Germany
it	Italy
jp	Japan
no	Norway
uk	United Kingdom
us	United States

Perhaps the most well-known example of an international top-level domain is

username@well.sf.ca.us.

indicating a user on the Whole Earth 'Lectronic Link (the WELL) in San Francisco (sf), California (ca), USA (us).

Note that the segments of Internet addresses are separated by periods. It's always that way. (Well, *almost* always. The Net's an anarchy, after all, and you will occasionally see other address formats. They're rare, however, and assuredly the exception to the rule.)

US Top-Level Domains

At the risk of sounding politicocentric again, most domains are within the United States, and the "us" top-level domain is typically omitted for activity within this country, just as it is for paper mail that's to stay within our borders. Instead, top domains for US users typically identify the type of system they're using. Figure 14-5 identifies the common US top-level domains.

Figure 14-5: US top-level domains identify the nature of the user's affiliation.

Abbreviation	Affiliation
com	business and commercial
edu	educational institutions
gov	government institutions
mil	military installations
net	network resources
org	other (typically nonprofit)

My Internet address, as mentioned in Chapter 4, is majortom@aol.com. Anyone looking at my top-level domain can determine that I'm affiliated with a commercial organization—in this case, America Online.

Domain Names & Computer Names

To the immediate left of the top-level domain is the name of the location of the host computer and associated network domain that's actually connected to the Internet. Thus, a domain name such as uoregon.edu implies that there's a network named "uoregon" somewhere, and it has a direct line to the Internet.

Many institutions—especially educational ones—have more than one local area network (LAN). Most of my academic associates work at the University of Oregon, but the U of O has at least seven satellite networks connected to the University's central mainframe. One of those networks is located within a building called Oregon Hall, and the users on that network add to the string their identifier, oregon.uoregon.edu, which identifies the Oregon Hall (oregon) LAN, which is connected to the University of Oregon domain (uoregon), which is an educational institution (edu).

User Names

Most Internet activity takes the form of e-mail, and e-mail is sent to individuals. To identify an individual, the format *pdwilliams@oregon.uoregon.edu* is used. Everything to the left of the "at" symbol (@) in an Internet address is the user's name. Internet user names aren't subject to the 10-character limit that AOL screen names are subject to, so they can become quite elaborate.

Most people on the Net use their first initial and last name as their Internet name. This format is usually unique (at least to the domain), and it's not gender-specific (an issue which many Net users prefer to avoid). Spaces aren't allowed (so you'll often see underscores in their place: fred_morgan@mit.edu), and Internet addresses are not case sensitive. None of this should make a whit of difference to you, as your screen name (minus any spaces) automatically becomes your Internet user name. Your domain (sounds regal, doesn't it?) is aol.com.

The World Wide Web

Cultivated in UNIX and nurtured by computer professionals, the Internet became a variegation of disjointed fragments: USENET, Gopher, WAIS, telnet and mail. The Internet almost seemed to take pride in its incoherence. Now that the Net has evolved from its experimental stage, coherence, convenience—even hospitality—are not only appropriate, but essential.

Apparently, the scientists at CERN—the European Particle Physics Laboratory in Geneva, Switzerland—agree, for in 1989 they set out to advance the Internet an order of magnitude up the evolutionary ladder. The result of their endeavors, introduced in 1990, is the *World Wide Web*, a department store-like gathering of ftp, Gopher, WAIS gateways, e-mail and newsgroups. It's like a department store in that the Web puts all of these things under one roof, in familiar, convenient surroundings. If you can use a mouse, you can use the Web. Indeed, the Web is so obliging it might become your only use of the Internet (other than e-mail) from now on.

Hypermedia

The Web's cosmos is comprised of *hypermedia*. In my experience, the use of polysyllabic buzzwords usually indicates that the words' true meanings are obtuse and opaque. "Hypermedia" is no exception, but it's the heart of the Web, and an understanding of hypermedia is pivotal. Perhaps Figure 14-6 will help.

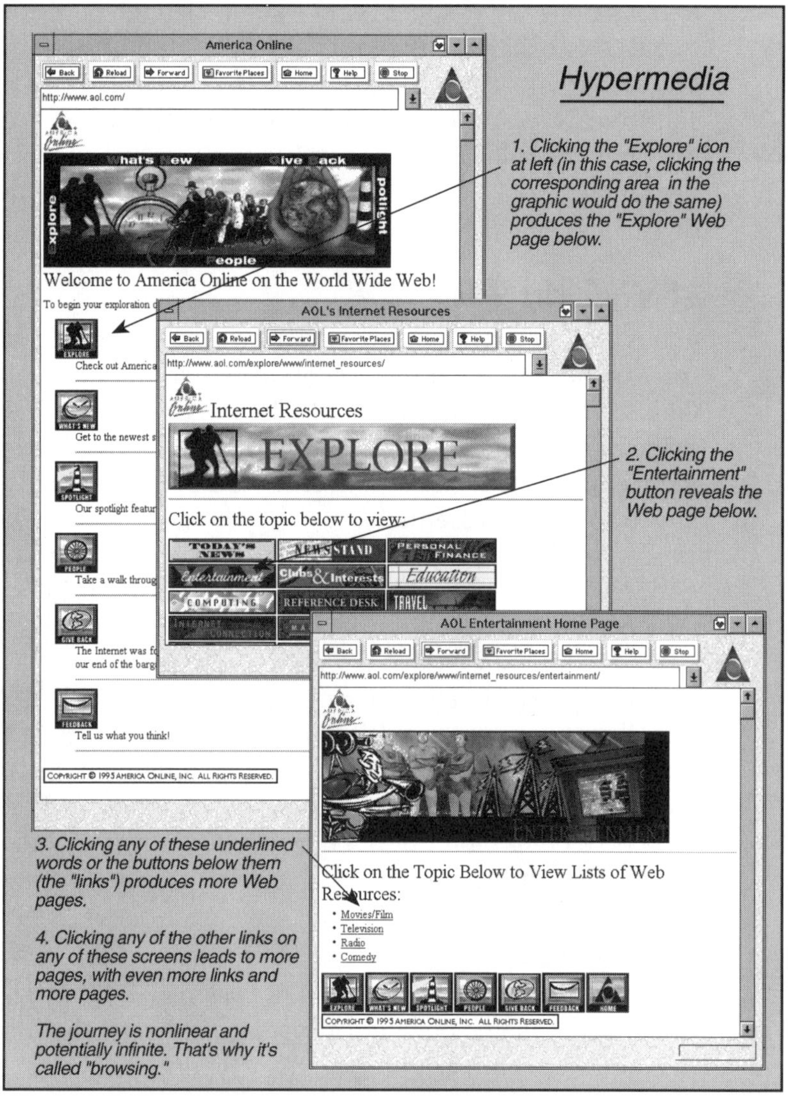

Figure 14-6: Hypermedia provides a nonlinear pathway to the infinite potential of the World Wide Web.

Hypermedia

1. Clicking the "Explore" icon at left (in this case, clicking the corresponding area in the graphic would do the same) produces the "Explore" Web page below.

2. Clicking the "Entertainment" button reveals the Web page below.

3. Clicking any of these underlined words or the buttons below them (the "links") produces more Web pages.

4. Clicking any of the other links on any of these screens leads to more pages, with even more links and more pages.

The journey is nonlinear and potentially infinite. That's why it's called "browsing."

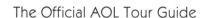

Each Web *page* consists of text and graphics (and more—like sound and video—if it's a really ambitious page), usually marked with *links* (*hyperlinks*, actually), or areas on the page that, when clicked, lead to something else. Links can produce more Web pages, graphics, sounds or videos: there's no limitation other than the capability of your hardware and the designer's imagination. The path shown in Figure 14-6 is only one of an infinite number of paths we could have explored. A click on the Spotlight or What's New buttons on AOL's Welcome page would fork to other paths, just as fertile and just as infinite as the one in the illustration. Indeed, the Web is a vast cosmos of resources, linked almost capriciously. This, perhaps, is why it's called the World Wide Web.

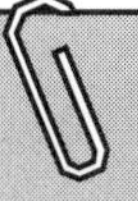

Nomenclature

So far, we've defined the *World Wide Web*, *page* and *link*, but there are a few other terms that require interpretation before we continue.

- A *Web browser* is software designed to browse the World Wide Web. Your AOL software contains a Web browser; you don't need anything else to browse the Web.
- *URL* is the Uniform Resource Locator, or the address for each article of text and each graphic, sound or video on the Web. There are millions of them, thus their addresses are lengthy and specific. URLs can be typed directly into the text field just below the FlashBar in AOL's Web window. They can be pasted there, too, which is probably a better idea.
- *HTTP* is HyperText Transfer Protocol. Appearing at the left end of a URL, http tells the browser to expect a hypertext Web document.
- *HTML* is HyperText Markup Language, the programming language that's used to create Web pages.

Favorite Places

As you explore the Web, you'll discover pages you'll want to return to, and when you return, you won't want to type URLs from the keyboard. That's what the *Favorite Places* feature is for.

I've enlarged a section of the AOL screen in Figure 14-7 to identify the two icons you need to know about with regard to Favorite Places. Most Web pages have a little heart-shaped icon on the title bar that serves as a bookmark. If you want to "mark" a page by adding it to your list of Favorite Places, simply click its little heart icon or drag it to the Favorite Places icon on the FlashBar (see 14-7).

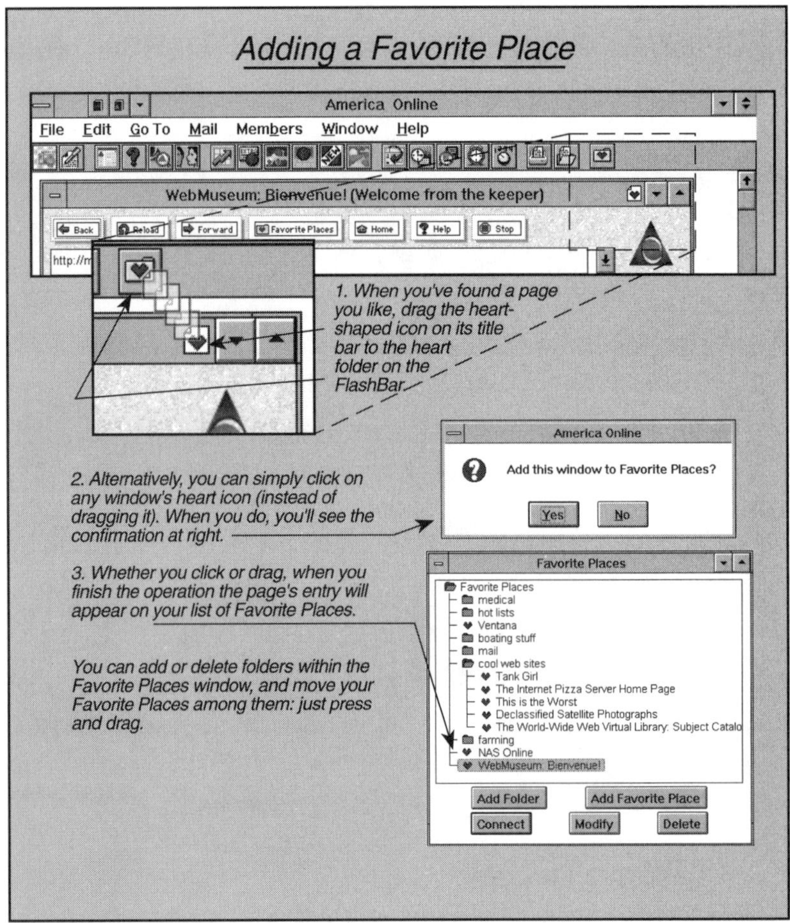

Figure 14-7: Adding Favorite Places is as simple as click or drag.

This technique doesn't apply only to Web-page windows: many areas within AOL offer a heart icon on their title bars; whenever you see one you can add your current location to your list of personal Favorite Places.

To open the Favorite Places window, click the Favorite Places icon on the FlashBar at any time, whether you're online or off. To go to one of your favorite places, just press and drag it to the World Wide Web window to replace the page currently displayed, or—if it's not a Web site, or you're not online—double-click it.

Browsing

This is not a place to become mired in procedural details. As the AOL software presents it, the Web really requires little explaining. It's a place for leisurely browsing, like an art gallery (try the French Louvre's Web Museum at http://mistral.enst.fr/louvre/) or the shelves of books in a public library (try the World Wide Web Virtual Library at http://info.cern.ch/hypertext/DataSources/bySubject/Overview.html). Be prepared for wandering and wondering at all of the remarkable rewards the Web has to offer. Add to your list of Favorite Places when you find places you want to return to, and surf the sea of the Internet the way the people at CERN intended. (The people at AOL hope you'll make extensive use of the Web, too: look at Figure 14-8.) This is the Internet at its best; it will bring you back time after time.

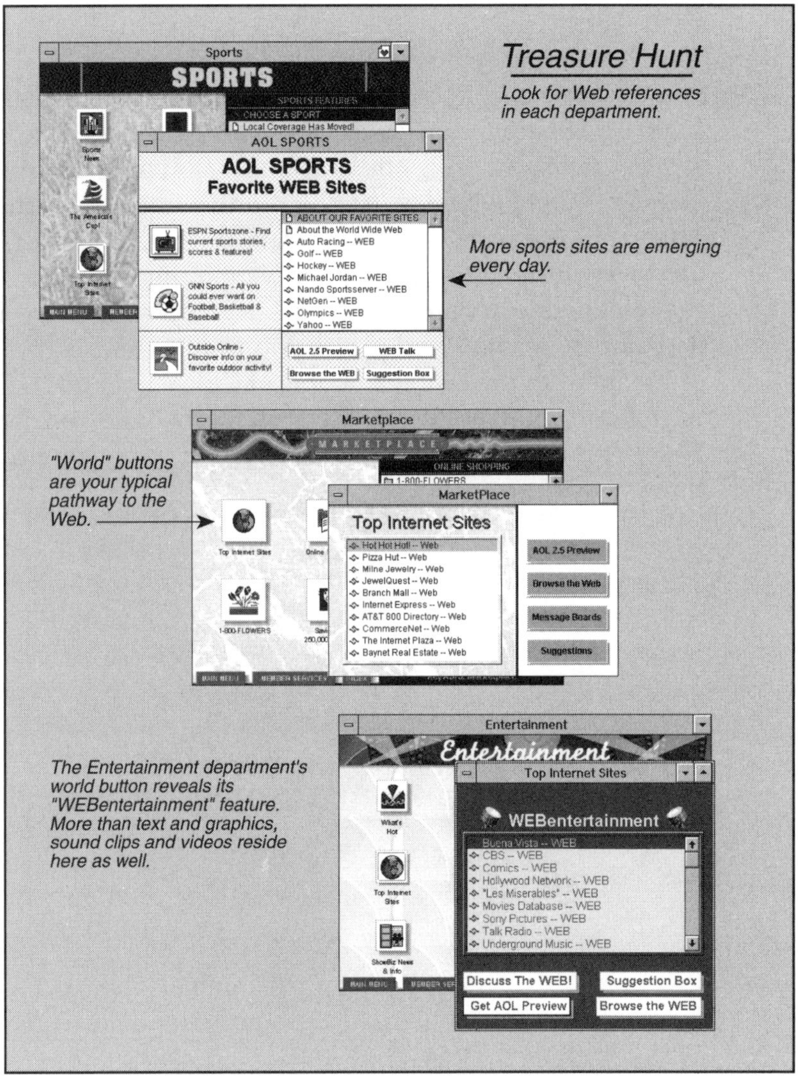
Treasure Hunt
Look for Web references in each department.
More sports sites are emerging every day.
"World" buttons are your typical pathway to the Web.
The Entertainment department's world button reveals its "WEBentertainment" feature. More than text and graphics, sound clips and videos reside here as well.
Sports
SPORTS
AOL SPORTS
AOL SPORTS Favorite WEB Sites
Marketplace
MarketPlace
Top Internet Sites
Entertainment
Top Internet Sites
WEBentertainment

Figure 14-8: The World Wide Web is integrated throughout America Online. Look for "world" buttons.

Mailing Lists

Internet mailing lists are something of a cross between Ed McMahon and Rush Limbaugh (a vivid, if not particularly adept, analogy if there ever was one).

Mailing lists are like Ed McMahon in that they arrive in your mailbox frequently and seemingly unbidden. They're like Rush Limbaugh in that they accept material from listeners (subscribers, in this case) and broadcast those contributions to everyone else on the list.

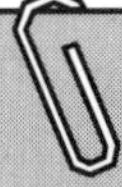

Shameless Plug

This chapter's description of mailing lists and the Web is necessarily abbreviated. Other Internet features will be abbreviated in this book as well. This is a tour of AOL, after all, not the Internet. If you want to become acquainted with the Net and AOL's gateway to it, read my *America Online's Internet*, also available from Ventana Press. Use the keyword: AOL Store, or look for it at your local bookstore.

Think of AOL's message boards. Mailing lists, like boards, are where people discuss issues of a common interest. There are thousands of lists, and the issues range from ablation to zymurgy.

Lists are often called *reflectors*: mail you send to a list is broadcast (reflected) to everyone else who subscribes to the list. Conversely, you will automatically receive—as Internet mail—every message sent to the list by each of the other subscribers.

In that way, mailing lists are similar to the AOL address book feature. Using an address book, you can associate a number of screen names with a single address book entry; when you select that entry, multiple screen names are plugged into the To (or CC) field of an outgoing mail form. An Internet mailing list is the same way: mail sent to it is received by every subscriber to the list. One name represents many.

America Online offers a direct line to its Internet mailing list feature; just use the keyword: MailingLists (see Figure 14-9).

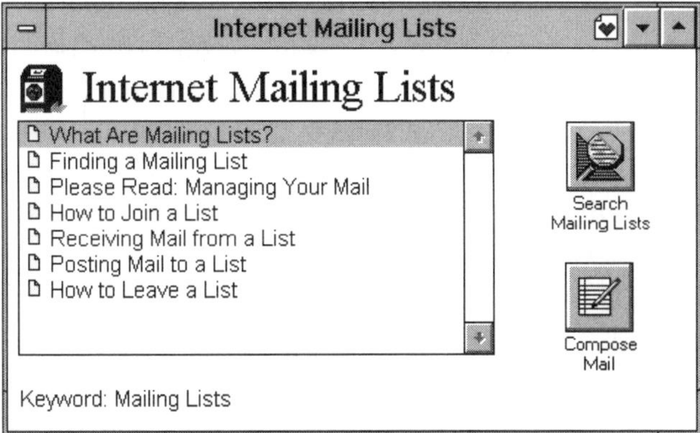

Figure 14-9: The keyword: MailingLists provides access to Internet mailing list information, including a searchable database of lists currently available.

Subscribing to a good mailing list can be entertaining, stimulating, enlightening and overwhelming. You should subscribe to one, just for the experience. Before you do, however, understand a few mailing list basics:

- It's not unusual for a list to generate a prodigious volume of mail. For this reason, it is important that you manage your mail box to avoid losing your mail. Your AOL mailbox is limited to 500 pieces of mail, including both read and unread mail. Unread mail disappears five weeks after the date it was sent. Read mail disappears one week after the date it was sent—even sooner when the mail load at AOL is heavy. If your total mailbox mail count (both read and unread) exceeds 500 pieces, the AOL system starts to delete excess mail, starting with read mail and then unread mail.
- Don't subscribe to a mailing list unless you plan to read it.
- When reading a list's description, be sure to note how to "unsubscribe" in case you change your mind about receiving it.
- If you subscribe to any mailing lists, sign on regularly to read your mail and clear your mailbox.
- Some lists are "moderated," some are not. Moderated lists are comparable to AOL's hosted chat rooms in that their content never strays too far off the subject and rarely becomes offensive. Unmoderated lists embody the anarchistic nature of the Internet and can become quite idiosyncratic and incautious.

America Online offers a searchable database of lists (review Figure 14-9). Again, the keyword: MailingLists will take you there. Don't be surprised if the subject you have in mind isn't listed. Do spend some time exploring the database: it searches the list descriptions by content, rather than by keyword. A search using the criterion "flying," for instance, produces all lists with the word "flying" in their descriptions, including "high-flying" and "flying by the seat of your pants." While searches like this can drift off the subject quickly, you never know what you'll unearth.

Newsgroups

Newsgroups are similar to mailing lists in that they're a free exchange of ideas, opinions and comments, usually confined to a specific field of interest. You visit a newsgroup, read the messages that are there, reply to those that inspire a response, post new messages when you have a new topic to propose, and come back another day to see what responses you've provoked.

Unlike mailing lists, no mail is involved with newsgroups. Most activity occurs while you're online, including reading and responding to postings. Thus, some will say that newsgroups are more immediate, more interactive and more conversational than mailing lists. Newsgroups or mailing lists: for most it's a matter of preference. You will probably want to dabble in both of them for a while.

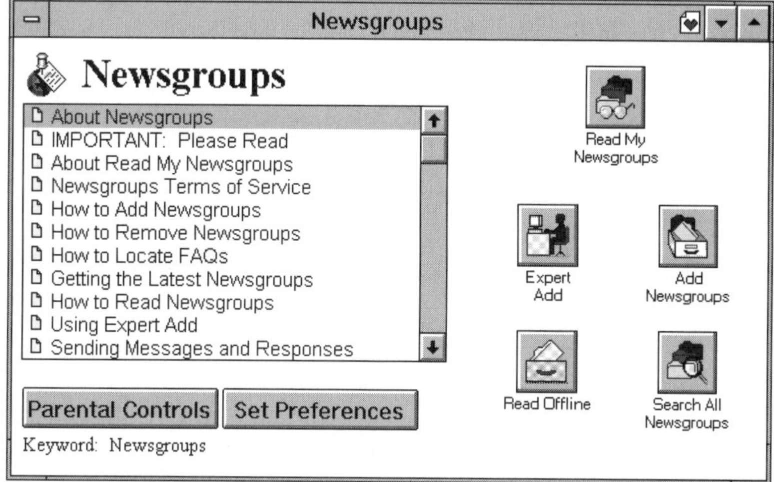

Figure 14-10: The America Online Newsgroups screen. To reach it, use the keyword: Newsgroups.

At the moment, over 18,000 newsgroups flood the Internet. This figure is more than quadruple the 4,000 mentioned in Adam Engst's *Internet Starter Kit* (copyright 1993), and that figure is more than double the 1,500 mentioned in Ed Krol's *The Whole Internet* (First Edition, copyright 1992). If the number of newsgroups keeps doubling every year, we'll have more than half a million of them by the turn of the century.

Because newsgroups are an Internet resource, AOL's own internal Terms of Service (TOS) don't apply. There are guidelines, however, and AOL's USENET Newsgroups TOS is a codification of these guidelines. The USENET TOS is always available in the list box at the keyword:

Newsgroups, where it's called Newsgroups Terms of Service (review Figure 14-10). Read it. Doing so might save you considerable newsgroup face, and AOL doesn't charge for the time when you do.

Getting Help

As I mentioned earlier, space considerations forbid the description of operational details for AOL's Internet features here. I have another book for that. Fortunately, however, help is never far away when you're using AOL's Internet features. A number of methods are available for accessing help from AOL, from other members and from the Internet community at large.

Online Help

Nearly every Internet window on AOL offers a potential for online help. Figure 14-11 shows a sampling.

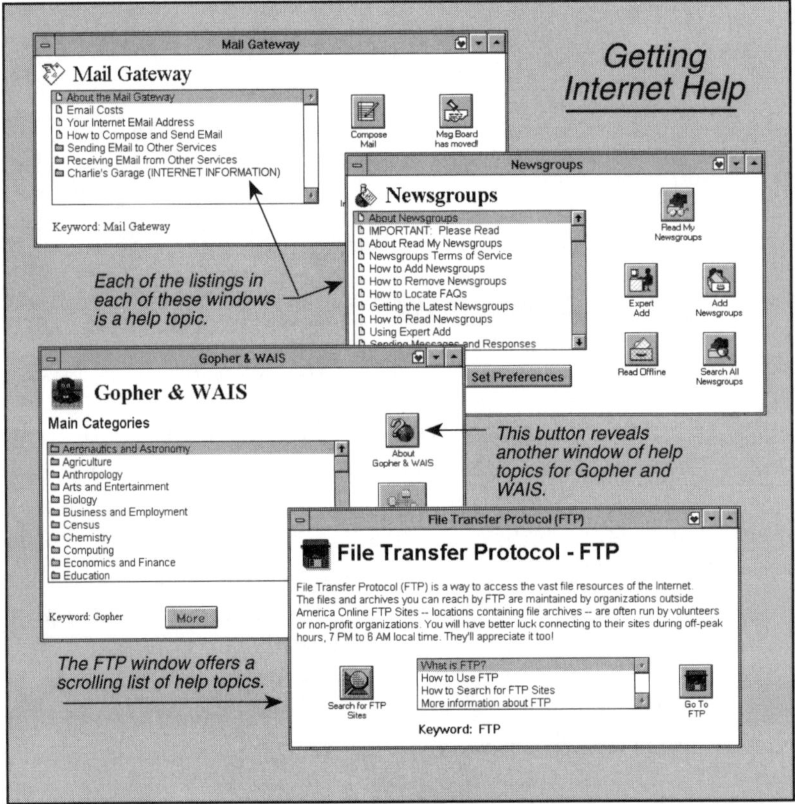

Figure 14-11: Help topics abound at the Internet Connection.

The good news is that because the newsgroup help files are stored at AOL (and not on your hard disk), they can be changed whenever the Internet staff wants to change them. These help files, in other words, always reflect changes made in response to suggestions from users or changes in the Net itself.

The bad news is that you have to be online to access them, and for that you pay.

Here's a tip: print 'em. Whenever a help window is open, all you have to do is choose Print from the File menu and you'll have a hard copy of the online help file that's currently open. You can print them all in this manner if you like.

Peer Assistance

I'm a firm believer in peer assistance. America Online members are usually your best source of help because they can empathize; they understand your needs. Experts are often too far removed from your situation (and have too many other things to do) to help the way other members can. In other words: if you have a question, ask around.

You might start with the Internet Connection message boards. Use the keyword: Internet, then double-click the Internet Message Board listing in the main window. Though the contents of all boards change, this one will, no doubt, always offer a folder (see Figure 14-12) where you can post questions and receive replies from others who've experienced a similar situation.

An ambitious team of *CyberJockeys* patrols these boards as well, answering especially difficult questions. You can recognize CyberJockeys by the leading *CJ* in their screen names.

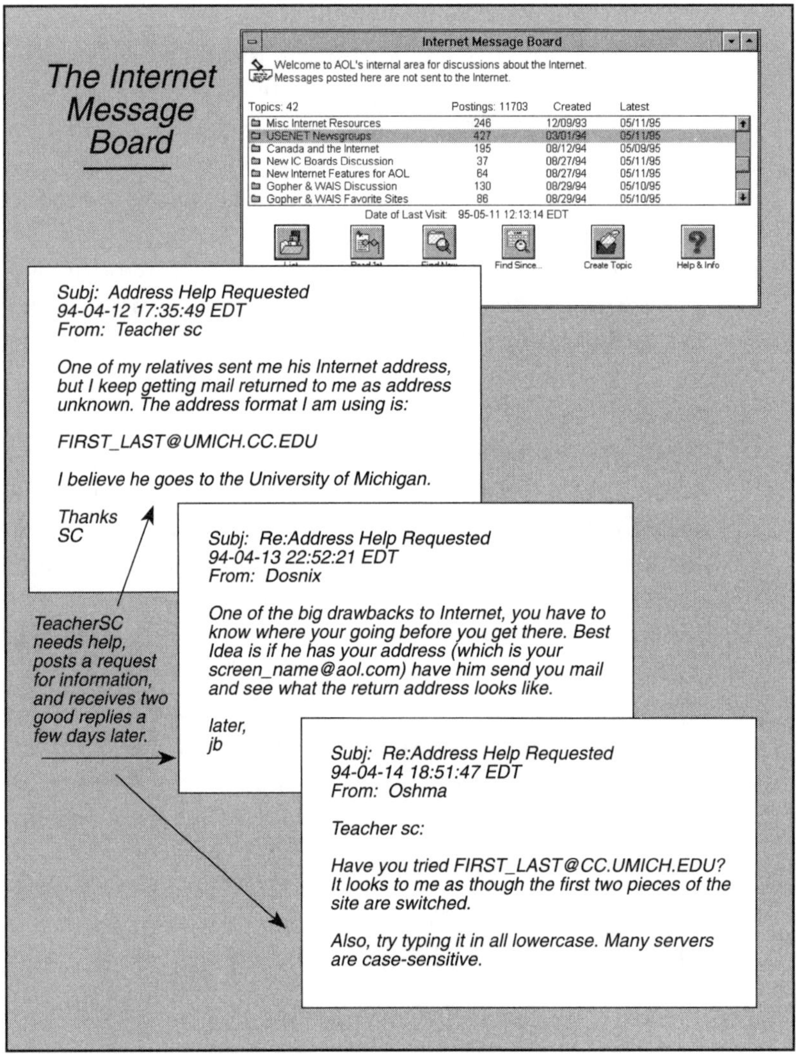

Figure 14-12: The Internet Connection message boards offer excellent help from fellow AOL members.

The Internet Message Board

Internet Message Board

Welcome to AOL's internal area for discussions about the Internet. Messages posted here are not sent to the Internet.

Topics: 42	Postings: 11703	Created	Latest
Misc Internet Resources	246	12/09/93	05/11/95
USENET Newsgroups	427	03/01/94	05/11/95
Canada and the Internet	195	08/12/94	05/09/95
New IC Boards Discussion	37	08/27/94	05/11/95
New Internet Features for AOL	64	08/27/94	05/11/95
Gopher & WAIS Discussion	130	08/29/94	05/10/95
Gopher & WAIS Favorite Sites	86	08/29/94	05/10/95

Date of Last Visit: 95-05-11 12:13:14 EDT

Find Since... Create Topic Help & Info

Subj: Address Help Requested
94-04-12 17:35:49 EDT
From: Teacher sc

One of my relatives sent me his Internet address, but I keep getting mail returned to me as address unknown. The address format I am using is:

FIRST_LAST@UMICH.CC.EDU

I believe he goes to the University of Michigan.

Thanks
SC

TeacherSC needs help, posts a request for information, and receives two good replies a few days later.

Subj: Re:Address Help Requested
94-04-13 22:52:21 EDT
From: Dosnix

One of the big drawbacks to Internet, you have to know where your going before you get there. Best Idea is if he has your address (which is your screen_name@aol.com) have him send you mail and see what the return address looks like.

later,
jb

Subj: Re:Address Help Requested
94-04-14 18:51:47 EDT
From: Oshma

Teacher sc:

Have you tried FIRST_LAST@CC.UMICH.EDU? It looks to me as though the first two pieces of the site are switched.

Also, try typing it in all lowercase. Many servers are case-sensitive.

aol.newsgroups.help

Finally, be sure to subscribe to the aol.newsgroups.help newsgroup (it, too, is part of the default newsgroup subscription list—you're probably already subscribed). This is the most active location for newsgroup assistance, and it's local. It's not broadcast throughout the Internet—your questions are seen only by fellow AOL members, and your responses will come from fellow AOL members.

Netiquette

Nowhere is the etiquette of online conduct more critical (or more abused) than in newsgroups. Most faux pas are committed by newbies—people like you and me. The Internet is a community, after all: one with a particularly stalwart camaraderie and an intense adherence to an iconoclastic propriety. Most specialized social organizations are that way, and to become a member of one without first becoming familiar with its catechism is fishing for disgrace. A minicourse in Netiquette, then, might help:

- Having stung myself a number of times, I've taken to writing my missives and *not* posting them for at least a couple of hours. Rather, I save them and recall them the next time I sign on. For some reason, this obliges me to read them again before I click the post button—and it has often saved me considerable newsgroup face.
- There are people on the other end of the line: people with emotions and feelings. Honor them.
- Honor yourself as well. You are known on the Net by what you write. Project the image you want others to see.
- Brevity is admirable; verbosity is disfavored. If you say what you have to say succinctly, your words will carry greater authority and impact.
- Read before writing. Add something to the conversation; don't simply repeat what's already been said. Subscribe to the news.answers newsgroup and read the Frequently Asked Questions file (FAQ) for your newsgroup before posting. By reading before you write you'll have a better sense of the tenor and conventions of the newsgroup to which you are posting.
- Quote the messages to which you're responding. Edit the quoted material to oblige brevity (and indicate when you've done so), use the quoting fashion you see in other messages and always acknowledge the person you're quoting.

- Contribute something. Some people speak simply to be heard; these same people post simply to see their material online. Don't contribute to the tedium: look for a new perspective, ask a probing question, make an insightful comment. If none come to mind, wait for another opportunity. There are plenty of opportunities on the Net; we all have something worthy to contribute eventually.
- Use help. If the help files described in this chapter don't answer your question, post a message in aol.newsgroups.help. Lots of people are willing to help you if you ask.

WAIS Databases & Gopher

Growth on the Internet is a stupendous thing. Most everyone agrees that it exceeds 100 percent a year; some contend that it's as high as 20 percent *per month.* Regardless of the figure, navigating the Net has become about as convenient as navigating the Atlantic Ocean: relatively easy if you have the right tools, but impractical—some might say perilous—if you don't.

Gopher

One solution to the dilemma is *Gopher*. Originating at the University of Minnesota (where the school mascot is the Golden Gopher), Gopher is a system that knows where things are on the Net and presents that knowledge as a series of nested menus. All you have to do is keep choosing menu items until you find what you're after, then Gopher "goes for" (it's kind of a double pun: mascot and "gofer") your material on the Net.

The Gopher system (keyword: Gopher) is actually composed of a number of *Gopher servers* located around the world. Each server is like a good librarian: it organizes content for your convenience. (Librarians organize libraries with card files; Gophers organize the Internet's content with menus.) When you find what you're looking for, it retrieves the information for you. Better yet, Gophers reference other Gophers: AOL's Gopher, for example, offers access to hundreds of others. It's as if you were given access to a librarians' convention, and the librarians, every one, brought their card files with them.

Though there are a number of Gopher servers, we're rarely made aware of them individually: AOL simply groups them into one massive menu tree that we're free to peruse as we wish. In a way, that's too bad, because you're usually unaware of the vast distances you're traveling when you access the various Gopher servers on AOL's menus. You might be in Switzerland one moment and Germany the next. That's the nature of the Net: distance has no meaning in cyberspace.

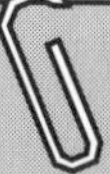

The Comics Come to the Net

The original Gopher server at the University of Minnesota was established to bring convenience to the Net. Since copies of all of the Internet sites' directories were stored on the server, searching was local. No time was spent connecting to and disconnecting from the individual sites until data was located.

In time, more Gopher servers came along. There are scores of them now, and searching the *servers* has become a task.

Enter *Veronica*, a tool that searches databases. Veronica is simply a database of the Gophers' directories and menu item names.

Computer programmers are an iconoclastic lot, and many of them relax by reading comic books. The Archie comics are big in cyberspace, so the Veronica resource was named for the Veronica comic book character. (Searching for a name for your latest creation? Pick up the nearest literature.) Betty and Jughead can't be far behind.

To access Veronica, click the Search all Gophers button in the main Gopher and WAIS window.

Gopherspace is a crowded place during the academic year, especially during finals. Because of the crowding, don't be surprised if you receive connect errors. Crowded or not, Gopherspace is a wonderful place to browse. Browsing is what Gopher is all about. Plan to spend a lot of time here.

WAIS

Gopher isn't the only way to search for data on the Net; *WAIS* (pronounced "wayz") is another. While Gopher is best suited for browsing, or poking around with no particular destination in mind, WAIS is best suited for searching, rather than browsing.

The Subtlety of Icons

Take a moment to look at Figure 14-13. Note the variety of icons pictured to the left of the menu topics.

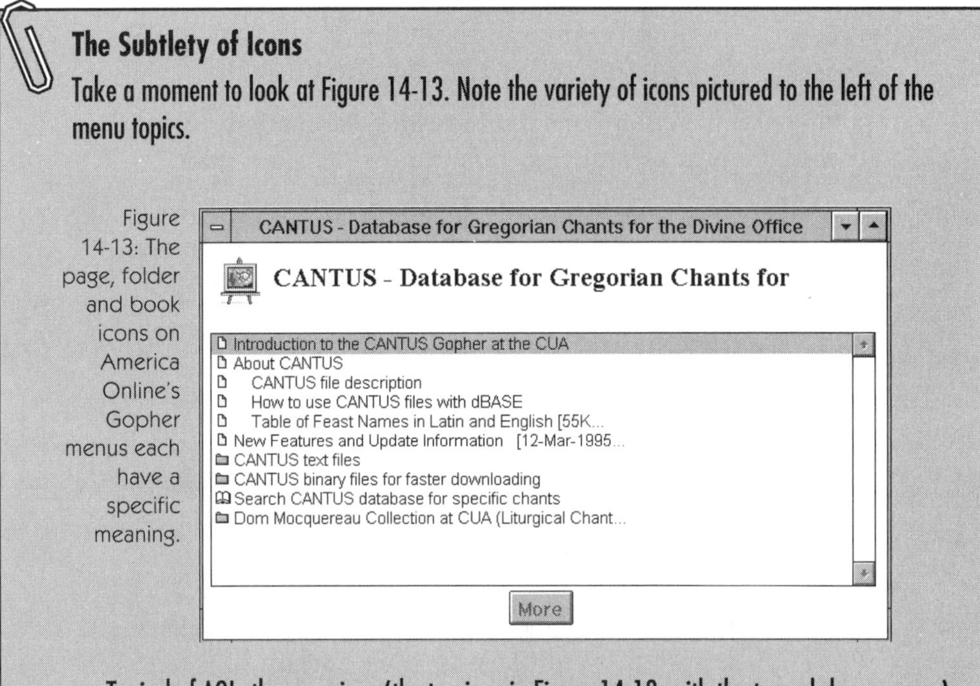

Figure 14-13: The page, folder and book icons on America Online's Gopher menus each have a specific meaning.

Typical of AOL, the page icon (the top icon in Figure 14-13, with the turned-down corner) represents an *article*: a text document suitable for reading onscreen or for saving or printing.

The folder icon represents another menu. Double-click a folder, and you get another menu of choices. This is the nesting that's endemic to Gopher-based information.

The open-book icon is a WAIS database. When you double-click it, you will see a criteria entry form (pictured later, in Figure 14-14). You'll then be able to enter search criteria and conduct the search itself.

WAIS servers contain custom indexes of data on the Internet, often limited to a single topic. Gopher indexes are more comprehensive, analogous to the card file in a public library. WAIS indexes are more like a private library; there are WAIS servers for computer science, molecular biology and literature, for example.

WAIS servers also offer a different "face" than Gophers do; while Gophers offer menus, WAIS servers offer a query form not unlike that of a database. You enter the criteria you're searching for, and the WAIS server responds with data that match your query.

Conducting a WAIS Search

One of the Internet's finest jewels is its exhaustive collection of so-called "e-texts"—electronic texts of the world's literature. While there will always be a place for the smell of old books and the crackle of stiff pages, there are occasions when the immediacy of e-text retrieval makes the difference between reading the text or not.

There are so many e-texts now on the Internet that a number of searching mechanisms have emerged, including the ALEX retrieval system pictured in Figure 14-14.

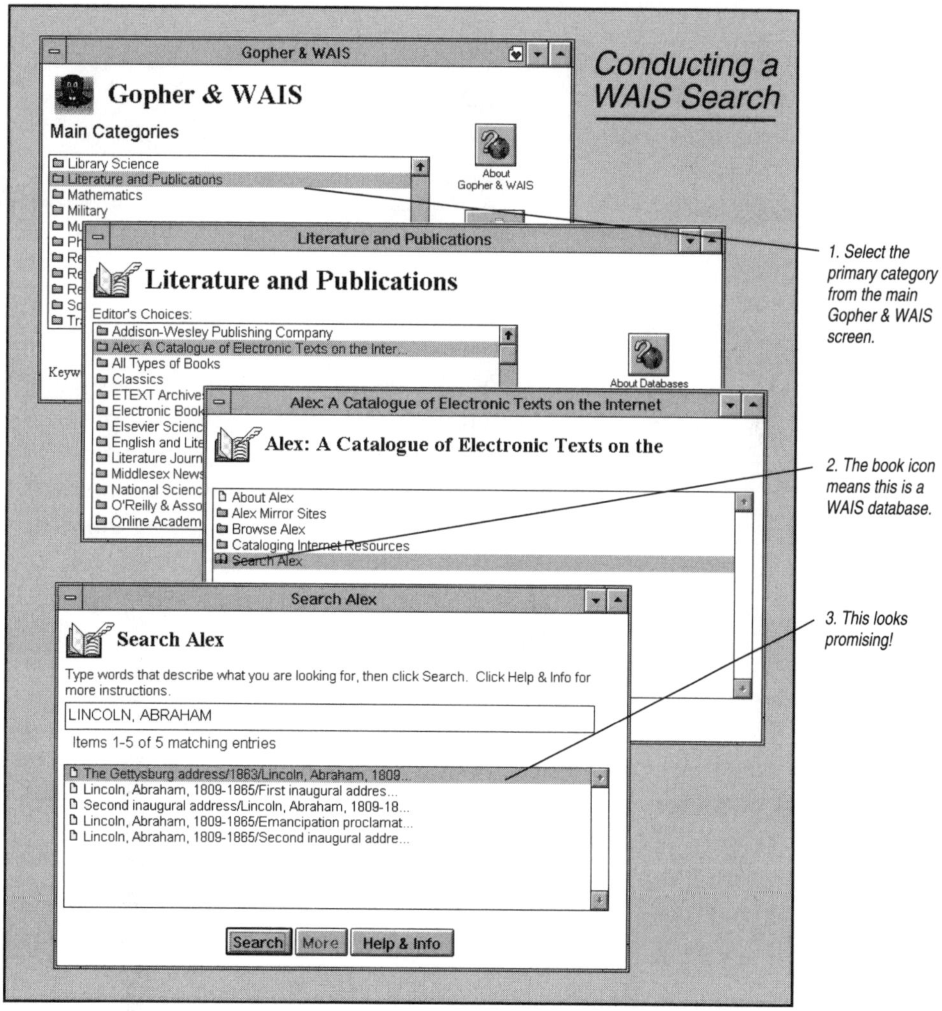

Figure 14-14: Searching the ALEX retrieval system for the electronic text of Lincoln's Gettysburg Address.

1. Select the primary category from the main Gopher & WAIS screen.

2. The book icon means this is a WAIS database.

3. This looks promising!

Note that I had to know about ALEX, and I had to know to find ALEX in the Literature and Publishing section of AOL's Gopher. WAIS is for searching the Internet when you know what you're after and know where to look for it. Developing an awareness of these things takes time. Don't expect to become a WAIS expert in a visit or two. Good things take time.

Editor's Choices

If you look carefully at the second window in Figure 14-14, you'll see the words "Editor's Choices." Each of the selections in the main Gopher and WAIS window leads to the Editor's Choices of resources available for that top menu item. These resources usually prove to be especially adroit: typically, they're comprehensive, intriguing and functional.

If you're browsing the Net, always try the Editor's Choices first. This is some of the best stuff the Internet has to offer.

FTP

Gopher, WAIS and the Web are nifty tools, but what if you want more direct access? What if you want to log on to another machine on the Net, see a directory of its files and download a few? We're talking now about the engine room of the Internet, where you directly access other computers' holdings as if they were your own hard drive. FTP, or *File Transfer Protocol,* is that kind of access; it's how you download files from other machines, and files can be anything: programs, sounds, video and graphics.

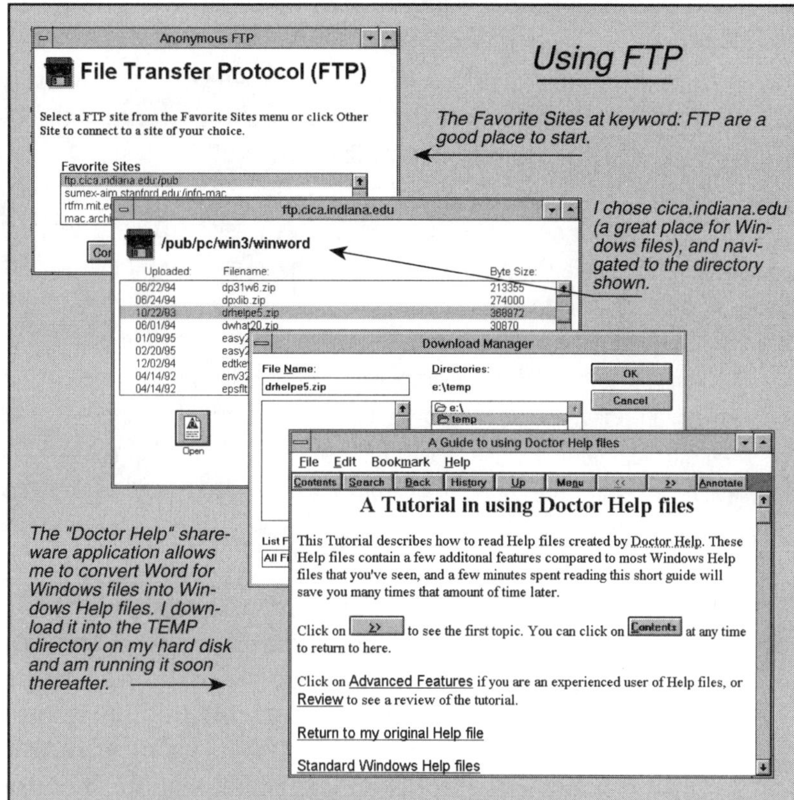

Figure 14-15: Using FTP to download a Microsoft Word utility from the Center for Innovative Computer Applications.

FTP is two things, actually. First, it's a protocol, allowing machines on the Net to exchange data (files) without concern for the type of machine that originated the file, the file's original format or even the operating systems of the machines involved. FTP is also a program—in which case it's called *ftp*, without the capitalization—that enables FTP. Just as the word *telephone* denotes both a device you hold in your hand and a system for international communications, ftp is both the message and the medium.

The term is also used as both a noun ("It's available via ftp") and a verb ("FTP to sri.com and look in the netinfo directory"). It's hard to misuse the term, in other words. Just don't try to pronounce it: this is one acronym that's always spelled out.

Anonymous FTP

Originally, most FTP sessions occurred between a site and a person at a remote location who had an account at that site. The person would log on by supplying an account name and a password, then conduct the appropriate file activities.

The need soon became apparent, however, for less restrictive access. What if a site wanted to post a file for *anyone* to download? A number of publicly funded agencies require such an arrangement. NASA's space images, as an example, are funded by public money, thus the public should have access to them.

The solution is *anonymous FTP*. During an anonymous FTP session, the user logs on to the remote site using the account name "anonymous" (AOL does this for you unless you supply a specific user name). The password for anonymous login, typically, is the user's Internet address—a common courtesy so the people at the remote site can determine who is using their system if they wish. Again, AOL does this for you unless you supply a specific password.

Operating FTP successfully and acquiring a library of fertile FTP locations (and when to access them) is a skill worthy of development, but it *does* require time to develop. Begin by reading the help files available at the keyword: FTP (and pictured in Figure 14-11), and practice for a while using AOL's "favorite sites," pictured in Figure 14-15. If you feel you need more help, post questions on the Internet Connection message boards. AOL's community is always ready to help you learn.

Moving On

Each of the Internet resources described on these pages is an existing AOL feature. Others will no doubt come along. That's part of the fun of telecommunications: this is just the beginning, and there's always more to come. Becoming a member of AOL (and exploring the Internet) is a little like planting a fruit tree: there's lots of diversity (blossoms, bees, fruit, firewood), and each year there's more than there was the year before.

It's positively organic. ;-)

Internet aside, our most precious resource as a society is our children, and AOL certainly hasn't forgotten them. In fact, there's an entire department dedicated to kids, and it's as palatial as the Internet itself. Shall we take a look? Turn the page....

CHAPTER 15

Kids Only

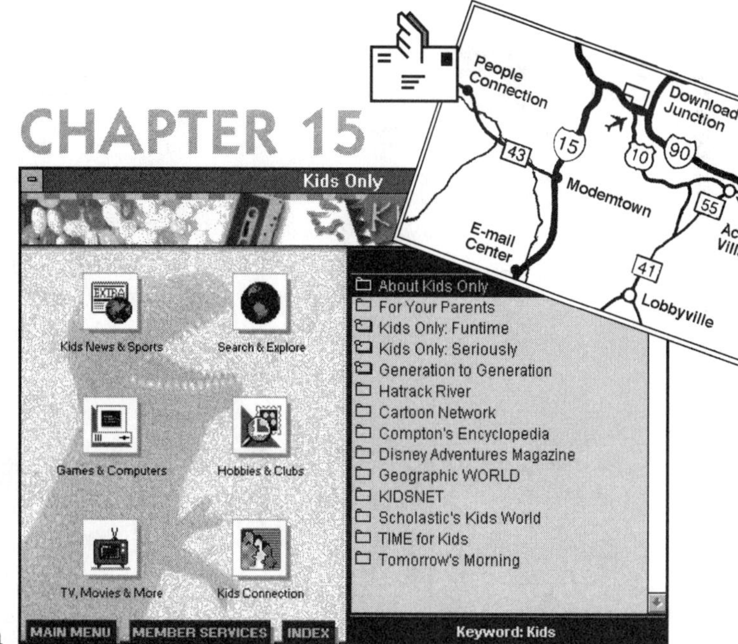

The introduction to Chapter 13 described the Clubs & Interests Department "...as multiethnic as Ellis Island and as variegated as a harlequin's tights." It then went on to mention the African American, Asian, Hispanic, senior and gay boards and in so doing left out an entire segment of our society—kids.

Don't worry: kids get equal time in this book, and on AOL. In fact, they have an entire department. Kids Only was a mere forum a few months ago and now, deservedly, it's a department (see Figure 15-1).

This makes sense. Perhaps no other segment of our society adapts as well to computers as our kids do, and kids have no qualms about striking up a new online friendship, uploading original art or speaking their minds on a board topic.

Kids Only is made up of six departments: Kids News & Sports, Search & Explore, Games & Computers, Hobbies & Clubs, TV, Movies & More and Kids Connection. *Kids News & Sports* contains the weekly Kids Magazine, Tomorrow's Morning and the Kids Only 'zine created by kids, for kids online. *Search & Explore* contains educational forums such as the Encyclopedia, Homework Help, Teacher Pager, Smithsonian and National Geographic World Magazine. *TV, Movies & More* contains Cartoon Network, Disney Adventures magazine, and searchable Television Listings. *Games & Computers* contains software reviews, cartoons, comics and game libraries.

Kids Only is AOL's Riviera for kids aged 6 to 13. Though adults occasionally drop by, this *is* the Kids Only Department, and kids are the ruling class. Click the Kids Only button on the Main Menu, or use the keyword: Kids.

Kids Only is cohosted by Jack Powell—a kid person by choice and by profession. When he's not at home with his four daughters, he works as a pediatrician and pediatric cardiologist. Jack's wife Jean is a pediatric nurse, and cohost Genevieve Kazdin is a critic and reviewer of media for children. Gen has twin granddaughters to occupy her time when she's not online.

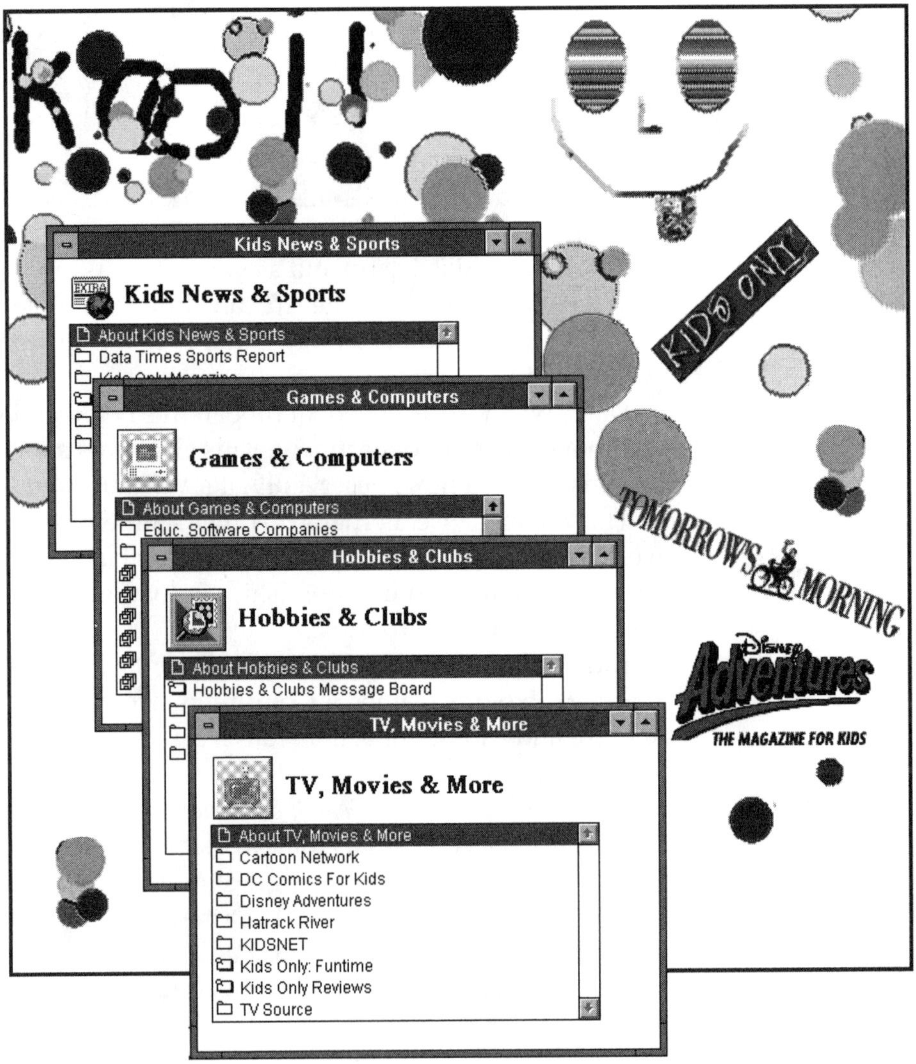

Figure 15-1: A montage of Kids Only forums appears against a background by Chaz Pabst.

The Boards

Kids love to talk, so much so that Kids Only offers not one, but five message boards for their comments. *Funtime* offers folders on annoying siblings, dinosaurs and the unexplained (among others); *Seriously* offers folders on AIDS, sexism and drugs; and *Generation to Generation* is the only board in the department where adult participation is encouraged. These boards are lively, unpredictable and often insightful. Even if you're not a kid, you'll enjoy reading the kids' comments. Kids Only Reviews is a place where children state their opinions about movies, books, magazines, games, software and more. There's even a message board devoted to hobbies and club discussions.

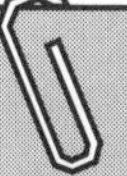

Silly Putty

Sometimes you'll find the most interesting material in the least likely place. This most certainly was the case when I explored Kids Only's Seriously board. Andy Baird, an AOL forum consultant in the graphics library, responded to a New Hampshire high school student's request for information about a now-famous synthetic rubber with the following piece:

"Silly Putty was indeed invented more or less by accident in the 1940s. A Scottish engineer named James Wright was working in the laboratories of General Electric in an attempt to create a superior synthetic rubber. (The battles in the Pacific had cut off the supplies of natural rubber from the Far East, so synthetic rubber was a hot priority during WWII.)

"Wright combined boric acid and silicone oil in a beaker, which resulted in a gooey mass. When he dropped a blob of the stuff, Wright was surprised to find that it bounced back and hit him in the face! Yet it could be stretched like putty, and if left to itself, would flow like a liquid. GE sent samples of the strange substance to engineers and researchers, hoping someone would find a use for it...but no one could.

"Six years later, an unemployed advertising executive named Peter Hodgson found out about the putty and tried selling it as a novelty gift item through a book catalog. To everyone's surprise, the putty outsold almost everything else in the catalog. Deeply in debt, Hodgson borrowed $147 and bought a big batch of the glop from GE; then he packaged it in plastic eggs, added the name Silly Putty and took some samples to the annual Toy Fair in New York. That led to an article in the *New Yorker* magazine, which in turn set off an avalanche of sales—250,000 orders came in in three days!

More

"The rest is history. Binney and Smith, the product's owners, say that over 200,000,000 eggs—that's 3,000 tons of Silly Putty!—have been sold over the years. (They're currently produced at the rate of 12,000 eggs a day at a putty plant in Pennsylvania.) Peter Hodgson died in 1975, leaving an estate of $140,000,000—and many happy Silly Putty owners!"

Andy Baird has his own folder in the Seriously board, called Ask Andy. If you have a science question that needs answering, Andy's the one to ask!

The Libraries

A colleague of mine—Craig Hickman from the University of Oregon's math department—loves to dabble with his computer. He also has kids of his own, and in his spare time he writes programs for his kids to use. He brought a little paint program he had written with him when he taught programming classes in my department at the University of Oregon in Portland. It was a great example of multimedia programming, but aside from his kids' use and the classroom example, he didn't have any plans for the program. He was just filling idle time when he wrote the program.

Until the software publisher Broderbund made him an offer he couldn't refuse. Almost overnight *KidPix* went from a plaything to one of the most successful painting programs for the Macintosh ever sold. It's cheap, it's colorful and makes lots of noise, and it has the kind of tools kids love to use.

KidPix is such a hit that today it has its own Kids Only library—the *KidPix Trading Post*. There are others as well: *The Kids Only Library* offers sounds, GIFs, smileys, morphs, HyperCard stacks, QuickTime movies, stories and icons; *Cartoon Images* are all GIF files, which display as they're downloaded (if you're using version 1.5 or later of the AOL software); *Apps for Kids* are all computer applications, including spelling checkers, typing tutors, word processors and trivia programs.

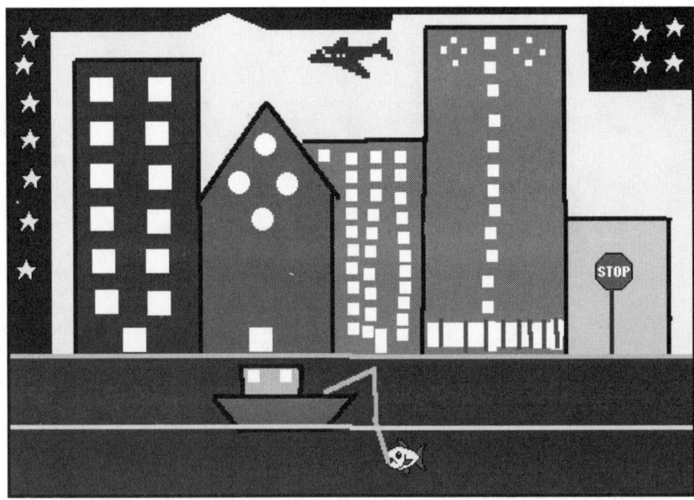

Figure 15-2: A KidPix illustration by Scott Ostermiller, uploaded to Kids Only's KidPix Trading Post.

Hatrack River

Orson Scott Card has long been committed to online computer networks. His most famous novel, *Ender's Game*, not only showed many of the future possibilities of online services like AOL, but was quite possibly the first novel ever published online before it appeared in print.

Now on AOL, Orson Scott Card has opened his fictional town of Hatrack River. Hatrack River figures prominently in his series of American frontier fantasies called *The Tales of Alvin Maker*; it is also the name of a publishing company that Card and his wife, Kristine, own and operate.

Hatrack River is a particularly erudite and prophetic community—one of those niches marked by passion and intelligence that resonate with a number of onliners who can't find serendipity elsewhere. Hatrack River is founded on a healthy respect for the dignity and beliefs of others. We're all welcome at Hatrack, whether we choose to speak or simply to listen.

I mention Hatrack here because one of its libraries—the Dragon's Tale—is devoted to the writings of those who are under 18 (see Figure 15-3). If you're the parent of a youngster (or if you're under 18 yourself) with a literary penchant, take a moment to visit Hatrack River. The keyword: Hatrack will get you there in a hurry.

Figure 15-3: Russell Miller's (age 15) "Killing of the Veggies" appears in the Dragon's Tale library at Hatrack River.

The Killing of the Veggies

by Russell Miller

The end is near, the cabbage cried,
the judgement is at hand
our time is done, the jig is up
now we're to be salads on demand.

The end is near, the cabbage cried,
the vegetarians' knives will swiftly fly
into our tender, ripening flesh
and I fear we all will die.

Hark unto sweet salvation,
cried the cabbage with loud and fierce voice
now we will die, but our souls all will live
if in religion we all do rejoice.

Bah said the carrot
Are you really so stupid you think we have souls?
That your god, he will hear us?
And save us from bowls?

Said the tomato: god's a veggie too
and protects us all from the knives
so that we never end up in salad bowls
and there forfeit our lives.

Wrong! said an olive, although god is up there
and god may just be a veggie too
but god, himself is a deist
and does not care one whit about you!

Or! said the carrot
what if you're half-right, and there is a god above,
but one who is human, however
and who looks on vegetables with no great love?

O swift was the blade and the cuts that it made
and like a vorpal sword it did go snicker-snack
and the vegetables were all brutally killed
their bodies split open and cracked.

Upon the large counter the bodies were strewn
no yard site; save bowls, for final bed.
Then they were tossed, and more insults ensued,
as then there was dressing for the dead.

An orange on the table had heard the whole talk
and had watched as they hawwed and they hemmed.
The talk on god had been quite impressive,
but in the end where had it got them?

What moral then was learned you ask
as the salad is interred,
eaten by hungry vegetarians,
with great gusto and nary a word.

As for the the orange, nothing at all.
He already knew that to be one must do.
And depending for help on a god who might be
is a path that is stupid and dangerous too.

As for the rest some had believed some had not
and really what more can be said?
Perhaps they'd been sinners, perhaps they'd been saints
but now they all were just dead.

And the souls? Well, not much is known
perhaps they were saved perhaps not.
But I don't think we'll ever truly know if they exist
and if so, where they go after veggie bodies rot.

The Tree House

The Tree House is Kids Only's chat room (chat rooms are discussed in Chapter 12, "People Connection"), and it's one of the busiest—and most feature-packed—chats on AOL.

During the week that I'm writing this chapter, the Tree House discusses weather on Friday night, plays real-time games on Saturday and Sunday nights, offers a Star Trek simulation on Monday night, plays trivia on Tuesday, and offers video-game tips and tricks on Wednesday. Other times of the week are set aside for specific age groups.

Double-click the Tree House listing in the Kids Connection menu and read the Tree House Calendar for the latest schedule.

TIME Online

Throwing its considerable weight behind the conviction that kids are our most precious resource, *TIME* magazine launched TIME Online in late 1993. It has since become something of a *au fait* online community for kids—and kids only: participation by those over 14 years of age is discouraged. The topics are often substantial, the philosophies insightful, and the opinions articulate.

TIME Online's purpose is to see what young people think about *TIME* magazine and the subjects of its stories in the context of kids' interests and kids' perceptions. Perhaps most significantly, it provides kids with an opportunity to talk directly to *TIME's* writers and editors. If you want to glimpse tomorrow's hopes and ambitions, read this board (see Figure 15-4).

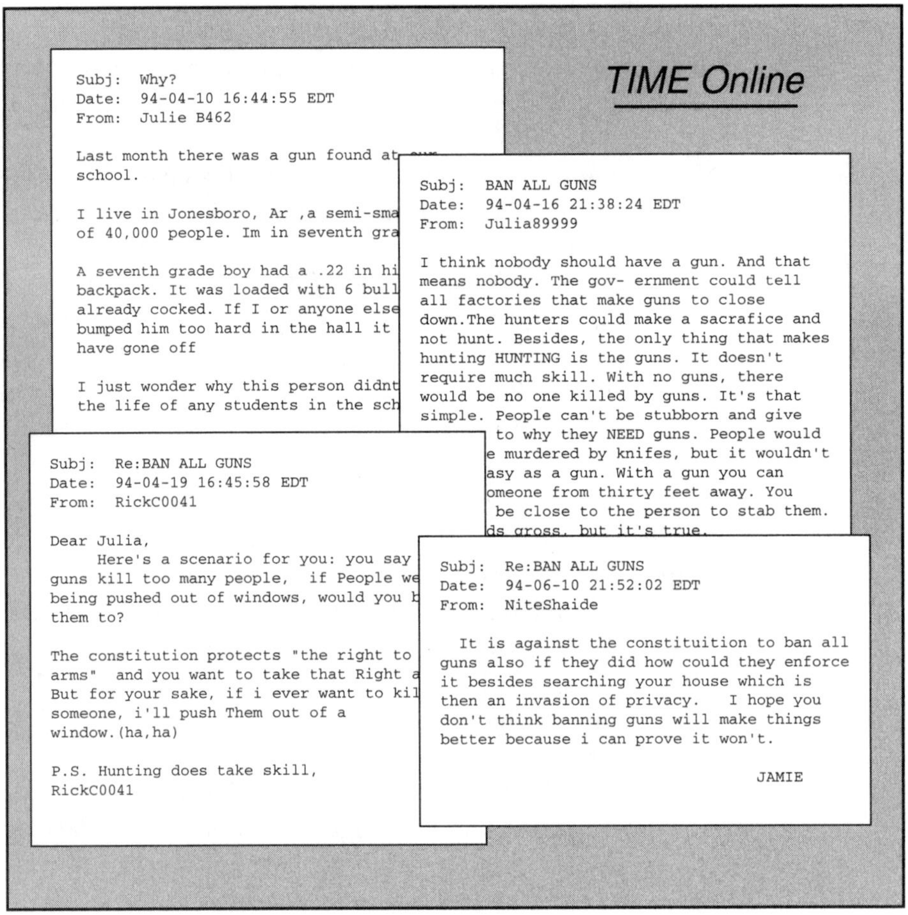

Figure 15-4: Gun control isn't just an adult issue. The kids at TIME Online have resolute opinions too.

TIME Online

```
Subj:  Why?
Date:  94-04-10 16:44:55 EDT
From:  Julie B462

Last month there was a gun found at
school.

I live in Jonesboro, Ar ,a semi-sma
of 40,000 people. Im in seventh gra

A seventh grade boy had a .22 in hi
backpack. It was loaded with 6 bull
already cocked. If I or anyone else
bumped him too hard in the hall it
have gone off

I just wonder why this person didnt
the life of any students in the sch
```

```
Subj:  BAN ALL GUNS
Date:  94-04-16 21:38:24 EDT
From:  Julia89999

I think nobody should have a gun. And that
means nobody. The gov- ernment could tell
all factories that make guns to close
down.The hunters could make a sacrafice and
not hunt. Besides, the only thing that makes
hunting HUNTING is the guns. It doesn't
require much skill. With no guns, there
would be no one killed by guns. It's that
simple. People can't be stubborn and give
 to why they NEED guns. People would
e murdered by knifes, but it wouldn't
asy as a gun. With a gun you can
omeone from thirty feet away. You
 be close to the person to stab them.
ds gross, but it's true.
```

```
Subj:  Re:BAN ALL GUNS
Date:  94-04-19 16:45:58 EDT
From:  RickC0041

Dear Julia,
     Here's a scenario for you: you say
guns kill too many people,  if People we
being pushed out of windows, would you b
them to?

The constitution protects "the right to
arms"  and you want to take that Right a
But for your sake, if i ever want to kil
someone, i'll push Them out of a
window.(ha,ha)

P.S. Hunting does take skill,
RickC0041
```

```
Subj:  Re:BAN ALL GUNS
Date:  94-06-10 21:52:02 EDT
From:  NiteShaide

  It is against the constituition to ban all
guns also if they did how could they enforce
it besides searching your house which is
then an invasion of privacy.   I hope you
don't think banning guns will make things
better because i can prove it won't.

                                   JAMIE
```

A Word to Parents

Though it occurs throughout the service, harassment and exploitation are particularly obstructive in Kids Only. To be effective, Kids Only must be a place where kids are made to feel welcome: it's their online home, and a home—above all—must always be comfortable.

TOS

America Online's Terms of Service (keyword: TOS) clearly define the rules of acceptable online behavior. Parents should become familiar with them and share an understanding of them with their children before the kids first sign on.

When your child witnesses a TOS violation, he or she should be encouraged to use the keyword: GuidePager and ask a Guide to enter the room where the violation is occurring. Not only will the offender encounter the significance of TOS enforcement (that's as politely as I can put it), your child will see what happens when these rules are broken. A witness to a "TOS event" rarely forgets the experience.

Instant Messages

Instant Messages often arrive unbidden, and when kids are involved they're occasionally unwelcome as well. Your child should know how to turn Instant Messages off (send an Instant Message to the screen name: $im_off) and back on again (send an Instant Message to the screen name: $im_on). Instant Messages are discussed in Chapter 12, "People Connection." Read about them if you haven't already.

Online Time

A friend of mine once recounted her horror when she discovered that her daughter had fallen asleep for two hours while making a call to a 900 number. While 900 numbers usually charge by the minute and AOL charges by the hour, AOL's charges can nonetheless add up quickly when a child—who can hardly be expected to understand the significance of a month of six-hour Saturdays in the Kids Only Tree House—is left unattended online. The Kids Only staff suggests you teach your children how to use FlashSessions for collecting and posting mail (FlashSessions are discussed in Chapter 19). Set limits on the amount of time they are allowed online much in the way television viewing is limited. Kids Only should be a fun electronic clubhouse, but not a financial burden. America Online cannot be held responsible for charges you might deem excessive.

Parental Control

Finally, become familiar with AOL's Parental Control feature (keyword: ParentalControl). It's discussed in Chapter 12 (see the sidebar on page 252) and it offers parents the ability to determine where their children can go online and under what conditions they're allowed there.

Moving On

I don't want to become mired in negativity. Above all, Kids Only is a place for kids. Shyness, introversion, even autism aren't uncommon in the ages between 6 and 13, and the anonymity offered by the online milieu is often therapeutic to these conditions. Shy kids nurture here; aggressive kids pacify; challenged kids thrive. Heck, even well-rounded kids like it. So do adults. Don't tell the kids.

If Kids Only is the clubhouse in our online community, there must be a schoolhouse somewhere, and there is. It's called the Education Department and, delightfully, it's one of the most kaleidoscopic departments AOL offers. It's described in the next chapter. Don't miss it.

CHAPTER 16

Education

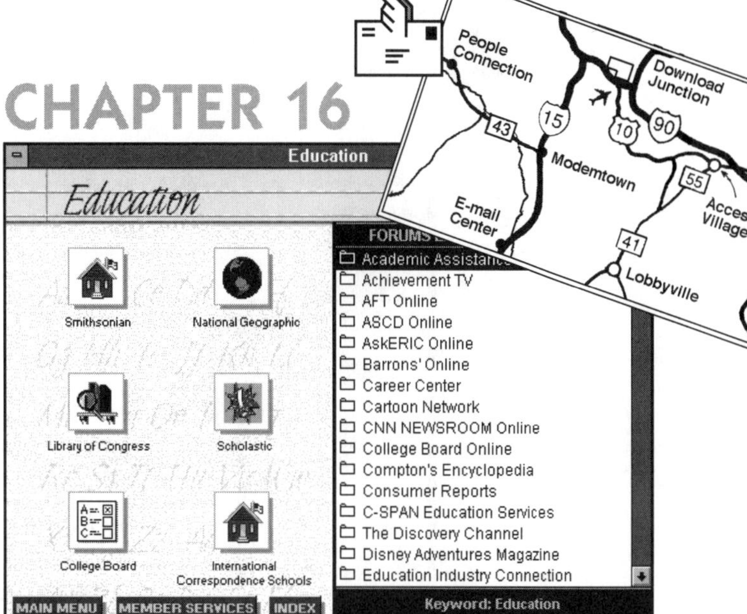

I've read your letters. Many of you skip this department and this chapter. You're here to have fun, and education isn't your idea of a joyride on the infobahn.

Too bad, because the rewards in the Education Department are as abundant as, well, June graduates in search of jobs.

Don't get me wrong: the emphasis here is on learning. Yes, the inquisitive browser will find scores of treasures here, but students, teachers and parents of students (or students-to-be) are especially well served by this department. If you fall into any of these categories, you should investigate the Education Department. Use the keyword: Education, or click on the Department button on the Main Menu. Before you do, however, read this chapter. It's a big department, and this chapter will help you to refine your investigation and offer some tips as well.

Education for Everyone

While teachers and students are exceptionally well served by this department, the rest of us are not overlooked. There's a Career Center; *National Geographic* and *Disney Adventures* magazines; the Smithsonian Institution; NPR, CNN and C-SPAN; and the Online Campus. Imagine having access to such resources without paying for magazine or cable subscriptions, or private tutoring fees!

This may be the most surprising department of them all. You expect to find students and teachers here, but mad Russians, giant lizards and supersonic spy planes? They're all in the Education Department (keyword: Education), and so is much, much more.

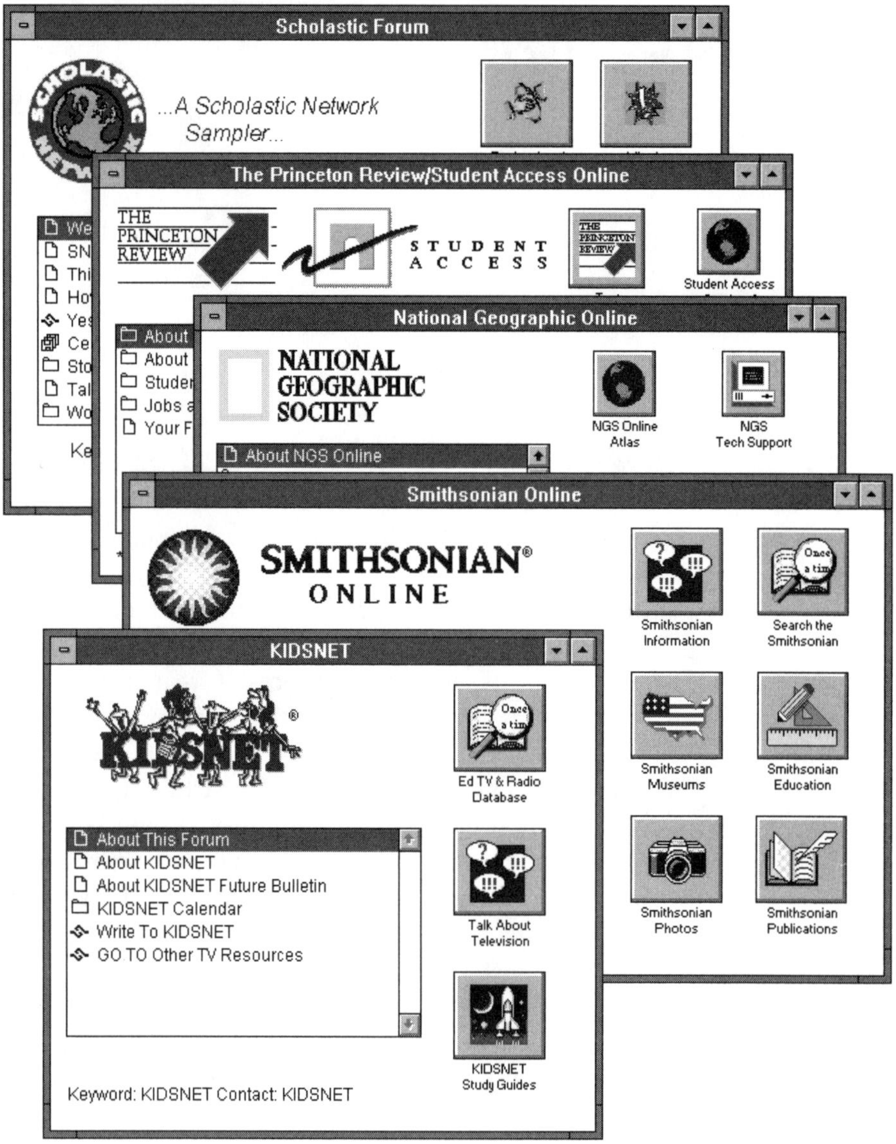

Figure 16-1: The Education Department offers a wealth of resources.

National Geographic Online

Here you will find selections from *National Geographic* magazine and National Geographic's *Traveler* and *World* magazines, as well as a variety of news stories and press releases (keyword: Geographic). The television program is also featured in the Geographic TV Forum (see Figure 16-2).

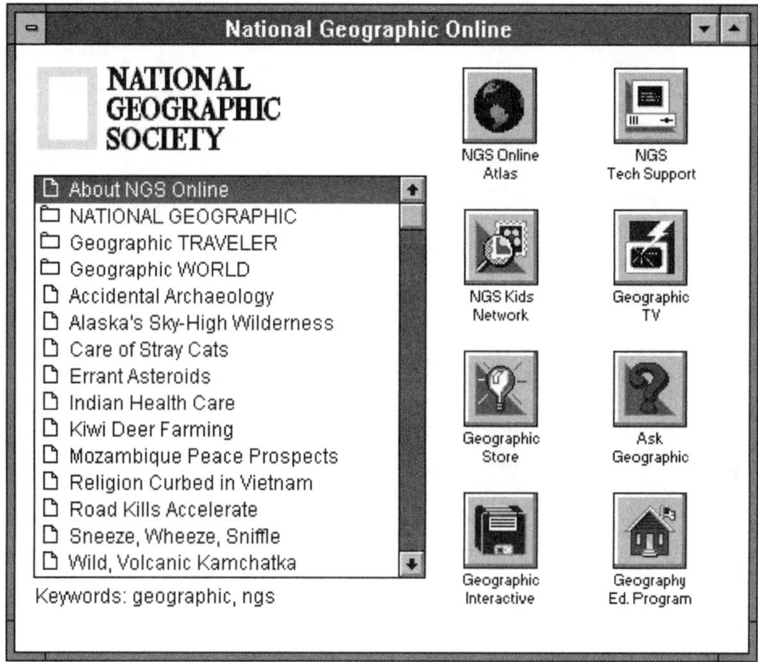

Figure 16-2: *National Geographic, Traveler* and *World* magazines are all included in National Geographic Online.

National Geographic's *Earth Almanac* tracks events on earth of particular interest to the Geographic reader. Written in the traditional Geographic style, the stories are always intriguing and often a little unusual. On the afternoon that I looked in, two stories struck me as particularly interesting—especially one recounting the adventures of ten-foot-long serpents intent on decimating the US territories in the South Pacific (see Figure 16-3).

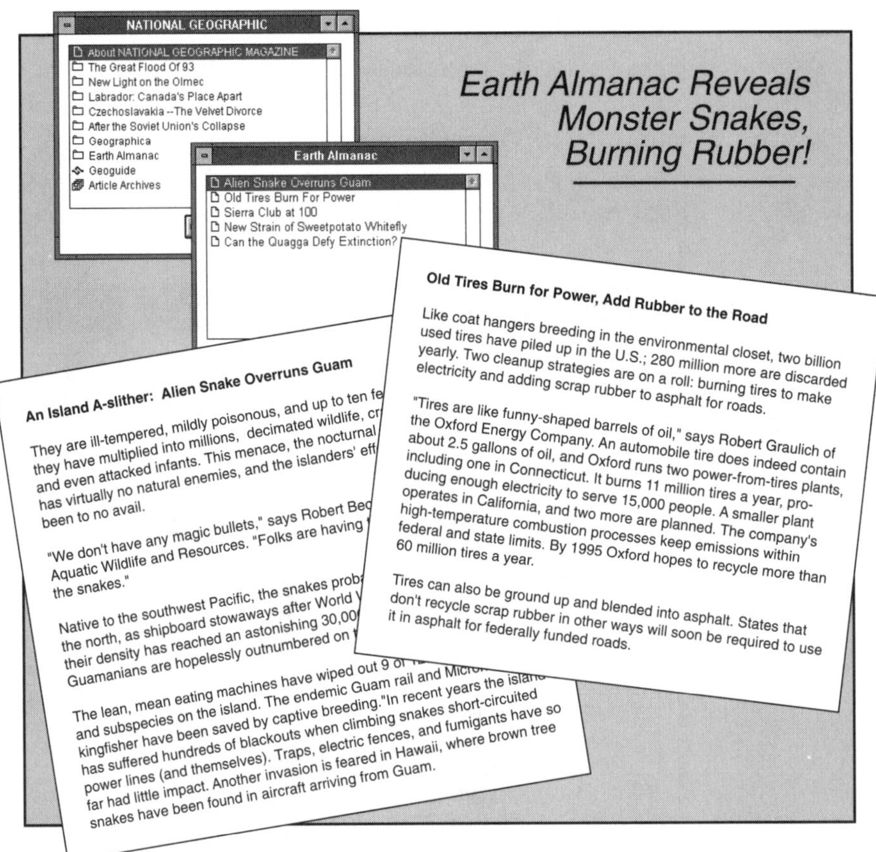

Figure 16-3: National Geographic's *Earth Almanac* regales the reader with reports on rapacious reptiles and recycled rubber.

Constant Change

Perhaps you've noticed: this is not a conservative, tranquil industry. The waters of telecommunications are about as placid as an Atlantic storm. For this reason, America Online is in a state of constant change.

Case in point: as I write this, AOL has just announced an alliance with Simon & Schuster, the world's largest educational publisher. The service, called College Online, will create a new interactive experience for college professors and students—the first nationwide set of interactive services geared specifically to the higher education market.

Simon & Schuster will become a huge presence in the Education Department. Don't let changes like this annoy you. Seek them out and rejoice in their significance: AOL is always improving and we're the reason. To stay abreast of the changes, use the keyword: New.

The Library of Congress Online

The *Online Secret Soviet Archives* are a temporary "exhibit" in the Education Department, not unlike the exhibit upon which they are based in the Library of Congress (keyword: Library). In the museum business, temporary (or traveling) exhibits don't stay in any one museum permanently; after an appropriate stay, they move on to other museums where others may see them. Indeed, the Library of Congress returned the Russian Archives exhibit to Moscow in July of 1992.

I include the Online Secret Soviet Archives as an example of the topical material endemic to this department and to impress you with the quality and opulence of its "traveling" exhibits. It also represents the world's first online version of a major national exhibit, and it appeared on America Online.

The Online Secret Soviet Archives (more properly, *Revelations from the Russian Archives*) is a collection of documents culled from several declassified secret files of the former Soviet Union. The full exhibit of some 300 Soviet documents, photographs and films—which were on display in the Library of Congress in the spring of 1992—is the first such exhibition in the West. It shed new light on some of the major events of the 20th century, from the Russian Revolution to recent times. Included in the exhibit are materials relating to such topics as Stalin's reign of terror, the Gulag system, censorship, the workings of the secret police, substandard construction practices at the Chernobyl nuclear plant and the 1962 Cuban Missile Crisis.

The online exhibit consists of excerpts from 25 of the 250 documents in the museum exhibit. Scans of the original documents are posted in GIF format (GIF is a graphics format which we'll discuss in Chapter 19, "FlashSessions & the Download Manager").

Each scanned original is accompanied by an English translation (which you can read online or save to your hard drive for further study) and a piece providing the appropriate historical background. Reading these documents is an experience never to be forgotten—a John Le Carre novel come to life, an event best illuminated by the Russian originals, downloaded and displayed on your screen, in heirloom color and Cyrillic mystery (see Figure 16-4).

The Secret Soviet Archives have been placed on exhibit on America Online "indefinitely." They make up a unique and most rewarding area on the service. Don't pass this one by!

КМ-3 40

Секретно

КОМИТЕТ
ГОСУДАРСТВЕННОЙ БЕЗОПАСНОСТИ СССР
21.02.79г. № 346-А
Москва

ЦК КПСС

О недостатках в строительстве
Чернобыльской АЭС

По имеющимся в КГБ СССР данным, на отдельных участках строительства второго блока Чернобыльской атомной электростанции имеют место факты отступления от проектов, а также нарушения технологии ведения строительных и монтажных работ, что может привести к авариям и несчастным случаям.

Колонны карк
от разбивочных осей д
отсутствуют горизонт
нением от осей до 15
отступлением от пред
тормозные площадки и
клонени до 8 градусо
Заместитель
дал указание на прои
где во многих местах
ные нарушения с ведо
лекса т. Матвеева Ю.
ства. Повреждение ги

Revelations from the Russian Archives

CHERNOBYL
Central Committee of the CPSU
USSR COMMITTEE OF STATE SECURITY [KGB]
February 21, 1979 No. 346
Moscow

Construction Flaws at the Chernobyl Nuclear Power Plant [AES]

According to data in the possession of the KGB of the USSR, design deviations and violations of construction and assembly technology are occurring at various places in the construction of the second generating unit of the Chernobyl AES, and these could lead to mishaps and accidents.

The structural pillars of the generator room were erected with a deviation of up to 100 mm from the reference axes, and horizontal connections between the pillars are absent in places. Wall panels have been installed with a deviation of up to 150 mm from the axes. The placement of roof plates does not conform to the designer's specifications. Crane tracks and stopways have vertical drops of up to 100 mm and in places a slope of up to 8.

Deputy head of the Construction Directorate, Comrade V. T. Gora, gave instructions for backfilling the foundation in many places where vertical waterproofing was damaged. Similar violations were permitted in other sections with the knowledge of Comrade V. T. Gora and the head of the construction group, Comrade IU. L. Matveev. Damage to the waterproofing can lead to ground water seepage into the station and radioactive contamination of the environment.

The leadership of the Directorate is not devoting proper attention to the foundation, on which the quality of the construction largely depends. The cement plant operates erratically, and its output is of poor quality.Interruptions were permitted during the pouring of especially heavy concrete causing gaps and layering in the foundation. Access roads to the Chernobyl AES are in urgent need of repair.

Construction of the third high-voltage transmission line is behind schedule, which could limit the capacity utilization of the second unit.
As a result of inadequate monitoring of the condition of safety equipment, in the first three quarters of 1978, 170 individuals suffered work-related injuries, with the loss of work time totalling 3,366 worker-days.

The KGB of Ukraine has informed the CPSU Central Committee of these violations. This is for your information.

Chairman of the Committee [KGB]
[signed] IU. Andropov...Secret

Figure 16-4: The Chernobyl report exceeded 1,000 words and occupied nearly six pages. The page shown here, which documents early construction flaws, was written in early 1979. The plant exploded at 1:21 A.M. on April 26, 1986—a little over seven years later.

As I write this, the Library of Congress features three additional online exhibits, including the Columbus Quincentenary, the Scrolls from the Dead Sea and Treasures of the Vatican. The Vatican exhibit includes such rare delights as love letters from Henry VIII to Anne Boleyn, Galileo's diaries and much more. The Library of Congress Online is not only fascinating and educational, it's a capital example of the benefits online access has to offer.

The Electronic University Network

The word "University" in academic circles implies accreditation and baccalaureate degrees recognized across the nation. The word also implies an accredited program of graduate studies leading to post-baccalaureate degrees. The Electronic University Network (keyword: EUN) offers both, each available without leaving your computer.

The University is based on the belief that quality education can be made available to people where they are—the home, the work place, the barracks, the hotel room, the hospital; the belief that it's the quality of the dialog between the teacher and the student, not the distance between them, that determines the quality of education; the belief that reading, writing and thinking are at the heart of the educational process.

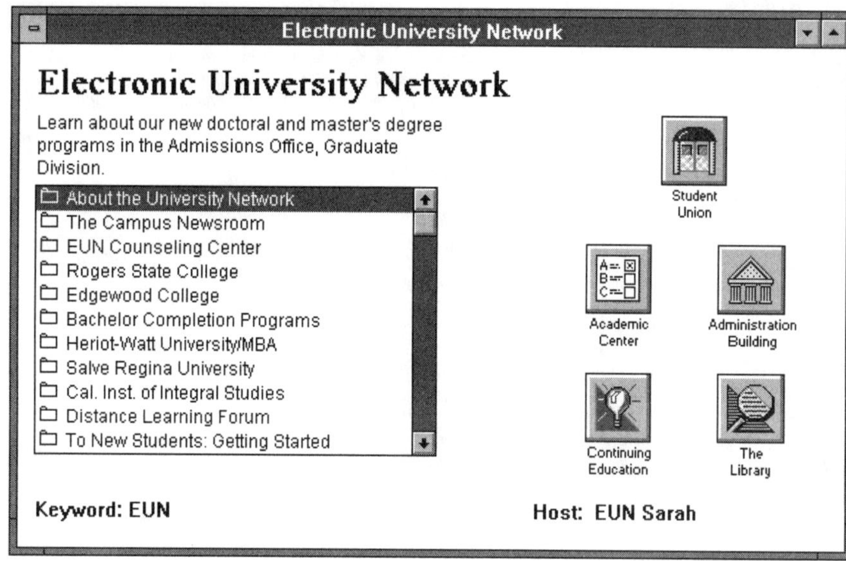

Figure 16-5: The Electronic University Network offers accredited learning, ranging from Associate's to Master's degrees.

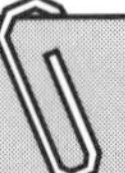

Core Courses in the EUN MBA Program

SV 612 *Accounting for Management Decisions*
The uses of accounting information as it relates to decision making in business. Emphasizes current planning and control models, long-range decision making techniques, performance evaluation and accounting information for special decisions. The course may include current readings and case analysis.

SV 622 *Microeconomic Analysis*
Analysis of the behavior of consumers and business firms. Topics covered: the theory of demand, production, and supply, competitive and monopolistic markets, factor markets, general equilibrium and welfare economics, externality problems and public goods.

SV 604 *Financial Planning and Control*
Advanced application of selected finance topics to case studies. Specific topics include capital budgeting, dividend policy, leverage and working capital management. Current topics in finance, such as mergers and multinational corporations, will also be covered.

SV 620 *Quantitative Analysis for Decision Making*
The application of quantitative methods to managerial decision making with emphasis upon problem formulation, the analysis of the effects of changes in parameters and other aspects of model interpretation. The application of technique is emphasized.

SV 621 *Organizational Behavior*
Analysis of the effects of organizational roles in the behavior of people in organizations using an open system perspective. Through the analysis of research findings, the managerial implications of perception, communication, influence processes, technology and the motivational basis of behavior are examined.

SV 631 *Marketing Administration*
Analysis of marketing concepts and problems from the point of view of the business executive engaged in problem solving and decision making in formulating an effective marketing program. Emphasis on planning, organizing and controlling international as well as domestic marketing activities and their integration with objectives and policies of the firm.

SV 690 *Social Environment of Business*
An interdisciplinary course designed to develop students' ability to recognize, interpret and respond to major exogenous forces of concern in business. Topics include: ethical considerations, public policies, laws and regulations, economic environment, political and social influences, accounting practices, multinational corporations and other current concerns of national and international dimensions.

SV 695 *Executive Policies and Planning*
The study of the business enterprise from a top management point of view, emphasizing the formulation of strategies and policies for adapting to external influences and opportunities. The course requires the student to integrate knowledge of the functional areas in the development of comprehensive plans and policies. This course is taken after all other Core courses have been completed.

The University offers nearly 100 undergraduate courses that earn college credit and enable students to receive an Associate's or Bachelor's degree. You can also earn a Master of Business Administration (MBA) through the University. The MBA is offered in association with Saginaw Valley State University; the program is comprehensive (see sidebar) and nationally recognized.

Speaking of home study, be sure to investigate International Correspondence Schools (keyword: ICS), the oldest and largest accredited home study school in the nation. Using ICS online, you can not only e-mail your instructors for overnight replies, you can talk to fellow students as well. AOL brings a new immediacy to correspondence schools, and ICS is a premier example of that potential.

Smithsonian Online

The Smithsonian Institution in Washington, DC, is probably America's most popular museum. Occupying a significant percentage of the District, the Institution is really a collection of 17 museums and galleries, including a zoo.

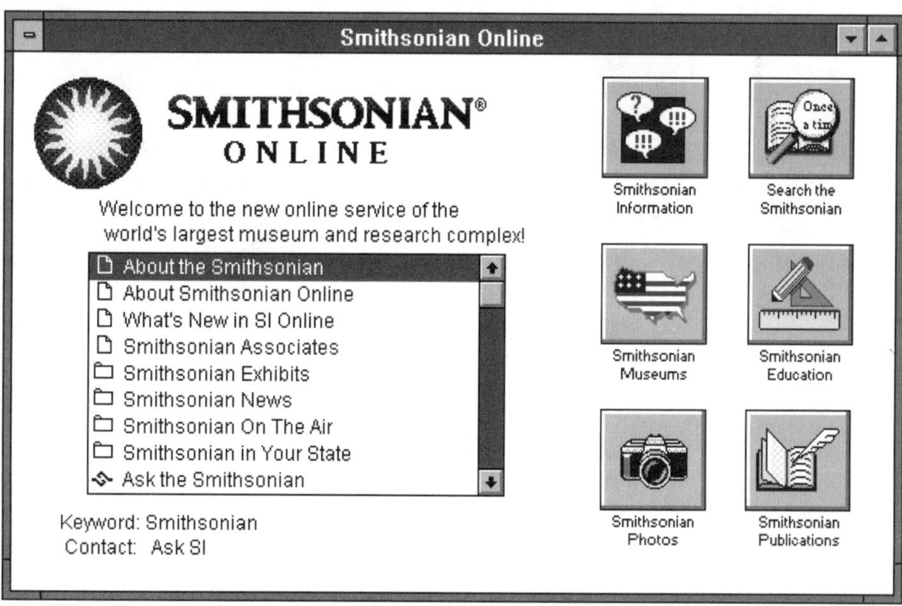

Figure 16-6: Smithsonian Online offers electronic, round-the-clock access to one of America's most comprehensive resources.

Smithsonian Online offers not only descriptions, articles, and photos from many of these museums, it also offers a comprehensive planning guide for anyone planning to visit the Institution. Visiting the Smithsonian is not a casual event; planning is not only recommended, it's essential. And you can do all of your planning using America Online.

Figure 16-7: The SR-71 Blackbird spy plane touches down on the runway at Dulles International Airport near Washington, DC, having just set a new cross-country speed record on its way to being donated to the Smithsonian Institution. The photo is available online and appears here courtesy of the Smithsonian Institution.

The thousands of Smithsonian Online images are scrupulously indexed; the Smithsonian Education Services area offers ideas, outlines, and publications for the teacher; and the Education Resource Guide catalogs educational materials available from the Smithsonian and several affiliated organizations. This is one of the richest environments available on the service, and it warrants your exploration.

Education for the Student

As you can assume from its title, the emphasis in this department is education: learning more about it, getting more out of it and exploring new avenues. For the student, perhaps that last opportunity is the most valuable. Of all the online opportunities AOL provides for the student, three deserve specific mention here: Student Access, the Academic Assistance Center and College Board Online.

Princeton Review/Student Access

A number of resources are available to help students get more out of college, expand graduate school and career options, and network with other students nationwide. The Princeton Review, the nation's most effective test-prep company, has brought them together as an AOL service called Princeton Review/Student Access Online (see Figure 16-8).

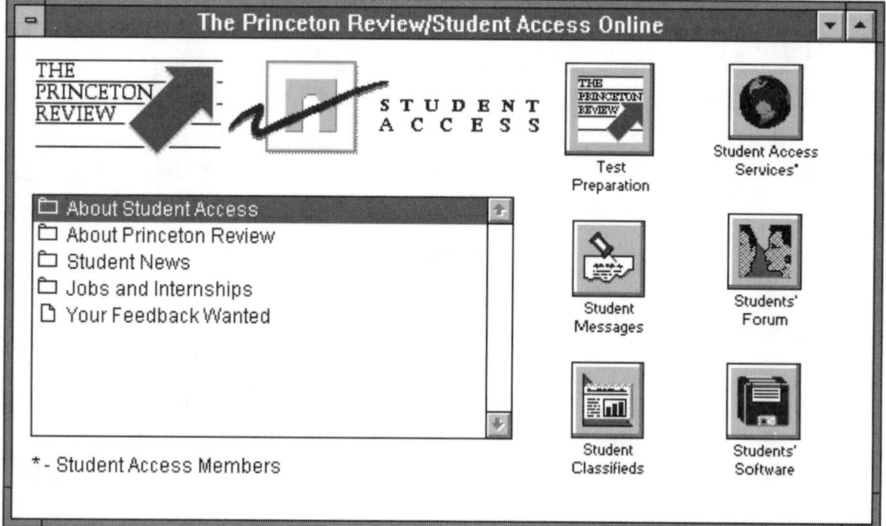

Figure 16-8: Student Access Online offers a number of educational, financial and career services.

Membership in Student Access enables the student to take advantage of a variety of exclusive educational, financial and career services, including the following:

- Financial planning
- Internship opportunities
- Admissions counseling
- Job-placement services
- Group buying power offering hundreds of products and services at discounted rates

- The service's greatest asset—the Student Access members themselves. Student Access forums and trips connect thousands of college students nationwide.

Student Access represents an almost unfair advantage to the student, yet membership is open to anyone.

Tom de Boor

Tom de Boor's office is devoid of ornamentation. The only break in the monotonous white sheetrock is a lone corkboard, suspended by a single nail at the upper left corner. The other nail—the one intended to hold the upper right corner—pulled out of the wall some time ago. The corkboard dangles at a 45 degree angle above Tom's IBM-PS1. Two other computers are present in the room, a host terminal and a Macintosh SE. Neither is turned on; both are shrouded in opaque layers of dust. The host terminal has been recently used: the dust has been wiped away from the area on the screen that Tom wanted to see.

Tom frequently brushes unruly hair from his eyes as he talks. And talking is something he's good at: animated, enthusiastic talk. In contrast to the disarray in Tom's office, his thinking is organized and methodical, and his conversation is compelling and ardent. As Manager/Senior Producer of Educational Services, Tom oversees AOL's most ambitious and scholarly effort, and he doesn't take this work lightly.

Tom's challenges are magnitude and access. An online service confronts two conflicting necessities: depth and convenience. The Education department is not unlike an immense public library: so diverse that it stimulates, but so large that it intimidates. Tom's solution is an environment that's more exploratory than linear. How often do you go to a video store in search of a specific movie and come home with something entirely different? People like to browse. Tom's objective is what he calls "Information Art": a browsing (rather than searching) environment—rich in graphics, sound and video—where education is as entertaining and diverse as a stroll down a midway or a visit to a mall: nonlinear and personal. It's about time education became fun.

Few can equal Tom's ambition, and that ambition is outwardly directed: Tom couldn't care less about the charm of his office or the pedigree of his coiffeur. He's singularly devoted to his department. Students, teachers, parents and administrators would have to search far and wide for a service that's as comprehensive, convenient and affordable as the Education Department, and Tom de Boor is the man to thank for it.

The Academic Assistance Center

The Academic Assistance Center (keyword: Homework) is designed for students who need additional reinforcement of the concepts they're learning, help with their homework or help with skills that have become rusty. In particular, this is the place to find teachers—teachers online and dedicated to the pursuit of academic goals.

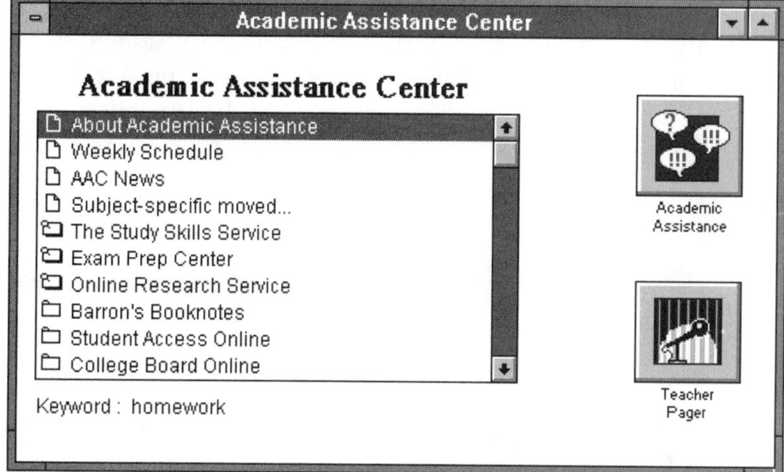

Figure 16-9: The Academic Assistance Center is where students find teachers and professionals to help with academic issues.

The Academic Assistance Center is dedicated to providing the student with academic assistance—online, without surcharge and guaranteed: all the message boards mentioned below are closely monitored—if a student posts a message on any of them and doesn't receive a response within 48 hours, AOL credits the student with an hour of free time.

- Live, real-time help with a general or specific subject area can be obtained in the Academic Assistance help area, where students can post questions, attend one of many regularly scheduled sessions in a variety of subjects, or sign up for a special individual instruction session with one of AOL's instructors.
- During the evening, the "Teacher Pager" is ready to connect a student with a teacher online and live; all a student needs to do is use the keyword: TeacherPager. (The Teacher Pager is discussed in Chapter 17, "Reference Desk.")

- Help with research or term papers can be obtained through the Academic Research Service.
- Special help with end-of-term exams is available through the Exam Prep Center.
- Help in preparing for a standardized exam—like the GED and SAT exams—is available in the Study Skills Instruction area.

Homework is one area that's often foremost on the student's mind, and it's the subject that provokes most students to discover the Academic Assistance Center in the first place. Figure 16-10 identifies a few of the subject areas that were active when I visited—and I visited in the summer, when activity on these boards is slow in comparison to that of the school year.

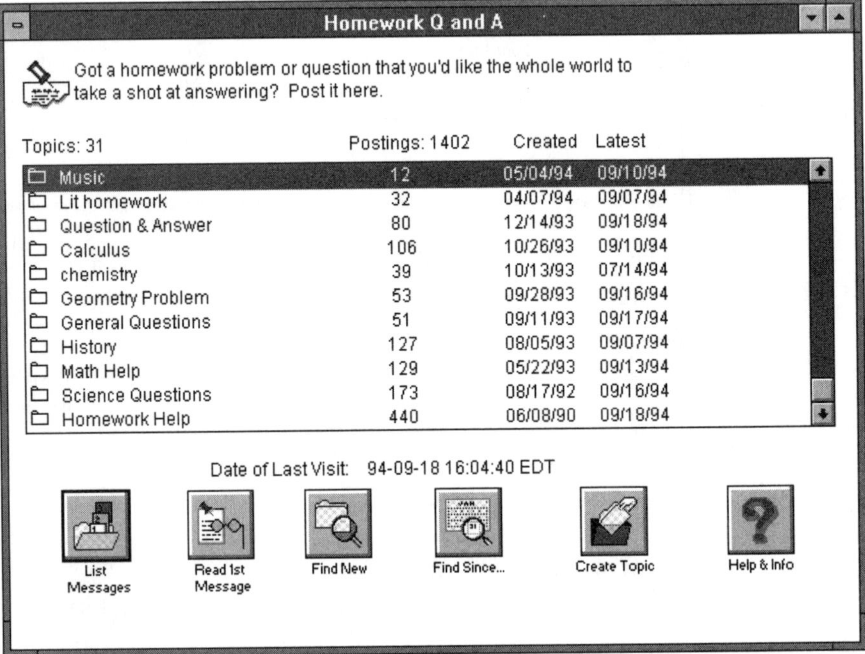

Figure 16-10: At the beginning of the academic year, over 1,400 messages populate the Homework Q & A message board.

College Board Online

Founded in 1900, the College Board is a national, nonprofit association of more than 2,500 institutions and schools, systems, associations and agencies serving both higher and secondary education. The College Board assists students who are making the transition from high school to college through services that include guidance, admissions, placement, credit by examination and financial aid. In addition, the board is chartered to sponsor research, provide a forum to discuss common problems of secondary and higher education, and address questions of educational standards.

Which is a mouthful. This means that the College Board Online (keyword: CollegeBoard) is an invaluable service to the student faced with all the college-related questions: Where should I go? How much will it cost? What are the admission requirements? What are my chances of getting in?

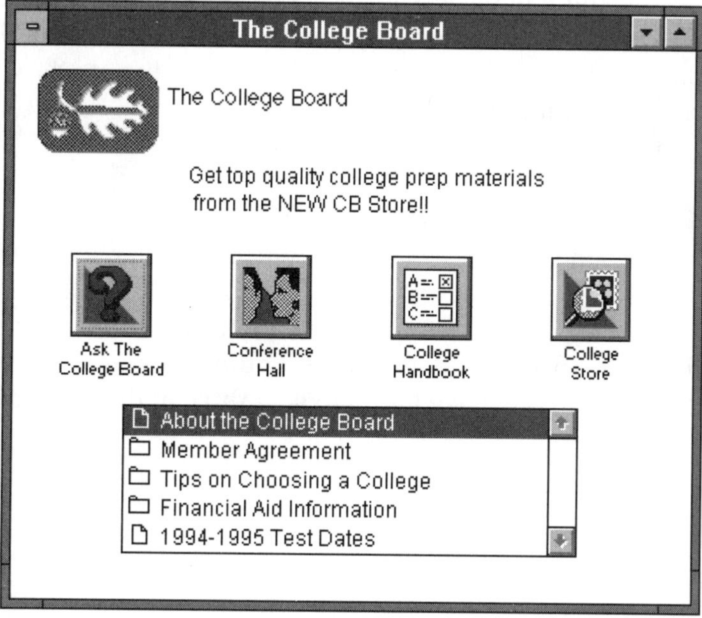

Figure 16-11: The College Board Online is invaluable for the student contemplating a college education.

Perhaps the best way to introduce the College Board is to play the part of a prospective student and query the College Board Handbook. The handbook contains descriptions of over 3,100 colleges and universities. Information about each school includes majors offered, academic programs, freshman admissions, student life and athletics. The Handbook can be searched either by topic or college name.

Let's say I'm interested in journalism and black history, and I've decided to pursue the combination of the two as a career. For this, I need an education. Perhaps the College Board Handbook has the answer (see Figure 16-12).

My search criteria for Figure 16-12 were "journalism" and "black studies." In response to these criteria, the College Handbook found 114 colleges that matched my criteria, one of which is the University of North Carolina at Chapel Hill. By selecting the UNC listing, I received all the text pictured in Figure 16-12. This is a profusion of information, and it's available for each of the other 113 candidates as well.

One thing I notice as I read the UNC admission requirements is that this is one tough school to get into. My credentials will have to be *sterling*. For this I need help, and for help I turn to the College Board Store (see Figure 16-13).

Education for the Teacher

Education is not an isolated activity. Education involves the transfer of knowledge, and the transfer of knowledge typically begins with a teacher. The people at America Online know that; that's why the Education Department features a number of areas specifically intended for teachers. Here we take a look at three of the service areas.

Figure 16-12: A query of the College Handbook identifies the University of North Carolina at Chapel Hill as a possible candidate for my interests in journalism and black studies.

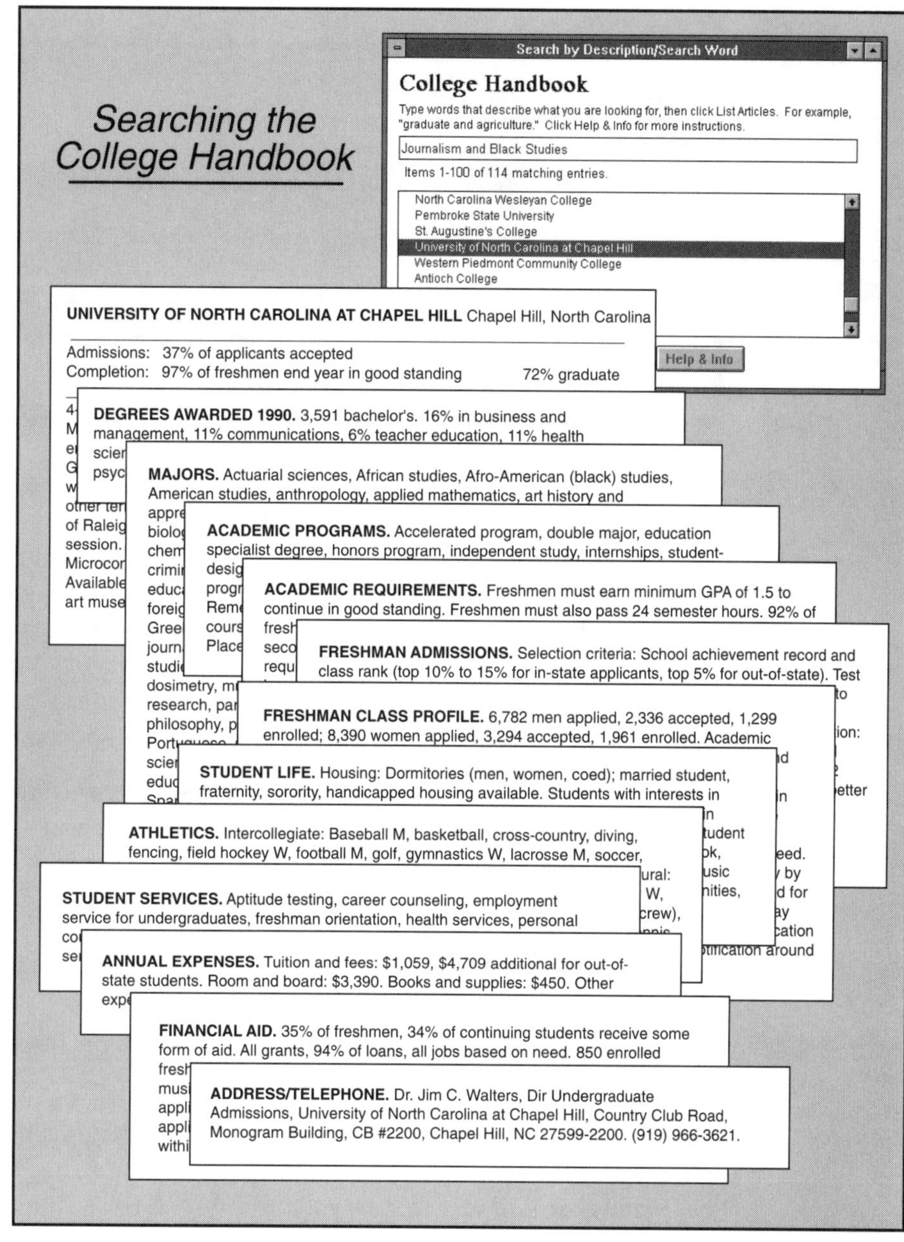

Searching the College Handbook
Search by Description/Search Word
College Handbook
Type words that describe what you are looking for, then click List Articles. For example, "graduate and agriculture." Click Help & Info for more instructions.
Journalism and Black Studies
Items 1-100 of 114 matching entries.
North Carolina Wesleyan College
Pembroke State University
St. Augustine's College
University of North Carolina at Chapel Hill
Western Piedmont Community College
Antioch College
Help & Info
UNIVERSITY OF NORTH CAROLINA AT CHAPEL HILL Chapel Hill, North Carolina
Admissions: 37% of applicants accepted
Completion: 97% of freshmen end year in good standing 72% graduate
DEGREES AWARDED 1990. 3,591 bachelor's. 16% in business and
MAJORS. Actuarial sciences, African studies, Afro-American (black) studies,
ACADEMIC PROGRAMS. Accelerated program, double major, education
ACADEMIC REQUIREMENTS. Freshmen must earn minimum GPA of 1.5 to
continue in good standing. Freshmen must also pass 24 semester hours. 92% of
FRESHMAN ADMISSIONS. Selection criteria: School achievement record and
class rank (top 10% to 15% for in-state applicants, top 5% for out-of-state). Test
FRESHMAN CLASS PROFILE. 6,782 men applied, 2,336 accepted, 1,299
STUDENT LIFE. Housing: Dormitories (men, women, coed); married student,
fraternity, sorority, handicapped housing available. Students with interests in
ATHLETICS. Intercollegiate: Baseball M, basketball, cross-country, diving,
STUDENT SERVICES. Aptitude testing, career counseling, employment
service for undergraduates, freshman orientation, health services, personal
ANNUAL EXPENSES. Tuition and fees: $1,059, $4,709 additional for out-of-
state students. Room and board: $3,390. Books and supplies: $450. Other
FINANCIAL AID. 35% of freshmen, 34% of continuing students receive some
form of aid. All grants, 94% of loans, all jobs based on need. 850 enrolled
ADDRESS/TELEPHONE. Dr. Jim C. Walters, Dir Undergraduate
Admissions, University of North Carolina at Chapel Hill, Country Club Road,
Monogram Building, CB #2200, Chapel Hill, NC 27599-2200. (919) 966-3621.

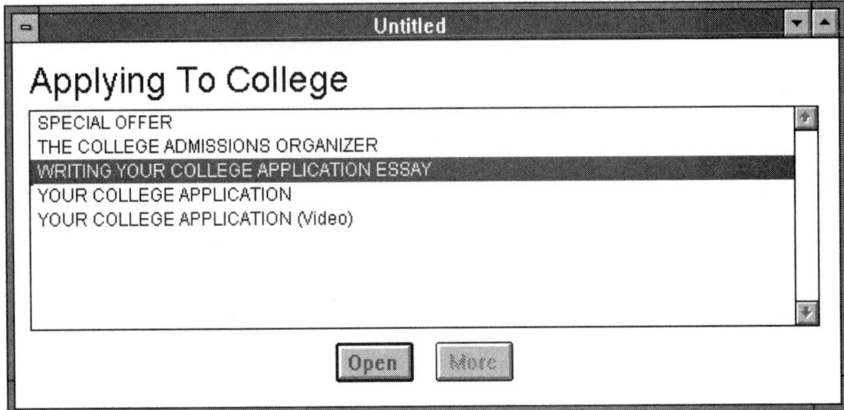

Figure 16-13: Shopping the College Board Store, I discover the perfect book and book/tape combination to help me hone my verbal communication skills so that I can submit a winning application.

Teachers' Information Network

The Teachers' Information Network (keyword: TIN) not only provides information pertaining to education; it also provides a gathering place where teachers can exchange information, ideas and experience (see Figure 16-14).

The Teachers' Information Network includes many more features than those pictured in Figure 16-14. Some of the sources:

- *KIDSNET* is a non-profit organization widely recognized as the most respected provider of information about and supplementary materials for educational television and radio programs. KIDSNET offers the only computerized clearinghouse devoted exclusively to children's programming, primarily through the use of three searchable databases: cassette, on-air and home video. The databases are updated on a monthly basis. Use the keyword: KIDSNET. (KIDSNET is also found in the Kids Only Department. See Chapter 15: "Kids Only.")
- *The Newsstand*, containing educational news items hot off the wires, regular feature articles from prestigious magazines such as Scholastic's *Electronic Learning* and the NSBA's *American School Board Journal*, articles of interest to educators from smaller presses, software reviews and a searchable database of information about more than 300 magazines.

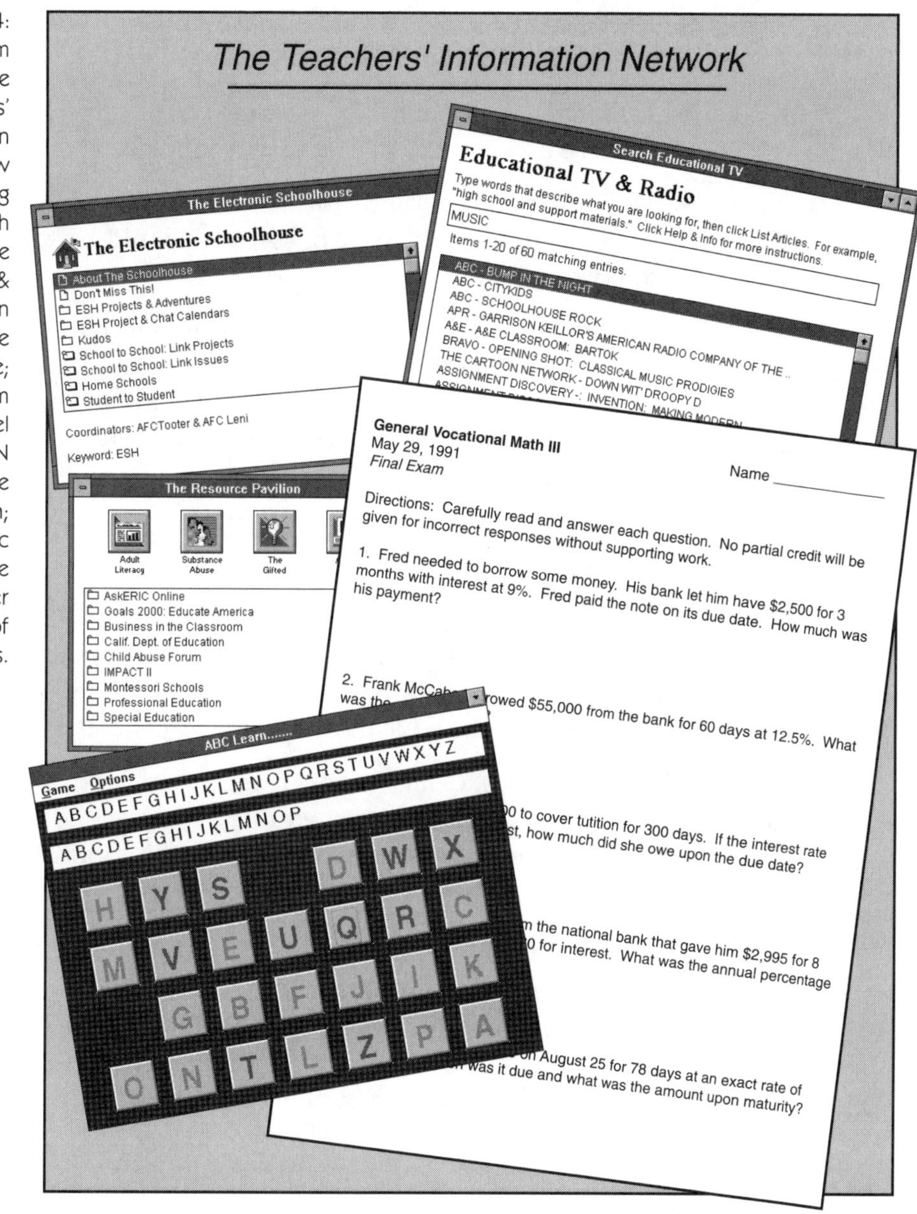

Figure 16-14: Clockwise from the top: the Teachers' Information Network window is full of promising titles; a search through the KidsNet TV & Radio listings; an exam from the Exam Exchange; "ABC Learn," from Dave Schoeffel and the TIN libraries; the Resource Pavilion; and The Electronic Schoolhouse. See the text for further descriptions of these services.

- *The Resource Pavilion*, where experts and educational organizations with particular specialties wait to answer teachers' questions.
- *The Idea Exchange*, the TIN message board center, used for the creative exchange of information and ideas on a variety of topics.
- *The Multimedia Exchange*, for the development of joint multimedia projects and the exchange of software, building the education of tomorrow today.
- *The Electronic Schoolhouse*, dedicated to the creative use of telecommunications in education, where a variety of innovative telecommunications projects are posted or unfolding, and where teachers can arrange for joint connects with other schools or with home-schooling students.
- *Teachers' Libraries*, containing a rich array of public domain educational software programs, files, graphics, sounds, lesson plans and exams.
- *Teachers' University*, teachers teaching teachers in live seminar-style classes, an opportunity to learn new skills from old pros and to contribute to the education of the next generation of educators.
- *The Convention Center*, where teachers can learn about education conferences and events scheduled by various educational boards, associations and organizations across the country, and receive live reports from major conventions.

CNN NEWSROOM Online

In the past few months, CNN NEWSROOM Online has become one of America Online's most popular features (Figure 16-15). CNN (Cable News Network) is the largest news-gathering organization in the world, and CNN NEWSROOM Online brings the power of CNN to the classroom, complete with ready-to-use outlines and materials for the teacher.

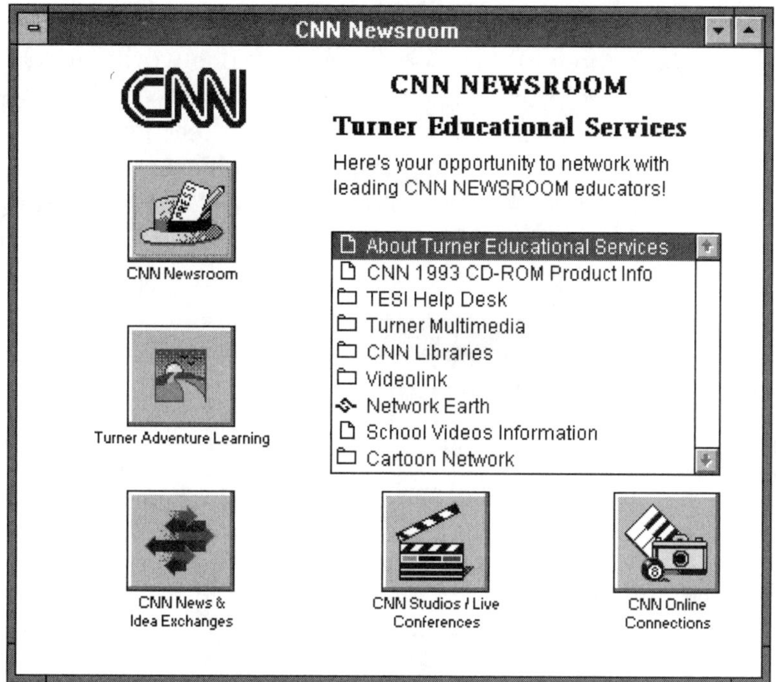

Figure 16-15: CNN NEWSROOM Online not only offers the Newsroom, but access to CNN reporters, an idea exchange, and newsroom guides for the teacher.

Much of CNN NEWSROOM Online is directed toward the teacher. Newsroom Guides offer classroom activities tied to *CNN NEWSROOM*, a daily 15-minute television news program that highlights the top stories of the day, presents student interest segments and features special newsroom "desks." The desks focus on science, international and business events. A Future Desk ponders events yet to happen, and Friday's Editor's Desk offers opinion for students to analyze. Each day's program is accompanied by an online Classroom Guide which provides teachers with key terms, suggested discussion topics, short- and long-term activities, and additional resources for easy follow-ups to viewing and discussion. The NEWSROOM is an extraordinary resource for the teacher. Who but CNN could offer a better look at current events? And who but AOL could bring it to the teacher in such a timely and convenient fashion?

NEA and ASCD Online

The National Education Association (keyword: NEA Public) is a teachers' union providing benefits, support, networking and—through related associations—accreditation for teachers and institutions. NEA Online is an ideal communications vehicle for the association: most teachers have access to a computer, and communication of this sort is best handled quickly, efficiently and bilateral. AOL excels at this.

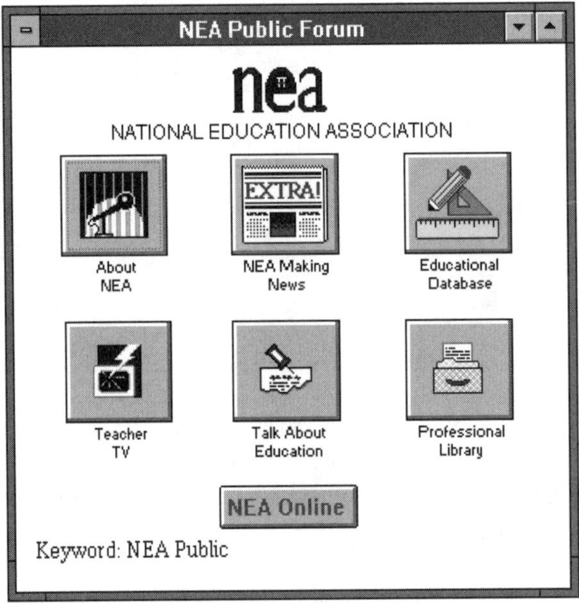

Figure 16-16: NEA Online offers a number of services for the teacher. Most of these services are available to anyone (including parents and students), not just NEA members.

ASCD's online area brings the resources of the association to members and the general public. Featured are articles from *Educational Leadership* (ASCD's flagship publication), catalogs of information about new ASCD products and services, an Ask ASCD research service, articles from *ASCD Update* and the *CTRC Quarterly*, and an opportunity to discuss curriculum issues on the area's "Talk About Curriculum" message board.

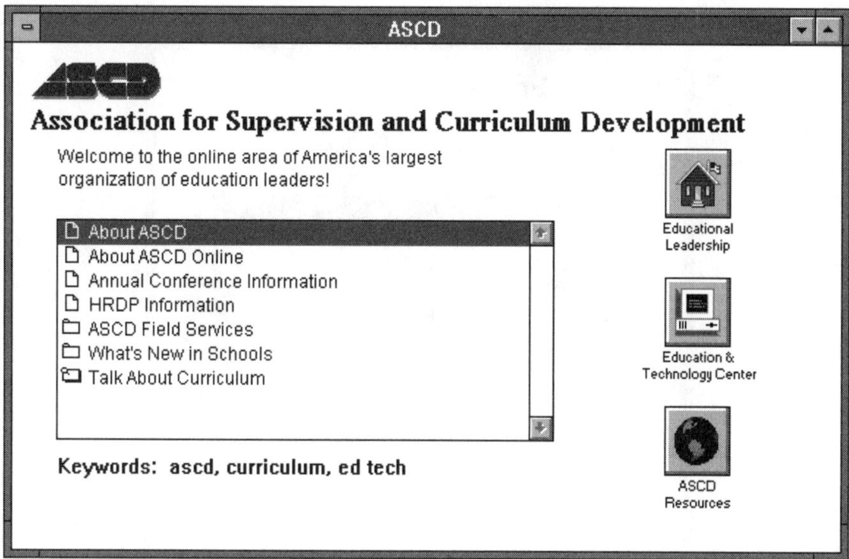

Figure 16-17: ASCD Online offers numerous resources for the educational administrator.

Education for the Parent

The Parents' Information Network (keyword: PIN) is an integrated full-service set of online services for parents, offering interactive forums on issues of importance to parents, articles from educational periodicals, databases of useful information, real-time conferencing opportunities and parent-oriented guides to other parts of America Online.

Of particular interest is the Parents' System Map—a guide to AOL from the parent's perspective. This is an innovative service, and a necessary one: AOL—as you have no doubt discovered—is huge. Learning the locations of forums, databases and libraries is a challenge, one that's well met by the Parents' System Map. If it is useful to a parent, it's no doubt on the map, including its title, brief description and location.

Look again at the forums in Figure 16-18: child abuse, giftedness, home schooling—here's where you can meet other parents who share the same interests as you and exchange concerns, techniques, successes and failures. When you need an empathetic friend, the Parents' Forum is the place to look.

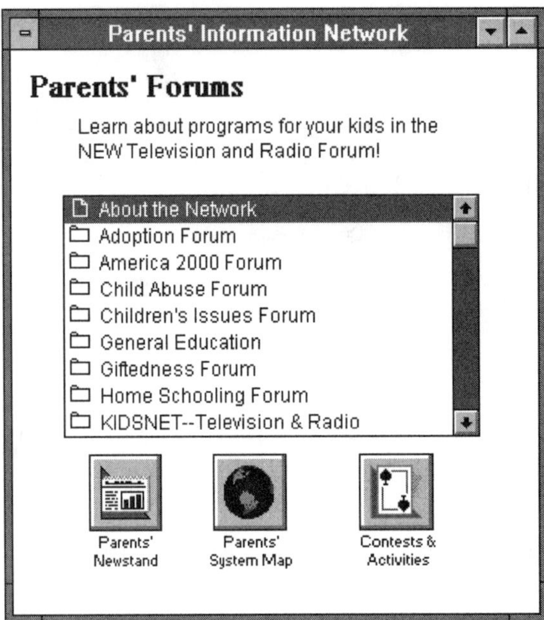

Figure 16-18: The Parents' Information Network gathers features from throughout the service and incorporates them into one easy-to-use resource.

The Broadcast Media

Though I've already mentioned CNN, there are two other broadcast services that should be of interest to you: National Public Radio Outreach and C-SPAN. An article I once read (found in WIRED Magazine—see Chapter 14: "The Internet") discussed the future of broadcast media and suggested that the era of passive, one-way broadcast communication was rapidly drawing to a close. I agree. We want more, and AOL's broadcast (and magazine) forums are burgeoning answers to that need.

National Public Radio Outreach Online

This is NPR's avenue of communication with educators and listeners alike. Educators will find a wealth of teacher's guides, newsletters and brochures which tie in with NPR programs—not unlike the strategy employed by CNN. The rest of us will find press releases, biographies (and photos) of on-air personalities, programming schedules and member station listings.

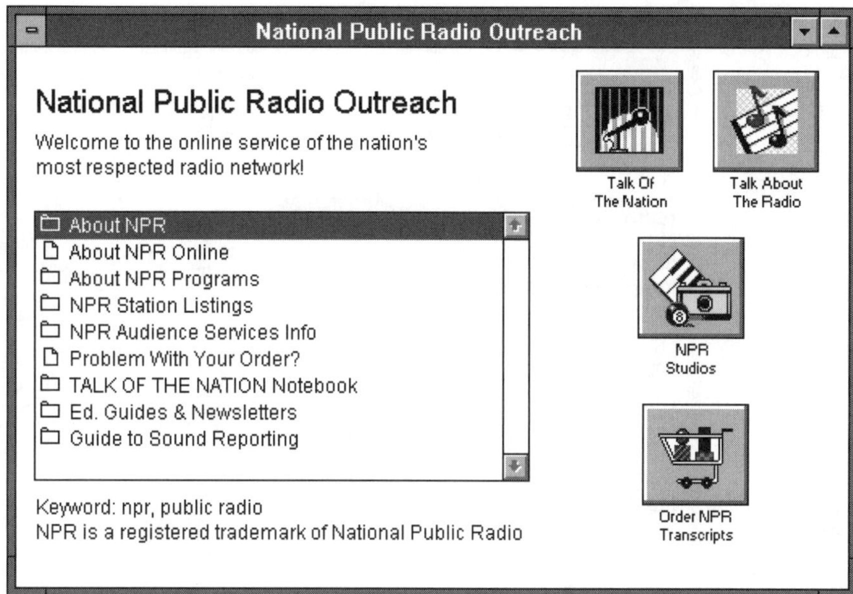

Figure 16-19: National Public Radio Outreach Online offers services for educators and listeners alike.

Two items are of particular interest: 1) "Talk About the Radio" provides direct access to NPR's listener-feedback loop. You're not only assured that your comment will be read, but you may receive a reply as well. 2) The Audience Services Information Area provides information on books, music and films reviewed on NPR's *All Things Considered*, *Morning Edition* and *Talk of the Nation*. Typically, contact information is included for individuals and organizations discussed in program features. The keyword? NPR, of course!

C-SPAN Online

Former House Speaker Jim Wright once called C-SPAN (Cable-Satellite Public Affairs Network) "America's Town Hall." Indeed, since 1977, C-SPAN has been providing live, unedited, balanced views of government forums that's unmatched in the broadcast industry. Now C-SPAN Online brings C-SPAN's viewers even closer to cable television's public-affairs network.

Perhaps the most significant part of the online service is its program descriptions and long-range scheduling information: finally, we can tell what's coming up next!

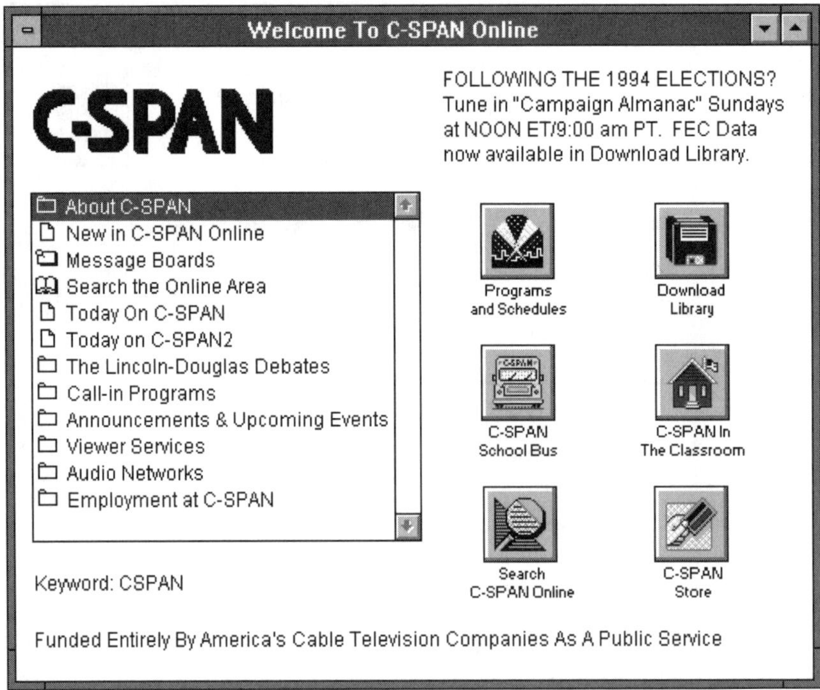

Figure 16-20: C-SPAN Online offers schedules, feedback, educational services and a searchable database for its viewers.

Educators who are interested in using C-SPAN as a teaching resource can join the network's free membership support service: C-SPAN in the Classroom. This service offers teaching guides, access to C-SPAN's archives, a toll-free educators' hotline and special issues of the *C-SPAN Digest*. Together with CNN and NPR, the C-SPAN Classroom offers a gold mine of current-affairs study material that's professionally produced, contemporary and—not to be forgotten—almost free. I wish my teachers had access to this material when I was in school.

Just Desserts

At the end of a heavy meal—your plate now emptied of consequences such as Chernobyl and post-graduate degrees—I like to serve a refreshing dessert. Something light, with a refreshing aftertaste. And what better than Disney Adventures Magazine (see Figure 16-21).

Figure 16-21: Disney Adventures Magazine offers a searchable database of articles, a library of pictures and sounds, and a chat room where kids can gather every Monday, Wednesday, and Friday evenings.

Disney Adventures is a magazine for kids, covering science, sports, entertainment, comics and puzzles. It's available at newsstands or grocery store checkout stands throughout the United States, or by subscription (you can subscribe online). More than four million kids read the magazine each month, and thousands of others visit the online forum every day.

Today I searched the Disney libraries and found the title song to Disney's film *Beauty and the Beast* in MIDI format. MIDI (Musical Instrument Digital Interface) is a hobby of mine, so naturally I downloaded the music and much to my delight, discovered not one but three versions of an arrangement of the Oscar-winning tune. The restrictions of the printed medium interfere here, or I'd play them for you. They're from Disney, after all, and they're exquisite.

(If you're interested in MIDI as I am, check out the PC Music & Sound Forum, keyword: PCMusic.)

Disney Adventures is AOL's lemon creme pie. It's rich and delicious, and the perfect end to a heavy online session. You don't have to be a kid to enjoy fresh pie, and the same's true for the Disney Adventures forum. Give it a try, and bring your appetite. Use the keyword: Disney.

Moving On

The Education Department is a vast collection of resources: a joint venture by professionals, parents and students alike. Coupled with America Online's ease of use and graphical interface, it's not only one of the most comprehensive online resources available, it's really fun. Educators will tell you that learning is most effective when it's enjoyable—an experience that encourages the student's return. The Education Department is that kind of experience.

Anyone will tell you, however, that research is a significant portion of education. And research is rapidly becoming an electronic medium. There's good reason for that. Find out by turning the page....

CHAPTER 17

Reference Desk

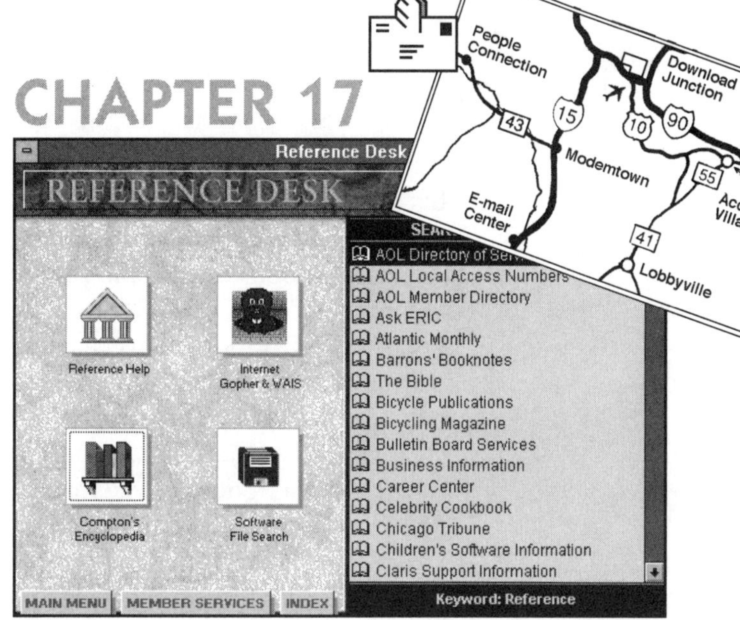

If ever there was a message in search of a medium, it's reference. The printed medium—home to reference works for centuries—is simply too inconvenient, too wasteful and too tardy to suit the information age. A printed encyclopedia, for example, might have made sense 60 years ago, but in order to describe every aspect of today's society—especially today's technological society—a comprehensive encyclopedia would have to fill a room, not a shelf. Even if you had the room, you would hesitate to use the thing: searching—especially cross-referencing—would be too tedious; it would probably be out of date by the time it was printed (it most certainly would by the time you paid for it); and its perpetual revisions would make indexing a nightmare.

Forget the printed encyclopedia. Forget the room to house it. Forget the payments and revisions. Turn on your computer, punch up AOL and click the Reference Desk button on the Main Menu, or use the keyword: Reference. It's all here, it's all topical, it's all affordable and not a single tree fell to make it all possible.

Compton's Encyclopedia

Compton's Encyclopedia is published by Compton's New Media, Inc. It features more than 9,000,000 words; 5,274 full-length articles; 29,322

The Reference Desk is America Online's access point to scores of online databases, reference works, and information librarians. If you have a question, the Reference Desk probably has the answer. Click the Reference Desk button on the Main Menu, or use the keyword: Reference.

capsule articles; and 63,503 index entries. The multimedia version of this encyclopedia took top honors at the 1991 Software Publisher's Association awards ceremony, taking the annual prize awarded for the best stand-alone educational product, and a Critic's Choice award as Best Education Program. The online version (keyword: Encyclopedia) is continually updated and easy to search. Finding all the references—including cross references—to the word "mammal" takes only moments, and nothing is inadvertently omitted.

I love trains. I love the sound and smell—and the romance—of trains. I ride a light rail system to work (Metropolitan Area Express [MAX] in Portland, Oregon; voted America's Best in 1989), and Amtrak's most popular route—the Coast Starlight—passes within a few miles of my house. To test Compton's Encyclopedia as an effective resource, I searched for the word "railroad" and was more than gratified with the results (Figure 17-1).

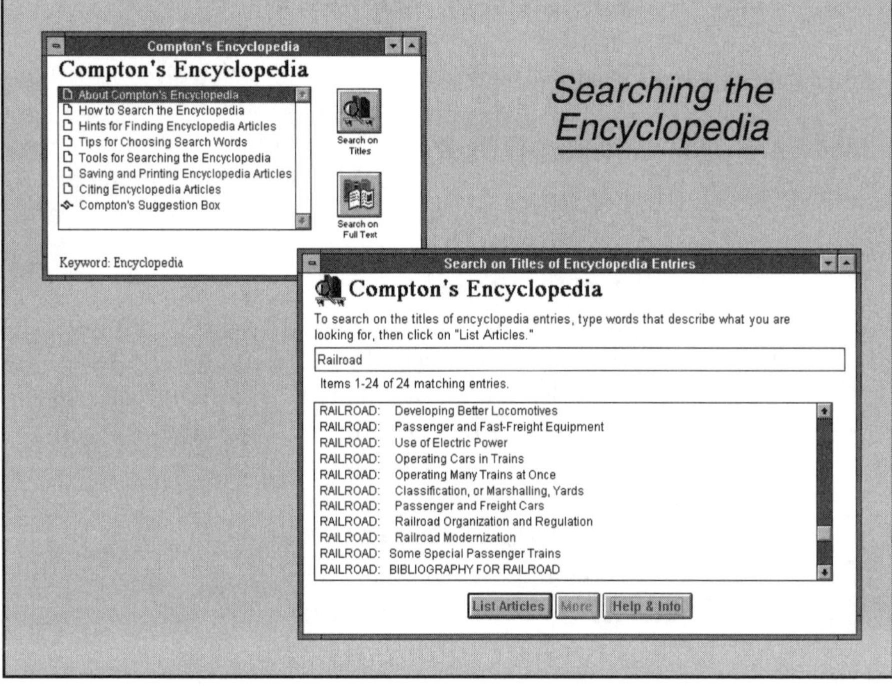

Figure 17-1: Twenty-four references to railroads! Elysian Fields for the railhead.

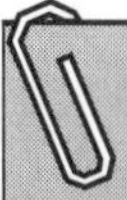

Notable Passenger Trains

These are the trains I want to travel in someday. The text below is extracted from Compton's Encyclopedia, Online Edition, and downloaded from AOL.

- Blue Train, South Africa.
  Said to be the most luxurious train in the world, the Blue Train makes a leisurely 1,000-mile, 26-hour trip once or twice a week between Pretoria and Cape Town.
- Coast Starlight, United States.
  Though I've already indicated that this is Amtrak's most popular train, it warrants a second mention here. The Coast Starlight crosses the Cascade Mountains and follows the coastline of California in a 1,400-mile, 33-hour trip between Seattle and Los Angeles. Save your pennies and get a sleeper.
- Indian Pacific, Australia.
  Another luxury train, the Indian Pacific crosses the Australian continent, from Sydney to Perth, in less than three days.
- Orient Express, Europe.
  Europe's first transcontinental express, for years unmatched in luxury and comfort. From 1883 to 1977 (with interruptions during WWI and WWII), it ran from Paris, France, to Constantinople (now Istanbul), Turkey. Short runs are still made over portions of the original route.
- Rheingold, West Germany.
  One of Europe's finest trains, the Rheingold runs between Amsterdam, The Netherlands, and Basel, Switzerland, following the Rhine River and stopping at such cities as Cologne, Mainz and Munich.
- Rossiya, Trans-Siberian Railway.
  The Rossiya runs daily between Moscow and Vladivostok. The trip takes a week. Call your travel agent before you pack: things are changing over there.
- TGV, France.
  This is the fastest train in the world, cruising at 180 miles per hour and covering the 267 miles between Paris and Lyon in two hours.

Whoa! One hundred and eighty miles an hour! Few cars can reach that speed—in fact, few private aircraft can reach that speed. Let's hope no cows wander onto the tracks....

Reference Help

Forgive my rambling. I got sidetracked when the subject of trains came up. I was talking about antiquated media and another has just come to our attention: the reference librarian. With apologies to my readers who are reference librarians, I suggest this is another service that's near the end of its run, at least in the form we've come to know. The reason? Online reference. It's convenient, it's unbounded, it's inexpensive, and it's online 24 hours a day.

The Academic Research Service

America Online's Academic Research Service (ARS) provides research support for students at the high school, college, or graduate level. It's populated by real people (Dr. Michael W. Popejoy is the administrator—he's also a professor, researcher, and writer) who accept your emailed questions and respond with emailed replies (guaranteed within 24 to 72 hours). The service is especially effective at reducing research time for students who must conduct online research. Coupled with AOL's Internet gateway (the Internet is discussed in Chapter 14), a student's research potential is boundless.

AskERIC Online

This is the Academic Research Service for educators. The Educational Resources Information Center (ERIC) is a national information system designed to provide educators with ready access to an extensive body of education-related literature. It's funded by the US Department of Education.

AskERIC is ERIC's online information clearinghouse for teachers. It performs the same service as the ARS, but it's educator (rather than student) oriented and even more comprehensive. AskERIC is an Internet domain, and the staff is drawn from the faculties of institutions all over the world. As with the ARS, you submit your questions to the staff via email and receive a reply 24 to 72 hours later.

Though the AskERIC service is an Internet gateway (gateways are described in Chapter 10, "Personal Finance"), you won't even know you're on the Internet when you pose a question or receive a reply.

But there's more: AOL also offers a local (non-Internet) database of ERIC's digests, news, and information centers. There's no waiting when you query this database, the answers are stored on the host computer hard disks, so the response is immediate (see Figure 17-2).

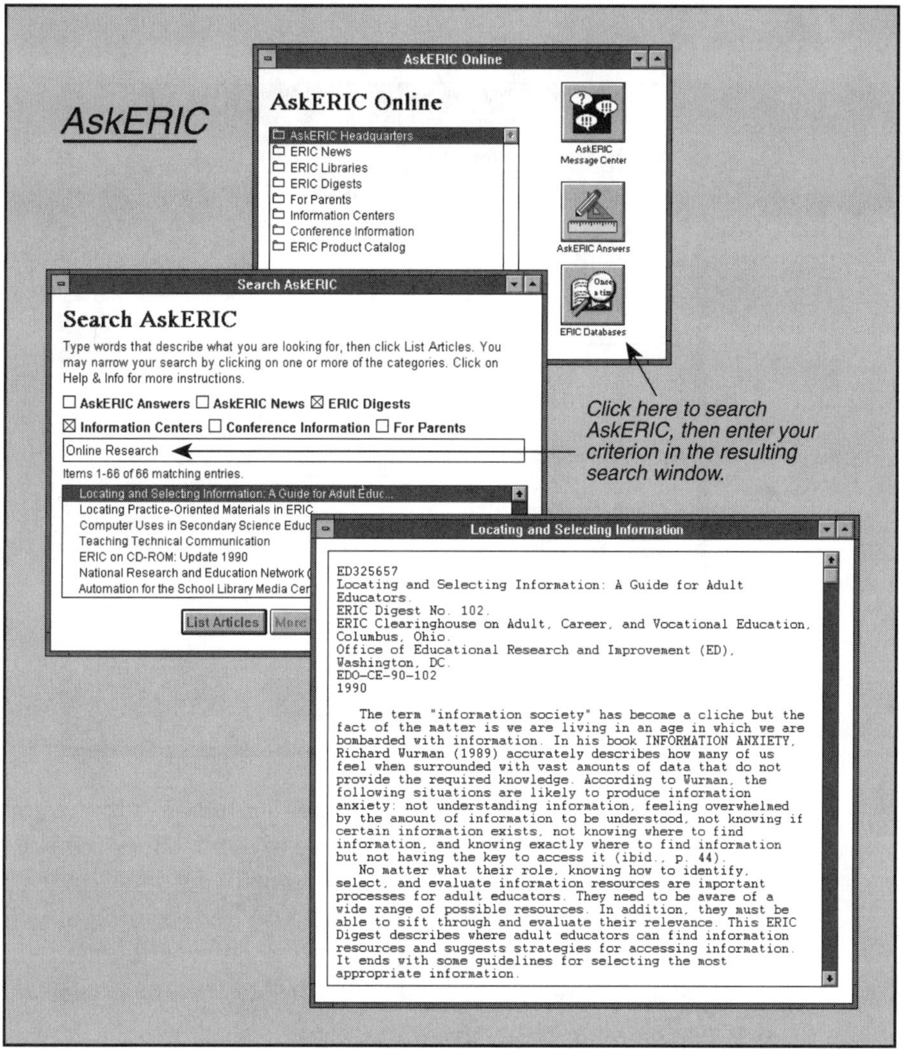

Figure 17-2: It only seems appropriate to search AskERIC Online for information regarding online research, and it found 66 references to the topic! In fact, the paper shown here should be required reading for any educator who is contemplating the online research potential.

AskERIC

AskERIC Online

AskERIC Headquarters
ERIC News
ERIC Libraries
ERIC Digests
For Parents
Information Centers
Conference Information
ERIC Product Catalog

AskERIC Message Center
AskERIC Answers
ERIC Databases

Search AskERIC

Type words that describe what you are looking for, then click List Articles. You may narrow your search by clicking on one or more of the categories. Click on Help & Info for more instructions.

☐ AskERIC Answers ☐ AskERIC News ☒ ERIC Digests
☒ Information Centers ☐ Conference Information ☐ For Parents

Online Research

Items 1-66 of 66 matching entries.

Locating and Selecting Information: A Guide for Adult Educ...
Locating Practice-Oriented Materials in ERIC
Computer Uses in Secondary Science Educ
Teaching Technical Communication
ERIC on CD-ROM: Update 1990
National Research and Education Network
Automation for the School Library Media Cen

List Articles | More

Click here to search AskERIC, then enter your criterion in the resulting search window.

Locating and Selecting Information

ED325657
Locating and Selecting Information: A Guide for Adult Educators.
ERIC Digest No. 102.
ERIC Clearinghouse on Adult, Career, and Vocational Education, Columbus, Ohio.
Office of Educational Research and Improvement (ED), Washington, DC.
EDO-CE-90-102
1990

The term "information society" has become a cliche but the fact of the matter is we are living in an age in which we are bombarded with information. In his book INFORMATION ANXIETY, Richard Wurman (1989) accurately describes how many of us feel when surrounded with vast amounts of data that do not provide the required knowledge. According to Wurman, the following situations are likely to produce information anxiety: not understanding information, feeling overwhelmed by the amount of information to be understood, not knowing if certain information exists, not knowing where to find information, and knowing exactly where to find information but not having the key to access it (ibid., p. 44).

No matter what their role, knowing how to identify, select, and evaluate information resources are important processes for adult educators. They need to be aware of a wide range of possible resources. In addition, they must be able to sift through and evaluate their relevance. This ERIC Digest describes where adult educators can find information resources and suggests strategies for accessing information. It ends with some guidelines for selecting the most appropriate information.

Like the Academic Research Service, AskERIC is free of extra charge on AOL. Just use the keyword: AskERIC.

Teacher Pager

While ARS is intended for the use of secondary and college students, and ERIC is a service primarily intended for educators, the Teacher Pager is intended for the use of students of all ages, and it's even more personal. To access the Pager, use the keyword: TeacherPager (Figure 17-3).

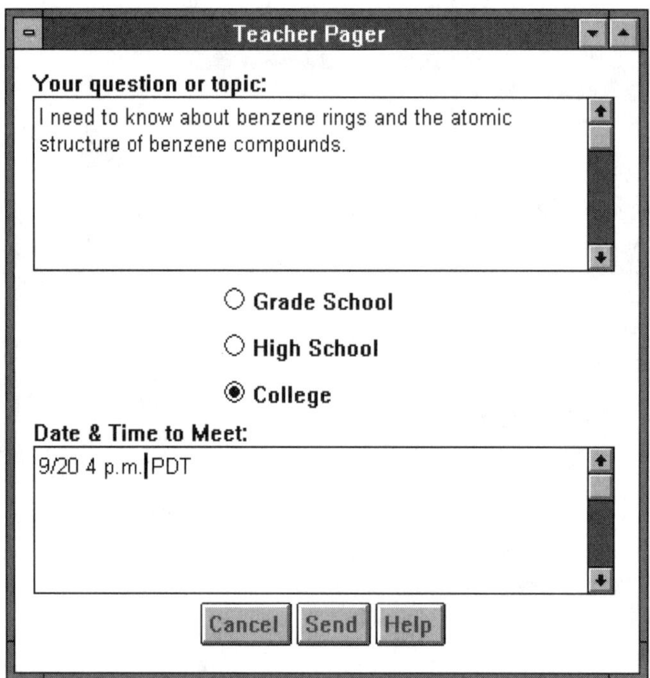

Figure 17-3: The Teacher Pager puts students in direct, one-on-one contact with a teacher online.

When the pager appears, type in your question or topic, select your grade level and a time you'd like to meet. When you click the Send button your message will automatically be sent to the Teacher Pager Coordinator, who will either get you help immediately (you should remain online for at least five minutes) or will email you later. Over 500 teachers and professionals are on staff for this purpose.

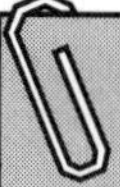

There's More

The services mentioned here aren't the only reference services AOL offers. Be sure to investigate Ask Smithsonian, Ask Geographic, and Ask NMAA (the Smithsonian's National Museum of American Art). There's a universe of professionals online, ready to help. All you have to do is ask.

File Search

You don't have to visit the Reference Desk in order to access AOL's file search. You can do this at any time, from any location, by using the keyword: FileSearch.

File Search (you might hear it called "Quickfinder"—either term is accurate and the keyword: Quickfinder works just as well) is AOL's mechanism for searching its list of online files. When you use the keyword, the File Search dialog box will appear (see Figure 17-4).

Figure 17-4: The File Search dialog box.

File Search

List files released since: (Click one)

All dates | Past month | Past week

List files in the following categories: (Click one or more)

All Categories

Applications | Games | OS/2
Development | Graphics & Animation | Telecommunications
DOS | Hardware | Windows
Education | Music & Sound

List files pertaining to the following keywords: (Optional)

List Matching Files | Get Help & Info

Most searches of AOL's online files are successful, but you might encounter situations where the search fails (no files are found) even though you know there are files online that meet your criteria, or where the search is too successful (wading through a hundred or more matches is just too much effort).

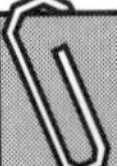

How Many Files Are Available?

One way of tracking AOL's growth is to make a periodic check of the total number of files available online. When I first joined the service (I'm a "charter member," having first signed on in early 1990), there were less than 10,000 files. When I checked today, there were over 60,000!

How did I determine the number of files available online? It's easy: just leave the file search dialog box empty (as it's pictured in Figure 17-4). Don't check any of the check boxes and don't put any criteria in the text box. Just leave the dialog as it appears when you first summon it, be sure the All Dates button is selected, then click the List Matching Files button.

America Online will respond with a listing of all of the files available online, and a number indicating their total. With this many files, you won't want to even browse the list, but the total number might be informative. Do this occasionally and watch AOL grow.

Let's say that you received a file from a friend who is using a Mac rather than a PC. It's common to compress files before sending them, and your friend used Stuffit to do so (indicated by the .sit filename extension). Stuffit is built into the Macintosh version of the AOL software, and most online files for Macs are "stuffed," as they say, so this isn't uncommon.

Unfortunately, you've got a PC, and PCs usually use the PKZIP compression software, not Stuffit. (StuffIt and PKZIP are discussed in Chapter 5, "Computing.") Needing a PC utility that will decompress every imaginable Mac stuffed file, you sign on and use File Search to locate the utility.

Your first temptation is to simply type the category (or name) of the program you're looking for in the criteria text box, as shown at the top of Figure 17-5. You don't really want Stuffit itself, it only runs on Macs. You want something that will unstuff Mac stuffed files on the PC, so the generic term "Mac" is about the best criterion for your purpose.

Figure 17-5: Honing in on an unstuffing program for the PC.

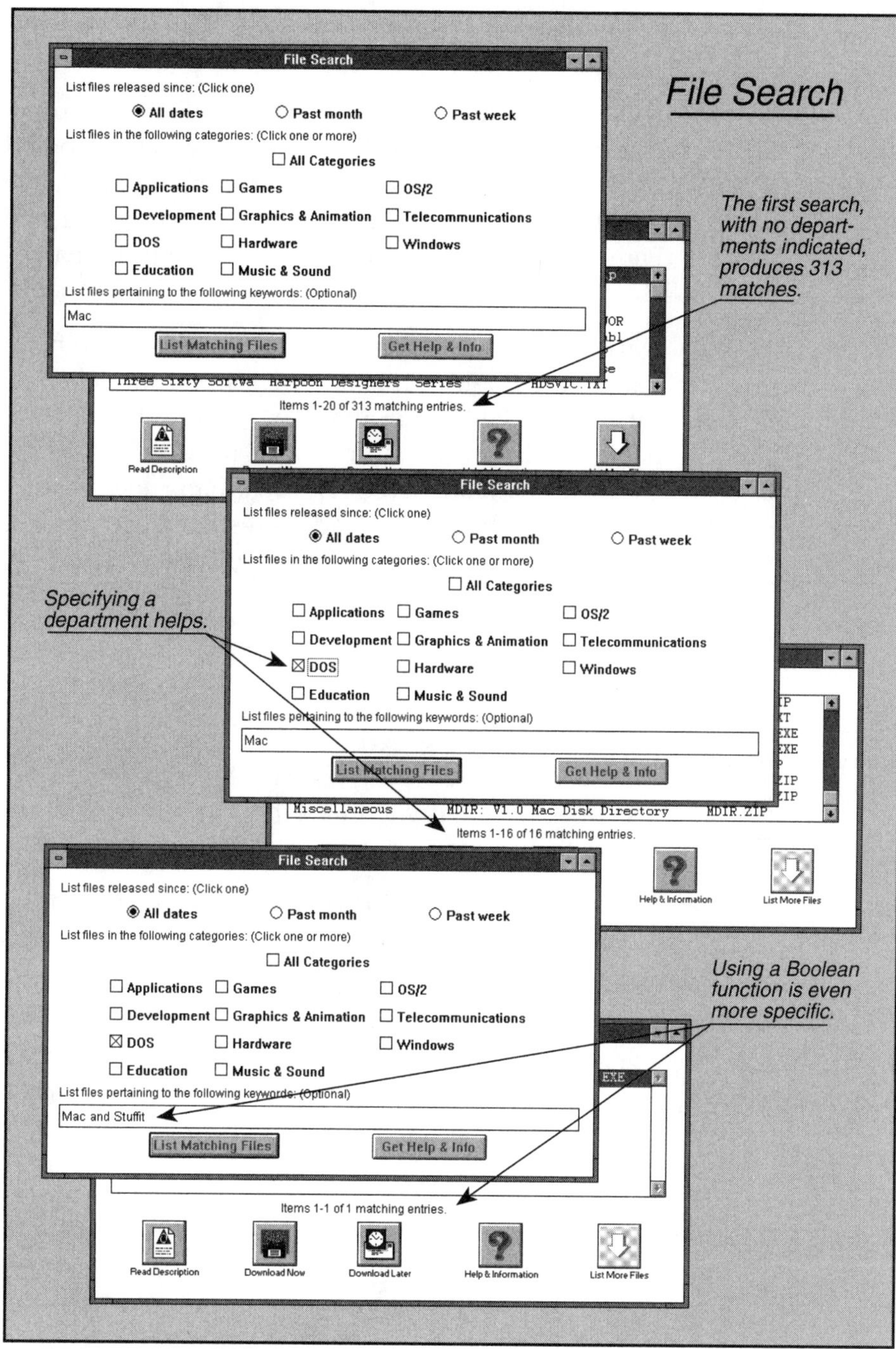

Notice the results of the first search: 313 files! Indeed, a few file searching tips seem in order:

- Use check boxes to narrow your search. It's tempting to ignore the check boxes in the middle of the file search dialog box. If you do, All Categories is the default condition, even if it's not checked. By specifying a check box (I specified DOS in the second example in Figure 17-5), my file search produced only 16 matches, a manageable number.
- Narrow your search with *ands*, *ors*, and *nots*. To further narrow a search, use Boolean functions (*ands*, *ors*, and *nots*). I used an *and* function in the third example pictured in Figure 17-5 and eliminated all of the other Mac-related files—whatever they are—that cluttered my results. (Be careful: mixing *ands* with *ors* or *nots* can sometimes produce misleading results. Read more about Boolean searches in Chapter 13, "Clubs & Interests.")
- Don't specify version numbers. You might have heard that UnStuff 1.0.1 is the latest version. Searching with the criterion: UnStuff 1.0.1 would not produce the latest version, UnStuff 1.1.
- Criteria are not case-sensitive. Don't worry about upper and lower case when you're typing criteria. America Online doesn't care. It also doesn't care if you make things plural or singular: "Mac" works no better or worse than "Macs."
- Use whole words. Abbreviations won't work, nor will wild cards. "UnS" (for UnStuff) or "UnS*" (using a wild card) won't find UnStuff.
- Search specific libraries if File Search fails. Using File Search to find "MajorTom," for example, will fail. Since MajorTom is a graphic, and since it's stored in the Gallery (discussed in Chapter 12, "People Connection"), go to the Gallery and conduct your search there.
- To find the latest files, leave everything blank and specify "Past week." This finds all of the files posted in just the past week.

Online Databases

With the fall 1994 release of the Reference Desk, AOL has effectively consolidated all of its online databases into one place. If you want information on water, for example, you can search over 70 databases, ranging from the Bible (317 references, including 80 for "holy water") to the White House (159 references, including 23 for "whitewater"). It's no longer necessary to roam all over the service, searching for databases and hoping you haven't missed one. They're all here; just use the keyword: Reference.

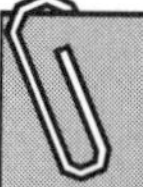

Print the List

If you conduct much online research, it helps to have a printed listing of AOL's online databases, one that you can consult whether you're online or off. Just click the Index button on the bottom of the Reference Desk window and choose Print from the File menu.

We've explored many of AOL's databases in previous chapters, and others are highly specialized. But two warrant our attention here.

AOL Local Access Numbers

The listing of telephone numbers with which you can contact AOL is a prodigious database in itself. America Online serves all of North America, after all, and that's a lot of territory (and a lot of access numbers). If you plan to travel with your computer, search this database for a list of access numbers for the localities you'll be visiting. Print the list, pack it with your modem, and take it along. You can access the database from the Reference Desk, or by using the keyword: Access.

If you are a frequent traveler, you'll want to read Appendix D, "On the Road." There are lots of tips there for the AOL road warrior.

BBS Search

America Online isn't the only electronic bulletin board system (BBS) available to you. Thousands of others dot the country. Few offer the breadth of service AOL does, but many offer the online community spirit, enhanced by their proximity to their members.

How do you find those that are near you? Search AOL's database of BBSs. It's available at the Reference Desk through Bulletin Board Services, or via the keyword: BBS.

Moving On

With our explorations of the Education and Reference Departments, we've had a substantive experience. Though the online environment is an ideal platform for education and reference it's well suited to a number of others, including commerce.

You can buy (and sell) everything from art to videotapes online, from other members or from retail merchants. It all happens at the Marketplace, coming up next.

CHAPTER 18

The Marketplace

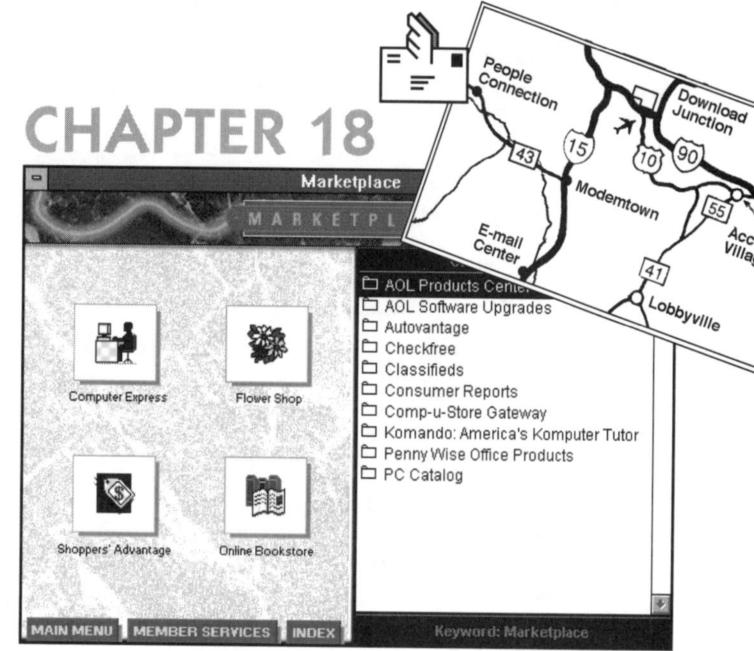

If the X-generation is to be believed, this is a material world. "Mall" is our mantra. But malls are a day's drive for some of us; others don't care for the crowds; still others would just as soon stay at home and do their shopping from there.

Forget the mall. Forget the shopping channel. Forget glossy catalogs. The Marketplace is as close as your computer.

Classifieds Online

This wouldn't be a fully operative communications medium without classified ads, and AOL has them—at no extra charge. Just select the Classifieds from the main Marketplace window, or use the keyword: Classifieds (see Figure 18-1).

Classifieds Online offers, among other things, a library that adds unique value to the classifieds: ZIP and area code directories; UPS, FedEx and US Mail rate charts; a UPS manifest printing program; and the complete American Computer Exchange used computer pricing guide.

The Marketplace is AOL's emporium—its flea market and bazaar, its supermarket and shopping mall. Leave the car in the driveway and the kids in the yard. We're ready to lend a little support to the private sector, and we don't even have to leave the comfort of home. Click the Marketplace button on the Main Menu or use the keyword: Marketplace and *shazam!*, we're ready to pursue Acquisition Mode.

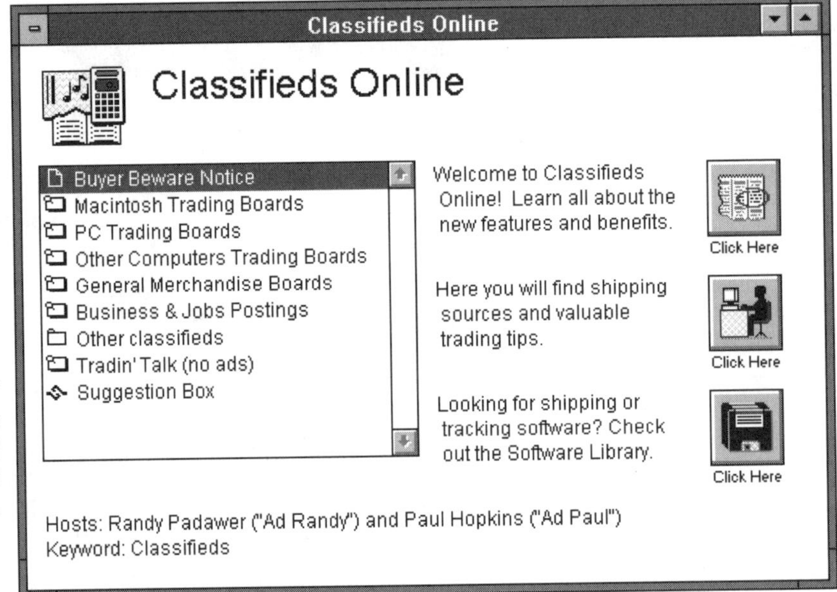

Figure 18-1: Classifieds Online, where you can buy and sell computers and components, advertise your professional services, search the job postings, exchange computer games and software, and take advantage of business opportunities—all without extra charges.

The Hard Sell

Browsing the Classifieds Online library the other day, I came across the following excerpt from Direct-Marketing Firepower, an intriguing book by Jonathan Mizel. He's describing his friend Joe, who placed an ad on a local bulletin board system—a similar situation (though much more parochial) to AOL's Classifieds Online:

"So he decided this local BBS would be just the place to advertise it (the hard disk) since they allowed free classifieds for computer items. Joe placed the ad for this item on a Monday. I think he said he was selling it for $120.00. Guess how many responses Joe got by Wednesday. Go on, guess.

"Within 48 hours, Joe had received 220 responses to his little classified ad on a system that was only used by San Francisco technical computer people. The total number of people who are on the system is probably less than 5,000. He was freaked out, even mad because people kept emailing him and calling him to get this damn piece of equipment (which, by the way, sold immediately)...

"Too bad old Joe didn't have 220 hard drives!"

Joe's experience occurred on a system with less than 5,000 members. America Online has over a million. When I last checked, over 11,000 classifieds were running, with more coming in every day. There's a portentous potential here.

And it's all free. All you pay is your regular AOL connect time.

Shoppers' Advantage

Speaking of numbers, approximately 3.1 million members (over one percent of the United States population!) shop through Shoppers' Advantage. This is a little like the shopping "clubs" that have sprouted up nationwide: you pay a small annual membership fee and you're rewarded with a warehouse full of products, attractively priced, in stock and ready for shipment. Shoppers' Advantage not only offers the convenience of online shopping, it guarantees the lowest prices anywhere, or it will refund the difference.

You can browse the store whether or not you're a member of Shoppers' Advantage—a significant advantage over local shopping clubs—and you can enroll online at any time.

Look at the benefits Shoppers' Advantage offers:

- Discounts of 10 to 50 percent on all manufacturers' list prices.
- Over 250,000 name-brand products, all in a searchable online database. If a product you're looking for is not on the database you can contact the Product Research team, and they will try to obtain the product for you.
- Automatic two-year free warranty extension. Even if there is only a three- or six-month manufacturer's warranty, Shoppers' Advantage will extend the warranty on any product purchased through them to two years, at no cost.
- Merchandise from name-brand manufacturers, including Panasonic, GE, JVC, Nikon, Sony, Pioneer, AT&T, Nintendo, Whirlpool, Quasar, Jordache, Hoover, Pentax, Timex, Memorex, Rayban, Radio Shack, Pierre Cardin, Singer, Magnavox—an all-star roster of manufacturers.
- The Department Store, where browsing—rather than searching—is the order of the day, and the Best Buys section, where the staff

posts their best bargains. If you want to compare prices and features for yourself, Shoppers' Advantage can compare up to 50 similar items at the same time and display the results for your consideration.

 Lowest price guarantee. If, within 30 days of buying something through Shoppers' Advantage, you find the same piece of merchandise being sold for a lower price by an authorized dealer, send Shoppers' Advantage a copy of the ad and they will send you the difference.

- A money-back guarantee. If you are not fully satisfied with Shoppers' Advantage, all you need do is call their toll-free number to cancel your membership. Your current membership fee will be refunded in full.

Mozart Mania

Searching the Shoppers' Advantage database the other day, I discovered the set of compact discs shown in Figure 18-2.

Figure 18-2: He only lived to see 37: Mozart was precocious, powdered and prolific. Now he is inexpensive as well.

```
Compact discs(STDK) Delta (DELT)
Model#: 358559 Title: 30 CD Mozart Collection
----------------------------------------------------
Enjoy Mozart's timeless music over a lifetime with
this 30-CD commemorative collection. Features selec-
tions of Don Giovanni, Magic Flute, and Marriage of
Figaro; Violin Concerti 1, 2, and 3; early Symphonies
1, 2, and 3; Symphonies 21, 34, 35, 36, 38, 39, and
40; Piano Concerti 1, 2, and 3; Clarinet Concerto,
four horn concerti; the Flute Concerto, 21 songs,
piano sonatas, quintets and quartets, dances and
minuets, 11 marches and more.
----------------------------------------------------
List Price:               open
Our Price:               $109.00
With Regular Delivery: $118.95 (delivery in 2-3 weeks)
```

Now there's a feast for Mozart mania!, at less than four bucks a disc, delivered to your door. There's probably a law against this, but I won't tell anyone if you don't.

Moving On

I've only scratched the surface of the Marketplace. You can order flowers online via AOL's electronic florist, or buy discounted books at the Online Bookstore. You not only can sell your old adding machine in the Classifieds, but you can buy a new one at the Penny Wise Office Products Store. Of course, you don't really need an adding machine because you have a computer, but isn't it time for a new one? Computer Express has not only computers, but components and software as well.

The pursuit of materialism, however, is no longer our concern. It's time to roll out the heavy armament. The next chapter explores AOL's Strategic Defense Initiative: FlashSessions and the Download Manager. America Online can sign on automatically, send and receive your mail, then sign back off—at any time of the day or night. It can queue files for later downloading and resume downloading files that have been interrupted.

Many of these features are unique to AOL. They're unprecedented, inconceivable and almost magical, but they're not indescribable. And describe them is what we're about to do. Read on....

CHAPTER 19

FlashSessions & the Download Manager

I've been getting a lot of email lately. I've made a number of online friends and we correspond a lot, and I get tons of mail from readers. If I read all this mail online, they would have to deliver my AOL bill with a forklift.

There's an additional challenge to my finances: I'm a downloading zealot. I beta test a lot of software, all of which has to be downloaded. I collect utilities, fonts and graphics for my desktop-publishing ventures. I'm constantly downloading snippets from the Writers' Forum. I probably download three or four hours' worth of material a week. Starting a 58-minute download is one thing; remembering to return to the computer 58 minutes later is another. If I go outside to mow the lawn during a long download, there's a high probability I won't remember the computer when the download is finished. When I do remember it—usually about 20 minutes after the download is finished—I've just paid for 20 minutes of idle connect time. This is not frugal.

Happily, AOL offers two solutions to these problems: FlashSessions and the Download Manager.

What Are FlashSessions?

Rather than try to explain FlashSessions, let me tell you about my typical morning. After fixing coffee, I sit down at my PC and run AOL.

Mike Keefe's editorial cartoons (keyword Keefe) are a regular feature of America Online. His material is an ideal candidate for FlashSessions and the Download Manager, the two rat race–relieving features described in this chapter.

I do not sign on; rather, I choose Read Incoming Mail from the Mail menu. All the mail I've received in the past 24 hours appears there. I read it all, forwarding, replying and composing new mail. Then I check the Download subdirectory on my hard disk. A few downloaded files usually appear there, and I move them elsewhere on my hard drive, wherever I want them to be. All of this happens off-line, at my leisure: there are no clocks running. My PC, you see, signed on at 4:00 A.M. It sent the mail I had prepared the previous day, retrieved and stored any mail AOL was holding for me, and downloaded the files I had requested. It did all this while I slept the sleep of innocence, while system activity was light and nobody wanted to use the phone.

On many days, that's all the computing I do. I'm sound asleep when the PC is online, and my connect time is reduced to the absolute minimum: about a minute a day when I'm not downloading. This kind of absentee management is called a FlashSession. FlashSessions sign on, send and receive mail, download predesignated files, and sign off, all without human participation. You can schedule a FlashSession to occur at a predetermined (and unattended) time, you can invoke a FlashSession manually (whether you're online or off), or you can conclude an online session with a FlashSession. They do their work quickly, efficiently and without complaint. This is what computing is supposed to be.

Futility Revisited

In Chapter 4, I had you send yourself a letter. Yes, it was an exercise in futility, but you saw email in action. We're about to repeat the exercise, but this time we'll have the computer do it for us. We'll not only experience futility, we'll experience automated futility. This is not what computing is supposed to be, but it might prove to be enlightening.

- Do not sign on. Rather, choose Compose Mail from the Mail menu. As you did in Chapter 4, prepare a short message to yourself. Your Compose Mail window should look something like that pictured in Figure 19-1. (Be sure to put your screen name in the To box, not mine. You have no idea how many people sent me FlashSession tests based on these instructions in the first edition of this book.)

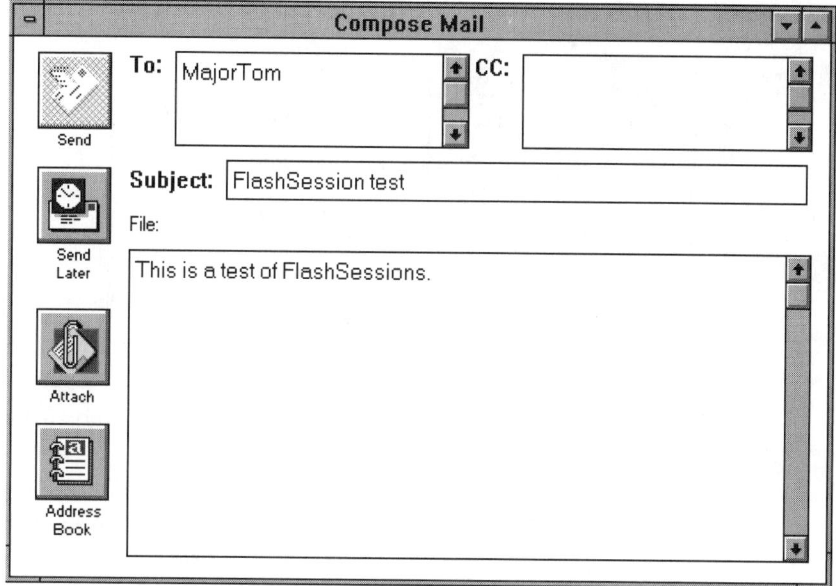

Figure 19-1: Compose a message to yourself, substituting your screen name in the To field.

Note that the Send Now button is dimmed. Since you're not online, this command is not available. Instead, click the Send Later button. America Online will reply with the message pictured in Figure 19-2.

Figure 19-2: America Online confirms your request to Send Later.

- Note that the dialog box in Figure 19-2 suggests that you "...select FlashSessions from the Mail menu." Do that now.

- A FlashSession window will appear (see Figure 19-3), including all of the check boxes. All of your check boxes should be checked, as shown in Figure 19-3.

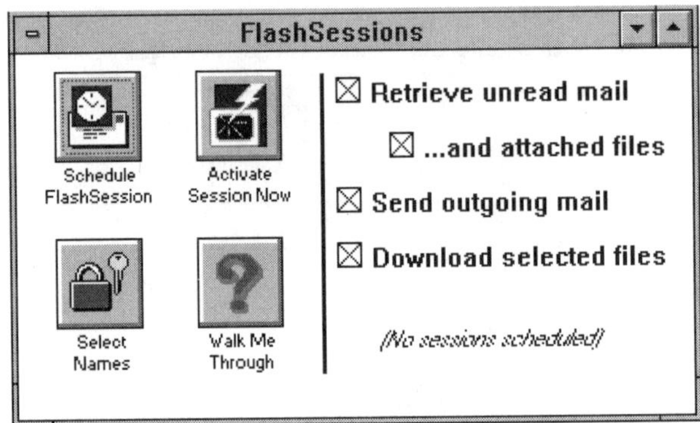

Figure 19-3: Configure FlashSessions in the FlashSession window.

- Click the button marked Select Names and complete the resulting form as pictured in Figure 19-4. Select the screen name you want to use (if you are using more than one) and enter the password you use (for that screen name) when you sign on to AOL. Your screen name will appear in place of mine, and the number of characters in your password will probably differ as well. (Notice that your password isn't displayed as you type: asterisks representing each letter in your password appear instead. That's as it should be. You never know who's looking over your shoulder.)

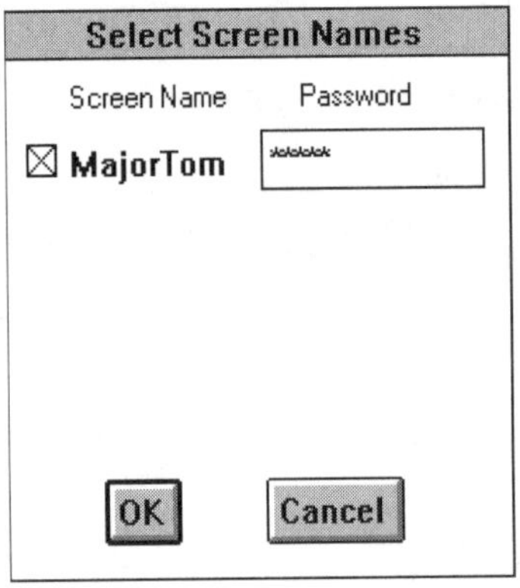

Select Screen Names

Screen Name Password

☒ MajorTom *****

OK Cancel

Figure 19-4: Complete the Select Screen Names form.

- When you have completed the Select Screen Names form, click the OK button. Back at the FlashSession window, click the Activate Session Now button. America Online will respond with the form pictured in Figure 19-5.

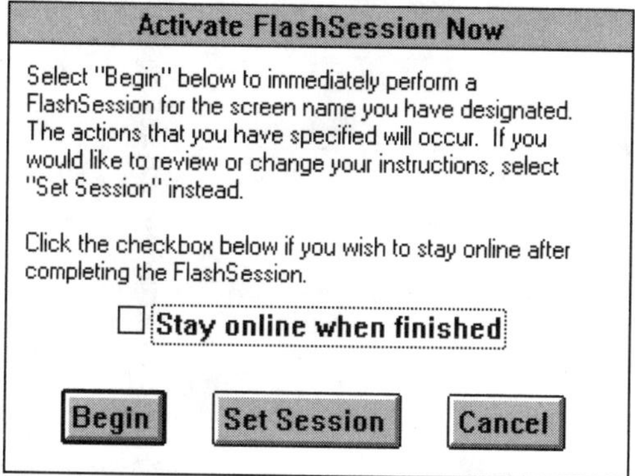
Activate FlashSession Now
Select "Begin" below to immediately perform a FlashSession for the screen name you have designated. The actions that you have specified will occur. If you would like to review or change your instructions, select "Set Session" instead.
Click the checkbox below if you wish to stay online after completing the FlashSession.
Stay online when finished
Begin
Set Session
Cancel

Figure 19-5: If this is your first FlashSession, read these instructions carefully and review your FlashSession actions if you want.

- The Stay online when finished feature allows you to run a FlashSession—sending and receiving mail, uploading and downloading files—then stay online for more events after the FlashSession concludes. That's not our intention at the moment. For the purposes of this exercise, be sure the Stay online when finished feature is cleared, as shown in Figure 19-5.

- Click the button marked Begin. America Online takes over (Figure 19-6).

- Because of AOL's rapid email turnaround, this FlashSession has resulted in both an upload and a download. Not only did you send mail to yourself, you also received it. Whether you noticed it or not, you've got mail and you need to read it. But you're not online. How do you read mail when you're off-line?

- Pull down the Mail menu. The Read Incoming Mail command should be available (see the top portion of Figure 19-7). Choose it.

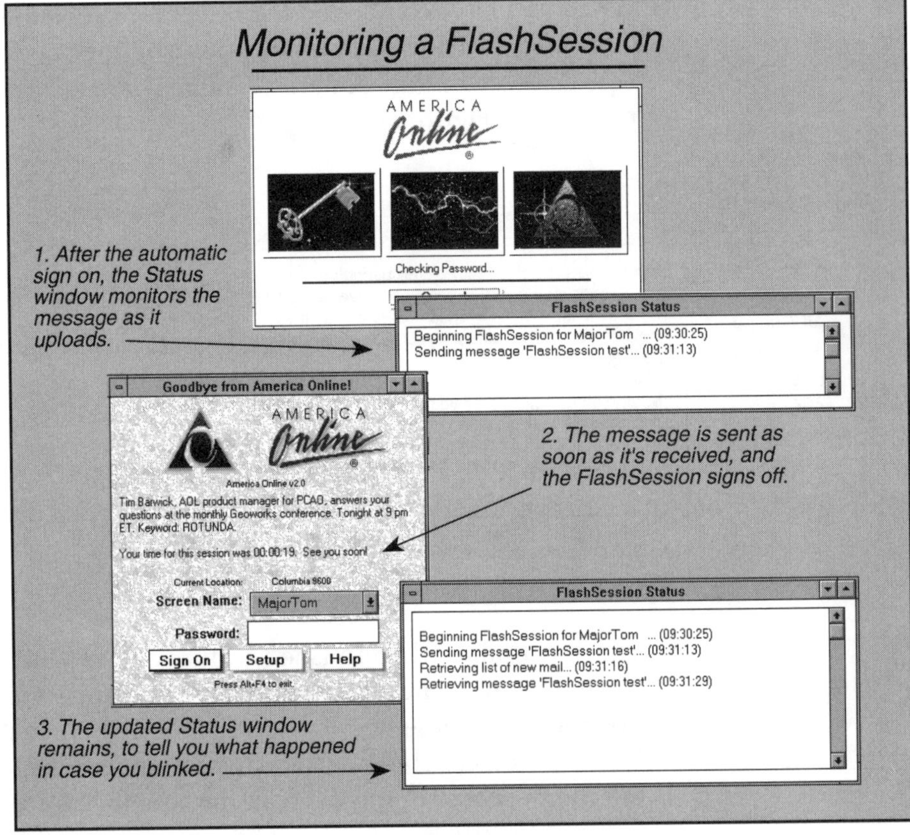

Figure 19-6: The FlashSession "flashes" your mail to America Online headquarters in Virginia and back in seconds.

- The Incoming Mail window will appear (see the middle portion of Figure 19-7). Double-click the entry representing your test.

- A second window will open (Figure 19-7, bottom), containing the text of your test. After you've read it, delete it by clicking the Delete button in the lower right corner.

I'm reminded of a big Mercedes sedan I read about the other day. In an irrational effort to remain the technological leader among motorcars, Mercedes equipped the car with motorized headrests! Now that's technology. Our exercise was a little like that. We threw technology at a task that was no doubt best left undone. At least we're in good company.

Figure 19-7: You can read mail off-line when it's convenient for you and the clock's not running.

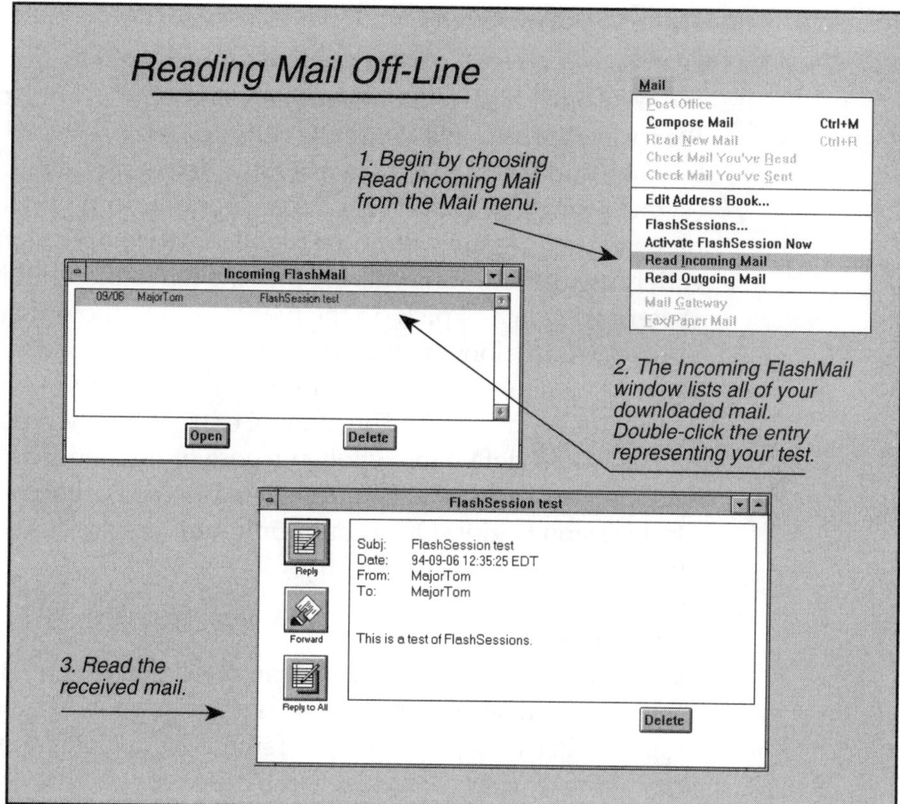

Scheduling FlashSessions

You can invoke a FlashSession at any time, whether you're online or off-line. Alternatively, you can schedule FlashSessions to occur at predetermined intervals: every day, every hour—whenever you please. Before any FlashSession can get under way, however, you have to tell AOL some things it needs to know.

FlashSession Setup

I can hear it now: it's 4 A.M. and the AOL voice calls from the other room. "Tom," it says, "come out here and type in your password!" Bleary eyed, I stumble to my PC and type my password. I crawl back into bed and start to drift off when the voice calls again. "Tom," it says (Is that a smirk in the voice?), "come out here and tell me which screen name to use!" Again, I stumble to the PC, tripping over the dog, who, rudely awakened, runs yelping into the hall table, spilling the Waterford crystal. I pick up the pieces, hiding those that don't seem to fit together any longer, and Band-Aid the laceration that has developed across the dog's nose. I do all this smiling, of course. Always smiling.

Do I make my point? The manual entry of passwords and screen names would defeat the whole purpose of unattended FlashSessions. These things have to be communicated to the PC before the first FlashSession begins. Once communicated, they're stored on disk, eliminating the need for reentry.

Using Multiple Screen Names

Many AOL members use more than one screen name. Perhaps more than one member of your family uses the service. Maybe you have an alter ego. Perhaps you're shy, or famous, or reclusive, and you don't want anyone to see your real name on-screen. Whatever the reason, if you use more than one screen name, you have to tell your PC which of these names to use for its FlashSessions, and you'll have to enter a password for each screen name.

Selecting Names & Entering Passwords

Selecting names and entering passwords is easy, and once it's done you won't need to do it again unless you want to reconfigure your FlashSessions. I won't linger here, as we've already selected a name and entered a password during the exercise that led off this chapter. Figure 19-8 shows you how to do it.

Figure 19-8: The FlashSessions command under the Mail menu takes you to the entry form for selecting names and entering passwords.

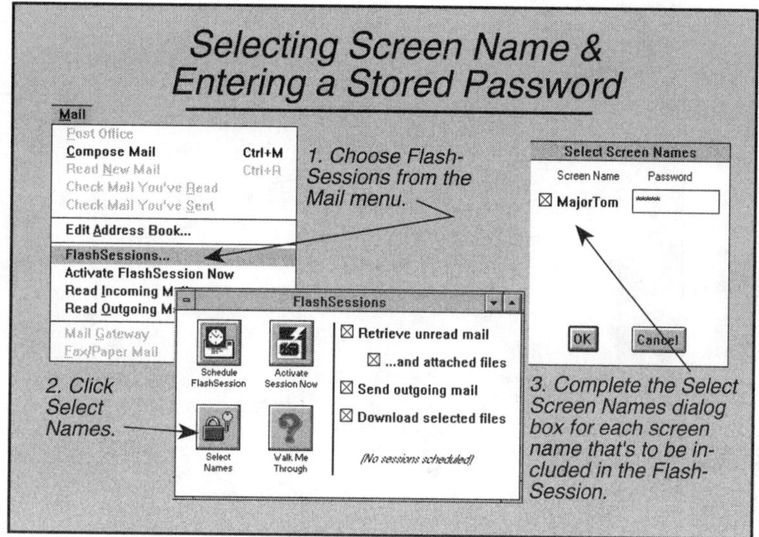

Though Figure 19-8 illustrates the entry of a single password for a single screen name, the Select Screen Names form can accommodate a number of each. Enter as many passwords as you wish for your various screen names—the same passwords you use when you sign on.

Walk Me Through

Look at the center window pictured in Figure 19-8. There's a button there marked Walk Me Through that should prove comforting.

The Walk Me Through feature performs as promised, walking you through the FlashSession setup process with extensive instructions. Even if you're an infrequent FlashSession user and prone to absent-mindedness, this feature always stands ready to serve.

Declaring the Download Destination

One more setup task remains before you can start a FlashSession: you must declare a destination for downloaded files. Figure 19-9 illustrates the process and offers a brief glimpse of the Download Manager, a subject we will discuss later in this chapter.

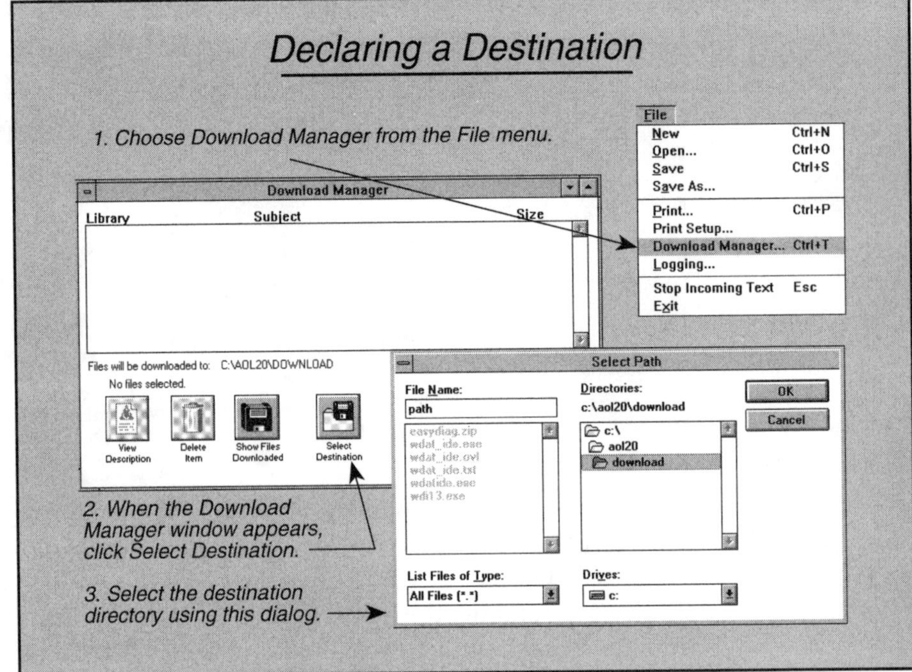

Figure 19-9: The Download Manager lets you specify where you want downloaded files saved. The Download subdirectory in your AOL20 directory is the default.

Attended FlashSessions

Now that you've stored your screen names, passwords and destinations, you're ready to run a FlashSession. The exercise that began this chapter describes an attended FlashSession: one that occurs when you issue a FlashSession command. Let's examine attended FlashSessions first.

Many FlashSessions occur when you're about to wrap up an online session. There's something organic about the flow of an online session: after a couple of months online, you'll glide from one task to another with all the fluidity of warm honey. The last thing you'll want to do is interrupt a session with a download or the transmission of a piece of mail. Instead, schedule a FlashSession to take care of these things when your session has concluded. More about this in a moment.

Another kind of attended FlashSession occurs when you're off-line and want your PC to sign on, transfer files and sign off. As you saw during the earlier exercise, the advantage here is speed. FlashSessions know exactly what they're doing; they waste no time, they waste no money, and you don't have to stick around while they're under way.

Off-line Attended FlashSessions

This is exactly what we did during the exercise that began this chapter. You begin an off-line FlashSession not by signing on, but by choosing Activate FlashSession Now from the Mail menu (shown at the top of Figure 19-10). When the Activate Session Now form appears (see the bottom of Figure 19-10), select the Stay online when finished check box if that's what you want to do, then click the Begin button.

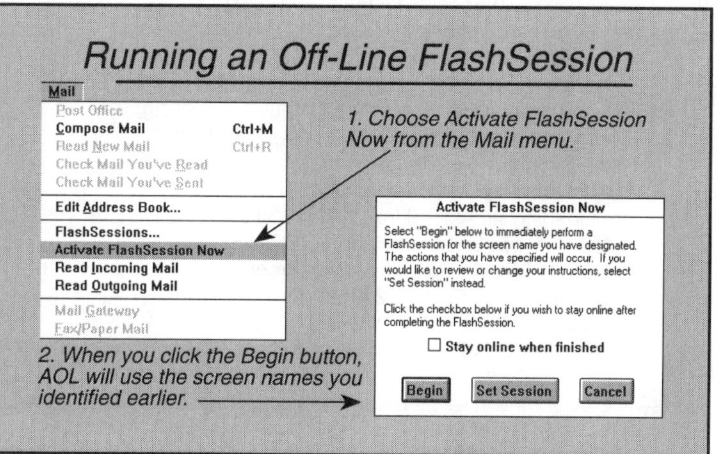
Running an Off-Line FlashSession
Mail
Post Office
Compose Mail Ctrl+M
Read New Mail Ctrl+R
Check Mail You've Read
Check Mail You've Sent
Edit Address Book...
FlashSessions...
Activate FlashSession Now
Read Incoming Mail
Read Outgoing Mail
Mail Gateway
Fax/Paper Mail
1. Choose Activate FlashSession Now from the Mail menu.
Activate FlashSession Now
Select "Begin" below to immediately perform a FlashSession for the screen name you have designated. The actions that you have specified will occur. If you would like to review or change your instructions, select "Set Session" instead.
Click the checkbox below if you wish to stay online after completing the FlashSession.
Stay online when finished
Begin
Set Session
Cancel
2. When you click the Begin button, AOL will use the screen names you identified earlier.

Figure 19-10: Once your screen name and password are stored, a menu selection and a mouse click are all it takes to run an off-line attended FlashSession.

Do You Know Who You Are?

There's a bit of a trap waiting for you if you follow the two steps illustrated in Figure 19-10 and aren't paying attention. What's not apparent are the screen names that AOL will use during the upcoming FlashSession. Review the Select Screen Names window in Figure 19-9 if necessary, and note that AOL will run a FlashSession for each name that's selected in the Select Screen Names window, not just the screen name that's currently appearing in the Welcome window. Be sure you know which names are selected in the Select Screen Names window before you allow your FlashSessions to run.

Normally, this is all you need to do to run an off-line attended FlashSession. When you click the Begin button, your PC signs on, does everything it's been told to do, then signs off. It repeats the process for as many screen names as you've indicated. When the dust settles, a

FlashSession Status window remains on your screen to inform you of what happened (Figure 19-11). This is more a necessity than a convenience. Without the FlashSession Status window, you might have to perform some major sleuthing to find out what happened during a FlashSession, especially one that occurred in your absence.

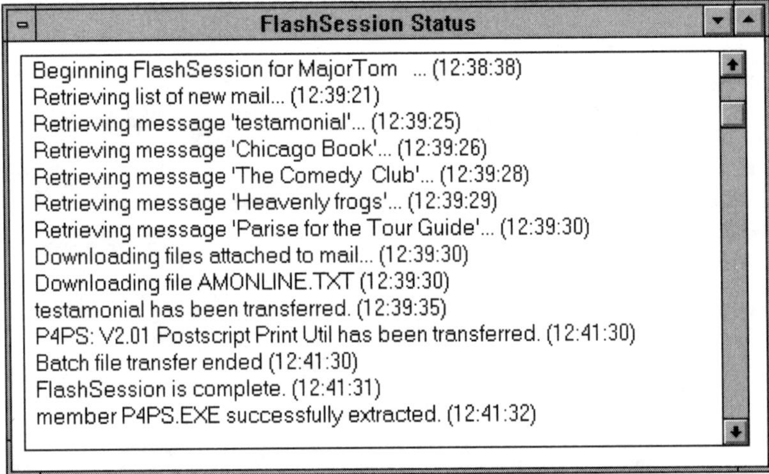

Figure 19-11: The FlashSession Status window lets you know what happened during a FlashSession, just in case you weren't watching.

Look again at Figure 19-11. I received five pieces of new mail (one with an attached file) and downloaded a file I scheduled for download earlier. The AOL software even extracted (decompressed) my downloaded file for me.

It isn't uncommon for only two entries to appear there, representing the start and finish of a FlashSession. This isn't as meaningless as it might seem. If a no-activity session occurs in the middle of the night, I would know the next morning that nothing happened during my 4 A.M. FlashSession, and I wouldn't waste my time looking for mail or files that weren't there. Of additional benefit is notification of errors. If I misaddressed some mail or if the session was interrupted for some reason, I'd read about it here.

Online Attended FlashSessions

Another form of attended FlashSession is the one that occurs at sign-off. During a typical online event you might visit a forum or two, mark some files for downloading, reply to some mail and perhaps compose some new mail. Downloads in particular can be disruptive to the flow of an online session. Sitting at your PC watching a thermometer tally your tedium is not the best use of your time. That's why AOL provides sign-off FlashSessions.

When you've finished everything you want to do online, choose Activate FlashSession Now from the Mail menu rather than selecting Sign Off from the Go To menu (see the top of Figure 19-12), click Sign off when finished, then click the Begin button (see the bottom of Figure 19-12). This is one alternative to the Sign Off command; the other is the Download Manager, which I'll discuss later in this chapter. Either one will work if activity remains that doesn't require your involvement.

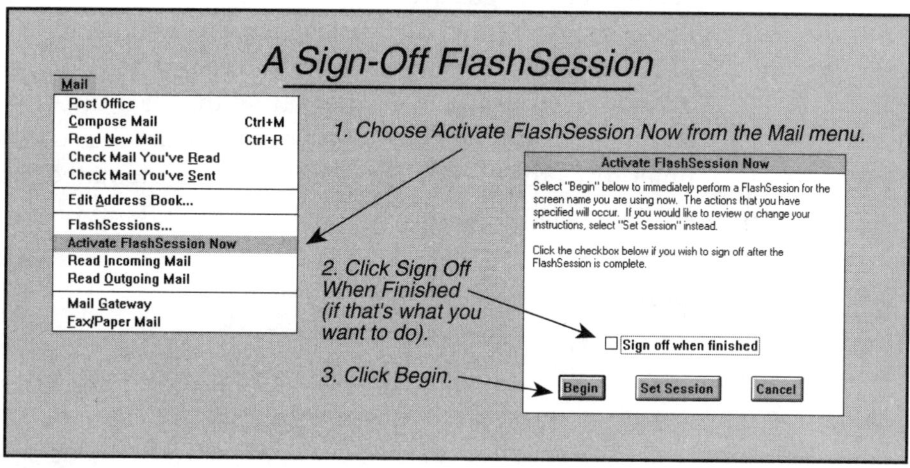
A Sign-Off FlashSession
Mail
Post Office
Compose Mail Ctrl+M
Read New Mail Ctrl+R
Check Mail You've Read
Check Mail You've Sent
Edit Address Book...
FlashSessions...
Activate FlashSession Now
Read Incoming Mail
Read Outgoing Mail
Mail Gateway
Fax/Paper Mail
1. Choose Activate FlashSession Now from the Mail menu.
Activate FlashSession Now
Select "Begin" below to immediately perform a FlashSession for the screen name you are using now. The actions that you have specified will occur. If you would like to review or change your instructions, select "Set Session" instead.
Click the checkbox below if you wish to sign off after the FlashSession is complete.
2. Click Sign Off When Finished (if that's what you want to do).
Sign off when finished
3. Click Begin.
Begin
Set Session
Cancel

Figure 19-12: Rather than choose Sign Off from the Go To menu, choose Activate FlashSession Now from the Mail menu. All of your queued downloads and mail routines will become a part of the sign-off routine.

Note that you can either elect to stay online after the FlashSession concludes (which is the default, as shown in Figure 19-12), or the software can automatically sign off after your FlashSession activities have ended (see Figure 19-13). You will have to specifically activate the Sign Off When Finished option if it's your preference.

Activate FlashSession Now
Select "Begin" below to immediately perform a FlashSession for the screen name you are using now. The actions that you have specified will occur. If you would like to review or change your instructions, select "Set Session" instead.
Click the checkbox below if you wish to sign off after the FlashSession is complete.
Sign off when finished
Begin
Set Session
Cancel

Figure 19-13: Turn on the Sign off when finished option to sign off automatically.

Delayed FlashSessions

A few months ago I went to the hardware store and purchased one of those timers that turns electrical appliances on and off at preset times. I plugged my PC into it and set it to come on at 4 A.M. I declared AOL as a start-up application (see the Setting the Start-up Application sidebar) and instructed it to sign on and run my FlashSession soon after the timer turns the PC on. The key to all this automated profundity is the delayed FlashSession, our final FlashSession topic.

Setting the Start-up Application

Buying a timer from the hardware store isn't enough. Normally, Windows starts with the Program Manager running, and the Program Manager can't sign on to AOL. If you want a FlashSession to run when a timer turns on your machine, you must declare AOL as the start-up application. Windows makes it easy:

- Working in the Program Manager, click once (don't double-click) on the AOL icon to make it active.
- Choose Copy from the Program Manager's File menu. A Group box will appear with the name of one of your Program Manager windows selected within.

More

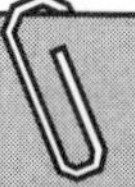

- Click the downward-pointing arrow to the right of the list box and scroll, if necessary, until you see the name of the StartUp group.
- Select the StartUp group, then click the Copy window's OK button.

Unless your StartUp window is displayed within the Program Manager, you won't see the results, but the next time you start Windows, your AOL software will start as well. If you've instructed the AOL software to run an unattended FlashSession, it will do so soon thereafter.

Note: To remove AOL from your startup applications, use the Program Manager to display the StartUp window, select the AOL button, then choose Delete from the Program Manager's File menu. Don't worry: you won't delete the AOL application itself, you'll just delete its icon from the StartUp group.

This is only half of the task, however. Unless you've changed things, your PC probably starts with DOS, not Windows. If that's your situation, add a line to your AUTOEXEC.BAT file. It should be the last line, and all it should say is "Win" (without the quotes). You can use the Notepad accessory to edit your AUTOEXEC.BAT file.

Scheduling the Date & Time

One more task remains before AOL will conduct its FlashSessions unattended: scheduling the time of day and the days of the week that you want AOL to conduct its FlashSessions. Figure 19-14 illustrates the procedure.

I've assumed here that you've checked all the activities you want AOL to carry out during a FlashSession using the FlashSession window (pictured at the top of Figure 19-14). Usually you'll want to select all three activities (files incoming, mail outgoing, mail incoming) shown in the illustration.

I've also assumed that you have declared the appropriate screen names for which you want the FlashSession to apply. Review Figure 19-4 if you're unsure.

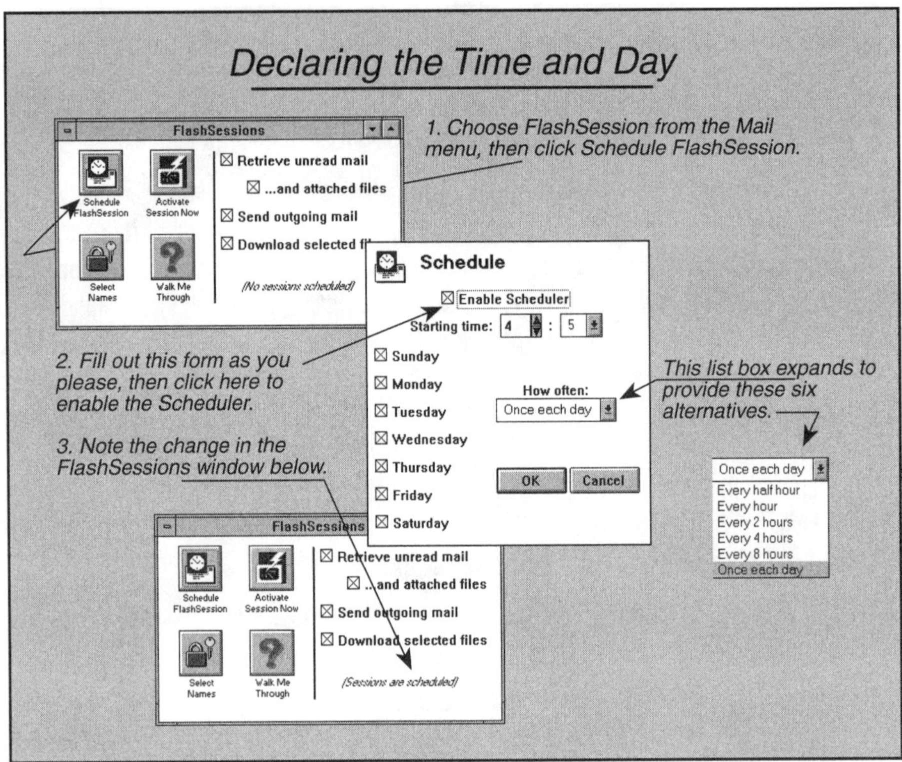

Figure 19-14: The Schedule FlashSession window lets you declare the days and times to be used for unattended FlashSessions. Be sure to check the Enable Scheduler box or the FlashSession won't run.

Excepting Incoming Files

Just last week, I attempted to send some email to a friend. Attached to the message was a 270k file. Unfortunately, I misspelled his name in the To box of the Compose Mail form. Even more unfortunately, the misspelling was a legitimate AOL member screen name, and the mail was sent to the wrong address. Although I re-sent the mail to the proper person later, the person who was on the receiving end of the misaddressed mail was no doubt quite displeased with me if he downloaded my file. My error might have cost him a half hour or more of connect time.

In other words, to protect yourself from encountering a mistake like the one I inadvertently inflicted on that unsuspecting AOL member, you might want to deactivate the ...and attached files option in the FlashSessions window (see the top window in Figure 19-14). The default is on; you might want to change that. After all, you can always sign back on to download files, but you can't undo the cost of a 40-minute download once it's done.

Look again at Figure 19-14. Note that my FlashSessions are scheduled for 5 minutes after the hour. In fact, I only have two choices: 5 or 35 minutes after the hour. America Online arbitrarily assigned these times when I joined. Yours will differ from mine, and so will everyone else's. America Online staggers FlashSession times to distribute the load on the host computer. If given our druthers, most of us would probably choose to run our FlashSessions on the hour or the half-hour—that's human nature. But the host computer would bog down, answering thousands of simultaneous phone calls. Offering random times is AOL's way of avoiding FlashSession overload.

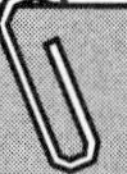

Leave It On

If you follow my lead and elect to use a timer to turn on your PC, it's probably best that you not instruct the timer to turn the PC off a while later. Some hard disks aren't fond of having the rug pulled out from beneath them. Leave the PC running until you shut it down manually.

Reading Flashmail

It only makes sense that AOL lets you read incoming Flashmail. What's interesting is that you can read outgoing Flashmail as well. This is especially comforting for those of us who suffer from occasional bouts of uncertainty. Until it's actually sent, mail is ours to edit, append, or wad up and throw away. (Now that I think about it, you can edit, append, or wad up and throw away mail even after it's sent—as long as no one has read it. Refer to Chapter 4, "Electronic Mail," if you're not familiar with this feature.)

Reading Incoming Mail

Incoming Flashmail is stored in a file in the IDB subdirectory of your AOL20 directory. The file's name is XXX.MAL (where "XXX" is the first eight characters of your screen name). This file is not intended for use by software other than AOL. The Read Incoming Mail command is active whenever a FlashSession has received incoming mail. Typically, this is the first command you'll choose after a FlashSession is finished. To read incoming mail, follow the steps illustrated in Figure 19-15.

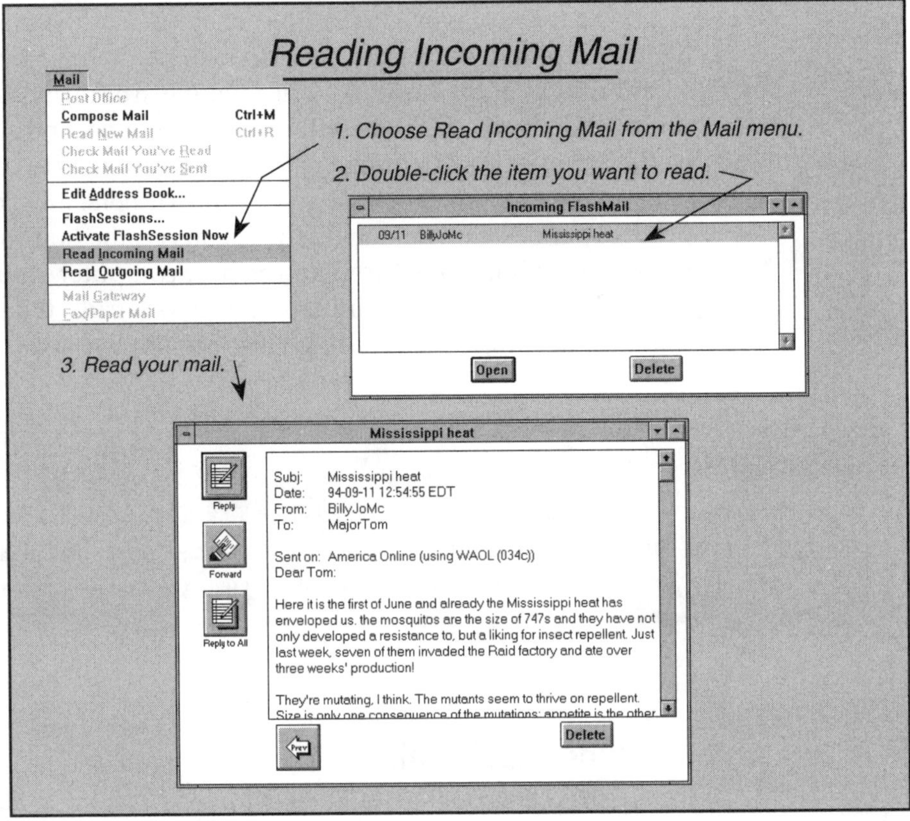

Figure 19-15: Reading incoming mail is easy. Save it if you want, but don't forget to delete it (note the Delete button at the bottom of the illustration) after you read it!

> **Watch Those Screen Names!**
>
> It's important to note that the only mail appearing in the Read Incoming Mail window is that which is addressed to the screen name currently appearing in the window that was on-screen when you signed on. If you've used a FlashSession to download mail for more than one screen name, you must change the screen name in the Welcome window (or the Goodbye window, if you've signed on and signed off earlier) to identify incoming mail for each of your screen names. Only then will you find all the mail that came in during the session.

Don't confuse the Read Incoming Mail command with the Check Mail You've Read command, which also appears under the Mail menu. Check Mail You've Read is an online command that allows you to review mail you've already read. The Read Incoming Mail command discussed here is usually issued off-line, after a FlashSession has concluded. (Again, review Chapter 4 for a thorough explanation of email commands.)

Avoid Clutter

Incoming Flashmail is stored in a file in your IDB subdirectory. All incoming mail messages are stored there until they're deleted, even after they have been read. In other words, if you don't delete incoming mail (by using the Delete button pictured at the bottom of Figure 19-15) after you've read it, the Read Incoming Mail command will remain active, and all incoming mail—past and present—will appear in the Incoming Flashmail window. This is confusing, to say the least. Save incoming Flashmail elsewhere on your hard drive if you wish, but always delete it from your Flashbox after you've read it.

Reading Outgoing Mail

The Read Outgoing Mail command allows you to read outgoing Flashmail before you send it. It can be invoked either online or off, as long as you've prepared FlashMail for sending but haven't sent it yet.

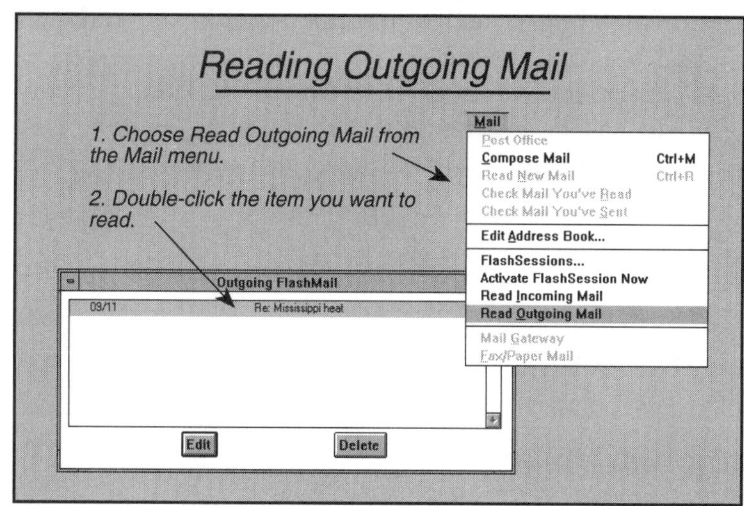

Figure 19-16: The Read Outgoing Mail command is available only when mail has been scheduled for delivery but hasn't been sent.

Again, don't confuse this command with the Check Mail You've Sent command. Check Mail You've Sent is an online command letting you review mail you've sent during the past week. The Read Outgoing Mail command pertains only to mail you've scheduled for delivery that hasn't been sent yet.

The Download Manager

Downloads probably offer more potential than any other AOL feature. Tens of thousands of files reside on AOL's hard disks, and every one of them can be downloaded to your computer. Using the Download Manager, you can establish a queue of files while you're online, reading descriptions and estimating time. When your session is almost over, you instruct the Download Manager to download the files and sign off. Once the process has begun, you can walk away.

Let's watch a typical Download Manager session to see what the screens look like. We'll schedule two files for downloading; then we'll instruct the Download Manager to handle the downloading process and sign off automatically.

Selecting Files for Downloading

Figure 19-17 illustrates the process of selecting a stock chart from the Decision Point Forum (discussed in Chapter 10, "Personal Finance") for downloading. Even if you don't invest in the market, these charts can be quite enlightening.

We might as well give the Download Manager more than one thing to do, so let's select another file to add to the download queue. A Mike Keefe political cartoon seems appropriate (Figure 19-18).

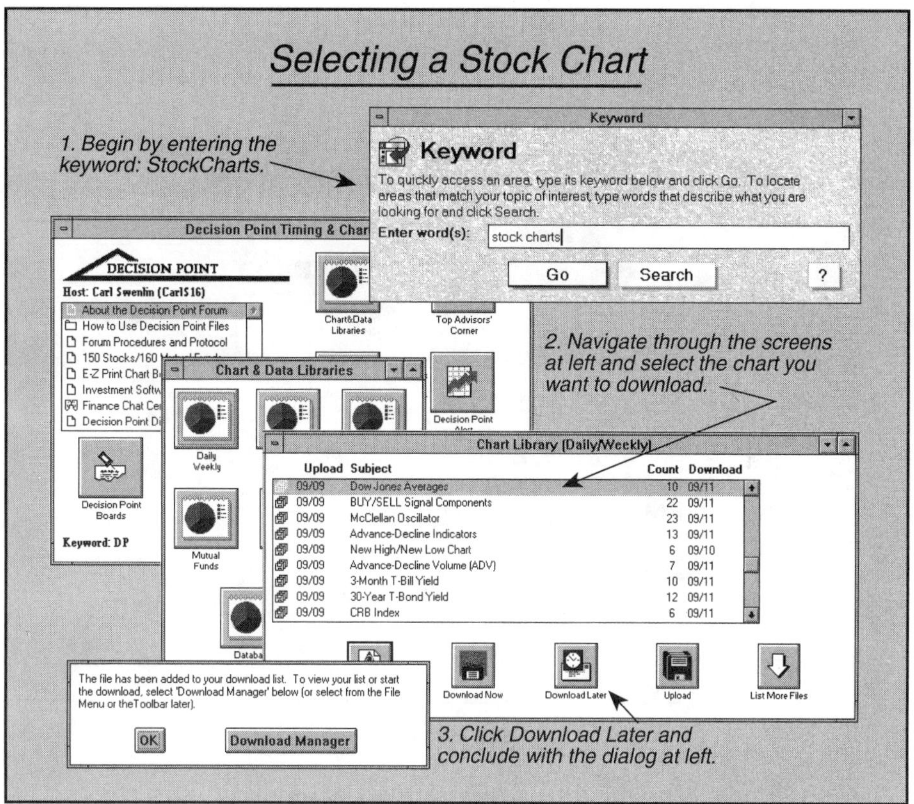

Figure 19-17: The last step in selecting a stock chart for delayed downloading is to click the Download Later button, which results in the dialog box at the bottom of the illustration.

He's a Blues Musician too

Mike Keefe has been drawing political cartoons for the Denver Post for 15 years. He won the 1991 Fischetti Editorial Cartoon Award, and has been recognized by Sigma Delta Chi and the National Headliners Club, winning their highest honors. His work also appears in *USA Today, The New York Times, The Washington Post, TIME, Newsweek* and *U.S. News and World Report*. His online cartoons are available every Monday, Wednesday and Friday by 9 P.M. (Eastern time). You can reach him online via the screen name dePIXion. You can find his cartoons by using the keyword Keefe. One graces the first page of this chapter.

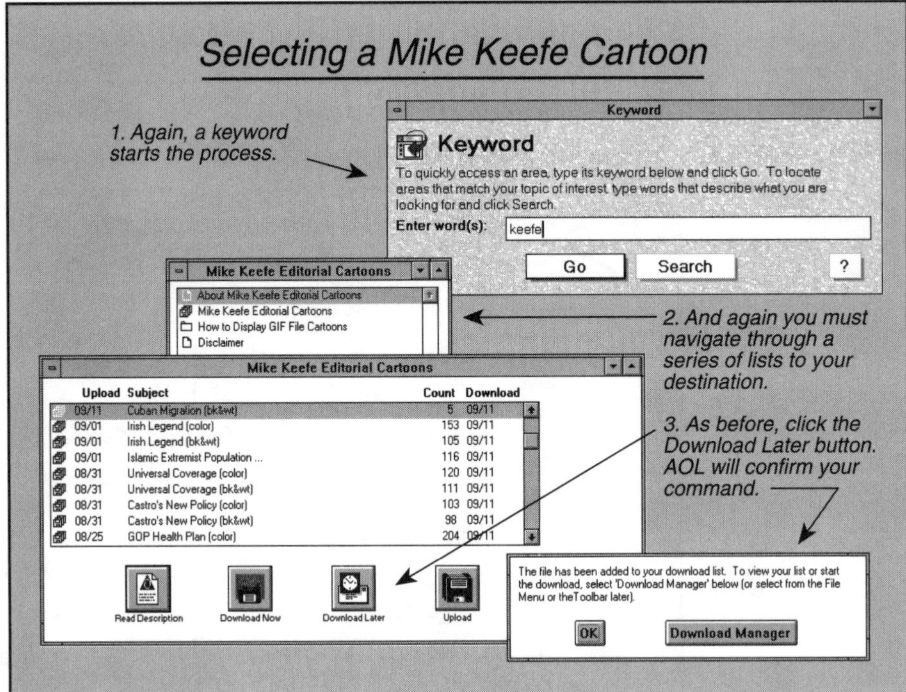

Figure 19-18: Selecting a Mike Keefe cartoon for delayed downloading.

Running the Download Manager

Meanwhile, back at the keyboard, we've decided to call it a day. Rather than sign off, we choose Download Manager from the File menu. This is a second alternative to the Sign Off command (the first being Activate FlashSession Now—under the Mail menu—described earlier in this chapter). The Activate FlashSession Now command accommodates both delayed mail and downloading activities, but it doesn't offer the control that the Download Manager does. The Download Manager—under the File menu—doesn't send queued mail, but it offers access to all of the options pictured in Figure 19-19. If you have mail to send and files to download when you sign off, choose Activate FlashSession Now (and configure the Download Manager ahead of time). If you have only files to download, choose the Download Manager.

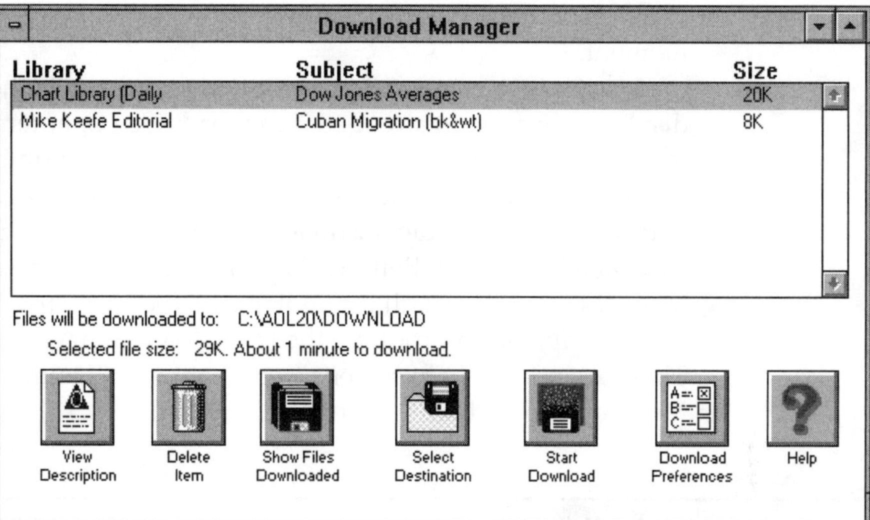

Figure 19-19: The Download Manager window lists all files scheduled for download, including sizes, destinations and the estimated amount of time required to download the entire queue.

Note the buttons across the bottom of Figure 19-19. This is an impressive array of commands. America Online wants you to have complete control over the downloading process, especially now that it's about to begin.

View Description is the same as the View Description button when you're browsing a file library. It's handy to have this command here. Although you probably read a file's description half an hour ago, chances are you remember nothing about it now that you've reached the Download Manager window. Lots of things could have happened in the interim. This button saves a long trip back to the file's original location to review its description.

Delete Item allows you to remove a file (or two, or three) from the list. Sometimes, enthusiasm exceeds resources.

Show Files Downloaded lets you review your past downloads. The number of downloads available for review is set with the Download Preferences button (which we'll discuss in a moment). There's no value in downloading the same file twice. Though AOL will warn you if you try to download a file you've already downloaded, you can save yourself the trouble by checking this list first.

Select Destination allows you to declare a destination directory other than the Download subdirectory, which is the default.

Note: All the files in the queue must download to the same directory.

Start Download begins the download process. We'll use it in a moment.

Download Preferences allows you to determine whether images are displayed during an attended download. (See Chapter 4, "Computing," for a discussion of the online graphics viewer.) A number of compression options are presented here (again, see Chapter 4), as is the number of downloads available for review when you click the Show Files Downloaded button. Refer to Appendix E, "Preferences," for a comprehensive discussion of all the AOL preference options.

The *Help* button produces the Download Manager help screens. These are off-line help screens (see Chapter 3, "Online Help & the Members" for a discussion of off-line help).

Pick Up Where You Left Off

Occasionally the downloading process is interrupted. Lightning strikes. A power cord gets tripped over. The phone line develops a stutter. These kinds of things don't happen often; but when they do, they always occur when you're 80 percent through a 47-minute download. Poof! There goes 35 minutes of connect time.

Don't worry about it. If a file is interrupted during a download, your AOL software makes a note of it and resumes the download queue where you left off the next time you return to the Download Manager.

The downloading process commences when the Start Download button is clicked.

Look at Figure 19-20. When the Sign Off After Transfer option is selected, you can walk away from the computer while all this is going on, secure in the knowledge that the Download Manager will sign off when everything has been downloaded satisfactorily.

When it's all over, you have two nice, big graphics to tack to the wall (Figure 19-21).

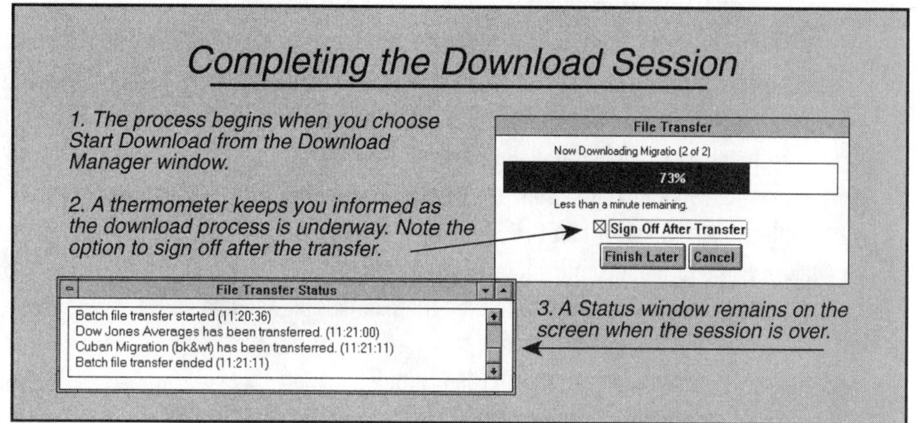

Figure 19-20: The FlashSession ends with a display of the information above.

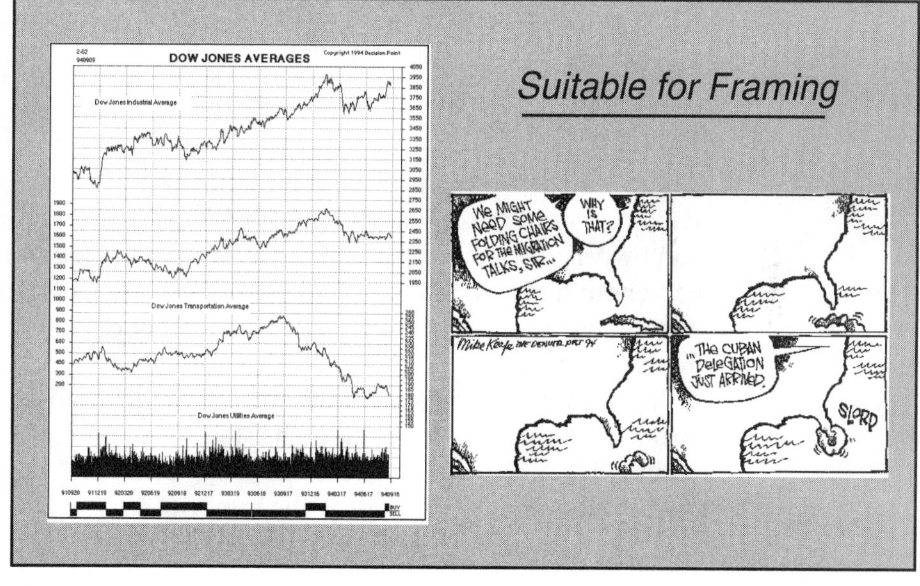

Figure 19-21: Tack the Dow Jones Averages and a political cartoon to your wall each day; people will think you're clever, erudite and urbane.

GIF Files

Widows programs are fond of BMP and PCX graphics. Unfortunately, no other brand of computer is, and AOL serves a half-dozen different brands of computers.

Fortunately, a number of generic graphic formats have emerged, including TIFF, EPS and GIF. Perhaps you noticed that the stock charts and cartoons we just discussed were GIF files. Graphics Interchange Format (GIF) files were developed specifically for the telecommunications industry. The format accommodates color, grayscale, and black-and-white graphics with equal aplomb. It's also a very efficient format: more data is packed into each GIF byte than practically any other graphics format.

It makes little difference to you what format an online graphic is in, because the AOL software reads and displays most of them. It will convert them from one format to another as well; just choose Save from AOL's File menu whenever a graphic is displayed on-screen. You'll have a number of formats to choose from when you do.

Moving On

All this time spent talking about FlashSessions and the Download Manager might make you feel like a real yahoo if you don't use them. Don't worry about it: not all AOL members get enough mail or download enough files to make FlashSessions and the Download Manager worthwhile. In other words, you've got plenty of company: the yahoos are the majority.

There's a political statement there, I'm sure; but to explore it would hardly be the way to conclude a chapter. Instead, reward yourself for reading this far by turning the page. The "Ten-Best" chapter follows. It's the pot of gold at the end of the rainbow.

CHAPTER 20

Ten Best

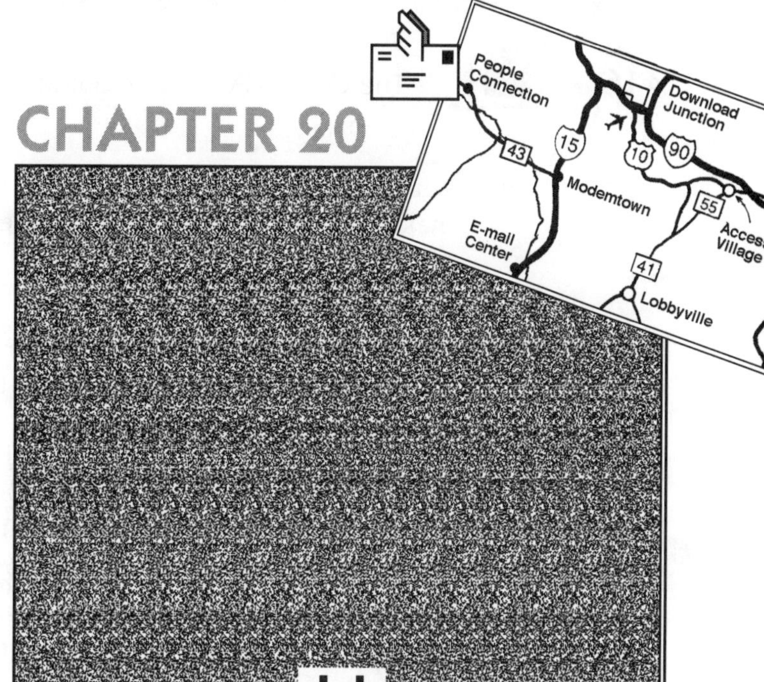

When I was a boy, I believed that if I remained quiet and cooperative all day and all night Christmas Eve, Santa would be especially generous to me. For one 24-hour period every year, I was a model child. I did everything that was asked of me, exactly as requested. I must have been right: nowadays I receive paperweights and paisley ties on Christmas mornings rather than the electric trains and red wagons I received back in the days of deference.

Have you been naughty or nice? You haven't turned to this chapter first, have you? This chapter is a reward for faithful readers only. This is my Ten Best chapter, and I award it only to those who have read all of the preceding 19 chapters. If that's you, read on . . . .

Ten Best Tips

Since we're discussing honor and privilege, let's begin with a list of the Ten Best Tips for using AOL. Most of these tips represent methods by

---

Frontispiece graphic by Kai Krause, generated by his KPT 3D Stereo Noise filter for Photoshop. To find out more about Kai's filters, use the keyword PhotoShop and follow the path Software Libraries > KPT section. To find the graphic for downloading, use the keyword FileSearch, then search the graphics files using the criterion 3D. To see the encoded image, stare at the two squares at the bottom of the graphic, allowing your eyes to go out of focus, until the two squares become three. Maintaining that focus (or lack of it), shift your gaze upward. You will see a familiar object in three dimensions. This is arguably one of the ten best graphics posted on AOL.

which you can save time online (so you save money); all of them will make your online experience more efficient and effective; and not a one of them is dishonorable.

1. **Read this book.**
   If you're reading this paragraph in spite of the admonition on the previous page, at least plan to read the rest of the book eventually. It's full of insights and techniques—not only mine, but those of scores of other members as well. You don't have to be online to use this book. Take it on your next blue-water cruise: people will think you're very erudite, recondite and jocose.

2. **Use keywords and keyboard shortcuts.**
   This tip is so important that I've included two appendices—Appendix A and B—listing AOL's keywords and keyboard shortcuts, respectively. Keywords can save you tons of time. Don't worry about committing them all to memory, just memorize those you use often. (Your most frequently used keywords should be added to your Go To menu, which is explained in Chapter 13, "Clubs & Interests.") Keywords take you to locations that normally require the navigation of menus within menus within menus, and they do it in less than a second. To enter a keyword, press Ctrl+K. To search the online list of keywords, press Ctrl+K, enter your topic and click the Search Help button.
   America Online's keyboard shortcuts are so Windows-like that only a few require additional thought. A few are unique, and they're worth memorizing: Ctrl+K to enter a keyword, Ctrl+M to compose new mail, Ctrl+F to find a member, Ctrl+I to send an Instant Message—that's only four. It won't take long to learn them.

3. **Use Escape and hoodwink the hourglass.**
   All of this talk about Control+key combinations may dilute your memory of the Escape key. This is not my intention. Escape disconnects sluggish sign-ons; halts printing; and halts long articles, downloads and lists as they are received online. That's important: sometimes you'll double-click an article icon (articles are discussed in Chapter 13) only to find that you got yourself into a four-minute feed that you don't want to read after all. No problem: press Escape. The same goes for lists: Escape stops my list of Mail You've Read, for instance, which contains hundreds of entries.

The ability to circumvent the hourglass cursor is a little-known AOL feature, known to only a few regular users. Whenever you see the hourglass cursor, try using it to manipulate various controls on the screen. This is especially convenient when you want to manipulate scroll bars and menu bars. When you're receiving a long list of items, you can start scrolling through that list using the hourglass cursor without having to wait for the hourglass to go away. All you have to do is explore a bit: move that hourglass around, click your mouse and watch what happens.

4. **Use FlashSessions, and read and compose mail off-line.**

   The Compose Mail command (Mail menu) works off-line as well as on. You can compose all your mail off-line while the clock's not running, perfecting every phrase. You can even attach files while you're composing mail off-line. When you have finished composing a piece of mail, click the Send Later icon at the left of the new mail (Untitled) window. America Online will store it (and any mail you compose) on your disk for transmission either later when you're online (choose Read Outgoing Mail from the Mail menu, then click the Send All button) or more likely via a FlashSession (discussed in Chapter 19).

   Likewise, resist the urge to read new mail online. Rather, wait until you've finished all your other online activity, then choose Activate FlashSession Now from the Mail menu. America Online will download all of your incoming mail, then sign off. Once you're off-line, choose Read Incoming Mail from the Mail menu and read your mail at your own pace.

5. **Use help.**

   Read the sidebar on page 49 and follow the tips there, in the order in which they appear.

6. **Keep track of your time and money.**

   It's easy to lose track of time and money when you're online, but no one—neither you nor AOL—benefits from unexpected charges when the bill arrives. You can always check your current (and previous) month's bill by using the keyword Billing (which is free). The keyword Clock tells you how long you've been online during any particular session.

7. **Log your sessions and save to disk.**

   Don't spend time reading material online that can just as easily be saved and read later while off-line. Logging is a mechanism that allows you to capture all the text you encounter online without stopping to read it, whether it's text from the encyclopedia, messages on a board, or a discussion in a conference room. Any text that appears on your screen will be saved to a log if you open one before you start your online journey. (See Chapter 6, "Today's News," for a discussion of logging procedures.)

   Logging is particularly valuable for new members. Start a log, sign on and visit a few areas, then sign off. Once you're off-line, review the log (use the Open command under the File menu to open logs). You'll learn a lot about AOL when you can review an online session at your leisure.

   Of course, it's not easy to remember to open a log for each session, and sometimes you don't know you're going to run across something you want to save until you're there. Fortunately, all text received on AOL can be saved onto your hard drive for later review off-line. Simply go to the File menu and select Save. This causes all the text in the article or message in the front-most window on your screen to be transferred to any disk drive you specify, where it is saved as a plain text file that you can read using AOL or the word processor of your choice. Note that it isn't necessary for you to scroll through the entire article in order to save it. Even though you haven't seen the entire text of the article, your computer has, and everything is saved when you issue the Save command.

8. **Multitask and download when system activity is minimal.**

   Your AOL software can download in the background while you're working on a spreadsheet or using your word processor. If you start a long download—even if it's via a FlashSession—and you have something else to do with your PC, use the procedures described in Chapter 13, "Clubs & Interests," to activate another application and do what's got to be done.

   Here's another downloading tip: the AOL system—the host computer and the long-distance carrier in your local area—gets very busy in the evenings and on weekends. Your time on the system is allocated in slices, and these time slices get smaller as the system becomes more active. Your computer spends more of its time waiting in line for data when these time slices get small, yet the clock keeps running regardless.

Whenever you're planning a long download—say, anything over 10 minutes—plan it for the time of day when the system is least active. Typically, that's the morning: the earlier the better. Read about FlashSessions and the Download Manager in Chapter 19, and use both of them to tame your download time.

9. **Look for More buttons.**
   Lots of AOL windows include buttons or folders marked More. Don't neglect them. America Online doesn't tie up your system feeding you all 500 matching entries to a database search, for instance. Rather, it offers the first 20, then waits to see if you want more. You might want to cancel at that moment, or you might want to see more. When the conditions are appropriate, AOL always offers the More option, but it's only useful if you choose to exercise it. America Online users who neglect the More buttons online never know what they're missing.

10. **Manage your windows.**
    America Online's "modeless" strategy allows you to wander all over the service, leaving a litter of windows behind you. A mess like this quickly becomes unmanageable. You might spend needless time cleaning up after yourself or searching for a specific window on screen while the online clock keeps running. Moreover, some of AOL's windows—the Main Menu and the Spotlight, in particular—are slow to redraw, and there's no need to pay for these windows' redrawing time while you're online. A number of techniques aid window management:

    - The Windows menu offers the Close All, Cascade and Tile commands. The Cascade command arranges all of your windows in a cascade, filing them like folders in a file cabinet. Very tidy. Life could use a command like this.
    - The Close All command closes all windows, and Ctrl+F4 closes only the front-most window. Alternatively, you can double-click the top window's control-menu box (the one in the window's upperleft corner) to close it.

- The bottom of the Windows menu lists the titles of all open windows. Use this menu to find the one you want quickly and easily, no matter how messy the screen becomes.

Ten Best Downloads

This list is hardly objective and is most certainly in no particular order. It is exclusive of fonts and graphics: you will have to explore those on your own. This is just a list of really great and useful stuff, all of which is available online for the cost of your connect time and perhaps a small shareware fee.

To find any of the downloads mentioned, use the keyword FileSearch, then specify the name of the file—excluding the version number (see the searching tips in Chapter 17, "Reference Desk")—as your search criteria. If you find more than one version of a particular program available, be sure to download the one with the highest version number, since it's the most recent release of that program.

1. **PKZIP and WinZip**
   PKZIP is offered as a commercial product, as shareware, and as an integral feature of your AOL software. PKZIP is a DOS-based product, however, so its commands are arcane and difficult to remember for the casual user. WinZip's interface is as easy to learn as they come. It's a Windows product, so you lose some speed—not much—but it's fully compatible with PKZIP files. One or both of these utilities should be on every Windows-user's shelf, especially when you consider the minimal shareware fee. File compression is discussed in Chapter 4, "Electronic Mail," and again in Chapter 5, "Computing."

2. **VirusScan**
   This is the popular virus detection (and eradication) shareware package from Chris McAfee and McAfee Associates. Virus protection software is only as good as its most recent release—new viruses are hatched every day—and updates to VirusScan are posted on McAfee's own area on AOL.

The latest release of VirusScan includes two programs: *Scan* scans both memory and disks, looking for and (optionally) eradicating known viruses it finds; *Vshield* is a memory-resident program that continuously monitors system activities, detecting viruses as they're introduced. Both Windows and DOS interfaces are available in the same package. Use the keyword McAfee for more information.

3. **PaintShop Pro**

Most of the really spectacular graphics available on AOL are in a format that your AOL software can open and display. Occasionally, however, you might run into one that chokes AOL's software, or won't import into your word-processing or desktop-publishing program. For those occasions, you need a Swiss Army knife of a graphics program—one that opens anything (including GIF, JPG, TIFF, BMP and PCX) and saves in formats that are useful to you. That program is PaintShop Pro, from JASC, Inc. PaintShop's new filters and resampling routines elevate it far above the average format-conversion program. It's a great capture program for screen shots, but it's also one of the most expensive shareware packages available online. Use the keyword FileSearch, then search with the criterion Paint Shop.

4. **Makin' Waves**

Makin' Waves by Geoff Faulkner is a Windows sound conversion utility and WAV file player. It converts the major sound formats: .VOCC, .SOU and .SND to the .WAV format required by most sound-savvy Windows applications (including AOL). It also converts the sounds found on the Macintosh Music & Sound forum (keyword: MMS) and there are thousands of those. File search using the criterion: Faulkner.

As mentioned in Chapter 12, you must have a sound card and speakers to make effective use of AOL's sounds. Microsoft's driver for your machine's internal speaker is incompatible with the AOL software.

5. **UUCODE**

UUCODE is Windows shareware that converts binary files (including graphics) to text files (and vice versa) through a process known as *uuencoding*. The conversion allows you to send and receive binary files via e-mail or the Internet (newsgroups make extensive use of uuencoded data).

You may recall from discussions in Chapter 4 ("Electronic Mail") that Internet mail does not support attachments. In other words, you can't send files via the Internet unless you use UUCODE or a program like it. Getting the hang of uuencoding takes a while (send some uuencoded mail to yourself first, as a test), but it's just about the only solution to a chronic Internet imperfection. File search: UUCODE.

6. **WAOL Express**

Bill Pytlovany is not only a skilled Windows programmer, he's also one of the most personable people you'll ever meet online. He has written Windows software for a number of clients, including AOL. Thus, when I discovered Whale Express online (and saw that Bill was its programmer), I eagerly downloaded it.

Whale Express is a Windows-based scripting language designed specifically for AOL. Using Whale Express you can write "scripts" (macros) that run your WAOL (Windows AOL—pronounced "whale") software automatically and unattended. Whale Express will sign on, get your mail, and sign off—all by itself. You can then compose replies (off-line) and run another Whale script to sign back on, send the mail, and sign back off. This feature alone will save you enough money to pay for Bill's shareware.

There's a NewScreenName command that allows you to change screen names automatically, scripts can call other scripts, and the help file serves as a complete reference to the utility. File search using the keyword Whale Express.

7. Smileys

There are lots of lists of smileys posted online. Use the keyword FileSearch, then search with the criterion Smileys. You'll find SMILEY.TXT, a venerable introduction to smiley etiquette; and you'll find SMILEYS.ZIP, a comprehensive (nearly 100k) smiley anthology with a frivolous little DOS application that displays a smiley and its meaning each time you enter SMILEY at the DOS prompt. Great stuff for your AUTOEXEC.BAT file. ;-)

8. WinSpell

This is a spell-checking addition that's ideal for WAOL users. It checks each word against its internal dictionary *as you type*, alerting you to spelling errors as they're made (a feature that can be turned off, if you can't stand the nagging). It works well with Windows AOL, checking your mail and message-board postings before you commit them to the scrutiny of the online proletariat. File search using the keyword WinSpell.

9. Dazzle

I suppose you could call Dazzle a screen saver but who needs another screen saver when Windows comes with one of its own?

I was skeptical. Dazzle isn't a Windows program—you have to stoop to DOS to use it—and it's not a screen saver (actually, it is—if you send in your shareware fee, otherwise it's a stand-alone program), so why bother?

Because it's so *good!* Dazzle can calm fierce beasts, smooth turbulent waters and lift tormented spirits. It's better than LSD and perfectly legal. You've gotta see this thing. File search using the keyword Dazzle.

10. Fairy Godmom

Fairy Godmom is a rarity: a great computer game with no carnage. Armed only with a magic wand, Godmom can temporarily convert your pursuers (most take the form of befuddled crabs) into things like brick walls. The games features 50 levels of play and should challenge even the most experienced arcade-game player. It has good sound and great graphics and animation. Try animating a Godmom as she ascends a ladder in a full-length gown and you'll see what I mean. It's shareware from John Blackwell. File search using the keyword Fairy Godmother.

11. I Laughed So Hard I Cried

I know this is number 11 on a list of 10, but it's not really a download either. Rather, "I Laughed So Hard I Cried" is a series of humorous stories and anecdotes discovered online and compiled by Sandy Brockman (AFLSandyB). To find it, visit Sandy's Beginners Forum (keyword Beginners) and investigate the Beginners Software Libraries. This is spirit-lifting stuff, and we can all use a lift of spirits now and again.

Many thanks to Kate Chase (PC Kate) for her assistance with this list. If you're a download enthusiast, make it a point to visit the Windows Shareware 500 forum, where the top 500 shareware packages are posted and continuously updated. Use the keyword Win500.

Ten Most-Frequently Asked Questions of Customer Relations

As you might expect, the people in Customer Relations spend 90 percent of their time answering the same questions over and over again. Perhaps it will help if I answer them for you here. It might save you the trouble of contacting Customer Relations (and save them the trouble of replying).

1. **Where can I get help?**

   Read Chapter 3, "Online Help & the Members." Also, look up the topic in the index of this book to see if your question is answered here.

   - Read the sidebar on page 49 and follow the tips in the order in which they appear.
   - Run the AOL software and choose Help from the menu bar.
   - Go online and choose the Member Services command from the Members menu (or use the keyword Help). The Member Services area provides information on how to access online and off-line help sources. Member Services is free. Spend as much time there as you like.
   - Ask a Guide for help. Press Ctrl+L and look for someone in the Lobby with the word "Guide" in his or her screen name.

- Ask the Technical Representatives in TechLive who supply live, online support. Press Ctrl+K and use the keyword TechLive.
- Get assistance from your fellow AOL members. Use the keyword MHM, which takes you to the Members Helping Members message boards.
- Send an e-mail message with your question to the AOL staff. Use the keyword Help, then click the EMail to the Staff button.
- If you have another telecom application (such as Windows Terminal), call the AOL bulletin board service. The BBS is open 24 hours a day, and can be accessed at baud rates up to 14.4 bps. The call is free; dial 1-800-827-5808. Set your telecom software for 8 data bits, no parity, and 1 stop bit.
- If you have a fax machine or fax modem, call the AOL FaxLink service. This service provides information via fax concerning connectivity problems or error messages and software and hardware incompatibilities. This number is also toll free: 1-800-827-5551.
- Call AOL Technical Support at 1-800-827-3338. This should be your last resort.

2. **How can I get AOL to multitask?**

- Multitasking is a fancy word for doing more than one activity at a time on your computer, and it's never more appropriate than it is in telecommunications software like AOL. Some downloads, for instance, can take quite a bit of time, and you will tire quickly of watching the thermometer which monitors downloading progress.
- To switch to another Windows application during a download, press Alt+Tab or Ctrl+Esc. These traditional Windows commands switch among active applications and allow you to access any one of them while AOL is working in the background.
- *Note:* Version 2.5 (but not the earlier versions) is capable of multitasking within itself. Once a download has begun, you can compose and send mail, visit forums—just about anything you

can do when you're not downloading. Be aware, however, that performance might be sluggish, and that tasks involving other downloads (or uploads) may not function at all.

Final Note: America Online does not recommend that you launch other applications that require a lot of disk access. This could affect the AOL downloading process running in the background and cause it to halt.

3. **How do I find additional or closer access numbers?**

   SprintNet (discussed in Chapter 1, "Starting the Tour") is always adding additional access numbers. To stay in touch, use the keyword Access. If you're away from your normal location, read Appendix C.

4. **Can I use the same AOL account from multiple computers?**

   No problem, even if they're different kinds of computers. All you need is AOL software for each (which is free). Use the keyword Upgrade to request additional copies of AOL software. Or, if you have another telecom application, you can download the software from the AOL BBS. (For details on connecting to the BBS, see item 1.)

   When you receive the additional copy of the software, do *not* use the certificate number and password in the packet. Rather, enter the screen name and password you normally use when you're asked for the certificate number and password. This will configure the new software to your existing account. But remember, only one screen name from each AOL account can be signed on at a time.

5. **Where do I begin?**

   Try the Beginners Forum. Use the keyword Beginners.

   If you're using Version 2.0, begin at the Main Menu (if it's not displayed, select the Main Menu command from the Go To menu). From there, click any of the 14 Department buttons that closely match your interests. Also, click the Discover America Online button to find popular and new AOL areas.

   The New Member Lounge in People Connection is also a good place to start. Choose Lobby from the Go To menu, then click the Rooms button.

You might also visit the Clubs & Interests and Computing Departments. Find a forum there that interests you, read and reply to messages posted on the boards, and visit the forum's chat room when it's available.

Perhaps most important, though, is to do what you enjoy. There's no right or wrong place to begin your AOL travels. Feel free to explore uncharted territory. You can hardly get lost when you never leave home.

6. **How can I see how much time I have used and check my bill?**

   The keyword Clock displays the online clock; the keyword Billing displays your current charges, exclusive of the current session. You can get a complete explanation of charges here, and change your billing method if you want. The keyword Billing is a free area.

7. **How do I change my screen name?**

   Though you cannot change your original screen name, you can add up to four additional names and use them as you wish—including deleting them and adding others. Use the keyword Names. This is a free area as well.

   Note: Once you delete a screen name, you cannot reinstate it.

8. **How do I change my profile?**

   Use the keyword Help, then click the Billing Information icon. Alternatively, choose Edit Your Online Profile from the Members menu. The first method is free; the second is not.

9. **How do I disable Call Waiting?**

   Call Waiting can disrupt online sessions, often resulting in a disconnect. To disable it, choose Setup from the Welcome window when you're not online. At the network and modem setup window select Edit Location. In most areas, you need only check the box labeled "Use the following command to disable call waiting." If you have a pulse line, you may need to change the command from "*70," to "1170,". If you have trouble, consult your local phone company or ask Technical Support (see item 1 of this list).

10. How do I turn off my modem's speaker when dialing?

- While off-line, click the Setup button in the Sign On window.
- At the Modem and Network Setup window, select Setup Modem and then select Edit Commands.
- Type "M0" (that's "M-zero") just before the ^M in the Setup Modem String box. (that is, AT&FE1QV1&D2X4&C1M0^M).
- Click the OK button and keep doing so until you return to the Sign On window.

Thanks to Mary Daffron, Brian Weston and the AOL Technical Support Help Desk for help with this list.

Ten Best Ways to Make Friends Online

Perhaps above all, AOL is a community. If you're not a part of it, you're missing a wealth of opportunity. Like any community, you're ahead of the game if you know how to break into it. Here's how:

1. **Visit the Lobby.**
   Read Chapter 12 ("People Connection"), then press Ctrl+L for the Lobby. Say hello when you arrive. The Lobby is probably the greatest resource for online friends.

2. **Find a favorite room and hang out there.**
   Chapter 12 describes the Event Rooms Guide (keyword PC Studio). Look it over, find a room that interests you, and visit that room when it's available. You might also find a favorite room by visiting any of AOL's forums (forums are described in Chapter 13, "Clubs & Interests").

3. **Visit the New Member Lounge.**
   If you're new to AOL, you'll find comfort in numbers in the New Member Lounge. Press Ctrl+L, click the Rooms button, then select New Members Lounge from the Public Rooms list.

4. **Post your profile.**
   Don't neglect to post a profile for yourself. Use the keyword Help, then click the Billing Information icon. (You can also edit your profile by using the appropriate command under the Members menu, but the keyword method is free.) Talk about yourself. Make your personality irresistible. People in chat rooms often peek at other occupants' profiles, and if you haven't posted a profile, you're a persona non grata.

5. **Use an effective screen name.**
   You can use the Help keyword technique described earlier to add a screen name to your account if the one you're using now isn't very effective in a social situation. People have a hard time relating to a screen name like "Tlich6734," but many find "MajorTom" worthy of comment. If nothing else, include your first name or your nickname in your screen name so people can address you like the friend you want to be.

6. **Search the membership for others with similar interests.**
   Use the keyword Directory to search the Member Directory for others with interests similar to yours. Read their profiles and send them email. You'll be surprised at the number who reply.

7. **Read messages and reply.**
   Find a forum that interests you (see Chapter 13, "Clubs & Interests"), go to its message boards, and start reading messages. Eventually you'll see some that provoke a response. Go ahead: post your comment. It gives you a great sense of purpose the next time you sign on: you'll scramble to that message board to see if anyone responded to your posting.

8. **Post a message soliciting replies.**
   Members Helping Members (keyword MHM; see Chapter 3, "Online Help & the Members") is a great place for message posting, but any forum will do. Post a message asking for help or an opinion. People love to help, and everyone has an opinion.

9. **Read articles and reply.**
   This is similar to item 7. In forums like the Writer's Forum, people pour their hearts out in their articles, and they're always hoping for a little positive feedback.

10. **Download a file posted by another member and reply.**
    This goes especially for fonts and graphics. Download a few files (downloading is discussed in Chapter 5, "Computing") and reply to the originator via email. In selecting the graphics for this book, I sent e-mail to dozens of online artists, and every one of them replied within a day or two—most with two or three pages of enthusiastic banter.

Ten Best Smileys

I posted my own list of smileys in the first edition of this book, but I've since received mail from many readers with smileys of their own. Invariably, theirs are better. Perhaps the most charming was the list from Spencer Soloway, which appears below. For a complete list of smileys, use the keyword FileSearch, then use the criterion Smiley.

1. };^)' "lil devil"
2. B) "wearing shades"
3. :c) "pig headed"
4. [:-I] "robot"
5. $-) "lotto fever"
6. I-) "cyborg"
7. :-() "stubbed my toe"
8. @-->-->-- "a rose"
9. O:) "Angel"
10. <:-) "I'm a dunce"

Everybody Out of the Bus!

Our tour has concluded. Typical of tours everywhere, ours has been an abridgment, a synopsis of things I find most interesting about AOL. You will find your own favorites, and in so doing discover things that I not only didn't mention, but didn't know myself. Moreover, AOL is a moving target: like most online services, AOL is almost a fluid—flowing from opportunity to opportunity, conforming to trends and advances, relentlessly expanding to fill new voids. I'll try to keep up, and no doubt there will be another edition of this book someday to describe an even bigger and better AOL than the one we know today.

Meanwhile, this edition has reached its end. While you're waiting for the next one, sign on to AOL and send me some e-mail. Tell me what you want included (or excluded) in the next edition. Tell me what you liked or disliked about this book. Send me logs, files, articles—anything you think might complement the *America Online Tour Guide*. I look forward to hearing from you.

—MajorTom

APPENDIX A
Keywords

Keywords are the fastest way to get from one place to another on America Online. To go to a specific forum or area, you just select Keyword from the Go To menu (or type Ctrl+K), and enter the keyword.

Of course, you need to know the keyword before you can enter it. The most current list of keywords is always available by clicking the Keyword Help button in the Go To Keyword window. It's a long list, so long that it's divided into sub-lists by department. Because of its length, you might have trouble finding the keyword you're after by consulting the list online. (Printing it is an option.)

Allow me to suggest two alternatives: 1) Use the keyword: Services (or choose Search Directory of Services from the Go To menu). The Directory of Services is a searchable database of services offered by America Online (and it's discussed in Chapter 3, "Online Help and the Members"). Because it's searchable, the Directory is a faster method of locating an online area than reading through the list of keywords, and the Directory always lists keywords when they're available. 2) Use the lists of keywords appearing below. They're alphabetical: one by keyword, the other by subject. They may save you the trouble of printing a list of your own.

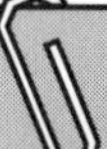

Keyword tips

The three little keyword tips below may be of help to you.

- Like screen names, keywords are neither case nor space-sensitive. "directoryofservices" works just as well as "Directory of Services."
- Many of AOL's windows identify their associated keywords in the lower-left corner of the window. Look for these.
- Add frequently-used keywords to your Go To menu. Editing the Go To menu is described in Chapter 13, "Clubs & Interests."

The keyword lists below were compiled by Jennifer Watson (screen name: Jennifer) on August 17, 1994. Please e-mail changes or additions to her, as she maintains the lists on a continuing basis. You can download the latest keyword lists by using the keyword: FileSearch, then specifying the criterion: Keyword List. Thanks, Jennifer!

Entries with asterisks (*) are within free areas. Entries with daggers (†) are platform dependent. Some are for the Mac; some are for the PC. Mac platform-dependent entries may not be available to PC users.

Alphabetical by Keyword

Keyword	Area
@TIMES	@times/The New York Times Online
3DSIG	3D Special Interest Group
5.0	DOS Forum
5THGENERATION	Fifth Generation
25REASONS	Best of America Online showcase
9600	9600 Baud Access Center*
9600ACCESS	9600 Baud Access Center*
9600CENTER	9600 Baud Access Center*
A2APPLEWORKS	Apple Productivity Forum
A2ART	Apple Graphics and Sound Forum
A2DEVELOPMENT	Apple Development Forum
A2EDUCATION	Apple Education Forum
A2GAMES	Apple Games and Entertainment Forum
A2GRAPHICS	Apple Graphics and Sound Forum
A2HARDWARE	Apple Hardware Forum
A2MUSIC	Apple Graphics and Sound Forum
A2PERIPHERALS	Apple Hardware Forum
A2PRODUCT	Apple Hardware Forum
A2PRODUCTIVITY	Apple Productivity Forum
A2TELECOM	Apple Communications Forum
A2UTILITIES	Apple Utilities & Desk Accessories Forum
A2WORDPROCESSING	Apple Productivity Forum
AAII	AAII Online
AATRIX	Aatrix Software, Inc.
AAW	Apple Productivity Forum
ABBATEVIDEO	Abbate Video
ABF	Beginners' Forum
ABM	Adventures by Mail
ACADEMY	Starfleet Academy
ACCESS	Local access numbers*
ACCESSERIC	AskERIC
ACCESSNUMBERS	Local access numbers*
ACCESSSOFTWARE	Access Software
ACCOLADE	Accolade, Inc.
ACER	Acer America Corporation
ACHIEVEMENTTV	Achievement TV
ACM	Apple Communications Forum
ACOT	Apple Classrooms of Tomorrow
ACTIVISION	Activision
AD&D	AD&D Neverwinter Nights
ADD	AD&D Neverwinter Nights
ADOPTION	Adoption Forum
ADS	auto*des*sys, Inc.
ADSIG	Advertising Special Interest Group
ADV	Apple Development Forum
ADVANCED	Advanced Software, Inc.
ADVANCEDGRAVIS	Advanced Gravis
ADVENTURE	Games Forum†
ADVENTURESBYMAIL	Adventures by Mail
ADVERTISING	Advertising Special Interest Group
ADVERTISINGSIG	Advertising Special Interest Group
ADVICE	Advice & Tips
AECSIG	Architects, Engineers and Construction SIG
AED	Apple Education Forum
AFFINITY	Affinity Microsystems
AFRICANAMERICAN	The Exchange
AFT	American Federation of Teachers
AFTERWARDS	Afterwards Coffeehouse
AGM	Apple Games and Entertainment Forum
AGR	Apple Graphics and Sound Forum
AGS	Apple Graphics and Sound Forum
AHW	Apple Hardware Forum
ALADDIN	Aladdin Systems, Inc.
ALDUS	Aldus Corporation
ALPHATECH	Alpha Software Corporation
ALTSYS	Altsys Corporation
ALVIN	Hatrack River Town Meeting
ALYSIS	Alysis Software
AMATEURRADIO	Ham Radio Club
AMBROSIA	Ambrosia Software
AMERICANAIRLINES	EAASY SABRE
AMERICANDIALOGUE	American Dialogue
AMERICANINDIAN	The Exchange
AMS	Graphics and Sound Forum
ANALOG	Science Fiction Forum
ANIMATEDSOFTWARE	Animated Software

ANIMATION	Graphic Forum†
ANOTHERCO	Another Company
AOLBEGINNERS	Beginners' Forum
AOLPRODUCTS	AOL Products Center
APDA	Apple Professional Developer's Association
APOGEE	Apogee Software
APPLE	Apple II/Mac Computing & Software Department†
APPLE2	Apple II Computing & Software Department
APPLEII	Apple II Computing & Software Department
APPLEIIDEVELOPMENT	Apple Development Forum
APPLEIIEDUCATION	Apple Education Forum
APPLEIIGAMES	Apple Games and Entertainment Forum
APPLEIIGRAPHICS	Apple Graphics and Sound Forum
APPLEIIHARDWARE	Apple Hardware Forum
APPLEIIMUSIC	Apple Graphics and Sound Forum
APPLEIIPRODUCTIVITY	Apple Productivity Forum
APPLEIISOFTWARE	Apple II Software Center
APPLESCRIPT	AppleScript SIG
APPLEWORKS	Apple Productivity Forum
APPLICATIONS	Apple Applications Forum
APPLICATIONS	Apple Business Forum
APPMAKER	Bowers Development
APPS	Applications/Business Forum†
APR	Apple Productivity Forum
ARCADE	Games Forum†
ARES	Ares Microdevelopment, Inc.
ARGOSY	Argosy
ARIEL	Ariel Publishing
ARM	Real Estate Online
ART	Graphics Forum†
ARTICULATE	Articulate Systems
ARTIFICE	Artifice, Inc.
ARTS	Afterwards Coffeehouse
ASCD	Assoc. for Supervisor & Curriculum Development
ASCTECH	Alpha Software Corporation
ASCTS	Alpha Software Corporation
ASI	Articulate Systems
ASIAN	The Exchange
ASIMOV	Science Fiction Forum
ASKAMERICAONLINE	Member Services
ASKANDY	Advice & Tips
ASKANITA	Advice & Tips
ASKAOL	Member Services
ASKCS	Member Services
ASKERIC	AskERIC
ASKTHEDOCTOR	Advice & Tips
ASKTHEDR	Advice & Tips
ASKTHELAWYER	Advice & Tips
ASSEMBLY	Development Forum†\
ASTRONOMY	Astronomy Club
ASYMETRIX	Asymetrix Corporation
ATC	Apple Communications Forum
ATTIMES	@times/The New York Times Online
ATLANTIC	The Atlantic Monthly Online
ATLANTICMONTHLY	The Atlantic Monthly Online
ATLANTICONLINE	The Atlantic Monthly Online
ATTICUS	Atticus Software
AUDIO	Stereo Review Online magazine
AUDIO/VIDEO	Dolby Audio/Video Forum
AUDITORIUM	Center Stage auditorium
AUG	User Group Forum
AUT	Apple Utilities & Desk Accessories Forum
AUTO	AutoVantage
AUTOEXEC	Tune Up Your PC
AUTORACING	The Grandstand
AUTOS	Road & Track Magazine
AUTOVANTAGE	AutoVantage
AVIATION	Aviation Club
AVID	Avid DTV Group
AVIDDTV	Avid DTV Group
AVOCAT	Avocat Systems
AVT	Apple Utilities & Desk Accessories Forum
AW	Apple Productivity Forum
AWGS	Apple Productivity Forum
AWP	Apple Productivity Forum
AWS	Apple Productivity Forum
BABYBOOMERS	Baby Boomers area
BACKCOUNTRY	Backpacker Magazine
BACKPACKER	Backpacker Magazine
BARRONS	Barrons Booknotes
BASEBALL	The Grandstand
BASELINE	Baseline Publishing
BASEVIEW	Baseview Products, Inc.
BASIC	Development Forum†
BASKETBALL	The Grandstand
BBS	BBS Corner
BBSCORNER	BBS Corner
BCS	Boston Computer Society
BEER	Wine & Dine Online
BEGINNER	Beginners' Forum
BEGINNERS	Beginners' Forum
BERKELY	Berkeley Systems
BERKSYS	Berkeley Systems
BERKSYSWIN	Berkeley Systems
BESTOFAOL	Best of America Online showcase
BETHESDA	Bethesda Softworks
BETHESDA	Bethesda Softworks, Inc.
BEYOND	Beyond, Inc.
BFA	The Bicycle Network
BI	Gay & Lesbian Community Forum
BICMAG	Bicycling Magazine
BICYCLE	The Bicycle Network
BICYCLING	Bicycling Magazine
BICYCLINGMAGAZINE	Bicycling Magazine
BIKENET	The Bicycle Network
BILL	Billing Information and Changes

BILLING	Account and Billing*
BIOSCAN	OPTIMAS Corporation
BISEXUAL	Gay & Lesbian Community Forum
BITJUGGLERS	Bit Jugglers
BLIND	DisABILITIES Forum
BLOCDEVELOPMENT	TIGERDirect, Inc.
BMUG	Berkley Macintosh Users Group
BOARDWATCH	Boardwatch Magazine
BOATING	The Exchange
BOOKBESTSELLERS	Book Bestsellers area
BOOKNOTES	Barrons Booknotes
BOOKS	Book Bestsellers area
BOOKSTORE	Online Bookstore
BOWERS	Bowers Development
BOXING	The Grandstand
BRAINSTORM	Brainstorm Products
BREW	Wine & Dine Online
BREWING	Wine & Dine Online
BRODERBUND	Broderbund
BUDDHISM	Religion & Ethics Forum
BULLMOOSE	Bull Moose Tavern
BULLSANDBEARS	Bulls and Bears Game
BUNGIE	Bungie Software
BUSINESS	Business News area
BUSINESSFORUM	Applications/Business Forum†
BUSINESSKNOWHOW	Business Strategies
BUSINESSNEWS	Business News area
BUSINESSSENSE	Business Sense
BUSINESSSTRATEGIES	Business Strategies
BYTE	ByteWorks
BYTEBYBYTE	Byte By Byte Corporation
BYTEWORKS	ByteWorks
C	Development Forum†
C&S	Computing Department†
CAD	Graphics Forum†
CAERE	Caere Corporation
CAERECORPORATION	Caere Corporation
CALLISTO	Callisto Corporation
CAMERA	Kodak Photography Forum
CAMERAS	Popular Photography Online
CAMPING	Backpacker Magazine
CAMPUS	Interactive Education Services
CANCEL	Cancel Account*
CARANDDRIVER	Car and Driver Magazine
CARDINAL	Cardinal Technologies, Inc.
CAREER	Career Center
CAREERNEWS	USA Today Industry Watch section
CAREERS	Career Center
CARS	Road & Track Magazine
CARTOONNETWORK	Cartoon Network
CARTOONS	Cartoon collection
CARUSO	Inside Technology
CASABLANCA	Casa Blanca
CASADY	Casady & Greene
CASINO	RabbitJack's Casino
CB	College Board
CBD	Commerce Business Daily
CELEBRITYCOOKBOOK	Celebrity Cookbook
CENTERSTAGE	Center Stage auditorium
CENTRAL	Central Point Software
CENTRALPOINT	Central Point Software
CESOFTWARE	CE Software
CHANGEPASSWORD	Change your password*
CHANGES	Account and Billing*
CHANNELC	CNN Newsroom Online
CHAT	People Connection
CHECKFREE	CheckFree
CHESS	Play-By-Mail & Strategy Gaming Forum
CHICAGO	Chicago Online
CHICAGOONLINE	Chicago Online
CHICAGOTRIBUNE	Chicago Tribuone
CHICO	California State University
CHRISTIAN	Religion & Ethics Forum
CHRISTIANS	Religion & Ethics Forum
CKFREE	CheckFree
CLARIS	Claris
CLASSES	Interactive Education Services
CLASSIFIED	Classifieds Online
CLASSIFIEDS	Classifieds Online
CLASSIFIEDSONLINE	Classifieds Online
CLINTON	White House Forum
CLOCK	Time of day and length of time online
CLUBPERFORMA	Apple Club Performa
CLUBS	Lifestyles & Interests Department
CMT	Coda Music Tech
CNN	CNN Newsroom Online
CNNNEWSROOM	CNN Newsroom Online
COBOL	Development Forum†
CODA	Coda Music Tech
CODAMUSIC	Coda Music Tech
COINS	The Exchange
COL	Chicago Online
COLCHAT	Chicago Online Chat
COLLIFESTYLES	Chicago Online Lifestyles
COLEDUCATION	Chicago Online Education
COLMARKETPLACE	Chicago Online Marketplace
COLNEWS	Chicago Online News, Business & Weather
COLPLANNER	Chicago Online Planner
COLSPORTS	Chicago Online Sports
COLLECTING	The Exchange
COLLEGE	College Board
COLLEGEBOARD	College Board
COLORIMAGING	Advanced Color Imaging Forum
COLORWEATHERMAPS	Color Weather Maps
COLUMNISTS	Columnists & Features Online

COLUMNS	Columnists & Features Online
COMMANDO	Kim Komando's Komputer Clinic
COMMUNICATIONS	Communications/Telecom/Networking Forum†
COMMUNITYCENTER	Lifestyles & Interests Department
COMPANIES	Industry Connection
COMPANY	Hoover's Handbook of Company Profiles
COMPANYPROFILES	Hoover's Handbook of Company Profiles
COMPAQ	Compaq
COMPOSER	Composer's Coffeehouse
COMPOSERS	Composer's Coffeehouse
COMPTONS	Encyclopedia
COMPUSTORE	Comp-u-Store Gateway
COMPUTE	Compute
COMPUTER	Computing Department†
COMPUTERAMERICA	Craig Crossman's Computer America
COMPUTEREXPRESS	Computer Express
COMPUTERLAW	CyberLaw, Cyberlex
COMPUTERPERIPHERALS	Computer Peripherals, Inc.
COMPUTERTERMS	Dictionary of Computer Terms
COMPUTING	Computing Department†
COMPUTOON	CompuToon area
COMPUTOON	CompuToon area
CONFERENCE	Weekly calendar of forum activity
CONFERENCECENTER	Weekly calendar of forum activity
CONFIG	Tune Up Your PC
CONNECTIX	Connectix
CONSERVATION	Backpacker Magazine
CONSUMER	Consumer Reports
CONSUMERREPORTS	Consumer Reports
CONSUMERS	Consumer Reports
CONTACTS	Employer Contacts
COOKBOOK	Celebrity Cookbook
COOKING	Cooking Club
COOPER	JLCooper Electronics
COSA	Company of Science and Art
COSN	Consortium for School Networking
COSTAR	CoStar
COURSES	Interactive Education Services
COURTROOMTELEVISION	Court TV
COURTTV	Court TV
COWLES	Cowles/SIMBA Media Information Network
COWLESSIMBA	Cowles/SIMBA Media Information Network
CPI	Computer Peripherals, Inc.
CPS	Central Point Software
CRAFTS	The Exchange
CRAIGCROSSMAN	Craig Crossman's Computer America
CREDIT	Credit for connect problems*
CREDITREQUEST	Credit for connect problems*
CRITICS	Critic's Choice
CRITICSCHOICE	Critic's Choice
CROSSMAN	Craig Crossman's Computer America
CRYSTALBALL	Advice & Tips
CSLIVE	Tech Help Live*
CSPAN	C-SPAN
CSPANCLASSROOM	C-SPAN Educational Services
CSPANONLINE	C-SPAN
CSUC	California State University
CURRICULUM	Assoc. for Supervisor & Curriculum Development
CUSTOMERSERVICE	Member Services*
CYBERLAW	CyberLaw, Cyberlex
CYBERLEX	CyberLaw, Cyberlex
DACEASY	DacEasy, Inc.
DANCINGRABBIT	Dancing Rabbit Creations
DARTS	Darts [Apple II only]
DATABASE	Database Support SIG
DATABASES	Database Support SIG
DATAPAK	DataPak Software
DATAWATCH	Datawatch
DATING	Romance Connection message boards
DAVIDSON	Davidson & Associates
DAYNA	Dayna Communications
DAYSTAR	Daystar Digital
DCCOMICS	DC Comics Online Preview
DCOPREVIEW	DC Comics Online Preview
DEAD	Grateful Dead Forum
DEADSEA	Library of Congress Online
DEAF	DisABILITIES Forum
DEBATE	Express Yourself
DEBATEFORUM	Issues and Debate Forum
DECISION	Decision Point Forum
DECISIONPOINT	Decision Point Forum
DELL	Dell Computer Corporation
DELRINA	Delrina Corporation
DELTAPOINT	Delta Point
DELTATAO	Delta Tao
DEMOCRACY	CNN Newsroom Online
DENEBA	Deneba Software
DES	DeskMate
DESKMATE	DeskMate
DESKTOPPUBLISHING	Desktop Publishing area†
DEV	Development Forum†
DEVELOPER	Development Forum†
DEVELOPMENT	Development Forum†
DEVELOPMENTFORUM	Development Forum†
DFFOOD	Destination Florida: Restaurants and Nightlife
DFOUT	Destination Florida: Outdoors
DFPARKS	Destination Florida: Attractions
DFROOMS	Destination Florida: Places to Stay
DFSHOP	Destination Florida: Shopping
DFSPORTS	Destination Florida: Sports
DFX	Digital F/X
DIALOGUE	American Dialogue
DIAMOND	Diamond Computer Systems
DIGISOFT	DYA/Digisoft Innovations
DIGITAL	Digital Vision
DIGITALECLIPSE	Digital Eclipse

DIGITALF/X	Digital F/X
DIGITALRESEARCH	Novell Desktop Systems
DIGITALRESEARCHINC	Novell Desktop Systems
DIGITALTECH	Disney Technologies
DILBERT	Dilbert Cartoon area
DILBERTCOMICS	Dilbert Cartoon area
DINE	Wine & Dine Online
DIPLOMATS	Diplomats in the Classroom
DIRECT	Direct Software
DIRECTORY	Member Directory
DIRECTORYOFSERVICES	Directory of Services
DIROFSERVICES	Directory of Services
DIROFSVCS	Directory of Services
DIS	DisABILITIES Forum
DISABILITIES	DisABILITIES Forum
DISABILITY	DisABILITIES Forum
DISCOVER	Discover AOL area
DISNEY	Disney Adventures Magazine
DISNEYADVENTURES	Disney Adventures Magazine
DISNEYMAGAZINE	Disney Adventures Magazine
DISNEYSOFTWARE	Disney/Buene Vista Software
DOLBY	Dolby Audio/Video Forum
DOLBYAUDIO/VIDEO	Dolby Audio/Video Forum
DONTMISS	Directory of Services
DOS	DOS Forum
DOS5.0	DOS Forum
DOS6	MS-DOS 6.0 Resource Center
DOS60	MS-DOS 6.0 Resource Center
DOSFORUM	DOS Forum
DOSOMETHING	Do Something!
DOWNLOAD	Software Center†
DOWNLOADCREDIT	Credit for connect problems*
DOWNLOADGAMES	Free online game downloading*
DOWNLOADING	Software Center†
DP	Decision Point Forum
DPA	Decision Point Forum
DRDOS	DOS Forum
DREAMWORLD	Dreamworld
DRI	Novell Desktop Systems
DRIVING	Car and Driver Magazine
DTP	Desktop Publishing area†
DTSPORTS	DataTimes Sports Reports
DUBLCLICK	Dubl-Click Software
DYNAWARE	Dynaware USA
DYNAWAREUSA	Dynaware USA
DYNO	Portfolio Systems, Inc.
EAASY	EAASY SABRE
EARTH	Environmental Forum
EARTH	Network Earth
EASSYSABRE	EAASY SABRE
EASYSABRE	EAASY SABRE
EBBS	EBBS
ECON	Econ Technologies
ECOTOURISM	Backpacker Magazine
ECS	Electronic Courseware
EDFORUM	Education Forum
EDITPROFILE	Edit your member profile*
EDMARK	Edmark Technologies
EDTECH	Assoc. for Supervisor & Curriculum Development
EDTV	KIDSNET Forum
EDUCATION	Education Department
EFF	Electronic Frontier Foundation
EFORUM	Environmental Forum
ELECTRIC	Electric Image
ELECTRICIMAGE	Electric Image
ELECTRONICCOURSEWARE	Electronic Courseware
ELECTRONICS	Gadget Guru Electronics Forum
EMERGENCY	Emergency Response Club
EMERGENCYRESPONSE	Emergency Response Club
EMIGRE	Emigre Fonts
EN/X	Energy Express
ENCYCLOPEDIA	Encyclopedia
ENDER	Hatrack River Town Meeting
ENDNOTE	Niles and Associates
ENERGYEXPRESS	Energy Express
ENGLISH	Nat'l Council of Teachers of English
ENTERTAINMENT	Entertainment Department
ENVIRONMENT	Environmental Forum
ERC	Emergency Response Club
ERIC	AskERIC
ESH	Electronic Schoolhouse
ETHICS	Ethics and Religion Forum
EUN	Electronic University Network
EXAMPREP	Exam Prep Center
EXCHANGE	The Exchange
EXPERT	Expert Software, Inc
EXPERTSOFT	Expert Software, Inc
EXPRESSMUSIC	Bose Express Music
EXPRESSYOURSELF	Express Yourself
FANTASYFOOTBALL	The Grandstand
FANTASYLEAGUES	The Grandstand
FARALLON	Farallon
FAX	Fax/Paper Mail
FEATURES	Columnists & Features Online
FEEDBACK	Member Services*
FELLOWSHIP	Fellowship of Online Gamers/RPGA Network
FFGF	Free-Form Gaming Forum
FIFTH	Fifth Generation
FILESEARCH	Search database of files
FINANCE	Personal Finance Department
FLIGHT	Flight Sim Resource Center
FLIGHTSIMS	Flight Sim Resource Center
FLIGHTSIMULATIONS	Flight Sim Resource Center
FLORIDA	Destination Florida
FLOWERSHOP	Flower Shop

FLY	Aviation Club
FLYING	Flying Magazine
FLYINGMAGAZINE	Flying Magazine
FOCUS	Focus Enhancements
FOCUSENHANCEMENTS	Focus Enhancements
FOG	Fellowship of Online Gamers/RPGA Network
FONTBANK	FontBank
FOOD	Cooking Club
FOOTBALL	The Grandstand
FORMZ	auto*des*sys, Inc.
FORUM	Computing Department†
FORUMAUD	Rotunda Forum Auditorium
FORUMAUDITORIUM	Rotunda Forum Auditorium
FORUMROT	Rotunda Forum Auditorium
FORUMS	Computing Department†
FRACTAL	Fractal Design
FRACTALDESIGN	Fractal Design
FRANKLIN	Franklin Quest
FREE	Member Services
FRIEND	Sign on a friend to AOL*
FSRC	Flight Sim Resource Center
FULLWRITE	FullWrite
FUND	Morningstar Mutual Funds
FUNDS	Morningstar Mutual Funds
FUTURELABS	Future Labs, Inc.
GADGETGURU	Gadget Guru Electronics Forum
GALLERY	Portrait Gallery
GAMEBASE	Game Base
GAMEDESIGN	Game Designers Forum
GAMEDESIGNER	Game Designers Forum
GAMEDESIGNERS	Game Designers Forum
GAMEROOMS	Games Parlor
GAMES	Entertainment Department
GAMES&ENTERTAINMENT	Entertainment Department
GAMESDOWNLOADING	Free online games downloading*
GAMESFORUM	Games and Entertainment Forum
GAMESFORUM	Games Forum†
GAMESPARLOR	Games Parlor
GAMING	Online Gaming Forums
GARDENING	The Exchange
GATEWAY	Gateway 2000, Inc
GATEWAY2000	Gateway 2000, Inc
GAY	Gay & Lesbian Community Forum
GCC	GCC Technologies
GCS	Gaming Company Support
GENEALOGY	Genealogy Club
GENEALOGYCLUB	Genealogy Club
GENERALMAGIC	General Magic
GEO	GeoWorks
GEOGRAPHIC	National Geographic Online
GEOWORKS	GeoWorks
GERALDO	The Geraldo Show
GERALDOSHOW	The Geraldo Show

GETTINGSTARTED	Beginners' Forum
GETTINGSTARTEDFORUM	Beginners' Forum
GFL	The Grandstand
GIFCONVERTER	GIF Converter
GIFTED	Giftedness Forum
GIX	Gaming Information Exchange
GLCF	Gay & Lesbian Community Forum
GLOBAL	Global Village Communication
GLOBALVILLAGE	Global Village Communication
GOLF	Sport News area
GOLFCOURSES	Golf Courses & Resort Information
GOLFRESORTS	Golf Courses & Resort Information
GOLFIS	Golf Courses & Resort Information
GOPHER	Internet Gopher & WAIS
GOSCUBA	Scuba Club
GOTAX	Tax Forum
GRANDSTAND	The Grandstand
GRAPHICARTS	Graphics Forum†
GRAPHICS	Graphics Forum†
GRAPHICSFORUM	Graphics Forum†
GRAPHICSIMULATIONS	Graphic Simulations
GRAPHISOFT	Graphisoft
GRATEFULDEAD	Grateful Dead Forum
GRAVIS	Advanced Gravis
GROUPWARE	GroupWare SIG
GRYPHON	Gryphon Software
GRYPHONSOFTWARE	Gryphon Software
GSMAG	GS+ Magazine
GSS	Global Software Suport
GTSF	Beginners' Forum
GUIDEPAGE	Page a Guide
GUIDEPAGER	Page a Guide
GUILD	Online Gaming Forums
HALLOFFAME	Downloading Hall of Fame
HAM	Ham Radio Club
HAMRADIO	Ham Radio Club
HANDLE	Add, change or delete screen names
HARDWARE	Hardware Forum†
HARDWARECOMPANIES	Industry Connection
HARDWAREFORUM	Hardware Forum†
HATRACK	Hatrack River Town Meeting
HATRACKRIVETTOWN	Hatrack River Town Meeting
HBSPUB	Harvard Business School Publishing
HCSSOFTWARE	HSC Software
HDC	hDC Corporation
HDCCORPORATION	hDC Corporation
HEADLINES	Top News area
HEALTH	Better Health & Medical Forum
HELIOS	Helios USA
HELIOSUSA	Helios USA
HELP	Member Services*
HELPDESK	The Help Desk
HELPWANTED	Search Help Wanted USA

Keyword	Area
HERITAGEFOUNDATION	Heritage Foundation area
HIGHLIGHTS	AOL Highlights Tour
HIKER	Backpacker Magazine
HIKING	Backpacker Magazine
HISPANIC	The Exchange
HOBBIES	Clubs & Interests Department
HOCKEY	The Grandstand
HOLIDAY	AOL Holiday Central
HOLLYWOOD	Hollywood Online
HOLLYWOODONLINE	Hollywood Online
HOME	Homeowner's Forum
HOMEBREW	Wine & Dine Online
HOMEBREWING	Wine & Dine Online
HOMEEQUITYLOAN	Real Estate Online
HOMEOFFICE	Home Office Computing Magazine
HOMEOWNER	Homeowner's Forum
HOMEOWNERSFORUM	Homeowner's Forum
HOMEPC	HomePC Magazine
HOMEREFINANCING	Real Estate Online
HOMETHEATER	Stereo Review Online magazine
HOMEWORK	Academic Assistance Center
HOOVERS	Hoover's Handbook of Company Profiles
HOROSCOPE	Horoscopes
HOROSCOPES	Horoscopes
HORSERACING	The Grandstand
HOT	What's Hot This Month showcase
HOTLINE	Members' Online Support*
HROSSPEROT	Ross Perot/United We Stand area
HSC	HSC Software
HYPERCARD	HyperCard Forum
IBM	IBM Connection
IBMOS2	OS/2 Forum
IBVA	IBVA Technologies
IC	Industry Connection
ICF	International Corporate Forum
ICOM	Viacom New Media
ICOMSIMULATIONS	Viacom New Media
ICS	International Correspondence Schools
IES	Interactive Education Services
IIN	Redate/IIN Online
IMAGING	Advanced Color Imaging Forum
IMH	Issues in Mental Health
IMPACTII	IMPACT II: The Teachers Network
IMPROV	The Improv Forum
IMPROVCLUB	The Improv Forum
IMPROVCLUBS	The Improv Forum
IMPROVFORUM	The Improv Forum
INCIDER	inCider
INDUSTRY	Industry Connection
INDUSTRYCONNECTION	Industry Connection
INFOCOM	Infocom
INFORMATION	Member Services
INLINE	Inline Design
INLINESOFTWARE	Inline Design
INSIDEMEDIA	Cowles/SIMBA Media Information Network
INSIDETECH	Inside Technology
INSIDETECHNOLOGY	Inside Technology
INSIGNIA	Insignia Solutions
INTEL	Intel Corporation
INTELLIMATION	Intellimation
INTERACTIVEDUCATION	Interactive Education Services
INTERACTIVEED	Interactive Education Services
INTERCON	InterCon Systems Corporation
INTEREST	Clubs & Interests Department
INTERNATIONAL	International House
INTERNET	Internet Center
INTERNETCENTER	Internet Center
INTERPLAY	Interplay
INTHENEWS	Mercury Center In the News area
INVESTING	Investors Network
INVESTMENTS	Investors Network
INVESTORS	Investors Network
INVESTORSNETWORK	Investors Network
IOMEGA	Iomega Corporation
IPA	Advanced Color Imaging Forum
ISIS	ISIS International
ISISINTERNATIONAL	ISIS International
ISLAM	Religion & Ethics Forum
ISLANDGRAPHICS	Island Graphics Corporation
ISSUES	Issues and Debate Forum
ISSUESANDDEBATE	Issues and Debate Forum
IYM	IYM Software Review
IYMSOFTWAREREVIEW	IYM Software Review
JLCOOPER	JLCooper Electronics
JOBS	Job Listings Database
JPEGVIEW	JPEGView
JUDAISM	Religion & Ethics Forum
KAPLAN	Kaplan Online
KEEFE	Mike Keefe Cartoons
KENSINGTON	Kensington Microware, Ltd.
KENTMARSH	Kent*Marsh
KIDDESK	Edmark Technologies
KIDNET	KIDSNET Forum
KIDSNET	KIDSNET
KIDSONLY	Kids Only Online
KITCHEN	Cooking Club
KIWI	Kiwi Software, Inc.
KNOWLEDGEBASE	Microsoft Knowledge Base
KOALA	Koala/MacVision
KODAK	Kodak Photography Forum
KOMANDO	Kim Komando's Komputer Clinic
KOMPUTERTUTOR	Kim Komando's Komputer Clinic
KOOL	Kids Only Online
KPT	HSC Software
LABNET	TERC LabNet
LAMBDA	Gay & Lesbian Community Forum

LANGUAGESYS	SYS Language Systems
LAPIS	Lapis Technologies
LAPISTECHNOLOGIES	Lapis Technologies
LAPUB	LaPub
LAWRENCE	Lawrence Productions
LEADER	Leader Technologies
LEADERTECH	Leader Technologies
LEADERTECHNOLOGIES	Leader Technologies
LEADINGEDGE	Leading Edge
LEARN	Education Department
LEARNING	Education Department
LEARNING&REFERENCE	Education Department
LEARNINGANDREFERENCE	Education Department
LEARNINGCENTER	Education Department
LEGAL	Legal SIG
LEGALSIG	Legal SIG
LESBIAN	Gay & Lesbian Community Forum
LETRASET	Letraset
LETTER	A Letter From Steve Case*
LIBERTARIAN	Libertarian Party Forum
LIBRARIES	Software Center†
LIBRARY	Library of Congress Online
LIBS	Software Center†
LIFESTYLES	Clubs & Interests Department
LIFESTYLES&HOBBIES	Clubs & Interests Department
LIFESTYLES&INTEREST	Clubs & Interests Department
LIFESTYLES&INTERESTS	Clubs & Interests Department
LIFETIME	Lifetime Television
LIFETIMETELEVISION	Lifetime Television
LIFETIMETV	Lifetime Television
LINKS	Access Software
LINKSWARE	LinksWare, Inc.
LISTINGS	TMS TV Source
LITERACY	Adult Literacy Forum
LITERATURE	Saturday Review Online
LOC	Library of Congress Online
LOCALNEWSPAPERS	Local Newspapers
LUCAS	LucasArts Games
LUCASARTS	LucasArts Games
MAC	Mac Computing & Software department
MAC500	Mac Shareware 500
MACART	Graphic Art & CAD Forum
MACBIBLE	The Macintosh Bible/Peachpit Forum
MACBUSINESS	Business Forum
MACCOMMUNICATION	Mac Communications Forum
MACCOMMUNICATIONS	Mac Communications Forum
MACCOMPUTING	Mac Computing & Software department
MACDESKTOP	Mac Desktop Publishing/WP Forum
MACDEVELOPMENT	Mac Development Forum
MACDTP	Mac Desktop Publishing/WP Forum
MACEDUCATION	Mac Education Forum
MACGAME	Mac Games Forum
MACGAMES	Mac Games Forum

MACGRAPHICS	Mac Graphic Art & CAD Forum
MACHARDWARE	Mac Hardware Forum
MACHOME	MacHome Journal
MACHOMEJOURNAL	MacHome Journal
MACHYPERCARD	Mac HyperCard Forum
MACINTOSH	Mac Computing & Software department
MACINTOSHBIBLE	The Macintosh Bible/Peachpit Forum
MACLIBRARIES	Mac Software Center
MACMULTIMEDIA	Mac Multimedia Forum
MACMUSIC	Mac Music & Sound Forum
MACO/S	Mac Operating Systems Forum
MACOPERATINGSYSTEMS	Mac Operating Systems Forum
MACOS	Mac Operating Systems Forum
MACPROGRAMMING	Mac Development Forum
MACROMEDIA	MacroMedia, Inc.
MACROMIND	MacroMedia, Inc.
MACSOFTWARE	Mac Software Center
MACSOUND	Mac Music & Sound Forum
MACSPEAKERZ	True Image Audio
MACTECH	MacTech Magazine
MACTECHMAG	MacTech Magazine
MACTECHMAGAZINE	MacTech Magazine
MACTELECOM	Mac Communications Forum
MACTELECOMM	Mac Communications Forum
MACTIVITY	Mactivity '94 Forum
MACUTILITIES	Mac Utilities Forum
MACVISION	Koala/MacVision
MACWORLD	MacWorld Magazine
MACWORLDEXPO	MacWorld Expo Center
MACWORLDPROCESSING	Mac Desktop Publishing/WP Forum
MADA	MacApp Developers Association
MAGAZINES	The Newsstand
MAILGATEWAY	Mail Gateway
MAIN	Reset Department menu to initial department [Apple II users only]*
MAINSTY	Mainstay
MALL	Marketplace
MALLARD	Mallard Software
MANHATTANGRAPHICS	Manhattan Graphics (RSG)
MANUAL	Members' Online Support*
MARKET	Market Master
MARKETFIELD	Marketfield Software
MARKETMASTER	Market Master
MARKETNEWS	Market News area
MARKETS	Market News area
MARTINSEN	Martinsen's Software
MASS	Massachusetts Governor's Forum
MASSACHUSETTS	Massachusetts Governor's Forum
MASTERWORD	MasterWord
MAXIS	Maxis
MBS	Business Forum
MC	Military City Online
MCAFEE	McAfee Associates

MCBUSINESS	Mercury Center Business & Technology area
MCCLASSIFIEDS	Mercury Center Advertising
MCENTERTAINMENT	Mercury Center Entertainment area
MCLIBRARY	Mercury Center Newspaper Library
MCLIVING	Mercury Center Bay Area Living area
MCM	Communications Forum
MCMARKET	Mercury Center Advertising
MCNEW	Mercury Center In the News area
MCNEWS	Mercury Center In the News area
MCO	Military City Online
MCSPORTS	Mercury Center Sports area
MCTALK	Mercury Center Conference area
MDP	Mac Desktop Publishing/WP Forum
MDV	Mac Development Forum
MECC	MECC
MED	Mac Education Forum
MEDIAINFORMATION	Cowles/SIMBA Media Information Network
MEDICINE	Better Health & Medical Forum
MEMBERDIRECTORY	Member Directory
MEMBERPROFILE	Edit your member profile*
MEMBERS	Member Directory
MEMBERSGUIDE	Members' Online Support*
MEMBERSONLINEGUIDE	Members' Online Support*
MEN	The Exchange
MENSA	Giftedness Forum
MERCURY	Mercury Center
MERCURYCENTER	Mercury Center
MERIDIAN	Meridian Data
MESSAGEPAD	Personal Digital Assistants Forum
METROWERKS	Metrowerks
METZ	Metz
MGM	Mac Games Forum
MGR	Mac Graphic Art & CAD Forum
MGX	Micrografx, Inc.
MHC	Mac HyperCard Forum
MHM	Members Helping Members message board*
MHW	Mac Hardware Forum
MICHAELREAGAN	The Michael Reagan Show Online
MICHAELREAGANSHOW	The Michael Reagan Show Online
MICHIGAN	Michigan Governor's Forum
MICHIGANGOVERNOR	Michigan Governor's Forum
MICRODYNAMICS	Micro Dynamics, Ltd.
MICROFRONTIER	MicroFrontier, Ltd.
MICROGRAFX	Micrografx, Inc.
MICROJ	Micro J Systems, Inc.
MICROMAT	MicroMat Computer Systems
MICRON	Xceed Technology
MICROPROSE	MicroProse
MICROSEEDS	Microseeds Publishing, Inc.
MICROSOFT	Microsoft Resource Center
MIDI	Graphics and Sound Forum
MIDI	Mac Music & Sound Forum
MIDI	PC Music and Sound Forum
MILITARY	Military and Vets Club
MILITARYCITYONLINE	Military City Online
MIRROR	Mirror Technologies
MLS	Real Estate Online
MMM	Mac Multimedia Forum
MMS	Mac Music & Sound Forum
MMW	Multimedia World Online [PC platform only]
MMWORLD	Multimedia World Online [PC platform only]
MOBILE	Mobile Office Online
MODEMHELP	Modem Help area* [PC platform only]
MOG	Members' Online Support*
MONEY	Business News area
MONSTERISLAND	Adventures by Mail
MONTESSORI	Montessori Schools
MOO	Gateway 2000, Inc
MORAFFWARE	MoraffWare
MORNINGSTAR	Morningstar Mutual Funds
MORPH	Gryphon Software
MORTAGE	Real Estate Online
MORTAGERATES	Real Estate Online
MORTGAGES	Real Estate Online
MOS	Mac Operating Systems Forum
MOUNTAINBIKE	Bicycling Magazine
MOVIEREVIEWS	Movies menu
MOVIES	Movies menu
MOVIES	Movies menu
MS-DOS	DOS Forum
MS-DOSFORUM	DOS Forum
MSA	Management Science Associates
MSDOS6	MS-DOS 6.0 Resource Center
MSDOS60	MS-DOS 6.0 Resource Center
MSFORUM	Microsoft Product Support
MSKB	Microsoft Knowledge Base
MSSUPPORT	Microsoft Resource Center
MSTATION	Bentley Systems, Inc.
MTC	Communications Forum
MTV	MTV Online
MUG	AOL Products Center
MULTIMEDIA	The Multimedia Exchange
MUSIC	Rocklink
MUSIC&SOUND	Graphics and Sound Forum†
MUSICANDSOUNDFORUM	Graphics and Sound Forum†
MUSICFORUM	Graphics and Sound Forum†
MUSTANG	Mustang Software
MUSTANGSOFTWARE	Mustang Software
MUT	Mac Utilities Forum
MUTUALFUND	Morningstar Mutual Funds
MUTUALFUNDS	Morningstar Mutual Funds
MVT	Mac Utilities Forum
MW	MasterWord
MWORD	MasterWord

NAESP	National Principals Center
NAME	Add, change or delete screen names
NAMES	Add, change or delete screen names
NAMI	National Alliance of Mentally Ill
NAPC	Employment Agency Database
NAQP	National Association of Quick Printers area
NATIONALGEOGRAPHIC	National Geographic Online
NBC	NBC Online
NBR	The Nightly Business Report
NBRREPORT	The Nightly Business Report
NCTE	Nat'l Council of Teachers of English
NEAONLINE	National Education Association
NEAPUBLIC	National Education Association
NEC	NEC Technologies
NECTECH	NEC Technologies
NEOLOGIC	NeoLogic
NETWORKEARTH	Network Earth
NETWORKING	Communications/Telecom/Networking Forum†
NETWORKINGFORUM	Communications/Telecom/Networking Forum†
NEVERWINTER	AD&D Neverwinter Nights
NEW	New Features & Services showcase
NEWAGE	Relgion & Ethics Forum
NEWERA	Tactic Software
NEWLINK	Beginners' Forum
NEWMAIL	New Mail Information area*
NEWREPUBLIC	The New Republic Magazine
NEWS	Today's News Department
NEWS&FINANCE	Today's News Department
NEWS/SPORTS/MONEY	Today's News Department
NEWSANDFINANCE	Today's News Department
NEWSBYTES	Newsbytes
NEWSGROUPS	Internet Usenet Newsgroup area
NEWSLINK	Top News area
NEWSPAPER	Local Newspapers
NEWSPAPERS	Local Newspapers
NEWSROOM	News & Finance Department
NEWSSEARCH	Search News Articles
NEWSSTAND	The Newsstand
NEWSTEXT	Top News area
NEWSWATCH	Search News Articles
NEWTON	Personal Digital Assistant's Forum
NEWWORLD	New World Computing
NEWYORK	@times/The New York Times Online
NEWYORKCITY	@times/The New York Times Online
NEWYORKTIMES	@times/The New York Times Online
NGLTF	Nation Gay & Lesbian Task Force
NGS	National Geographic Online
NIKON	Nikon Electronic Imaging
NILES	Niles and Associates
NINTENDO	Video Games area
NLF	Beginners' Forum
NMAA	National Museum of American Art
NMSS	National Multiple Sclerosis Society
NOHANDS	No Hands Software
NOMADIC	Nomadic Computing Discussion SIG
NORTON	Symantec
NOVELL	Novell Desktop Systems
NOW	Now Software
NOWPLAYING	Directory of Services
NPR	National Public Radio Outreach
NSDC	National Staff Development Council
NSS	National Space Society
NUMBERS	Local access numbers*
NWN	AD&D Neverwinter Nights
NYC	@times/The New York Times Online
NYT	@times/The New York Times Online
NYTIMES	@times/The New York Times Online
OADD	AD&D Neverwinter Nights
OBJECTFACTORY	Object Factory
ODEON	Odeon Auditorium
OFFICE	Penny Wise Office Products Store
OFFICEPRODUCTS	Penny Wise Office Products Store
OGF	Online Gaming Forums
OLDUVAI	Olduvai Software, Inc.
OLT	OnLine Tonight
OMNI	OMNI Magazine Online
OMNIMAGAZINE	OMNI Magazine Online
ON	ON Technology
ONLINEBOOKSTORE	Online Bookstore
ONLINEGAMING	Online Gaming Forums
ONLINEGUIDE	Members' Online Support
ONLINETONIGHT	OnLine Tonight
ONYX	Onyx Technology
OPCODE	Opcode Systems, Inc.
OPCODESYSTEMS	Opcode Systems, Inc.
OPTIMAGE	OptImage Interactive Services
OPTIMAS	OPTIMAS Corporation
ORIGIN	Origin Systems
ORIGINSYSTEMS	Origin Systems
ORSONSCOTTCARD	Hatrack River Town Meeting
OS2	OS/2 Forum
OSTWO	OS/2 Forum
OTTER	Otter Solution
OTTERSOLUTION	Otter Solution
OURWORLD	Top News area
OUTDOORGEAR	Backpacker Magazine
OUTDOORS	The Exchange
PACEMARK	PaceMark Technologies, Inc.
PACKER	Packer Software
PAGAN	Religion & Ethics Forum
PALM	Palm Computing
PALMCOMPUTING	Palm Computing
PALMTOP	Personal Digital Assistants Forum
PAP	Applications Forum
PAPERMAIL	Fax/Paper Mail
PAPYRUS	Papyrus

Keyword	Destination
PARENT	Parents' Information Network
PARENTALCONTROL	Parental Controls
PARLOR	Games Parlor
PASCAL	Development Forum†
PASSPORT	Passport Designs
PASSWORD	Change your password*
PBM	Play-By-Mail & Strategy Gaming Forum
PC	People Connection
PCANIMATION	PC Graphics Forum
PCAPPLICATIONS	PC Applications Forum
PCAPPLICATIONSFORUM	PC Applications Forum
PCAPS	PC Applications Forum
PCAUD	Center Stage auditorium
PCBEGINNERS	Beginners' Forum
PCBG	Beginners' Forum
PCCATALOG	PC Catalog
PCCATALOG	PC Catalog
PCCLASSIFIEDS	Browse the PC Catalog
PCCLASSIFIEDS	PC Catalog
PCDESKMATE	DeskMate
PCDEV	PC Development Forum
PCDEVELOPMENT	PC Development Forum
PCDEVELOPMENTFORUM	PC Development Forum
PCDM	DeskMate
PCEXPO	Redgate Online > PC Expo area
PCFORUMS	PC Computing & Software department
PCGAMES	PC Games Forum
PCGAMESFORUM	PC Games Forum
PCGRAPHICS	PC Graphics Forum
PCGRAPHICSFORUM	PC Graphics Forum
PCHARDWARE	PC Hardware Forum
PCHARDWAREFORUM	PC Hardware Forum
PCHELP	Beginners' Forum
PCHQ	Tandy Headquarters
PCLIBRARIES	PC Software Center
PCM	PC Telecom/Networking Forum
PCMU	PC Music and Sound Forum
PCMUSIC	PC Music and Sound Forum
PCMUSICANDSOUNDFORUM	PC Music and Sound Forum
PCMUSICFORUM	PC Music and Sound Forum
PCNOVICE	PC Novice & PC Today Online
PCPC	Personal Computer Peripherals
PCSECURITY	Computing & Software department†
PCSOFTWARE	PC Software Center
PCSOFTWARE	PC Software Center
PCSOUND	PC Music and Sound Forum
PCSOUNDFORUM	PC Music and Sound Forum
PCSTUDIO	PC Studio
PCSW	PC Software Center
PCTELECOM	PC Telecom/Networking Forum
PCTELECOMFORUM	PC Telecom/Networking Forum
PCTODAY	PC Novice & PC Today Online
PCUTILITIES	DOS Forum
PCWONLINE	PCWorld Online
PCWORLD	PCWorld Online
PCWORLDONLINE	PCWorld Online
PDA	Personal Digital Assistant's Forum
PDV	PC Development Forum
PEACHPIT	The Macintosh Bible/Peachpit Forum
PEACHTREE	Peachtree Software
PENNY	Penny Wise Office Products Store
PENNYWISE	Penny Wise Office Products Store
PENPAL	Edmark Technologies
PENTIUM	Intel Corporation
PEOPLE	People Connection
PEOPLECONNECTION	People Connection
PERFORMA	Apple Club Performa
PERFORMACENTER	Apple Club Performa
PERFORMARESOURCE	Apple Club Performa
PEROT	Ross Perot/United We Stand area
PERSONALFINANCE	Personal Finance area
PET	Pet Care Club
PETCARE	Pet Care Club
PETERNORTON	Symantec
PETITIONS	Local access numbers*
PETS	Pet Care Club
PF	Personal Finance area
PGM	PC Games Forum
PGR	PC Graphics Forum
PHANTASYGUILD	Online Gaming Forums
PHOTO	Kodak Photography Forum
PHOTOS	Popular Photography Online
PHOTOGRAPHY	Photography Area
PHOTOSHOP	Photoshop SIG
PHOTOSHOPSIG	Photoshop SIG
PHW	PC Hardware Forum
PHYSICALLYDISABLED	DisABILITIES Forum
PICTURES	Pictures of the World
PIN	Parents' Information Network
PIXAR	Pixar
PIXEL	Pixel Resources
PIXELRESOURCES	Pixel Resources
PLAY-BY-MAIL	Play-By-Mail & Strategy Gaming Forum
PLAYMATION	Playmation
PMM	PC Multimedia Forum
PMU	PC Music and Sound Forum
POLITICS	Bull Moose Tavern
POPPHOTO	Popular Photography Online
POPULARPHOTOGRAPHY	Popular Photography Online
PORTABLE	Mobile Office Online
PORTABLECOMPUTING	Mobile Office Online
PORTFOLIO	Your Stock Portfolio
PORTFOLIOSOFTWARE	Portfolio Systems, Inc.
POWERBOOK	PowerBook Reserouce Center
POWERMAC	Power Mac Resource Center
POWERPC	Power Mac Resource Center

POWERUP	Power Up Software
PPI	Practical Peripherals, Inc.
PRACTICALPERIPHERALS	Practical Peripherals, Inc.
PRAIRIESOFT	PrairieSoft, Inc.
PRC	Apple Club Performa
PRESS	AOL Press Release Library
PRESSRELEASE	AOL Press Release Library
PREVENTION	Substance Abuse Forum
PRINCETONREVIEW	Student Access Online
PRINCIPALS	National Principals Center
PRODIGY	Prodigy Refugees' Forum
PRODIGYFORUM	Prodigy Refugees Forum
PRODIGYREFUGEES	Prodigy Refugees Forum
PRODUCTIVITY	Applications/Business/Productivity Forum†
PRODUCTIVITYFORUM	Applications/Business/Productivity Forum†
PROFILE	Edit your member profile*
PROGRAMMERU	Programmer University
PROGRAMMING	Development Forum†
PROGRAPH	Prograph International, Inc.
PROVUE	ProVUE Development
PS1	IBM Connection
PSION	Psion
PSL	IBM Connection
PSYCHICLABS	IBVA Technologies
PTC	PC Telecom/Networking Forum
PU	Programmer University
PUBLICRADIO	National Public Radio Outreach
PUBLISHERS	Industry Connection
PUNCHLINE	Comedy Club and Punchlines
QMMS	Mac Music & Sound Forum
QMODEM	Mustang Software
QUALITAS	Qualitas
QUARK	Quark, Inc.
QUE	The Quantum Que and Graffiti community message boards
QUEST	Adventures by Mail
QUICKFIND	Search database of files†
QUICKFINDER	Search database of files†
QUICKPRINTERS	National Association of Quick Printers area
QUOTE	Stock Market Timing & Charts area
QUOTES	Stock Market Timing & Charts area
RABBITJACKSCASINO	RabbitJack's Casino
RACING	Car and Driver Magazine
RADIO	Ham Radio Club
RADIUS	Radius, Inc.
RAILROADING	The Exchange
RASTEROPS	RasterOps
RAY	Ray Dream
RAYDREAM	Ray Dream
RDI	Free-Form Gaming Forum
REACTOR	Reactor
READ	Adult Literacy Forum
READING	Saturday Review Online
READUSA	Online Bookstore
REAGAN	The Michael Reagan Show Online
REALESTATE	Real Estate Online
RECCENTER	Entertainment Department
RECREATION	Entertainment Department
RECREATIONCENTER	Entertainment Department
REDGATE	Redgate/IIN Online
REFERENCE	Reference Desk
REFERENCEDESK	Reference Desk
REGISTER	IES Registration Center
REGISTRATION	IES Registration Center
RELIGION	Ethics and Religion Forum
RENDERMAN	Pixar
REPRISE	Warner/Reprise Records Online
RESEARCH	Academic Assistance Center
RESNOVA	ResNova Software (RESNOVASOFTWARE)
RESTAURANT	Wine & Dine Online
RESTAURANTS	Wine & Dine Online
RICKILAKE	The Ricki Lake Show
ROAD	Road & Track Magazine
ROADANDTRACK	Road & Track Magazine
ROCK	Rocklink
ROCKLAND	Rockland Software
ROCKLANDSOFTWARE	Rockland Software
ROCKLINK	Rocklink
ROGERWAGNER	Roger Wagner Publishing
ROLEPLAYING	Role-Playing Forum
ROMANCE	Romance Connection message boards
ROOTS	Genealogy Club
ROSSPEROT	Ross Perot/United We Stand area
ROTUNDA	Rotunda Forum Auditorium
RPG	Role-Playing Forum
RPGA	Fellowship of Online Gamers/RPGA Network
RPGANETWORK	Fellowship of Online Gamers/RPGA Network
SABRE	EAASY SABRE
SALIENT	Salient Software
SANJOSE	Mercury Center
SATELLITES	Ham Radio Club
SATREVIEW	Saturday Review Online
SATURDAYREVIEW	Saturday Review Online
SCHOLASTIC	Scholastic Network/Scholastic Forum
SCHOOLHOUSE	Electronic Schoolhouse
SCI-FI	Science Fiction Forum
SCIENCEFICTION	Science Fiction Forum
SCIFI	Science Fiction Forum
SCIFICHANNEL	The Sci-Fi Channel
SCOUTING	Scouting Forum
SCOUTS	Scouting Forum
SCREENNAME	Add, change or delete screen names
SCREENNAMES	Add, change or delete screen names
SCUBA	Scuba Club
SEGA	Video Games area
SENIOR	SeniorNet

Keyword	Destination
SERIUS	Serius
SERVICE	Member Services
SERVICES	Directory of Services
SERVICESDIRECTORY	Directory of Services
SF	Science Fiction Forum
SHAREWARE500	Mac Shareware 500
SHAREWARESOLUTIONS	Shareware Solutions
SHIVA	Shiva Corporation
SHOPPING	Marketplace
SHOPPING&TRAVEL	Marketplace
SHOPPINGANDTRAVEL	Marketplace
SHORTHAND	Online Shorthands
SHORTHANDS	Online Shorthands
SHOWS	Center Stage auditorium
SI	Smithsonian Online
SIERRA	Sierra On-Line
SIFS	Computing & Software department†
SIGNUP	IES Registration Center
SIGS	Computing & Software department†
SILICON	Hardware
SIMBA	Cowles/SIMBA Media Information Network
SIMULATOR	Games Forum†
SKI	Ski Reports
SKICONDITIONS	Ski Reports
SKIREPORTS	Ski Reports
SKIWEATHER	Ski Reports
SMITHSONIAN	Smithsonian Online
SOCEITY	Saturday Review Online
SOFT	Software Center†
SOFTARC	SoftArc
SOFTDISK	Softdisk Superstore [PC platform only]
SOFTSYNC	Expert Software, Inc
SOFTWARE	Software Center†
SOFTWARECENTER	Software Center†
SOFTWARECOMPANIES	Industry Connection
SOFTWARECREATIONS	Software Creations
SOFTWAREDIRECTORY	Software Center†
SOFTWAREHELP	Software Center†
SOFTWARELIBRARIES	Software Center†
SOFTWARELIBRARY	Software Center†
SOFTWAREPUBLISHERS	Industry Connection
SOFTWARETOOLWORKS	Software Toolworks
SOLIII	Sol III Play-by-Email Game
SOPHCIR	Sophisticated Circuits
SOS	Wall Street SOS Forum
SOVARC	Library of Congress Online
SOVIET	Library of Congress Online
SOVIETARCHIVES	Library of Congress Online
SPACE	National Space Society
SPECIALINTERESTS	Clubs & Interests Department
SPECTRUM	Spectrum HoloByte
SPECULAR	Specular International
SPORTS	Sport News area

Keyword	Destination
SPORTSLINK	Sport News area
SPORTSNEWS	Sport News area
SRO	Saturday Review Online
SSI	Strategic Simulations
SSSI	SSSi
STAC	STAC Electronics
STAMPS	The Exchange
STARTER	Beginners' Forum
STARTREK	Star Trek Club
STEREO	Stereo Review Online magazine
STEREOREVIEW	Stereo Review Online magazine
STF	STF Technologies
STFTECHNOLOGIES	STF Technologies
STOCK	Stock Market Timing & Charts area
STOCKCHARTS	Decision Point Forum
STOCKLINK	Stock Market Timing & Charts area
STOCKPORTFOLIO	Your Stock Portfolio
STOCKQUOTES	Stock Market Timing & Charts area
STOCKS	Stock Market Timing & Charts area
STOCKTIMING	Decision Point Forum
STORE	Marketplace
STORES	Marketplace
STRATA	Strata, Inc.
STRATEGIC	Strategic Simulations
STRATEGY	Play-By-Mail & Strategy Gaming Forum
STUDENT	Student Access Online
STUDENTACCESS	Student Access Online
STUDY	Study Skills Service
STUDYSKILLS	Study Skills Service
STUFFIT	Aladdin Systems, Inc.
STUMP	Rotunda Forum Auditorium
SUBSTANCEABUSE	Substance Abuse Forum
SUGGESTION	Suggestion boxes*
SUGGESTIONS	Suggestion boxes*
SUPERCARD	Hardware
SUPERDISK	Alysis Software
SUPERMAC	SuperMac
SUPPORT	Member Services
SURVIVOR	Survivor Software
SURVIVORSOFTWARE	Survivor Software
SWC	Software Creations
SYMANTEC	Symantec
SYNEX	Synex
SYSOP	Member Services
SYSTEM7	Mac Operating Systems Forum
SYSTEM7.0	Mac Operating Systems Forum
SYSTEM7.1	Mac Operating Systems Forum
SYSTEM71	Mac Operating Systems Forum
TACTIC	Tactic Software
TALENT	Talent Bank
TALK	People Connection
TALKSHOW	Future Labs, Inc.

TANDY	Tandy Headquarters
TANDYHANDQUARTERS	Tandy Headquarters
TANDYHQ	Tandy Headquarters
TAROT	Advice & Tips
TAX	Tax Forum [seasonal]
TAXES	Tax Forum [seasonal]
TEACHER	Teachers' Information Network
TEACHERPAGER	Teacher Pager
TEACHERS	Teachers' Information Network
TEACHERU	Teachers' University
TECHHELPLIVE	Tech Help Live*
TECHNOLOGY	Computing Department†
TECHNOLOGYWORKS	Technology Works
TECHWORKS	Technology Works
TEEN	Teen Scene message boards
TEENS	Teen Scene message boards
TEENSCENE	Teen Scene message boards
TEKNOSYS	Teknosys Works
TELECOM	Communications/Telecom/Networking Forum†
TELECOMFORUM	Communications/Telecom/Networking Forum†
TELECOMMUNICATIONS	Communications/Telecom/Networking Forum†
TELEPORT	Global Village Communication
TELESCAN	Telescan Users Group Forum
TELEVISION	Soap Opera Summaries
TENNIS	The Grandstand
TERMS	Terms of Service*
TERMSOFSERVICE	Terms of Service*
TESTPREP	Kaplan Online
TEXASINSTRUMENTS	Texas Instrument
TGS	Prograph International, Inc.
THEATER	Saturday Review Online
THEATRE	Saturday Review Online
THEDEAD	Grateful Dead Forum
THEEXCHANGE	The Exchange
THEMALL	Marketplace
THENEWREPUBLIC	The New Republic Magazine
THEWHITEHOUSE	White House Forum
THREESIXTY	Three-Sixty Software
THRUSTMASTER	Thrustmaster
THUNDERWARE	Thunderware
TI	Texas Instrument
TIA	True Image Audio
TICKET	Ticketmaster
TICKETMASTER	Chicago Online Ticketmaster
TIGER	TIGERDirect, Inc.
TIGERDIRECT	TIGERDirect, Inc.
TIME	Time Magazine Online
TIMES	@times/The New York Times Online
TIMESART	@times: Art & Photography
TIMESARTS	@times: The Arts
TIMESBOOKS	@times: Books of The Times
TIMESDINING	@times: Dining Out & Nightlife
TIMESLEISURE	@times: Leisure Guide

TIMESMOVIES	@times: Movies & Video
TIMESMUSIC	@times: Music & Dance
TIMESNEWS	@times/The New York Times Online
TIMESREGION	@times: In The Region
TIMESSPORTS	@times: Sports & Fitness
TIMESSTORIES	@times: Top Stories
TIMESTHEATER	@times: Theater
TIMESLIPS	Timeslips Corporation
TIMEWORKS	Timeworks
TIN	Teachers' Information Network
TIPS	Advice & Tips
TITF	Daily calender of forum activity
TMAKER	T/Maker
TMS	TMS TV Source
TNEWS	Teachers' Newsstand
TNPC	The National Parenting Center
TNR	The New Republic Magazine
TOMORROW	Tomorrow's Morning newspaper
TOMORROWSMORNING	Tomorrow's Morning newspaper
TOOLWORKS	Software Toolworks
TOPNEWS	Top News area
TOS	Terms of Service*
TOSADVISOR	Terms of Service*
TOTN	National Public Radio Outreach
TOUR	AOL Highlights Tour
TOURGUIDE	AOL Products Center
TRAILGUIDES	Backpacker Magazine
TRAILS	Backpacker Magazine
TRAINING	Career Development Training
TRAVEL	Travel Department
TRAVELER	Travel Forum
TRAVELERSCORNER	Traveler's Corner
TRAVELFORUM	Travel Forum
TRAVELHOLIDAY	Travel Holiday Magazine
TREK	Star Trek Club
TRIB	Chicago Tribuone
TRIBADS	Chicago Online Classifieds
TRIBCLASSIFIED	Chicago Online Classifieds
TRIBUNE	Chicago Tribune
TRIVIA	Trivia Club
TRUEIMAGEAUDIO	True Image Audio
TSENG	Tseng
TSHIRT	AOL Products Center
TTALK	Teachers' Forum
TUNEUP	Tune Up Your PC
TUNEUPYOURPC	Tune Up Your PC
TUTORING	Academic Assistance Center
TV	Television
TVGOSSIP	TV Gossip
TVGUIDE	TMS TV Source
TVLISTINGS	TMS TV Source
TVSOURCE	TMS TV Source
UA	Unlimited Adventures

Keyword	Area
UCPA	United Cerebral Palsy Association, Inc.
UGC	User Group Forum
UGF	User Group Forum
UHA	Homeowner's Forum
UNIQUE	Best of America Online showcase
UNIVERSITIES	Electronic University Network
UNIVERSITY	Electronic University Network
UNLIMITEDADVENTURES	Unlimited Adventures
UPGRADE	Upgrade to the latest version of AOL*
USENET	Internet Usenet Newsgroup area
USERGROUP	User Group Forum
USERGROUPS	User Group Forum
USERLAND	Userland
USERNAME	Add, change or delete screen names
USF	University of San Francisco
USMAIL	Fax/Paper Mail
USNEWS	U.S. & World News area
UTAH	Utah Forum
UTAHFORUM	Utah Forum
VACATIONS	Backpacker Magazine
VATICAN	Library of Congress Online
VDISC	Videodiscovery
VENTANA	Mac Shareware 500
VENTANA500	Mac Shareware 500
VERTISOFT	Vertisoft
VETERANS	Military and Vets Club
VETS	Military and Vets Club
VETSCLUB	Military and Vets Club
VIACOM	Viacom New Media
VIDEODISC	Videodiscovery
VIDEODISCOVERY	Videodiscovery
VIDEOGAMES	Video Games area
VIDEOSIG	Video SIG
VIDEOTOOLKIT	Abbate Video
VIDI	VIDI
VIEWPOINT	Viewpoint DataLabs
VIREX	Datawatch
VIRTUALREALITY	Virtual Reality Resource Center
VIRTUS	Virtus Walkthrough
VIRUS	Virus Information Center SIG
VISIONARY	Visionary Software
VOYAGER	The Voyager Company
VOYETRA	Voyetra Technologies
VR	Virtual Reality Resource Center
VRLI	Virtual Reality Labs, Inc.
WAIS	Internet Gopher & WAIS
WALKTHROUGH	Virtus Walkthrough
WARNER	Warner/Reprise Records Online
WARNERMUSIC	Warner/Reprise Records Online
WEATHER	Weather
WEATHERMAPS	Color Weather Maps
WEIGAND	Weigand Report
WEISSMANN	Traveler's Corner
WESTWOOD	Westwood Studios
WESTWOODSTUDIOS	Westwood Studios
WHATSHOT	What's Hot This Month showcase
WHITEHOUSE	White House Forum
WILDCAT	Mustang Software
WILDCATBBS	Mustang Software
WILDERNESS	Backpacker Magazine
WIN	Windows Forum
WIN500	Windows Shareware 500
WINDOWS	Windows Forum
WINDOWS500	Windows Shareware 500
WINDOWSFORUM	Windows Forum
WINDOWSMAG	Windows Magazine
WINDOWSMAGAZINE	Windows Magazine
WINDOWWARE	Wilson Windowware
WINE	Wine & Dine Online
WINE&DINEONLINE	Wine & Dine Online
WINERIES	Wine & Dine Online
WINFORUM	Windows Forum
WINMAG	Windows Magazine
WINNEWS	Windows News area
WIRED	Wired Magazine
WOMEN	The Exchange
WOODSTOCK	Woodstock Online
WORDLIBRARY	MasterWord
WORDPERFECT	WordPerfect Support Center
WORKING	Working Software
WORLDNEWS	U.S. & World News area
WORTH	Worth Magazine Online
WORTHMAGAZINE	Worth Magazine Online
WORTHONLINE	Worth Magazine Online
WORTHPORTFOLIO	Worth Magazine Online Portfolio
WPMAG	WordPerfect Magazine
WRITER'S	Writer's Club
WRITERS	Writer's Club
WRITERSMARKET	Writers' Market Forum
WWIR	Washington Week in Review magazine
WWW	Wilson Windowware
XAOS	Xoas Tools
XAOSTOOLS	Xoas Tools
XCEED	Xceed Technology
YOURMONEY	Your Money area
YOURTOONS	Cartoon collection
ZEDCOR	Zedcor, Inc.

Alphabetical by Subject

@times/The New York Times Online	@TIMES
@times/The New York Times Online	ATTIMES
@times/The New York Times Online	NEWYORK
@times/The New York Times Online	NEWYORKCITY
@times/The New York Times Online	NEWYORKTIMES
@times/The New York Times Online	NYC
@times/The New York Times Online	NYT
@times/The New York Times Online	NYTIMES
@times/The New York Times Online	TIMES
@times/The New York Times Online	TIMESNEWS
@times: Art & Photography	TIMESART
@times: Books of The Times	TIMESBOOKS
@times: Dining Out & Nightlife	TIMESDINING
@times: In The Region	TIMESREGION
@times: Leisure Guide	TIMESLEISURE
@times: Movies & Video	TIMESMOVIES
@times: Music & Dance	TIMESMUSIC
@times: Sports & Fitness	TIMESSPORTS
@times: The Arts	TIMESARTS
@times: Theater	TIMESTHEATER
@times: Top Stories	TIMESSTORIES
3D Special Interest Group	3DSIG
9600 Baud Access Center*	9600
9600 Baud Access Center*	9600ACCESS
9600 Baud Access Center*	9600CENTER
A Letter From Steve Case*	LETTER
AAII Online	AAII
Aatrix Software, Inc.	AATRIX
Abbate Video	ABBATEVIDEO
Abbate Video	VIDEOTOOLKIT
Academic Assistance Center	HOMEWORK
Academic Assistance Center	RESEARCH
Academic Assistance Center	TUTORING
Access Software	ACCESSSOFTWARE
Access Software	LINKS
Accolade, Inc.	ACCOLADE
Account and Billing*	BILL
Account and Billing*	BILLING
Account and Billing*	CHANGES
Acer America Corporation	ACER
Achievement TV	ACHIEVEMENTTV
Activision	ACTIVISION
AD&D Neverwinter Nights	AD&D
AD&D Neverwinter Nights	ADD
AD&D Neverwinter Nights	NEVERWINTER
AD&D Neverwinter Nights	NWN
AD&D Neverwinter Nights	OADD
Add, change or delete screen names	HANDLE
Add, change or delete screen names	NAME
Add, change or delete screen names	NAMES
Add, change or delete screen names	SCREENNAME
Add, change or delete screen names	SCREENNAMES
Add, change or delete screen names	USERNAME
Adoption Forum	ADOPTION
Adult Literacy Forum	LITERACY
Adult Literacy Forum	READ
Advanced Color Imaging Forum	COLORIMAGING
Advanced Color Imaging Forum	IMAGING
Advanced Color Imaging Forum	IPA
Advanced Gravis	ADVANCEDGRAVIS
Advanced Gravis	GRAVIS
Advanced Software, Inc.	ADVANCED
Adventures by Mail	ABM
Adventures by Mail	ADVENTURESBYMAIL
Adventures by Mail	MONSTERISLAND
Adventures by Mail	QUEST
Advertising Special Interest Group	ADSIG
Advertising Special Interest Group	ADVERTISING
Advertising Special Interest Group	ADVERTISINGSIG
Advice & Tips	ADVICE
Advice & Tips	ASKANDY
Advice & Tips	ASKANITA
Advice & Tips	ASKTHEDOCTOR
Advice & Tips	ASKTHEDR
Advice & Tips	ASKTHELAWYER
Advice & Tips	CRYSTALBALL
Advice & Tips	TAROT
Advice & Tips	TIPS
Affinity Microsystems	AFFINITY
Afterwards Coffeehouse	AFTERWARDS
Afterwards Coffeehouse	ARTS
Aladdin Systems, Inc.	ALADDIN
Aladdin Systems, Inc.	STUFFIT
Aldus Corporation	ALDUS
Alpha Software Corporation	ALPHATECH
Alpha Software Corporation	ASCTECH
Alpha Software Corporation	ASCTS
Altsys Corporation	ALTSYS
Alysis Software	ALYSIS
Alysis Software	SUPERDISK
Ambrosia Software	AMBROSIA
American Dialogue	AMERICANDIALOGUE
American Dialogue	DIALOGUE
American Federation of Teachers	AFT
Animated Software	ANIMATEDSOFTWARE
Another Company	ANOTHERCO
AOL Highlights Tour	HIGHLIGHTS
AOL Highlights Tour	TOUR
AOL Holiday Central	HOLIDAY
AOL Press Release Library	PRESS
AOL Press Release Library	PRESSRELEASE
AOL Products Center	AOLPRODUCTS

AOL Products Center	MUG
AOL Products Center	TOURGUIDE
AOL Products Center	TSHIRT
Apogee Software	APOGEE
Apple Applications Forum	APPLICATIONS
Apple Business Forum	APPLICATIONS
Apple Classrooms of Tomorrow	ACOT
Apple Club Performa	CLUBPERFORMA
Apple Club Performa	PERFORMA
Apple Club Performa	PERFORMACENTER
Apple Club Performa	PERFORMARESOURCE
Apple Club Performa	PRC
Apple Communications Forum	A2TELECOM
Apple Communications Forum	ACM
Apple Communications Forum	ATC
Apple Development Forum	A2DEVELOPMENT
Apple Development Forum	ADV
Apple Development Forum	APPLEIIDEVELOPMENT
Apple Education Forum	A2EDUCATION
Apple Education Forum	AED
Apple Education Forum	APPLEIIEDUCATION
Apple Games and Entertainment Forum	A2GAMES
Apple Games and Entertainment Forum	AGM
Apple Games and Entertainment Forum	APPLEIIGAMES
Apple Graphics and Sound Forum	A2ART
Apple Graphics and Sound Forum	A2GRAPHICS
Apple Graphics and Sound Forum	A2MUSIC
Apple Graphics and Sound Forum	AGR
Apple Graphics and Sound Forum	AGS
Apple Graphics and Sound Forum	APPLEIIGRAPHICS
Apple Graphics and Sound Forum	APPLEIIMUSIC
Apple Hardware Forum	A2HARDWARE
Apple Hardware Forum	A2PERIPHERALS
Apple Hardware Forum	A2PRODUCT
Apple Hardware Forum	AHW
Apple Hardware Forum	APPLEIIHARDWARE
Apple II Computing & Software Department	APPLE2
Apple II Computing & Software Department	APPLEII
Apple II Software Center	APPLEIISOFTWARE
Apple II/Mac Computing & Software Department†	APPLE
Apple Productivity Forum	A2APPLEWORKS
Apple Productivity Forum	A2PRODUCTIVITY
Apple Productivity Forum	A2WORDPROCESSING
Apple Productivity Forum	AAW
Apple Productivity Forum	APPLEIIPRODUCTIVITY
Apple Productivity Forum	APPLEWORKS
Apple Productivity Forum	APR
Apple Productivity Forum	AW
Apple Productivity Forum	AWGS
Apple Productivity Forum	AWP
Apple Productivity Forum	AWS
Apple Professional Developer's Association	APDA
Apple Utilities & Desk Accessories Forum	A2UTILITIES
Apple Utilities & Desk Accessories Forum	AUT
Apple Utilities & Desk Accessories Forum	AVT
AppleScript SIG	APPLESCRIPT
Applications Forum	PAP
Applications/Business Forum†	APPS
Applications/Business Forum†	BUSINESSFORUM
Applications/Business/Productivity Forum†	PRODUCTIVITY
Applications/Business/Productivity Forum†	PRODUCTIVITYFORUM
Architects, Engineers and Construction SIG	AECSIG
Ares Microdevelopment, Inc.	ARES
Argosy	ARGOSY
Ariel Publishing	ARIEL
Articulate Systems	ARTICULATE
Articulate Systems	ASI
Artifice, Inc.	ARTIFICE
AskERIC	ACCESSERIC
AskERIC	ASKERIC
AskERIC	ERIC
Assoc. for Supervisor & Curriculum Development	ASCD
Assoc. for Supervisor & Curriculum Development	CURRICULUM
Assoc. for Supervisor & Curriculum Development	EDTECH
Astronomy Club	ASTRONOMY
Asymetrix Corporation	ASYMETRIX
Atticus Software	ATTICUS
auto*des*sys, Inc.	FORMZ
auto*des*sys, Inc.	ADS
AutoVantage	AUTO
AutoVantage	AUTOVANTAGE
Aviation Club	AVIATION
Aviation Club	FLY
Avid DTV Group	AVID
Avid DTV Group	AVIDDTV
Avocat Systems	AVOCAT
Baby Boomers area	BABYBOOMERS
Backpacker Magazine	BACKCOUNTRY
Backpacker Magazine	BACKPACKER
Backpacker Magazine	CAMPING
Backpacker Magazine	CONSERVATION
Backpacker Magazine	ECOTOURISM
Backpacker Magazine	HIKER
Backpacker Magazine	HIKING
Backpacker Magazine	OUTDOORGEAR
Backpacker Magazine	TRAILGUIDES
Backpacker Magazine	TRAILS
Backpacker Magazine	VACATIONS
Backpacker Magazine	WILDERNESS
Barrons Booknotes	BARRONS
Barrons Booknotes	BOOKNOTES
Baseline Publishing	BASELINE
Baseview Products, Inc.	BASEVIEW
BBS Corner	BBS
BBS Corner	BBSCORNER
Beginners' Forum	ABF

Beginners' Forum	AOLBEGINNERS
Beginners' Forum	BEGINNER
Beginners' Forum	BEGINNERS
Beginners' Forum	GETTINGSTARTED
Beginners' Forum	GETTINGSTARTEDFORUM
Beginners' Forum	GTSF
Beginners' Forum	HELPDESK
Beginners' Forum	NEWLINK
Beginners' Forum	NLF
Beginners' Forum	PCBEGINNERS
Beginners' Forum	PCBG
Beginners' Forum	PCHELP
Beginners' Forum	STARTER
Bentley Systems, Inc.	MSTATION
Berkeley Systems	BERKELY
Berkeley Systems	BERKSYS
Berkeley Systems	BERKSYSWIN
Berkley Macintosh Users Group	BMUG
Best of America Online showcase	25REASONS
Best of America Online showcase	BESTOFAOL
Best of America Online showcase	UNIQUE
Bethesda Softworks	BETHESDA
Bethesda Softworks, Inc.	BETHESDA
Better Health & Medical Forum	HEALTH
Better Health & Medical Forum	MEDICINE
Beyond, Inc.	BEYOND
Bicycling Magazine	BICMAG
Bicycling Magazine	BICYCLING
Bicycling Magazine	BICYCLINGMAGAZINE
Bicycling Magazine	MOUNTAINBIKE
Bit Jugglers	BITJUGGLERS
Boardwatch Magazine	BOARDWATCH
Book Bestsellers area	BOOKBESTSELLERS
Book Bestsellers area	BOOKS
Bose Express Music	EXPRESSMUSIC
Boston Computer Society	BCS
Bowers Development	APPMAKER
Bowers Development	BOWERS
Brainstorm Products	BRAINSTORM
Broderbund	BRODERBUND
Browse the PC Catalog	PCCLASSIFIEDS
Bull Moose Tavern	BULLMOOSE
Bull Moose Tavern	POLITICS
Bulls and Bears Game	BULLSANDBEARS
Bungie Software	BUNGIE
Business Forum	MACBUSINESS
Business Forum	MBS
Business News area	BUSINESS
Business News area	BUSINESSNEWS
Business News area	FINANCE
Business News area	FINANCIALDISTRICT
Business News area	MONEY
Business Sense	BUSINESSSENSE

Business Strategies	BUSINESSKNOWHOW
Business Strategies	BUSINESSSTRATEGIES
Byte By Byte Corporation	BYTEBYBYTE
ByteWorks	BYTE
ByteWorks	BYTEWORKS
C-SPAN	CSPAN
C-SPAN	CSPANONLINE
C-SPAN Educational Services	CSPANCLASSROOM
Caere Corporation	CAERE
Caere Corporation	CAERECORPORATION
California State University	CHICO
California State University	CSUC
Callisto Corporation	CALLISTO
Cancel Account*	CANCEL
Car and Driver Magazine	CARANDDRIVER
Car and Driver Magazine	DRIVING
Car and Driver Magazine	RACING
Cardinal Technologies, Inc.	CARDINAL
Career Center	CAREER
Career Center	CAREERS
Career Development Training	TRAINING
Cartoon collection	CARTOONS
Cartoon collection	YOURTOONS
Cartoon Network	CARTOONNETWORK
Casa Blanca	CASABLANCA
Casady & Greene	CASADY
CE Software	CESOFTWARE
Celebrity Cookbook	CELEBRITYCOOKBOOK
Celebrity Cookbook	COOKBOOK
Center Stage auditorium	AUDITORIUM
Center Stage auditorium	CENTERSTAGE
Center Stage auditorium	PCAUD
Center Stage auditorium	SHOWS
Central Point Software	CENTRAL
Central Point Software	CENTRALPOINT
Central Point Software	CPS
Change your password*	CHANGEPASSWORD
Change your password*	PASSWORD
CheckFree	CHECKFREE
CheckFree	CKFREE
Chicago Online	CHICAGO
Chicago Online	CHICAGOONLINE
Chicago Online	COL
Chicago Online Chat	COLCHAT
Chicago Online Classifieds	TRIBADS
Chicago Online Classifieds	TRIBCLASSIFIED
Chicago Online Education	COLEDUCATION
Chicago Online Lifestyles	COLLIFESTYLES
Chicago Online Marketplace	COLMARKETPLACE
Chicago Online News, Business & Weather	COLNEWS
Chicago Online Planner	COLPLANNER
Chicago Online Sports	COLSPORTS
Chicago Online Ticketmaster	TICKETMASTER

Service	Keyword
Chicago Tribune	TRIBUNE
Chicago Tribuone	CHICAGOTRIBUNE
Chicago Tribuone	TRIB
Claris	CLARIS
Classifieds Online	CLASSIFIED
Classifieds Online	CLASSIFIEDS
Classifieds Online	CLASSIFIEDSONLINE
Clubs & Interests Department	CLUBS
Clubs & Interests Department	COMMUNITYCENTER
Clubs & Interests Department	HOBBIES
Clubs & Interests Department	INTEREST
Clubs & Interests Department	LIFESTYLES
Clubs & Interests Department	LIFESTYLES&HOBBIES
Clubs & Interests Department	LIFESTYLES&INTEREST
Clubs & Interests Department	LIFESTYLES&INTERESTS
Clubs & Interests Department	SPECIALINTERESTS
CNN Newsroom Online	CHANNELC
CNN Newsroom Online	CNN
CNN Newsroom Online	CNNNEWSROOM
CNN Newsroom Online	DEMOCRACY
Coda Music Tech	CMT
Coda Music Tech	CODA
Coda Music Tech	CODAMUSIC
College Board	CB
College Board	COLLEGE
College Board	COLLEGEBOARD
Color Weather Maps	COLORWEATHERMAPS
Color Weather Maps	WEATHERMAPS
Columnists & Features Online	COLUMNISTS
Columnists & Features Online	COLUMNS
Columnists & Features Online	FEATURES
Comedy Club and Punchlines	PUNCHLINE
Commerce Business Daily	CBD
Communications Forum	MCM
Communications Forum	MTC
Communications/Telecom/Networking Forum†	COMMUNICATIONS
Communications/Telecom/Networking Forum†	NETWORKING
Communications/Telecom/Networking Forum†	NETWORKINGFORUM
Communications/Telecom/Networking Forum†	TELECOM
Communications/Telecom/Networking Forum†	TELECOMFORUM
Communications/Telecom/Networking Forum†	TELECOMMUNICATIONS
Comp-u-Store Gateway	COMPUSTORE
Company of Science and Art	COSA
Compaq	COMPAQ
Composer's Coffeehouse	COMPOSER
Composer's Coffeehouse	COMPOSERS
Compute	COMPUTE
Computer Express	COMPUTEREXPRESS
Computer Peripherals, Inc.	COMPUTERPERIPHERALS
Computer Peripherals, Inc.	CPI
Computing Department†	C&S
Computing Department†	COMPUTING
Computing Department†	COMPUTER
Computing Department†	FORUM
Computing Department†	FORUMS
Computing Department†	PCSECURITY
Computing Department†	SIFS
Computing Department†	SIGS
Computing Department†	TECHNOLOGY
CompuToon area	COMPUTOON
CompuToon area	COMPUTOON
Connectix	CONNECTIX
Consortium for School Networking	COSN
Consumer Reports	CONSUMER
Consumer Reports	CONSUMERREPORTS
Consumer Reports	CONSUMERS
Cooking Club	COOKING
Cooking Club	FOOD
Cooking Club	KITCHEN
CoStar	COSTAR
Court TV	COURTROOMTELEVISION
Court TV	COURTTV
Cowles/SIMBA Media Information Network	COWLES
Cowles/SIMBA Media Information Network	COWLESSIMBA
Cowles/SIMBA Media Information Network	INSIDEMEDIA
Cowles/SIMBA Media Information Network	MEDIAINFORMATION
Cowles/SIMBA Media Information Network	SIMBA
Craig Crossman's Computer America	COMPUTERAMERICA
Craig Crossman's Computer America	CRAIGCROSSMAN
Craig Crossman's Computer America	CROSSMAN
Credit for connect problems*	CREDIT
Credit for connect problems*	CREDITREQUEST
Credit for connect problems*	DOWNLOADCREDIT
Critic's Choice	CRITICS
Critic's Choice	CRITICSCHOICE
CyberLaw, Cyberlex	COMPUTERLAW
CyberLaw, Cyberlex	CYBERLAW
CyberLaw, Cyberlex	CYBERLEX
DacEasy, Inc.	DACEASY
Daily calender of forum activity	TITF
Dancing Rabbit Creations	DANCINGRABBIT
Darts [Apple II only]	DARTS
Database Support SIG	DATABASE
Database Support SIG	DATABASES
DataPak Software	DATAPAK
DataTimes Sports Reports	DTSPORTS
Datawatch	DATAWATCH
Datawatch	VIREX
Davidson & Associates	DAVIDSON
Dayna Communications	DAYNA
Daystar Digital	DAYSTAR
DC Comics Online Preview	DCCOMICS
DC Comics Online Preview	DCOPREVIEW
Decision Point Forum	DECISION
Decision Point Forum	DECISIONPOINT
Decision Point Forum	DP

Decision Point Forum	DPA
Decision Point Forum	STOCKCHARTS
Decision Point Forum	STOCKTIMING
Dell Computer Corporation	DELL
Delrina Corporation	DELRINA
Delta Point	DELTAPOINT
Delta Tao	DELTATAO
Deneba Software	DENEBA
DeskMate	DES
DeskMate	DESKMATE
DeskMate	PCDESKMATE
DeskMate	PCDM
Desktop Publishing area†	DTP
Desktop Publishing area†	DESKTOPPUBLISHING
Destination Florida	FLORIDA
Destination Florida: Attractions	DFPARKS
Destination Florida: Outdoors	DFOUT
Destination Florida: Places to Stay	DFROOMS
Destination Florida: Restaurants and Nightlife	DFFOOD
Destination Florida: Shopping	DFSHOP
Destination Florida: Sports	DFSPORTS
Development Forum†	DEV
Development Forum†	DEVELOPER
Development Forum†	DEVELOPMENT
Development Forum†	DEVELOPMENTFORUM
Development Forum†	BASIC
Development Forum†	C
Development Forum†	COBOL
Development Forum†	PASCAL
Development Forum†	PROGRAMMING
Development Forum†\	ASSEMBLY
Diamond Computer Systems	DIAMOND
Dictionary of Computer Terms	COMPUTERTERMS
Digital Eclipse	DIGITALECLIPSE
Digital F/X	DFX
Digital F/X	DIGITALF/X
Digital Vision	DIGITAL
Dilbert Cartoon area	DILBERT
Dilbert Cartoon area	DILBERTCOMICS
Diplomats in the Classroom	DIPLOMATS
Direct Software	DIRECT
Directory of Services	DIRECTORYOFSERVICES
Directory of Services	DIROFSERVICES
Directory of Services	DIROFSVCS
Directory of Services	DONTMISS
Directory of Services	NOWPLAYING
Directory of Services	SERVICES
Directory of Services	SERVICESDIRECTORY
DisABILITIES Forum	BLIND
DisABILITIES Forum	DEAF
DisABILITIES Forum	DIS
DisABILITIES Forum	DISABILITIES
DisABILITIES Forum	DISABILITY
DisABILITIES Forum	PHYSICALLYDISABLED
Discover AOL area	DISCOVER
Disney/Buene Vista Software	DISNEYSOFTWARE
Disney Adventures Magazine	DISNEY
Disney Adventures Magazine	DISNEYADVENTURES
Disney Adventures Magazine	DISNEYMAGAZINE
Disney Technologies	DIGITALTECH
Do Something!	DOSOMETHING
Dolby Audio/Video Forum	AUDIO/VIDEO
Dolby Audio/Video Forum	DOLBY
Dolby Audio/Video Forum	DOLBYAUDIO/VIDEO
DOS Forum	5.0
DOS Forum	DOS
DOS Forum	DOS5.0
DOS Forum	DOSFORUM
DOS Forum	DRDOS
DOS Forum	MS-DOS
DOS Forum	MS-DOSFORUM
DOS Forum	PCUTILITIES
Downloading Hall of Fame	HALLOFFAME
Dreamworld	DREAMWORLD
Dubl-Click Software	DUBLCLICK
DYA/Digisoft Innovations	DIGISOFT
Dynaware USA	DYNAWARE
Dynaware USA	DYNAWAREUSA
EAASY SABRE	AMERICANAIRLINES
EAASY SABRE	EAASY
EAASY SABRE	EASSYSABRE
EAASY SABRE	EASYSABRE
EAASY SABRE	SABRE
EBBS	EBBS
Econ Technologies	ECON
Edit your member profile*	EDITPROFILE
Edit your member profile*	MEMBERPROFILE
Edit your member profile*	PROFILE
Edmark Technologies	EDMARK
Edmark Technologies	KIDDESK
Edmark Technologies	PENPAL
Education Department	EDUCATION
Education Department	LEARN
Education Department	LEARNING
Education Department	LEARNING&REFERENCE
Education Department	LEARNINGANDREFERENCE
Education Department	LEARNINGCENTER
Education Forum	EDFORUM
Electric Image	ELECTRIC
Electric Image	ELECTRICIMAGE
Electronic Courseware	ECS
Electronic Courseware	ELECTRONICCOURSEWARE
Electronic Frontier Foundation	EFF
Electronic Schoolhouse	ESH
Electronic Schoolhouse	SCHOOLHOUSE
Electronic University Network	EUN

Service	Keyword
Electronic University Network	UNIVERSITIES
Electronic University Network	UNIVERSITY
Emergency Response Club	EMERGENCY
Emergency Response Club	EMERGENCYRESPONSE
Emergency Response Club	ERC
Emigre Fonts	EMIGRE
Employer Contacts	CONTACTS
Employment Agency Database	NAPC
Encyclopedia	COMPTONS
Encyclopedia	ENCYCLOPEDIA
Energy Express	EN/X
Energy Express	ENERGYEXPRESS
Entertainment Department	ENTERTAINMENT
Entertainment Department	GAMES
Entertainment Department	GAMES&ENTERTAINMENT
Entertainment Department	RECCENTER
Entertainment Department	RECREATION
Entertainment Department	RECREATIONCENTER
Environmental Forum	EARTH
Environmental Forum	EFORUM
Environmental Forum	ENVIRONMENT
Ethics and Religion Forum	ETHICS
Ethics and Religion Forum	RELIGION
Exam Prep Center	EXAMPREP
Expert Software, Inc	EXPERT
Expert Software, Inc	EXPERTSOFT
Expert Software, Inc	SOFTSYNC
Express Yourself	DEBATE
Express Yourself	EXPRESSYOURSELF
Farallon	FARALLON
Fax/Paper Mail	FAX
Fax/Paper Mail	PAPERMAIL
Fax/Paper Mail	USMAIL
Fellowship of Online Gamers/RPGA Network	FELLOWSHIP
Fellowship of Online Gamers/RPGA Network	FOG
Fellowship of Online Gamers/RPGA Network	RPGA
Fellowship of Online Gamers/RPGA Network	RPGANETWORK
Fifth Generation	5THGENERATION
Fifth Generation	FIFTH
Flight Sim Resource Center	FLIGHT
Flight Sim Resource Center	FLIGHTSIMS
Flight Sim Resource Center	FLIGHTSIMULATIONS
Flight Sim Resource Center	FSRC
Flower Shop	FLOWERSHOP
Flying Magazine	FLYING
Flying Magazine	FLYINGMAGAZINE
Focus Enhancements	FOCUS
Focus Enhancements	FOCUSENHANCEMENTS
FontBank	FONTBANK
Fractal Design	FRACTAL
Fractal Design	FRACTALDESIGN
Franklin Quest	FRANKLIN
Free online game downloading*	DOWNLOADGAMES
Free online games downloading*	GAMESDOWNLOADING
Free-Form Gaming Forum	FFGF
Free-Form Gaming Forum	RDI
FullWrite	FULLWRITE
Future Labs, Inc.	FUTURELABS
Future Labs, Inc.	TALKSHOW
Gadget Guru Electronics Forum	ELECTRONICS
Gadget Guru Electronics Forum	GADGETGURU
Game Base	GAMEBASE
Game Designers Forum	GAMEDESIGN
Game Designers Forum	GAMEDESIGNER
Game Designers Forum	GAMEDESIGNERS
Games and Entertainment Forum	GAMESFORUM
Games Forum†	ADVENTURE
Games Forum†	ARCADE
Games Forum†	GAMESFORUM
Games Forum†	SIMULATOR
Games Parlor	GAMEROOMS
Games Parlor	GAMESPARLOR
Games Parlor	PARLOR
Gaming Company Support	GCS
Gaming Information Exchange	GIX
Gateway 2000, Inc	GATEWAY
Gateway 2000, Inc	GATEWAY2000
Gateway 2000, Inc	MOO
Gay & Lesbian Community Forum	BI
Gay & Lesbian Community Forum	BISEXUAL
Gay & Lesbian Community Forum	GAY
Gay & Lesbian Community Forum	GLCF
Gay & Lesbian Community Forum	LAMBDA
Gay & Lesbian Community Forum	LESBIAN
GCC Technologies	GCC
Genealogy Club	GENEALOGY
Genealogy Club	GENEALOGYCLUB
Genealogy Club	ROOTS
General Magic	GENERALMAGIC
GeoWorks	GEO
GeoWorks	GEOWORKS
GIF Converter	GIFCONVERTER
Giftedness Forum	GIFTED
Giftedness Forum	MENSA
Global Software Suport	GSS
Global Village Communication	GLOBAL
Global Village Communication	GLOBALVILLAGE
Global Village Communication	TELEPORT
Golf Courses & Resort Information	GOLFCOURSES
Golf Courses & Resort Information	GOLFRESORTS
Golf Courses & Resort Information	GOLFIS
Graphic Art & CAD Forum	MACART
Graphic Forum†	ANIMATION
Graphic Simulations	GRAPHICSIMULATIONS
Graphics and Sound Forum	AMS
Graphics and Sound Forum	MIDI

Graphics and Sound Forum†	MUSIC&SOUND
Graphics and Sound Forum†	MUSICANDSOUNDFORUM
Graphics and Sound Forum†	MUSICFORUM
Graphics Forum†	ART
Graphics Forum†	CAD
Graphics Forum†	GRAPHICARTS
Graphics Forum†	GRAPHICS
Graphics Forum†	GRAPHICSFORUM
Graphisoft	GRAPHISOFT
Grateful Dead Forum	DEAD
Grateful Dead Forum	GRATEFULDEAD
Grateful Dead Forum	THEDEAD
GroupWare SIG	GROUPWARE
Gryphon Software	GRYPHON
Gryphon Software	GRYPHONSOFTWARE
Gryphon Software	MORPH
GS+ Magazine	GSMAG
Ham Radio Club	AMATEURRADIO
Ham Radio Club	HAM
Ham Radio Club	HAMRADIO
Ham Radio Club	RADIO
Ham Radio Club	SATELLITES
Hardware	SILICON
Hardware	SUPERCARD
Hardware Forum†	HARDWARE
Hardware Forum†	HARDWAREFORUM
Harvard Business School Publishing	HBSPUB
Hatrack River Town Meeting	ALVIN
Hatrack River Town Meeting	ENDER
Hatrack River Town Meeting	HATRACK
Hatrack River Town Meeting	HATRACKRIVETTOWN
Hatrack River Town Meeting	ORSONSCOTTCARD
hDC Corporation	HDC
hDC Corporation	HDCCORPORATION
Helios USA	HELIOS
Helios USA	HELIOSUSA
Heritage Foundation area	HERITAGEFOUNDATION
Hollywood Online	HOLLYWOOD
Hollywood Online	HOLLYWOODONLINE
Home Office Computing Magazine	HOMEOFFICE
Homeowner's Forum	HOME
Homeowner's Forum	HOMEOWNER
Homeowner's Forum	HOMEOWNERSFORUM
Homeowner's Forum	UHA
HomePC Magazine	HOMEPC
Hoover's Handbook of Company Profiles	COMPANY
Hoover's Handbook of Company Profiles	COMPANYPROFILES
Hoover's Handbook of Company Profiles	HOOVERS
Horoscopes	HOROSCOPE
Horoscopes	HOROSCOPES
HSC Software	HCSSOFTWARE
HSC Software	HSC
HSC Software	KPT
HyperCard Forum	HYPERCARD
IBM Connection	IBM
IBM Connection	PS1
IBM Connection	PSL
IBVA Technologies	IBVA
IBVA Technologies	PSYCHICLABS
IES Registration Center	REGISTER
IES Registration Center	REGISTRATION
IES Registration Center	SIGNUP
IMPACT II: The Teachers Network	IMPACTII
inCider	INCIDER
Industry Connection	COMPANIES
Industry Connection	HARDWARECOMPANIES
Industry Connection	IC
Industry Connection	INDUSTRY
Industry Connection	INDUSTRYCONNECTION
Industry Connection	PUBLISHERS
Industry Connection	SOFTWARECOMPANIES
Industry Connection	SOFTWAREPUBLISHERS
Infocom	INFOCOM
Inline Design	INLINE
Inline Design	INLINESOFTWARE
Inside Technology	CARUSO
Inside Technology	INSIDETECH
Inside Technology	INSIDETECHNOLOGY
Insignia Solutions	INSIGNIA
Intel Corporation	INTEL
Intel Corporation	PENTIUM
Intellimation	INTELLIMATION
Interactive Education Services	CAMPUS
Interactive Education Services	CLASSES
Interactive Education Services	COURSES
Interactive Education Services	IES
Interactive Education Services	INTERACTIVEDUCATION
Interactive Education Services	INTERACTIVEED
InterCon Systems Corporation	INTERCON
International Corporate Forum	ICF
International Correspondence Schools	ICS
International House	INTERNATIONAL
Internet Center	INTERNET
Internet Center	INTERNETCENTER
Internet Gopher & WAIS	GOPHER
Internet Gopher & WAIS	WAIS
Internet Usenet Newsgroup area	NEWSGROUPS
Internet Usenet Newsgroup area	USENET
Interplay	INTERPLAY
Investors Network	INVESTING
Investors Network	INVESTMENTS
Investors Network	INVESTORS
Investors Network	INVESTORSNETWORK
Iomega Corporation	IOMEGA
ISIS International	ISIS
ISIS International	ISISINTERNATIONAL

Island Graphics Corporation	ISLANDGRAPHICS
Issues and Debate Forum	DEBATEFORUM
Issues and Debate Forum	ISSUES
Issues and Debate Forum	ISSUESANDDEBATE
Issues in Mental Health	IMH
IYM Software Review	IYM
IYM Software Review	IYMSOFTWAREREVIEW
JLCooper Electronics	COOPER
JLCooper Electronics	JLCOOPER
Job Listings Database	JOBS
JPEGView	JPEGVIEW
Kaplan Online	KAPLAN
Kaplan Online	TESTPREP
Kensington Microware, Ltd.	KENSINGTON
Kent*Marsh	KENTMARSH
Kids Only Online	KIDSONLY
Kids Only Online	KOOL
KIDSNET	KIDSNET
KIDSNET Forum	EDTV
KIDSNET Forum	KIDNET
Kim Komando's Komputer Clinic	COMMANDO
Kim Komando's Komputer Clinic	KOMANDO
Kim Komando's Komputer Clinic	KOMPUTERTUTOR
Kiwi Software, Inc.	KIWI
Koala/MacVision	KOALA
Koala/MacVision	MACVISION
Kodak Photography Forum	CAMERA
Kodak Photography Forum	KODAK
Kodak Photography Forum	PHOTO
Lapis Technologies	LAPIS
Lapis Technologies	LAPISTECHNOLOGIES
LaPub	LAPUB
Lawrence Productions	LAWRENCE
Leader Technologies	LEADER
Leader Technologies	LEADERTECH
Leader Technologies	LEADERTECHNOLOGIES
Leading Edge	LEADINGEDGE
Legal SIG	LEGAL
Legal SIG	LEGALSIG
Letraset	LETRASET
Libertarian Party Forum	LIBERTARIAN
Library of Congress Online	DEADSEA
Library of Congress Online	LIBRARY
Library of Congress Online	LOC
Library of Congress Online	SOVARC
Library of Congress Online	SOVIET
Library of Congress Online	SOVIETARCHIVES
Library of Congress Online	VATICAN
Lifetime Television	LIFETIME
Lifetime Television	LIFETIMETELEVISION
Lifetime Television	LIFETIMETV
LinksWare, Inc.	LINKSWARE
Local access numbers*	ACCESS
Local access numbers*	ACCESSNUMBERS
Local access numbers*	NUMBERS
Local access numbers*	PETITIONS
Local Newspapers	LOCALNEWSPAPERS
Local Newspapers	NEWSPAPER
Local Newspapers	NEWSPAPERS
LucasArts Games	LUCAS
LucasArts Games	LUCASARTS
Mac Communications Forum	MACCOMMUNICATION
Mac Communications Forum	MACCOMMUNICATIONS
Mac Communications Forum	MACTELECOM
Mac Communications Forum	MACTELECOMM
Mac Computing & Software department	MAC
Mac Computing & Software department	MACCOMPUTING
Mac Computing & Software department	MACINTOSH
Mac Desktop Publishing/WP Forum	MACDESKTOP
Mac Desktop Publishing/WP Forum	MACDTP
Mac Desktop Publishing/WP Forum	MACWORLDPROCESSING
Mac Desktop Publishing/WP Forum	MDP
Mac Development Forum	MACDEVELOPMENT
Mac Development Forum	MACPROGRAMMING
Mac Development Forum	MDV
Mac Education Forum	MACEDUCATION
Mac Education Forum	MED
Mac Games Forum	MACGAME
Mac Games Forum	MACGAMES
Mac Games Forum	MGM
Mac Graphic Art & CAD Forum	MACGRAPHICS
Mac Graphic Art & CAD Forum	MGR
Mac Hardware Forum	MACHARDWARE
Mac Hardware Forum	MHW
Mac HyperCard Forum	MACHYPERCARD
Mac HyperCard Forum	MHC
Mac Multimedia Forum	MACMULTIMEDIA
Mac Multimedia Forum	MMM
Mac Music & Sound Forum	MACMUSIC
Mac Music & Sound Forum	MACSOUND
Mac Music & Sound Forum	MIDI
Mac Music & Sound Forum	MMS
Mac Music & Sound Forum	QMMS
Mac Operating Systems Forum	MACO/S
Mac Operating Systems Forum	MACOPERATINGSYSTEMS
Mac Operating Systems Forum	MACOS
Mac Operating Systems Forum	MOS
Mac Operating Systems Forum	SYSTEM7
Mac Operating Systems Forum	SYSTEM7.0
Mac Operating Systems Forum	SYSTEM7.1
Mac Operating Systems Forum	SYSTEM71
Mac Shareware 500	MAC500
Mac Shareware 500	SHAREWARE500
Mac Shareware 500	VENTANA
Mac Shareware 500	VENTANA500
Mac Software Center	MACLIBRARIES

Mac Software Center	MACSOFTWARE
Mac Utilities Forum	MACUTILITIES
Mac Utilities Forum	MUT
Mac Utilities Forum	MVT
MacApp Developers Association	MADA
MacHome Journal	MACHOME
MacHome Journal	MACHOMEJOURNAL
MacroMedia, Inc.	MACROMEDIA
MacroMedia, Inc.	MACROMIND
MacTech Magazine	MACTECH
MacTech Magazine	MACTECHMAG
MacTech Magazine	MACTECHMAGAZINE
Mactivity '94 Forum	MACTIVITY
MacWorld Expo Center	MACWORLDEXPO
MacWorld Magazine	MACWORLD
Mail Gateway	MAILGATEWAY
Mainstay	MAINSTY
Mallard Software	MALLARD
Management Science Associates	MSA
Manhattan Graphics (RSG)	MANHATTANGRAPHICS
Market Master	MARKET
Market Master	MARKETMASTER
Market News area	MARKETNEWS
Market News area	MARKETS
Marketfield Software	MARKETFIELD
Marketplace	MALL
Marketplace	SHOPPING
Marketplace	STORE
Marketplace	STORES
Marketplace	THEMALL
Martinsen's Software	MARTINSEN
Massachusetts Governor's Forum	MASS
Massachusetts Governor's Forum	MASSACHUSETTS
MasterWord	MASTERWORD
MasterWord	MW
MasterWord	MWORD
MasterWord	WORDLIBRARY
Maxis	MAXIS
McAfee Associates	MCAFEE
MECC	MECC
Member Directory	DIRECTORY
Member Directory	MEMBERDIRECTORY
Member Directory	MEMBERS
Members Helping Members message board*	MHM
Members' Online Support	ONLINEGUIDE
Members' Online Support*	ASKAMERICAONLINE
Member Services*	ASKAOL
Member Services*	ASKCS
Member Services*	CUSTOMERSERVICE
Member Services*	FEEDBACK
Member Services*	FREE
Member Services*	HELP
Member Services*	HOTLINE
Member Services*	INFORMATION
Members' Online Support*	MANUAL
Members' Online Support*	MEMBERSGUIDE
Members' Online Support*	MEMBERSONLINEGUIDE
Members' Online Support*	MOG
Member Services*	SERVICE
Member Services*	SUPPORT
Member Services*	SYSOP
Mercury Center	MERCURY
Mercury Center	MERCURYCENTER
Mercury Center	SANJOSE
Mercury Center Advertising	MCCLASSIFIEDS
Mercury Center Advertising	MCMARKET
Mercury Center Bay Area Living area	MCLIVING
Mercury Center Business & Technology area	MCBUSINESS
Mercury Center Conference area	MCTALK
Mercury Center Entertainment area	MCENTERTAINMENT
Mercury Center In the News area	INTHENEWS
Mercury Center In the News area	MCNEW
Mercury Center In the News area	MCNEWS
Mercury Center Newspaper Library	MCLIBRARY
Mercury Center Sports area	MCSPORTS
Meridian Data	MERIDIAN
Metrowerks	METROWERKS
Metz	METZ
Michigan Governor's Forum	MICHIGAN
Michigan Governor's Forum	MICHIGANGOVERNOR
Micro Dynamics, Ltd.	MICRODYNAMICS
Micro J Systems, Inc	MICROJ
MicroFrontier, Ltd.	MICROFRONTIER
Micrografx, Inc.	MGX
Micrografx, Inc.	MICROGRAFX
MicroMat Computer Systems	MICROMAT
MicroProse	MICROPROSE
Microseeds Publishing, Inc.	MICROSEEDS
Microsoft Knowledge Base	KNOWLEDGEBASE
Microsoft Knowledge Base	MSKB
Microsoft Product Support	MSFORUM
Microsoft Resource Center	MICROSOFT
Microsoft Resource Center	MSSUPPORT
Mike Keefe Cartoons	KEEFE
Military and Vets Club	MILITARY
Military and Vets Club	VETERANS
Military and Vets Club	VETS
Military and Vets Club	VETSCLUB
Military City Online	MC
Military City Online	MCO
Military City Online	MILITARYCITYONLINE
Mirror Technologies	MIRROR

Mobile Office Online	MOBILE
Mobile Office Online	PORTABLE
Mobile Office Online	PORTABLECOMPUTING
Modem Help area* [PC platform only]	MODEMHELP
Montessori Schools	MONTESSORI
MoraffWare	MORAFFWARE
Morningstar Mutual Funds	FUND
Morningstar Mutual Funds	FUNDS
Morningstar Mutual Funds	MORNINGSTAR
Morningstar Mutual Funds	MUTUALFUND
Morningstar Mutual Funds	MUTUALFUNDS
Movies menu	MOVIEREVIEWS
Movies menu	MOVIES
Movies menu	MOVIES
MS-DOS 6.0 Resource Center	DOS6
MS-DOS 6.0 Resource Center	DOS60
MS-DOS 6.0 Resource Center	MSDOS6
MS-DOS 6.0 Resource Center	MSDOS60
MTV Online	MTV
Multimedia World Online [PC platform only]	MMW
Multimedia World Online [PC platform only]	MMWORLD
Mustang Software	MUSTANG
Mustang Software	MUSTANGSOFTWARE
Mustang Software	QMODEM
Mustang Software	WILDCAT
Mustang Software	WILDCATBBS
Nat'l Council of Teachers of English	ENGLISH
Nat'l Council of Teachers of English	NCTE
Nation Gay & Lesbian Task Force	NGLTF
National Alliance of Mentally Ill	NAMI
National Association of Quick Printers area	NAQP
National Association of Quick Printers area	QUICKPRINTERS
National Education Association	NEAONLINE
National Education Association	NEAPUBLIC
National Geographic Online	GEOGRAPHIC
National Geographic Online	NATIONALGEOGRAPHIC
National Geographic Online	NGS
National Multiple Sclerosis Society	NMSS
National Museum of American Art	NMAA
National Principals Center	NAESP
National Principals Center	PRINCIPALS
National Public Radio Outreach	NPR
National Public Radio Outreach	PUBLICRADIO
National Public Radio Outreach	TOTN
National Space Society	NSS
National Space Society	SPACE
National Staff Development Council	NSDC
NBC Online	NBC
NEC Technologies	NEC
NEC Technologies	NECTECH
NeoLogic	NEOLOGIC
Network Earth	EARTH
Network Earth	NETWORKEARTH
New Features & Services showcase	NEW
New Mail Features*	NEWMAIL
New World Computing	NEWWORLD
Newsbytes	NEWSBYTES
Nikon Electronic Imaging	NIKON
Niles and Associates	ENDNOTE
Niles and Associates	NILES
No Hands Software	NOHANDS
Nomadic Computing Discussion SIG	NOMADIC
Novell Desktop Systems	DIGITALRESEARCH
Novell Desktop Systems	DIGITALRESEARCHINC
Novell Desktop Systems	DRI
Novell Desktop Systems	NOVELL
Now Software	NOW
Object Factory	OBJECTFACTORY
Odeon Auditorium	ODEON
Olduvai Software, Inc.	OLDUVAI
OMNI Magazine Online	OMNI
OMNI Magazine Online	OMNIMAGAZINE
ON Technology	ON
Online Bookstore	BOOKSTORE
Online Bookstore	ONLINEBOOKSTORE
Online Bookstore	READUSA
Online Gaming Forums	GAMING
Online Gaming Forums	GUILD
Online Gaming Forums	OGF
Online Gaming Forums	ONLINEGAMING
Online Gaming Forums	PHANTASYGUILD
Online Shorthands	SHORTHAND
Online Shorthands	SHORTHANDS
OnLine Tonight	OLT
OnLine Tonight	ONLINETONIGHT
Onyx Technology	ONYX
Opcode Systems, Inc.	OPCODE
Opcode Systems, Inc.	OPCODESYSTEMS
OptImage Interactive Services	OPTIMAGE
OPTIMAS Corporation	BIOSCAN
OPTIMAS Corporation	OPTIMAS
Origin Systems	ORIGIN
Origin Systems	ORIGINSYSTEMS
OS/2 Forum	IBMOS2
OS/2 Forum	OS2
OS/2 Forum	OSTWO
Otter Solution	OTTER
Otter Solution	OTTERSOLUTION
PaceMark Technologies, Inc.	PACEMARK
Packer Software	PACKER
Page a Guide	GUIDEPAGE
Page a Guide	GUIDEPAGER
Palm Computing	PALM
Palm Computing	PALMCOMPUTING
Papyrus	PAPYRUS
Parental Controls	PARENTALCONTROL

Parents' Information Network	PARENT
Parents' Information Network	PIN
Passport Designs	PASSPORT
PC Applications Forum	PCAPPLICATIONS
PC Applications Forum	PCAPPLICATIONSFORUM
PC Applications Forum	PCAPS
PC Catalog	PCCATALOG
PC Catalog	PCCATALOG
PC Catalog	PCCLASSIFIEDS
PC Computing & Software department	PCFORUMS
PC Development Forum	PCDEV
PC Development Forum	PCDEVELOPMENT
PC Development Forum	PCDEVELOPMENTFORUM
PC Development Forum	PDV
PC Games Forum	PCGAMES
PC Games Forum	PCGAMESFORUM
PC Games Forum	PGM
PC Graphics Forum	PCANIMATION
PC Graphics Forum	PCGRAPHICS
PC Graphics Forum	PCGRAPHICSFORUM
PC Graphics Forum	PGR
PC Hardware Forum	PCHARDWARE
PC Hardware Forum	PCHARDWAREFORUM
PC Hardware Forum	PHW
PC Multimedia Forum	PMM
PC Music and Sound Forum	MIDI
PC Music and Sound Forum	PCMU
PC Music and Sound Forum	PCMUSIC
PC Music and Sound Forum	PCMUSICANDSOUNDFORUM
PC Music and Sound Forum	PCMUSICFORUM
PC Music and Sound Forum	PCSOUND
PC Music and Sound Forum	PCSOUNDFORUM
PC Music and Sound Forum	PMU
PC Novice & PC Today Online	PCNOVICE
PC Novice & PC Today Online	PCTODAY
PC Software Center	PCLIBRARIES
PC Software Center	PCSOFTWARE
PC Software Center	PCSOFTWARE
PC Software Center	PCSW
PC Studio	PCSTUDIO
PC Telecom/Networking Forum	PCM
PC Telecom/Networking Forum	PCTELECOM
PC Telecom/Networking Forum	PCTELECOMFORUM
PC Telecom/Networking Forum	PTC
PCWorld Online	PCWONLINE
PCWorld Online	PCWORLD
PCWorld Online	PCWORLDONLINE
Peachtree Software	PEACHTREE
Penny Wise Office Products Store	OFFICE
Penny Wise Office Products Store	OFFICEPRODUCTS
Penny Wise Office Products Store	PENNY
Penny Wise Office Products Store	PENNYWISE
People Connection	CHAT
People Connection	PC
People Connection	PEOPLE
People Connection	PEOPLECONNECTION
People Connection	TALK
Personal Computer Peripherals	PCPC
Personal Digital Assistant's Forum	NEWTON
Personal Digital Assistant's Forum	PDA
Personal Digital Assistants Forum	MESSAGEPAD
Personal Digital Assistants Forum	PALMTOP
Personal Finance Department	PERSONALFINANCE
Personal Finance Department	PF
Pet Care Club	PET
Pet Care Club	PETCARE
Pet Care Club	PETS
Photography Area	PHOTOGRAPHY
Photoshop SIG	PHOTOSHOP
Photoshop SIG	PHOTOSHOPSIG
Pictures of the World	PICTURES
Pixar	PIXAR
Pixar	RENDERMAN
Pixel Resources	PIXEL
Pixel Resources	PIXELRESOURCES
Play-By-Mail & Strategy Gaming Forum	CHESS
Play-By-Mail & Strategy Gaming Forum	PBM
Play-By-Mail & Strategy Gaming Forum	PLAY-BY-MAIL
Play-By-Mail & Strategy Gaming Forum	STRATEGY
Playmation	PLAYMATION
Popular Photography Online	CAMERAS
Popular Photography Online	PHOTOS
Popular Photography Online	POPPHOTO
Popular Photography Online	POPULARPHOTOGRAPHY
Portfolio Systems, Inc.	DYNO
Portfolio Systems, Inc.	PORTFOLIOSOFTWARE
Portrait Gallery	GALLERY
Power Mac Resource Center	POWERMAC
Power Mac Resource Center	POWERPC
Power Up Software	POWERUP
PowerBook Reserouce Center	POWERBOOK
Practical Peripherals, Inc.	PPI
Practical Peripherals, Inc.	PRACTICALPERIPHERALS
PrairieSoft, Inc.	PRAIRIESOFT
Prodigy Refugees Forum	PRODIGYFORUM
Prodigy Refugees Forum	PRODIGYREFUGEES
Prodigy Refugees' Forum	PRODIGY
Programmer University	PROGRAMMERU
Programmer University	PU
Prograph International, Inc.	PROGRAPH
Prograph International, Inc.	TGS
ProVUE Development	PROVUE
Psion	PSION
Qualitas	QUALITAS
Quark, Inc.	QUARK
RabbitJack's Casino	CASINO

Service	Keyword
RabbitJack's Casino	RABBITJACKSCASINO
Radius, Inc.	RADIUS
RasterOps	RASTEROPS
Ray Dream	RAY
Ray Dream	RAYDREAM
Reactor	REACTOR
Real Estate Online	ARM
Real Estate Online	HOMEEQUITYLOAN
Real Estate Online	HOMEREFINANCING
Real Estate Online	MLS
Real Estate Online	MORTAGE
Real Estate Online	MORTAGERATES
Real Estate Online	MORTGAGES
Real Estate Online	REALESTATE
Redate/IIN Online	IIN
Redgate Online > PC Expo area	PCEXPO
Redgate/IIN Online	REDGATE
Reference Desk	REFERENCE
Reference Desk	REFERENCEDESK
Relgion & Ethics Forum	NEWAGE
Religion & Ethics Forum	BUDDHISM
Religion & Ethics Forum	CHRISTIAN
Religion & Ethics Forum	CHRISTIANS
Religion & Ethics Forum	ISLAM
Religion & Ethics Forum	JUDAISM
Religion & Ethics Forum	PAGAN
Reset Department menu to initial department [Apple II users only]*	MAIN
ResNova Software (RESNOVASOFTWARE)	RESNOVA
Road & Track Magazine	AUTOS
Road & Track Magazine	CARS
Road & Track Magazine	ROAD
Road & Track Magazine	ROADANDTRACK
Rockland Software	ROCKLAND
Rockland Software	ROCKLANDSOFTWARE
Rocklink	MUSIC
Rocklink	ROCK
Rocklink	ROCKLINK
Roger Wagner Publishing	ROGERWAGNER
Role-Playing Forum	ROLEPLAYING
Role-Playing Forum	RPG
Romance Connection message boards	DATING
Romance Connection message boards	ROMANCE
Ross Perot/United We Stand area	HROSSPEROT
Ross Perot/United We Stand area	PEROT
Ross Perot/United We Stand area	ROSSPEROT
Rotunda Forum Auditorium	FORUMAUD
Rotunda Forum Auditorium	FORUMAUDITORIUM
Rotunda Forum Auditorium	FORUMROT
Rotunda Forum Auditorium	ROTUNDA
Rotunda Forum Auditorium	STUMP
Salient Software	SALIENT
Saturday Review Online	LITERATURE

Service	Keyword
Saturday Review Online	READING
Saturday Review Online	SATREVIEW
Saturday Review Online	SATURDAYREVIEW
Saturday Review Online	SOCEITY
Saturday Review Online	SRO
Saturday Review Online	THEATER
Saturday Review Online	THEATRE
Scholastic Network/Scholastic Forum	SCHOLASTIC
Science Fiction Forum	ANALOG
Science Fiction Forum	ASIMOV
Science Fiction Forum	SCI-FI
Science Fiction Forum	SCIENCEFICTION
Science Fiction Forum	SCIFI
Science Fiction Forum	SF
Scouting Forum	SCOUTING
Scouting Forum	SCOUTS
Scuba Club	GOSCUBA
Scuba Club	SCUBA
Search database of files	FILESEARCH
Search database of files†	QUICKFIND
Search database of files†	QUICKFINDER
Search Help Wanted	HELPWANTED
Search News Articles	NEWSSEARCH
Search News Articles	NEWSWATCH
SeniorNet	SENIOR
Serius	SERIUS
Shareware Solutions	SHAREWARESOLUTIONS
Shiva Corporation	SHIVA
Sierra On-Line	SIERRA
Sign on a friend to AOL*	FRIEND
Ski Reports	SKI
Ski Reports	SKICONDITIONS
Ski Reports	SKIREPORTS
Ski Reports	SKIWEATHER
Smithsonian Online	SI
Smithsonian Online	SMITHSONIAN
Soap Opera Summaries	TELEVISION
SoftArc	SOFTARC
Softdisk Superstore [PC platform only]	SOFTDISK
Software Center†	DOWNLOAD
Software Center†	DOWNLOADING
Software Center†	LIBRARIES
Software Center†	LIBS
Software Center†	SOFT
Software Center†	SOFTWARE
Software Center†	SOFTWARECENTER
Software Center†	SOFTWAREDIRECTORY
Software Center†	SOFTWAREHELP
Software Center†	SOFTWARELIBRARIES
Software Center†	SOFTWARELIBRARY
Software Creations	SOFTWARECREATIONS
Software Creations	SWC
Software Toolworks	SOFTWARETOOLWORKS

Software Toolworks	TOOLWORKS
Sol III Play-by-Email Game	SOLIII
Sophisticated Circuits	SOPHCIR
Spectrum HoloByte	SPECTRUM
Specular International	SPECULAR
Sport News area	GOLF
Sport News area	SPORTS
Sport News area	SPORTSLINK
Sport News area	SPORTSNEWS
SSSi	SSSI
STAC Electronics	STAC
Star Trek Club	STARTREK
Star Trek Club	TREK
Starfleet Academy	ACADEMY
Stereo Review Online magazine	AUDIO
Stereo Review Online magazine	HOMETHEATER
Stereo Review Online magazine	STEREO
Stereo Review Online magazine	STEREOREVIEW
STF Technologies	STF
STF Technologies	STFTECHNOLOGIES
Stock Market Timing & Charts area	QUOTE
Stock Market Timing & Charts area	QUOTES
Stock Market Timing & Charts area	STOCK
Stock Market Timing & Charts area	STOCKLINK
Stock Market Timing & Charts area	STOCKQUOTES
Stock Market Timing & Charts area	STOCKS
Strata, Inc.	STRATA
Strategic Simulations	SSI
Strategic Simulations	STRATEGIC
Student Access Online	PRINCETONREVIEW
Student Access Online	STUDENT
Student Access Online	STUDENTACCESS
Study Skills Service	STUDY
Study Skills Service	STUDYSKILLS
Substance Abuse Forum	PREVENTION
Substance Abuse Forum	SUBSTANCEABUSE
Suggestion boxes*	SUGGESTION
Suggestion boxes*	SUGGESTIONS
SuperMac	SUPERMAC
Survivor Software	SURVIVOR
Survivor Software	SURVIVORSOFTWARE
Symantec	NORTON
Symantec	PETERNORTON
Symantec	SYMANTEC
Synex	SYNEX
SYS Language Systems	LANGUAGESYS
T/Maker	TMAKER
Tactic Software	NEWERA
Tactic Software	TACTIC
Talent Bank	TALENT
Tandy Headquarters	PCHQ
Tandy Headquarters	TANDY
Tandy Headquarters	TANDYHANDQUARTERS

Tandy Headquarters	TANDYHQ
Tax Forum	GOTAX
Tax Forum [seasonal]	TAX
Tax Forum [seasonal]	TAXES
Teacher Pager	TEACHERPAGER
Teachers' Forum	TTALK
Teachers' Information Network	TEACHER
Teachers' Information Network	TEACHERS
Teachers' Information Network	TIN
Teachers' Newsstand	TNEWS
Teachers' University	TEACHERU
Tech Help Live*	CSLIVE
Tech Help Live*	TECHHELPLIVE
Technology Works	TECHNOLOGYWORKS
Technology Works	TECHWORKS
Teen Scene message boards	TEEN
Teen Scene message boards	TEENS
Teen Scene message boards	TEENSCENE
Teknosys Works	TEKNOSYS
Telescan Users Group Forum	TELESCAN
Television	TV
TERC LabNet	LABNET
Terms of Service*	TERMS
Terms of Service*	TERMSOFSERVICE
Terms of Service*	TOS
Terms of Service*	TOSADVISOR
Texas Instrument	TEXASINSTRUMENTS
Texas Instrument	TI
The Atlantic Monthly Online	ATLANTIC
The Atlantic Monthly Online	ATLANTICMONTHLY
The Atlantic Monthly Online	ATLANTICONLINE
The Bicycle Network	BFA
The Bicycle Network	BICYCLE
The Bicycle Network	BIKENET
The Exchange	AFRICANAMERICAN
The Exchange	AMERICANINDIAN
The Exchange	ASIAN
The Exchange	BOATING
The Exchange	COINS
The Exchange	COLLECTING
The Exchange	CRAFTS
The Exchange	EXCHANGE
The Exchange	GARDENING
The Exchange	HISPANIC
The Exchange	MEN
The Exchange	OUTDOORS
The Exchange	RAILROADING
The Exchange	STAMPS
The Exchange	THEEXCHANGE
The Exchange	WOMEN
The Geraldo Show	GERALDO
The Geraldo Show	GERALDOSHOW
The Grandstand	AUTORACING

The Grandstand	BASEBALL
The Grandstand	BASKETBALL
The Grandstand	BOXING
The Grandstand	FANTASYFOOTBALL
The Grandstand	FANTASYLEAGUES
The Grandstand	FOOTBALL
The Grandstand	GFL
The Grandstand	GRANDSTAND
The Grandstand	HOCKEY
The Grandstand	HORSERACING
The Grandstand	TENNIS
The Improv Forum	IMPROV
The Improv Forum	IMPROVCLUB
The Improv Forum	IMPROVCLUBS
The Improv Forum	IMPROVFORUM
The Macintosh Bible/Peachpit Forum	MACBIBLE
The Macintosh Bible/Peachpit Forum	MACINTOSHBIBLE
The Macintosh Bible/Peachpit Forum	PEACHPIT
The Michael Reagan Show Online	MICHAELREAGAN
The Michael Reagan Show Online	MICHAELREAGANSHOW
The Michael Reagan Show Online	REAGAN
The Multimedia Exchange	MULTIMEDIA
The National Parenting Center	TNPC
The New Republic Magazine	NEWREPUBLIC
The New Republic Magazine	THENEWREPUBLIC
The New Republic Magazine	TNR
The Newsstand	MAGAZINES
The Newsstand	NEWSSTAND
The Nightly Business Report	NBR
The Nightly Business Report	NBRREPORT
The Quantum Que and Graffiti community message boards	QUE
The Ricki Lake Show	RICKILAKE
The Sci-Fi Channel	SCIFICHANNEL
The Voyager Company	VOYAGER
Three-Sixty Software	THREESIXTY
Thrustmaster	THRUSTMASTER
Thunderware	THUNDERWARE
Ticketmaster	TICKET
TIGERDirect, Inc.	BLOCDEVELOPMENT
TIGERDirect, Inc.	TIGER
TIGERDirect, Inc.	TIGERDIRECT
Time Magazine Online	TIME
Time of day and length of time online	CLOCK
Timeslips Corporation	TIMESLIPS
Timeworks	TIMEWORKS
TMS TV Source	LISTINGS
TMS TV Source	TMS
TMS TV Source	TVGUIDE
TMS TV Source	TVLISTINGS
TMS TV Source	TVSOURCE
Today's News Department	NEWS
Today's News Department	NEWS&FINANCE
Today's News Department	NEWS/SPORTS/MONEY
Today's News Department	NEWSANDFINANCE
Today's News Department	NEWSROOM
Tomorrow's Morning newspaper	TOMORROW
Tomorrow's Morning newspaper	TOMORROWSMORNING
Top News area	HEADLINES
Top News area	NEWSLINK
Top News area	NEWSTEXT
Top News area	OURWORLD
Top News area	TOPNEWS
Travel Department	SHOPPING&TRAVEL
Travel Department	SHOPPINGANDTRAVEL
Travel Department	TRAVEL
Travel Forum	TRAVELER
Travel Forum	TRAVELFORUM
Travel Holiday Magazine	TRAVELHOLIDAY
Traveler's Corner	TRAVELERSCORNER
Traveler's Corner	WEISSMANN
Trivia Club	TRIVIA
True Image Audio	MACSPEAKERZ
True Image Audio	TIA
True Image Audio	TRUEIMAGEAUDIO
Tseng	TSENG
Tune Up Your PC	AUTOEXEC
Tune Up Your PC	CONFIG
Tune Up Your PC	TUNEUP
Tune Up Your PC	TUNEUPYOURPC
TV Gossip	TVGOSSIP
U.S. & World News area	USNEWS
U.S. & World News area	WORLDNEWS
United Cerebral Palsy Association, Inc.	UCPA
University of San Francisco	USF
Unlimited Adventures	UA
Unlimited Adventures	UNLIMITEDADVENTURES
Upgrade to the latest version of AOL*	UPGRADE
USA Today Industry Watch section	CAREERNEWS
User Group Forum	AUG
User Group Forum	UGC
User Group Forum	UGF
User Group Forum	USERGROUP
User Group Forum	USERGROUPS
Userland	USERLAND
Utah Forum	UTAH
Utah Forum	UTAHFORUM
Vertisoft	VERTISOFT
Viacom New Media	ICOM
Viacom New Media	ICOMSIMULATIONS
Viacom New Media	VIACOM
Video Games area	NINTENDO
Video Games area	SEGA
Video Games area	VIDEOGAMES
Video SIG	VIDEOSIG
Videodiscovery	VDISC

Videodiscovery	VIDEODISC
Videodiscovery	VIDEODISCOVERY
VIDI	VIDI
Viewpoint DataLabs	VIEWPOINT
Virtual Reality Labs, Inc.	VRLI
Virtual Reality Resource Center	VIRTUALREALITY
Virtual Reality Resource Center	VR
Virtus Walkthrough	VIRTUS
Virtus Walkthrough	WALKTHROUGH
Virus Information Center SIG	VIRUS
Visionary Software	VISIONARY
Voyetra Technologies	VOYETRA
Wall Street SOS Forum	SOS
Warner/Reprise Records Online	REPRISE
Warner/Reprise Records Online	WARNER
Warner/Reprise Records Online	WARNERMUSIC
Washington Week in Review magazine	WWIR
Weather	WEATHER
Weekly calendar of forum activity	CONFERENCE
Weekly calendar of forum activity	CONFERENCECENTER
Weigand Report	WEIGAND
Westwood Studios	WESTWOOD
Westwood Studios	WESTWOODSTUDIOS
What's Hot This Month showcase	HOT
What's Hot This Month showcase	WHATSHOT
White House Forum	CLINTON
White House Forum	THEWHITEHOUSE
White House Forum	WHITEHOUSE
Wilson Windowware	WINDOWWARE
Wilson Windowware	WWW
Windows Forum	WIN
Windows Forum	WINDOWS
Windows Forum	WINDOWSFORUM
Windows Forum	WINFORUM
Windows Magazine	WINDOWSMAG
Windows Magazine	WINDOWSMAGAZINE
Windows Magazine	WINMAG
Windows News area	WINNEWS
Windows Shareware 500	WIN500
Windows Shareware 500	WINDOWS500
Wine & Dine Online	BEER
Wine & Dine Online	BREW
Wine & Dine Online	BREWING
Wine & Dine Online	DINE
Wine & Dine Online	HOMEBREW
Wine & Dine Online	HOMEBREWING
Wine & Dine Online	RESTAURANT
Wine & Dine Online	RESTAURANTS
Wine & Dine Online	WINE
Wine & Dine Online	WINE&DINEONLINE
Wine & Dine Online	WINERIES
Wired Magazine	WIRED
Woodstock Online	WOODSTOCK
WordPerfect Magazine	WPMAG
WordPerfect Support Center	WORDPERFECT
Working Software	WORKING
Worth Magazine Online	WORTH
Worth Magazine Online	WORTHMAGAZINE
Worth Magazine Online	WORTHONLINE
Worth Magazine Online Portfolio	WORTHPORTFOLIO
Writer's Club	WRITER'S
Writer's Club	WRITERS
Writers' Market Forum	WRITERSMARKET
Xceed Technology	XCEED
Xceed Technology	MICRON
Xoas Tools	XAOS
Xoas Tools	XAOSTOOLS
Your Money area	YOURMONEY
Your Stock Portfolio	PORTFOLIO
Your Stock Portfolio	STOCKPORTFOLIO
Zedcor, Inc.	ZEDCOR

APPENDIX B
Keyboard Guide

Some online services expect you to learn complex commands and cryptic code words to get around. Not America Online!

Like any graphical user interface (GUI) application, America Online has been designed for use with a mouse, and you should definitely take advantage of AOL's mouse capabilities if you intend to get the most out of your time online. If you don't have a mouse, you can still navigate the service from your keyboard; even if you do have a mouse, there will be times when it makes sense to use the keyboard instead. Some simple guidelines are provided here for quick reference.

Remember, you can press the Esc key at any time to cancel a long listing, a print job or most other time-consuming activities that you may not want to wait through while you're online.

To Pull Down A Menu Without Using the Mouse

The menu bar appears at the top of the America Online window. The File, Edit, Go To, Mail, Members, Windows and Help menus appear with an underlined letter. To pull down a menu, hold down the Alt key and press the underlined letter on the keyboard. A selection rectangle appears around the first menu item on the pulled-down menu. Press the Down arrow key to move the rectangle to the menu option.

Note: Some items on pulled-down menus offer underlines under key characters. Once a menu is pulled down, you can choose these items by pressing the appropriate key on the keyboard. Close All Windows, for instance, is Alt+W, then A.

Dialog Boxes

You can select every option in every dialog box without a mouse as well. It takes a keen eye, but sometimes it's faster than lifting your fingers from the keyboard and grabbing the mouse.

Once a dialog box appears on the screen, start tapping on the Tab key and watch the dialog box carefully. You will see a faint dotted rectangle or line skipping around within the box. Whenever it's on a button, just press the Enter key or spacebar. When it's in a scroll box (a list of file names, for instance), use the arrow keys to find the item you're after, then press the Enter key.

Note: You can cancel most dialog boxes by pressing the Esc key.

Scrolling Text

You can always scroll text within a text window by pressing on Up and Down arrow keys. To scroll larger amounts of text, use the Pg Up and Pg Dn keys. This is often superior to scrolling with the mouse, even if a mouse is available.

Keyboard shortcuts

Some menu items have an associated keyboard shortcut denoted with a caret (^) and a letter. To use the keyboard shortcut, hold down the Ctrl key and press the appropriate letter on your keyboard. (For example, instead of pulling down the Edit menu to cut a section of text, highlight the text you want to cut, then press Ctrl+X.) A listing of Ctrl+key shortcuts follows, in the order in which they appear on the menus.

Note: You don't need to press the Shift key, even though the letters are shown here in upper case.

Control menu	
Close a window	Ctrl+F4
Task List	Ctrl+Esc
File menu	
New	Ctrl+N
Open	Ctrl+O
Save	Ctrl+S
Print	Ctrl+P
Download Manager	Ctrl+T
Exit (Sign Off)	Alt+F4
Stop incoming text	Esc
Edit menu	
Undo	Ctrl+Z
Cut	Ctrl+X
Copy	Ctrl+C
Paste	Ctrl+V
Select All	Ctrl+A
Go To menu	
Departments	Ctrl+D
Keyword	Ctrl+K
Lobby	Ctrl+L
Personal Go To menu items	Ctrl+1 through Ctrl+0
Mail menu	
Compose mail	Ctrl+M
Read new mail	Ctrl+R
Members menu	
Send an instant message (New)	Ctrl+I
Transmit an instant message	Ctrl+Enter
Get a member's profile	Ctrl+G
Locate a member online	Ctrl+F
Preferences	Ctrl+=

APPENDIX C
Locations, Modems & CCL Files

America Online's custom software is not only user-friendly, it's modem-friendly. The first time you sign on to America Online, the software asks you several questions as part of the initial installation process. Your answers determine such things as modem speed and type, local access telephone numbers to use and so on. This information automatically configures your America Online software to connect effortlessly. However, you may need to modify this information: for example, if you change your location, upgrade your modem, or discover that your non-standard modem needs special configuration. This appendix will show you how to create and save multiple setups and how to modify your configuration. Modem files and CCL scripts as they relate to successful America Online connection are also covered.

Location Setups

Your America Online software allows you to create and store multiple sets of network setup and connection information. These sets of information are known as "location setups" and while these are handy for folks who move from location to location, they are also very useful for those who like to stay put. You can store configurations for different connection speeds as well as access numbers for various locations.

Think of location setups as coats. If you live in a temperate region of the country, you may only own one light windbreaker. On the other hand, if you call a more diverse climate your home, you may collect an entire wardrobe of coats for any weather condition. Location setups are no different: they allow you to successfully step out into the world of

America Online, regardless of where you are, what time it is or what you wish to accomplish. Best of all, creating and choosing your location setup before signing on is easier than purchasing and deciding which coat to wear.

New location setups are simple to create. Launch the America Online software and instead of signing on as you normally would, click the Setup button on the Welcome (sign on) window and click the Create Location button that appears to the right. In the new window that appears, enter your information (described below in Changing your setup). When you're finished, save your new location setup by clicking the Save button in the lower left hand corner of the window. When you're prompted to name the location setup, choose a title that reflects the function of the new information, such as "Ann Arbor" (for a different location) or "9600 Access" (for a different connection speed). To use the location setup you've just created, simply select it in the Network and Modem Setup window. The next time you sign on, your software will use the setup information in the chosen location setup.

Changing Your Location Setup

To create or modify location setups, you need to change your network options. Creation is simple, as described earlier in this appendix. To modify a setup, click the Setup button in the Welcome (sign on) window, then choose the location you wish to alter from the Network & Modem Setup list. In either creating or editing a setup, your software displays a window titled "Network Setup" with a number of options (see Figure C-1). Be sure to make a note of your current settings in case you need to return to them. You can use this screen to change any of a number of options, all described below.

Below, we'll look at each one of the variables pictured in Figure C-1.

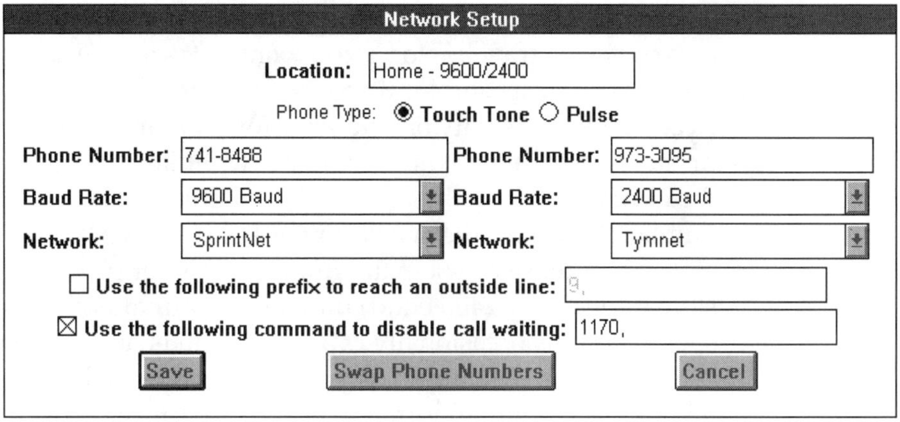

Network Setup

Location: Home - 9600/2400

Phone Type: ◉ Touch Tone ○ Pulse

Phone Number:	741-8488	Phone Number:	973-3095
Baud Rate:	9600 Baud	Baud Rate:	2400 Baud
Network:	SprintNet	Network:	Tymnet

☐ Use the following prefix to reach an outside line: 9,

☒ Use the following command to disable call waiting: 1170,

Save | Swap Phone Numbers | Cancel

Figure C-1: Working off-line, click the Setup button in the Welcome (sign on) window and choose either Edit Location or Create Location to access your network setup information.

Location

The Location field gives you the option of editing or creating a name for the Network Setup. Choose an appropriate name that allows for immediate recognition, as described earlier.

Phone Type

Touch-Tone phones are standard equipment today in homes and hotels. However, there are still a few local phone exchanges (or homes) that do not support tone-dialing; they use pulse dialing. If your America Online software seems to be having trouble when first dialing the local access number, select the Pulse option.

Phone Number

This field contains the phone number your America Online software uses to connect with the host computer. You'll notice that this field, and the associated Baud Rate and Network fields, are represented twice in the window. AOL automatically uses the second set of information if the first try with the primary information is unsuccessful. This allows you to set up an alternate access number and have it dialed if the primary is busy or unavailable.

You will need to change these numbers if you're moving to a new area, if you're traveling or if you want to try a different local access number. You can find local access numbers online via the keyword: Access. If there is only one number for your area, use that as both your primary and alternate number to allow for automatic redialing should the number be busy the first try. If you don't want to dial a second number, leave the alternate number field empty.

Tip: If you use a 9600-baud number for your primary number, list a slower (probably 2400 baud) number as your alternate number. High-speed access is occasionally capricious; 2400-baud access is not.

Another Tip: In some areas you may need to dial an area code, even for a local call. If you normally need to do this when you place voice calls, you will need to do it for America Online access as well.

Note: Remember, any long-distance charges you incur reaching the America Online access number are your responsibility. They're not included as a part of your monthly America Online fee. If you have to dial the number 1 before you can reach AOL's nearest access number, you're no doubt incurring long-distance charges.

Baud Rate

You'll most likely only need to change this if you get a new modem with a speed different than your usual modem, or if you're currently using a local access node that doesn't take full advantage of your modem's speed capabilities. For instance, you may use a local access number that can only handle 2400 baud. But if you later switch to a different number that can serve 9600 baud modems and you have a 9600 baud modem, you need to change the baud rate setting that your America Online software uses. Use the Baud Rate pop-up menu to set the baud rate to the highest speed your modem and node can handle.

Network

This pop-up menu is used to select which phone carrier handles your calls from the local access node to America Online's host computers. SprintNet is the most widely used carrier for America Online in the US; Datapac is used in Canada. You can use the Network pop-up menu to select the appropriate network as specified for your access number. (The keyword: Access—available only when you're online—lists all of AOL's access numbers.)

Outside Line Prefix

Some telephone systems, particularly those in hotels, offices and schools, require that you dial a "9" or other prefix to get an outside line. Enter the number you want America Online to dial; then enter a comma. The comma tells the modem to wait two seconds before dialing the next number. If it takes longer than two seconds for your phone system to access an outside line and generate a dial tone, you might want to add a second comma just to be sure. Note that the America Online software has already entered "9," for you in the Outside Line Prefix field. To use this prefix whenever you dial America Online, all you have to do is click this check box.

Disable Call Waiting

When you're connected to America Online and someone tries to call you, he or she would normally get a busy signal. If you have Call Waiting, however, the caller hears a normal ring and your modem hears the beep that normally lets you know you've got a call waiting. As you can imagine, this tends to confuse your PC (not to mention the host computers). That which is a convenience for voice communications is an interference for telecommunications and will cause your modem to disconnect from America Online. If you use Call Waiting, you can (and should) temporarily disable it on most phone systems by entering a code such as "1170," or "*70," before dialing America Online. Be sure to include the comma after the string of numbers: it tells the modem to wait two seconds before dialing the next number. Note that the America Online software has already entered "1170," for you in the Disable Call Waiting field. To configure your software to turn off Call Waiting whenever you dial America Online (but not any other time), all you have to do is click this check box. If you aren't sure what numbers you should enter to disable Call Waiting, check with your local telephone company or look in the front section of your local phone book, under Call Waiting.

Swap Phone Numbers

This handy button allows you to easily swap the information that you've set for your primary and alternate numbers. This is useful when the primary number is giving you difficulties and you'd rather use the alternate number initially.

Modem Files

For the majority of members, America Online has made it unnecessary to worry about such things as data bits, stop bits or parity. All your connection information is collected when you initially run America Online. Should you need to change your modem setup for any reason, follow the steps below:

- Click the Setup button at the bottom of the Welcome (sign on) window.
- Click the Setup Modem button. It makes no difference which location is selected in the Choose Location list box: it's assumed that your modem configuration is the same for each one.
- The Modem Selection and Customization window will appear. Select your modem from the extensive list that appears there. If your modem doesn't appear there, read on.
- America Online's user-friendliness doesn't stop there, though. They've gone the extra step of allowing you to customize your modem setup should you need it. If you use a modem that's not included in America Online's pre-configured modem settings, you may need to create a custom modem file. A modem file is simply information that allows your modem and the America Online software to work together smoothly. It tells the modem how to set itself up for dialing out, how to place a call and how to behave once it is connected. Fortunately, you hardly ever need to alter your modem file, but the option is available on those rare occasions when it is necessary. In these cases, a number of simple solutions are available:
- If you are able to sign on, drop by the free Tech Help Live area online (use the keyword: TechLive), available both weekdays and weekends. An America Online representative will guide you through the process of configuring the software for your modem.
- If it is after hours for Tech Help Live (and you're able to sign on), you may be able to find a pre-configured file for your modem

already available. Go to keyword: ModemHelp and click the Modem Drivers button. The well-stocked Modem Drivers library is very likely to contain what you need. If you find a file for your modem, download it to the MPM subdirectory located in your AOL directory. After you've downloaded the file, sign off and click Setup in the Welcome window (actually, it'll be the Goodbye window if you've just signed off), click Modem Setup, and your modem type will appear in the list for selecting.

- If you are unable to sign on, call America Online Technical Support at 1-800-827-3338. Like the Tech Help Live area, this service is available seven days a week and the representatives can offer considerable guidance.
- If you are unable to sign on to America Online but you can sign on to other services, you can access the same Modem Drivers library described above through the America Online Technical Support BBS. Just dial 1-800-827-5808 with a standard telecommunications program (such as Terminal which comes with Windows). Your settings should be: 8 data bits, no parity, 1 stop bit. You can access the BBS at modem speeds up to 14,400 bps. Complete instructions for dialing the BBS and using the Terminal program are available under AOL's Help menu.
- If you are an advanced user, you can create a custom modem file suited to your own needs. Please note that even as an expert telecommunicator, you are advised to consult your modem's manual or technical support line for the features you can enable or disable before making changes. If you'd like to give this option a go, read on...

Customizing your modem file

To customize your modem file, follow the steps below:

- Working off-line, choose Open from the File menu.
- Find the MPM subdirectory located in your AOL directory.

- Select a pre-configured modem file from those that appear in the MPM subdirectory. Use the one that's closest to describing your modem make and model.
- Make a copy of this file by choosing Save As from the File menu and giving your file a distinctive name. While you could simply make changes to the original file, making a copy first allows you to revert back should it be necessary.
- Open your new file up and scroll to the top of the document. Under [ID], you'll see lines beginning with Name and Title. Change the text following "Name=" and "Title=" to something different so you can recognize it later. For example, try adding " — my version" to the end of the name and title already given. Once you've made the change, select Save from the File menu.
- Now click on Setup at the bottom of the Welcome (sign on) window and choose Modem Setup. Select your modem file from the Modem Selection and Customization list. To customize, select one of the three buttons to the right of the window (see Figure C-2).

The three Modem File editors each display a window with a number of fields. You can use these editors to customize any of the modem commands. Consult your modem manual before making changes.

Don't overlook the Modem Port option in the Modem Selection and Customization window. This tells the software where to look for the modem's physical connection to your computer, with the default being COM 1. If you want to use a modem connected to a port other than COM 1, select the appropriate port here. If you aren't sure which port your modem uses, check the actual ports on the back of the computer.

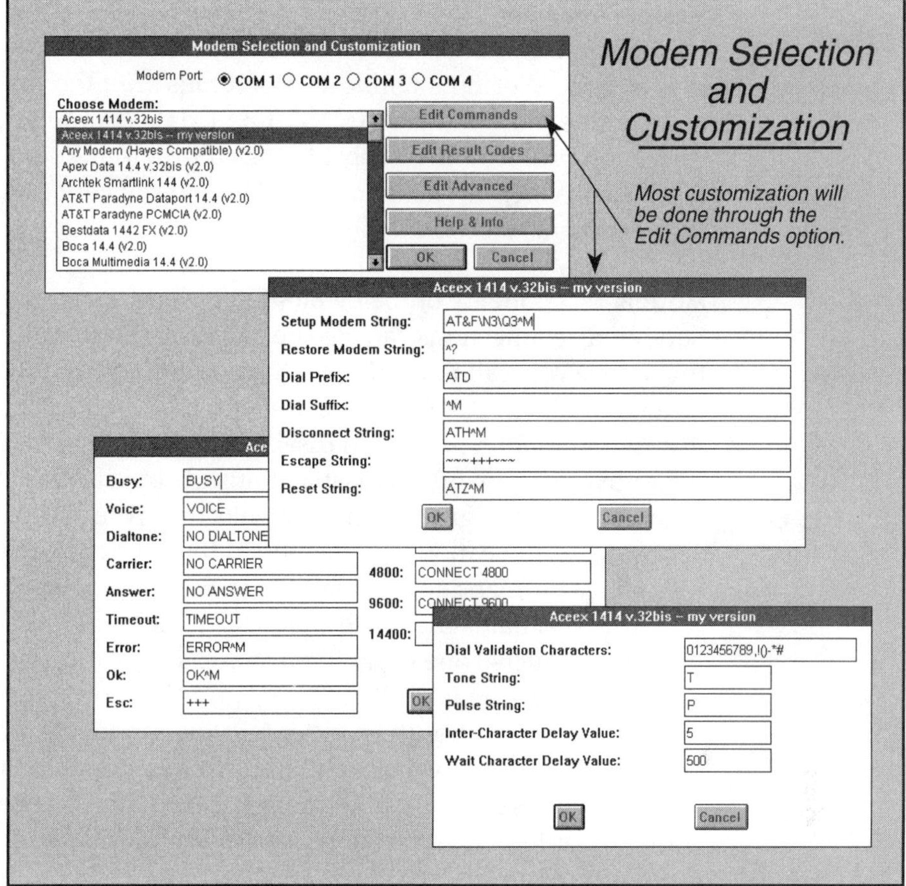

Figure C-2: America Online offers built-in editors to customize a modem file.

Solving Common Modem Problems

Here are some common modem problems and solutions:

Modem Won't Dial

America Online's software requires certain commands to connect properly to the host computer. To verify that these commands are included, click Edit Commands in the Modem Setup area and check the command strings. You may want to try including "ATQ0V1E0" to your Setup Modem String, if something similar isn't already present. You should also check your Dial Prefix field—for most modems this should read "ATV1 S11=55 Q0 E0 D" (those 0's are zeros).

Modem Dials But Won't Connect

If your connection fails at some point between the high-pitched carrier tone and the Welcome window, or if it fails after the first thing you try to do online, flow control (XON/XOFF), data compression or error-correction protocols are probably the culprit. Make sure that these are disabled: "AT&F" in the front and "^M" at the very end of your Setup Modem String should do the trick.

Modem Disconnects on Call Waiting

Sudden disconnections can also be caused by Call Waiting. The click that indicates a call is waiting on the line sounds like a "break" (disconnect immediately) signal to the modem, which obligingly hangs up. If this is a problem, you should disable Call Waiting when you connect to America Online. You can disable it off-line by clicking the Setup button in the Welcome (sign on) window, selecting your location in the list, choosing Edit Location and clicking in the check box marked "Use the following command to disable call waiting." The input field to the right of this line contains the pulse code to disable Call Waiting which also works for Touch-Tone users in most areas. In some areas, you may need to change the default of "1170," to "*70," for Touch-Tone use. Include a comma after the code: it tells the modem to wait two seconds before dialing the next number. If you aren't sure what numbers you should enter to disable Call Waiting, check with your local telephone company or look in the front section of your local phone book under Call Waiting.

Modem Disconnects Frequently

If you have problems with line noise (static on your phone line while signed on to America Online), the result may be file-transfer errors, strange characters on the screen or occasional disconnections from America Online. One step you can take to cut down on line noise is to temporarily set your baud rate to a lower speed. Try the speed one step down from your current setting. You can also try another local access number (if available).

Another common cause of frequent disconnects is a phone cord with a bad connector (or jack) on one or both ends, or a faulty wall jack. If you hear lots of static when you're talking on the phone, odds are the same amount of static (line noise) is present when you use America

Online. Check with your telephone company or an electrician to find out what can be done to improve your line quality.

Modem Speaker Stays On

To disable your modem speaker, click on Edit Commands in the Modem Setup area and add "M0" (the letter M and zero) to the Setup Modem String. If there are already characters present, add "M0" immediately before the characters "^M" which fall at the end. For example, if you are using a Zyxel modem, your Setup Modem String would appear as "AT&FM0^M."

Alternatively, "M1" will enable the speaker until a connection is made and "M2" will keep the speaker turned on after a connection has been established.

CCL Files

The dysfunctionally curious will note the CCL subdirectory in the AOL directory. Normally, you won't need to worry about this, but to satisfy your curiosity, here is a brief description of CCLs and what they are all about.

A CCL file (Communication Control Language) is a modem "script" that allows your modem to talk to certain communication systems. Your America Online software comes with CCLs for networks like SprintNet, Tymnet and Datapac, enabling them to work with America Online. CCL scripts are written in a programming language and can be modified with a simple text editor. The CCLs come pre-configured and already in place; you needn't do anything to take advantage of these other than verify that the appropriate CCL for your access number is selected in the Network pop-up menu in the Network Setup screen. Additionally, it is unlikely you will need to alter a CCL script as modem files can handle virtually all of your needs. There may be times when the connection process is too complicated for a modem file, however. If you find a modified or custom modem file is not able to solve your problems, contact America Online Technical Support for further details.

APPENDIX D
On The Road

Your access to America Online need not end where your wanderlust begins. Whether you travel across the country or use a notebook PC at work and at home, America Online is only a phone call away. This appendix gives you tips for calling America Online while traveling, finding local access numbers and signing on using a computer other than your own.

Using America Online on the Road

Using America Online when you are traveling is easy with these few preparations and helpful hints:

- Inexpensive kits are available that help in setting up your modem when traveling. It's also a good idea to travel with an extra length of standard phone line with modular (RJ-11) jacks on each end, and a phone splitter. These items are available at many phone and electronics stores.
- If you're going to be staying in a hotel, ask for a "computer-ready" room: one with an extra phone jack for your modem. If the hotel doesn't have phones set up for computer users, you can usually remove the phone cable from its phone jack and connect your modem cable.
- If you need to dial a long distance access number and want to avoid the hotel's long distance charges or accruing charges on a friend's phone bill, you can use your calling card. Edit your location's network setup (detailed in Appendix C) by inserting the following in the Phone Number field:

  ```
  <Long distance carrier number, if needed> + 0 + <area code> +
  <access number> + ,,,,, + <calling card number> + PIN (personal
  identification number, which may be optional)
  ```

For example: 10333-0-313-665-2900,,,,,12312312341234#

Those five commas cause AOL to wait ten seconds while your long-distance carrier comes on the line and asks for your calling-card number.

Note that your long-distance carrier number may be needed to override the default carrier for the phone you are calling from: AT&T is 10288, MCI is 10222, and Sprint is 10333. Call Waiting may cause problems with this procedure, so disable it if you are having difficulties.

- Use America Online to back up your work while traveling. Send mail to yourself and attach the file you want to save. If you need to restore the file, you can read the mail and download the saved file. If you lose your work while you're on the road, or even after you return, you'll have a backup waiting online when you get home.
- In your travels, you may find yourself using America Online in places where loud sounds could be disruptive to others around you, such as a friend's guest room or a waiting room. In these situations, you can disable your America Online sounds (check your General Preferences under the Members menu) or turn your modem speaker off (refer to Chapter 20, "Top Ten," or check your modem manual).
- Look up the local access numbers (by using the keyword: Access) for the area you'll be visiting. Do this before you leave: it's much easier. Create individual locations (discussed in Appendix C) for your most frequent destinations and name them appropriately. Now when you need to sign on you can simply select your location, say Work, Branch Office, Home or Cottage, through the Setup button on the Welcome (sign on) window and you're ready!

General help with signing on is available in the America Online Software under the Help menu.

Finding Local Access Numbers Off-line

If you discover you need a new access number while you're on the road but you are unable to get online to search the number directory, you aren't alone. Many others have traveled down this path before and a variety of options have opened up:

- Sign on with the NewLocal# option in the Screen Name pop-up menu on the Welcome (sign-on) window. With this option enabled, America Online will automatically call a toll-free number and present you with a list of access numbers to choose from.
- Call America Online's Technical Support Hotline at 1-800-827-3338 (within USA) or 1-703-893-6288 (from Canada or overseas), open seven days a week from 6 a.m. to 4 a.m. Eastern Time.
- Phone the carrier network: Tymnet can be reached at 1-800-336-0149; SprintNet at 1-800-877-5045 ext. 5 and SprintNet's automatic access number listings at 1-800-473-7983.
- If you have a fax modem or access to a fax machine, call America Online's FAXLink service at 1-800-827-5551 and request a list of access numbers be faxed to you. An automated voice menu will guide you through the choices.
- Connect to America Online's Technical Support BBS at 1-800-827-5808 with a standard telecommunications program (such as Terminal which comes with Windows). Your settings should be: 8 data bits, no parity, 1 stop bit. You can access the BBS at modem speeds up to 14,400 bps. Complete instructions for dialing the BBS and using the Terminal program are available under AOL's Help menu.
- If you're within the US, you can connect to SprintNet's Local Access Numbers Directory with a standard telecommunications program. To access, simply dial any SprintNet node directly and once connected, type "@D" and press the Return key twice. At the @ prompt given, type "c mail" and press Return, then type "PHONES" for the username and "PHONES" again for the password. You can look up any local SprintNet number available.

Signing on as a Guest

In your travels you are likely to visit others who have America Online on their computers. While your screen names won't appear in their software, you can still use their machine to sign on with your account. Just select the "Guest" screen name from the pop-up menu on the Welcome (sign on) window and then click the Sign On button. (The "Guest" name always appears in the list of screen names, no matter whose machine you're using or what kind of computer it is.) The software will dial the local access number and connect to America Online.

After you've made the connection, you'll see a dialog box that asks for a screen name and the password. Enter your screen name and password. America Online will connect using your account. Charges (other than long-distance charges, if any) you accrue during the session will be billed to your account rather than your friend's.

Note: Data such as your Address Book and FlashSession information is stored locally in your America Online software rather than on AOL's host machines. As a result, you will not be able to see this information when signed on as a Guest on another computer. You are also unable to edit your screen names while signed on as a Guest.

To sign off from a Guest session, simply choose Sign Off from the Go To menu as you normally would.

APPENDIX E
Preferences

Like all good software, America Online for Windows offers the opportunity to configure the program to your liking via a group of user preferences. What if you work in a crowded office and don't want to hear sounds like "You have mail!" broadcast for all to hear? What if you get tired of typing in your password every time you sign on? Why does AOL close your Compose Mail window after you've sent mail?

All of these things—and a number of others—are covered by AOL's member preferences. Preferences can be set online or off, so you're best advised to set them off-line when the meter isn't running.

Begin by choosing Set Preferences from the Member menu or use the keyboard shortcut Ctrl+=. Five categories of preferences will appear in the form of the five buttons pictures in Figure E-1.

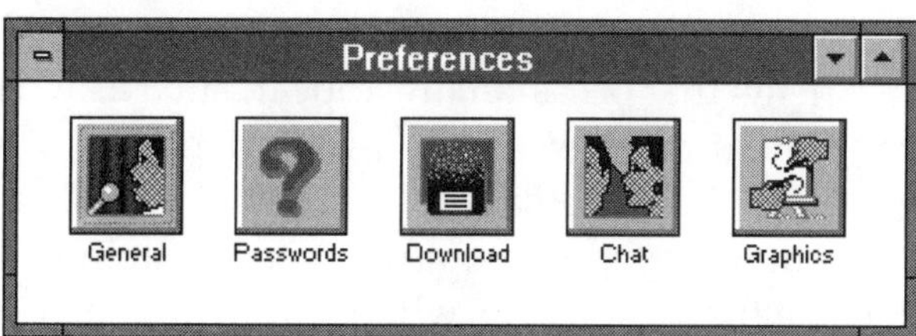

Figure E-1: The five categories of preferences. Click any one of these buttons to make changes.

Here are the functions you can change with the Preferences command:

General Preferences

Here's where you have control over sounds, text and Network News (see Figure E-2).

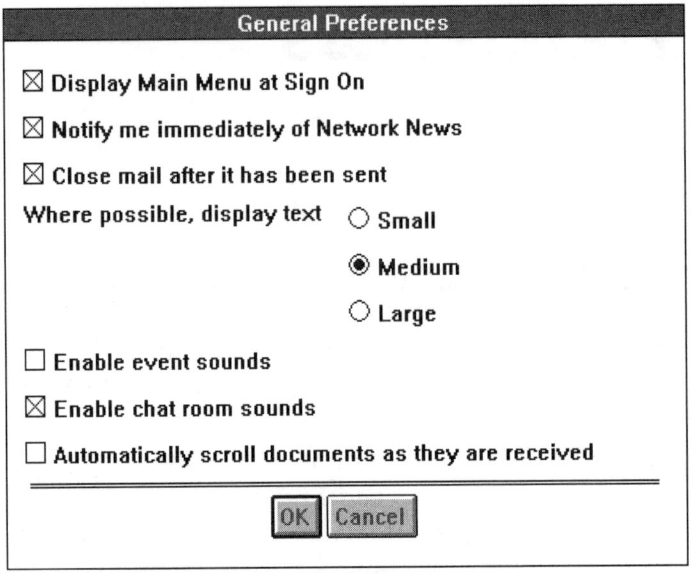

General Preferences

☒ Display Main Menu at Sign On

☒ Notify me immediately of Network News

☒ Close mail after it has been sent

Where possible, display text ○ Small ◉ Medium ○ Large

☐ Enable event sounds

☒ Enable chat room sounds

☐ Automatically scroll documents as they are received

OK Cancel

Figure E-2: The General Preferences window provides control over the most frequently changed options in the program.

Display Main Menu at Sign On shows the departments window (the Main Menu) when you first come online. If you don't use the Main Menu to navigate AOL, you may prefer to turn this option off. (The default setting is On.)

Notify me immediately of Network News turns on the Network News announcements that occasionally appear, such as when AOL goes down for regular maintenance. If this option is on, you don't need to do anything to get these messages—they automatically appear on your screen, and they don't interrupt what you're doing. If you would prefer not to receive these messages while you're online, turn off this option. (The default setting is On.)

Close mail after it has been sent does just that. AOL is automatically set to close a mail document after you've sent it to the recipient. If you would like to keep a document you have already sent open on your screen, turn this preference off. (The default setting is On.)

Where possible, display text as... provides control over the size of most text that's received online. If you're using an SVGA monitor—800 by 600, for example—incoming text may be too small for you to read. Some people have trouble with small text regardless of their monitor's size. No matter what causes the problem, this control offers the fix. (The default setting is Medium.)

Enable event sounds activates the sounds like "Welcome" when you sign on, and "You've got mail!" when mail is waiting for you. If your machine can play these sounds (many machines can't — read Chapter 12, "People Connection," for details on this subject) and you don't want to hear them, turn this control off. (The default setting is On.)

Enable chat room sounds activates member-sent sounds in chat rooms. Some chat rooms are especially sound-oriented. Try LaPub for an example. These people love to laugh out loud and slap one another on the back—quite aurally. To hear these sounds, you must have them installed on your machine, your machine must be sound-compatible and you must leave this preference turned on. (For more about chat room sounds, read Chapter 12, "People Connection.") (The default setting is On.)

Automatically scroll documents as they are received scrolls articles as they are received online. At 9600 baud, you can't read this fast, so scrolling incoming text is of no particular value. It makes the screen a busy place to watch, and in some cases, may actually slow down the transmission speed of text transfers. That's why the default is off. It's always better to log incoming text (logging is discussed in Chapter 6, "Today's News"), and read your logged text after you sign off. However, if you prefer to have articles scroll as they are received for whatever reason, turn this preference on.

Edit Stored Preferences

Passwords keep other people from using your account when you're not around. Once a password is stored, anyone using that machine can sign on and spend hours online, at your expense.

Note: this preference pertains only to the *computer* that's in use when you set the preference, not to the account. If the account is also used on another machine, stored passwords won't be available there (unless you make them so).

On the other hand, there are those of us for whom that potential simply doesn't exist. Perhaps you lock your computer when you're away, or the other people in your office or home are trustworthy beyond reproach. I sign on 5 or 10 times a day, and my computer is in my studio, which is sanctified ground. Typing my password 5 or 10 times a day is not only unnecessary, it's counterproductive. For this reason, I store my password (Figure E-3) and never have to type it in.

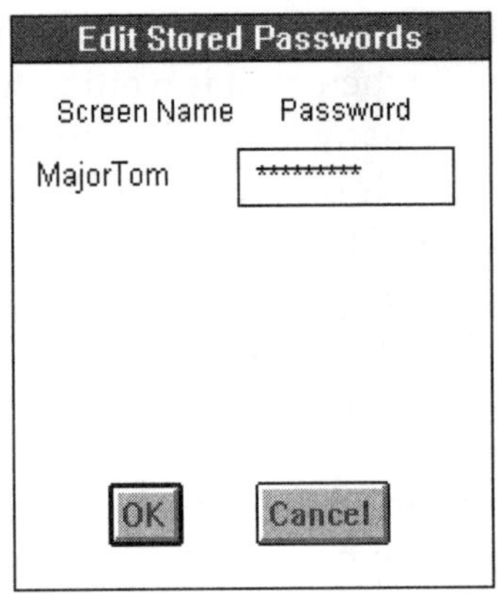

Figure E-3: You can't read my stored password. AOL displays only asterisks. The password, nonetheless, is there, and I don't have to type it in when I sign on.

Use this option with care! AOL shows no pity when members call with unexpected bills run up by fellow office workers or members of the family. If there's a possibility that someone might access your account while you're away, don't utilize this feature. (The default is Off.)

Download Preferences

If you do much downloading, you should (1) use the Download Manager, and (2) examine these preferences. (Downloading & the Download Manager are discussed in Chapter 19.)

Download Preferences

☒ Display image files on Download

☒ Automatically decompress files at sign-off

☐ Delete ZIP and ARC files after decompression

☒ Confirm additions to my download list

☒ Retain information about my last 20 downloads

OK Cancel

Figure E-4: The Download Preferences dialog box provides control over your downloading configuration.

Display image files on Download allows you to view most graphics as they're received. Viewing them online allows you to abort the download if you don't like (or need) what you see. It's best to leave this preference on unless your PC is very low on memory, or very slow. (The default setting is On.)

Automatically decompress files at sign-off uses AOL's built-in version of PKUnZip (PKZip and PKUnZip are discussed in Chapter 5, "Computing") to decompress any zipped files you have downloaded. AOL automatically unzips these files when you sign off. If you would prefer that these files not be unzipped, turn this preference off. If you download to floppies (a practice I recommend), you will want to turn this preference off. (The default setting is On.)

Delete ZIP and ARC files after decompression removes the archive from your disk after it's decompressed. Since most of us prefer to store the archive on a floppy as a form of backup, this option defaults to the off condition.

Confirm additions to my download list causes the dialog box pictured in E-5 to appear whenever you add a file to your queue of files to be downloaded.

The file has been added to your download list. To view your list or start the download, select 'Download Manager' below (or select from the File Menu or theToolbar later).
OK
Download Manager

Figure E-5: AOL displays this dialog box whenever you add a file to your download queue. If you don't want to bother with it, turn the appropriate preference off.

This dialog box is a convenience if you like to visit the Download Manager every time you add a file to its list. It's an annoyance if you do not. If it annoys you, turn the preference off. (The default setting is On.)

Retain information about my last XX downloads determines how many files are listed when you click the Download Manager's Show Files Downloaded button. Each file that's retained consumes about 2k of your hard disk's storage space. You're the only one who knows how much of your hard disk you can afford to dedicate to this feature, so give this number some thought before changing it.

On the other hand, if you do much downloading this feature is a godsend, as it monitors your downloads and tells you if you've already downloaded a file *before* you unnecessarily download it a second time. The larger this number, the more apt you are to catch your forgetfulness.

Chat Preferences

If you're fond of chat rooms, look these preferences over carefully. Chat rooms are discussed in Chapter 12, "People Connection."

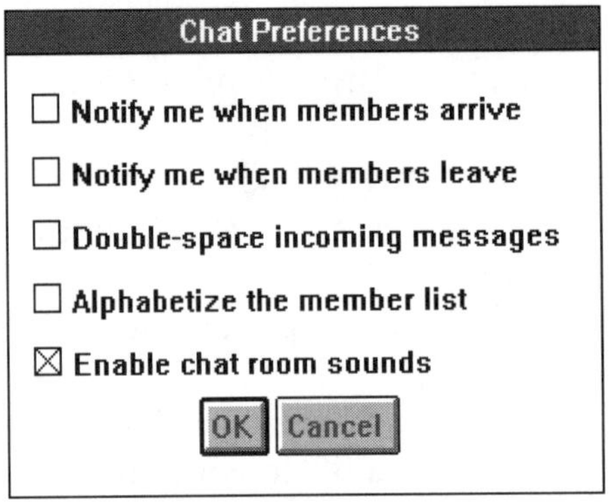

Figure E-6: The Chat Preferences provide control over your chat room environment.

Chat Preferences

☐ Notify me when members arrive

☐ Notify me when members leave

☐ Double-space incoming messages

☐ Alphabetize the member list

☒ Enable chat room sounds

OK Cancel

Notify me when members arrive causes the "OnlineHost" to place a line in your chat room window announcing the entrance of every arriving member. Host and Guides love this feature, and it's helpful for all of us when we're in a room that doesn't have a lot of comings and goings. If the members in a room are transitory—as people in lobbies, for instance, tend to be—you will probably want to leave this preference off. (The default setting is Off.)

Notify me when members leave is the same as the preference described above, except the notification is provided when the member leaves, rather than arrives in, the room. Again, it's helpful for Hosts and Guides. (The default setting is Off.)

Double-space incoming messages just makes them easier to read. It also halves the amount of conversation that's displayed on your screen at any one time. It's a compromise, but the decision is yours. (The default setting is Off.)

Alphabetize the member list offers you the choice of viewing the member list (the little scroll box of member names in the upper right corner of chat windows) in alphabetical order or in the order in which members arrive in the chat room. If you want to watch comings and goings (and the Notify preferences are turned off), leave this preference turned off. If you tend to refer to the list often—perhaps to look up the profiles of or send Instant Messages to other members in the room—alphabetizing it may help. (The default setting is Off.)

Enable chat room sounds is simply a second offering of the preference discussed earlier. It's listed under the General Preferences (see Figure E-2) as well. You may turn it on or off in either place. (The default setting is On.)

Graphics Preferences

These preferences pertain to the online viewing of graphics as they're received. Downloading graphics and the online graphics viewer are discussed in Chapter 5, "Computing."

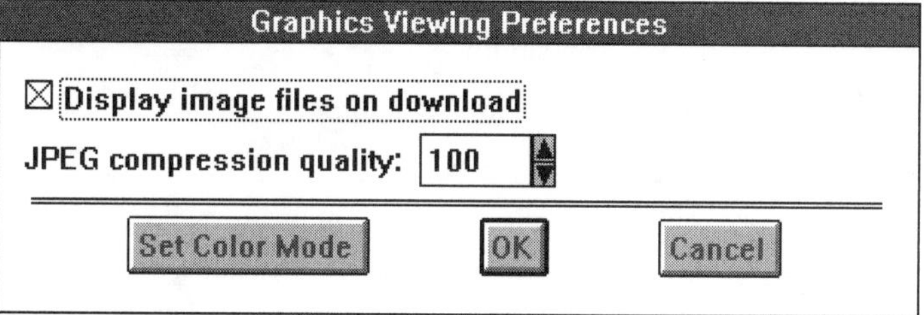

Figure E-7: The Graphics Preferences provide control over graphics that are received online.

Display image files on download is a second offering of the preference discussed earlier under Download Preferences (see Figure E-4). Again, this preference allows you to view most graphics as they're downloaded. (The default setting is On.)

JPEG compression quality allows you to set the rate of compression for graphics when you save them to disk using JPEG compression. The higher the compression quality, the better the quality of the image; but the higher the compression quality, the more space the image will take on your disk. It's best to leave this set at the highest quality level (100) unless you are low on disk space or don't mind the quality loss. (The default setting is 100.)

If you have a question, experiment a bit with a favorite image of yours. Save it three or four times in the JPEG format using different compression quality settings, then open each version you've saved to see how the compression quality setting affected them.

Set Color Mode, available through the button on the bottom of the window, gives you the option of choosing the correct number of colors that your monitor can display (see Figure E-8). Normally AOL can detect this automatically, but not all monitors accurately report their capabilities. If you are noticing problems displaying images, you may try adjusting this control. (The default setting is Detect Automatically.)

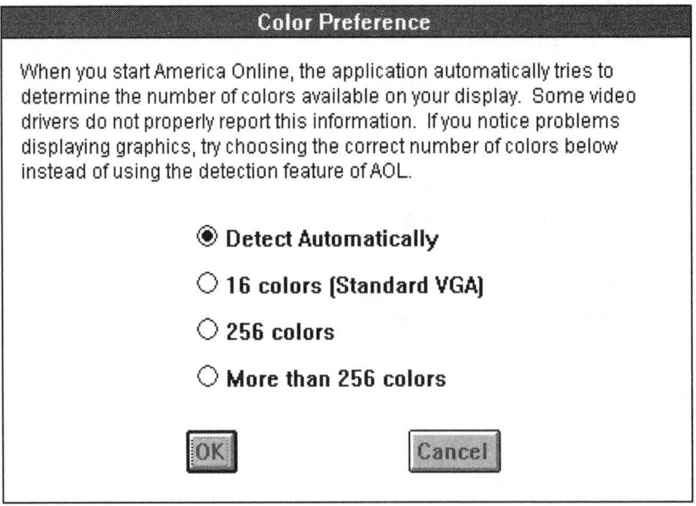

Figure E-8: The Set Color Mode preference gives control over the number of colors AOL displays. Leave this at Detect Automatically unless you are experiencing problems.

Explore these preferences. Alter every one of them and live with the changes for a week. You may discover something you didn't know about yourself!

Glossary

This glossary was prepared by Jennifer Watson (screen name: Jennifer) and George Louie (screen name: NumbersMan) of the America Online staff (to whom I express my heartfelt thanks for a job very well done). It's updated regularly and posted online. To find it, use the keyword FileSearch, then search with the criterion VirtualLingo.

access number — A phone number (usually local) your modem uses to access America Online. To find an access number online, go to keyword: ACCESS. If you aren't signed on to AOL, there are a number of ways to get access numbers:

- Sign on with the "New Local#" (Windows version of AOL) or "Get Local#" (Mac AOL 2.1 or higher) option in the "Set Up & Sign On" window.
- Delete all your numbers in Setup; AOL will automatically call the 800 number and let you choose from the list of access numbers.
- Phone the network: Call SprintNet at 1-800-877-5045 ext. 5 or SprintNet's automatic access number listings at 1-800-473-7983; call Tymnet at 1-800-336-0149.
- Dial up SprintNet's Local Access Numbers Directory: Using a general telecommunications program, you can call in to a SprintNet node directly. Once connected, type "@D" and hit the Enter key twice. At the @ prompt given, type "c mail" and hit Enter, then type "PHONES" for the username and "PHONES" again for the password. You can look up any local SprintNet number available.
- Call America Online's Technical Support Hotline at 1-800-827-3338 (within U.S.) or 1-703-893-6288 (from Canada or overseas), open from 6 a.m. to 4 a.m. ET, seven days a week.
- Call AOL's FAXLink service at 1-800-827-5551 and request that a list of access numbers be faxed to you. An automated voice menu will guide you through the choices.
- Dial up AOL's Technical Support BBS with a standard telecommunications program at 1-800-827-5808 (settings: 8 data bits, no parity, 1 stop bit, up to 14.4K).

If you don't have a local access number, read the information in the Access Number area (keyword: HELP) on how to obtain one. See also Datapac, SprintNet, Tymnet and node.

Address Book — An AOL software feature that allows you to store screen names for easy access. Your Address Book may be created, edited or used through the Address Book icon available when composing mail. You can also create or edit them with the Edit Address Book option under your Mail menu. See also e-mail and screen names.

afk — Common shorthand for "away from keyboard." It's most often used in chat and IMs when it's necessary to leave the keyboard for an extended length of time. See also shorthands, abbreviations and chat.

America Online, Incorporated (AOL) — The Vienna, Virginia-based parent company of the three online services—America Online, PC-Link and Q-Link. PC-Link and Q-Link are going offline fall 1994, however. Formerly known as Quantum Computer Services and founded in 1985, AOL has grown rapidly in both size and scope. AOL has over 1 million members and dozens of alliances with major companies. America Online's stock exchange symbol is AMER. To contact AOL headquarters, call 703-448-8700. See also AOL.

analog — Information composed of continuous and varying levels of intensity, such as sound and light.

AOL — Abbreviation for America Online, Inc. Occasionally abbreviated as AO. See also America Online, Incorporated.

AOLiversary — A date celebrated yearly on which a member first became an active on America Online. Considered an accurate yardstick by some to determine their state of addiction. See AOLoholic.

AOLoholic — A member of AOL who begins to display any of the following behaviors: spending most of their free time online; thinking about AOL even when off-line (evidenced by the addition of shorthands to non-AOL writings); attempting to bring all their friends and family online; and/or thinking AOL is the best invention since the wheel. A 12-step plan is in development. Many, but not all AOLoholics, go on to become remote staff. See also member and remote staff.

archive (ARC) — (1) A file that has been compressed smaller with file compression software. See also file, file compression, PKZIP, and StuffIt. (2) A file that contains message board postings that may be of value, but have been removed from a message board due to their age, inactivity of topic, or lack of message board space. These messages are usually bundled into one document, and placed in a file library for retrieval later. See also file and library.

article — A text document intended to be read online, but may be printed or saved for later examination offline. On MacAOL, the limit is 25k; if longer it will scroll off the top of the window (the "More" feature is not available on MacAOL). See also document.

ASCII — Acronym for American Standard for Computer Information Interchange (or American Standard Code for Information Interchange). ASCII is the numeric code used to represent computer characters on computers around the world.

Ask the Staff button — See Comment to Staff button.

asynchronous — Data communication via modem of the start-stop variety where characters do not need to be transmitted constantly. Each character is transmitted as a discrete unit with its own start bit and one or more stop bits. AOL is asynchronous. See also synchronous.

attached file — A file that hitches a ride with e-mail. Be the file text, sound or pictures of your hamster "Bruno," it is said to be attached if it has been included with the e-mail for separate downloading by the recipient (whether addressed directly, carbon copied, forwarded or blind carbon copied.) See also archive, download, e-mail and file.

auditorium — Auditoriums are specially equipped online "rooms" that allow large groups of AOL members (up to 300–500) to meet in a structured setting. Currently, there are four auditoriums: The Coliseum, a.k.a. Center Stage (for special and general events), Rotunda (for computing-related topics or computing company representatives), the Odeon (for Information Providers) and Tech Live (for questions and help on AOL — this is in the free area). The auditoriums are divided into two parts: the stage, where the emcee and the guest speaker(s) are located, and the chat rows, where the audience is located. More information on auditoriums can be found at keyword: SHOWS or ROTUNDA. See also emcee, OnlineHost, Coliseum, Odeon, Rotunda and Tech Live.

bandwidth — A measure of the amount of information that can flow through a given point at any given time. To use a popular analogy, a low bandwidth is a two-lane road while a high bandwidth is a six-lane superhighway.

baud rate — A unit for measuring the speed of data transmission. Technically baud rates refer to the number of times the communications line changes states each second. Strictly speaking, baud and bits per second (bps) are not identical measurements, but most non-technical people use the terms interchangeably. See also bps.

BBS (Bulletin Board Service) — A system offering information that can be accessed via computer, modem and phone lines. For more information online, go to keyword: BBS.

blind carbon copy (bcc) — A feature of the AOL e-mail system that allows you to send e-mail to a member or members without anyone other than you being aware of it. See also e-mail.

board — An abbreviated reference to a message board or bulletin board service (BBS). See also message board and BBS.

bps (bits per second) — A method of measuring data transmission speed. Currently, 1200, 2400 and 9600 bps are supported on AOL. 14,400 may be available in larger cities, but unreliably as it is still in testing. See also baud.

brb — Common shorthand for "be right back." It is used by AOL members when participating in chat/conference rooms or talking in IMs (Instant Messages). See also shorthands, abbreviations and chat.

browse — To casually explore rather than examine in detail. Typically used in reference to message boards and file libraries.

btw — Common shorthand for "by the way." It is used in IMs, chat/conference rooms, e-mail and message postings. See also shorthands, abbreviations and chat.

bulletin board — See message board and BBS.

carbon copy (cc) — A feature of the AOL e-mail system that allows you to address e-mail to a member for whom the e-mail is not directly intended or is of secondary interest. See also e-mail.

CCL (Communication Control Language) — A script that allows you to control your modem. CCL scripts are most useful when the connection process is more complicated than can be handled by a modem file. See also modem files.

Center Stage — See Coliseum.

chat — To engage in real-time communications with other members. See also Instant Message, chat room, conference room and auditorium.

chat rooms — Online areas where members may meet to communicate and interact with others. There are two kinds of chat areas — public and private. Public chat areas can be found in the People Connection area (keyword: PEOPLE) or in the many forums around AOL. Public rooms may either be officially-sanctioned rooms or member-created rooms (which are listed separately). All public rooms are governed by AOL's Terms of Service (TOS) and are open to anyone interested. See also private room, chat, host, Guide, TOS and People Connection.

chat sounds — Sounds may be played and broadcast to others in chat areas by selecting "Chat Sounds..." under the "Chat" menu. You can also play them by typing: {S <sound>} and sending it to the chat area. Be sure to type it exactly as shown and insert the exact name of the sound you wish to play where <sound> appears in the example. See also chat room and library.

CIS — Short for CompuServe Information Service. May also be abbreviated as CI$. See also Compuserve.

client — A computer that requests information from another.

close box — The small box in the upper-left corner of your window. Clicking on this box closes the window. Not to be confused with a shoe box, boom box or even clothes box. See also window.

club — See forum.

Coliseum — Previously known as Center Stage, The Coliseum is an auditorium located in People Connection or via the keyword: SHOWS. See also auditorium and emcee.

Command key — Usually located near the Spacebar, you'll find printed on it either an open Apple symbol or a clover-leaf symbol (or both). Holding down the Command key while another key is pressed will often activate a special function. See also Option key and Open-Apple key.

Comment to Staff button — A button available in file libraries that will allow you to send a note to the managers of the library. See also download and library.

CompuServe (CIS) — A large, established commercial online service similar to America Online. While CompuServe Information Service (CIS) has more databases available, their service is priced higher and is less user-friendly than AOL. CIS is owned by H&R Block. May be referred to as "CIS" or "CI$" in shorthand during chat.

conference room — A specific kind of chat area found in forums all around AOL where members can meet, hold conferences and interact in real-time. Conference rooms can hold up to 23 or 48 members at any one time (depending on location), and are located outside of the People Connection. See also host, moderator and protocol.

corporate staff — Members who are usually company or IP (information provider) employees and work at the corporate offices of the company. In-house AOL, Inc. staff is often referred to in this manner as well. See also in-house and IP.

CS Live — See Tech Live.

Customer Relations — America Online's Customer Relations Hotline is open from 9 a.m. to 2 a.m. Eastern time Monday through Friday, and noon to 1 a.m. on weekends. Call 1-800-827-6364 during these hours. See also Tech Live.

cyberpunk — First used to designate a body of speculative fiction literature focusing on marginalized people in technologically-enhanced cultural "systems." Within the last few years, the mass media has used this term to catergorize the denizens of cyberspace. Cyberpunks are known to cruise the information landscapes with alacrity, or lacking that, eagerness.

cyberspace — An infinite world created by our computer networks. Cyberspace is no less real than the real world—people are born, grow, learn, fall in love and die in cyberspace. These effects may or may not be carried over into the physical world. America Online is an example of cyberspace created through interaction between the energies of the members, staff and computers. See also online community.

daemon — An automatic program that performs a maintenance function on AOL. For example, a board daemon may run at 3 A.M. and clean up old posts on a message board.

database — A collection of information, stored and organized for easy searching. A database can refer to something as simple as a well-sorted filing cabinet, but today most databases reside on computers because they offer better access. See also Directory of Services, Member Directory and searchable.

Datapac — A packet-switching network operated by Bell Canada that provides local access numbers for Canadian members at an extra fee. See also packet-switching network and access number.

Delete — An AOL e-mail system feature that allows you to permanently remove a piece of mail from any and all of your mailboxes. See also e-mail and Status.

demoware (demonstration software) — These are often full-featured versions of commercial software, with the exception being that the Save or Print features are often disabled. Some demos are only functional for certain periods of time. Like shareware, demonstration software is a great way to try before you buy.

department — This is the broadest category of information into which America Online divides its material. There are 14 departments, corresponding with the departmental organization of this book.

digital — Information that is represented by two discrete states (either 1 or 0) and also referred to as binary information. Most information in the real world is not digital, but must be converted into this form to be used by computers.

Directory of Services — A searchable database that allows AOL members to quickly locate AOL's available services. This is available at keyword: SERVICES. See also database and searchable.

document — An information file, usually relating specific details on a topic. See also article and file.

DOD — Abbreviation for Data On Demand, a method of receiving artwork updates. AOL is unique in that as it grows and new areas are added, the custom artwork associated with new services and areas can be added on the fly. At the time of this writing, DODs are only available on the Mac AOL and WAOL platforms; PC/GEOS users receive artwork updates via UDOs.

download — The transfer of information stored on a remote computer to a storage device on your personal computer. This information can come from AOL via its file libraries, or from other AOL members via attached files in e-mail. See also archive, attached file, file, library, download count and download manager.

download count — The download count (often abbreviated "Cnt" in a library window) refers to the number of times that file has been downloaded. This is often used as a gauge of the file's popularity. See also file, library and download.

download manager — An AOL software feature that allows you to keep a queue of files to download at a later time. You can even set up your software to automatically sign off when your download session is complete. You can schedule your software to sign on and grab files listed in the queue at times you specify. See also download and file.

e-mail — Short for electronic mail. One of the most popular features of online services, e-mail allows you to send private communications electronically from one person to another. See also attached file, carbon copy, blind carbon copy, return receipt, Keep As New, Delete, Status, e-mail address and gateway.

e-mail address — A cyberspace mailbox. On AOL, your e-mail address is simply your screen name; for folks outside of AOL, you address is yourscreenname@aol.com. For mail outgoing from AOL, check out the Internet Center (keyword: INTERNET) for more information. See also e-mail and screen name.

echo — A rare AOL system bug that rapidly repeats a person's chat over and over in a chat or conference room. Also known as a system scroll. If this occurs, you should leave the room immediately and page a Guide using keyword: GUIDEPAGER.

emcee — A member who has been trained to moderate and host events held in auditoriums. See also auditorium.

emoticons — Symbols consisting of characters found on any keyboard which are used to give and gain insight on emotional states. For example, the symbol :) is a smile — just tilt your head to the left and you'll see the : (eyes) and the) (smile). A brief list of emoticons is available at keyword: SHORTHANDS. See also shorthands and chat.

eWorld — Apple Computer's newest online service. Based on AOL's client system, eWorld is expected to be a popular service with its stylized graphics and Apple support. eWorld opened to the public on June 20, 1994.

FAQ — Short for "Frequently Asked Questions." FAQs may take the form of an informational file containing questions and answers to common concerns/issues. See also message board and library.

fax (facsimile) — A technique for sending graphical images (such as text or pictures) over phone lines. While faxes are usually sent and received with a stand-alone fax machine, faxes may also be sent to or from computers using fax software and a modem. You can also send a fax through AOL at keyword: FAX.

file — Any amount of information that is grouped together as one unit. On AOL, a file can be anything from text to sounds and can be transferred to and from your computer via AOL. See also download, library and software file.

file compression — A programming technique by which many files can be reduced in size. Files are usually compressed so that they take up less storage space, can be transferred quicker and/or can be bundled with others. See also file and download.

file name extensions — These are usually three-character codes found suffixing a file name, and are primarily used for PC files.

flame — Made popular on the Internet, this means to chat, post messages, or send e-mail about something that is considered inflammatory by other members, and may cause fires among those who read and respond to it. Harassment and vulgarity are not allowed on America Online, and if you see this occurring, you may report the occurrence at keyword: TOS. See also chat, message board, e-mail and TOS.

flashmail — On the Mac, this is a feature of the AOL software that allows you to save your outgoing e-mail to disk to send at a later time, or save your incoming e-mail so you can look at it later, online or off-line. These e-mails are stored in your flashbox, and the outgoing files are sent with FlashSessions. See also e-mail.

folder — Groupings of messages by topic within message boards are termed "folders" on America Online. See also message and message boards.

form — A window for an area online—usually comprised of a text field, a list box (scrollable), and one or more icons. See also icon and window.

forum — A place online where members with similar interests may find valuable information, exchange ideas, share files and get help on a particular area of interest. Forums (also known simply as areas or clubs) are found everywhere online, represent almost every interest under the sun, and usually offer message boards, articles, chat rooms and libraries, all organized and accessible by a keyword. Forums are moderated by forum hosts or forum leaders. See also form and keyword.

freeware — A file that is completely free and often made available in libraries of online services like AOL for downloading. Unlike public domain files, you are not able to modify it and the author retains the copyright. Since the author or programmer usually posts freeware and the user downloads it, distribution is direct and nearly without cost. See also file, shareware and public domain.

gateway — A link to another service, such as the Internet, EAASY SABRE or StockLink. Gateways allow members to access these independent services through AOL. See also Internet.

GIF (Graphic Interchange Format) — A type of graphic file that can be read by most platforms; the electronic version of photographs. GIFs can be viewed with a GIF viewer utility, which are located at keyword: GALLERY.

Gopher — A feature of the Internet that allows you to browse huge amounts of information. The terms implies that it will "go-pher" you to retrieve information. It also refers to the way in which you "tunnel" through the various menus, much like a gopher would. See also WAIS and Internet.

GUI — Graphical User Interface. Some examples of GUIs include the Mac Operating System, OS/2 and Windows. See also operating system, system, OS/2 and Windows.

Guide — Experienced AOL members who have been specially chosen and trained to help other members enjoy their time online. All on-duty Guides wear their "uniforms"—the letters "Guide" followed by a space and a two- or three-letter suffix in all caps. See also Guide Pager, Lobby and uniform.

Guide Pager — A feature of AOL that allows you to page a Guide when there is a problem in a chat or conference room. Simply go to keyword: GUIDEPAGER, and you will be presented with a simple form to complete regarding the problem. See also Guide and TOS.

hacker — Not to be confused with hamsters, hackers are self-taught computer gurus who take an unholy delight in discovering the well-hidden secrets of computer systems. Blighted by a bad reputation of late, hackers do not necessarily denote those who intend harm or damage. There are those, however, who feed upon the pain inflicted by viruses. See also virus.

hamster — Unbeknownst to most users, AOL's host computers are actually powered by these small, efficient creatures with large cheek pouches. They are notorious for being temperamental workers. When things slow down or troubles mount online, it is a sure sign that an AOL employee forgot to feed the hamsters.

help room — Online "rooms" where members can go to get live help with the AOL software/system as well as assistance in finding things online. See also Guide, Help, MHM and Tech Live.

host — (1) The AOL computer system. (2) An AOL member who facilitates discussion in chat rooms. You can find hosts all over the system, and they will often be wearing "uniforms" —letters in front of their names (usually in all caps) to designate the forum they host for. See also Guide, chat room, conference room and uniform.

hot chat — A safe, euphemistic term which means to chat about (read "flirt") and engage in the popular online dance of human attraction and consummation. Virtually, of course. And usually in private rooms or IMs.

icon — A graphic image of a recognizable thing or action that leads to somewhere or initiates a process. See also keyboard shortcuts.

Ignore — (1) Chat blinders; a way of blocking a member's chat from your view in a chat/conference room window. Ignore is most useful when the chat of another member becomes disruptive in the chat room. (2) An AOL e-mail system feature that allows you to ignore mail in your New Mail box, causing it to be moved to your Old Mail box without having to read it first. See also e-mail and Status.

in-house — Used to describe those employees that actually work at AOL in Vienna, Virginia. May also be referred to as corporate staff. This is contrasted with remote staff, many of whom are actually volunteers and work from their homes. See also corporate staff and remote staff.

IP (Information Provider) — A person or party supplying material for use on AOL's services, and/or responsible for the content of an area on America Online's services. See also corporate staff and remote staff.

interactive — Having the ability to act on each another. AOL is interactive in the sense that you can send information and, based upon that, have information sent back (and vice versa). The chat rooms are an excellent example.

insertion point — The blinking vertical line in a document marking the place where text is being edited. The insertion point may be navigated through a document with either the mouse or the arrow keys.

IM (Instant Message) — AOL's equivalent of passing notes to another person during a meeting, as opposed to speaking up in the room (chat) or writing out a letter or memo (e-mail). Instant Messages (IMs) may be exchanged between two AOL members signed on at the same time and are useful for conducting conversations when a chat room isn't appropriate, available or practical.

Internet — The mother of all networks is not an online service itself, but rather serves to interconnect computer systems and networks all over the world. The Internet is managed by the National Science Foundation (NSF). AOL features an Internet Center which includes access to e-mail service to and from Internet addresses, USENET Newsgroups, and Gopher & WAIS Databases, among other features. FTP and Telnet access will be offered within 1994. AOL has even provided "Net Guides" who rove among the areas helping members out. To receive mail through the Internet gateway, you need to give others your Internet mailing address which consists of your AOL screen name (without any blank spaces) followed by the "@" symbol and "aol.com" (i.e., jennilynn@aol.com). To obtain more information about the Internet, use the keyword: INTERNET to go to the Internet Center. For information about TCP/IP access to America Online, see TCP/IP. See also gateway, gopher, newsgroups and WAIS.

Keep As New — An AOL e-mail system feature that allows you to keep mail in your New Mail box, even after you've read or ignored it. See also e-mail.

keyboard shortcuts — The AOL software provides us with keyboard command equivalents for menu selections. For example, rather than selecting "Send Instant Message" from the menu, you could type Command-I on the Mac or Open-Apple-I on the Apple II. For a complete list of these keyboard shortcuts, see the Keyboard Shortcuts Chart included as a supplement to the VirtuaLingo Glossary.

keyword — (1) A fast way to move around within America Online. To use a keyword, type Command-K on the Mac and then the keyword, followed by the Enter key. Keywords are communicated to others in a standard format: Keyword: NAME. An updated list of all public keywords is available in the AOL file libraries by searching for "keyword surf" (don't include the quotes) at keyword: FILESEARCH. (2) A single word you feel is likely to be included in any database on a particular subject. A keyword is usually a word that comes as close as possible to describing the topic or piece of information you are looking for. Many of AOL's software libraries can be searched for keywords.

library — An area online in which files may be uploaded to and downloaded from. The files may be of any type: text, graphics, software, sounds, etc. To search libraries available for your platform, go to keyword: FILESEARCH. See also file, download, upload, search and browse.

line noise — Extraneous noise on telephone lines that is often heard as clicks or static. While line noise is usually only a nuisance to voice communications, it means trouble for data being transmitted through modems. If you are having problems remaining connected, it may be the result of line noise. Signing off, redialing and getting a new connection will often help this problem.

Lobby — Often seeming more like the Grand Central Station of AOL rather than a sedate hotel foyer, the Lobby is the default chat room of the People Connection. See also chat, chat room and Guide.

LOL — Shorthand for "Laughing Out Loud," often used in chat areas and Instant Messages. Another variation is ROFL, for "Rolling On Floor Laughing." See also shorthands, abbreviations and chat.

lurk — To sit in a chat room or read a message board, yet contribute little or nothing at all. Hamsters are known lurkers. See also chat and conference room.

Mac AOL — The Apple Macintosh version of the AOL client software. The current version is 2.5. May also be referred to as MAOL.

macro — A "recording" of keystrokes or mouse movements/clicks on a computer that allows you to automate a task. Macros are usually created with shareware and commercial software and can be initiated with a single key.

megabyte — 1,048,576 bytes of data.

member — An AOL subscriber. The term "member" is embraced because AOLers are members of the online community. See also Online Community.

Member Directory — The database of AOL member screen names that have profiles. To be included in this database, the member only needs to have created a Member Profile. The Member Directory is located at keyword: MEMBERS. See also member, Member Profile, database and searchable.

Member Profile — A voluntary online information document that describes oneself. Name, address information, birthday, sex, marital status, hobbies, computers used, occupation and a personal quote may be provided. This is located at keyword: MEMBERS or PROFILE. See also member and Member Directory.

message — A note posted on a message board for others members to read. A message may also be referred to as a post. See also message board.

message board — An area where members can post messages to exchange information, ask a question or reply to another message. All AOL members are welcome and encouraged to post messages in message boards (or boards). Message boards are occasionally called bulletin boards. See also message, folder, thread and Message Center.

message board pointer — An automatic place-marker for message boards. AOL keeps track of the areas you have visited by date, allowing you to pick up where you left off upon your return. Once you've visited a message board, clicking on the "Find New" button will show you only the new messages that have been posted since your last visit. The pointers are updated each time you return. These pointers stay in effect for 60 days after your last visit.

Message Center — A collection of message boards in one convenient area. See also message board.

MHM (Members Helping Members) — A message board in the free area where America Online members can assist and get assistance from other members. Located at keyword: MHM.

modem — An acronym for modulator/demodulator. This is the device that translates the signals coming from your computer into a form that can be transmitted over standard telephone lines. A modem also translates incoming signals into a form that your computer can understand.

modem file — An information file which stores your modem settings for connecting to AOL. As modems differ, you often need to use a modem file configured specifically for your modem. See also CCL.

moderator — Typically a host who facilitates a discussion during a conference. The moderator usually manages protocol, if used. See also host, conference room and protocol.

MorF — Acronym for Male or Female. To ask another member their sex. This happens frequently in Lobbies and chat rooms in the People Connection, but it is considered ill-mannered by most seasoned onliners. BorG (Boy or Girl?) is another manifestation of this virus that seems to infect some members. See also Lobby, chat room and People Connection.

netiquette — 'Net manners. Cyberspace is a subculture with norms and rules of conduct all its own—understanding of these will often make your online life more enjoyable and allow you to move through more smoothly. Online etiquette includes such things as proper capitalization (don't use all caps unless you mean to shout). Basically, the most important rule to keep in mind is one we learned offline and in kindergarten of all places: Do unto others as you'd have them do unto you (a.k.a. The Golden Rule). See keyword: SHORTHANDS for a primer in AOL etiquette.

Network News — AOL maintenance broadcasts and feedback that are displayed in a small window. Network News can be enabled or disabled with the AOL software (select Preferences under the Members menu).

newbie — Affectionate term for a new member (under six months). The New Member Lounge in the People Connection is a popular haunt for the newly initiated.

newsgroups — Internet's version of a public message board. Available on AOL at keyword: NEWSGROUPS. See also Internet.

node — A single computer or device accessible via a phone number and used by one or more persons to connect to a telecommunications network, such as AOL. See also packet-switching network, access number, Datapac, SprintNet and Tymnet.

Odeon — An auditorium which focuses on conferences for media providers online, such as OMNI Magazine Online or NBC Online. The Odeon is accessible through individual forums or through keyword: ODEON. See also Auditorium.

online — The condition of a computer when it is connected to another machine via modem.

online community — A group of people bound together by their shared interest or characteristic of interacting with other computer users through online services, BBSes or networks. Because of the pioneer aspects of an online community, established onliners will welcome newcomers and educate them freely, in most cases. See also cyberspace.

OnlineHost — The screen name of AOL's host computer used to send information and usually seen in chat rooms, conference rooms and auditoriums. See also chat room, conference room and auditorium.

Open-Apple key — A special function key on the Apple II series keyboard. Usually located near the Spacebar, with an outline of the Apple Computer Logo on the key. Holding down the Open-Apple key while another key is pressed will often activate a special function. See also Command key, Option key and keyboard shortcuts.

OS (operating system) — The software that is used to control the basic functions of a computer. Operating systems are generally responsible for allocation and control of a computer's resources. Some common operating systems are: System 7, MS-DOS, UNIX, and OS/2. See also System, UNIX and Windows.

Option key — A special function key commonly found on Mac keyboards. Usually located on the bottom row of keys and labeled "Option." Holding down the Option key while another key is pressed will often activate a special function.

OS/2 — IBM's 32-bit operating system which offers a Macintosh-like interface for IBM PC and compatible machines. The current release of OS/2, version 2.1, runs Windows 3.1, Dos and OS/2 specific applications. See also operating system and Windows.

P* — shorthand for Prodigy Service. See also Prodigy Service.

packet-switching network (PSN) — The electronic networks that enable you to access a remote online service by dialing a local phone number. See also access number, node, Datapac, SprintNet and Tymnet.

palmtop — See PDA.

parental chat controls — Parental Control enables the master account holder to restrict access to certain areas and features on AOL (such as blocking IMs and rooms). It can be set for one or all screen names on the account; once Parental Control is set for a particular screen name, it is active each time that screen name signs on. Changes can be made by the master account holder at any time. To access controls, go to keyword: PARENTALCONTROL.

PDA — Short for Personal Digital Assistant. A hand-held computer that performs a variety of tasks, including personal information management.

People Connection (PC) — The AOL department dedicated to real-time chat. Many different rooms can be found here: Lobbies, officially-sanctioned rooms, member-created rooms, private rooms, the Center Stage auditorium and PC Studio. You can access this area with keyword: PEOPLE. Feel free to surf PC, but please obey hamster crossing signs. See also department, chat room.

PKZIP — A compression utility for PCs to compress one file, or multiple files, into a smaller file (called an archive), which will make for shorter up/downloading. The latest version is 2.04g. See also archive, download, file, file compression, archive and StuffIt.

post — (1) The act of putting something online, usually into a message board. (2) A message in a message board. See also message board and message.

private — The state of being in a private room. It is considered taboo by some members to be "seen" in a private room because this is often the communication channel of choice for "hot chatters." In reality, however, private rooms are a convenient way to meet with someone when IMs would get in the way. See also private room and hot chat.

private room — A chat room which is created by a member via an option in People Connection where the name is not public knowledge.

Prodigy — An information service founded as a joint venture between IBM and Sears. It is currently one of the larger competitors that AOL faces. Prodigy is marred by continuous online advertising, screening of messages before they're allowed to be posted, and other quirks. For all it's drawbacks, Prodigy still has a enormous subscriber base. For those members who defected from Prodigy to AOL, there is a Prodigy Refugees Forum online (keyword: PRODIGY). See also P*.

profile — AOL allows each screen name to have a "profile" attached to it. A profile tells a bit about who you are, where you live, what your interests are — anything you want others to know about you. A profile can be created or updated at keyword: PROFILE. See also member, Member Directory and screen name.

protocol — A system used in conference rooms to keep order and facilitate a discussion. When you have a question, you type "?," when you have a comment, you type "!" and when you are finished, you type "/ga" A queue of those waiting with questions and answers is displayed at regular points throughout the conference, and members will be invited to speak by the moderator or host. It is considered impolite and a breach of protocol to speak out of turn. See also conference room, host and moderator.

public domain — A file that's completely free, uncopyrighted, and typically posted on services like AOL for distribution (via downloading) directly to the user. Since the producer (or programmer) usually posts this and the user downloads it, distribution is direct and nearly without cost.

punt — The act of being disconnected from AOL often as a result of difficulties at AOL or interference on your node (such as line noise). See also node and line noise.

punt pillows — Virtual "pillows" given, via chat or IMs, to cushion the posterior of a member who was punted. Often depicted as () () () () or [] [] [] [] (the harder, concrete variety). See also chat, IMs and punt.

'puter — An affectionate abbreviation for one's computer; often employed by enthusiasts and AOLoholics.

Q-Link — AOL's service for Commodore 64 and 128 users.

Q-Pons — Points Q-Link members may win through participation in special events. These may be accrued and "traded in" for free time or collectibles (5000 Q-Pons are the equivalent of one free hour of online access on Q-Link). There is no equivalent on America Online or PC-Link. See also Q-Link.

quoting — To include parts of an original message in a reply. One or two greater-than characters > is the standard method for setting off a quote from the rest of the message. They are usually placed to the left of the sentence, followed by a space, but may also be placed on the right as well.

release — To make something available to the general public, such as a file in a file library. See also file and library.

remote staff — AOL members who staff the various forums and areas. They usually work from their homes, not AOL headquarters, hence "remote." Often these are Guides, Hosts, Forum leaders/assistants/consultants, etc. See also IP, corporate staff, in-house, Guide and host.

return receipt — A feature available with the Mac AOL software that returns a piece of e-mail acknowledging that mail you sent to another AOL member (or members) has been received. To enable this function, you must check the "Return Receipt" box on the e-mail window before it is sent. See also e-mail, carbon copy, blind carbon copy and status.

revolving door — A chat or conference room has a "revolving door" when members are quickly moving in and out of the room. Lobbies and many popular chat rooms in the People Connection will often have "revolving doors." See also chat room, conference room and Lobby.

Rotunda — An auditorium that features conferences with companies or areas in the Computing & Software department. Accessible via keyword: ROTUNDA. See also auditorium.

screen name — The names—pseudonyms, more often than not—that identify AOL members online. Screen names may contain no fewer than three and no more than ten characters, must be unique, and cannot contain vulgarity or vulgar references. Also, some combinations of letters are reserved for online staff (such as "Guide" or "OMNI"). Screen names may not start with a number. See also member and e-mail address.

scroll — (1) Refers to the movement of incoming text and other information on your computer screen. See scroll bar. (2) The act of repeatedly typing similar words on screen, or spacing out the letters of a word. See keyword: TOS for more information.

scroll bar — The bar on the right hand side of a window which allows you to move the contents up and down, or on the bottom of a window for moving things to the left or right. The area on the scroll bar between the up and down arrows is shaded if there is more information than fits in the window, or white if the entire content of the window is already visible. See also scroll (1).

search — Typically used in association with libraries and other searchable databases, the term search refers to a specific exploration of files or entries themselves, rather than a causal examination done line by line. See also searchable, database, file and library.

searchable — A collection of logically related records or database files which serve as a single central reference; a searchable database accepts input and yields all matching entries containing that character string. The Members Directory is an example of a searchable database. See also search, database, Directory of Services and Members Directory.

self-extracting archive — A compressed file that contains instructions to automatically decompress itself when opened; the software that decompressed it originally is not needed. On the Mac, these files can be decompressed simply by double-clicking on the icon. Self-extracting archive files are usually identifiable by the ".sea" extension. See also file compression and StuffIt.

shareware — A fully-functional file that is distributed with the promise of "try before you buy." Made available with the downloader's good conscience in mind, the authors of shareware ask that if you continue to use their product, you pay the fee requested in their documentation. See also file.

ShrinkIt — A compression utility for Apple IIs to compress one or more files into a smaller file, called an archive. See also archive, file, file compression, archive, PKZIP and StuffIt.

shorthands — The collective term for the many emoticons and abbreviations used during chat. These devices were developed by members over time to give information on the writer's emotional state when ASCII text only is available. A brief list of these is available at keyword: SHORTHANDS. See also emoticons, abbreviations and chat.

sign-on kit — The free software, registration codes and directions for creating a new AOL account. There are a number of ways to obtain sign-on kits. Online, go to keyword: FRIEND and follow the directions there to have kit sent via snail mail. Off-line, you can always find a "free offer" card in a magazine, particularly those magazines which have online forums like OMNI Magazine. You may also find the sign-on kits themselves bundled in one or more newsstand magazines, such as *MacWorld,* or with commercial software, modems and computers. Sign-on kits can also be ordered via phone (1-800-827-6364, ext. 7776). Of course, you can always purchase *The Official America Online Membership Kit & Tour Guide* from your local bookstore; a sign-on kit is included in the back of the book. If you simply need new AOL software but not a entirely new account, you can download the latest software for your platform at keyword: UPGRADE or use the AOL Support BBS (see the access number entry for information regarding the AOL Support BBS).

simulchat — A chat held simultaneously with a radio call-in broadcast. Online chat participants listen to the broadcast and discuss the same topics being discussed on the air. The radio broadcast takes questions and comments from the online chat as well as from callers. See also chat.

smileys — See shorthands and emoticons.

snail mail — Mail that is sent via the U.S. Postal Service. Not meant as derogatory, but to point out the difference between nearly instantaneous e-mail versus the delivery of tangible packages. See also e-mail.

snert — Acronym for Sexually Nerdishly Expressive Recidivistic Trolls. A member who is disruptive or annoying.

software file — A file available in an AOL software library. Often, a software file online is actually multiple files (a program, its documentation, etc.) which are compressed together for shorter uploading or downloading. Every file posted online for download must meet AOL's Terms of Service standards and be checked for functionality and viruses. See also archive, file, file compression, library, TOS, virus, ARC, PKZIP, ShrinkIt and StuffIt.

sounds — See chat sounds.

Spam — A luncheon meat produced by the Hormel Foods Corporation. Spam is frequently the butt of many online jokes originally due to Monty Python's use of Spam as the topic of some of their skits. Lately, Spam jokes have taken on a life of their own online and you may see references to it in chat rooms or message boards. Fortunately, hamsters consider Spam a delicacy. See chat, chat rooms and message boards.

SprintNet — Formerly known as Telenet, SprintNet is a packet-switching network that provides members with 1200, 2400 and 9600 bps local access numbers to America Online. SprintNet networks are owned and operated by US Sprint. See also packet-switching and access number.

StuffIt — A popular compression program for the Apple Macintosh currently published by Aladdin Software and written by Raymond Lau. Stuffit is the standard method of compressing Mac files for uploading to AOL's file libraries. See also archive, file compression, self-extracting archive, download and shareware.

Status (of e-mail) — An AOL feature that allows you to check if e-mail has been read yet and, if read, when. The status for an e-mail message will be either "(not yet read)," "(ignored)," or will show the precise date and time when the mail was read. See also e-mail, carbon copy, blind carbon copy and return receipt.

surf — To cruise in search of information not readily evident in the hope of discovering something new. Usually paired with another word to describe the type of information being sought.

synchronous — Data communication technique in which bits are transmitted and received at a fixed rate. Used to transmit large blocks of data over special communications lines. Much more complex than asynchronous communication, this technique has little application for most personal computer users. See also asynchronous.

sysop — Abbreviation for system operator. The individual who operates and maintains a computer service — usually including a message board, a library or collection of libraries, and a chat room. Pronounced "sis-op." See also forum.

system — Short for operating system, this refers to the software that controls the basic operations of a computer. System can also refer to the collection of components that have a functional existence when combined. Some examples of this include your computer system, the telephone system, or the AOL system. See also operating system, OS/2 and Windows.

TCP/IP — Acronym for Transmission Control Protocol/Internet Protocol. The protocol language that Internet machines use to communicate. AOL announced that they are testing a version of the AOL client software that allows users to use TCP/IP to sign on to AOL. To get this beta software, apply at keyword: TCP on AOL, or get it from ftp.aol.com. Note that beta software is not supported by AOL's Technical Support Staff. See also Internet.

Tech Live — Also known as CS Live, this is a free area where you can ask questions of AOL staff live. The Tech Live Auditorium is open from 9 a.m. to 2 a.m. Eastern time, Monday through Friday, and 12 noon to 1 a.m. Saturday and Sunday. Here you can get live help from experienced Customer Relations staff working in-house at AOL headquarters. This service is available in the Free Area through keyword: CSLIVE. You can get to Tech Live without entering the Free Area if you are on a Mac or PC; simply go to keyword: PEOPLE, click on Rooms, go to the Members Rooms list and create a room called "Tech Live" — you'll be taken to the Tech Live auditorium. See also Customer Relations.

thread — In general terms, a discussion that travels along the same subject line. More specifically, a thread refers a group of posts in a message board under the same subject and (hopefully) topic. See also message board.

thwapp — To hit someone upside their screen name; a virtual slap. For example you may be ::thwapped:: for requesting an age/sex check in a chat room.

timeout — (1) What happens when you've got two computers connected online and one gets tired of waiting for the other (i.e., when the hourglass [PC] or beachball [Mac] cursor comes up and the "host fails to respond"). (2) The result of remaining idle for a certain amount of time while signed on to AOL. This timeout time is usually thirty minutes, but may vary with different modems. In this case, AOL's computers are tired of waiting for you. It's also protection against staying signed on all night when an AOLoholic falls asleep at the keyboard.

title bar — The portion of a window where the name of the window is displayed. On the Mac the title bar also may include the close box and the zoom box. See also close box, window and zoom box.

TOS — Short for America Online's Terms of Service—the terms of agreement everyone agrees to when registering for and becoming a member of America Online. These terms apply to all accounts on the service(s). The areas covered include General Information, Payment Information, Third Party Sales and Service, Termination Information, Disclaimer and Liability Notices, Online Conduct, America Online Software License, Copyright Notices, Information Supplied By Members, Electronic Mail, Other Provisions. You can read these terms at keyword: TOS. Also included are avenues of reporting TOS violations to AOL. See TOSAdvisor and TOS warning.

TOSAdvisor — In days of olde, this was the screen name to which all TOS violations observed by members are sent to. These days, if you feel something violates TOS, you should go to keyword: TOS to report it (with the exception of Apple and PC-Link members — they still e-mail TOSAdvisor). The Terms of Service Staff area can also be reached at keyword: PCSTUDIO > Terms of Service/Parental Controls > Write to Terms of Service Staff. See TOS, TOS warning and OSW.

TOSsable — The state of being likely to receive a TOS warning. For example, a TOSsable word is one which a TOS warning could be given to if typed online. See TOS and TOS warning.

TOS warning — An on screen warning given by a trained Guide or Host for violating AOL's Terms of Service. These warnings are reported to AOL who takes action (or not, depending on the severity of the breach). See TOS.

Tour Guide — Short for *The Official America Online Membership Kit & Tour Guide*—this book.

troll — An online wanderer that often leaves a wake of disgruntled members before crawling back under their rock. It is unclear why trolls find AOL a popular watering hole, but it could be because they consider hamsters a delicacy. See also snert.

Tymnet — A packet-switching network that provides members with 1200 and 2400 bps local access numbers to America Online. Tymnet networks are owned and operated by BT Tymnet. To find Tymnet local access numbers, go to keyword: ACCESS or call 1-800-336-0149. See also packet-switching network and access number.

typo — (1) A typographical error. (2) A dialect that many onliners have mastered with the advent of keyboards and late nights.

UDO — A method of receiving updates to the AOL software. Upon signing-on to AOL, the UDO sends all the necessary updates to your computer before you can do anything else.

uniform — The screen name that's often "worn" by a staff member, either in-house or remote, when working online. The screen name usually consists of a identifiable prefix and a personal name or initials. See also Guide and Host. Some current uniforms include:

AFL	Apple/Mac Forum Leader
AFA	Apple/Mac Forum Assistant
AFC	Apple/Mac Forum Consultant
CNR	CNN News Room staff
CSS	Company Support Staff
GLCF	Gay and Lesbian Community Forum staff
Guide	General system guide
GWRep	GeoWorks Representative
IC	Industry Connection
NPR	National Public Radio Outreach staff
OMNI	OMNI Magazine Online staff
PC	PC Forum Leader
PCA	PC Forum Assistant
PCC	PC Forum Consultant
PCW	PC World Online
PS1	PS1 Connection staff
Teacher	IES Teacher
TECHLive	Tech Live representative
VGS	Video Game Systems staff
WCC	Chicago Online/Windy City Chat staff

UNIX — An easy-to-use operating system developed by Ken Thompson, Dennis Ritchie and coworkers at Bell Laboratories. Since it also has superior capabilities as a program development system, UNIX should become even more widely used in the future. AOL does not currently have software for the UNIX platform. See also operating system.

Unsend — An AOL e-mail system feature that allows you to retrieve mail that has been sent but not yet read. See also e-mail.

upload — (1) The transfer of information from a storage device on your computer to a remote computer, such as AOL's host computer. This information may be uploaded to one of AOL's file libraries or it may be uploaded with a piece of e-mail as an attached file. See also file, file compression and library. (2) The file or information which is sent or uploaded.

virus — Computer software that has the ability to attach itself to other software or files, does so without the permission or knowledge of the user, and is generally designed with one intent—to propagate themselves. They *may* also be intentionally destructive, however not all virus damage is intentional. Some benign viruses suffer from having been poorly written and have been known to cause damage as well. Virus prevention software and information may be found at keyword: VIRUS (on the Mac platform) or keyword: MCAFEE (on the PC platform).

WAIS — (Wide Area Information Server) A database that allows you to search through huge amounts of information on the Internet, similar in some respects to a Gopher. WAIS databases are now widespread through the Internet. See also Gopher and Internet.

WAOL — The PC platform's Windows version of the AOL client software. The current version is 1.1 — rev. 38.

weeding — (Yes, that's "weeding" as in a garden of bliss.) An online wedding. Often held in the People Connection chat rooms like Romance Connection or in the LaPub. Nuptial announcements and well-wishes can be found in The Que message board at keyword: QUE.

window — A portion of the computer screen in which related information is contained, usually with a graphical border to distinguish it from the rest of the screen.

Windows — A graphical extension to the DOS operating system used on IBM PCs and compatibles. Developed by Microsoft, the Windows environment offers drop-down menus, multitasking and mouse-oriented operation. See also system and UNIX.

ZIP — see PKZIP.

zoom box — The zoom box is the small box in the upper-right corner of the window. Clicking on the zoom box will cause a reduced window to zoom up to fill the entire screen; clicking on the zoom box of a maximized window will cause it to zoom down to its reduced size.

Bibliography

Aboba, Bernard. *The BMUG Guide to Bulletin Boards and Beyond.* Berkeley, CA: BMUG, 1992.
Though BMUG is an acronym for the Berkeley Macintosh Users' Group, this book is not particularly Macintosh-specific. Aside from the 100 or so pages devoted to use of the BMUG Bulletin Board System (BBS), this book is a thorough presentation of telecommunications subjects, including a quick-start chapter; using USENET UUCP and FidoNew netmail; a BBS Network Guide; sending mail around the world; jargon; buying a modem; how to save money on your phone bill; file transfer between Macs, PCs and Unix; and file compression. Excellent basic reference for any telecomunicator, especially the Internet user.

Dvorak, John C. *Dvorak's Guide to PC Connectivity.* New York: Bantam, 1991. 3 disks.
As its title suggests, this book is more about connectivity, not telecommunications (Dvorak's telecommunications book appears below). It is divided into four parts: cables, hardware (modems, fax, scanners, storage, printers), connectivity software and networks.

Dvorak, John C. and Nick Anis. *Dvorak's Guide to PC Telecommunications.* Berkeley, CA: Osborne-McGraw Hill, 1990. 2 disks.
A comprehensive examination of telecommunications divided into four parts: layman's view, technical view, user guides (to the programs on the enclosed disks) and appendices.

Frey, Donnalyn. *A Directory of Electronic Mail Addressing & Networks.* 4th ed. Cambridge, MA: O'Reilly & Associates, 1994.

Glossbrenner, Alfred. *The Complete Handbook of Personal Computer Communications: Everything You Need to Know to Go Online With the World* (3rd ed.). New York: St. Martin's Press, 1989.
This is the book to get if you're after a listing of all the commercial online services available and what they have to offer. Includes CompuServe, Delphi, Dow Jones, Huttonline, Investor's Express, NewsMet, MCI Mail and, of course, America Online.

Pournelle, Jerry and Michael Banks. *Pournelle's PC Communications Bible*. Redmond, WA: Microsoft Press, 1992.
More of a practical view of telecommunications than a technical one, this book features chapters on online research, doing business by modem and international communications (with emphasis on Japan and Europe).

Prevost, Ruffin and Rob Terrell. *The Mac Shareware 500: The Last Word on the Best Virus-free Macintosh Shareware*. Chapel Hill, NC: Ventana Press, 1992. 4 disks (including AOL software).
The heart of this book is its Macintosh shareware reviews: games, fonts, graphics, utilities, sound and music, education and more. The book includes five hours of connect time on AOL for new or existing members, which nearly offsets the purchase price. If you download data for your Macintosh, you must have this book.

Rittner Don. *EcoLinking: Everyone's Guide to Online Environmental Information*. Berkeley, CA: Peachpit Press, 1992.
The first guide to the growing phenomenon of activists and researchers using computers to link up with each other. Excellent guide to online research—including the Internet—in the layperson's lexicon.

Robinson, Phillip. *Delivering Electronic Mail*. San Mateo, CA: M&T Books, 1992.
A thorough treatise on electronic mail, including chapters on terminology, security, choosing an e-mail system, using an e-mail system, managing an e-mail system, LAN e-mail programs, public e-mail systems and the Internet. Excellent resource for the person in charge of a local e-mail system.

Stoll, Cliff. *The Cuckoo's Egg*. New York: Pocket Books (Simon & Schuster), 1990.
Reads like a spy novel, but it's a true story of computer espionage via the Internet. This is great reading, regardless of whether you're interested in telecommunications. It's required reading if you want to know more about the Internet. Cliff nailed the spy (after three years of tracking—when the CIA, FBI and NSA could not) and made the front page of the *New York Times*.

Index

A

B

C

D

E

F

G

H

I

N

P

Q

R

S

T

U

V

W

X

Y

Z

Colophon

This book was produced on several different Macintosh Quadras using PageMaker 5.0. It was output directly to film using a Linotronic 330 imagesetter.

The body text is set in Palatino. Subheads, running heads and folios are set in varying weights of DTC Kabel. The sidebars are set in Adobe Futura Condensed. Some of the illustrations were produced in Aldus Freehand 3.1.

FOR WINDOWS
SMARTSUITE
VERSION 4.0
DESKTOP COMPANION
WITH DISK!
1-2-3
Ami Pro
Approach
Freelance Graphics
Organizer
Patrick J. Burns
Jan Weingarten
Robert Bixby
VENTANA PRESS
The VISUAL GUIDE to
MICROSOFT ACCESS
FOR WINDOWS 95
WITH DISK!
The VISUAL GUIDE to
PARADOX
FOR WINDOWS
WITH DISK!

Insightful Guides

CUTTING-EDGE TOOLS & TECHNIQUES

Photoshop f/x

$39.95, 360 pages, illustrated

Push Photoshop's creative limits with this essential idea sourcebook! Full color throughout, *Photoshop f/x* takes users step by step through an impressive gallery of professional artists' illustrations. Explores techniques for using third-party filters, customizing filters, masking, advanced channels and more. The companion CD-ROM features a free copy of Paint Alchemy 1.0, animated recreations of step by steps, and Andromeda third-party filters from Kai's Power Tools plus demos, photos, shareware and more!

Advertising From the Desktop

$24.95, 464 pages, illustrated

Advertising From the Desktop offers unmatched design advice and helpful how-to instructions for creating persuasive ads. With tips on how to choose fonts, select illustrations, apply special effects and more, this book is an idea-packed resource for improving the looks and effects of your ads.

Looking Good in Color

$29.95, 272 pages, illustrated

Low prices and high power offer colorful DTP possibilities. But color without concept is pale indeed. This cross-platform guide starts with basics—the color wheel, how much is enough, how much is too much—and offers proven techniques for showing your true colors! Generously illustrated in full color.

The Gray Book, Second Edition

$24.95, 280 pages, illustrated

This "idea gallery" for desktop publishers offers a lavish variety of the most interesting black, white and gray graphic effects that can be achieved with laser printers, scanners and high-resolution output devices. The *Second Edition* features new illustrations, synopses and steps, added tips and an updated appendix.

Looking Good in Print, Third Edition

$24.95, 464 pages, illustrated

For use with any software or hardware, this desktop design bible has become the standard among novice and experienced desktop publishers alike. With more than 300,000 copies in print, *Looking Good in Print, Third Edition*, is even better—with new sections on photography and scanning. Learn the fundamentals of professional design along with tips on resources and reference materials.

Newsletters From the Desktop, Second Edition

$24.95, 392 pages, illustrated

Now the millions of desktop publishers who produce newsletters can learn how to improve the designs of their publications. Filled with helpful design tips and illustrations, as well as hands-on tips for building a great-looking publication. Includes an all-new color gallery of professionally designed newsletters, offering desktop publishers at all levels a wealth of ideas and inspiration.

Books marked with this logo include a free Internet *Online Companion*™, featuring archives of free utilities plus a software archive and links to other Internet resources.

A Great Gift Idea!

Give your friends or relatives everything they need to join the digital revolution and juice up their online literacy. With *The Official America Online Membership Kit & Tour Guide, Second Edition*, they can explore the nation's fastest-growing commercial online service **at no risk**.

The Tour Guide shows readers how to

- **Get news** from dozens of online wire services, newspapers and magazines.
- **Exchange e-mail** with friends on the other side of the world.
- **Explore the Internet** through America Online's new Internet services.
- **Download** tens of thousands of software files for a Macintosh or PC.
- **Get expert computing advice** from top hardware and software companies.
- **Access stock quotes**, buy and sell stocks online and track investments with an online portfolio management system.
- **Discuss politics** and current affairs in AOL's chat rooms.
- **And much more!**

Get the most from your time online! This readable, richly illustrated "traveling companion" includes the America Online starter disk and **20 FREE hours of online time** for new members!

Find your place in the emerging digital global village. While you're at it, find a place for a friend, too—a great gift for novice and experienced online users alike!

Kits available for Windows and Macintosh.

To order, use the form on the order page, or contact your local book or computer store.

To order any Ventana Press title, complete this order form and mail or fax it to us, with payment, for quick shipment.

TITLE	ISBN	QUANTITY	PRICE	TOTAL
Advertising From the Desktop	1-56604-064-7	________	x $24.95 =	$ ________
The Gray Book, 2nd Edition	1-56604-073-6	________	x $24.95 =	$ ________
HTML Publishing on the Internet for Windows	1-56604-229-1	________	x $49.95 =	$ ________
Looking Good in Color	1-56604-219-4	________	x $29.95 =	$ ________
Looking Good in Print, 3rd Edition	1-56604-047-7	________	x $24.95 =	$ ________
Newsletters From the Desktop, 2nd Edition	1-56604-133-3	________	x $24.95 =	$ ________
The Official America Online for Macintosh Membership Kit & Tour Guide	1-56604-127-9	________	x $27.95 =	$ ________
The Official America Online for Windows Membership Kit & Tour Guide	1-56604-128-7	________	x $27.95 =	$ ________
Photoshop f/x	1-56604-179-1	________	x $39.95 =	$ ________
SmartSuite Desktop Companion	1-56604-184-8	________	x $24.95 =	$ ________
The Visual Guide to Microsoft Access for Windows 95	1-56604-286-0	________	x $34.95 =	$ ________
The Visual Guide to Paradox for Windows	1-56604-150-3	________	x $29.95 =	$ ________
Voodoo Windows 95	1-56604-145-7	________	x $24.95 =	$ ________
Windows, Word & Excel Office Companion, 2nd Edition	1-56604-083-3	________	x $21.95 =	$ ________
			Subtotal =	$ ________
			Shipping =	$ ________
			Total =	$ ________

SHIPPING

For all standard orders, please ADD $4.50/first book, $1.35/each additional.
For "two-day air," ADD $8.25/first book/$2.25/each additional.
For orders to Canada, ADD $6.50/book.
For orders sent C.O.D., ADD $4.50 to your shipping rate.
North Carolina residents must ADD 6% sales tax.
International orders require additional shipping charges.

Name ______________________ Daytime telephone ______________________
Company ______________________
Address (No PO Box) ______________________
City ______________________ State ________ Zip ________
Payment enclosed ___VISA ___MC ___ Acc't # ______________________ Exp. date ________
Signature ______________________ Exact name on card ______________________

Mail to: Ventana Press • PO Box 13964 • Research Triangle Park, NC 27709-3964 ☎ 800/743-5369 • Fax 919/544-9472

Check your local bookstore or software retailer for these and other bestselling titles, or call toll free: **800/743-5369**